Constitutional Law in Venezuela

Constitutional Law in Venezuela

Third Edition

Allan R. Brewer-Carías

This book was originally published as a monograph in the International Encyclopaedia of Laws/Constitutional Law.

Founding Editor: Roger Blanpain
General Editor: Frank Hendrickx
Volume Editors: André Alen & David Haljan

Wolters Kluwer

Published by:
Kluwer Law International B.V.
PO Box 316
2400 AH Alphen aan den Rijn
The Netherlands
E-mail: lrs-sales@wolterskluwer.com
Website: www.wolterskluwer.com/en/solutions/kluwerlawinternational

Sold and distributed by:
Wolters Kluwer Legal & Regulatory U.S.
920 Links Avenue
Landisville, PA 17538
United States of America
Email: customer.service@wolterskluwer.com

Printed on acid-free paper

ISBN 978-94-035-1407-9

e-Book: ISBN 978-94-035-1417-8
web-PDF: ISBN 978-94-035-2797-0

The Author

Prof. Dr Iur. Allan R. Brewer-Carías had his Law Degree (*Summa Cum Laude*) from the *Central University of Venezuela* (1962). After following postgraduate courses with Professors M. Waline, Ch. Eisenmann and R. Charlier at the *Université de Paris* between 1962 and 1963, he obtained his Doctor of Laws title (*Summa Cum Laude*) in 1964 at the *Central University of Venezuela*.

Since 1963, he has been a Professor at the *Central University of Venezuela*, where he was Director of the *Public Law Institute* (1978–1989), Head of the *Administrative Law Chair* and Head of the *Public Law Department* of the same University. He has been a Professor in postgraduate courses in the Law Faculty of the University of *Cambridge* (*LLM*), *UK*; in the *Université de Paris II*; in the *Universidad de el Rosario*: in the *Universidad del Externado de Colombia* in Bogotá; and in the Columbia Law School, *Columbia University in the city of* New York.

In 1981, he was awarded the *National Sciences Prize* of Venezuela for his achievements in law and institutional studies.

He was Vice President of the International Academy of Comparative Law (The Hague) (1982–2010), a Member of the Board of Directors of the Inter-American Institute of Human Rights, and a Member of the Venezuelan National Academy of Political and Social Sciences, where he served as President in 1997–1999.

In Venezuela, he has been a *Senator* for the Federal District; Head of the *Presidential Commission on Administrative Reform*, and *Minister for Decentralization*; and was elected as an independent Member of the *National Constituent Assembly* in 1999, participating in the drafting of the 1999 Constitution.

Since 1980, he has been the Director of the *Public Law Journal* (*Revísta de Derecho Público*) published by the Editorial Jurídica Venezolana, and has extensively published, more than 250 books and more than 1,200 articles on Constitutional and Administrative Law, Political Sciences, Public Administration and Constitutional and Urban History. All the references can be found at www.allanbrewercarias.com.

Since 1974, he has been a partner of the Law Firm *Baumeister & Brewer*, Caracas, and is currently working and residing in New York.

The Author

Table of Contents

List of Abbreviations

OAS	Organization of American States
ICJ	International Court of Justice
OGEL	Oil, Gas & Energy Law
PSUV	Partido Socialista Unido de Venezuela
RCTV	Radio Caracas Televisión
UCV	Universidad Central de Venezuela
UGMA	Universidad Gran Mariscal de Ayacucho
VAT	Value-added Tax
QBD	Commercial Court

General Introduction

Chapter 1. An Outline of Venezuelan Constitutional History

1. The Venezuelan State, located in the northern territories of South America, was created in 1811 after a General Congress of the representatives of the 'United Provinces of *Caracas, Cumaná, Barinas, Margarita, Barcelona, Mérida y Trujillo*' on 5 July 1811 solemnly proclaimed the 'Declaration of the Independence' from Spain, establishing the 'American Confederation of Venezuela in the Meridian Continent'. The work of the Congress,[1] after almost one year, resulted in the sanctioning on 21 December 1811 of the 'Federal Constitution for the United States of Venezuela'.[2] Venezuela was, thus, the first country that adopted the trends of modern constitutionalism derived from the American (1776) and French (1789) Revolutions, and to adopt the federal form of State following the principles adopted a few decades before in the United States of America.[3]

2. These initial constituent decisions were the immediate outcome of the political rebellion initiated the previous year on 19 April 1810 in the Province of Caracas (created in 1528),[4] against the authority of the Spanish Crown. Among the facts that ignited such rebellion was the extreme political instability affecting the Spanish government since 1808, due to the absence of Ferdinand VII from Spain, who with his father, the former Carlos IV, was held captive in France by Emperor Napoleon Bonaparte. The invasion of the Peninsula by the French Army, and the appointment of Joseph Bonaparte as King of Spain by the Emperor after enacting a new Constitution for the Realm, in Bayonne, was another contributory factor. This situation

1. *See* Ramón Díaz Sánchez (ed.), *Libro de Actas del Supremo Congreso de Venezuela 1811–1812* (Caracas: Academia Nacional de la Historia, 1959).
2. *See* Caraccciolo Parra Pérez (ed.), *La Constitución Federal de Venezuela de 1811 y Documentos afines* (Caracas: Academia Nacional de la Historia, 1959), 79 et seq.; and Allan R. Brewer-Carías, *Las Constituciones de Venezuela*, vol. I (Caracas: Academia de Ciencias Políticas y Sociales, 2008), 553–581.
3. *See* Allan R. Brewer-Carías, *Reflexiones sobre la Revolución Norteamericana (1776), la Revolución Francesa (1789) y la Revolución Hispanoamericana (1810–1830) y sus aportes al constitucionalismo moderno* (Bogotá: Universidad Externado de Colombia, 2008).
4. *See* the relevant constitutional documents of the Independence in Allan R. Brewer-Carias, *Documentos constitucionales de la Independencia/Constitucional Documents of the Independence* 1811, (Caracas, Editorial Jurídica Venezolana, 2012), and in *El 19 de Abril de 1810* (Caracas: Instituto Panamericano de Geografía e Historia, 1957). *See* Juan Garrido Rovira, *La Revolución de 1810* (Caracas: Universidad Monteávila, 2009); Enrique Viloria Vera & Allan R. Brewer-Carías, *La Revolución de Caracas de 1810* (Caracas: Centro de Estudios Ibéricos y Americanos de Salamanca, 2011).

and the war of independence that spread all over the Spanish Peninsula, originated a de facto political situation affecting the government of the Monarchy, provoking the creation of provisional provincial governments (*Juntas*) spontaneously established during the war. The Central board (*Junta Suprema*) of these provisional local governments by 1810 was forced to be concentrated on the Island of Cádiz, in the extreme south of Andalucía, and there it appointed a Regency board to govern the Realm in the absence of the Monarch, convening the elections for the *Cortes* (Parliament) in order to draft a new Constitution, which is known as the 1812 Cádiz Constitution.

This situation, and the fear of being subjected to France, originated the political rebellion in the colonies, in particular in the Municipality of Caracas, whose councilmen decided to ignore the Spanish colonial authorities, and to establish in substitution of the colonial Governor and the Provincial Council (*Ayuntamiento*), a *Junta Suprema de Venezuela Conservadora de los Derechos de Fernando VII*, following the same pattern of the *Juntas* that were established in almost all the provinces of Spain during the war of independence. The example given by the Province of Caracas was immediately followed by almost all the Provinces that since 1777 were integrated for military purposes in the General Captaincy of Venezuela. These Provinces were *Cumaná* (created in 1568), *Barinas* (created in 1786), *Margarita* (created in 1525), *Barcelona* (created in 1810), *Mérida* (created in 1676) and *Trujillo* (created in 1810). All of them during 1810 and 1811 declared their independence and adopted their own provincial constitutions.[5]

The 21 December 1811 Federal Constitution, adopted by the elected representatives of these Provinces in General Congress,[6] left open the possibility for the other Provinces which, although having been part of the General Captaincy of Venezuela, had not participated in the independence movement, as was the case of the provinces of *Maracaibo* (created in 1676) and the city of Coro, and of *Guayana* (created in 1568), to seek their future incorporation in the new State (Article 128).

3. By the time in which this independent and constituent process began in Venezuela, the political and constitutional effects of the American (1776) and French (1789) Revolutions had begun to spread toward many of the Hispanic-American Colonies, directly influencing the drafting of the 1811 Constitution.[7] Consequently, as already mentioned, modern constitutionalism principles were adopted in Venezuela before the sanctioning of the March 1812 Cádiz Constitution of the Spanish

5. *See* Ángel F. Brice (ed.), *Las Constituciones Provinciales* (Caracas: Academia Nacional de la Historia, 1959); Allan R. Brewer-Carías, *La Constitución de la Provincia de Caracas de 31 de enero de 1812* (Caracas: Academia de Ciencias Politicas y Sociales, 2011).
6. *See* Juan Garrido R, *El Congreso Constituyente de Venezuela, Bicentenario del 5 de julio de 1811* (Caracas: Universidad Monteávila, 2010).
7. *See* Pedro Grases (Compilador), *El pensamiento político de la Emancipación Venezolana* (Caracas: Ediciones Congreso de la República, 1988); Tulio Chiossone, *Formación Jurídica de Venezuela en la Colonia y la República* (Caracas: UCV, 1980).

Monarchy.[8] Nonetheless, this Constitution, although not having had influence in the initial constitution-making process of Venezuela, had an important influence in other constitution-making processes held after 1820 in other former Spanish colonies of Latin America and in Italy and Portugal.[9]

Consequently, it can be said that Venezuela was the first country in constitutional history that, after the American and French Revolutions, sanctioned a modern constitution based on the principles of constitutional supremacy, sovereignty of the people, political representation and republicanism. An extended declaration of fundamental rights of Man and Society[10] that organized the State according to the principle of separation of powers with a system of checks and balances and the superiority of the law as an expression of the general will was also key to its formation. This has resulted in a presidential system of government and elected representatives to the senate and the representatives' chamber (*diputados*). The government was of a federal form, according to which the former colonial Provinces became federated sovereign states, within which the Constitution set forth the establishment of a local government system. The Judicial Power was integrated by judges imparting justice in the name of the nation with judicial review powers.

4. Since the 1811 Constitution, and during the last 200 years, the Venezuelan-independent State has been subjected to twenty-six Constitutions sanctioned successively in 1811, 1819, 1821, 1830, 1857, 1858, 1864, 1874, 1881, 1891, 1893, 1901, 1904, 1909, 1914, 1922, 1925, 1928, 1929, 1931, 1936, 1945, 1947, 1953, 1961 and 1999.[11] This excessive number of 'constitutions' was the product of the absence of the 'amendment' constitutional revision technique, so in their great majority, they were mere partial and punctual reforms generally provoked by circumstantial political factors. That is, this number of constitutions does not correspond to a similar number of fundamental political pacts originating new political regimes and forms of constitutional government. The fact has been, on the contrary, that in Venezuelan history, between 1811 and 2015, *four* great constitutional periods and political changes can be distinguished, each one distinct in its political characteristic, form of government, leadership and programmes.[12] Each of these periods developed according to a new leadership that assumed the government, reached

8. *See* Allan R. Brewer-Carías, *Los inicios del proceso constituyente Hispano y Americano, Caracas 1811 – Cádiz 1812* (Caracas: bid & co. Editor, 2012); Allan R. Brewer-Carías, *Sobre el constitucionalismo hispanoamericano pre-gaditano 1811–1812* (Caracas: Editorial Jurídica Venezolana, 2013) 25 et seq.
9. *See* Allan R. Brewer-Carías, *Reflexiones sobre la Revolución Norteamericana (1776), la Revolución Francesa (1789) y la Revolución Hispanoamericana (1810–1830) y sus aportes al constitucionalismo moderno* (Bogotá: Universidad Externado de Colombia, 2008), 204 et seq.
10. *See* Allan R. Brewer-Carías, *Las declaraciones de derechos del pueblo y del hombre de 1811* (Caracas: Academia de Ciencias Políticas y Sociales, 2011).
11. *See* the texts of all the Venezuelan Constitutions since 1811, in Ulises Picón Rivas, *Índice Constitucional de Venezuela* (Caracas, 1944); Luis Mariñas Otero, *Las Constituciones de Venezuela* (Madrid, 1965); Allan R. Brewer-Carías, *Las Constituciones de Venezuela*, 2 vols (Caracas: Academia de Ciencias Políticas y Sociales, 2008).
12. *See* Allan R. Brewer-Carías, *Historia Constitucional de Venezuela* (Caracas, 2 vils. Editorial Alfa, 2008). 2d ed. (Caracas: Colección Tratado de Derecho Constitucional, vol. I, Editorial Jurídica Venezolana, 2013).

exhaustion after entering into decay and inexorably arrived at a final crisis. This, in each case, needed the work of more than a generation in order to build and establish a new political project in lieu of the previous institutional collapsed framework.[13] Since 1999, a *fifth* constitutional period has been in the process of being conformed, after the approval of the currently in force 1999 Constitution, a period that, nonetheless, is still in the first phase of being shaped. The political crisis initiated in 1989, which provoked the collapse of the previous period, has not yet concluded.[14]

§1. First Constitutional Period (1811–1864): The Independent, Autonomous, Semi-Decentralized State

5. The *first* of these great political-constitutional periods in the history of the country is the one of the *Independent Semi-Decentralized State* established by the 'Federal Constitution for the Venezuelan States' of 21 December 1811 that lasted up to 1864, which was dominated by the generation that fought for independence from Imperial Spain. The defining political project that characterized this historical period was the effort to create a brand-new State on the former Spanish colonial territory,[15] organizing the government in a federal state with the former colonial Provinces integrated in 1777, for military purposes, in the General Captaincy of Venezuela. The territories of Venezuela, being very poor, had no other colonial integration and were under the general authority of two Viceroyalties (New Spain and Peru) and of two *Audiencias* (*Santo Domingo* and *Nueva Granada*) that were the most important instruments of colonial government. Consequently, the Captaincy General, created only thirty years before the Independence, was composed of highly autonomous and decentralized provincial entities developed under the Spanish Crown to govern these extremely isolated and poor provincial colonies. It was precise because of the dispersion and autonomy of the government and the territorial organization of these former Provinces that a federal constitutional system was chosen in 1811 to create the Venezuelan State.

13. *See* on the identification of these five political periods in Venezuelan history, in *Informe sobre la descentralización en Venezuela 1993, Memoria del Dr Allan R. Brewer-Carías, Ministro de Estado para la Descentralización (junio 1993–febrero1994)* (Caracas, 1994), 17 et seq.; and Allan R. Brewer Carías, *Instituciones Políticas y Constitucionales, vol. I, Evolución histórica del Estado* (Caracas, 1996); 'La conformación político-constitucional del Estado Venezolano', in *Las Constituciones de Venezuela, cit.*, vol. I, 23–526; and in *Historia Constitucional de Venezuela*, vol. I (Caracas: Editorial Alfa, 2008), 220 et seq.
14. *See* Allan R. Brewer-Carías, *Dismantling Democracy. The Chávez Authoritarian Experiment* (New York: Cambridge University Press, 2010); *La mentira como política de Estado. Crónica de una crisis política permanente: 1999–2015* (Caracas 2015); *La dictadura judicial y la perversión del Estado de derecho. El juez constitucional y la destrucción de la democracia en Venezuela* (Madrid, Editorial IUSTEL, 2017; *The Collapse of the Rule of Law and the Struggle for Democracy in Venezuela. Lectures and Essays (2015–2020),* (Miami Dade College, 2020); *La Constitución de plastilina y vandalismo constitucional. La ilegítima mutación de la Constitución por el Juez Constitucional al servicio del autoritarismo* (Caracas, Editrorial Jurídica Venezolana, 2022).
15. *See* Tomás Polanco, 'Interpretación jurídica de la Independencia', in *El Movimiento Emancipador de Hispanoamérica, Actas y Ponencias* (Caracas: Academia Nacional de la Historia, 1961). *See* the relevant text in *Textos oficiales de la Primera República de Venezuela*, vol. I (Caracas: Academia Nacional de la Historia, 1959), 105.

However, it must be borne in mind that by the time of the independence of Venezuela and the adoption of the republican federal form of government, the Republic had already been suppressed in France (1808), and no other form of government, different to the Monarchical regime against which the revolution of independence was conducted, could inspire the framing of the new State except the new Republican Federal one that at that time had begun to be shaped in North America, allowing former colonies to gain independence within a new State. The 'Confederation de Venezuela' was therefore based on a scheme taken from the experience of the United States in order to try to unify territories that had never before been united, except militarily during the previous thirty years through the Captaincy General. As aforementioned, in all other aspects, the Venezuelan provinces experienced no other form of integration, remaining isolated provinces, virtually without communication with one another.

6. This constitutional period developed between 1811 and 1864 through various stages marked by constitutional changes: first, with the Constitution of the primary process of constitution building of the State, the 1811 Constitution, that as aforementioned was preceded by Provincial Constitutions adopted by each Province between 1810 and 1811, configuring what was called the 'First Republic',[16] as a civic Republic, ruled by civilians until the military Spanish invasion in 1812;[17] second, the constitution-making process that developed since 1813 during the liberation wars against Spain, influenced by the ideas of Simón Bolívar, the Liberator and political and military leader of the country's struggle for liberation and independence;[18] third, with the 1819 Constitution, adopted after a prolonged seven years wars against another important expeditionary Spanish Army that was sent in 1814 to crush the rebellion, called the *Angostura* Constitution, drafted by Simón Bolívar himself;[19] fourth, with the Constitution of 1821, the first Constitution of the 'Colombian' State formed by the Venezuelan territories and those of the former provinces of the *Virreinato de Nueva Granada*, following the proposals made by Simón Bolívar;[20] and fifth, with the 1830 Constitution that re-established the Venezuelan State

16. *See* Caracciolo Parra Pérez, *Historia de la Primera República de Venezuela*, vol. I (Caracas: Academia Nacional de la Historia, 1959).
17. *See* Allan R. Brewer-Carías, Enrique Viloria Vera y Asdrúbal Aguiar (Coordinadores), *La Independencia y el Estado constitucional en Venezuela: como obra de civiles (19 de abril de 1811, 5 de julio de 1811, 2 de diciembre de 1811)*, (Caracas, Editorial Jurídica Venezolana, 2018); and Allan R. Brewer-Carías 'La independencia de Venezuela y el inicio del constitucionalismo hispanoamericano en 1810–1811, como obra de civiles, y el desarrollo del militarismo a partir de 1812, en ausencia de régimen constitucional', *Revista de Historia Constitucional,* 14 (Oviedo, Revista Electrónica, file:///C:/Users/Allan%20Brewer/Downloads/Dialnet-LaIndependenciaDeVenezuelaYElInicioDelConstitucion-4393208%20(1).pdf 2013), 405–424.
18. *See* Simón Bolívar, *Escritos Fundamentales* (Caracas: Monte Ávila Editores, 1982); *Proclamas y Discursos del Libertador* (Caracas, 1939); *Los Proyectos Constitucionales de Simón Bolívar, El Libertador 1813–1830* (Caracas, 1999); Pedro Grases & Tomás Polanco (eds), *Simón Bolívar y la Ordenación del Estado en 1813* (Caracas, 1979).
19. *See* Pedro Grases (ed.), *El Libertador y la Constitución de Angostura de 1819* (Caracas, 1970).
20. *See* Allan R. Brewer-Carías, *La Constitución de la República de Colombia de 30 de agosto de 1821. producto de la unión de los pueblos de Venezuela y de la Nueva Granada. Sus antecedentes y condicionantes* (Caracas. Editorial Jurídica Venezolana, Bogotá, Editorial Temis, 2021).

separated from the State of Nueva Granada that the same year adopted its own Constitution. This 1830 Constitution was the one with the longest period of continuous enforcement (1830–1857) with two reforms made to it in 1857 and in 1858, particularly because of the struggle between the central and provincial governments.[21]

7. The most distinguished trend of this first constitutional period (beginning with the 1811 Constitution) was the configuration of a more or less decentralized State resulting from a 'federative pact' entered by sovereign and independent provinces after having also approved their own provincial constitutions. During this first period (except during the wars of liberation), the dominant pattern of the government was the important local-federated power which was even designed in 1830 against the ideas of Simón Bolívar, with the political power located at the Province-Cities level with a very weak central government. This feature, at the beginning of the institution building of the country, initiated its also long process of institutional disarticulation, mainly provoked by the regional *caudillos* that governed the country during the nineteenth century. This pattern was only eliminated at the beginning of the twentieth century when the *Caudillista* federation was definitively buried.

8. Also in this period, the bitter war fought since 1813 to liberate from Spain the territories of the new State that were invaded and consolidate the independence (1813–1821), was not only a political one but a social one between the dominant Creole white population that had control over the local government and the economy, and the lower working classes including the former slaves instigated by the caudillos supporting the Royalist forces. After changing the pattern of the war through extreme measures (*Decreto de Guerra a Muerte*), gaining control of the territory, and having sanctioned the 1819 Constitution in Angostura, Simón Bolivar proposed the conformation of a great State integrating the territories of what today is Venezuela, Colombia, Panama and Ecuador. In this framework, Venezuela disappeared as an independent State up to 1830 and was a Department of so-called Great Colombia.

9. The separation of Venezuela from that great State took place in 1830, in a secessionist process lead by José Antonio Páez, one of the distinguished military leaders of the independence, which coincided with the death of Bolívar. It was a political reaction of the military *caudillos* of Venezuela against the centralized government of Bogotá, provoking the sanctioning of the 1830 Constitution of Venezuela, which was the result of a central-federal pact. The resulting 'Centralized Federation' (*see infra* paragraphs 200 et seq.) has been one of the main trends of the subsequent constitutional history of the country.

10. Thus, from the beginning of constitutionalism in 1811, in one way or another, the federal form of the State and the pendulum movement between centralization and decentralization have marked the entire political history of Venezuela, even in current times. With such form, the regional political *caudillismo* found its

---

21. *See* Eleonora Gabaldón, *La Constitución de 1830 (El debate parlamentario y la opinión de la prensa)* (Caracas: Instituto Biblioteca Nacional, ed. Turnes, 1991).

place in the Constitution, and even if in the years after 1819, the term 'federal' disappeared from the constitutional texts, the same political trend of regional and local autonomy continued assuring the authority of the military *caudillos*. Thus, towards the end of the decade of the 1850s, the struggle between the central power, which had itself been built by the regional leaders, and regional Powers, provoked a rupture of the constitutional system culminating in the Federal Wars of 1858–1863, or *Guerras Federales*.[22]

11. The 1830 Constitution was reformed in 1857 in a constitution-making process that did not satisfy the regional political claims against the central government that had begun to take shape during the previous two decades. This provoked a *coup d'état*, the first in Venezuelan constitutional history, that led to the sanction in 1858 of a new Constitution by a Constituent Assembly with more federal elements than the previous one.[23] As has been the general pattern in Venezuelan history, these reforms were a prelude to the collapse of the constitutional order.

After these constitutional reforms of 1857 and 1858, in the midst of the war, it appeared that there was no other solution to the political crisis than to bring out one of the leaders of the independence war who had been present and active in the political life of the country since Independence and had completely dominated it after Bolívar. This was José Antonio Páez, who was called in as the 'saviour' of the country. Although invested in dictatorial powers, the reality is that he did not last as President for more than a few months. The first political period of Venezuelan constitutional history definitively concluded with the Federal Wars, which like the independence war, were also wars of social character, which left profound consequences in the political history of the country. From the political point of view, it resulted in the triumph of regional and local powers regarding central government, being the federation, the political form used to reaffirm the power of the regional *caudillos* and the politico-federal disintegration of the Republic. Also, from the social point of view, the wars gave rise to a second social revolution, in continuation of the one that took place with the war of independence, but still more anarchic than the latter, even provoking the physical disappearance of the land owner class, under popular resentment, but giving rise to social equalitarianism that was later reaffirmed by the *mestizaje*.

§2. SECOND CONSTITUTIONAL PERIOD (1864–1901): THE FEDERAL STATE AND THE UNITED STATES OF VENEZUELA

12. With the end of the independent semi-decentralized state government period, in the aftermath of the federal wars, a new political cycle began with a new form of government, a new leadership, and a new political programme, giving rise to the period of the *Federal State* (1864–1901). The change was a radical one, although a few years earlier, the new leaders of the *Federación* were only hardly recognized as

22. *See* José S. Rodríguez, *Contribución al Estudio de la Guerra Federal en Venezuela*, 2 vols (Caracas, 1960); Emilio Navarro, *La Revolución Federal, 1859 a 1863* (Caracas, 1963).
23. *See* Eleonora Gabaldón, *La Convención de Valencia (la idea federal), 1858* (Caracas, 1988).

local leaders, with no national projections. Moreover, Antonio Guzmán Blanco himself, who dominated this period but was not seen at that time as the leader, was called to command the second great constitutional historical period as he effectively did, defining the cast of national politics from 1863 up to the beginning of the twentieth century.[24]

In 1863, through a constitution-making process developed by a Constituent Assembly,[25] the remains of the prior state system had vanished and the new order was being built, formally covered with the form of a federal State based on an extreme system of territorial distribution of public power. This system was based on autonomous federal entities or states with their own governments elected by universal and direct suffrage and confined the 'National Power' to a Federal District, a neutral territory that was 'temporarily' placed in Caracas.

13. The Constitution of 14 April 1864 established the 'United States of Venezuela', 'reuniting' twenty provinces that declared themselves 'independent', recognizing their 'autonomy' reciprocally, and adopting the denomination of 'States'.[26] Antonio Guzmán Blanco was elected President of the Republic, acting as *primus inter pares* regarding the regional *caudillos* in a political system initially controlled by the latter. In the first years of his tenure, among other governing institutions, Guzmán Blanco made use of 'Conferences of Plenipotentiaries' which were nothing more than formal meetings of the regional *caudillos* in Caracas to resolve common political problems of national scope. He also tried to define a 'bolivarian doctrine' in order to attain, through the cult of Bolivar, some sort of political unity to his regime (*see infra* paragraphs 17, 35, 53, 262, 357). The country continued to be very poor, with a large public debt, and increasingly subjected to the new autocracy installed in the Central Power led by Guzmán Blanco, named the 'Great Civilizator'.[27] He established the complete separation between the Catholic Church and the State regarding public affairs (*see infra* paragraphs 118 et seq.) After twice reforming the Constitution, in 1874 and in 1881, the latter called the 'Swiss Constitution' because of the creation of a 'Federal Council',[28] mainly tending to accommodate it to his way of exercising power, he converted many of the traditional states (former Provinces) into 'Sections' of larger new states with aggregated territories, one of them called 'Great Guzman Blanco State'. In 1881 he retired to France, progressively contributing to the deterioration and weakening of his own authority.

---

24. *See* Germán Carrera Damas, *Formulación definitiva del Proyecto Nacional: 1870–1900* (Caracas: Cuadernos Lagoven, 1988).
25. *See* Rafael Lugo Felice, 'Proceso Constituyente de 1863', in *Procesos Constituyentes y Reformas Constitucionales en la Historia de Venezuela: 1811–1999*, ed. Elena Plaza y Ricardo Combellas (Coord.), vol. I (Caracas: UCV, 2005), 225–264.
26. *See* J. Gabaldón Márquez (ed.), *Documentos Políticos y Actos Ejecutivos y Legislativos de la Revolución Federal* (Caracas, 1959).
27. *See* R.A. Rondón Márquez, *Guzmán Blanco. El Autócrata Civilizador o Parábola de los Partidos Políticos Tradicionales en la Historia de Venezuela*, 2 vols (Caracas, 1944).
28. *See* Elide Rivas, 'El proceso constituyente y la Constitución de 1881. Un federalismo a la Suiza', in *Procesos Constitu yentes y Reformas Constitucionales en la Historia de Venezuela: 1811–1999*, ed. Elena Plaza y Ricardo Combellas (Coord.) vol. I (Caracas: UCV, 2005), 317–339.

14. The last decade of the nineteenth century was also marked by constitutional reforms in 1892 and 1893, initiating a frequent historical constitutional change recurrence of seeking to extend the tenure of the President of the Republic. However, the political crisis derived from the interminable struggles between the Central Powers and the regional *caudillos* could not be stemmed by just constitutional reforms, particularly because of the general degradation of the political system, which eventually provoked its collapse.

This period came to an end with the *Revolución Liberal Restauradora* (23 October 1899) led by Cirpiano Castro, one of the Andean *caudillos*,[29] which originated in defence of the sovereignty of states and as a reaction against the decision of the Congress to give the National Executive the power to provisionally appoint its Governors, once the traditional territories of the traditional states were restored.

§3. Third Constitutional Period (1901–1945): The Centralized Autocratic State

15. This Liberal Restoration Revolution of 1899, launched in defence of federalism, ironically consolidated Cipriano Castro into power as President of the Republic, by means of the approval of a new Constitution by a Constituent Assembly in 1901 which reversed all of the remaining general trends of a federal State.[30] During his tenure, he resisted the attempts of European Navies (Great Britain, Germany and Italy) to blockade the Venezuelan coast seeking payment of debts by the country (*see infra* paragraphs 111, 347). His Vice President, Juan Vicente Gómez, was his revolutionary companion, who at the beginning of the twentieth century led the last war against the remaining regional *caudillos*, consolidating the hegemonic presence of the Andean rulers in the central national government. He concluded with the traditional nineteen century Liberal and Conservative political parties and with the basis of the federal form of the State. Gómez also initiated the process of political integration of the country after forming, for the first time in the country's history, a National Army substituting the former traditional States' militias, and got rid of Castro, using for such purpose a ruling of the Federal and Cassation Court accusing Castro of criminal offences.[31] He controlled State and military power from 1908 up to his death in 1935, consolidating the new political period of the *Centralized Autocratic State,* which finished in 1945.[32]

---

29. *See* Domingo A. Rangel, *Los Andinos en el Poder* (Caracas, 1964); Ramón J. Velásquez, *La Caída del Liberalismo Amarillo, Tiempo y Drama de Antonio Paredes* (Caracas, 1973).
30. *See* Mariano Picón Salas, *Los días de Cipriano Castro* (Caracas: Barquisimeto, 1955); Ángel Zerpa Aponte, 'El primer proceso constituyente del Siglo XX: La Constituyente de 1901', in *Procesos Constituyentes y Reformas Constitucionales en la Historia de Venezuela: 1811–1999*, ed. Elena Plaza y Ricardo Combellas (Coord.), vol. II (Caracas: UCV, 2005), 419–449.
31. *See* R.J. Velásquez, *La caída del Liberalismo Amarillo. Tiempo y Drama de Antonio Paredes* (Caracas, 1973), 206 et seq., and 242 et seq.
32. *See* Ramón J. Velásquez (Director), *El Pensamiento Político Venezolano en el Siglo XX*, 10 vols (Caracas, 1983); Ángel Ziemn, *El Gomecismo y la formación del Ejército Militar* (Caracas, 1979); Allan R. Brewer-Carías, 'El desarrollo institucional del Estado Centralizado en Venezuela (1899–1935) y sus proyecciones contemporáneas', in *Revista de Estudios de la Vida Local y*

16. During this period, the true integration among the regions of the nation began, and the Nation State was consolidated, a process which had occurred in many Latin American nations far earlier, towards the mid-nineteenth century. After the initial 1901 Constitution, various constitutional reforms took place in 1904, 1909, 1914 and 1922, ending this first part of the period with the 1925 Constitution, in which the autocratic centralized State was consolidated, although without abandoning the federal framework. This latter Constitution was subsequently also reformed, due to Gómez political and military circumstantial motives, in 1928, 1929 and 1931, and after his death, in 1936 and 1945, without changing substantially the constitutional provisions regarding the progressive centralization of State powers at the national level in all its scopes: political, military, fiscal, administrative and legislative. In this task, the dictatorship of Gómez was decisive, inspired by the authoritarian idea of the 'necessary guardian' (*Gendarme Necesario*),[33] fed with the new public income wealth that precisely began to pour into the public coffers due to the beginning of the oil exploitation in the country, through concessions given to foreign companies.

17. After the death of Gómez, with a constitutional reform sanctioned by Congress in 1936, his Defence Minister, Eleazar López Contreras, succeeded him in the Presidency of the Republic, and a gradual process of transition from autocracy to democracy began, which was continued within the Presidency of Isaías Medina Angarita, also Lopez's Minister of Defence. López Contreras was the other political ruler in the country's history that profited from the 'Bolivarian' doctrine in order to give some basis to his policies (*see supra* paragraph 13; *infra* paragraphs 35, 53, 269, 263, 357, 557).

This period witnessed the birth of workers' and mass movements, and of political organizations that initiated the contemporary political parties which had originated in the student movements of 1928.[34] Nonetheless, after finishing centralizing power and progressively finishing with the federal vestiges, except for the use of the term, eventually, the Andean political leadership did not fully understand the changes that had been taking place in the Venezuelan society, and also in the world as a consequence of the World Wars, particularly regarding the general democratizing tendencies. In this regard, for instance, the two successors of Juan Vicente Gómez failed to understand that in 1945 and after the Second World War, direct elections, and secret and universal suffrage were essential elements in the consolidation of the democracy that was beginning to be born.

Autonómica (Madrid, 1985), Nos 227, 483–514; and Nos 228, 695–726; and Naudy Suárez Figueroa (ed.), *Programas Políticos Venezolanos de la Primera Mitad del siglo XX* (Caracas, 1977).

33. *See* Laureano Vallenilla Lanz, *Cesarismo Democrático. Estudios sobre las bases sociológicas de la Constitución efectiva de Venezuela* (Caracas, 1952); *El sentido americano de la democracia. Cesarismo democrático y otros textos* (Caracas: Biblioteca Ayacucho, 1991).

34. *See* Vicente Magallanes, *Los Partidos Políticos en la Evolución Histórica Venezolana* (Caracas, 1973).

The Constitution was finally reformed in 1945,[35] but despite the clamour of new political actors, who were the products of nascent syndicalism and the democratic opening, direct elections and universal suffrage was not established. Instead, the Constitution sanctioned only a limited form of 'universal' suffrage in which women were excluded from all national elections and restricted to municipal voting, and the indirect system for the election of the National President was left unchanged. Such a timid democratic opening was not sufficient; so despite the extremely important legal reforms promoted by Medina to organize the mining and petroleum industries and ensure that the oil concessions were really taxed, and despite the fact that Venezuela was a country more open to the world on the eve of the wave of contemporary democratization that followed the Second World War, the *Medinista* leadership still failed to see the significance of the need for a direct and universal presidential election for the succession of Medina Angarita. Unfortunately, here again, as in so many instances in history, the incomprehension of the historical juncture blinded the leadership, which was lost in trying to impose succession by an Andean candidate through the three-tiered system of indirect Congressional elections, while being overshadowed by López Contreras who threatened them with his own candidacy.

18. In the 1945 constitutional reform, the key components of the regime remained untouched, with the result that the constitutional text together with the remaining of authoritarian political system initiated at the beginning of the twentieth century, lasted only a few more months until the October Revolution of 1945. This was led by the social-democratic party, *Acción Democratica*, beginning the democratization process not only of the State but also of society; and sweeping away the autocratic regime with its leadership and the generation that undertook its political programme at the beginning of the twentieth century. As it can be clearly deduced from the Constituent Act of the Revolutionary *Junta,* the principal constitutional idea motivating the Revolution, among its other causes, was the institution of secret, direct and universal suffrage.

§4. Fourth Constitutional Period (1945–1999): The Democratic Centralized State of Parties

19. In 1945, and as a consequence of the democratic revolution that followed, a new political period was opened, one of the *Democratic Centralized State of Parties* that found its foundations in the Constitution of 5 July 1947, sanctioned by a Constituent Assembly.[36] This Constitution laid the foundations of the democratic regime that lasted until 1999, based on two fundamental pillars: the democratic

35. *See* Linda Núñez, 'El reforma constitucional del 1945', in *Procesos Constituyentes y Reformas Constitucionales en la Historia de Venezuela: 1811–1999*, ed. Elena Plaza y Ricardo Combellas (Coord.), vol. II (Caracas: UCV, 2005), 563–585.

36. *See* Ingrid Jiménez Monsalve, 'Asamblea Nacional Constituyente 1946–1947. Logros y fracasos de un programa político', in *Procesos Constituyentes y Reformas Constitucionales en la Historia de Venezuela: 1811–1999*, ed. Elena Plaza y Ricardo Combellas (Coord.), vol. II (Caracas: UCV, 2005), 587–621.

regime through political parties but based on a dominant party; and a centralized constitutional structure of the State. The Constitution was only in force for one year (1947–1948) when the system was broken by a military coup, which led to one decade of dictatorship conducted by General Marcos Pérez Jimenez (1948–1958), who promoted in 1953 the sanctioning of a new Constitution[37] that eliminated the denomination itself of the State as 'United States of Venezuela'.

20. After trying to be re-elected in 1957, Pérez Jiménez was overthrown by a new democratic revolution that took place in 1958, restoring the democratic system again. That year the leaders of the political parties signed a very important political pact known as '*Pacto de Punto Fijo*',[38] which formed the basis for the restoration of democracy in the country. Unfortunately, a decade of military dictatorship had to be suffered in order for the political leadership to arrive at the conclusion that a pluralistic system of parties and political compromises and a consensus was needed in order to establish democracy; and for Rómulo Betancourt,[39] who was the leader of the failed October 1945 Revolution, to admit and understand that democracy could not and cannot function on the basis of the hegemony of a single party excluding all other political groups. The *Pacto de Punto Fijo* of 1958 was the profoundly distilled product of the painful experience of militarism of the 1950s, and its focused objective was precisely to implant a democracy that would amply bear fruit in the following decades.[40]

21. This Pact conditioned the drafting of the 1961 Constitution, which has been the one with the longest term in force in the country from 1961 to 1999.[41] In this Constitution, the main role was given to the political parties who monopolized political representation, political participation, and State power, following the principles of the electoral system of proportional representation (d'Hondt model), which

37. *See* Andrés Stambouli, *Crisis Política Venezuela 1945–1958* (Caracas, 1980); José Rodríguez Iturbe, *Crónica de la Década Militar* (Caracas, 1984).
38. *See* Juan Carlos Rey, *El sistema de partidos venezolano 1830–1999* (Caracas 2015), and 'El sistema de partidos venezolano', in *Problemas socio políticos de América Latina* (Caracas, 1980), 255 a 338; Naudy Suárez Figueroa, *Punto Fijo y otros puntos. Los grandes acuerdos políticos de 1958*, Serie Cuadernos de Ideas Políticas No. 1 (Caracas: Fundación Rómulo Betancourt, 2006); Allan R. Brewer-Carías, 'El "Pacto de Punto Fijo" de 1958 como punto de partida para el establecimiento y consolidación del sistema democrático y del Estado constitucional de derecho en Venezuela' in *Libro Homenaje a Humberto Romero Muci* (Caracas, Academia de Ciencias Políticas y Sociales, 2022).
39. *See* R. Betancourt, *La Revolución Democrática en Venezuela* (Caracas, 1968); Roberto J. Alexander, *The Venezuela Democratic Revolution. A Profile of the Regime of Rómulo Betancourt* (New Jersey, 1964).
40. *See* D.H. Blank, *Politics in Venezuela* (1973); Manuel Rachadell, *Evolución del Estado venezolano 1958–2015. De la conciliación de intereses al populismo autoritario* (Caracas, Ediorial Jurídica Venezolana, 2015).
41. *See La Constitución de 1961 y la evolución constitucional de Venezuela*, 2 vols (Caracas: Ediciones del Congreso de la República, 1972–1973); *Estudios sobre la Constitución. Libro Homenaje a Rafael Caldera*, 4 vols (Caracas: UCV, 1980); and Allan Brewer-Carías, La Constitución y sus Enmiendas (Caracas: Editorual Jurídica Venezolana, 1991).

remained unaltered until after the electoral reform of 1993.[42] The resulting political project conditioned the life of the generations that led the country during the last four decades of the twentieth century, based on the compromise to establish and maintain a democratic government, and to promote the democratization of the society and of the economy. During the period, the country lived under a democratic representative regime, with a succession of nine Presidents who, for the first time in Venezuelan political history, were all elected by universal, direct and secret suffrage.

22. Regarding the form of the State, the federal form was kept, but covered a very centralized state in which the states were kept but lacked effective political power, due to the fact that all power; political, economic, legislative, taxing, administrative and labour, was concentrated at the national level of government. This centralism of the state was accompanied by other centralisms, that of the political parties, internally organized in a 'centralized democratic' scheme, similar to the one developed in the labour unions, which became another fundamental element of the system.[43] Nonetheless, the Constitution, due to its democratic foundations, expressly established the possibility to promote the decentralization of the Federation by empowering the National Assembly to revert the centralization framework of the country, by transferring powers and competencies from the national level to the states. At the beginning of the political crisis of the 1990s, that process began through the sanctioning of the Organic Law on the Transfer, Distribution and Decentralization of competencies among public entities,[44] which began to be implemented.[45] Unfortunately, since 1994 and particularly after 1999, the decentralization efforts were abandoned (*see infra* paragraphs 200 et seq.).

23. The 1961 Constitution, when enacted, was one of the more advanced of its time, having served as a model in many aspects of later Latin American Constitutions. As aforementioned, its text was the result of a consensus attained among the various political actors, being considered an authentic political pact of the Venezuelan society, conceived by the leaders of a generation that at the time had more than two decades of political struggle, and in a historical moment in which the spirit of unity and concord prevailed, resulting from the overthrow of the Perez Jimenez dictatorship.

During the last four decades of the twentieth century, political parties dominated the political scene. This meant that when they entered, during the 1990s, into the

42. *See* Allan R. Brewer-Carías, *Cambio Político y Reforma del Estado en Venezuela*, ed. Tecnos (Madrid, 1975), 178 et seq.

43. *See* Allan R. Brewer-Carías, *El Estado. Crisis y Reforma* (Caracas: Academia de Ciencias Políticas y Sociales, 1983); *El Estado Incomprendido. Reflexiones sobre el sistema político y su reforma* (Caracas: Vadell hermanos, 1985); *Problemas del Estado de Partidos* (Caracas: Editorial Jurídica Venezolana, 1989); *Cinco siglos de Historia y un País en Crisis* (Caracas: Academia de Ciencias Políticas y Sociales y Comisión Presidencial del V Centenario de Venezuela, 1998), 95 a 117.

44. The Law was sanctioned in 1989. *See* Allan R. Brewer-Carías et al., *Leyes y reglamentos para la Descentralización Política de la Federación* 94 (Caracas, 1990). *See* in *Gaceta Oficial* No. 39.140 of 17 Mar. 2009.

45. *See Informe sobre la descentralización en Venezuela 1993. Informe del Ministro de Estado para la Descentralización* (Caracas, 1994).

profound political crisis that affected their leadership,[46] particularly because they failed to understand the democratic advances they helped to complete, the political vacuum they left provoked the take-over of the State and its institutions by an authoritarian and militaristic government. This government was led by an anti-party leader that appeared in the middle of the political vacuum, the late Hugo Chávez Frias, a former Lieutenant-Colonel who led a military attempt of a *coup d'état* in 1992. Chávez was elected in 1998, promoting the collapse of the democratic political system designed in 1958, and tried to begin a new political system that nonetheless is still in the process of being conformed, characterized by a status of permanent *coup d'Etat* given by all the Branches of Government[47] (*see infra* paragraphs 26, 249 et seq.).

§5. The Beginning of a Fifth Constitutional Period after 1999: The Centralized, Military and Authoritarian State

24. The main political offer Chávez made during the 1998 presidential campaign, besides the anti-party slogans and the promise of change, was the convening of a Constituent Assembly in order to 'redound' the State and to sanction a new Constitution with a new democratic and participatory order, in substitution of the 1961 Constitution and of the *Pacto de Punto Fijo* framework (*see supra* paragraph 20; *infra* paragraph 186). For the sanctioning of the new Constitution, after bitter political and legal disputes, a National Constituent Assembly, not established in 1961 as a constitutional review procedure, was convened and elected in 1999, exclusively promoted by the new President of the Republic. This became the main institutional tool he used to materialize a complete take-over of all the branches of government of the State and to reinforce the centralization of the Federation. According to the then-in-force 1961 Constitution, the only way to elect such Assembly in 1999 was after a previous constitutional reform incorporating it in the Constitution, unless a constitutional judicial interpretation of the 1961 Constitution allowed the election. The latter was precisely what the Supreme Court of Justice did

46. *See* Pedro Guevara, *Estado v. Democracia* (Caracas, 1997); Miriam Kornblith, *Venezuela en los 90. Crisis de la Democracia* (Caracas, 1998); and Allan R. Brewer-Carías, *El Estado, Crisis y Reforma* (Caracas: Academia de Ciencias Políticas y Sociales, 1983); *El Estado Incomprendido. Reflexiones sobre el sistema político y su reforma* (Caracas, 1985); *La crisis de las instituciones: responsables y salidas Revista de la Facultad de Ciencias Jurídicas y Políticas*, No. 64 (1985), 129–155; *Problemas del Estado de Partidos* (Caracas: Editorial Jurídica Venezolana,1989); and 'Reflexiones sobre la crisis del sistema político, sus salidas democráticas y la convocatoria a una Constituyente', in *Los Candidatos Presidenciales ante la Academia* (Caracas: Academia de Ciencias Políticas y Sociales, 1998), 11 a 66.

47. *See*, for instance, Allan R. Brewer-Carías, *Golpe de Estado y proceso constituyente* (México, Instituto de Investigaciones Jurídicas, 2002); *Golpe de Estado Constituyente, Estado Constitucional y Democracia*, Caracas: Editorial Jurídica Venezolana, Colección Tratado de Derecho Constitucional, vol. VIII, 2015; *El golpe a la democracia dado por la Sala Constitucional* (Caracas: Editorial Jurídica Venezolana, 2014); 'El golpe de Estado dado en diciembre de 2014, con la inconstitucional designación de las altas autoridades del poder público', *Revista de Derecho Público*, 140 (Caracas: Editorial Jurídica Venezolana, 2014); Asdrúbal Aguiar (Compilador), *El Golpe de Enero en Venezuela (Documentos y testimonios para la historia)*, (Caracas, Editorial Jurídica Venezolana, 2013).

in January 1999, although in a very ambiguous way,[48] trying to resolve the then-existing dilemma between popular sovereignty willing to be expressed and constitutional supremacy. It eventually decided in favour of the former.[49]

25. The Constituent Assembly was then elected in July 1999 after a consultative referendum that took place in April 1999, which was completely controlled by Chávez supporters with more than 95% of its seats. This method of the constitution-making process was not the first of its kind in Venezuelan constitutional history. After the two initial ones creating the independent and autonomous State of Venezuela (1811 and 1830), seven other constitution-making processes were carried out in 1858, 1863, 1893, 1901, 1914, 1946 and 1953 through Constituent Assemblies or Constituent Congresses, but in each case, as a consequence of a de facto rejection of the existing constitution, through a *coup d'état*, a revolution, or a civil war.

The constitution-making process of 1999, in contrast, had a peculiarity that made it different from all the previous ones in Venezuelan history, in the sense that it was not the result of a de facto rejection of the 1961 Constitution, through a revolution, a war or a *coup d'état.* Rather it had its origin in a democratic process, and without involving a de facto rupture of the previous political regime,[50] it eventually resulted in the 'death of the Constitution'.[51]

The process took place in the context of a severe political crisis that was affecting the functioning of the democratic regime's centralized political parties established in 1958, resulting from the lack of its evolution. That is why the call for the referendum consulting the people on the establishment of the Constituent National Assembly, as expressed in the February 1999 Decree issued by the President, intended to ask the people their opinion on a Constituent National Assembly 'aimed at transforming the State and creating a new legal order that allows the effective functioning of a social and participative democracy'. That was the formal *raison d'être* of the constitutional process of 1999, and that is why, with few exceptions, it would have been difficult to find anyone in the country who could have disagreed with those stated purposes.

26. The Constituent Assembly, far from dedicating itself to writing off the new Constitution, was the main tool the newly elected President had, in order to assault and control all the branches of government, violating the same 1961 Constitution

---

48. *See* Allan R. Brewer-Carías, 'La configuración judicial del proceso constituyente en Venezuela de 1999 o de cómo el guardián de la Constitución abrió el camino para su violación y para su propia extinción', in *Revista de Derecho Público*, No. 77–80 (Caracas: Editorial Jurídica Venezolana, 1999), 453–514. *See* the text of the Supreme Court rulings in the same *Revista*
49. *See* Allan R. Brewer-Carías, 'El desequilibrio entre soberanía popular y supremacía constitucional y la salida constituyente en Venezuela en 1999', in *Revista Anuario Iberoamericano de Justicia Constitucional, No. 3 1999* (Madrid: Centro de Estudios Políticos y Constitucionales, 2000), 31–56.
50. *See* Allan R. Brewer-Carías, 'On the making process and the 1999 Constitution in Venezuela, en el Symposium on "Challenges to Fragile Democracies in the Americas: Legitimacy and Accountability"', *Texas International Law Journal* 36 (Austin: University of Texas at Austin, 2001): 333–338.
51. *See also* Alessandro Pece, 'Morte di una Costituzione' in *Giurisprudenza Costituzionale*, XVIV Fasc. 2 1999 (Milano, Giuffrè Editore, 1999, pp. 154–155; Allan R. Brewer-Carías (editor), *La muerte de una Constitución. El proceso constituyente de 1999 desencadenado por dos sentencias de la Corte Suprema* (Caracas, Editorial Jurídica Venezolana, 2022).

whose interpretation helped to create it. Consequently, the elected Constituent Assembly technically gave a *coup d'état,*[52] unfortunately with the consent and complicity of the former Supreme Court of Justice, which, as it always happens in these illegitimate institutional complicity cases, was inexorably the first victim of the authoritarian government which it had helped to grab power. Just a few months later, in December 1999, that Supreme Court was erased from the institutional scene.

However, unfortunately, Chavez did not formally conceive the constitutional process conducted by the National Assembly as an instrument of conciliation aimed at reconstructing the democratic system and assuring good governance. That would have required the political commitment of all components of society and the participation of all sectors of society in the design of a new, functioning democracy, which did not occur. The constitutional process of 1999, on the contrary, served to facilitate the total take-over of State power by a new political group that crushed all the others, including the then-existing political parties. As a result, almost all of the opportunities for inclusion and public participation vanished, and the constitution-making process became an endless *coup d'état* when the Constituent Assembly, elected in July of 1999, began violating the existing Constitution of 1961 by intervening and assuming all branches of government, over which it had no power, according to the referendum mandate that created the Assembly. The Constituent Assembly also intervened in the federated states without any legitimate authority by eliminating their Legislative Assemblies.

27. The general result of the 1999 constitution-making process[53] was its failure as an instrument for political reconciliation, and the stated democratic purposes of the process were not accomplished. No effective reform of the State was accomplished, except for the purpose of authoritarian institution building, and for the election of a populist government that has concentrated all branches of government and crushed political pluralism. Thus, if it is true that political changes of great importance were made, some of them have contributed to the aggravation of the factors that provoked the crisis in the first place. New political actors assumed power, but far from implementing a democratic conciliation policy, they have accentuated the differences among Venezuelans, worsening political polarization, and making conciliation increasingly difficult. The seizure of power which characterized the process has opened new wounds, making social and political rivalries worse than they

52. *See* Allan R. Brewer-Carías, Golpe de Estado y proceso constituyente en Venezuela (Mexico, Guayaquil: Universidad Nacional Autónoma de México, 2002, 2006).

53. *See* Allan R. Brewer-Carías, 'The 1999 Venezuelan Constitution-Making Process as an Instrument for Framing the development of an Authoritarian Political Regime', in Laura E. Miller (Editor), *Framing the State in Times of Transition. Case Studies in Constitution Making,* (Washington, United States Institute of Peace Press, 2010), pp. 505–531; 'Constitution Making in Defraudation of the Constitution and Authoritarian Government in Defraudation of Democracy. The Recent Venezuelan Experience', *Lateinamerika Analysen* 19, No. 1 (2008), GIGA, German Institute of Global and Area Studies, Institute of Latin American Studies, Hamburg 2008, 119–142; *Asamblea Constituyente y Proceso Constituyente 1999, Colección Tratado de Derecho Constitucional*, Tomo VI, (Caracas, Fundación de Derecho Público, Editorial Jurídica Venezolana, 2013).

have been for more than a century. Despite Venezuela's extraordinary oil wealth during the first years of the twenty-first century, the social problems of the country have increased.

28. The violations of the 1961 Constitution that continued to be in force at the time the National Constituent assembly was elected were subsequently followed by the violation of the new 1999 Constitution voted on November 1999 by the same Constituent Assembly, and approval by referendum was held on 15 December 1999.[54] The violation began on 22 December 1999, a week later, when the Constituent Assembly enacted a 'Transitional Constitutional Regime' Decree, which was not authorized in the new Constitution, and which was not submitted to, nor approved by, popular vote.[55] It was that extra-constitutional regime which allowed the Constituent Assembly to continue the endless *coup d'état* initiated a few months earlier, affecting the separations of powers, and allowing the new National Assembly elected in 2000 to legislate outside the constitutional framework.

The final result of that 1999 constitution-making process was the omission of provisions in the new Constitution to undertake the democratic changes that were most needed in Venezuela, namely, the effective separation of powers, the political decentralization of the Federation and the reinforcement of states and municipal political powers.[56]

Nonetheless, and in spite of these absences of democratic reforms, in 1999, a new constitutional period in Venezuelan history began to be configured, establishing the framework of an *Authoritarian and Centralized State*, based on populist policies of socialist trends, which have been developing during the first decade of the twenty-first century. This State has been erected by demolishing the rule of law principles, the separation of powers and the federation; by weakening the effectiveness of the protection of constitutional rights; by subjecting the judicial review system and other check and balance institutions to the Executive, and by progressively destroying representative democracy itself in the name of a supposedly 'participatory democracy'. Nonetheless, the Constitution formally establishes a general framework of a democratic political regime and the rule of law, which in political practice has been distorted.

29. But the 1999 constitution-making process governed by the National Constituent Assembly did not finish with the final proclamation of the new Constitution

---

54. *See* in *Gaceta Oficial* No. 5.453 Extra. of 24 Mar. 2000. The text was originally published in *Gaceta Oficial* No. 36.860 of 30 Dec. 1999. Arts 160, 162, 174, 192 and 230 of the 1999 Constitution were amended by referendum held on 14 Feb. 2009. *See Gaceta Oficial* No. 5.908 Extra. of 19 Feb. 2009.
55. *Gaceta Oficial* No. 36.859 of 29 Dec. 1999.
56. *See* on the initial critical comments of the Constitution in Allan R. Brewer-Carías, 'Reflexiones críticas sobre la Constitución de Venezuela de 1999' in *Constitucionalismo Iberoamericano del Siglo XXI*, ed. Diego Valadés & Miguel Carbonell (Coordinadores) Cámara de Diputados. LVII Legislatura (México: Universidad Nacional Autónoma de México, 2000), 171–193; in *Revista Facultad de Derecho, Derechos y Valores* III, No. 5 (Universidad Militar Nueva Granada, Santafé de Bogotá, D.C., Colombia, Julio 2000), 9–26; in the collective book, *La Constitución de 1999* (Caracas: Academia de Ciencias Políticas y Sociales, 2000), 63–88; and in *Revista de Derecho Público,* No. 81 (Caracas: Editorial Jurídica Venezolana, 2000), 7–21.

on 20 December 1999, and the Constituent Assembly continued to act as a constituent power, even ignoring the new Constitution, particularly sanctioning the aforementioned constitutional transitory regime after the popular approval of the Constitution.

In effect, the text approved by the National Constituent Assembly in November of 1999, and submitted to a referendum for popular approval on 15 December 1999, contained just twenty-eight Transitory Provisions intended to assure the immediate legal effect of the Constitution and to regulate the legislative programme to execute the Constitution. These were the provisions approved by the people, in which no solution was given with respect to the possible immediate transition of titular officials of the State organs elected a year before, under the 1961 Constitution, in relation to the new organs established under the Constitution of 1999. That is, the people, when approving the Constitution, did not vote for any termination of the mandate of the previously elected authorities. The consequence of this omission was that in order, for instance, to substitute the former Congress with the new National Assembly, their members needed to be elected according to the new Constitution. After the election of the new National Assembly, it could begin to elect the new head of the Branches of Government, like the Supreme Tribunal or the Officers of the Citizen and Electoral power. The only transitory provision of the 1999 Constitution on these matters of electing new officers to high public offices was the immediate provisional appointment of the People's Defender, an office created by the new Constitution (Ninth Transitory Provision) until the new National Assembly to be elected in 2000 could make the definitive election.

30. Notwithstanding, the Constituent Assembly, without having any power for such purpose, as aforementioned, after the Constitution was approved by the people, on 22 December 1999 sanctioned the Decree on 'The Regimen of Transition for the Public Powers', creating a constitutional vacuum by dismissing the senators and representatives to the former Congress, the representatives to the State Legislative Assemblies and intervening in the Municipal Councils, all elected in 1998; the magistrates of the former Supreme Court of Justice, the General Comptroller of the Republic, the members of the former Supreme Electoral Council and of the then-existing Council of the Judiciary, and the General Prosecutor of the Republic.

The consequence of the created institutional vacuum was the 'need' for the same Constituent Assembly to fill it, and without any power to do so, it 'created' a new organ, not provided for in the new Constitution. In order to act as Legislative Power, the 'National Legislative Commission' called the 'Little Congress' (*Congresillo*), 'until representatives to the National Assembly are elected and in office' (Article 5), appointed its members in a discretionary way. The same happened at the state level, with the dismissals of the former representatives to the Legislative Assemblies and the subsequent appointment of members of new organs not established in the Constitution, the State Legislative Commissions. Regarding the Municipal Councils, they were subjected to the supervision and control of the National Constituent Assembly or the National Legislative Commission, violating their autonomy.

The Constituent Assembly also determined the number of Magistrates of each of the Chambers of the new Supreme Tribunal of Justice, appointing them, due to the vacuum that the same Assembly, without any constitutional authority created, by dismissing the Magistrates of the former Supreme Court of Justice; and creating a new organ that existed until 2010, the 'Commission on the Functioning and the Re-structuring of the Judicial System (Article 21) that substituted the former Council of the Judiciary.' In 2010 this Commission was eliminated, once the Judicial Disciplinary Jurisdiction began to function (*see infra* paragraph 424).

The result of this usurpation of the popular will by the National Constituent Assembly was the beginning of an endless constitutional transitory regime in defraudation of the new Constitution, governed by new provisional authorities designated by the Assembly, which in many cases, as is the case of the Judiciary, continues to exist one decade after the sanctioning of the Constitution.

§6. The Outgoing Constitutional Process in Defraudation of the Constitution and of Democracy (1999–2015)

31. After the sanctioning of the 1999 Constitution by the National Constituent Assembly through a constitution-making process that began with the violation of the 1961 Constitution and finished with the violation of the new 1999 Constitution by the same Constituent Assembly, after its popular approval, the constitutional process in Venezuela during the first fifteen years of the twenty-first century, could be globally characterized as a process developed in continuous defraudation of the Constitution and of the democratic regime.

As aforementioned, the 1999 National Constituent Assembly was the instrument used by the newly elected President to dissolve and intervene in all branches of government (particularly the Judiciary) and to dismiss all the public officials that had been elected just a few months before (November 1998) with the sole exception of the President of the Republic itself. In addition, the Constitutional Assembly intervened in all the other branches of government, among them, and above all, the Judiciary, whose autonomy and independence were progressive and systematically demolished.[57] The result has been the tight Executive control over the Judiciary, particularly regarding the newly appointed Supreme Tribunal of Justice, with its Constitutional Chamber the most ominous instrument for the consolidation of authoritarianism in the country[58] (*see infra* paragraphs 73, 251 et seq., 433 et seq., 715 et seq.).

57. *See* Allan R. Brewer-Carías, 'The Government of Judges and Democracy. The Tragic Situation of the Venezuelan Judiciary', in *Venezuela. Some Current Legal Issues 2014, Venezuelan National Reports to the 19th International Congress of Comparative Law, International Academy of Comparative Law, Vienna, 20–26 Jul. 2014* (Caracas: Academia de Ciencias Políticas y Sociales, 2014), 13–42; 'La progresiva y sistemática demolición de la autonomía e independencia del Poder Judicial en Venezuela (1999–2004)', in *XXX Jornadas J.M Dominguez Escovar, Estado de derecho, Administración de justicia y derechos humanos* (Barquisimeto: Instituto de Estudios Jurídicos del Estado Lara, 2005), 33–174.

58. *See* Allan R. Brewer-Carías, *Authoritarian Government v. The Rule Of Law. Lectures and Essays (1999–2014) on the Venezuelan Authoritarian Regime Established in Contempt of the* Constitution (Caracas: Fundación de Derecho Público, Editorial Jurídica Venezolana, 2014); Manuel Rachadell, *Evolución del Estado venezolano 1958–2015. De la conciliación de intereses al populismo autoritario* (Caracas, Ediorial Jurfidica Venezolana, 2015).

32. After the initial defraudation of the Constitution in order to control all the State branches of government, another defraudation process began, this time of democracy, led by the authoritarian government that emerged from the 1999 constituent process, which used representative democracy for the purpose of progressively eliminating it, and supposedly substituting it by a 'participative democracy', among others aspects, based on the establishment of popular councils of a new Popular Power controlled by the Head of the State (*see infra* paragraphs 175, 283, 666).

33. But notwithstanding the purpose, the outcome has been that all the essential elements of democracy (*see infra* paragraphs 52, 167) are precisely the ones that have unfortunately been ignored or fractured in Venezuela, in the name of that supposed participative democracy. Never before, has there been more violation of human rights as can be deduced from the numerous petitions filed before the Inter-American Commission on Human Rights. The access to power has been achieved contrary to the rule of law, by violating the separation and independence of the Judicial, Citizen and Electoral Powers, and the last political reforms creating the Communal Councils, tend to substitute electoral representation by supposed citizens assemblies and councils whose members are not elected but appointed from the summit of the Popular Power controlled by the National Executive.[59] The plural regime of parties has been destroyed, and an official single Socialist Party has been created by the State itself, completely imbricated in its apparatus and controlled by the President of the Republic. Since everything depends on the oil-rich State, only those who are part of the Single Party are able to have a political, administrative, economic and social life.[60]

One crucial step in this process took place in December 2010, through the sanctioning by the National Assembly, in contempt of the Constitution, of a group of Organic Laws established in parallel to the Constitutional State of a so-called Communal State. This State exercised not the Public Power as established in the Constitution, but a so-called Popular Power, through the organization of Communes, Communal Councils, Social Control entities, and socio-productive entities. All these entities work within an economic system of 'communal economy' that has affected the constitutional structure of the State[61] (*see infra* paragraphs 233 et seq.; 264 et

59. *See* Allan R. Brewer-Carías, 'El inicio de la desmunicipalización en Venezuela: La organización del Poder Popular para eliminar la descentralización, la democracia representativa y la participación a nivel local', in *AIDA, Opera Prima de Derecho Administrativo. Revista de la Asociación Internacional de Derecho Administrativo* (Universidad Nacional Autónoma de México, Facultad de Estudios Superiores de Acatlán, Coordinación de Postgrado, Instituto Internacional de Derecho Administrativo 'Agustín Gordillo', Asociación Internacional de Derecho Administrativo, México, 2007), 49 a 67.

60. *See* Allan R. Brewer-Carías, *Estado Totalitario y desprecio a la ley. La desconstitucionalización, desjuridificación, desjudicialización y desdemocratización de Venezuela* (Caracas: Fundación de Derecho Público, Editorial Jurídica Venezolana, 2d ed., 2015).

61. *See* these Organic Laws on the Popular Power, the Communes, the Communal Counils, the Communal Economic System, and the Social Comprollership in *Gaceta Oficial* No. 6.011 Extra. of 21 Dec. 2010. *See* the comments in Allan R. Brewer-Carías et al., *Leyes Orgánicas sobre el Poder Popular y el Estado Comunal (Los Consejos Comunales, las Comunas, la Sociedad* Socialista y el Sistema Económico Comunal) (Caracas: Editorial Jurídica Venezolana, 2011).

seq. and 664 et seq.) implementing through statutes (organic laws), all that the government could not achieve through the constitutional reform project that was rejected by the people in 2007[62] (*see infra* paragraphs 36 et seq. and 261 et seq., 623).

This entire institutional distortion has been established without the existence of separation or independence between the public powers, not only in their horizontal division due to the control that the Executive Power has over them; but also in their vertical distribution, where the Federation has been progressively dismantled. Consequently, the federated states and the municipalities have been minimized, by means of eliminating every trace of political decentralization, that is, of autonomous entities in the territory, preventing any real possibility for democratic participation.

Another crucial step in the process of dismantling the rule of law took place in January 2013, after the announcement of the death of President Hugo Chávez, through the appointment to succeed him by means of an unconstitutional interpretation made by the Constitutional Chamber of the Supreme Tribunal, of a non-democratic elected official, as was the Executive Vice president, Nicolás Maduro, who was later elected as President of the Republic in the electoral process that took place in March 2013.[63]

34. The result has been that the fundamental components of democracy (*see infra* paragraphs 50, 167) have also been ignored or fractured, in the sense that the governmental activity deployed by the rich and suddenly wealthy State ceased to be transparent due to the lack of any sort of control and check and balance, it not being possible to demand any kind of accountability or responsibility from the government for the public interests management, so a rampant corruption has developed in a way never seen before. In addition, the freedom of speech and press has been systematically threatened, imposing in many cases self-censorship, as reporters and dissidents are persecuted.[64]

The consequence has been that all the essential elements and fundamental components of democracy have been progressively dismantled, particularly the separation of powers. On the contrary, what the country is facing is an excess of concentration and centralization of power, as it occurs in any authoritarian government, despite the electoral origin they can have. In such cases, as history has shown,

62. *See* Allan R. Brewer-Carías, *Estudios sobre el Estado Comunal o Estado del Poder Popular. O de cómo se desconstitucionaliza al Estado en fraude a la Constitución y a la voluntad popular,* (Caracas, Editorial Jurídica Venezolana, 2021).

63. *See* Allan R. Brewer-Carías, 'El juez constitucional y la demolición del principio democrático de gobierno. O de cómo la Jurisdicción Constitucional en Venezuela impuso arbitrariamente a los ciudadanos, al inicio del período constitucional 2013–2019, un gobierno sin legitimidad democrática, sin siquiera ejercer actividad probatoria alguna, violentando abiertamente la Constitución', *Revista de Derecho Público*, No. 133 (Caracas: Editorial Jurídica Venezolana, 2013), 179–212.

64. *See* as an example, the case of the shout down of RCTV, in Allan R. Brewer-Carías, 'El juez constitucional en Venezuela como instrumento para aniquilar la libertad de expresión y para confiscar la propiedad privada: el caso RCTV' (I de III), in *Gaceta Judicial* (mayo: Santo Domingo, República Dominicana, 2007), 24–27.

an inevitable tendency toward tyranny develops, particularly when there are no efficient controls over those who govern, and even worse if they have or believe in having popular support. In the case of Venezuela, the authoritarian government that has taken roots during the last decade against the principle of separation of powers has led to the concentration of all powers in the hands of the Executive Power which in its turn controls the National Assembly, and consequently all the other branches of government (*see infra* paragraphs 216 et seq., 236).

35. All these authoritarian trends were intended to be constitutionalized through a Constitutional Reform proposal in 2007, aimed to radically transform the Decentralized, Democratic, Pluralistic rule of law and Social State into a Socialist, Centralized, Repressive and Militaristic State, grounded in a so-called Bolivarian doctrine, identified with 'XXI Century Socialism', and a communal economic system of State capitalism.[65] These constitutional reforms were proposed in defraudation of the Constitution due to the fact that the proposed changes, because of their importance regarding the structure of the State, needed the convening of a national Constituent Assembly (Article 347), and not just to be approved by the constitutional reform procedure. The intention was to consolidate a Communist and Socialist State based on State capitalism or, as was announced by the then Vice President of the Republic in January 2007, the instalment of 'the dictatorship of democracy';[66] of course, a contradiction in itself because in a democracy no dictatorship is acceptable, whether of democracy or 'of the proletariat' as was proposed ninety years ago (1918) in the old Soviet Union through the same sort of 'councils' then called 'soviets' of soldiers, workers and countrymen.

But even without succeeding in the proposed constitutional reform, the fact is that in defraudation of democracy, since 2010, a new model of authoritarian State of a supposed Popular Power has taken shape in Venezuela, having its immediate origin in popular elections, providing the regime with a camouflage suit with 'constitutional' and 'elective' shapes, designed for the destruction of the representative democracy itself.[67]

---

65. *See* Allan R. Brewer-Carías, *La Reforma Constitucional de 2007 (Comentarios al proyecto inconstitucionalmente sancionado por la Asamblea Nacional el 2 de noviembre de 2007)* (Caracas: Editorial Jurídica Venezolana, 2007); Manuel Rachadell, *Socialismo del Siglo XXI. Análisis de la Reforma Constitucional propuesta por el Presidente Chávez en agosto de 2007* (Caracas: Fundación Estudios de Derecho Administrativo, FUNEDA, 2007).
66. Jorge Rodríguez, Vice President of the Republic, in January 2007, expressed: 'Of course we want to install a dictatorship, the dictatorship of the true democracy and the democracy is the dictatorship of everyone, you and us together, building a different country. Of course we want this dictatorship of democracy to be installed forever', in *El Nacional* (Caracas, 2 Jan. 2007), A-2.
67. *See* Allan R. Brewer-Carías, *Authoritarian Government v. The Rule Of Law. Lectures and Essays (1999–2014) on the Venezuelan Authoritarian Regime Established in Contempt of the Constitution* (Caracas: Fundación de Derecho Público, Editorial Jurídica Venezolana, 2014); 'El autoritarismo establecido en fraude a la Constitución y a la democracia y su formalización en Venezuela mediante la reforma constitucional. (De cómo en un país democrático se ha utilizado el sistema eleccionario para minar la democracia y establecer un régimen autoritario de supuesta "dictadura de la democracia" que se pretende regularizar mediante la reforma constitucional)', in *Temas constitucionales. Planteamientos ante una Reforma* (Caracas: Fundación de Estudios de Derecho Administrativo, FUNEDA, 2007), 13–74.

36. In effect, in August 2007, the President of the Republic filed before the National Assembly, at his own initiative, a 'Constitutional Reform' draft that after the corresponding discussions was sanctioned by the Assembly on 2 November 2007, formally approving to 'Reform' the 1999 Constitution, in the following aspects: abandoning the Democratic Rule of Law State, a Centralized, Socialist and Militaristic State, based on a Socialist Bolivarian Doctrine; changing the Armed Force into a Bolivarian Armed Force, and creating a new component of it, the Bolivarian Popular Militia; dismantling the Federation and all that remained of political decentralization by giving the President and his regional authorities power over the states; dismantling the Municipal government by consolidating below them the Communal Councils for the Popular Power, controlled directly by the President of the Republic and composed by non-elected members, eliminating representative democracy at the lower lever of the State; reinforcing Presidentialism, concentrating all powers in the hands of the President, establishing the possibility of his indefinite re-election, and expanding his powers in 'states of exception' (emergency situations); eliminating economic freedom, establishing the pre-eminence of public property over private property, and consolidating the State capitalism already in place; eliminating the autonomy of the Central Bank; and limiting political participation of civil society in the election of High officials of the non-elected branches of government and of Citizenship in the referendums; and reducing participation to institutions with socialist purposes.[68]

All these reform proposals were formulated and discussed by the National Assembly in defraudation of the Constitution, due to the fact that they seek to modify essential elements of the State and political system that could only be transformed through the constitutional review procedure of a 'National Constituent Assembly' and not by means of the 'constitutional reform' procedure (Articles 342, 347) (*see infra* paragraphs 128 seq.). It was an attempt, proposed by the President of the Republic and approved by the National Assembly, to introduce essential changes in the Constitution evading the procedure established in the 1999 Constitution for such fundamental changes; that is, a constitutional review proposed in defraudation of the Constitution, being sanctioned through a procedure established for other purposes, in order to deceive the people.

A change of the nature of the one that was proposed, according to Article 347 of the 1999 Constitution, required the convening and election of a National Constituent Assembly, and could not be undertaken by means of the 'constitutional reform' procedure, which, as it has been mentioned, is exclusively reserved for a 'partial revision of the Constitution and a substitution of one or several of its norms without modifying the structure and fundamental principles of the Constitutional text'. Consequently, by following this procedure in order to achieve substantial constitutional changes, it was to act fraudulently with respect to the Constitution, in a process that

---

68. *See* Allan R. Brewer-Carías, 'El sello socialista que se pretendía imponer al Estado', in *Revista de Derecho Público*, No. 112 *(Estudios sobre la Reforma Constitucional)* (Caracas: Editorial Jurídica Venezolana, 2007), 71–76.

can be considered as accomplished in defraudation of the Constitution.[69] This occurs when existing institutions are used in a manner that appears to adhere to constitutional form and procedure in order to proceed towards the creation of a new political regimen, a new constitutional order, without altering the established legal system.

Fortunately, the 2007 Constitutional Reform, although sanctioned by the National Assembly, was rejected by popular vote in the referendum held on 2 December 2007,[70] but again, in a new defraudation of the Constitution process,[71] Chávez reacted aggressively against the will of the people, breaching the Constitution and imposing the rejected constitutional reform by means of ordinary legislation.[72] As already mentioned, he enacted several decrees – laws and legislation sanctioned by the National Assembly between 2008 and 2011 that created the framework for a Cuban-style Communal State.[73] Claims for judicial review were raised in vain and ended up hidden in the files of a Supreme Tribunal that never processed the requests.[74] As a result, the government was able to implement unconstitutional laws with total impunity, without any sort of control or judicial review,[75] in particular, due to the absence of an independent Constitutional Chamber of the Supreme Tribunal made futile any judicial review action (*see* paragraphs 422 seq.).

37. One of the constitutional consequences of the popular rejection of a constitutional reform proposed at the initiative of the President of the Republic, in accordance with Article 345, is that it 'cannot be submitted again before the Assembly in

69. *See* Allan R. Brewer-Carías, 'El juez constitucional vs. la supremacía constitucional O de cómo la jurisdicción constitucional en Venezuela renunció a controlar la constitucionalidad del procedimiento seguido para la "reforma constitucional" sancionada por la Asamblea Nacional el 2 de noviembre de 2007, antes de que fuera rechazada por el pueblo en el referendo del 2 de diciembre de 2007', in Eduardo Ferrer Mac Gregor and César de Jesús Molina Suárez (Coordinators), *El juez constitucional en el Siglo XXI*, vol. I (Mexico, 2009), pp. 385–435.
70. Allan R. Brewer-Carías, 'La reforma constitucional en Venezuela de 2007 y su rechazo por el poder constituyente originario', in *Revista Peruana de Derecho Público*, Año 8, No. 15 (Lima, Julio-Diciembre 2007), 13–53.
71. *See* the comments on the 2008 Decree-laws, in 'Estudios sobre los decretos leyes Julio-Agosto 2008', *Revista de Derecho Público*, No. 115 (Caracas: Editorial Jurídica Venezolana, 2008). *See* Allan R. Brewer-Carías, '¿Reforma constitucional o mutación constitucional?: La experiencia venezolana', *Revista de Derecho Público,* No 137 (Caracas: Editorial Jurídica Venezolana, 2014), 19–65.
72. *See* the articles published in the Monographic issued of the *Revista de Derecho Público, 'Estudios sobre los Decretos Leyes'* No. 115 (Caracas, Editorial Jurídica Venezolana, 2008), pp. 9–435.
73. *See* Allan R. Brewer-Carías, 'Introducción General al Régimen del Poder Popular y del Estado Comunal (O de cómo en el siglo XXI, en Venezuela se decreta, al margen de la Constitución, un Estado de Comunas y de Consejos Comunales, y se establece una sociedad socialista y un sistema económico comunista, por los cuales nadie ha votado), *in Allan R. Brewer-Carías et al., Leyes Orgánicas sobre el Poder Popular y el Estado Comunal (Los consejos comunales, las comunas, la sociedad socialista y el sistema económico comunal*, (Caracas, Editorial Jurídica Venezolana, 2011), pp. 11–182.
74. *See* the text of the claim for Judicial Review filed against the Organic Laws of the Popular Power, which was never considered by the Constitutional Chamber of the Supreme Tribunal, in *Allan R. Brewer-Carías et al., Leyes Orgánicas ... supra* note 73, at 509–596.
75. *See* Allan R. Brewer-Carías, *Estado Totalitario y Desprecio a la Ley: La Desconstitucionalización, Desjuridificación, Desjudicialización y Desdemocratización de Venezuela* (Caracas, Editorial Jurídica Venezolana, 2015), pp. 152–53.

the same constitutional term' (*see infra* paragraphs 96, 721), which in the case of the President, having been elected in 2006 endures up to 2012. Nonetheless, after the official party lost regional and local elections in the most important state and municipal entities of the country on November 2008, the President of the Republic formally announced that he was going to seek again the review of the Constitution, in order to establish the possibility of his indefinite re-election, first by 'authorizing' his official Party to formulate a 'constitutional amendment' proposal by popular initiative, and after, due to the celerity problems of this review procedure, asking the National Assembly to take the initiative to formulate proposal for a reform of the Constitution again in order to allow his indefinite re-election.[76] The Assembly approved the 'amendment' on January 2009, eliminating the limits for the re-election of all elected public officials established in Articles 160, 162, 174, 192 and 230 of the Constitution, and again, in defraudation of the Constitution, an already popular rejected reform was submitted to a new referendum held on 14 February 2009, in the same constitutional period, contrary to Article 345 of the Constitution, using fraudulently this time the constitutional 'amendment' procedure[77] (*see infra* paragraphs 96, 721).

38. Two questions with constitutional implications resulted from this new 'amendment' proposal that was the object of constitutional discussions: first, the possibility to use a 'constitutional amendment' procedure through which no fundamental constitutional principle can be changed, in order to alter and change the principle of alternating government that is a fundamental republican principle formulated in Article 6 of the Constitution; and second, the possibility to use the 'constitutional amendment' procedure to include the continuous election of the President of the Republic, changing the limits imposed in the Constitution (re-election only once, for the next period), which was a proposal previously submitted to a referendum in December 2007, and rejected by the people. On these matters, the Constitutional Chamber of the Supreme Tribunal of Justice on 3 February 2009 issued two decisions (Nos 46 and 53)[78] in which a binding interpretation of the Constitution was established: first, regarding the possibility of submitting to popular vote a modification of the Constitution via 'constitutional amendment' on the same matter already rejected by the people in a 'constitutional reform' procedure held during the same constitutional term. The Constitutional Chamber argued that the limit imposed in the Constitution was directed only to the National Assembly to discuss a constitutional reform again on the same subject once rejected by the people, without considering the substantive aspect of the prohibition regarding the limits to

76. *See* the President speeches in *El Universal* (Caracas, 30 Nov.–5 Jan. 2008)
77. The amendment was approved in the referendum by 54% of the votes, and was published in *Gaceta Oficial* No. 5.908 Extra. of 19 Feb. 2009.
78. *See* the Constitutional Chamber of the Supreme Tribunal of Justice Decision No. 53, of 3 Feb. 2009 (*Interpretation of Arts 340, 6 and 345 of the Constitution* Case), in www.tsj.gov.ve/ decisions/scon /Febrero/53-3209-2009-08-1610.html. *See* the comments on that decision in Allan R. Brewer-Carías, 'El Juez Constitucional vs. La alternabilidad republicana (La reelección continua e indefinida)', in *Revista de Derecho Público*, no. 117 (enero-marzo 2009) (Caracas, 2009), 205–211. Also published in www.analitica.com/va/politica/opinion/6273405.asp.

ask again and again the people, to express in an endless way their will, through referenda (*see infra* paragraph 128). Second, regarding the possibility of using the 'constitutional amendment' procedure in order to change the fundamental principle of alternating (*alternabilidad*) government, which means that public offices must be occupied by turns, and not continuously by the same elected person, the Constitutional Chamber said that what the principle of *alternabilidad* imposed was 'for the people as sovereign to have the possibility to periodically elect their representatives', confusing alternating government (*gobierno alternativo*) with 'elected government' (*gobierno electivo*), that is, the principle that elected public offices must be occupied by turns, with the principle of election of representatives, considering that the principle of alternating (*alternabilidad*) government can only be infringed if the possibility to have elections is impeded. With these decisions, what the Supreme Tribunal made, in addition to resolving the constitutional challenges to the 15 February 2009 referendum was, through a constitutional interpretation, to modify or mutate the text of the Constitution, changing the sense of the prohibition of subsequent calling for a referendum on the same matters, and also changing the sense of a constitutional principle like the principle of alternating government considering it similar to the principle of elective government, ignoring the difference established in the Constitution (Article 6) (*see infra* paragraphs 128, 721).

§7. The Suffocation of the Legislative Power (National Assembly) by the Constitutional Chamber of the Supreme Tribunal, and the Unconstitutional Covenant of a New Constitutional Assembly to Usurp Legislative Powers (2016–2020)

39. By 2015, the political, economic and social destruction of the Venezuelan democracy and Constitutional State was almost complete, provoking a popular reaction through the parliamentary election held in December of that year, which surprised everybody, including the controlled electoral body, which was unable to manipulate the overwhelming results. After such an election, the government lost control of the majority it held in the National Assembly, and the opposition obtained a qualified majority of representatives. This reversal was the second most important political setback of the authoritarian regime since 1999, after the defeat of the 2007 constitutional reform.[79]

However, as the regime had become accustomed to exercising absolute power without any sort of checks and balances, an autonomous National Assembly was of course intolerable for the Government which began to systematically obstruct the opposition from carrying out its legislative agenda and gradually began to strip the legislature of all its powers and functions, which was possible because of the cooperation between the Executive Branch and the Supreme Tribunal of Justice.[80]

---

79. *See* Allan R. Brewer-Carías, 'The Collapse of the Rule of Law in Venezuela 1999–2019', in, *Journal of International Law and Politics,* vol. 52, No. 3, (New York, New York University, Summer 2020) pp. 741–775.

80. *See* generally, Allan R. Brewer-Carías, *El Golpe a la Democracia Dado por la Sala Constitucional,* (Caracas, Editorial Jurídica Venezolana, 2015), pp. 35–53.

In only two days (29 and 30 December 2015), the outgoing National Assembly enacted more than thirty statutes stripping away all legal powers from the newly elected Assembly and appointing new Supreme Tribunal justices, packing it entirely with members of the governing party.[81] All this happened even before the newly elected National Assembly could hold its first session on 5 January 2016.

40. Filled with members of the governing party, the Supreme Tribunal acted to prevent the Assembly from exercising its functions, issuing more than one hundred rulings that transformed the political system into a judicial dictatorship.[82] The new system was characterized by the ability of the Executive to use the subdued Supreme Tribunal as his main instrument to neutralize the National Assembly, eliminating all its functions in order to consolidate power.[83]

The Constitutional Chamber of the Supreme Tribunal declared unconstitutional practically all the laws and statutes sanctioned by the new National Assembly.[84] The Chamber even went so far as to reform the Assembly's internal regulations of functioning and debates in order to subject the exercise of its legislative functions to prior approval by the Executive Branch,[85] an unthinkable abuse of executive power in any democratic state. Further reducing the Assembly's political power to control the government and the Public Administration, the Chamber imposed a rule that requires prior approval by the Executive Vice President before a Minister can be questioned by the Assembly; eliminated the possibility for the Assembly to oppose and disapprove the states of emergency that the Executive has successively decreed; prohibited the National Assembly from approving votes of no-confidence against the Ministers; ignored the constitutional obligation of the President to submit his Annual Address on the State of the Nation before the National Assembly, deciding instead for the President to deliver it before the same Supreme Tribunal; did away with the requirement of legislative approval of the national budget law, transforming it into a mere executive decree to be approved by the Tribunal; abolished the Assembly's power to review its own decisions and repeal them, as it would have

81. *See* Allan R. Brewer-Carías, *Dictadura judicial y perversión del Estado de derecho: La Sala Constitucional y la destrucción de la democracia en Venezuela* (Caracas, Editorial Jurídica Venezolana, second ed., 2016), pp. 116–135.
82. *See* Carlos M. Ayala Corao & Rafael J. Chavero Gazdik, *El Libro Negro del TSJ de Venezuela: Del Secuestro de la Democracia y la Usurpación de la Soberanía Popular a la Ruptura del Orden Constitucional (2015–2017)* (Caracas, Editorial Jurídica Venezolana, 2017); José Vicente Haro, 'Las 111 decisiones inconstitucionales del TSJ ilegítimo desde el 6D-2015 contra la Asamblea Nacional, los partidos políticos, la soberanía popular y los DDHH', in *Buscando el Norte* (10 Jul. 2017), http://josevicenteharogarcia.blogspot.com/2016/10/las-33-decisiones-del-tsj.html (listing all the rulings of the Constitutional Chamber against the National Assembly).
83. *See* Allan R. Brewer-Carías, *Dictadura judicial y perversión del Estado de derecho: La Sala Constitucional y la destrucción de la democracia en Venezuela* (Caracas, Editorial Jurídica Venezolana, second ed., 2016), pp. 137–400.
84. *See* Allan R. Brewer-Carías, *Consolidación de la tiranía judicial. El Juez Constitucional controlado por el Poder Ejecutivo, asumiendo el Poder Absoluto*, (Caracas/New York, Editorial Jurídica Venezolana International 2017).
85. *See* Allan R. Brewer-Carias, 'El fin del Poder Legislativo: la regulación por el Juez Constitucional del régimen interior y de debates de la Asamblea Nacional, y la sujeción de la función legislativa de la Asamblea a la aprobación previa por parte del Poder Ejecutivo' in *Revista de Derecho Público*, No. 145–146 (Caracas, Editorial Jurídica Venezolana, 2016), pp. 428–443.

been able to do for the unconstitutional appointment of the justices of the Supreme Tribunal made in December 2015; prevented the National Assembly from expressing its political opinion during debates; and annulled all major bills, resolutions and declarations adopted by the Assembly.[86]

Finally, based on decisions issued in 2017 and following an alleged contempt of court ruling by the Electoral Chamber of the same Supreme Tribunal, the Constitutional Chamber systematically declared null and void all 'present and future decisions' of the National Assembly, on some occasions, even threatening to revoke the popular mandate of its members and to imprison them.[87]

41. However, the process did not end here. In one of its most notorious actions, the Constitutional Chamber issued two decisions in March 2017 (No. 155 of 27 March 2017, and No. 156 of 29 March 2017), wherein it unconstitutionally declared a state of emergency, eliminated the parliamentary immunity of the representatives, and arbitrarily assumed all parliamentary powers of the National Assembly.[88] Further, the Tribunal went so far as to delegate legislative powers to the President of the Republic, allowing him to reform laws and codes, including the Criminal Code and the Organic Code of Criminal Procedure, at his own discretion.[89] It was these decisions that finally triggered Venezuela's application to the Inter-American Democratic Charter by the Organization of American States (OAS).[90]

These decisions gave birth to a new model of authoritarian government that did not have its origin in a military *coup*, as was common in Latin America, but rather in the manipulation of popular elections, the degradation of judicial review processes, and the abuse of democratic tools. The result of this model was to ultimately give de facto control of the country to the military and destroy the rule of law and democratic principles, all under the convenient camouflage of constitutional and elective processes.

86. *See* generally, Allan R. Brewer-Carías, *Dictadura judicial y perversión del Estado de derecho: La Sala Constitucional y la destrucción de la democracia en Venezuela* (Caracas, Editorial Jurídica Venezolana, 2016), pp. 195–213; 259–313.
87. On 30 Dec. 2015, in order to prevent the opposition gaining control of the qualified majority of the National Assembly, the Electoral Chamber of the Supreme Tribunal issued a precautionary measure suspending the proclamation of the four elected representatives of the Amazon State. Notwithstanding, the Assembly, having the power to qualify its own members, decided to incorporate the elected representatives. Instead of sending the case to the criminal courts in order to declare the representatives that disobeyed the judicial order in contempt, the Constitutional Chamber directly declared the whole Assembly, as an institution, in contempt, declaring the nullity of all its past and future decisions in an unconstitutional way. *See* Allan R. Brewer-Carias, *Consolidación de la tiranía judicial. El Juez Constitucional controlado por el Poder Ejecutivo, asumiendo el Poder Absoluto*, (Caracas/New York, Editorial Jurídica Venezolana International, 2017), pp. 83–144.
88. *Ibid.*, 145–228.
89. *Ibid.*, pp. 215–216.
90. The OAS decided in 2017, at the proposal of its Secretary General, that Venezuela had violated its Constitutional order and thus violated the Inter-American Democratic Charter of September 2001. Allan R. Brewer-Carías (ed.), *La crisis de la democracia en Venezuela, la OEA y la Carta Democrática Interamericana: Documentos de Luis Almagro (2015-2017),* (New York, Editorial Jurídica Venezolana, 2d. ed., 2017), pp. 20–27.

42. After all these developments, the 1999 Venezuelan Constitution today (2022) is a tragic example of a Constitution that was violated even before it was published. There is no other way to explain how a federal state was transformed into a centralized system of power. The separation between five branches of government (*see* paragraphs 438 et seq.) has been replaced by a political system of the total concentration of power and the principle of representativeness has been neglected. Political participation has been denied and ignored, economic liberty has been engulfed by strict nationalization of all activities, and state capitalism has emerged as a result of indiscriminate expropriation and confiscation.[91]

43. One of the most notorious acts of this constitutional tragedy began in July 2017, with the unconstitutional convening and functioning of a new Constituent Assembly with unlimited powers and duration. President Nicolás Maduro installed the Assembly in breach of the provisions of the Constitution that entrust the power to convene such an Assembly to the people only by means of a referendum.[92] The new Constituent Assembly, composed of more than five hundred members, was elected through an ad hoc electoral system contrary to the universal and direct suffrage guaranteed in the Constitution, based on a territorial (municipal) and corporate vote exercised by chosen sectors of the society, thus institutionalizing discrimination and exclusion. The purpose of the Assembly was supposed to construct a socialist, populist or communal state framework following the same trends that had been rejected by the people in 2007, and the same that has been unconstitutionally implemented through ordinary legislation since 2010.[93]

The unconstitutional convening of this fraudulent Constituent Assembly was again challenged before the Constitutional Chamber of the Supreme Tribunal, eventually being the result of the decision of that Chamber to consider that if it is true that a referendum is indeed needed in order to change a comma, word, or phrase in an article of the Constitution, nonetheless it is not necessary to ask for the people's approval when changing the entire Constitution, as it was intended.[94] With this nonsensical opinion, eight individuals (the President of the Republic and seven Justices of the Tribunal) imposed their will upon the people.

Based on this unconstitutional decision, the members of the Constituent Assembly were elected in July 2017, and all of them affiliated with the official party. The Assembly assumed an original constituent power, substituting the people's will and

91. In relation to the oil industry, *see*, e.g., Allan R. Brewer-Carías, *Crónica de una Destrucción: Concesión, Nacionalización, Apertura, Constitucionalización, Desnacionalización, Estatización, Entrega y Degradación de la Industria Petrolera,* (Caracas, Editorial Jurídica Venezolana, 2018), pp. 251–277.

92. *See* Allan R. Brewer-Carías, *Usurpación Constituyente 1999, 2017. La historia se repite: una vez como farsa y la otra como tragedia*, (Caracas, Editorial Jurídica Venezolana International, 2018).

93. *See* Allan R. Brewer-Carías and Carlos García Soto (ED.), *Estudios sobre la Asamblea Nacional Constituyente y su inconstitucional convocatoria en 2017* (Bogotá, Editorial Temis, 2017.

94. *See* on the Decisions Nos 378 of 31 May 2017 and 455 of 12 Jun. 2017 issued by the Constitutional Chamber of the Supreme Tribunal, the comments in: Allan R. Brewer-Carías, 'El Juez Constitucional vs. El pueblo como poder constituyente originario. De cómo la Sala Constitucional del Tribunal Supremo de Justicia avaló la inconstitucional convocatoria de una Asamblea Nacional Constituyente, arrebatándole al pueblo su derecho exclusivo a convocarla', in Allan R. Brewer-Carías and Carlos García Soto (ED.), *Estudios sobre la Asamblea Nacional Constituyente … supra,* pp. 481–494

sovereignty, acting with supra-constitutional powers, and imposing its will on all constituted powers, including the Supreme Tribunal. The judicial tyranny of the previous years was thus in part transformed into a constituent tyranny, whereby the Supreme Tribunal became completely subordinated to the Executive.[95]

Additionally, between 2017 and 2018, the Constituent Assembly acted as a sort of Caribbean reincarnation of the 1793 *Comité de Salut Public* of the Terror Regime in revolutionary France, which was established in order to prosecute any dissidence.[96] The Assembly declared, for instance, that elected members of the National Assembly were traitors to the motherland, particularly after they met with public officials and representatives in foreign countries in order to explain the situation in Venezuela. The persecution of members of the National Assembly reached new heights in August 2018 when the Supreme Tribunal, in collaboration with the Constituent Assembly, ordered the apprehension and incarceration of two representatives, unjustly indicting them of magnicide and other grave crimes against the state.[97]

§8. The Unconstitutional Presidential Election in 2018 and the Subsequent Enactment of the Transition Regime Aimed to Reestablish Democracy and the Reinforcement of the Constitution in 2019

44. The authoritarian feature of the regime conducted by President Maduro based on unconstitutional actions taken since 2017, was reinforced by the 2017 National Constituent Assembly's decision to supplant the National Electoral Council and illegitimately convene an advanced presidential election in order to re-elect Nicolás Maduro for a new term (2019–2025).[98]

That fraudulent re-election of Nicolás Maduro was held on 20 May 2018, through a process that did not meet the national and international standards set for democratic, free, fair, and transparent elections. Consequently, the National Assembly, as a political and legislative body that represents the sovereign will of the people and as the primary interpreter of the Constitution, approved a Resolution (22 May 2018) denouncing the farce of the elections process, stating that it:

> violated all the electoral guarantees recognized in Human Rights Treaties and Agreements, and in the Constitution of the Bolivarian Republic of Venezuela

95. *See* Allan R. Brewer-Carías, *Usurpación Constituyente 1999, 2017 … supra*, pp. 609–615 *See* generally Carlos Ayala Corao and Rafael Chavero Gazdik, La Asamblea Nacional Constituyente de Venezuela (2017–2019): El Leviatán de la Democracia (Caracas, Editorial Jurídica Venezolana, 2019).
96. *See* generally Committee of Public Safety, *Encyclopaedia Britannica,* https://www.britannica.com/topic/Committee-of-Public-Safety (last visited 13 Apr. 2020) (noting how the Committee used harsh measures against enemies of the Revolution).
97. *See* Allan R. Brewer-Carias, *Consolidación de la tiranía judicial. El Juez Constitucional controlado por el Poder Ejecutivo … supra*, pp. 133–144.
98. *See* Allan R. Brewer-Carías, 'Reflexiones sobre la dictadura en Venezuela, después de la fraudulenta "reelección" presidencial de mayo de 2018', in *Revista de Derecho Público*, Nos 153–154 (Caracas, Editorial Jurídica Venezolana International, 2018), pp. 177–216.

> and the Organic Law of Electoral Processes, considering the effective absence of the Rule of Law; the partiality of the electoral arbiter; the violation of the effective guaranties for exercising the right to vote and the right to be elected to office by popular vote; the lack of effective controls against acts of electoral corruption perpetrated by the government; the systematic breach of the freedom of expression, together with the partiality of mass media controlled by the government, the absence of effective and transparent mechanisms of electoral oversight.[99]

45. The National Assembly also stated that if the majority of the people of Venezuela refrained from participating in the illegitimate elections process, in which 68% of the Registered electors abstained, it was the people who:

> in defense of our Constitution and invoking Articles 333 and 350 sanctioned by the Constitution, decided to reject, disavow and not validate the farce called for on May 20, in spite of the government's pressure through mediums of social control.[100]

By virtue of the foregoing, the National Assembly resolved 'to declare as "non-existent" the farce that took place on May 20, 2018'; 'to disavow the alleged outcome announced by the National Electoral Council, especially the alleged election of Nicolás Maduro Moros as President of the Republic, who must heretofore be deemed a usurper of said office'; and to 'disavow any illegal and illegitimate acts of proclamation and swearing in of Nicolas Maduro for the 2019-2025 term'.[101]

The National Assembly also issued a Resolution on 13 November 2018, 'to promote a political solution for the national crisis', declaring that 'as of January 10, 2019, Nicolas Maduro continues to usurp the office of President of the Republic, in spite of not being the president-elect', and deeming 'all the decisions of the National Executive Branch ineffective as of that date, pursuant to the terms of Article 138 of the Constitution'.[102] This Resolution was a manifestation of civil disobedience and of resistance against illegitimacy. It disavowed the results of a fraudulent election, declaring it non-existent, and ignored the proclamation of the supposedly elected official.[103]

---

99. Acuerdo reiterando el desconocimiento de la farsa realizada el 20 de mayo de 2018 para la supuesta elección del Presidente de la República [Resolution reiterating the rejection of the farce carried out for the supposed election of the President of the Republic] Asamblea Nacional de la República Bolivariana de Venezuela (22 May 2018).
100. *Ibid*
101. *Ibid*
102. Acuerdo con el objeto de impulsar una solución política a la crisis nacional, fortaleciendo las fuerzas democráticas del pueblo de Venezuela con el respaldo de la comunidad internacional [Resolution to Propel a Political Solution to the National Crisis, Strengthening the Democratic Force of the People of Venezuela with the Support of the International Community], Asamblea Nacional de la República Bolivariana de Venezuela (13 Nov. 2018).
103. *See* Allan R. Brewer-Carías, *El Derecho Constitucional a la Desobediencia Civil: Estudios: Aplicación e Interpretación del Artículo 350 de la Constitución de Venezuela de 1999,* (Buenos Aires, Ediciones Olejnik, 2019), pp. 183–198 (2019).

46. The Resolution of 22 May 2018, specifically mentioned a Declaration of the '*Grupo de Lima*' issued on 21 May 2018, which was followed by other declarations of a similar tone expressed by more than forty-four governments of the Americas and Europe, all rejecting the legitimacy of the election.[104] The '*Grupo de Lima*', made up of representatives of the governments of Argentina, Brazil, Canada, Chile, Colombia, Costa Rica, Guatemala, Guyana, Honduras, México, Panamá, Paraguay, Perú, and Saint Lucia, agreed to contribute to 'preserve the attributions of the National Assembly', expressing that they:

> Do not recognize the legitimacy of the electoral process that took place in Venezuela and that ended on May 20, 2019, for failure to meet the international standards of a democratic, free, just and transparent electoral process.[105]

The same day, Mike Pompeo, Secretary of State of the United States, said simply that:

> The United States condemns the fraudulent election that took place in Venezuela on May 20. This so-called 'election' is an attack on constitutional order and an affront to Venezuela's tradition of democracy.[106]

On 23 May, the G7, which gathers the leaders of Germany, Canada, the United States, France, Italy, Japan, and the United Kingdom (UK), denounced the presidential election because it failed to 'meet accepted international standards' and did not safeguard 'basic guarantees for an inclusive, fair and democratic election'.[107] The statement rejected the 'Venezuelan presidential election, and its results, as it is not representative of the democratic will of the citizens of Venezuela.'[108]

47. The consequence of this rejection of Maduro's re-election was the lack of a legitimately elected president who could be sworn in on 10 January 2019. As a result, on 4 January 2019, the National Academy of Political and Social Sciences, Venezuela's highest consultative entity on institutional matters, issued a proclamation highlighting that due to the 'non-existence of the conditions necessary to hold

104. *See* Moises Rendon, 'Venezuela's Presidency in Jeopardy', Ctr for *Strategic & Int'l Studies* (22 Oct. 2018), https://www.csis.org/analysis/venezuelas-presidency-jeopardy (reporting that more than fifty countries did not recognize the results of the election).

105. Grupo de Lima, Declaración del Grupo de Lima sobre el fraudulento proceso electoral del 20 de mayo, Provea (21 May 2018),https://provea.org/actualidad/declaracion-del-grupo-de-lima-sobre-el-fraudulento-proceso-electoral-del-20-de-mayo/

106. Press Statement, Michael R. Pompeo, Secretary of State, U.S. Dep't of State, An Unfair, Unfree Vote in Venezuela, (21 May 2018), https://www.state.gov/an-unfair-unfree-vote-in-venezuela/.

107. Press Release, European Council, G7 Leaders' Statement on Venezuela (23 May 2018), https://www.consilium.europa.eu/en/press/press-releases/2018/05/23/g7-leaders-statement-on-venezuela/.

108. European Council, *supra* note 107; El G7 Denunció las Elecciones en Venezuela por 'no Cumplir los Estándares Internacionales' ni Asegurar 'Garantías Básicas' [The G7 Denounced the Elections in Venezuela for 'Failing to Comply with International Standards' and Ensure 'Basic Guarantees'], Infobae (23 May 2018), https://www.infobae.com/america/venezuela/2018/05/23/el-g7-denuncio-las-elecciones-en-venezuela-por-no-cumplir-los-estandares-internacionales-ni-asegurar-garantias-basicas/.

free and fair elections',[109] the illegitimate presidential re-election of May 2018 placed the country in an 'unprecedented situation'.[110] This conclusion was due to the fact – according to the Academy – that:

> the coming January 10th 2019, the date on which, as established in article 231 of the Constitution, the President of the republic for the term 2019–2025 is to be sworn, [Venezuela does] not have a president legitimately elected by means of free and just election.[111]

Consequently, the Academy, facing the grave situation confirmed by those facts, demanded that 'the different Branches of Government respect the Constitution', and take actions to achieve 'the full reestablishment of the constitutional and democratic order of the country'.[112] This message was addressed to the National Assembly, the only State organ with democratic legitimacy in the country, as all the other branches of government had been overcome by the Executive.

The National Assembly, as the people's representative and the primary interpreter of the Constitution, had no choice but to interpret the Constitution in such a way as to bring about a resolution of the political crisis. To fulfil the Article 231 requirement of having a legitimately elected president to fill the office for the 2019–2025 term, the Assembly analogized to Article 233 of the Constitution, which refers to cases of absolute absence of the president prior to taking office. In such instances, Article 233 provides the following:

> When an elected President is permanently unavailable to serve prior to his inauguration, a new election by universal suffrage and direct ballot shall be held within 30 consecutive days. Pending election and inauguration of the new President, the President of the National Assembly shall take charge of the Presidency of the Republic.

Interpreting the Constitution and applying this rule by analogy, the National Assembly determined that because there was no legitimately elected president that could be constitutionally sworn in for the upcoming term, Article 233 of the Constitution required that the president of the National Assembly had the duty to take charge of the presidency of the Republic. Because assuming the presidency of the Republic under such circumstances was one of the functions inherent in the President of the Assembly's duties, it was fully within the regular operation of law (*ex*

---

109. 'La Academia de Ciencias Políticas y Sociales, Ante el Diez de Enero de 2019: Fecha en la que ha de Juramentarse al Presidente de la República Conforme a la Constitución [Before 10 Jan. 2019: The Date on Which the President of the Republic Must Be Sworn in, According to the Constitution] (4 Jan. 2019), https://800noticias.com/academia-de-ciencias-politicas-y-sociales-desconocera-a-maduro-el-10-de-enero

110. *Ibid*

111. *Ibid*

112. *Ibid*

constitutione). There was no need for any additional swearing-in before the Assembly, for he had already done this when accepting the position as President of the Assembly on 5 January 2019.[113]

The National Assembly issued a Resolution explaining its interpretation of the Constitution on the same day as the swearing-in ceremony, which decreed that there was an 'emergency due to the total disruption of constitutional continuity', setting the path for the 'ceasing of the usurpation'.[114] As the president of the National Assembly stated on that same day, 'Today there is no Chief of State, today there is no commander in chief of the Armed Forces, today there is a National Assembly that represents the people of Venezuela.'[115]

A few days later, on 15 January 2019, the National Assembly completed its interpretation of the Constitution and issued another Resolution, reaffirming 'the usurpation of the Presidency of the Republic' by Nicolás Maduro Moros and the need to 'reestablish the Constitutional order', and adopting a set of 'decisions to proceed to restore the force of the constitutional order, on the basis of Articles 5, 187, 233, 333 and 350 of the Constitution'.[116]

The National Assembly specifically decided to restore the constitutional order based on Article 333, which give citizens the right to take necessary action to establish the validity of the constitution, and Article 350, which sanctions civil disobedience against Maduro's usurpations.[117] The Assembly resolved to effectively form a transition government that could proceed to organize free and transparent elections.[118]

In the same Resolution, the Assembly decided 'to formally declare the usurpation of the Presidency of the Republic by Nicolás Maduro Moros and, consequently, assume as legally ineffective the de facto status of Nicolás Maduro and declare all the alleged actions of the Executive Branch to be null and void, pursuant to Article 138 of the Constitution'.[119] The Assembly explained its plan:

> to adopt, within the framework of the application of Article 233, the measures that allow restoring the conditions of electoral integrity so that, once the usurpation ceases and a Transition Government is formed and installed, it will call

---

113. *See* Allan R. Brewer-Carías, *Transición hacia la Democracia en Venezuela. Bases Constitucionales y Obstáculos Usurpadores*, (Miami, Iniciativa Democrática de España y las Américas, Editorial Jurídica Venezolana, 2019); José Ignacio Hernández G., *Bases fundamentales de la transición en Venezuela*, (Caracas, Editorial Jurídica Venezolana, 2019).
114. Venezuela: Asamblea Nacional Se Declara 'En Emergencia' Por Jura de Nicolás Maduro [Venezuela: National Assembly Declares 'an Emergency' Over the Swearing In of Nicolás Maduro], T13 (10 Jan. 2019), https://www.dw.com/es/el-parlamento-venezolano-se-declara-en-emergencia-por-jura-de-maduro/a-47034572.
115. Juan Guaidó (@jguaido), Twitter (10 Jan. 2019, 2:44 PM), https://twitter.com/jguaido/status/1083449585232736256?lang=en.
116. *See* Acuerdo sobre la declaratoria de usurpación de la Presidencia de la República por parte de Nicolás Maduro Moros y el restablecimiento de la vigencia de la Constitución [Resolution on the declaration of usurpation of the Presidency of the Republic by Nicolás Maduro Moros and the restablesment of the enforcement of the Constitution] Asamblea Nacional de la República Bolivariana de Venezuela (15 Jan. 2019).
117. *Ibid*
118. *Ibid*
119. *Ibid*

and hold free and transparent elections within the shortest time possible, as provided in the Constitution and other Laws of the Republic and applicable treaties.[120]

48. For this transition process, the National Assembly also enacted a law on 5 February 2019, titled the '*Statute That Governs the Transition to Democracy in Order to Reinstate the Constitution*', which confirmed that 'the president of the National Assembly is the legitimate acting president of the Bolivarian Republic of Venezuela in accordance with Article 233 of the Constitution'.[121]

The National Assembly's constitutional interpretation in its 15 January Resolution and in the Statute for the Transition created an implicit understanding that as of 10 January 2019, representative Juan Guaidó, in his capacity as President of the National Assembly, by mandate of the Constitution was the interim President of the Republic (Article 14) until fair, just and free democratic election could take place to elect the President to complete the constitutional period 2019–2025. Juan Guaidó himself expressed the same message in various public statements, including a public rally held on 23 January 2019.

In assuming the interim presidency of the Republic in his capacity as President of the National Assembly, Guaidó merely fulfilled a duty imposed by the Constitution. As such, he did not self-proclaim himself to be the president, as was erroneously repeated in media reports.[122] He simply assumed one of the functions that were constitutionally vested in him as president of the National Assembly (Article 233).[123] Therefore, the 'oath' expressed by Guaidó at a rally on 23 January 2019, although an important political formality, did not replace the formal oath that he swore when becoming President of the National Assembly on 5 January 2019, which fulfilled, among other duties, that of assumption of the Presidency of the Republic.

The subsequent popular rallies and demonstrations within Venezuela indicated that citizens understood what had happened. The international community also

---

120. *Ibid*

121. Estatuto que rige la transición a la democracia para restablecer la vigencia de la Constitución de la República Bolivariana de Venezuela [Statute Governing the Transition to Democracy to Reestablish the Validity of the Constitution of the Bolivarian Republic of Venezuela], Asamblea Nacional de la República Bolivariana de Venezuela (5 Feb. 2019). *See* the comments in: Allan R. Brewer-Carías, *Transición hacia la Democracia en Venezuela. Bases Constitucionales y Obstáculos Usurpadores*, *supra*, p. 249.

122. *See* Allan R. Brewer-Carías, 'Juan Guaidó no se "autoproclamó". En su carácter de Presidente de la Asamblea Nacional, ante a ausencia de un Presidente Legítimamente electo para el período 2019-2025, Juan Guaidó quedó constitucionalmente encargado de la Presidencia de la República a partir del 10 de enero de 2019', in: http://allanbrewercarias.com/biblioteca-virtual/1003-juan-guaido-no-se-autoproclamo-caracter-presidente-la-asamblea-nacional-ante-la-ausencia-presidente-legitimamente-electo-periodo-2019-2025/.

123. *See*: Allan R. Brewer-Carías, *Transición hacia la Democracia en Venezuela, supra*, p. 227; and José Ignacio Hernández G., *Bases fundamentales de la transición en Venezuela*, (Caracas/New York, Editorial Jurídica Venezolana, 2020), p. 141.

understood, as was expressed in official statements issued by the foreign governments referring to the illegitimacy of the 2018 election and requesting the organization of free and transparent elections.[124]

For example, the Lima Group, in the statement issued on 4 January 2019,[125] ratified the illegitimacy of the 2018 presidential election because it 'did not comply with the necessary guarantees or international standards for a free, fair and transparent election';[126] and, the European Parliament in a Resolution of 31 January 2019 acknowledged Guaidó as 'the legitimate and democratically elected president of the National Assembly' and thus recognized him to be 'the legitimate interim president of the Bolivarian Republic of Venezuela, in accordance with the Venezuelan Constitution, as stated in Article 233, and express[ed] its full support for his roadmap'.[127]

Also, as an example, on 23 January 2019, the President of the United States issued a clear statement recognizing deputy Juan Guaidó as the Interim President of Venezuela, adding that 'In its role as the only legitimate branch of government duly elected by the Venezuelan people, the National Assembly invoked the country's constitution to declare Nicolas Maduro illegitimate, and the office of the presidency therefore vacant';[128] and on 4 February 2019, the UK Foreign Secretary gave a statement also recognizing Juan Guaidó 'as the constitutional interim President of Venezuela, until credible presidential elections can be held'.[129]

As mentioned, the Transition Statute ratified that 'The President of the National Assembly is, according to article 233 of the Constitution, the legitimate President in Charge of the Bolivarian Republic of Venezuela. The decisions of the President in Charge are to be subjected to parliamentary control of the National Assembly according to article 187.3 of the Constitution' (Article 14). The Transition Statute, in addition, regulated in its Article 15, various mechanisms for the 'defense of the rights of the Venezuelan people and government', providing for the possibility that the necessary decisions be 'taken to that end' 'in order to ensure the safeguarding of the assets, goods, and interests of the Government abroad'. For such purpose, the Statute authorized the Interim President, 'subject to the authoritative scrutiny of the National Assembly under the principles of transparency and accountability', to appoint a Special Attorney General 'to defend and represent the rights and interests

---

124. *See* list of countries in José Ignacio Hernández G., (2020), Bases fundamentales de la transición en Venezuela, cit., p. 164.
125. *See*: https://www.cancilleria.gov.co/en/news-room/news/declaracion-grupo-lima-1. The statement was subscribed by Argentine, Brazil, Canada, Chile, Colombia, Costa Rica, Guatemala, Guyana, Honduras, Panama, Paraguay, Peru and St. Lucia. An English translation of the statement can be seen here: https://www.international.gc.ca/world-monde/international_relations-relations_internationales/latin_america-amerique_latine/2019-01-04-lima_group-groupe_lima.aspx?lang=eng.
126. *Ibid.*
127. *See* text in European Parliament, 2014–2019, Approved Texts, P8_TA-PROV(2019)0061 Situation in Venezuela, available at: http://www.europarl.europa.eu/sides/getDoc.do?pubRef=-//EP//NONSGML+TA+P8-TA-2019-0061+0+DOC+PDF+V0//ES
128. *See* https://www.whitehouse.gov/briefings-statements/statement-president-donald-j-trump-recognizing-venezuelan-national-assembly-president-juan-guaido-interim-president-venezuela/.
129. *See* https://www.gov.uk/government/news/uk-recognises-juan-guaido-as-interim-president-of-venezuela.

of the Republic, State companies and other decentralized entities of the Public Administration abroad', and Ad-hoc Administrative Boards 'to assume the direction and administration of public institutes, autonomous institutes, State foundations, State associations and organizations, State own companies, including companies established abroad, and any other decentralized entity, for the purpose of appointing administrators and, in general, adopting the measures necessary to control and protect their assets'. Based on such powers, for instance, the Interim President with the authorization of the National Assembly, appointed the Special Attorney General and the Ad-Hoc Board of Directors, among others, of Petróleos de Venezuela S.A. and of the Central Bank of Venezuela, for the protection of the assets of the republic abroad. Those public officials and bodies have been acting abroad with the recognition of many foreign governments.[130]

In 2020, parliamentary elections were held to elect the new National Assembly for the constitutional period 2021–2025, but they were declared illegitimate and null by the National Assembly, not being recognized by many democratic countries in the International Community.[131] That led to the reform of the Transition Statute to extend for one year the constitutional functioning of the National Assembly elected in 2015, until January 2022.[132] Again, in January 2022, a new reform of the Transition Statute was also approved to extend the constitutional functioning of the National Assembly until January 2023.[133]

In parallel to the application of the regime established in the Transition Statute by the opposition-controlled National Assembly elected in 2015, in particular regarding the protection of foreign assets of the Republic, and in spite of all the international recognitions, the fact was also that during the Transition Regime, the de facto totalitarian government-controlled by Nicolás Maduro continued with its abuses and subjugation of the other branches of government, in particular the Judicial Power.[134]The only exception was the legislative branch represented by the National Assembly elected in 2015, which although controlled by the opposition, was eventually neutralized in its actions by the Constitutional Chamber of the Supreme Tribunal controlled by the government (*see supra* paragraphs 39–42).

---

130. *See* José Ignacio Hernández and Allan R. Brewer-Carías, *The Defense of the Rights and Interests of the Venezuelan State by the Interim Government Before Foreign Courts, and their International Recognition 2019–2020,* (New York, Editorial Jurídica Venezolana, 2021).
131. *See* Allan R. Brewer-Carías and José Ignacio Hernández G., *La ilegítima e inconstitucional convoctoria de las elecciones parlamentarias en 2020*, (Miami, Iniciativa Democrática de España y las Américas, Editorial Jurídica Venezolana International, 2020).
132. *See* all the documents in Allan R. Brewer-Carías, Asdrúbal Aguiar A., Román J. Duque Corredor and José Ignacio Hernández G., *La transición constitucional y su continuidad en Venezuela,*(Miami, Iniciativa Democrática de España y las Américas, Editorial Jurídica Venezolana International, 2021).
133. *See* all the documents and discussions in José Ignacio Hernández, (Coordinador), *Estudios sobre la reforma del Estatuto de Transición de 2022 y la continuidad constitucional del régimen de transición de 2019*, (Miami, Iniciativa Democrática España y las Américas, Editorial Jurídica Venezolana International 2022).
134. *See* Allan R. Brewer-Carías, 'Dismantling the Rule of Law by politically controlling the Judiciary in Venezuela and its harmful projection on the Inter-American judicial system for the protection of human rights', *European Review of Public Law/Revue Européenne de Droit Public*, vol. 33, No. 3, autumn/automne 2021 pp. 877–918; and La demolición de la independencia y autonomía del Poder Judicial en Venezuela 1999-2021, (Caracas, Editorial Jurídica Venezolana, 2021).

The previously referred constitutional process and political crisis that since the approval of the 1999 Constitution has characterized the functioning of the Venezuelan State, has undoubtedly affected all the constitutional foundations of the rule of law State as it was established in its provisions (principle of supremacy of the Constitution, representative government, separation of powers, principle of legality, entrenched declarations of human rights, judicial review). The Constitution has not been changed, but all its constitutional mandates have been ignored,[135] being the result of the complete collapse of the rule of law State.[136] Additionally, all the acts and decisions issued by the National Assembly and by Interim President Juan Guaidó since 2019 were declared null and void by the Constitutional Chamber of the Supreme Tribunal, in many cases acting ex officio, violating all the due process of law and fair trial principles, to an extent that such rulings have not been recognized by foreign courts, as was, for instance, the case of the British High Courts in 2022 (*see infra* paragraphs 740 et seq.).

49. On 30 December 2022, a new reform of the Transition Statute was sanctioned basically to extend the 'constitutional continuity' of the National Legislative Branch until 5 January 2024, exercised by the National Assembly elected in December 2015, which can also function through its Delegate Commission (Article 7) to which new and extended attributions were assigned (Article 8).[137]

Consequently, the reform, whose Draft submitted to the first discussion on 22 December 2022 was highly criticized,[138] can in fact be considered to be a 'new' Transition Statute, in which *no direct mention is made to the Interim President of the Republic*, a position that according to Article 233 of the Constitution and since January 2019 was occupied by Mr Juan Guaidó, who as President of the National Assembly began to exercise the Executive Branch as was later recognized in the same 2019 Transition Statute (Article 14).

In the 'new' 2022 Statute, mentions are made to the Interim President *only in and indirect way*, for instance, in Article 20, which was established, in an express way, that from the publication of the 'reform', '*all the entities and public officials appointed by the Interim President will cease to have effects*'. This provision applies, among others, to the Special Attorney General appointed by Mr Guaidó, and to the 'ambassadors' also appointed by Guaidó, as Interim President, before some foreign governments and some International Organizations.

---

135. *See* Allan R. Brewer-Carías, *La mentira como política de Estado. Crónica de una crisis política permanente. Venezuela 1999–2015* (Caracas, Editorial Jurídica Venezolana, 2015)
136. *See* Allan R. Brewer-Carías, *The Collapse of the Rule of Law and the struggle for Democracy in Venezuela. Lectures and Essays (2015–2020),* (Miami Dade College, 2020).
137. *See the text in Gaceta Legislativa, No. 66, 3 Jan. 2023. See all* the documents and discussions in Allan R. Brewer-Carías and Asdrúbal Aguiar, (Coordinadores), *F*in del regimen de *Transición en Venezuela,* (Miami, Iniciativa Democrática España y las Américas, Editorial Jurídica Venezolana International 2023).
138. *See*, among others, the comments in: Allan R. Brewer-Carías, 'La pretendida reforma del Estatuto de Transición a la Dmocracia que supuestamente "elimina" el Gobierno Interino, no es más que un gran e inconstitucional disparate, porque dicho Gobierno no fue "creado" por la Asamblea Nacional ni puede por tanto ser "eliminado" por la misma', Nuw York, 17 de diciembre, 2022. Available at: http://allanbrewercarias.com/wp-content/uploads/2022/12/A.R.-Brewer-Carias.-Sobre-la-reforma-del-Estatuto-de-Transicion-27-dic-2022.pdf.

Nonetheless, as established in Articles 20 and 22 of the new Statute, this provision does not apply to: (i) 'the Council of Administration and Protection of Assets, (ii) the Council for the Administration of the Expenses Program for the Security and Defense of Democracy, (iii) *the Ad-Hoc Board of PDVSA* and (iv) the *Ad-Hoc Board of the Central Banc of Venezuela*', which '*will continue to function* for 12 months, which is the period of enforcement of the Statute' (Articles 20, 22).

The direct consequence of all these provisions of the 'new' Transition Statute is the configuration of a sort of 'Parliamentary Government', due to the fact that all the functions and organs that were created attached to the Interim President (Interim Government) after the reform was assigned to the National Assembly (Article 8) and to a new 'Council for the Administration and Protection of Assets' appointed by the National Assembly (Article 9).[139]

This Council, in particular, was transformed and converted into a legislative body in charge of protecting and managing the assets of the Republic abroad, a sort of 'legislative public holding', with powers (i) to 'participate, when considered convenient, in the administration of such assets'; (ii) to 'represent the shares of the Republic in the entities in which it is a shareholder'; and (iii) to 'appoint or revoke judicial representatives of the Republic' to act in judicial processes abroad (Articles 9, 14).

Nonetheless, it was expressly clarified that the powers of attorney that were validly granted by the former Special Attorney General, according to the previous Transition Statute, will remain effective until revoked by the same Council (Article 9). Also, it must be pointed out that the transition regime established in the previous Statute regarding the state-owned enterprise Petroleso de Venezuela S.A. PDVSA, has been basically kept in the new Statute (Article 13).

It must also be mentioned that according to Article 11 of the new Transition Statute, the National Assembly or its Delegate Commission have the power to enact all the decision needed to implement the new Statute (Article 12), as well as the power to 'appoint international representatives to act before multilateral organizations on matters of Human Rights, migration or humanitarian crisis and the fight against corruption; and to act for the democratic protection of assets before the United States of America, the United Kingdom, and / or wherever required'. It is also provided that these officials 'may act in matters of organization and support for Venezuelan

139. The National Assembly received the recognition of Foreign Governments. For example, on 3 Jan. 2023, the Government of the United States expressed: 'The United States continues to recognize the National Assembly democratically elected in 2015 as the last remaining democratic institution in Venezuela, and we welcome the agreement reached to extend its authority.' *See* Ned Price, department of State, 3 Jan. 2023, available at: https://www.state.gov/translations/spanish/el-gobierno-interino-de-venezuela-y-la-asamblea-nacional-de-2015/. On 12 Jan. 2023 the Government of the United Kingdom expressed before Parliament that 'we continue to regard the National Assembly elected in 2015 as the last democratically elected National Assembly in Venezuela, and note the vote extending its mandate for another year' *See* David Rutley MP, Foreign, Commonwealth & Development Office, 12 Jan. 2023, available at https://www.gov.uk/government/speeches/uk-government-position-on-venezuela.es-419.

migrants and must be accountable to the National Assembly or the Delegate Commission'.[140] Now, bearing in mind all the variability of the constitutional process in the country that has taken place particularly after 2016, we will proceed to study and analyze in the following pages, the Constitutional Law in Venezuela according to what it is established in the 1999 Constitution.

140. *See* Allan R. Brewer-Carías and Asdrúbal Aguiar, *El final del encargado de la Presidencia y el Gobierno Parlamentario en Venezuela, Iniciativa Democrática España y las Américas*, Editorial Jurídica Venezolana, Caracas 2023.

Chapter 2. Some Basic Aspect of the Political System of Government According to the 1999 Constitution and Its Distortions

50. According to the Constitution of 1999, Venezuela has been formally organized as a democratic Republic that is expressly qualified as 'The Bolivarian Republic of Venezuela', conceived as an '*Etat de droit*', in the sense of the English expression 'rule of law', with an elected government organized according to the principles of separation of powers, a presidential system of government, and vertical division of powers following the federal form of government; all their actions being subjected to judicial review by the Courts when unconstitutional or illegal.

§1. The Democratic Republic

51. The 1999 Constitution, following the tradition initiated in 1811, has been politically organized as a Republic, where the 'sovereignty resides untransferably in the people', who exercise it 'directly' by means of referendum and other instruments established in the Constitution, 'and indirectly, through suffrage, by the organs that exercise State Powers' (Article 5). This provision consecrates the principles of popular sovereignty and the democratic regime, in particular the concept of political representation, adding in Article 62 the rights of all Citizens 'to participate freely in public matters directly or by means of their representatives'.

The important aspect of being stressed is the expression that sovereignty resides 'untransferable' *(intransferiblemente)* in the people; it resides only and always in the people, so that no man or entity may assume it, not even a Constituent Assembly, which of course could never be 'sovereign'. That is why the Constitution also indicates, when regulating the 'National Constituent Assembly' as a means for constitutional review, that 'the people of Venezuela are the repository of the original constituent power' (Article 347), which, for that reason, could never be transferred to an Assembly.

Of course, the consecration of the principle of popular sovereignty and its untransferability led, in the modern world, to the development of the principle of representative democracy, in the sense that the people, who are the holders of sovereignty, normally exercise it through representatives. Popular sovereignty and representative democracy are then consubstantial and indivisible principles.

52. However, as it has been conceived in the Inter-American Democratic Charter *(Carta Democratica Interamericana)* adopted by the OAS in 2001 after so many anti-democratic, militarist and authoritarian regimes disguised as democratic because of their electoral origin, democracy is not only a matter of electing governments, in the sense that it has many other *essential elements of the representative democracy.* That is, in addition to having periodic, fair and free elections, based on the universal and secret vote as an expression of the will of the people; democracy means the respect for human rights and fundamental liberties; the access to power and its exercise with subjection to the rule of law; the plural regime of the political parties and organizations; and the separation and independence of public powers (Article 3). In addition, democracy also has other *fundamental components*, like the transparency of governmental activities; the integrity, responsibility of governments in public management; the respect of social rights and freedom of speech and press; the constitutional subordination of all institutions of the State to the legally constituted civil authority; and the respect to the rule of law of all the entities and sectors of society.[141]

Without all such essential elements and fundamental components in force, it is difficult to consider that a political system is really a democratic one, notwithstanding the formal declarations in the Constitution.

53. Consequently, even though democracy as a political system of government and social life is much more than just representative democracy, the latter is an essential part of it and cannot be substituted by a supposedly 'participatory democracy', as it was intended to be drafted in the 1999 Constitution with the elimination of the word 'representative' from Article 6, which in order to characterize the democratic government, only uses the expressions: 'participative, elective, decentralized, alternating, pluralist, and of revocable mandates'. Notwithstanding, democracy is always 'representative',[142] and in addition, it can be more or less 'participative' according to the degree of direct participation of the people in public decision-making[143] (*see infra* paragraphs 167 et seq., 175 et seq.).

141. *See* Allan R. Brewer-Carías, *La crisis de la democracia venezolana. La Carta Democrática Interamericana y los sucesos de abril 2002* (Caracas: Ediciones El Nacional, 2002).

142. *See* Pedro L. Bracho Grand y Miriam Álvarez de Bozo, 'Democracia representativa en la Constitución Nacional de 1999', in *Estudios de Derecho Público: Libro Homenaje a Humberto J. La Roche Rincón,* vol. I (Caracas: Tribunal Supremo de Justicia, 2001), 235–254; and Ricardo Combellas, 'Representación vs. Participación en la Constitución Bolivariana. Análisis de un falso dilema', en *Bases y principios del sistema constitucional venezolano* (Ponencias del VII Congreso Venezolano de Derecho Constitucional realizado en San Cristóbal del 21 al 23 de Noviembre de 2001), vol. II San Cristóbal, 383–402.

143. *See* Manuel Feo La Cruz, 'La participación de la sociedad civil en el proceso de gestión pública. Retos y desafíos', in E*l Derecho Público a comienzos del siglo XXI. Estudios homenaje al Profesor Allan R. Brewer-Carías*, vol. I (Madrid: Instituto de Derecho Público, UCV, Civitas Ediciones, 2003), 415–429; Yusby S. Méndez-Apolinar, 'La obligación ciudadana de participar en los asuntos públicos, como expresión de la cultura democrática', in *El Derecho Público a comienzos del siglo XXI. Estudios homenaje al Profesor Allan R. Brewer-Carías*, vol. I (Madrid: Instituto de Derecho Público, UCV, Civitas Ediciones, 2003), 431–437; Ana P. Deniz, 'La participación ciudadana en la Constitución de 1999', in Revista de Derecho Constitucional, No. 7 (enero-junio) (Caracas: Editorial Sherwood, 2003), 115–124; Fernando Flores Jiménez, 'La participación ciudadana en la Constitución venezolana de 1999', in *Revista de Derecho Constitucional*, No. 5 (julio-diciembre) (Caracas: Editorial Sherwood, 2001), 75–88; Luis Salamanca, 'La Constitución venezolana de 1999: de la representación a la hiper-participación ciudadana', in *Revista de Derecho Público*, No. 82 (abril-junio) (Caracas: Editorial Jurídica Venezolana, 2000), 85–105; Humberto Njaim, 'Las implicaciones de la democracia participativa: un tema constitucional de nuestro tiempo', in *Constitución y Constitucionalismo Hoy* (Caracas: Editorial Ex Libris, 2000), 719–742; Allan R. Brewer-Carías, 'Democracia participativa, descentralización política y régimen municipal', in *Tendencias actuales del derecho público en Iberoamérica*, ed. Miguel Alejandro López Olvera y Luis Gerardo Rodríguez Lozano (Coordinadores) (México: Editorial Porrúa, 2006), 1–23; Ricardo Combellas, 'La democracia participativa y la Constitución de la República Bolivariana de Venezuela', in *Derecho Constitucional. General y Particular. Actualizado con la Constitución de la República Bolivariana de Venezuela del 24-03-2000*, vol. I (Caracas: Universidad Santa María), 279–305.

Nonetheless, the drafters of the Constitution of 1999 pretended to install a supposedly 'participative democracy', by confounding participation with direct democracy instruments like the referenda, which are established in all its forms: consultative, approbatory, abrogating, and revoking (Articles 71–74); and by defining a government political project based on a supposedly direct relation between the President of the Republic and the people, giving rise to an illusory 'participative' mechanism that is controlled from above (*see infra* paragraphs 232 et seq.). In this sense, in the name of such 'participatory democracy' and in parallel to the Democratic Constitutional State established in the Constitution, a 'Popular Power State' or 'Communal State' has been progressively implemented since 2006, based on Communal Councils not elected by universal and direct suffrage and controlled by the National Executive, dismantling the very notion of 'representative' democracy.[144] As such, the 'Communal State' monopolizes power and consolidates it hegemonically, in a concentrated and authoritarian manner, completely contrary to that which is required of a democratic regime.

The fact is that participation in democratic systems is only possible when a developed system of local government is established, with their own autonomous governments elected democratically, not in supposed 'communal councils' conceived in parallel to the municipalities, directly dependent on the President of the Republic, and directed by non-elected public officials, as it has been regulated by statute[145] (*see infra* paragraphs 232 et seq.). That is, political participation is only effectively possible in a decentralized system of government based on local authorities, which is contrary to the concentration of Power and centralism as it has been developed in Venezuela during the past years (*see infra* paragraphs 64, 203 et seq.).

§2. The 'Bolivarian' Republic of Venezuela

54. But regarding the Republic, one of the innovations incorporated in Article 1 of the Constitution, was the renaming of the Republic, changing the traditional expression 'Republic of Venezuela', for the 'Bolivarian Republic of Venezuela'; a change that can yield multiple interpretations. In the beginning, the motivation for the new name given to the country was formally to refer to the ideas and actions of Simón Bolívar, who as mentioned was not only the 'Liberator' of Venezuela at the beginning of the nineteenth century in the wars of independence against Spain (*see supra* paragraphs 1, 2) but also of other Latin American countries such as Colombia, Ecuador, Bolivia and Peru which were historically called the 'Bolivarian' Republics.

---

144. *See* Allan R. Brewer-Carías, *El 'nuevo constitucionalismo latinoamericano' y la destrucción del Estado democrático por el Juez Constitucional. El Caso de Venezuela* (Madrid, Ediciones Olejnik, 2018).

145. Communal Councils Law, Gaceta Oficial No. 5.806 Extra. of 10 Apr. 2006. *See* in general Allan R. Brewer-Carías, *Estudios sobre el Estado Comunal o Estado del Poder Popular. O de cómo se desconstitucionaliza al Estado en fraude a la Constitución y a la voluntad popular* (Caracas, Editorial Jurídica Venezolana, 2021).

Although it has not been the first time in Venezuela's political history that rulers, mainly of military and authoritarian roots, had evoked Simón Bolívar to attract followers and to give some 'doctrinal' basis to their regimes,[146] never before had the adherence to Bolivar led to changing the Republic's name and to the invention of a 'Bolivarian doctrine' to justify the government's policies, as Chávez did regarding his 'XXI century Socialism' one[147] (*see infra* paragraphs 262, 357).

In Venezuelan constitutional history, strictly speaking, the only 'Bolivarian Republic' that has existed as a State, has been the one resulting from the 'union of the peoples of Colombia' proposed by Simón Bolívar in 1819 and materialized in the 1821 Constitution of the Republic of Colombia (comprising the territories of today's Venezuela, Nueva Granada and Ecuador). With that constitution, the Republic of Venezuela just disappeared as an autonomous State,[148] a situation that endured up until 1830, until Bolivar's death.

---

146. It was the case of Antonio Guzmán Blanco in the nineteenth century and of Cipriano Castro, Juan Vicente Gómez, Eleazar López Contreras, and Marcos Pérez Jiménez in the twentieth century. John Lynch has pointed out: 'The traditional cult of Bolivar has been used as a convenient ideology by military dictators, culminating with the regimes of Juan Vicente Gómez and Eleazar López Contreras; these had at least more or less respected the basic thought of the Liberator, even when they misrepresented its meaning.' *See* John Lynch, *Simón Bolívar: A Life* (New Haven, CT: Yale University Press, 2007), 304. *See also* Germán Carrera Damas, *El culto a Bolívar, esbozo para un estudio de la historia de las ideas en Venezuela* (Caracas: UCV, 1969); Luis Castro Leiva, *De la patria boba a la teología bolivariana* (Caracas: Monteávila, 1987); Elías Pino Iturrieta, *El divino Bolívar. Ensayo sobre una religión republicana* (Caracas: Alfail, 2008); Ana Teresa Torres, *La herencia de la tribu. Del mito de la independencia a la Revolución bolivariana* (Caracas:Editorial Alfa, 2009). *See also* the historiography study on these books in Tomás Straka, *La épica del desencanto* (Caracas: Editorial Alfa, 2009).
147. John Lynch has pointed out: 'In 1999 Venezuelans were astonished to learn that their country had been renamed "the Bolivarian Republic of Venezuela" by decree of President Hugo Chávez, who called himself a "revolutionary Bolivarian". Authoritarian populist, or neocaudillos, or Bolivarian militarists, whatever their designation, invoke Bolívar no less ardently than did previous rulers, though it is doubtful whether he would have responded to their calls ... But the new heresy, far from maintaining continuity with the constitutional ideas of Bolívar, as was claimed, invented a new attribute, the populist Bolívar, and in the case of Cuba gave him a new identity, the socialist Bolívar. By exploiting the authoritarian tendency, which certainly existed in the thought and action of Bolívar, regimes in Cuba and Venezuela claim the Liberator as patron for their policies, distorting his ideas in the process.' *See* John Lynch, *Simón Bolívar: A Life* (New Haven, CT: Yale University Press, 2007), 304. *See* also A.C. Clark, *The Revolutionary Has No Clothes: Hugo Chávez's Bolivarian Farce* (New York: Encounter Books, 2009), 5–14. The last attempt to completely appropriate Simón Bolívar for the 'Bolivarian Revolution' was the televised exhumation of his remains that took place at the National Pantheon in Caracas on 26 Jul. 2010, conducted by President Chávez himself and other high officials, including the Prosecutor General, among other things, for the purpose of determining if Bolivar died of arsenic poisoning in Santa Marta in 1830, instead of from tuberculosis. *See* Simon Romero, 'Building a New History By Exhuming Bolívar', *The New York Times*, 4 Aug. 2010, A7.
148. *See* the text in Allan R. Brewer-Carías, *Las Constituciones de Venezuela*, vol. 1 (Caracas: Academia de Ciencias Políticas y Sociales, 2008), 643–46. *See also*: Allan R. Brewer-Carías, *La Constitución de la República de Colombia de 30 de agosto de 1821*. Producto de la unión de los pueblos de Venezuela y de la Nueva Granada. Sus Antecedentes y Condicionantes, (Bogotá, Caracas, Academia de Ciencias Políticas y Sociales de Venezuela; Academia Colombiana de Jurisprudencia, Editorial Jurídica Venezolana, Editorial Temis, 2021).

55. Consequently, the renaming of the Republic in 1999, this time without affecting the country's sovereignty, was explained as intent to give the Republic, although ignoring the past 200 years of history, a 'definitive' national doctrine supposedly based on the thoughts of Bolívar. Nonetheless, as it can now be appreciated, the truth was otherwise, being just a label used by the new rulers of the country in order to impose their own socialist doctrine disguised as a Bolivarian one.

For that purpose, the first step taken in order to give the country the name of Bolivar was an exclusive political or partisan one based on the name initially given in 1982 to the political movement used by the late President of the Republic (H. Chávez) to gain power, the 'Bolivarian Revolutionary Movement 200 (MBR-200)'. Because such an organization could not continue as a formal political party in order to lead the 'Bolivarian' revolution due to the legal prohibition for parties to use their denomination symbols of the motherland,[149] the decision was to incorporate the name in the Constitution by labelling the country,[150] and the party became the Fifth Republic Movement (*Movimiento v. República,* MVR) which was later transformed into the United Socialist Party of Venezuela (PSUV), which declared itself as a 'Marxist' party following the 'Bolivarian doctrine.'[151]

The consequence of the constitutional reform on this matter has been that everything related to the new political regime has been called Bolivarian, beginning, for instance, with the initial creation of the 'Bolivarian Circles' that were the first social or communal organizations promoted and supported by the government in order to react against any opposition to the government and to threaten anybody with views contrary to it.[152]

The fact has been that the partisan character of the use of the Bolivar's name applied to the Republic and to the government policies has initiated a bitter polarization of the country, between those who are 'Bolivarian' and those who are not and, consequently, supposedly, between patriots and anti-patriots, good people and bad people, pure people and corrupt people, revolutionary and anti-revolutionary or oligarchs; all that by manipulating history and popular feelings regarding the image of Bolivar.

56. The constant promotion of the 'Bolivarian Revolution' even led the President of the Republic himself, in 2007, to draft and propose a constitutional reform

149. According to the Political Parties Law, *Gaceta Oficial* No. 27.725, of 30 Apr. 1965, political parties cannot use the name of the founders of the country or homeland symbols. The political organization the President formed before campaigning for the 1998 election was Movimiento Bolivariano 200. That name could not be used to identify the political party he founded, which became *Movimiento v. República*

150. *Mutatis mutandi*, in a certain way it happened with the use of the name of Augusto C. Sandino in the name of the *Frente Sandinista de Liberación* and of the Sandinista Republic of Nicaragua.

151. *See* 'Declaration of Principles' of the PSUV (23 Apr. 2010), available at http://psuv.org.ve/files/tcdocumentos/Declaracion-de-principios-PSUV.pdf.

152. The general assembly of the OAS, in its Report of 18 Apr. 2002, said about the Bolivarian Circles, that they 'are groups of citizens or grassroots organizations which support the President's political platform. Many sectors consider them responsible for the human rights violations, acts of intimidation and looting'. *See* the reference in Allan R. Brewer-Carías, *La crisis de la democracia en Venezuela* (Caracas: Libros El Nacional, 2002).

before the National Assembly,[153] (*see supra* paragraphs 33, 36, *infra* paragraphs 261 et seq.) in order to express and formally incorporate in the text of the Constitution the socialist 'Bolivarian doctrine' as the fundamental doctrine of the State. For such purpose, 'Bolivarian socialism' was proposed to be incorporated into the Constitution as the State's guiding doctrine, even for international relations. This constitutional reform, based on the then so-called twenty-first-century socialism,[154] failed to be implanted, being rejected by the people through popular votes in the 2 December 2007 referendum.[155]

Nonetheless, and despite its rejection by the people's votes, in the following year (2008), the 2007 constitutional reform proposals began to be implemented by the authoritarian government in violation of the Constitution through a massive number of decree-laws issued by the President and by means of Organic Laws sanctioned by the National Assembly, changing in this way the Constitution but without formally reforming it. The last set of unconstitutional legislation implementing the 2007 rejected reform was approved in December of 2010, by formally creating a Communal State (or Socialist or Communist State) based upon the exercise of a Popular Power that has no constitutional basis, in parallel to the existing Constitutional decentralized State based upon the Public Power (National, state, municipal) expressly established in the Constitution.[156]

57. For such purpose, after the set of unconstitutional laws approved between 2008 and 2009 related to the implantation of Socialism as the doctrine of the new Communal State, in January 2010, Chávez himself confessed that the supposedly 'Bolivarian revolution', was no more than the phantasmagorical resurrection of the historically failed 'Marxist revolution', but in this case led by a President who has

153. *See* on the constitutional reforms proposals, Allan R. Brewer-Carías, *Hacia la consolidación de un Estado socialista, centralizado, policial y militarista. Comentarios sobre el sentido y alcance de las propuestas de reforma constitucional 2007* (Caracas: Editorial Jurídica Venezolana, 2007); *La reforma constitucional de 2007 (Comentarios al proyecto inconstitucionalmente sancionado por la Asamblea Nacional el 2 de noviembre de 2007)* (Caracas: Editorial Jurídica Venezolana, 2007).

154. *See* Rogelio Pérez Perdomo, 'La Constitución de papel y su reforma', in *Revista de Derecho Público* 112 *(Estudios sobre la reforma constitucional)* (Caracas: Editorial Jurídica Venezolana, 2007), 14; G. Fernández, 'Aspectos esenciales de la modificación constitucional propuesta por el Presidente de la República. La modificación constitucional como un fraude a la democracia', *ibid.*, 22; Alfredo Arismendi, 'Utopía Constitucional', in *ibid.*, 31; Manuel Rachadell, 'El personalismo político en el Siglo XXI', in *ibid.*, 66; Allan R. Brewer-Carías, 'El sello socialista que se pretendía imponer al Estado', in *ibid.*, 71–75; Alfredo Morles Hernández, 'El nuevo modelo económico para el Socialismo del Siglo XXI', in *ibid.*, 233–36.

155. The definitive voting figures in such referendum have never been informed to the country by the government-controlled National Electoral Council. *See* Allan R. Brewer-Carías, 'Estudio sobre la propuesta de Reforma Constitucional para establecer un estado socialista, centralizado y militarista (Análisis del anteproyecto presidencial, Agosto de 2007)', *Cadernos da Escola de Direito e Relações Internacionais da UniBrasil* 7 (Curitiba, 2007), 265–308.

156. *See* Gustavo Linares Benzo, 'Sólo un Poder Público más. El Poder Popular en la reforma del 2007', in *Revista de Derecho Público* 112 *(Estudios sobre la reforma constitucional)* (Caracas: Editorial Jurídica Venezolana, 2007), 102–105; Arturo Peraza, 'Reforma, Democracia participativa y Poder Popular', in *ibid.*, 107–113.

never even read Marx's writings.[157] This announcement provoked in April 2010, that the governmental PSUV of which the President presides, in its First Extraordinary Congress then adopted its 'Declaration of Principles' in which it officially declared itself as a 'Marxist', 'Anti-imperialist' and 'Anti-capitalist' party. According to the same document, the party's actions are to be based on 'scientific socialism' and on the 'inputs of Marxism as a philosophy of praxis', in order to substitute the 'Capitalist Bourgeois State' with a 'Socialist State' based on the Popular Power and the socialization of the means of production.[158] Of course, none of these ideas can be found in the works of Simón Bolivar, his name only being used as a pretext to continue to manipulate the Bolivar 'cult' to justify authoritarianism, as has occurred so many times before in the history of the country.[159]

With these declarations, it can be said, finally, that the so-called Bolivarian Revolution has been unveiled;[160] a revolution for which nobody in Venezuela has voted except for its rejection in the 2 December 2007 referendum, in which the President's proposals for constitutional reforms in order to establish a Socialist, Centralized, Police and Militaristic State received a negative popular response.[161]

§3. The Social and Democratic Rule of Law and Justice State

58. According to Article 2 of the Constitution of 1999, Venezuela is defined as an '*Estado democrático y social de derecho y de justicia*', that is, a 'social democratic rule of law and justice State'.[162]

---

157. In his annual speech before the National Assembly on 15 Jan. 2010, in which Chávez declared to have 'assumed Marxism', he also confessed that he had never read Marx's works. *See* María Lilibeth Da Corte, 'Por primera vez asumo el marxismo', in *El Universal* (Caracas, 16 Jan. 2010), www.eluniversal.com/2010/01/16/pol_art_por-primera-vez-asu_1726209.shtml.
158. *See* 'Declaración de Principios, I Congreso Extraordinario del Partido Socialista Unido de Venezuela', 23 Apr. 2010, at http://psuv.org.ve/files/tcdocumentos/Declaracion-de-principios-PSUV.pdf.
159. In Bolívar's writings, nothing can be found that could allow to identify his thoughts with any socialist ideas. Otherwise, Karl Marx himself would have detected it, in 1857, ten years after writing on Socialism and Communism in his book with Friedrich Engels, *The German Ideology* (*See* in www.educa.madrid.org/cms_tools/files/0a24636f-764c-4e03-9c1d-6722e2ee60d7/Texto%20Marx%20y%20Engels.pdf), when writing the very critical entry on 'Bolívar y Ponte, Simón', for the *New American Cyclopaedia*, vol. III, 1858., in which he observed nothing regarding possible socialists ideas that could be had derived from the writings of Bolívar. *See* the text in www.marxists.org/archive/marx/works/1858/01/bolivar.htm.
160. *See* Allan R. Brewer-Carías, 'The "Bolivarian Revolution" in Venezuela and the regime's contempt of Constitutional law', in Uwe Kischel und Christian Kirchner (Coord.), *Ideologie und Weltanschauung im Recht*, (Tübingern, Gesellschaft für Rechtsvergleichtung e.V., Rechtsvergleichung und Rechtsvereinheitlichung, Mohr Siebeck, 2012), pp. 121–148
161. *See* on the 2007 constitutional reforms proposals, Allan R. Brewer-Carías, *Hacia la consolidación de un Estado socialista, centralizado, policial y militarista. Comentarios sobre el sentido y alcance de las propuestas de reforma constitucional 2007* (Caracas: Editorial Jurídica Venezolana, 2007); *La reforma constitucional de 2007 (Comentarios al proyecto inconstitucionalmente sancionado por la Asamblea Nacional el 2 de noviembre de 2007)* (Caracas: Editorial Jurídica Venezolana, 2007).
162. *See* Luis Enrique Useche Díaz, 'El Estado Social y Democrático de Derecho y de Justicia. Utopía y Frustración', in *Tendencias Actuales del Derecho Constitucional. Homenaje a Jesús María Casal Montbrun*, ed. Jesús María Casal, Alfredo Arismendi & Carlos Luis Carrillo Artiles (Coords.), vol. I (Caracas: UCV/Universidad Católica Andrés Bello, 2008), 129–160; José M. Delgado Ocando,

Yet, the rule of law in the Venezuelan constitutional system is not only a deduction of the constitutional framework establishing the conception of the State as submitted to the Constitution and the law in which the citizens are not subjected to arbitrary rules. It is the result of an express provision of the Constitutions which have been included in it, following the contemporary constitutional trend as expressed in the Constitution of the Federal Republic of Germany (Article 20.1), in the Spanish Constitution (Article 1) and in the Constitution of Colombia (Article 1).

In this regard, the rule of law implies the subordination of the State and its officials to the authority of the law (Preamble), in the sense that all branches of government and the organs of the State are subjected to the 'Constitution and laws' (Article 137) and Public Administration must act completely subjected to the law (Article 141). This principle implies the existence in the Constitution of the systems of judicial review of legislation (Articles 334 and 336) and of administrative actions *(contencioso administrativo)* (Article 259) (*see infra* paragraphs 706 et seq.).

59. But in addition, the Constitution not only declared that Venezuela is a rule of law State (*Estado de derecho*), but that it is also a democratic and social justice State, which implies three different additional qualifications: social State, democratic State and justice State.

The idea of a 'social State' is that of a State with social obligations established to procure social justice, an objective which brings the State to intervene in social and economic activity as a welfare State. That is why this Social State must seek the application of the fundamental values of equality and solidarity, the pre-eminence of human rights (Preamble, Articles 1 and 21) and the achievement of 'social justice' as one of the bases of the economic system (Article 299)[163] (*see infra* paragraphs 84, 93, 664).

Regarding the 'democratic State', the expression refers to the grounds of the political organization of the Nation according to democratic principles (Articles 2, 3, 5 and 6), as a 'democratic society' (Preamble), of representative and participatory character (*see supra* paragraph 51, *infra* paragraphs 82, 160 et seq., 183).

Finally, the 'State of justice' refers to a State that must tend towards guaranteeing justice, specifically beyond procedural formalities. That is why, the value of justice is expressly proclaimed (Preamble and Article 1), for which the right of having access to justice is declared as well as the right to obtain the effective protection of

---

'El estado social de derecho', in *Lex. Revista del Colegio de Abogados del Estado Zulia* (Colegio de Abogados del Estado Zulia., 236, Maracaibo 2000, 17–27.

163. On the social values in the Constitution *see* Jacqueline Lejarza A., 'El carácter normativo de los principios y valores en la Constitución de 1999', in *Revista de Derecho Constitucional,* No. 1 (septiembre-diciembre) (Caracas: Editorial Sherwood, 1999), 195–220; Liliana Fasciani 'De la Justicia a la Justicia Social', in *Tendencias Actuales del Derecho Constitucional. Homenaje a Jesús María Casal Montbrun*, ed. Jesús María Casal, Alfredo Arismendi & Carlos Luis Carrillo Artiles Coords, vol. I (Caracas: UCV/Universidad Católica Andrés Bello, 2008), 161–196. *See also*: Allan R. Brewer-Carías, 'Global Values in the Venezuelan Constitution. Some Prioritizations and Several Incongruences', in *An Inquiry into the Existence of Global Values: Through the Lens of Comparative Constitutional Law*, eds Dennis Davis, Alan Richter & Cheryl Saunders (Hart Publishing Oxford 2015), pp. 417–447.

persons' rights and interests (Article 26),[164] the courts being obligated to guarantee the provision of justice without cost, assuring constant accessibility, impartiality, adequacy, transparency, autonomy, independence, responsibility, equanimity and expediency, absence of dilatory practices, and unnecessary formalities or annulments (Article 26) (*see infra* paragraphs 389 et seq.).

Unfortunately, the authoritarian government that took shape during the past years conducting the so-called Bolivarian Revolution, instead of developing the 'social democratic rule of law and justice State' formally declared in the Constitution, has consolidated a Totalitarian State that is in contradiction with what is provided in the Constitution.[165]

§4. SEPARATION OF POWERS

60. Article 136 of the Constitution establishes a double system of checks and balances regarding State powers and the branches of government. First, the vertical distribution of State power on a territorial basis, between the municipal, states and national powers, giving form to the Federal form of Government, organized into three levels of governments constituting the Republic at the national level, the states at the state level and the municipal at the local government level. The State, accordingly, is qualified in Article 4 as a Federal Decentralized State (*see infra* paragraphs 203 et seq.).

However, the same Article 136 establishes the horizontal separation of powers regarding the National Public Power, which is divided between the traditional Legislative, Executive and Judicial Powers, to which the Constitution now has added two new branches: the Citizen and the Electoral Powers, in a system of *penta* separation of powers (*see infra* paragraphs 239 et seq.). These branches of Public Power have their own functions, but the respective organs that exercise them must collaborate between them in the prosecution of the State aims.[166]

---

164. *See* José R. Duque Corredor, 'El acceso a la justicia como derecho fundamental en el contexto de la democracia y de los derechos humanos', in *Revista de derecho del Tribunal Supremo de Justicia*, No. 6 (Caracas, 2002), 379 a 389; Judith Useche, 'El acceso a la justicia en el nuevo orden constitucional venezolano', in *Bases y principios del sistema constitucional venezolano (Ponencias del VII Congreso Venezolano de Derecho Constitucional realizado en San Cristóbal del 21 al 23 de Noviembre de 2001)*, vol. II, 29–76; Lourdes Cortes de Arangon, 'El acceso de los administrados al sistema jurídico: ¿un derecho vivo?', in *Estudios de Derecho Administrativo: Libro Homenaje a la UCV*, vol. I (Caracas: Imprenta Nacional, 2001), 275–305.

165. *See Allan R. Brewer*-Carías, *Authoritarian Government v. The* Rule of Law. *Lectures and Essays (1999-2014) on the Venezuelan Authoritarian Regime Established in Contempt of the Constitution, (Caracas, New York, Editorial Jurídica Venezolana, 2014); Estado Totalitario y desprecio a la ley. La desconstitucionalización, desjuridificación, desjudicialización y desdemocratización de Venezuela* (Caracas: Fundación de Derecho Público, Editorial Jurídica Venezolana, 2014); 'El Estado Totalitario y la ausencia de Estado democrático y social de derecho y de justicia, de economía mixta y descentralizado', in Ramsis Ghazzaoui (Coordinador), *XVII Jornadas Centenario Internacionales. Constitución, derecho administrativo y proceso: vigencia, reforma e innovación (*Valencia, Colegio de Abogados del Estado Carabobo, Instituto de Estudios Jurídicos Dr José Ángel Castillo Moren, 2014), 31–151.

166. *See* Carlos Luis Carrillo Artiles, 'La composición del poder público en la Constitución de la República Bolivariana de Venezuela', in *Libro Homenaje a Enrique Tejera París, Temas sobre la*

61. It must be mentioned that since the 1947 Constitution, as in many other Latin American countries, the Constitution began to directly create new bodies with some kind of autonomy, beyond the three traditional powers, not subjected to the Legislative, the Executive or the Judiciary, conceived to accomplish certain control functions. These have included the Comptrollers General, Peoples' or Human Rights Defenders, Public Prosecutors or General Prosecutors, Judicial Councils or Councils of the Judiciary, and special organs for the control and administration of elections. This evolution of constitutional autonomous organs was the one that formally gained an important foothold in the Constitution of 1999, which not only regulates such entities but affords them the status of a constitutional 'power' or branch of government, thereby creating a penta separation of powers in which the Legislative Power is exercised by the National Assembly; the Executive Power by the President of the Republic and other officers of the government and its Administration; the Judicial Power by the Supreme Tribunal of Justice and other Courts; the Citizen Power by the Comptroller General of the Republic; the Prosecutor General (Public Prosecutor) and the Peoples' Defender; and the Electoral Power by the National Electoral Council and other organs of electoral power.

62. The essence of the principle of the separation of powers in the Constitution is that each constitutionally established organ of the State exercises its respective function with independence and autonomy, in a system of checks and balances in which no branch of government is to be or can be subject to that of another, except on matters of judicial review, audit controls or protection of human rights. Nonetheless, on the contrary, the *penta* division of powers under the Constitution of 1999 is deceiving because it, in fact, conceals the subjection of some of the principal branches of government to the legislator, in a very dangerous system regarding democracy and the rule of law that leaves an open the door to the concentration of power in the State and to authoritarianism,[167] to which the Constitutional Chamber of the Supreme Tribunal of Justice has contributed[168] (*see infra* paragraph 705).

The Constitution, in fact, contains an absurd distortion of the separation of power principle by giving the National Assembly the authority not only to elect but to dismiss the Judges of the Supreme Tribunal of Justice, the Prosecutor General, the General Comptroller, the People's Defender and the Members of the National Electoral Council from their positions (Articles 265, 279 and 296); and in some cases

---

Constitución de 1999 (Caracas: Centro de Investigaciones Jurídicas (CEIN), 2001), 51 a 76; Allan R. Brewer-Carías, 'Consideraciones sobre el régimen de distribución de competencias del Poder Público en la Constitución de 1999', in *Estudios de Derecho Administrativo. Libro Homenaje a la UCV*, ed. Fernando Parra Aranguren y Armando Rodríguez García Editores, vol. I (Caracas: Tribunal Supremo de Justicia, 2001), 107–136.

167. *See* Gustavo Tarre, *Solo el poder detiene al poder, La teoría de la separación de los poderes y su aplicación en Venenzuela* (Caracas: Editorial Jurídica Venezolana, 2014).

168. *See* Allan R. Brewer-Carías, 'Sobre la mutación del principio de la separación de poderes en la jurisprudencia constitucional', *Revista de Derecho Público*, No. 132 (Caracas: Editorial Jurídica Venezolana, 2012), 201–213; 'El principio de la separación de poderes como elemento esencial de la democracia y de la libertad, y su demolición en Venezuela mediante la sujeción política del Tribunal Supremo de Justicia', *Revista Iberoamericana de Derecho Administrativo, Homenaje a Luciano Parejo Alfonso,* 12 (San José, Costa Rica, Asociación e Instituto Iberoamericano de Derecho Administrativo Prof. Jesús González Pérez, 2012), 31–43.

established through legislation, even by a simple majority of votes (*see infra* paragraphs 438 et seq.). Even this latter solution was proposed to be formally constitutionalized in the rejected 2007 Constitutional reform proposals, which seek to eliminate the guarantee of the qualified majority of the members of the National Assembly for such dismissals and to establish a simple majority for that purpose.

63. It is really impossible to talk about the independence of separate powers, and mutual control when the tenure of the Head officials of the institutions depends on the political will of one of the branches of government.[169] The sole fact of the provision of such possibility for the National Assembly to dismiss makes futile the formal consecration of the independence of powers, since the High officials of the State are aware that they can be removed at any time precisely when they act effectively with independence. In Venezuela, in political practice, this has converted to a system of concentration of powers in the National Assembly, and because of the political control that the President of the Republic has exercised upon the Assembly, to the concentration of powers in the hands of the former (*see infra* paragraphs 246, 257). The consequence has been the total absence of fiscal or audit control made by the General Comptroller Office over the huge disposal of the oil wealth not always in accordance with budget discipline rules; the total absence of protection assured by the People's Defender, which has been perceived more as a defender of State power than of the people; and the indiscriminate use by the Public Prosecutor of the Judiciary and of judicial procedures as a tool to persecute any political dissidence; and the absolute control exercised by the Executive over the Judiciary.[170]

64. Besides the vertical distribution of State Powers (national power, states power and municipal power) and the horizontal Separation of Powers (Legislative, Executive, Judicial, Citizens and Electoral Powers), according to the Constitution, no other State Power can be conceived. Nonetheless, as already mentioned, in 2007, a proposed Constitutional Reform was rejected, proposing the creation of a new State Power, called the 'Popular Power', to be established in parallel to the Constitutional State and its Powers. Notwithstanding such rejection, the National Assembly in December 2010, by-passing the Constitution sanctioned a set of organic laws through which it has defined the legislative framework of such 'new State' called the 'Communal State', in parallel to the Constitutional State, conceived as a socialist, centralized, military and police State, acting in the exercise of a so-called Popular Power[171] (*see infra* paragraphs 232, 263, 279). This new State, for whose creation nobody has voted, is supposedly based on the exercise of the sovereignty of the people but exclusively in a 'direct' manner through the exercise

169. *See* Allan R. Brewer-Carías, 'Democracia: sus elementos y componentes esenciales y el control del poder', *Grandes temas para un observatorio electoral ciudadano, vol. I, Democracia: retos y fundamentos (Compiladora Nuria González Martín)* (México: Instituto Electoral del Distrito Federal, 2007), 171–220.
170. *See* Allan R. Brewer-Carías, *La demolición de la independencia y autonomía del Poder Judicial En Venezuela 1999–2021*, (Caracas, Editorial Jurídica Venezolana, 2021).
171. *See* the Organic laws on the Popular Power; the Communes; the Communal Economic System; the Public and Communal Planning; and the Social Comptrollership, in *Gaceta Oficial* No. 6.011 Extra. 21 Dec. 2010.

of the 'Popular Power' and subjected to a new 'socialist principle of legality'. For the organization of this 'Communal State', the communes are established as the fundamental unit, seeking to unconstitutionally supplant the municipalities as the 'primary political units of the national organization' (Article 168 of the Constitution). Through the organization of such Communes, the Popular Power is supposed to be exercised as an expression of the 'popular sovereignty' although not through representatives. As above-mentioned, it is, therefore, a political system in which representative democracy is ignored, openly violating the Constitution.

§5. Presidential System of Government

65. The Venezuelan system of government, following the general feature in Latin America, since the beginning of the Republic in 1811, has always been the Presidential system, which remains in the 1999 Constitution. The President of the Republic is then, at the same time, the Head of State and the Head of the Executive and the Public Administration, and is elected by universal, direct and secret suffrage (Articles 226, 228). Nonetheless, in the relationship between the National Executive and the National Assembly, the Constitution has adopted some elements of parliamentarianism based on provisions already introduced since the 1961 Constitution.[172]

But in the 1999 Constitution, the presidential framework of government has been exacerbated[173] by the combination of a few factors: first, by the extension of the presidential term from five to six years, and by the initial possibility for the immediate re-election of the President (Article 230). This provision has been reformed by a constitutional amendment approved in 2009, establishing the principle of the indefinite re-election of the President, eliminating the republican principle of

172. *See* Donato Lupidii, 'El sistema presidencial y la Constitución venezolana de 1999', in *El Derecho Público a comienzos del siglo XXI. Estudios homenaje al Profesor Allan R. Brewer-Carías*, vol. I (Madrid: Instituto de Derecho Público, UCV, Civitas Ediciones, 2003), 819–835; Miguel A. Gómez Ortiz, 'El régimen presidencial en Venezuela', in *Bases y principios del sistema constitucional venezolano (Ponencias del VII Congreso Venezolano de Derecho Constitucional realizado en San Cristóbal del 21 al 23 de Noviembre de 2001),* vol.II, 299–336; José Peña Solis, 'Notas sobre los Sistemas de Gobierno parlamentario y Presidencial. Breve Referencia al Sistema Venezolano', in *Tendencias Actuales del Derecho Constitucional. Homenaje a Jesús María Casal Montbrun*, ed. Jesús María Casal, Alfredo Arismendi y Carlos Luis Carrillo Artiles (Coord.), vol. I (Caracas: UCV/ Universidad Católica Andrés Bello, 2008), 405–430; Alfredo Arismendi A., 'El fortalecimiento del Poder Ejecutivo Nacional en la Constitución venezolana de 1999', in *El Derecho Público a comienzos del siglo XXI. Estudios homenaje al Profesor Allan R. Brewer-Carías*, vol. I (Madrid: Instituto de Derecho Público, UCV, Civitas Ediciones, 2003), 837–865; Ricardo Combellas, 'El Poder Ejecutivo en la Constitución de 1999', in *Revista UGMA Jurídica de la Facultad de Derecho de la Universidad Gran Mariscal de Ayacucho*, No. 1 (mayo-agosto) (Barcelona-Venezuela, 2002), 9–24.

173. *See* Allan R. Brewer-Carías, 'El sistema presidencial de gobierno en la Constitución de Venezuela de 1999', in Allan R. Brewer-Carías, *Estudios sobre el Estado Constitucional (2005–2006)* (Caracas: Editorial Jurídica Venezolana, 2007), 475–624.

alternate representation in government.[174] In any case, the illusory remedy for what originally was a long tenure of twelve years allowing only one immediate re-election was the provision of the possibility of a repealing referendum but conceived in such a complicated and complex way (Article 72) that it has been nearly inapplicable (*see infra* paragraph 178). Second, the loss of the checks and balances between the Executive and the Legislative Branches of Government, among other factors, due to the elimination of the Senate, that is, the elimination of the traditional legislative bicameralism that had existed in the country since 1811. Third, the possibility for the President of the Republic to dissolve the National Assembly, even in exceptional cases when three votes for the parliamentary censure of the Vice President of the Republic (Article 240), have been approved (*see infra* paragraph 292). Fourth, the possibility that through the approval of enabling laws (*leyes habilitantes*) the National Assembly can delegate the legislative power to the Executive, by means of which through Executive decrees-laws *(Decretos-leyes*), the President without any limits can legislate (Article 203), resulting in practice that with the enabling laws of 2001, 2002, 2007 and 2014 all the important statutes in the country have been sanctioned by the President of the Republic, although he has had (except during 2016–2020) the complete control of the National Assembly. In the 1961 Constitution, the possibility for the legislative delegation was limited to only economic and financial matters and in extraordinary circumstances (*see infra* paragraphs 148 et seq.)

66. Another element that should be mentioned with respect to the relations between the powers of the State is the attribution to decree, 'the removal from office of the President of the Republic' (Article 233), to the Supreme Tribunal of Justice without significant specific delineation or definition of conditions for exercising that power.

§6. ALTERNATING GOVERNMENT

67. Since the beginning of the Republic, the general restriction for elected officials to be re-elected in a continuous way, without limits, has been a tradition within the presidential system of government. The restriction to presidential re-election was first established in the 1830 Constitution, as a reaction to continuity in office (*continuísmo*), precisely in order to confront individuals' anxieties to perpetuate themselves in power and to avoid the advantages that public officials in office could have in electoral processes.[175]

174. *See* Allan R. Brewer-Carías, 'El Juez Constitucional vs. La alternabilidad republicana (La reelección continua e indefinida)', in *Revista de Derecho Público*, No. 117, (Caracas, Editorial Jurídica Venezolana 2009), pp. 205–211

175. The reaction against continuity in power was clearly expressed by Simón Bolívar in his famous Angostura Speech (1819) when he said: 'The continuation of the authority in the same individual has frequently been the end of democratic governments. Repeated elections are essentials in popular systems, because nothing is more dangerous than to leave for a long term the same citizen in power. The people get used to obey him, and he gets used to command them; from were usurpation and tyranny is originated ... .Our citizens must fear with more than enough justice that the same

This principle of limiting the term of elected officials called the principle of '*alternabilidad*' (alternating),[176] means that the public offices must be occupied by turns, and not continuously by the same elected person. It is in this same sense that the Supreme Tribunal of Justice of Venezuela, in a decision of 2002 issued by its Electoral Chamber, said that *alternabilidad* means 'the successive exercise of public offices by different persons' (Decision No. 51 of 18 March 2002).[177] The principle, consequently, is not the same as the 'elective' principle or to be elected for public offices. To be elected is one thing, and another is to occupy public offices by turns. The principle has always been established as a 'rock-like' or immutable constitutional clause (*Cláusula pétrea*), in the sense that it can never be changed. That is why Article 6 of the Constitution says that 'The government of the Republic and of its political entities is and will always be alternating' *(alternativo)*, in addition to 'democratic, participatory, elective, decentralized, responsible, plural and of repeal mandates', which mean that it cannot be changed.

The principle was included in almost all the Venezuelan Constitutions since 1830 (1830, 1858, 1864, 1874, 1881, 1891, 1893, 1901, 1904, 1909, 1936, 1845 and 1947), establishing a general prohibition for the immediate re-election of the President of the Republic for the next term. In the 1961 Constitution, the prohibition for re-election was extended up to two terms (ten years), and it was in the 1999 Constitution that the provision was made more flexible, by establishing for the first time in more than a century the possibility for the immediate re-election of the President, but only once, for the next term (Article 230). This limit was proposed to be eliminated in the rejected 2007 Constitutional Reform, and was finally eliminated, after a constitutional interpretation of the alternating principle,[178] through a constitutional amendment approved by referendum on February 2009 (*see supra* paragraph 65), violating the basis of the people's right to democracy.[179] In addition, the 2009 Constitutional Amendment also eliminated the limits established for the re-election of the representatives to the National Assembly and the States Legislative Councils, and for the re-election of the Governors of the states and the Mayors of the municipalities (Articles 160, 162, 174, 192) (*see infra* paragraphs 127, 172, 221, 711).

§7. The Centralized Federation

68. Venezuela was the first country to adopt since 1811, after the United States of America, a federal form of government politically uniting former colonial

---

Official, who has governed them for a long time, could perpetually command them.' *See* in Simón Bolívar, *Escritos Fundamentales* (Caracas, 1982).

176. From the Latin word '*alternatium*', which means 'interchangeably' or 'by turns'.

177. Quoted in the Dissenting Vote to the Constitutional Chamber of the Supreme Tribunal of Justice Decision No. 53, of 2 Feb. 2009 (*Interpretation of Arts 340, 6 and 345 of the Constitution* Case), in www.tsj.gov.ve/decisions/scon/Febrero/53-3209-2009-08-1610.html.

178. *See* Allan R. Brewer-Carías, 'El Juez Constitucional vs. La alternabilidad republicana (La reelección continua e indefinida)', in *Revista de Derecho Público*, No. 117, (Caracas, Editorial Jurídica Venezolana, 2009), pp. 205–211.

179. *See* Allan R. Brewer-Carías, *Derecho a la democracia y reelección presidencial indefinida. Tres Estudios*, (Santiago, Buenos Aires, Madrid, Ediciones Olejnik, 2021).

provinces (*see supra* paragraph 2). Those provinces were progressively transformed into the twenty-three states (*see infra* paragraph 115) which the territory of the Republic is divided, adding to them, a Capital District (the former Federal District, covering parts of the city of Caracas) (*see infra* paragraphs 115, 226), and federal dependencies that comprise almost all the islands located along the country's coast in the Caribbean Sea (*see infra* paragraph 116).

The consequence of the federal form of the State has been the establishment in the text of the constitutions of a system of the vertical distribution of State power in three-tier levels, as it is prescribed in the 1999 Constitution by setting forth that 'The Powers of the State shall be distributed between the Municipal Powers, the State Powers and the National Powers' which must collaborate and cooperate in the pursuit of the State objectives (Article 136) (*see infra* paragraphs 199, 213 et seq.).

69. The constitutional and political tendency since the beginning of the twentieth century has been a process of centralization of powers at the national level, so the territorial distribution of power and territorial autonomy of the states has almost disappeared (*see infra* paragraphs 219 et seq.) Nonetheless, according to the provisions of the 1961 Constitution, an initial political decentralization process sparked by the democratic practice began in 1989 with the transfer of powers from the central government to the federal states, and for the first time since the nineteenth century, with the direct elections of Governors of the states and Mayors, which provoked for regional political life the beginning of playing an important role in the country (*see infra* paragraph 201). But the 1999 Constitution, instead of undertaking the changes that were needed for reinforcing democracy, namely the effective political decentralization of the federation and the reinforcement of state and municipal political powers, has caused the pendulum to swing back, and to reinforce the centralization process[180] (*see infra* paragraph 203).

§8. Judicial Review System

70. Following a general Latin American feature, the judicial review system established in Venezuela since the nineteenth century has been mixed in nature, in which the concentrated method of judicial review is applied conjunctly with the diffuse method.[181] On the one hand, all courts are entitled to decide upon the constitutionality of legislation and of its inapplicability in a particular case, with *inter*

180. *See* Allan R. Brewer-Carías, 'El Estado federal descentralizado y la centralización de la federación en Venezuela. Situación y perspectiva de una contradicción constitucional', in *Federalismo y regionalismo*, ed. Diego Valadés and José María Serna de la Garza (Coordinadores) (Universidad Nacional Autónoma de México, Tribunal Superior de Justicia del Estado de Puebla, Instituto de Investigaciones Jurídicas, Serie Doctrina Jurídica No. 229, México 2005), 717–750; Allan R. Brewer-Carias and Jan Kleinheisterkamp, 'Venezuela: The End of federalism?', in Daniel Halberstam and Mathias Reimann (Editors), *Federalism and Legal Unification: A Comparative Empirical Investigation of Twenty Systems* (London, Springer, 2014), 523–543.

181. *See* Allan R. Brewer-Carías, *La Justicia Constitucional (Procesos y procedimientos constitucionales)* (México: Instituto Mexicano de Derecho Procesal Constitucional, ed. Porrúa), 2007; *Judicial Review in Comparative Law* (Cambridge: Cambridge Studies in International and Comparative

partes effects; and on the other hand, the Supreme Court or a Constitutional Court or Tribunal are empowered to declare always at the request of a party the total nullity of statutes contrary to the Constitution (*see infra* paragraphs 670 et seq.).

71. Article 7 of the 1999 Constitution declares that its text is 'the supreme law' of the land and 'the ground of the entire legal order'. This provision assigns to all judges the duty 'of guaranteeing the integrity of the Constitution' (Article 334) with the power to decide not to apply a statute that is deemed to be unconstitutional when deciding a concrete case. Article 335 of the Constitution also assigns the Supreme Tribunal of Justice the duty of guaranteeing 'the supremacy and effectiveness of the constitutional rules and principles', as 'the maximum and final interpreter of the Constitution', with the duty to seek for 'its uniform interpretation and application'.

72. Additionally, the Constitutional Chamber of the Supreme Tribunal of Justice (Articles 266.1 and 336) is the 'Constitutional Jurisdiction', exclusively empowered to declare the nullity of statutes and other State acts with similar rank and effects or issued in direct execution of the Constitution. The Tribunal also is empowered to judge the unconstitutionality of the omissions of the legislative organ.

Other State acts, such as administrative acts and regulations, are also subject to judicial review by the 'Contentious Administrative Jurisdiction' whose courts are empowered to annul administrative acts because of their illegality or unconstitutionality (Article 259) (*see infra* paragraph 706).

Also, according to Article 29 of the Constitution, the courts have a duty to protect all persons in their constitutional rights and guarantees when deciding an action for protection, or '*amparo*'. Such an action can be brought before the court against any illegitimate harm or threat to such Rights (*see infra* paragraphs 594 et seq.).

73. Of course, judicial review, above all, is an institutional tool which is essentially linked to democracy; democracy is understood as a political system not just reduced to the fact of having elected governments, but where separation and control of power and the respect and enforcement of human rights is possible through an independent and autonomous judiciary. It has been precise because of this process of reinforcement of democracy that judicial review of the constitutionality of legislation and other governmental actions has become an important tool in order to guarantee the supremacy of the Constitution, the rule of law, and the respect of human rights. It is in this sense that judicial review of the constitutionality of State acts has been considered the ultimate result of the consolidation of the *rule of law*, when precisely in a democratic system, the courts can serve as the ultimate guarantor of the Constitution, effectively controlling the exercise of power by the organs of the State.

On the contrary, as happens in all authoritarian regimes, even having elected governments, if such control is not possible, the same power can constitute the most

---

Law. New Series, Cambridge University Press, 1989), 406; *Études de droit public comparé* (Bruxelles: Académie International de Droit Comparé, Bruylant, 2001), 526–934; *Judicial Review. Comparative Constitucional Law Essays, Lectures and Courses (1985–2011)* (Caracas: Fundación de Derecho Público, Editorial Jurídica Venezolana, 2014).

powerful and diabolical instrument for the consolidation of authoritarianism, the destruction of democracy, and the violation of human rights.[182] Unfortunately, this is what has been happening in Venezuela, where after decades of democratic ruling through which we constructed one of the most formally complete systems of judicial review in South America, since 2000, that same system has been the instrument through which the politically controlled judiciary, and particularly the subjected Constitutional Chamber of the Supreme Tribunal, have been consolidating the authoritarian regime installed in the country (*see supra* paragraphs 39 et seq.; *infra* 251, 715 et seq.)

182. *See* Allan R. Brewer-Carías, *Crónica de la 'In' Justicia Constitucional. La Sala Constitucional y el autoritarismo en Venezuela* (Caracas: Editorial Jurídica Venezolana, 2007); *Práctica y distorsión de la justicia constitucional en Venezuela (2008–2012)* (Caracas: Editorial Jurídica Venezolana, 2012); and *La Patología de la Justicia Constitucional* (Caracas: Tercera edición ampliada, Editorial Jurídica Venezolana, 2014); *El golpe a la democracia dado por la Sala Constitucional (De cómo la Sala Constitucional del Tribunal Supremo de Justicia de Venezuela impuso un gobierno sin legitimidad democrática, revocó mandatos populares de diputada y alcaldes, impidió el derecho a ser electo, restringió el derecho a manifestar, y eliminó el derecho a la participación política, todo en contra de la Constitución),* (Caracas, Editorial Jurídica Venezolana, 2015).

Chapter 3. Global Values in the Constitution

74. As has been aforementioned, the 1999 Venezuelan Constitution contains not only an extensive number of articles devoted to enumerating human rights (120) but also a rich text full of values, principles and global declarations. The Constitutional Chamber of the Supreme Tribunal of Justice has said that the Constitution is 'an instrument with legal spirit that connects, according to the nature of the applicable precept, both the bodies of the State and the individuals'; and that imposes constitutional juridical situations 'with reference to indispensable values for the assurance of human freedom, equality and dignity' guaranteed by the judiciary.[183]

Constitutional values in the Venezuelan Constitution[184] are expressed not only in its Preamble but also in many of its articles, as goals intending to guide the state, society and general conduct of individuals.[185] Consequently, in Venezuela, global values and principles do not derive from the sole interpretation and application of the Constitution by the courts, but from provisions in the Constitution itself.[186] Nonetheless, by means of constitutional judicial decisions, the sense, scope and priority character of many of these constitutional principles and values have been defined and enriched; and also, unfortunately, in many cases, some constitutional incongruence has been established between the constitutional text and the political practice of government.

§1. Constitutional Values and Their Prioritization

75. The Preamble to the Constitution began by declaring that it was adopted by the representatives of the Venezuelan people, having in mind the achievement of a series of goals 'guided by social, economic, political and judicial values',[187] in order to inspire the action of the state, 'which must respond to equalitarian, international, democratic, moral and historical principles'.

In this context, the state is defined as a 'state of justice, federal and decentralized', that must develop its action to enforce the values of 'freedom, independence, peace, solidarity, common good, territorial integrity, cohabitation and the empire of

183. *See* Decision No. 963 dated 5 Jun. 2001. *José A Guía y otros v. Ministerio de Infraestructura, Revista de Derecho Público*, Nos 85–88 (Caracas: Editorial Jurídica Venezolana, 2001) 447.
184. *See* on the subject of these Part: Allan R. Brewer-Carías, 'Global Values in the Venezuelan Constitution. Some Prioritizations and Several Incongruences', in *An Inquiry into the Existence of Global Values: Through the Lens of Comparative Constitutional Law*, eds Dennis Davis, Alan Richter & Cheryl Saunders (Hart Publishing Oxford 2015), pp. 417–447.
185. *See* Allan R Brewer-Carías, 'La constitucionalizaci6n del derecho administrativo', in *Derecho Administrativo*, vol. I (Bogotá, Universidad Externado de Colombia, 2005) 215 ff.
186. *See* Allan R Brewer-Carías, *Principios fundamentales del derecho público* (Caracas: Editorial Jurídica Venezolana, 2005).
187. Regarding the nature of the Preamble and its constitutional value, *see* the decision of the former Supreme Court of Justice in its Political-Administrative Chamber, dated 8 Aug. 1989, *Revista de Derecho Público* No. 39 (Caracas: Editorial Jurídica Venezolana, 1989) 102.

the law for these and all future generations', in a society that is qualified as 'democratic, participatory, multi-ethnic and pluri-cultural', which is confirmed, for instance, by the express recognition in the Constitution of the indigenous populations' status (Articles 119 et seq.).

These goals represent the fundamental principles and constitutional values that inspire the constitutional text as a whole. They have the same binding quality as constitutional provisions, and consequently are enforceable. As affirmed by the Constitutional Chamber of the Supreme Tribunal, 'the statutes must have those values as their guide, so those that do not follow them or that are contrary to those objectives become unconstitutional'.[188]

76. Besides the values guiding the configuration of the state declared in the Preamble, the Constitution also enumerates as superior values of the legal system and of the whole state activity: 'life, freedom, justice, equality, solidarity, democracy, social responsibility and, in general, the pre-eminence of human rights, ethics and political pluralism' (Article 2).

Additionally, the Constitution identifies 'the defence and the development of the individual and the respect of his/her dignity, the democratic exercise of the popular will, the construction of a fair and peace-loving society, the promotion of the prosperity and wellbeing of the people and the guarantee of the fulfilment of all principles, rights and duties recognized and enshrined in the Constitution' as essential goals of the state, considering 'education and work' as fundamental processes to achieve those ends (Article 3).

The constitutional text also gave form to a series of social ends specified in the Preamble with the object of ensuring 'the right to a life, work, culture, education, social justice and equality without discrimination nor subordination of any kind'. Reference is also made in the Constitution regarding the social goals of society and of the state in order to achieve 'social justice'. The assurance of 'equality without discrimination nor subordination of any kind' is also specified as a fundamental social goal.

77. Referring to the Republic, particular further fundamental values are expressly emphasized in the Constitution: the principle that the nation's rights ('independence, freedom, sovereignty, immunity, territorial integrity and the national self-determination') cannot be renounced or abandoned (Article 1).

The Preamble sets out as one of the goals of the state, the 'peaceful cooperation between nations', which implies the commitment to look for a peaceful solution to controversies, and the rejection of war. This peaceful cooperation must be executed in accordance with the 'principle of the non-intervention' in the affairs of other countries, and the principle of 'self-determination of the people'. Also, it specifies that international cooperation must be carried out 'according to the universal and indivisible guarantee of human rights and the democratization of the international society'.

---

188. *See* Case: *Deudores hipotecarios v. Superintendencia de Bancos*, *Revista de Derecho Público*, No. 89–92 (Caracas: Editorial Jurídica Venezolana, 2002) 94 ff.

References are also made in the Constitution to other values that must guide the international relations of the Republic, including 'nuclear disarmament, the ecological balance and the environment considered as a common and non-renounceable patrimony of humanity'. In particular, according to the Preamble, another fundamental goal that must serve as guidance for the state's actions is 'the impulse and consolidation of Latin American integration' (Article 153).

78. Some of the values declared in the Constitution have been prioritized in political practice and through judicial decisions, in the sense that they have been considered as having some kind of superior hierarchy regarding other principles that are governed by the former. This is the case for human dignity; fairness/justice/the rule of law/state of justice; equality/respect/tolerance/diversity/multiculturalism; democracy/participation/decentralization/inclusion; compassion/caring/solidarity/social justice/social state; community/civil society; family; life; honesty/integrity; learning/education; freedom/liberty/independence; security; responsibility/account ability/transparency; environment.

79. Human Dignity: The value of 'human dignity' is considered by the courts 'as inherent to the human condition' that exists 'before the state' and imposes on all branches of government the need to be 'at the service of the human being'.[189] This implies not only the existence of constitutional rights considered 'inherent to human beings' but also the emergence of the 'principle of progressiveness' in their interpretation and enforcement. According to the criteria set out by the Constitutional Chamber of the Supreme Tribunal, the courts have an obligation 'to interpret the entire legal system in the light of the Right of the Constitution ... which also means, that they have to interpret the system congruently with the fundamental rights or human rights, that must be respected above all, making a progressive and complete interpretation'.[190]

The Constitution refers to this value in many articles when guaranteeing to anybody deprived of liberty the right to be 'treated with respect due to the inherent dignity of the human being' (Article 46); when guaranteeing that the judicial seizure of a person's home must be made 'always respecting human dignity' (Article 47); when imposing the obligation on the state's security offices to always 'respect the human dignity and rights of all persons' (Article 55); when establishing the duty of the state to protect senior citizens and disabled persons, always respecting their 'human dignity' (Articles 80, 81); and when guaranteeing that the salary of every worker must be 'sufficient to enable him or her to live with dignity' (Article 91).

The Constitutional Chamber of the Supreme Tribunal has considered human dignity as 'one of the values on which the Social rule of law and Justice State is based, and around which all the legal system and all the actions of the branches of government (public powers) must turn'. Based on this approach, the Chamber defined human dignity as 'the supremacy that persons have as an inherent attribute of their

189. *See* Decision of the First Court of the Administrative Jurisdiction dated 1 Jun. 2000, Case: *Julio Rocco A*, *Revista de Derecho Público*, No. 82 (Caracas: Editorial Jurídica Venezolana, 2000) 287 ff.

190. *Ibid*

rational being, which imposes on public authorities the duty to watch for the protection and safe-conduct of the life, freedom and autonomy of men and women for the sole fact of their existence, independently of any other consideration'. Thus, 'the sole existence of man grants him the right to exist and to obtain all the guarantees needed to assure him a dignified life, that is, his own existence, proportional and rational to the recognition of his essence as a rational being'. This concept of human dignity implies the imposition 'upon the State of the duty to adopt the necessary protective measures to safeguard the legal assets that define man as a person, that is, life, integrity, freedom, autonomy'.[191]

The Political-Administrative Chamber of the Supreme Tribunal of Justice has also emphasized the pre-eminent character of dignity, considering it the 'axiological' element representing 'the ideological base that supports the dogmatic order of the current Constitution', limiting the exercise of public power and establishing an effective judicial guarantee system. Hence this 'prevalent position of human dignity' is considered a 'superior value of the legal system'. It implies 'the obligation of the State and of all its bodies to protect and guarantee human rights as the main purpose and objective of its public action'. Consequently, the development of human dignity is considered by the Supreme Tribunal as 'one of the superior values of the legal system', seeing its 'defence and development' as 'one of the essential objectives of the State' (Articles 2 and 3).[192]

Human dignity also promotes the idea of the 'pre-eminence of human rights' (Preamble), which according to the 'principle of progressiveness' (Article 19) imposes the need for the interpretation of statutes in the most favourable way for their enjoyment. In this regard, Article 19 of the 1999 Constitution begins the Title on 'Duties, Rights and Constitutional Guarantees' by setting forth that the state must guarantee every person, 'according to the progressiveness principle and without discrimination whatsoever, the enjoyment and non-renounceable, indivisible and interdependent exercise of human rights'. The provision adds that 'the respect and the guarantee of the rights are mandatory to all State bodies in accordance with the Constitution, the treaties on human rights signed and ratified by the Republic and the statutes'.[193] As affirmed by the courts, 'the interpretation of the corresponding constitutional provisions and any future constitutional revision must be performed in the most favourable way for the exercise and enjoyment of the rights', adding that:

---

191. With this purpose, the Constitution, in its Art. 3, 'establishes that the recognition of the human dignity constitutes a structural principle of the Social rule of law State and for that, it forbids, in its Title III, Chapter III, the forced disappearances, the degrading treatments, the tortures or cruel treatments that could harm the life as an inviolable right, the degrading punishments and all other inherent rights of the human person (articles 43 ff)' *see* Decision No. 2442, dated 1 Sep. 2003, Case: *Alejandro Serrano López*, *Revista de Derecho Público*, Nos 83–96 (Caracas: Editorial Jurídica Venezolana, 2003) 183 ff.
192. *See* Decision No. 224 dated 24 Feb. 2000, *Revista de Derecho Público*, No. 81 (2000, Editorial Jurídica Venezolana, Caracas) 131 ff. *See also*, decision of the Constitutional Chamber of the Supreme Tribunal No. 3215 dated 15 Jun. 2004, *Revista de Derecho Público*, Nos 97–98 (Caracas: Editorial Jurídica Venezolana, 2004) 428.
193. About this principle, the Constitutional Chamber of the Supreme Tribunal of Justice, quoting Art. 2 of the American Convention on Human Rights, in Decision No. 1154, dated 29 Jun. 2001, based on the same principle, has ruled that it is necessary 'to adapt the legal system in order to ensure the efficiency of said rights, being unacceptable the excuse of the inexistence or unsuitability of the

> this principle is so important that its application obliges the State to update legislation in favour of the defence of the human rights and in view to dignify the human condition, adapting the interpretation of the norms 'to the sensibility, thought and needs of the new times in order to adapt them to the new established order and to reject any anachronistic precept that opposes their effective force'.[194]

In order to give human dignity its complete application, Article 23 of the 1999 Constitution ensured that international treaties on human rights signed and ratified by Venezuela, 'prevail in the internal order when containing more favourable provisions regarding their enjoyment than those contained in the Constitution and the laws of the Republic'. The same article provides for the immediate and direct application of these treaties by state bodies, particularly the courts.[195]

However, in order to reinforce the constitutional value of human dignity, the human rights that are guaranteed and protected are not only the ones enumerated in the Constitution but also those considered 'inherent to the human person' (Article 22).[196] The last phrase of Article 22 of the Constitution established that 'the lack of regulatory statutes regarding human rights do not diminish their exercise'; that is, their application cannot be conditioned by the existence of a statute developing it; on the contrary, the lack of legal instruments regulating them does not diminish their

---

means provided in the internal order for their protection and application'. *Revista de Derecho Público*, Nos 85–88 (Caracas: Editorial Jurídica Venezolana, 2001) 111 ff.

194. In this sense the First Court of the Administrative Jurisdiction has considered as its obligation 'to interpret the entire legal system in the light of the Right of the Constitution, even more, when acting in exercise of the constitutional power for protection, which also means, that we have to interpret the system congruently with the fundamental rights or human rights, that must be respected above all, making a progressive and complete interpretation'. *See* Decision dated 1 Jun. 2000, Case: *Julio Rocco A*, *Revista de Derecho Público*, No. 82 (Caracas: Editorial Jurídica Venezolana, 2000) 287 ff.

195. The Constitutional Court of the Supreme Tribunal has for instance applied this provision regarding due process rights, preferentially applying Art. 8 of the American Convention on Human Rights. *See* Decision dated 14 Mar. 2000 Case: *CA Electricidad del Centro and CA Electricidad de los Andes*, *Revista de Derecho Público*, No. 81 (Caracas: Editorial Jurídica Venezolana, 2000) 157–58; quoted also in Decision No. 328 dated 9 Mar. 2001, of the same Chamber, *Revista de Derecho Público*, Nos 85–88 (Caracas: Editorial Jurídica Venezolana, 2001) 108. The Political-Administrative Chamber of the Supreme Tribunal interpreted and developed the criteria established by the Constitutional Chamber regarding the lack of application of Art. 185 of the Organic Law of the Supreme Court of Justice in Decision No. 802 dated 13 Apr. 2000, Case: *Elecentro v. Superintendencia Procompetencia*, *Revista de Derecho Público* No. 82 (Caracas: Editorial Jurídica Venezolana, 2000) 270. On a similar matter, *see also*, Decision No. 449 dated 27 Mar. 2001, *Dayco de Construcciones v. INOS*, *Revista de Derecho Público*, No. 85–88 (Caracas: Editorial Jurídica Venezolana, 2001). Nonetheless, the Political-Administrative Chamber has denied giving prevalence to Art. 8 of the American Convention regarding the requests made by corporate persons, understanding that the Convention only refers to the 'human' rights of individuals. *See* Decision No. 278 dated 1 Mar. 2001, *Revista de Derecho Público*, Nos 85–88 (Caracas: Editorial Jurídica Venezolana, 2001) 104.

196. This open clause is more extensive in comparison with the original wording of the North American Constitution (Ninth Amendment), in the sense that it refers not only to the rights and guarantees not enumerated in the Constitution but also in the international instruments on human rights, which conforms a truly unlimited cast of unstated, but protected rights that are inherent to the human person.

exercise, being such rights 'of immediate and direct application by the courts and all other bodies of the State' (Articles 22, 23 Constitution).[197]

80. Fairness/Justice/Rule of Law/State of Justice: 'Justice' has also been considered as a global and 'fundamental value' that must contribute to 'the construction of a just and peace-loving society resulting from the democratic exercise of popular will' (Article 3). The Constitutional Chamber has considered that 'the power to administer justice must be exercised in the name of the Republic and come from the citizens (Article 253)', and 'must be executed with independence and impartiality' by judges 'free from subordinations and inadequate pressures' (Articles 254 and 256 of the Constitution). This has been considered as 'a new paradigm about values and constitutional principles connected to the justice', which has led to the conception of the 'State of Justice', considering the judiciary not just one more branch of government but 'the integrating and stabilizing State power with authority to control and even dissolve the rest of the branches of government' (Judicialist State).[198]

This conception of the 'State of Justice' (*Estado de Justicia*) not only flows from the provisions of the Preamble and of Article 1 that declares justice as a constitutional value but from the constitutional provisions establishing 'the prevalence of the notion of material justice over formalities and technicalities';[199] and providing for the 'effective judicial protection' of human rights by means of a system of justice that must be 'free, available, impartial, idoneous, transparent, autonomous, independent, responsible, fair and expeditious, without improper delays, formalisms or useless repositions' (Article 26).[200] To that effect, the procedural laws must establish the 'simplification, uniformity and efficiency of the proceedings and adopt a brief, oral and public procedure, without sacrificing justice because of omission of non-essential formalities' (Article 257).

81. Equality/Respect/Tolerance/Diversity/Multiculturalism: The Preamble to the Constitution also declares as a fundamental social value, 'equality without discrimination or subordination of any kind', which results from the traditional and

197. *See* Decision No. 723, dated 15 May 2001, *Revista de Derecho Público*, Nos 85–88 (Caracas: Editorial Jurídica Venezolana, 2001) 111.
198. *See* Decision No. 659 of the Political-Administrative Chamber dated 24 Mar. 2000, Case: *Rosario Nouel v. Consejo de la Judicatura y Comisión de Emergencia Judicial*, *Revista de Derecho Público* No. 81 (Caracas: Editorial Jurídica Venezolana, 2000) 103–04.
199. *See* Supreme Tribunal of Justice, Decision No. 949 of the Political-Administrative Chamber dated 26 Apr. 2000, *Revista de Derecho Público*, No. 82 (Caracas: Editorial Jurídica Venezolana, 2000) 163 ff.
200. This conception of the 'State of Justice' has also been analysed by the Constitutional Chamber of the Supreme Tribunal of Justice, particularly in Decision No. 389 dated 7 Mar. 2002, in which the principle of the informality of the process was repeated, also asserting the principle of *pro actione* as another principle of the State of Justice. *See Revista de Derecho Público*, Nos 89–92 (Caracas: Editorial Jurídica Venezolana, 2002) 175 ff.

historical egalitarian character of Venezuelan society, which rejects any kind of discrimination or servility (Articles 19, 21). This has also been considered 'as a fundamental principle of democracy'.[201]

The principle of equality has been defined in a very explicit way in Article 21 of the Constitution, stating that all persons are equal before the law, and consequently, no discrimination can be allowed based on race, sex, religion, social condition, or any other cause having the purpose or consequence of annulling or harming the recognition, enjoyment and exercise of rights and liberties in conditions of equality. For such purpose, the Constitution provides for the juridical and administrative conditions in order to effectively guarantee equality before the law; for instance, providing for positive measures in favour of persons or groups that could be discriminated, marginalized or vulnerable; protecting persons located in circumstance of manifest weakness and punishing abuses and harms inflicted against them.

On matters of religion and belief, the Constitution expressly declares that the state must guarantee the freedom of 'cult and religion' (Article 50); everybody having the right to profess religious faith and cults, and to express their beliefs in private or in public by teaching and other practices, provided that such beliefs are not contrary to moral, good customs or public order. No one shall invoke religious beliefs or discipline as a means for evading compliance with the laws or preventing another person from exercising his rights. The autonomy and independence of religious confessions and churches are likewise guaranteed in the Constitution, subject only to such limitations as may derive from the Constitution and the law. The Constitution also entitles parents to determine the religious education to be given to their children in accordance with their convictions.

The Constitution guarantees freedom of conscience, although conscientious objections cannot be invoked in order to evade compliance with laws or prevent others from complying with them or exercising their rights (Article 60).

Finally, the Preamble of the Constitution expressly declares the Venezuelan Society to be multi-ethnic and pluricultural.

82. Democracy/Participation/Decentralization/Inclusion: The Constitution guarantees 'democracy' (Preamble), not only as a political regime and as a condition of the government, but also as a way of life, founded in the ideas of political pluralism and equal 'participation' of everyone in the political processes. In this sense, the concept of the 'democratic state' (*Estado democrático*) is also identified as a constitutional principle that gives roots to the political organization of the nation, as it derives from the Preamble ('democratic society') and from Articles 2, 3, 5 and 6 of the Constitution. Democracy is also established in Article 6 of the Constitution as an immutable regime of the government of the Republic and of its political entities (states and municipalities), by declaring that it is and always will be 'democratic, participative, elective, decentralized, alternative, responsible, pluralist, and of revocable mandates'.

---

201. *See* Decision No. 439 of the Political-Administrative Chamber dated 6 Oct. 1992, *Revista de Derecho Público*, No. 52 (Caracas: Editorial Jurídica Venezolana, 1992) 91–92.

The Constitutional Chamber of the Supreme Tribunal of Justice, in a Decision No. 23 dated 22 January 2003 held that the intention of the 1999 Constitution was to:

> establish a democratic, participative and protagonist society, which implies that it is not just the State who has to adopt and submit its institutions to the ways and principles of democracy, but it is also the society (formed by Venezuelan citizens) who must play a decisive and responsible role in the conduct of the Nation.[202]

By establishing the concept of participation as a fundamental principle of democracy, the Constitution regulates it as a political-constitutional right 'considering individuals as member of a determined political community, in order to take part in the formation of public decisions or of the will of the public institutions'; a right that is related to other political rights established in the Constitution, like the right to vote (Article 63), petition (Article 51), have access to public offices (Article 62), a political association (Article 67), demonstration (Article 68), and be informed in due time and truthfully by public administration (Article 143). It is also related to social rights, like the right to health (Article 84), educational rights (Article 102) and environmental rights (Article 127).[203]

'Participative democracy', in addition to 'representative' and 'direct' democracy, is promoted in other constitutional instruments established for the direct intervention of citizens in the decision-making process of public affairs, and in particular, 'in political matter: the election of public office, the referendum, the revocation of the term of office, the initiative for legislation, for constitutional reforms and for the constituent process, the open municipal council and the citizens' assembly whose decisions will be of binding force' (Article 70).

83. The Constitution directly regulates some mechanisms in order to guarantee the direct participation of the representatives of the different sectors of society in the adoption of some public decisions, particularly through the integration of 'Nominating Committees' for the proposal of candidates for the election by the National Assembly of high public officials not popularly elected, namely, the Prosecutor General, the General Comptroller, the judges of the Supreme Court, and the members of the Electoral National Council, seeking to avoid the traditional agreements between political parties.[204] This was considered by the Constitutional Chamber of the Supreme Tribunal of Justice, in a Decision No. 23 dated 23 January 2003, as a result of the 'struggles to change the negative political culture generated by decades of a centralized state of political parties (Cfr. Allan R. Brewer-Carias, *Problemas del Estado de Partidos*, Caracas 1988, p. 39) that interfered with the development of democratic values, through the participation of the people which is no

202. *See* Case: *Interpretación del articulo 71 de la Constitución* in *Revista de Derecho Público*, Nos 93–96 (Caracas: Editorial Jurídica Venezolana, 2003) 530 ff.
203. *Ibid*
204. *See*, e.g, Allan R Brewer-Carías, *Los problemas del Estado de Partidos* (Caracas: Editorial Jurídica Venezolana, 1988).

longer limited to electoral processes', recognizing their 'intervention in the formation, formulation and execution of public politics as a means to overcome the deficits of governability that have affected our political system due to the lack of harmony between the State and the society'; and radically changing 'from the root, the relations between State and society in which the latter receives back its legitimate and undeniable protagonist role by means of the exercise of its fundamental political rights'.[205]

In order to ensure the enforcement of citizens' right to political participation, the principle of federalism is promoted so that public power is territorially distributed among various levels of government, each of them with autonomous, democratic political institutions.

Article 4 of the 1999 Constitution formally defines the Republic of Venezuela 'as a decentralized Federal State under the terms set out in the Constitution' governed by the principles of 'territorial integrity, solidarity, concurrence and co-responsibility'. In practice, Venezuela continues to be a contradictory 'centralized federation'.[206]

Article 136 of the 1999 Constitution states that 'public power is distributed among the municipal, state and national entities', establishing a federation with three levels of political governments and autonomy: a national level exercised by the Republic (federal level); the states level, exercised by the 23 states and a Capital District; and the municipal level, exercised by the 338 existing municipalities. At each of these levels, the Constitution requires a government that is 'democratic, participatory, elected, decentralized, alternative, responsible, plural and with revocable mandates' (Article 6). Regarding the Capital District, this has substituted the former Federal District, which was established in 1863, with the elimination of traditional federal interventions that existed regarding the authorities of the latter.

84. Compassion/Caring/Solidarity/Social Justice/Social State: Article 2 of the 1999 Constitution defines the Venezuelan state as a social and democratic rule of law state, in which the principle of 'social responsibility' (Preamble) prevails in guiding public policies, configuring the state as a 'Social State', with specific social duties regarding society. In particular, the Constitution refers to the social goal of society and of the state in order to ensure 'social justice', guaranteeing the equitable participation of all in the enjoyment of wealth, preventing its concentration in a few hands, avoiding unfair income differences, and seeking the guarantee of a dignified and prosperous existence for the community (Articles 112, 299).

This idea of a 'Social State' (*Estado Social*) refers to a State with social obligations that strives for social justice, which allows its intervention in social and economic activities, as a welfare state. Such social character mainly derives from the fundamental constitutional value of 'equality and non-discrimination' that comes from the Preamble, and from Article 1 of the Constitution which, besides declaring

205. *See* Case: *Interpretación del articulo 71 de la Constitución* in *Revista de Derecho Público*, Nos 93–96 (Caracas: Editorial Jurídica Venezolana, 2003) 530 ff.

206. *See* Allan R Brewer-Carías, *Federalismo y Municipalismo en la Constitución de 1999* (Caracas: Universidad Católica del Táchira-Editorial Jurídica Venezolana, 2001); 'Centralized Federalism in Venezuela' (2005) 43(4) *Duquesne Law Review* 629–43.

it as a fundamental right (Article 21), is the criterion of the performance of the state (Article 2), and of the principle of 'social justice' as the base of the economic system (Article 299).

This concept of a 'Social State' has been defined by the Constitutional Chamber of the Supreme Tribunal in a Decision No. 85 dated 24 January 2002, thus:

> The Social State must protect people or groups that regarding others are in a situation of legal weakness, regardless of the principle of equality before the law, which in practice does not resolve anything, because unequal situations cannot be treated with similar solutions. In order to achieve the balance, the Social State not only intervenes in the labour and social security factor, protecting the salaried workers not related to the economic or political power, but it also protects their health, housing, education and economic relations. That is why the Economic Constitution must be seen from an essentially social perspective.
>
> The State is obligated to protect the weak, defend their interests protected by the Constitution, particularly through the courts; and regarding the strong, its duty is to watch that their freedom is not a load for everybody. As a juridical value, there cannot be constitutional protection at the expense of the fundamental rights of others ....
>
> The Social State tries to harmonise the antagonistic interests of society, without allowing unlimited actions from social forces based on the silence of the statutes or their ambiguities, because otherwise that would lead to the establishment of an hegemony over the weak by those economically and socially stronger, in which the private power positions become an excessive diminution of the real freedom of the weak, in a subjugation that constantly encourages the social crisis.[207]

85. Community/Civil Society: The Constitution contains specific provisions that refer to the community, the family and civil society, implying the existence, in addition to personal and individual rights, of collective rights. These have been analysed by the Constitutional Chamber of the Supreme Tribunal in Decision No. 1395 dated 21 November 2000, as corresponding to the organized community (Article 84), like the right to participate in the decision-making process of the public health institutions; the Venezuelan people (Articles 99 and 347), cultural values; the community (Article 118), develop associations of social and participative character; the indigenous people (Articles 121, 123, and 125); maintain their ethnic and cultural identity, and maintain their own economic practices and to political participation. These are, according to the Chamber's doctrine, differentiated entities that are considered holders of collective rights by express order of the Constitution.[208]

---

207. *See* Case: *Deudores hipotecarios v. Superintendencia de Bancos*, *Revista de Derecho Público*, Nos 89–92 (Caracas: Editorial Jurídica Venezolana, 2002) 94 ff.
208. *Revista de Derecho Público*, No. 84 (Caracas: Editorial Jurídica Venezolana, 2000) 331 ff.

86. Family: The Constitution has established several personal rights to be protected by the state, beginning with the protection of the family and of families. Article 75 imposes on the state the obligation to protect families as a natural association in society, and as the fundamental space for the overall development of human beings. According to the same constitutional provision, family relationships must be based on equality of rights and duties, solidarity, common effort, mutual understanding and reciprocal respect among family members. In order to protect families, the state must guarantee protection to the mother, father or other person acting as head of a household.

87. Children and adolescents have the right to live, be raised and develop in their original families. When this proves to be impossible or contrary to their best interests, they shall have the right to have a substitute family, in accordance with the law. Article 76 of the Constitution provides for the full protection of motherhood and fatherhood, whatever the marital status of the mother or father. Couples have the right to decide freely and responsibly how many children they wish to conceive and are entitled to access to information and means necessary to guarantee the exercise of this right. The state guarantees overall assistance and protection for motherhood, in general, from the moment of conception, throughout pregnancy, delivery and the puerperal period, and guarantees full family planning services based on ethical and scientific values. The implication of this provision, particularly when protecting maternity from the moment of conception, limits abortion as a right.

Article 77 of the Constitution also expressly 'protects marriage between a man and a woman, based on free consent and absolute equality of rights and obligations of the spouses'; consequently, same-sex 'marriages' are not protected in the Constitution, and only a stable de facto union between a man and a woman that meets the requirements established by law shall have the same effects as marriage.

Children and adolescents are considered full legal persons whose rights shall be protected by specialized courts, organs and legislation. The rights flow from the Constitution, the Convention on Children's Rights and other international treaty that may have been executed and ratified by the Republic in this field. The state, families and society shall guarantee their full protection as an absolute priority, taking into account their best interest in actions and decisions concerning them. The state shall promote their progressive incorporation into active citizenship, and shall create a national guidance system for the overall protection of children and adolescents (Article 78).

88. Regarding senior citizens, Article 80 of the Constitution imposes on the state the duty to guarantee the full exercise of their rights and guarantees, providing that the state, with the participation of families and society, is obliged to respect their human dignity, autonomy and to guarantee them full care and social security benefits to improve and guarantee their quality of life. Pension and retirement benefits granted through the social security system shall not be less than the urban minimum salary. Senior citizens shall be guaranteed the right to proper work if they indicate a desire to work and are capable of work.

89. Life: The most important civil right according to the Constitution is the right to life, Article 43, as 'inviolable'. The Constitution thus prohibits the death penalty, providing that 'no law shall provide for the death penalty and no authority shall apply the same'. In addition, the article obliges the state to 'protect the life of persons who are deprived of liberty, are in military or civil services, or are subject to its authority in any other manner'. The right to life, therefore, is an absolute right that cannot be 'suspended' nor restricted in cases of states of exception decreed by the President of the Republic.

90. Learning/Education: A chapter in the Constitution is devoted to educational rights. In this respect, Article 102 establishes that 'education is a human right and a fundamental social duty that is democratic, cost-free, and mandatory'. The consequence of this provision is an obligation imposed on the state to provide education as a function of greatest interest, at all levels and in all modes, as an instrument of scientific, humanistic and technical knowledge at the service of society. Every person has the right to a full, high-quality, ongoing education under conditions and circumstances of equality, subject only to personal aptitude, vocation or aspiration limitations. According to the Constitution, education is obligatory at all levels, from day-care to the diversified secondary level.

Education is constitutionally declared to be a public service (Article 102), although it states that, 'the State will stimulate and protect private education imparted which accords with the principles established in this Constitution and the Laws'. The Constitution establishes that education offered in state institutions is free of charge up to the undergraduate university level. The state shall create and maintain institutions and services sufficiently equipped to ensure the admission process, ongoing education and programme completion in the education system (Article 103). The communications media, public and private, shall contribute to civil education. The state guarantees public radio and television services and library and computer networks, with a view to allowing universal access to information (Article 108).

91. Honesty/Integrity: The Preamble to the Constitution refers to the values of 'ethics'. Ethical values are expressly mentioned in the provisions regarding education. Consequently, beyond the legal provisions referred to as public ethics in public administration, there is a set of ethical norms that must guide society and state officials in the task of transforming the state and creating a new legal system. As for public administration, which must be 'at the service of the people', the Constitution also enumerates the principles and values on which it must be based: 'honesty, participation, celerity, efficiency, effectiveness, transparency, the accounting and responsibility in the execution of the public function, with complete subjection to the statutes and to the Law' (Article 141).

92. Impartiality. As for elections, the Constitution enumerates the following principles that must be guaranteed regarding the electoral processes: 'equality, reliability, impartiality, transparency and efficiency', besides the 'personalization of the vote and proportional representation' (Article 293).

Regarding public services, the Constitution enumerates a series of governing principles in this respect: regarding the national public health system, it states that it must be 'inter-sectorial, decentralized and participative, and managed by the principles of gratuitousness, universality, integrity, impartiality, social integration and solidarity' (Article 84); in respect of the social security system, it indicates that the system must be 'universal, integral, unified [*solidario*], unitary, efficient and participative financing, from direct or indirect contributions' (Article 86); and as for the education, the Constitution expresses that it must be:

> 'democratic, free and mandatory,' [...] 'based on the respect to all thought tendencies, in order to develop the creative potential of every human being and the complete exercise of his/her personality inside a democratic society based on the ethical valuation of labour and the active, conscientious and unified [*solidaria*] participation in the processes of social transformation related with the values of the national identity and with a Latin-American and universal vision.' (Article 102)

93. Social Economic Justice. Regarding the socioeconomic regime of the Republic, the Constitution enumerates the following principles on which the system must be based:

> 'social justice, democracy, efficiency, free competition, environmental protection, productivity and solidarity, in order to guarantee the integral human development, a dignified and prosperous existence for the collectivity, the generation of labour sources, high national added value, elevation of the standard of living of the people and to strengthen the economical supremacy of the country, guaranteeing juridical security, stability, dynamism, supportability, permanence and equity of the economic growth, in order to achieve a fair distribution of the wealth by means of a democratic, participative and of open consultation strategic planning'. (Article 299)

94. Freedom/Liberty/Independence: The Constitution establishes certain rights that cannot be renounced or waived, being 'independence, freedom, sovereignty, immunity, territorial integrity and national self-determination' (Article 1).

Regarding independence, in the provisions referred to the territorial organization of the state, particularly regarding the 'decentralised federal state' (Article 4), it is established that it must be configured following the principles of 'territorial integrity, cooperation, solidarity, concurrence and co-responsibility' (Article 4). As for the national statutes that can be sanctioned by the National Assembly regarding concurrent competences between the national, the states and municipal levels, Constitution prescribes that they must be oriented by 'the principles of independence, coordination, cooperation, co-responsibility and subsidiary' (Article 165).

'Independence' is also affirmed in the Preamble, in the sense of reaffirming the existence of the Republic itself, which attained its independence from the Spanish monarchy in 1810, not subjected to any nature of foreign domination. Consequently, the 'territorial integrity' of the nation is also conceived as another fundamental value of the country, which impedes the modification of its borders in any way. Regarding the aims of 'peace', as a fundamental value, it implies the existential rejection of war.

However, 'freedom', according to the Preamble, is also one of the most fundamental values, understood in its most classical expression as the right of every individual to do anything that does not harm others, to not be obliged to do what the law does not order nor to be impeded from doing what it does not forbid; that is, the right to the 'free development of the personality', which is also expressly regulated (Article 20) without any other limitation than those derived from the rights of others and the public and social order.

95. Security: According to Article 55 of the Constitution, 'every person has the right to be protected by the state, through the entities established by law for the protection of citizens from situations that constitute a threat, vulnerability or risk to the physical integrity of individuals, their properties, and the enjoyment of their rights or the fulfilment of their duties. The citizens' participation in programmes for purposes of prevention, citizen safety and emergency management shall be regulated by a special law'.

The Constitution guarantees that the state's security entities shall respect the human dignity and rights of all persons and sets forth expressly that the use of weapons or toxic substances by police and security officers shall be limited by the principles of necessity, convenience, opportunity and proportionality in accordance with the law.

The Constitution enumerates the following principles regarding the Nation's security: 'independence, democracy, equality, peace, freedom, justice, solidarity, promotion and conservation of the environment, the affirmation of the human rights and the progressive satisfaction of all individual and collective needs of the Venezuelan people' (Article 326).

96. Responsibility/Accountability/Transparency: The Constitution establishes the general principle providing for state liability, incorporated in an express way in Article 140, that 'The State is liable for the damages suffered by individuals in their goods and rights, provided that the injury be imputable to the functioning of Public Administration', being possible to comprise in the expression 'functioning of Public Administration' its normal or abnormal functioning. The Constitution provides for elected public officials to be subject to accountability (*rendición de cuentas*), establishing the possibility for them being subjected to repeal referendums for the revocation of mandates (Article 6), which according to Article 72, can only take place at the mid-point of a term in office. The corresponding petition for a repeal referendum can only be one of the popular initiatives that must be signed by at least 20% of the registered voters in the corresponding jurisdiction. In order for a mandate to be repealed or revoked, the concurrence of a number of voters equal to or greater than the number that originally elected the official is needed, and the voters must total at least 25% of the registered voters in the corresponding jurisdiction. If the repeal petition is approved, the substitute officer must be elected immediately according to the electoral procedures established in the Constitution and laws. This repeal referendum was distorted in 2004 regarding its application to the President of the Republic and was transformed against the constitutional provision into a 'ratifying' referendum[209] (*see infra* paragraph 718).

Article 143 of the Constitution guarantees the rights of citizens to be informed and to have access to administrative information. In the first place, it provides for the right of citizens to be promptly and truly informed by public administration regarding the situation of the procedures in which they have a direct interest, and to know about the definitive resolutions therein adopted, to be notified of administrative acts and to be informed on the courses of the administrative procedure.

The constitutional article also establishes the individual right everybody has to have access to administrative archives and registries, without prejudice of the acceptable limits imposed in a democratic society related to national or foreign security, a criminal investigation, the intimacy of private life, all according to the statutes regulating the matter of secret or confidential documents classification. The same article provides for the principle of prohibition of any previous censorship referring to public officials regarding the information they could give referring to matters under their responsibility.

97. Environment: The Constitution regulates the environment, declaring that each generation has the right and duty to protect and maintain the environment for its own benefit and that of the world of the future; and that everyone has the right, individually and collectively, to enjoy a safe, healthful and ecologically balanced life and environment.

The state shall protect the environment, biological and genetic diversity, ecological processes, national parks and natural monuments, and other areas of particular ecological importance. The genome of a living being shall not be patentable, and the field shall be regulated by the law relating to the principles of bioethics.

It is a fundamental duty of the state, with the active participation of society, to ensure to people their development in a pollution-free environment in which air, water, soil, coasts, climate, the ozone layer and living species receive special protection, in accordance with law (Article 127).

In order to guarantee the protection of the environment, Article 129 of the Constitution prescribes that any activities capable of generating damage to ecosystems must be preceded by environmental and socio-cultural impact studies. The state shall prevent toxic and hazardous waste from entering the country, as well as prevent the manufacture and use of nuclear, chemical and biological weapons. A special law shall regulate the use, handling, transportation and storage of toxic and hazardous substances.

As a matter of public policy, Article 128 of the Constitution imposes on the state the duty to develop a land use policy taking into account ecological, geographic, demographic, social, cultural, economic and political realities, in accordance with

209. *See* Allan R Brewer-Carías, 'El secuestro del Poder Electoral y la confiscación del derecho a la participación política mediante el referendo revocatorio presidencial: Venezuela 2000–2004' *Boletín Mexicano de Derecho Comparado* 112 (México, Instituto de Investigaciones Jurídicas, Universidad Nacional Autónoma de México, 2005), 11–73.

the premises of sustainable development, including information, consultation and male/female participation by citizens. An organic law shall develop the principles and criteria for this zoning.

Article 106 of the Constitution ensures that environmental education is obligatory in the various levels and modes of the education system, as well as in informal civil education.

§2. The Incongruences Between Declared Values and Political and Judicial Practice

I. Superior Values of the Constitution and the 'Political Project'

98. The superior character of the values enshrined in the Constitution has been transformed by the Constitutional Chamber of the Supreme Tribunal of Justice, in its Decision No. 23 of 22 January 2003. Thus, the universal meaning of the values has been eschewed by the Tribunal which has said that 'to interpret the legal system according to the Constitution, means to protect the Constitution itself from every diversion of principles and from every separation from the political project that it embodies by will of the people'. It added:

> [A] system of principles, assumed to be absolute and supra historical, cannot be placed above the Constitution, nor that its interpretation could eventually contradict the political theory that supports it. From this perspective, any theory that proposes absolute rights or goals must be rejected and … the interpretation or integration [of the Constitution] must be done according to the living cultural tradition whose sense and scope depends on the specific and historical analysis of the values shared by the Venezuelan people. Part of the protection and guarantee of the Constitution is established then, in an in fieri politic perspective, reluctant to the ideological connection with theories that can limit, under pretext of universal validities, the supremacy and the national self-determination, as demanded in Article 1° eiusdem.[210]

This doctrine of subjection of the global constitutional values to a political project was ratified in Decision No 1.939 of 18 December 2009 (*Gustavo Álvarez Arias y otros*) in which the Constitutional Chamber declared a decision of the Inter-American Court of Human Rights as non-enforceable in Venezuela, rejecting the existence of superior values which may trump government policy. The Chamber argued that the legal order 'is a normative theory at the service of politic defined in the axiological project of the Constitution'; that the standard in order to resolve conflicts between principles and provisions must be 'compatible with the political project of the Constitution', and such provisions 'cannot be affected with interpretations that could give prevalence to individual rights or that could give prevalence

210. *Interpretación del Article 71 de la Constitución*, *Revista de Derecho Público*, No. 93–96 (Caracas: Editorial Jurídica Venezolana, 2003) 530 ff.

to the international order regarding the national one affecting the State sovereignty'; that no system of principles 'supposedly absolute and supra-historic can be placed above the Constitution', and that 'theories based on universal values that pretend to limit the sovereignty and national auto-determination are unacceptable'.[211]

This rejection of superior and universal values has been followed by the rejection of the constitutional rank that the Constitution has given to international instruments of human rights and to their direct and immediate application by all courts.

In effect, Article 23 of the 1999 Constitution, one of the most important provisions for the protection of human rights, provides for constitutional ranking of international treaties on human rights and their prevalence when containing provisions more favourable to their enjoyment than those established in the internal legal order. Its inclusion in the new Constitution was a significant advance in the completion of the protective framework of human rights.

99. Nonetheless, in the judicial practice and particularly regarding the provisions of the American Convention of Human Rights, the doctrine of the Supreme Tribunal in this case has been progressively restrictive, eventually rejecting the constitutional ranking of the international instruments of human rights. This restrictive approach by the Constitutional Chamber, that has affected the role of the Inter-American institutions for the protection of human rights, began with a decision dated 5 May 2000, in which the Constitutional Chamber objected to the 'quasi-jurisdictional' powers of the Inter-American Commission when issuing provisional protective measures regarding a state, qualifying it as 'unacceptable', stating that they 'imply a gross intrusion in the country's judiciary, like the suspension of the judicial proceeding against the plaintiff, measures that can only be adopted by the judges exercising their judicial attributions and independence, according to what is stated in the Constitution and the statutes of the Republic'.[212]

The restrictive approach regarding the role and value of international institutions for the protection of human rights was also applied in Decision No 1.942 of 15 July 2003 (*Impugnación de artículos del Código Penal, Leyes de desacato*),[213] in which the Constitutional Chamber, when referring to International courts, stated that 'in Venezuela, in general, in relation to Article 7 of the Constitution, no jurisdictional organ could exist above the Supreme Tribunal of Justice, and even in such case, its decisions when contradicting constitutional provisions are inapplicable in the country'.

This approach was extended in the decision of the Constitutional Chamber No 1.939 of 18 December 2008 (*Abogados Gustavo Álvarez Arias y otros*), in which it

211. *See* at www.tsj.gov.ve/decisiones/scon/Diciembre/1939–181208–2008–08–1572.html.

212. *See Faitha M Nahmens L and Ben Ami Fihman Z* (*Revista Exceso*), Exp No. 00–0216, Decisión No. 386 dated 17 May 2000. *See* the reference in Carlos Ayala Corao, 'Recepción de la jurisprudencia internacional sobre derechos humanos por la jurisprudencia constitucional' *Revista del Tribunal Constitucional* 6 (Lima, 2004), 275 ff.

213. *See* en *Revista de Derecho Público*, No 93–96 (Caracas: Editorial Jurídica Venezolana, 2003) 136 ff.

declared a decision of the Inter-American Court on Human Rights as non-enforceable in Venezuela. The decision of the former of 5 August 2008 (*Apitz Barbera y otros (Corte Primera de lo Contencioso Administrativo) v. Venezuela*)[214] condemned the Venezuelan state for the violation of the judicial guarantees of three former judges of a First Contentious Administrative Court that was dismissed by a Special Commission of the Supreme Tribunal. The Constitutional Chamber in its decision rejected the supra-constitutional character of the provisions of the American Convention, considering that in the event of a contradiction of a provision of the Constitution and a provision of an international treaty, the judiciary should have the attribution to determine the applicable provisions.[215] The non-enforceability in Venezuela of the decisions of the Inter-American Court of Human Rights was ratified by the Supreme Tribunal of Venezuela in Decision No. 1547 of 17 October 2011 (*Estado Venezolano v. Corte Interamericana de Derechos Humanos*),[216] in which the Constitutional Chamber decided on the 'unconstitutionality' of the decision of the Inter-American Court on Human Rights of 1 September 2011 (*Leopoldo López v. Estado de Venezuela)*[217] (*see infra* paragraphs 735 et seq.)

The problem with the interpretative role of the Court is that the Constitutional Chamber, unfortunately, is overly controlled by the Executive.[218] This has resulted in the rejection of the power of all courts to apply, in a direct and immediate way, international instruments on human rights for the resolution of judicial cases.

II. Erosion of Public Participation in Political Decision-Making

100. The goal of participation requires some form of decentralization, the inclusion of instruments of direct democracy in a representative democratic framework and the possibility for the people to express their opinion on political decisions.

Referendums can be useful instruments in order to perfect democracy, but by themselves cannot satisfy the aim of participation. This is illustrated in the 2002–2004 process concerning the Venezuelan presidential repeal referendum (*see infra* paragraphs 102, 178, 194, 196, 364), which was converted into a presidential 'ratification' referendum of a plebiscitary nature.[219] A repeal referendum is a vote asking the people if the mandate of an elected official must be revoked or not; it is

214. *See* in www.corteidh.or.cr. Excepción Preliminar, Fondo, Reparaciones y Costas, Serie C No. 182.
215. Available at www.tsj.gov.ve/decisiones/scon/Diciembre/1939–181208–2008–08–1572.html.
216. Available at www.tsj.gov.ve/decisiones/scon/Octubre/1547–171011–2011–11–1130.html.
217. Available at www.corteidh.or.cr/docs/casos/articulos/resumen_233_esp.pdf. *See* the comments in Allan R Brewer-Carías, 'El ilegítimo "control de constitucionalidad" de las sentencias de la Corte Interamericana de Derechos Humanos por parte la Sala Constitucional del Tribunal Supremo de Justicia de Venezuela: el caso *Leopoldo López v. Venezuela, septiembre 2011*', *Revista de Derecho Público* 128 (Caracas: Editorial Jurídica Venezolana, 2011) 227–50.
218. *See* Allan R Brewer-Carías, 'El juez constitucional al servicio del autoritarismo y la ilegítima mutación de la constitución: el caso de la Sala Constitucional del Tribunal Supremo de Justicia de Venezuela (1999–2009)', *Revista de Administración Pública* 180 (Madrid, Centro de Estudios Constituionales, 2009), 383–418.
219. *See* Allan R Brewer-Carías, 'El secuestro del Poder Electoral y de la Sala Electoral del Tribunal Supremo y la confiscación del derecho a la participación política mediante el referendo revocatorio presidencial: Venezuela: 2000–2004' *Revista Costarricense de Derecho Constitucional*, Tomo V

not a vote asking if the elected official must remain or not be in office. In the first case, the vote of the people for *YES*, if reached the percentage established in the Constitution, it is the decision to revoke, independently of the number of people that could have voted for *NO*. In the second case, it would be a 'plebiscite', based only on the majority of votes for the *YES* or the *NO* that is not established in the Constitution. But in the 2004 repeal referendum, the National Electoral Council, when giving the voting results, converted it into a plebiscite ratifying the President.[220]

The result of the implementation of the 1999 Constitution is that Venezuelan democracy transformed from being a representative democracy with more or less competitive and pluralist parties which alternated in government (1958–1998), into a centralized plebiscite democracy, in which effectively all power lies with the President, supported by politically partisan votes of the National Assembly and the military, and more appropriate to a one-party system.

This plebiscite democracy system has created an illusion of popular participation, particularly by means of the uncontrolled distribution of state oil income among the poor through governmental social programmes that are not tailored to the promotion of investment and the creation of meaningful employment. This plebiscite democracy is less representative and less participatory than the traditional representative party democracy, which, notwithstanding all the warnings[221] that were raised, the traditional parties have failed to preserve.

101. However, the only two constitutional provisions establishing means for direct participation of the people in political decisions process, in practice, have been neutralized. This applies to the election of higher officials of the Branches of Government (Prosecutor General, Comptroller General, People's Defender, National Electoral Council, Justices of the Supreme Court) that according to the Constitution must be nominated by specific Committees composed of 'representatives of the various sectors of society' (Articles 270, 279, 295) (*see infra* paragraphs 168, 239, 294, 415 ff., 442, 445, 455). Nonetheless, the different statutes regulating their composition have organized such Committees as 'parliamentary commissions' subjected to the political party that control the majority if the National Assembly.[222]

(San José, Costa Rica, Instituto Costarricense de Derecho Constitucional, Editorial Investigaciones Jurídicas SA, 2004) 167–312; and in *Revista Jurídica del Perú* 55 (Lima, 2004), 353–96.

220. *See* in general Allan R Brewer-Carías, *Crónica sobre la 'in' justicia constitucional. La Sala Constitucional y el autoritarismo en Venezuela*, (Caracas, Editorial Jurídica Venezolana, 2007), pp. 349–378.

221. *See* in general Allan R Brewer-Carías, *El Estado. Crisis y reforma* (Caracas: Academia de Ciencias Políticas y Sociales, 1982); and *Problemas del Estado de partidos* (Caracas: Editorial Jurídica Venezolana, 1988); Allan R Brewer-Carías, 'La crisis de las instituciones: responsables y salidas', *Revista del Centro de Estudios Superiores de las Fuerzas Armadas de Cooperación*, 11 (Caracas, 1985), 57–83; *Revista de la Facultad de Ciencias Jurídicas y Políticas*, 64 (Caracas: Universidad Cebtral de Venezuela, 1985), 129–55. Also *see* Allan R Brewer-Carías, *Instituciones Políticas y Constitucionales*, vol. I, Evolución histórica del Estado (San Cristóbal-Caracas, Universidad Católica del Táchira, Editorial Jurídica Venezolana, 1996) 523–41.

222. *See* Allan R. Brewer-Carías, 'La participación ciudadana en la designación de los titulares de los órganos no electos de los Poderes Públicos en Venezuela y sus vicisitudes políticas', en *Revista*

The other provision for the direct participation of the people established in the 1999 Constitution, in decision-making processes, is the obligatory public consultation that has to be organized before sanctioning of the statutes (Article 211) (*see infra* paragraph 181). This provision, in practice, has generally been ignored because since 2001 almost all the statutes in the country have been issued by means of decree-laws or delegated legislation, and the Executive Branch has never organized any sort of popular participation in order to hear the opinion of the people. Even worst, the Constitutional Chamber of the Supreme Tribunal has expressly ruled in Decision No. 203, 25 March 2014 (*Impugnación del Decreto de la Ley Orgánica de la Administración Pública*), that popular participation is not guaranteed in the Constitution when the statutes are issued by the President of the Republic, but only when sanctioned by the National Assembly.[223]

III. The Erosion of the Democratic Principle

102. The democratic principle embedded in the Constitution as one of its most important values means that all high officials of the State must be elected by direct or indirect popular vote and that the will of the people manifested through an election must be respected, corresponding only to the people, directly or indirectly revoke the election made.

This implies that according to the Constitution, the representatives (*diputados*) to the National Assembly and the President of the Republic must always be elected by popular vote through a direct, secret and universal vote cast by the people (Articles 186, 228) and that only the vote of the people cast in a referendum organized by popular initiative, can revoke the democratic mandate of those elected to the Executive and Legislative Branches of Government (Articles 72, 198, 233). The same democratic principle applies regarding the election of the high official of the other Branches of Government (Judicial, Citizens and Electoral) in the sense that they only can be elected by an indirect popular vote made by a qualified majority of the elected representatives to the National Assembly acting as an electoral body, and that their mandates can only be revoked by the same Assembly with the same qualified vote (Articles 265, 279, 296) (*see infra* paragraph 249, 442).

Nonetheless, the incongruence in this case between the constitutional provisions and the practice of government has been notorious, basically resulting from

---

Iberoamericana de Derecho Público y Administrativo (San José, Costa Rica, Asociación Latinoamericana de Derecho Administrativo, 2005), 76–95.

223. Available in *Revista de Derecho Público*, *Revista de Derecho Público*, 137 (Caracas: Editorial Jurídica Venezolana, 2014), 100–103. *See* the comments on the decision in Allan R. Brewer-Carías, 'El fin de la llamada 'democracia participativa y protagónica' dispuesto por la Sala Constitucional en fraude a la Constitución, al justificar la emisión de legislación inconsulta en violación al derecho a la participación política', in *ibid.*, 157–164. *See also* Allan R. Brewer-Carías, 'El derecho ciudadano a la participación popular y la inconstitucionalidad generalizada de los decretos leyes 2010–2012, por su carácter inconsulto', *Revista de Derecho Público*, No. 130 (Caracas: Editorial Jurídica Venezolana, 2012), 85–88.

decisions of the Constitutional Chamber of the Supreme Tribunal[224] that, for instance, in January 2013, imposed a non-elected official (the then-acting Executive Vice President) to act as President of the Republic;[225] in 2014 revoked the popular electoral mandate of an elected representative to the National Assembly,[226] and of two elected municipal mayors;[227] and in 2014, it allowed the 'indirect election' of the Justices of the Supreme Tribunal, the Prosecutor General, the General Comptroller and the People's Defender by only simple majority of votes of the representatives present in the session of the Assembly, and even worst, the same Constitutional Chamber designated the members of the National Electoral Council, usurping the role of the National Assembly[228] (*see infra* paragraphs 456). In addition, the representative democratic principle has been relegated by the Constitutional Chamber, accepting that there is no need for universal and direct suffrage for the 'election' of the members of the Communal Councils.[229]

224. *See* in general on the Supreme Tribunal decisions: Allan R. Brewer-Carías, *El golpe a la democracia dado por la Sala Constitucional* (Caracas: Editorial Jurídica Venezolana, 2014).
225. Decisions No. No. 2 of 9 Jan. 2013, available at http://www.tsj.gov.ve/decisio-nes/scon/Enero/02-9113-2013-12-1358.html, and No. 141 of 8 Mar. 2013, available at http://www.tsj.gov.ve.decisio-nes/scon/Marzo/141-9313-2013-13-0196.html. *See* the comments in Asdrúbal Aguiar (Compi lator), *El Golpe de Enero en Venezuela (Documentos y testimonios para la historia) (*Caracas: Editorial Jurídica Venezolana, 2013), 85–90. 97–106, 133–148 y 297–314.
226. Decision No. 207 de 31 de marzo de 2014, available at en http://www.tsj.gov.ve/decisiones/scon/marzo/162546-207-31314-2014-14-0286.HTML Also published in *Gaceta Oficial*No. 40385 of 2 Apr. 2014. *See* the comments in Allan R. Brewer-Carías, 'La revocación del mandato popular de una diputada a la Asamblea Nacional por la Sala Constitucional del Tribunal Supremo de oficio, sin juicio ni proceso alguno (El caso de la Diputada María Corina Machado)', *Revista de Derecho Público,* 137 (Caracas: Editorial Jurídica Venezolana, 2014), 165–189.
227. Decision No. 138 of 17 Mar. 2014, available at http://www.tsj.gov.ve/decisiones/scon/marzo/162025-138-17314-2014-14-0205.HTML 2014; and Decision No. 245 of 9 Apr. 2014, available at: http://www.tsj.gov.ve/decisiones/scon/abril/162860-245-9414-2014-14-0205.HTML *See also* in *Gaceta Oficial*,40.391 de 10 de abril de 2014. *See* the comments in Allan R. Brewer-Carías, 'La ilegítima e inconstitucional revocación del mandato popular de alcaldes por la Sala Constitucional del Tribunal Supremo, usurpando competencias de la jurisdicción penal, mediante un procedimiento "sumario" de condena y encarcelamiento (El caso de los Alcaldes Vicencio Scarano Spisso y Daniel Ceballo)', *Revista de Derecho Público,* 138 (Caracas: Editorial Jurídica Venezolana, 2014), 176–210.
228. Decision No. 1864 of 22 Dec. 2014, available at: http://historico.tsj.gov.ve/decisiones/scon/diciembre/173494-1864-221214-2014-14-1341.HTML; and Decision No. 1865 of 26 December 26, 2014, available at: http://historico.tsj.gov.ve/decisiones/scon/diciembre/173497-1865-261214-2014-14-1343.HTML. *See* the comments in Allan R. Brewer-Carías, 'El golpe de Estado dado en diciembre de 2014, con la inconstitucional designación de las altas autoridades del Poder Público', *Revista de Derecho Público,* 40 (Caracas: Editorial Jurídica Venezolana, 2014).
229. *See* in general regarding the Erosion of the Democratic Principle, Allan R. Brewer-Carías, *The Collapse of the Rule of Law and the struggle for Democracy in Venezuela. Lectures and Essays (2015–2020),* (Miami, Miami Dade College, 2020); *Sobre la democracia,* (Caracas, New York, Editorial Juridica Venezolana, 2919); *Proyectos constitucionales del Chavismo: para desmantelar la democracia y establecer un Estado socialista en Venezuela (Del principio al fin: 1999–2019)* (Bogotá, Editorial Temis, Editorial Jurídica Venezolana, 2019); *El 'nuevo constitucionalismo latinoamericano' y la destruccion del Estado democrático por el Juez Constitucional. El Caso de Venezuela* (Buenos Aires, Ediciones Olejnik, 2018); *La justicia constitucional, la demolición del Estado democrático en Venezuela en nombre de un 'nuevo constitucionalismo', y una tesis 'secreta' de doctorado en la Universidad de Zaragoza* (Caracas, Madrid, Universidad Carlos III, Editorial Jurídica Venezolana, 2018).

IV. The Contradictory State Intervention in the Internal Life of Civil Society Entities

103. In some cases, the incongruence between constitutional provisions is not the product of judicial rulings or of political application of the Constitution, but of norms contained in the Constitution. In this context, the Constitution, contrary to its participative phraseology, creates scope for intervention in the organizations of civil society by establishing the jurisdiction of the National Electoral Council for 'the organisation of the elections of trade-unions, professional associations and organisations with political objectives' and in general, to guarantee 'the equality, reliability, impartiality, transparency and efficiency of the electoral processes' (Article 293.6).

According to this provision, the Constitution provides that the internal elections that can take place within political parties, trade unions and professional associations of any kind must be organized by the state through one of the branches of government. This represents a contradiction with the participatory feature attributed to the Constitution and with its declared goal of promoting citizens' participation.

Consequently, all the internal electoral processes within the political parties in Venezuela from 2000 are to be organized by the National Electoral Council, although this has not always been the case in practice.

State intervention has been active regarding civil society organizations. For example, even though the trade-unions are considered as not being 'inside the structure of the Venezuelan public organization',[230] the Electoral Chamber of the Supreme Court, in Decision No. 46 dated 11 March 2002, justified state intervention and supervision regarding social organizations, arguing that it tends:

> To guarantee [internal] democracy in said organisations through the transparency and celerity of their electoral processes and the selection of the legitimate authorities that are called to represent the interests and rights of those affiliated in the negotiations and collective conflicts of labour; in the procedures of conciliation and arbitrage; in the promotion, negotiation, celebration, revision and modification of collective labour conventions, and in everything necessary for the guarantee of the patrimony and the interests of the trade union organisation.[231]

The Electoral Chamber of the Supreme Tribunal of Justice has decided in many cases to participate in the internal functioning of other forms of civic associations, as happened within neighbourhood associations. In Decision No. 61 dated 29 May 2001, the Constitutional Chamber considered that the matter was about organizations 'that the constitutional text, itself, refers to as "civil society", being able to request, from the National Electoral Council, its intervention in order to organize

230. *Revista de Derecho Público*, 84 (Caracas: Editorial Jurídica Venezolana, 2000) 132 ff.
231. *Revista de Derecho Público*, Nos 89–92 (Caracas: Editorial Jurídica Venezolana, 2000) 148–49.

their internal elections'.[232] In a decision dated 1 November 2000, in which the Electoral Chamber ruled against the electoral regulations issued by the Electoral Commission of a social club, considering that, even though the club was an association, 'the constitutional text itself refers to as forming part of "civil society", with authority to be freely constituted by its members, providing for their own organisation, being nonetheless able to request the intervention of the National Electoral Council for the organisation of their internal elections'.[233]

As for other civil associations, such as businesses and industrial or commercial chambers, the Electoral Chamber of the Supreme Tribunal, in Decision No. 18, dated 15 February 2001, considered that a civil association called 'Cámara de Comercios e Industrias del Estado Aragua' by virtue of its objectives to 'encourage for the economic development and the social progress of the region, providing the collective effort of the sectors that form it', as well as 'the defence and the strengthening of the free initiative and the freedom of the enterprise', constituted an indirect participative mechanism – both economically and socially – of a sector of the people in national society life; thus 'even if the referred civil association is of a private character, its objectives transcend the core particular interest'. For this reason, the Chamber considered that it was 'justified to include it as one of the organisations of the "civil society" implicitly stated in Article 293.6 of the Constitution', a reason for which it declared its jurisdiction to resolve a dispute challenging the election held in the association 'independently of the nature of the entity from which these proceed'.[234]

But in other cases, the Electoral Chamber has recognized the obligatory intervention of the National Electoral Council in the electoral processes of civil associations like those of university professors, as occurred regarding internal elections in the professors' association of the Universidad Central de Venezuela (UCV). Regarding these associations, the Electoral Chamber ruled in a Decision No. 51 dated 19 May 2000 that Article 293.6 refers to those 'groups of people that in their condition of professionals, unite to defend their common interests and to achieve improvements also of common character, independently from the fact that their conformation is not done by expressed disposition of a statute, but by common agreement from its members, under a form of private right'. The Electoral Chamber thus included associations established inside the Universities, formed by the professionals of diverse disciplines or knowledge areas that are part of the institution in their condition of professors, teachers or instructors, imposing on them the intervention of the state to organize their internal electoral processes.[235]

232. *See* Exp 000064, *Asociación de Residentes de la Urbanización La Trinidad*. *See* the reference in Allan R Brewer-Carías, *Derecho Administrativo*, vol. I (Bogotá, Universidad Externado de Colombia, 2005) 413 ff.

233. *See* Exp 0115, *Asociación Civil Club Campestre Paracotos*. *See* the reference in Allan R Brewer-Carías, *Derecho Administrativo*, vol. I (Bogotá, Universidad Externado de Colombia, 2005) 413 ff.

234. *See* Exp 000017, *Cámara de Comercios e Industrias del Estado Aragua*. This jurisprudence was ratified by the same Chamber according to verdict No. 162, Exp 2002–000077 dated 10–17–02 (Cámara de Comercio e Industrias del Estado Bolívar). *See* the reference in Allan R Brewer-Carías, *Derecho Administrativo*, vol. I (Bogotá, Universidad Externado de Colombia, 2005) 413 ff.

235. *See Asociación de Profesores de la UCV*, in *Revista de Derecho Público*, No. 82 (Caracas: Editorial Jurídica Venezolana, 2000) 92 ff.

V. The Dangerous Expansion of Security and Defence Values

104. The Constitution made substantial departures from the provisions of the earlier 1961 Constitution regarding national security and defence and the military. The earlier Constitution contained only three provisions on the subject: Article 133, establishing restrictions regarding the possession of arms; Article 131, prohibiting the simultaneous exercise of civilian and military authority by any public official other than the President of the Republic as Commander in Chief of the Armed Forces; and Article 132, referring to the general regulation of the Armed Forces.

By contrast, the Constitution promotes a marked militarist shape to the state, with particular provisions regarding not only the military but also the security and defence establishment (*see infra* paragraphs 272, 354).

Article 322 of the Constitution begins by stating that the security of the nation falls within the essential competence and responsibility of the state, founded upon the state's 'integral development'; the defence of the state being the responsibility of Venezuelans, and of all natural and legal persons, whether of public or private law, within the geographic territory of the state.

In addition, Article 326 provides for general principles of national security, declaring that its preservation in 'economic, social, political, cultural, geographic, environmental and military areas' mutually corresponds ('co-responsibility') to the state and to civil society, in order to fulfil the principles of 'independence, democracy, equality, peace, liberty, justice, solidarity, promotion and conservation of the environment, the affirmation of human rights, and, the progressive satisfaction of the individual and collective needs of Venezuelans on the basis of sustainable and productive development fully covering the national community'. All of these principles are enumerated in the opening Articles 1, 2, and 3 of the Constitution of 1999.

For this purpose, the Constitution created a new council, the National Council of Defence (Article 323), as the nation's highest authority for defence planning, advice, and consultation to the state (public powers) on all matters related to the defence and security of the nation's sovereignty, territorial integrity, and strategic thinking. This Council is presided over by the President of the Republic and integrated by the Executive Vice President, the President of the National Assembly, the President of Supreme Tribunal of Justice, the President of the Moral Republican Council (Citizen Branch of government, Article 237), the Ministers of the defence sectors: interior security, foreign relations, and planning, and others whose participation is considered pertinent.

Under the Constitution, the traditional national armed forces (comprised of the Army, the Navy, the Air Force, and the National Guard) have become integrated into a single institution, named the 'National Armed Force', which nonetheless, according to Article 328, is comprised of the Army, the Navy, the Air Force, and the National Guard, each working within its area of competence to fulfil its mission, and with its own system of social security, as established by its respective organic legislation.

All these constitutional provisions reinforce a normative framework with clear marks of a militarist structure, which when combined with the centralization of state power and the concentration of state power in the President by his control over the National Assembly. The result is a system that has shown authoritarian tendencies.

In particular, in the Constitution's provisions on military matters, the idea of the subjection or subordination of military authority to civilian authority has disappeared. Instead, what has been created is a greater autonomy of the National Armed Forces, whose four branches (since 2008, five branches) have been unified into one institution with the possibility of intervention in civilian functions.

This militaristic tendency is evidenced by the following constitutional rules: first, the elimination of the traditional prohibition that military and civilian authority be exercised simultaneously, as was established by Article 131 of the 1961 Constitution; second, the elimination of control by the National Assembly of senior military promotions, as provided in Article 331 of the 1961 Constitution and throughout the country's traditional constitutionalism; third, the elimination of the constitutionally 'non-deliberative and apolitical' character of the military institution, as established in Article 132 of the 1961 Constitution, which has opened the way for the Armed Force, as a military institution, to deliberate politically, intervene, and give its opinion on matters under resolution within the civil organs of the state; fourth, the elimination of the obligation of the Armed Force to ensure the stability of democratic institutions required by Article 132 of the 1961 Constitution; fifth, the elimination of the obligation of the Armed Force to respect the Constitution and laws 'the adherence to which will always be above any other obligation' as was set forth in Article 132 of the 1961 Constitution; sixth, the express right of suffrage granted to members of the military in Article 330 of the 1999 Constitution, which in many cases has been politically incompatible with the principle of obedience; seventh, the submission of authority over the use of all weapons, for war or otherwise, to the Armed Force, while removing this authority from the civil administration of the state (Article 324); eighth, the general attribution of police administrative functions to the Armed Force (Article 329); ninth, the establishment of procedural privilege for generals and admirals in the sense that in order for them to be judged, the Supreme Tribunal of Justice must declare in advance of trial whether or not the proceeding has merit (Article 266.3); and tenth, the adoption in the Constitution of the concept of the 'doctrine of national security', as a global, totalistic, and omni-comprehensive doctrine in the sense that everything that happens in the state and in the nation concerns the security of the state, including economic and social development (Article 326); with the duty for the Armed Force to have an 'active participation in national development' (Article 328). All these provisions create a picture of militarism, unique in Venezuelan constitutional history, not found even in former military regimes.

As can be appreciated from the above-mentioned, the Venezuelan Constitution incorporated in its text an express and extensive list of constitutional values and principles defined as goals intended to guide the conduct and activities of the state, society and individuals. Thus, those global values and principles do not derive from the process of interpretation and application of the Constitution, particularly by the courts, but are expressly established in the text of the Constitution.

By means of constitutional interpretation, mainly through the Constitutional Chamber of the Supreme Tribunal of Justice, the sense, the scope and the priority character of many of the constitutional principles and values have been defined and enriched, even giving some of them a priority vis-à-vis others. Unfortunately, in practice, these have been distorted by legislative practice and by the same Supreme

Tribunal decisions[236] originating some constitutional incongruence between what is provided for in the Constitution and what has been decided in the political practice of government.

---

236. *See* Allan R Brewer-Carías, *La patología de la justicia constitucional* (San José, Costa Rica, Investigaciones Jurídicas, 2012; (Third edition: Caracas, Editgorial Jurídica Venezolana, 2014); *Golpe a la democracia dado por la Sala Constitucional* (Caracas: Editorial Jurídica Venezolana, 2d ed. 2015).

Chapter 4. State Territory

105. Venezuela is one of the largest Latin American countries located in the northern part of South America with an area of 916,445 kms^2. Its boundaries are with Colombia to the west, Brazil and Colombia to the south and Guyana to the east. To the north, it has 2,813 km of coast on the Caribbean Sea and the Atlantic Ocean.

106. The territory is defined in Article 10 of the Constitution, in similar terms as in all the previous Constitutions since 1821, by referring to the one that appertained to the General Captaincy of Venezuela (*see supra* paragraphs 2, 5) before the 19 April 1810 political transformation (independence) began (*see supra* paragraph 2), with the modifications resulting from the treaties and arbitral rulings not affected of nullity. The previous 1961 Constitution only referred to the modifications resulting from treaties 'validly adopted by the Republic' (Article 7), a phrase that was added 'in order to demonstrate in an unequivocal manner, the will of the Republic to only accept those modifications to its territorial *status* resulting from a free and valid determination'.[237] These provisions were the consequence of many boundaries the country had with its neighbours.

107. Since the separation of Venezuela from Great Colombia in 1830 (*see supra* paragraph 9), boundary problems were always present between the two countries, up to 1881 when the disputed boundaries were settled by means of an Arbitral Treaty (14 September 1881), in which, due to the fact that both countries 'could not reach an agreement regarding their respective rights or *uti possidetis juris,* of 1810', they agreed to submit the matter to the judgment and ruling by the Spanish King, as legal arbitrator, in order to establish the territory appertaining before 1810 to the General Captaincy of Venezuela, and to the Viceroyalty of Nueva Granada. Consequently, in March 1891, an Arbitral decision was signed establishing the respective boundaries, which was executed by a pact of 30 December 1898.

108. Regarding Brazil, on 5 May 1859, Venezuela signed a Boundary and River Navigation Treaty with the then Emperor of Brazil, in which the boundaries were determined, being later marked between 1879 and 1905.

109. Also, on 5 August 1857, an Arbitral Convention was signed between Venezuela and the Netherlands regarding the sovereignty over the Aves Island in the Caribbean, a matter that was submitted to the decision of Queen Elizabeth II of Spain, who ruled in 1865 that the island appertained to Venezuela.

110. Regarding the boundaries with the former British colony of Guyana, the aforementioned 1961 Constitution provision (Article 7) that opened the possibility for the country to formally challenge the validity of treaties or arbitral awards concerning its borders, acquired particular significance, particularly regarding the 1899

---

237. *See* José A. Zambrano Velazco, *Sumario Jurídico de la territorialidad* (Maracaibo-San Cristóbal, 1983); Allan R. Brewer-Carías, 'Territorio de Venezuela. Período Republicano', in *Diccionario de Historia de Venezuela*, vol. II (Caracas: Fundación Polar, 1989), 867–874.

Arbitration decision that established the border with British Guiana, which Venezuela considered had ignored its territorial rights derived from the incorporation of the Province of Guyana, created in 1868, in the General Captaincy of Venezuela (1777).

In effect, after the 13 August 1814, Anglo–Dutch Treaty, the colonial possessions of the Dutch in the Americas were returned to what they were at the beginning of the war in 1803, with the exceptions of the Cape of Good Hope and the South American settlements of Demerara, Essequibo and Berbice, which were ceded to the UK, being consolidated in 1831 as British Guiana. The Treaty did not define the western boundary of the British colony regarding the newly re-establish Venezuelan State (1830) and particularly with its province of Guyana, so after the British commissioned Robert Schomburgk to delineate that boundary (1835), the Venezuelan–Guyana Boundary Dispute officially began when in 1840 the Venezuelan Government protested British encroachment on Venezuelan territory, considering that the borders of the former Guyana Province of the General Captaincy of Venezuela extended as far east as the Essequibo River.[238]

After claims and protests, and due to the United States' threats of intervention, the UK agreed in 1897, by means of the Treaty of Washington entered into by the UK and Venezuela, to let an international tribunal arbitrate the boundary. On 3 October 1899, the Tribunal issued a decision determining the boundary line between the Colony of British Guiana and the United States of Venezuela, and without any written opinion or explanation, awarded more than 90% of the disputed territory of British Guiana to the UK, with Venezuela receiving the mouth of the Orinoco River and a short strait of the Atlantic coastline just to the east.

111. The 1899 Arbitral Award coincided with one of the main nineteenth-century internal political struggles of Venezuela, in which a Revolution (the Liberal Restorative Revolution) seized State power and consolidated the authoritarian government that controlled the country for almost the entire first half of the twentieth century (*see supra* paragraphs 15, 16). The newly established government was also involved in a bitter international struggle which arose because of unpaid loans, provoking Great Britain, Germany and Italy to send a joint naval expedition to the Venezuelan coast to blockade seaports and capture Venezuelan gunboats (*see supra* paragraph 15; *infra* paragraph 347).

112. In 1949, the *American Journal of International Law*[239] published, after his death, a Memorandum written by Severo Mallet-Prevost (11 August 1944), a lawyer who had acted as a junior counsel for Venezuela at the Paris 1899 Tribunal, adducing that the Arbitral Tribunal's president had coerced several of its members into assenting to the final decision, that was the result of a political deal between Britain and Russia. Consequently, under the 1961 Constitution, Venezuela claimed

---

238. *See* Tomás E. Carrillo Batalla (Coord.), *La Reclamación Venezolana sobre la Guayana Esequiba* (Caracas: Academia de Ciencias Políticas y Sociales, 2009); Allan R. Brewer-Carías, 'Guyana-Venezuela Border Dispute', in *Max Planck Encyclopedia of Public* International *Law* (Oxford University Press, 2008); Héctor Faundez and Rafael Badell (Coord.), *La controversia sobre el Esequibo (*Caracas: Academia de Ciencias Políticas y Sociales, 2022).

239. 'The Venezuela-British Guiana Boundary Arbitration of 1899', in *American Journal of International Law*, Vol. 43, July 1949, 523–530.

that their rights to the Essequibo territory had been ignored by a tribunal which had settled the frontier based not on a judicial process, but on a political deal, filing in 1962 a formal territorial reclaim before the UK.

In 1966, an 'Agreement to resolve the controversy between Venezuela and the UK of Great Britain and Northern Ireland regarding the Venezuela and British Guiana Borders' was signed in Geneva, in consideration that the independence of British Guiana was going to be proclaimed as it happened that same year. Venezuela recognized the new State of Guyana with the stipulation that it 'does not imply recognition or in any way renouncement or diminishment of the territorial rights that Venezuela is claiming'. Afterwards, Guyana became a State party of the Geneva Agreement (Article VII); Venezuela reiterated its claim that the Paris Tribunal Arbitral decision of 1899 was 'null and void', considering that the *Guayana* Essequibo territory claimed by Venezuela 'has its east border with the new State of Guyana, on the Essequibo river line, from its origins to its discharge on the Atlantic Ocean'.

On 18 June 1970, the governments of Venezuela, Britain, and Guyana signed the Protocol of Port-of-Spain, which suspended for a period of twelve years the application of Article IV of the Geneva Agreement, providing for the parties to explore the possibility of improving their understanding and to create a more convenient environment to continue with the procedures set forth in the Geneva Agreement. The protocol was to end on 18 July 1982, but one year before, the Venezuelan Government publicly announced its decision not to extend its term, provoking the reactivation of the Geneva Agreement provisions, in the sense that the claim would be regulated by its Article IV, which refers to the peaceful settlement means set forth in Article 33 of the United Nations Charter. Accordingly, the matter was eventually referred to the Secretary General of the United Nations, for the selection of a peaceful settlement means, being the dispute settlement in his hands between 1985 and 2017, through a United Nations-based Good Officer process.[240]

113. On 30 January 2018, the Secretary General, after having analysed the developments of 'the good offices process' 'concluded that significant progress has not been made towards arriving at a full agreement for the solution of the controversy', 'chose the International Court of Justice as the means to be used for the solution of the controversy'.[241] This Secretary-General decision was followed by a claim filed by Guyana before the International Court of Justice (ICJ) against Venezuela, requesting it to decide that the boundary between the two States was fixed by an 1899 Arbitral Award, which according to Guyana, remains valid and binding on the parties. The ICJ issued a ruling on 18 December 2020, deciding that 'it has jurisdiction to entertain Guyana's claims concerning the validity of the 1899 Award about the frontier between British Guiana and Venezuela and the related question of

240. Nonetheless, since 2004 the Venezuelan Government prevented to officially reject the Guyana's official decisions to pursue natural resources exploitations in the Essequibo claimed territory. In 2015, some tardy reactions from Venezuela were expressed. *See*, for instance: 'Venezuela impone sanciones diplomáticas a Guyana', in http://internacional.elpais.com/internacional/2015/07/07/actualidad/1436238555_401097.html.

241. *See* Press release: SG/SM/18879-ICJ/630. 30 Jan. 2018. 'Secretary General Chooses ICJ as Means for Peacefully Settling Long-Standing Guyana-Venezuela Border Controversy', available at: https://press.un.org/en/2018/sgsm18879.doc.htm

the definitive settlement of the dispute regarding the land boundary between the territories of the Parties'.[242] After initial reluctancy from Venezuela to participate in the judicial process, in 2022, it filed preliminary objections that were discussed by the parties in hearings held between 17 and 21 November 2022.[243]

114. Regarding the delimitation of Venezuelan territorial waters, the first Treaty on the matter in international history was the Treaty on Maritime Waters of the Paria Gulf, signed by Venezuela and Great Britain on 26 February 1942, establishing the delimitation of waters between the continental territory of Venezuela and the Island of Trinidad. This Treaty was later substituted by the Treaty signed between Venezuela and Trinidad and Tobago on Maritime and Submarines Waters in November 1990.

The national statutes related to Territorial Water, Contiguous Zone, and Continental Shell of 1956 and to Exclusive Economic Zone of 1978, set forth that in cases in which the limits established according to its provisions caused superposition regarding foreign waters, the matter must be resolved according to international law. Consequently, Venezuela has subscribed to International Treaties for the delimitation of maritime and submarines areas with all the States with boundaries of waters, except Colombia: on 28 March 1978, with the United States of America regarding the Islands of Puerto Rico and Saint Croix (Law 20 July 1978); on 30 March 1978, with the Netherlands regarding the Netherlands Antilles (Aruba, Bonaire and Curaçao) (Law 20 July 1978); on 3 March 1979, with Dominican Republic (Law 26 July 1979); on 19 July 1980, with France regarding the Islands of Guadalupe and Martinique and the Island of Aves (Law 15 July 1982).

115. The national territory, being the State organized as a Federal Decentralized one, is politically organized according to Article 16 of the Constitution, and divided into twenty-three states, one Capital District where the capital city of Caracas is located (*see infra* paragraph 226), Federal Dependencies that are the Venezuelan Islands in the Caribbean Sea, and Federal Territories.[244] The twenty-three states are the following: Amazonas, Anzoátegui, Apure, Aragua, Barinas, Bolívar, Carabobo, Cojedes, Delta Amacuro, Falcón, Guárico, Lara, Mérida, Miranda, Monagas, Nueva Esparta, Portuguesa, Sucre, Táchira, Trujillo, Vargas, Yaracuy and Zulia. The Capital District exists, which in 2000 substituted the former traditional Federal District founded in 1863, comprising part of the City of Caracas, which is the Capital of the

242. Available at: chrome-extension://efaidnbmnnnibpcajpcglclefindmkaj/https://www.icj-cij.org/public/files/case-related/171/171-20201218-JUD-01-00-EN.pdf.

243. *See* 'The International Court of Justice held Public Hearings in the case *Guyana v. Venezuela*', Production date 21 Nov. 2022, available at: https://media.un.org/en/asset/k16/k16zu3xpxs

244. *See* Armando Rodríguez, 'Las nuevas bases constitucionales de la estructura político territorial en Venezuela', in *Revista de Derecho Administrativo,* No. 10 (septiembre-diciembre) (Caracas: Editorial Sherwood, 2001), 169–200; Ramón Crazut, 'Comentarios al Título II de la Constitución de 1999 sobre el espacio geográfico y la división política', in *Revista de Derecho Público,* No. 81 (Caracas: Editorial Jurídica Venezolana, 2000), 40–46;. Tulio Álvarez, 'El concepto de territorio y su integración en el caso venezolano', in *Estudios de Derecho Público*, ed. en Román Duque Corredor, y Jesús María Casal (Coord.), vol. II (Caracas: Universidad Católica Andrés Bello, 2004), 1–50.

Republic. In 2009 the Capital District was organized but contrary to the Constitution, just as a 'national' entity dependent on the Central Government.[245] The Constitution also establishes Federal Dependencies, which comprise the Venezuelan islands in the Caribbean Sea, except those integrating the state of Nueva Esparta (Islands of Margarita, Coche and Cubagua). Following a tradition also initiated in 1864, the Constitution also provided for the Federal Territories (Article 16), which nonetheless are currently non-existent. The last two Federal Territories were the Delta Amacuro Federal territory in the Orinoco Delta and the Amazonas Federal territory in the south of the country, which was transformed into states in 1991 and 1992.[246] In 2011, the creation of a new federal territory was announced by the Government comprising some of the Islands near the coast (*Territorio Insular Miranda*).

---

245. *See* the Special Law on the Organization and Regime of the Capital District, *Gaceta Oficial* No. 39.156 of 13 Apr. 2009. *See* Allan R. Brewer-Carías, 'La problemática del régimen jurídico del "Distrito Capital" en la estructura federal del Estado en Venezuela, y su inconstitucional regulación legal', *AIDA Opera Prima de Derecho Administrativo*, No. 5 (México: Universidad Nacional Autónoma de México, enero-junio 2009, 2009), 81–119; and Allan R. Brewer-Carías et al., *Leyes sobre el Distrito Capital y el Área metropolitana de Caracas* (Caracas: Editorial Jurídica Venezolana, 2009).
246. *See* Allan R. Brewer-Carías, 'El régimen de los Territorios y Dependencias Federales', in *Revista de Derecho Público*, No. 18 (Caracas:Editorial Jurídica Venezolana, 1984), 85–98.

Chapter 5. Population (Demographic Data) and Language

116. The national population census of 2011 showed a total Venezuelan population of 28,946,101 (2014 estimated 30,206,307), mainly being concentrated in the coastal and mountain zones, which represent approximately 20% of the territory and more than 80% of the population. The region of the plains, with 30% of the territory, has only 10.2% of the total population, and the Guayana region, with 50% of the territory of the country, only has 6% of the population.

The density of the population is 25.2 inhabitants per km^2, the highest one in the Capital District (4,240 inhabitants per km^2), followed by the states of Carabobo, Nueva Esparta, Miranda and Aragua. The lowest density is located in the southern states of Amazonas, Delta Amacuro, Apure and Bolivar, where the indigenous people population (less than 1.5% of the total population) (*see infra* paragraphs 578 et seq.), is mainly concentrated.

The Venezuelan population is characterized by being an aggregation of mixed races, a product of the historical *mestizaje* of the country, whose origin is to be found in the colonial times with the unions of Indians and Spaniards and since the sixteenth century, with the African population. After Second World War, an important process of migration took place in the country, and the country received many Spanish, Portuguese and Italian migrants who were rapidly integrated into the country. During the 1970s, a similar process of migration took place with people from South American countries, mainly due to the development of the Venezuelan economy compared to the recession in other counties. All those processes of migration have given rise to a completely integrated population without any sort of interracial conflicts, in spite of the recurrent efforts made by the government since 2000 to provoke social class conflicts.

However, Venezuela being traditionally a country of immigrants, in the past years, particularly after 2012, due to the economic, social and political crisis provoked by the authoritarian regime imposing erroneous socialist policies that have destroyed the productive apparatus of the country, nationalizing and confiscating almost all private investments, the country has been transformed into a country of emigrants. This situation has originated a humanitarian crisis in a way never before seen and experienced in Latin America, reflected in an exodus of more than six million Venezuelan that have fled the country.[247] In the words of Luis Almagro, the Secretary-General of the OAS in 2018: 'the greatest exodus that has existed in the history of Western Hemisphere'.[248] An exodus that has changed the demography of the country in a way still to be determined.

247. *See*, for instance: 'The Crisis Next Door. Mass exodus of exasperated Venezuelan is overwhelming neighboring countries', The Washington Post, 2 Mar. 2018, in https://www.washingtonpost.com/news/world/wp/2018/03/02/feature/i-cant-go-back-venezuelans-are-fleeing-their-crisis-torn-country-en-masse/?noredirect=on&utm_term=.f0dbbb8f948d2.

248. *See*: 'Almagro: Crisis migratoria venezolana es el éxodo más grande del hemisferio', in Noticierodigital.com, Santo Domingo, EFE, 29 de agosto de 2018, en http://www.noticierodigital.com/2018/08/almagro-proxima-semana-se-hara-reunion-abordar-la-crisis-migratoria-sufre-venezuela/.

117. However, regarding language, the official language of the country is 'Castilian' (Spanish). Nonetheless, according to Article 9 of the Constitution, the indigenous languages are also of official use for the indigenous peoples and being part of national and humanity cultural heritage, must be respected in all the national territory[249] (*see infra* paragraph 580).

249. Indigenous Languages Law, *Gaceta Oficial* No. 38.981 of 28 Jul. 2008.

Chapter 6. Constitutional Relationship Between Church and State

118. The most important religion in Venezuela has always been Roman Catholic. Nonetheless, except in the 1811 Constitution, where the Catholic, Apostolic and Roman religion were declared the only and exclusive one of the population as well as the State's religion (Article 1), in no other Constitution has such a provision been included. In the 1857 constitutional reform, a provision establishing that the State was to protect the Catholic religion (Article 5) was in effect only for a few months (*see supra* paragraph 11). Since the 1864 Constitution (Articles 14, 13), religious freedom has been expressly declared and guaranteed in the country (*see infra* paragraphs 466, 524).

119. However, the separation between Church and State is the principle established in Venezuela since the nineteenth century, after decades in which the State had the right to be involved in Church affairs. In effect, since the Independence, the newly independent State assumed the Right to *Patronato Eclesiastico* that the Spanish Crown used to have regarding the Catholic Church. Consequently, on 25 July 1824, the Congress of the Republic of Colombia passed an Ecclesiastic *Patronato* Law, conferring to the State the power to be involved in the administration and organization of the Catholic Church, and even regarding the discipline of the Church and the administration of the Church properties.

During the presidency of Antonio Guzmán Blanco (*see supra* paragraph 13), the traditional conflicts between the State and the Church were exacerbated, when the government suspended the Seminars, imposing the laic character of education. In 1873, civil marriage was formally decreed, and the civil registry was organized out of the reach of the Church. All these provisions were incorporated in the first Civil Code approved that same year, substituting the former ecclesiastic provisions, and since then, have been the general regime of civil law applied in the country. In 1874 all Convents and Cloisters were dissolved, and the ecclesiastic properties were taken by the State.

120. Later, in 1911, a Decree was adopted on the Supreme Inspection of Cults, where references were made to the Ecclesiastic *Patronato* Law. These inspection powers were also included in the 1961 Constitution, which after establishing the freedom of religion (Article 65), expressly regulated the Ecclesiastic *Patronato* right, establishing with the same trend as the 1947 Constitution, that nonetheless, international agreements could be signed to regulate the relations between the Church and the State (Article 130).[250]

Based on this provision, a *Modus Vivendi* was signed in 1964 between the Saint Siege and the Venezuelan State regulating the relations between the Church and the State, substituting the old provisions referred to as the Ecclesiastic *Patronato*. In the 1999 Constitution, no reference at all is made to these matters, being limited to

250. *See* José Rodríguez Iturbe, *Iglesia y Estado en Venezuela 1824–1964* (Caracas, 1968); and Jesús Leopoldo Sánchez, 'El convenio Eclesiástico, las Constituciones Hispanoamericanas y los Códigos Nacionales', in *Estudios sobre la Constitución. Libro Homenaje a Rafael Caldera*, vol. III (Caracas: UCV, 1979), pp. 1723 ff

establishing the freedom of religion and cult that the State must guarantee. The Constitution also proclaimed the independence and autonomy of all churches and religions (Article 59).

Chapter 7. Constitutional Principles Regarding International Relations

121. The Preamble of the Constitution establishes the political, social, cultural and international goals of the State and the Society, and among the latter, it is defined as an essential goal of the State to pacifically cooperate with all nations, through pacific solutions of controversies, rejecting war. The international cooperation must be governed by the principles of non-intervention in other countries' affairs, and of the self-determination of peoples, according to the universal and indivisible international guarantee of human rights and the democratization of international society.

The Preamble also refers to the values that must govern the International relations of the Republic, like nuclear disarmament, environmental equilibrium as well as the healthy environment as a common and non-renounceable human heritage.

Another of the main goals of the State mentioned in the Preamble that must govern the action of the State is the promotion and consolidation of Latin American integration, which at that moment was referring to the Andean Community of Nations of which Venezuela was a member up to 2006.

122. In addition to the Preamble, Article 152 of the Constitution also refers to the international relations of the Republic, pointing out that they must coincide with the goals of the State regarding the exercise of its sovereignty and the people's interest. Those relations must be governed by the principles of independence, equality between States, free determination and non-intervention in internal matters of other States, the pacific solution of controversies, cooperation, human rights respect, solidarity among the people in their fight for emancipation and the welfare of humankind.[251] In addition, the same Article 152 provides that the Republic must maintain the most firm and decided defence of these principles and of the democratic practice in all international organs and institutions.

123. Regarding the Latin American integration process, the 1999 Constitution incorporated a major reform providing for a constitutional basis for such a process, giving foundations to the possibility of the transfer of State powers to supranational entities. The previous constitutional situation was precarious due to the provision of Article 108 of the 1961 Constitution, which in fact impeded Venezuela's ability to decide to enter with clear constitutional solutions into the process of integration.[252] On the contrary, and with the purpose of giving specific constitutional grounding to any supra-national integration process, Article 153 of the 1999 Constitution incorporated a new express clause on the subject, in which, in addition to

251. *See* in general, Juan Carlos Sainz Borgo, 'Régimen internacional de la Constitución de 1999', in *Revista de la Facultad de Ciencias Jurídicas y Políticas,* No. 121 (Caracas, 2001), 143–209.

252. *See* Allan R. Brewer-Carías, *Implicaciones constitucionales del proceso de integración económica regional* (Caracas, 1997); 'Las exigencias constitucionales de los procesos de integración y la experiencia latinoamericana', in *Congreso de Academias Iberoamericanas de Derecho* (Córdoba: Academia Nacional de Derecho y Ciencias Sociales de Córdoba, 1999), 279–317; 'Las implicaciones constitucionales de la integración económica regional', in *El Derecho Venezolano a finales del Siglo XX* (Caracas: Academia de Ciencias Políticas y Sociales, 1998), 407–511.

imposing on the Republic the duty to promote and favour the Latin American and Caribbean integration in order to advance towards the creation of a Community of Nations, it established the possibility for the Republic to participate by means of treaties, in the creation of supra-national organizations, to which powers may be attributed or transferred to conduct the processes of integration that the Constitution assigns to the branches of government. Accordingly, the same constitutional provision establishes that the resulting communitarian law *(derecho comunitario)*, not only has direct and immediate effect on internal law because it is considered to be an integral part of the existing legal order, but it also has to be preferred over national laws with which they could be in conflict.[253]

These provisions of the Constitution were very important regarding the only integration process in Latin America with a supra-national organization, that is, the Andean Community of Nations, which had its origin in the Cartagena Agreement (*Andean Pact*) of 1969, initially signed by Bolivia, Chile, Colombia, Ecuador and Peru, and to which Venezuela adhered to in 1973 as a Member State. In 1996 the Andean Pact of sub-regional integration was transformed into the Andean Community of Nations, conformed by supra-national organs such as the Commission, the Andean Court of Justice and the Andean Parliament.[254] Unfortunately, Venezuela withdrew from the Andean Community in 2006. In July of that same year, Venezuela was admitted to be part of Mercosur, an integration process initially established between Argentina, Brazil, Paraguay and Uruguay, from which, because of the rupture of the democratic order occurred in the country, in 2017, it has been suspended in all its rights and obligations as Member State.[255]

On matters of human rights, the Constitution (Article 23), not only establishes that the provisions of the International Treaties on Human Rights are immediately and directly applicable by the courts and any other organ exercising Public Powers

253. *See* in general, Jorge L. Suárez, 'La Constitución venezolana y el Derecho Comunitario', in *El Derecho Público a comienzos del siglo XXI. Estudios homenaje al Profesor Allan R. Brewer-Carías,* vol. III (Madrid: Instituto de Derecho Público, UCV, Civitas Ediciones, 2003), 253–276; Marianella Zubillaga, 'Los fundamentos del Derecho Comunitario y su soporte constitucional: la experiencia europea y andina', *ibid.,* 281–307; Jorge L. Suárez M., 'La Comunidad Andina, la responsabilidad del Estado y la Constitución venezolana', in *Estudios de Derecho Público: Libro Homenaje a Humberto J. La Roche Rincón,* vol. II (Caracas: Tribunal Supremo de Justicia, 2001), 489–648; Jorge L. Suárez M., 'La Constitución venezolana de 1999 y la integración regional', in *Estudios de Derecho Administrativo: Libro Homenaje a la UCV,* vol. I (Caracas: Imprenta Nacional, 2001), 440–472; Nelly Herrera Bond, 'El Derecho Comunitario en la nueva Constitución', in *Comentarios a la Constitución de la República Bolivariana de Venezuela* (Caracas: Vadell Hermanos Editores, 2000), 7–10; Jorge Petit, 'Los principios de auto–ejecutividad e inmediatez de los tratados internacionales en materia de integración a la luz de la Constitución Venezolana de 1999, en el marco de la Comunidad Andina de Naciones', in *Revista de la Facultad de Ciencias Jurídicas y Políticas de la UCV,* No. 122 (Caracas, 2001), 153–168; and Juan Carlos Sainz Borgo, 'La regulación constitucional del proceso de Integración Andino', in *Libro Homenaje a Enrique Tejera París, Temas sobre la Constitución de 1999* (Caracas: Centro de Investigaciones Jurídicas (CEIN), 2001), 241 a 271.

254. *See* Allan R. Brewer-Carías, 'El largo camino para la consolidación de las bases constitucionales de la integración regional andina y su abandono por el régimen autoritario de Venezuela', in André Saddy (Coordinador), *Dereito Público Econômico Supranacional* (Rio de Janeiro: Methoius Consultoría Jurídica Internacional, 2009).

255. *See* the text of the resolution dated 5 Aug. 2017, 'Suspensión de Venezuela en el MERCOSUR', in https://www.mercosur.int/suspension-de-venezuela-en-el-mercosur/.

but also assigns to them constitutional rank giving them preference over internal law if they are more favourable regarding the enjoyment or exercise of rights.[256] Unfortunately, and in spite of these important provisions, on these matters, the Supreme Tribunal in a few decisions issued between 2008 and 2011, declared the decisions of the Inter-American Court of Human Rights created by the Inter-American Convention of Human Rights as being non-enforceable in the country, requesting the Executive to withdrawal from the Convention which eventually occurred in 2012 (*see infra* paragraph 738).

124. Finally, it must be mentioned that according to Article 155 of the Constitution, in all international treaties, covenants and agreements signed by the Republic, a clause must be inserted according to which the parties are obliged to resolve the controversies that could arise between them, derived from their interpretation or execution, by the pacific means recognized in international law provided that it is possible in the procedure followed by the signing.

256. *See* Allan R. Brewer-Carías, 'Nuevas reflexiones sobre el papel de los tribunales constitucionales en la consolidación del Estado democrático de derecho: defensa de la Constitución, control del poder y protección de los derechos humanos', in *Dignidad de la persona, Derechos Fundamentales, Justicia Constitucional*, ed. Francisco Fernández Segado (coordinador) (Madrid: Dykinson, 2008), 761–826.

Part I. Sources of Constitutional Law

Chapter 1. The Constitution

§1. Supremacy and Rigidity

125. The principle of constitutional supremacy is expressly established in Article 7 of the 1999 Constitution sets forth that 'the Constitution is the supreme norm and the foundation of the legal order', and that, 'all persons and organs that exercise public power are subject to this Constitution'. For such purpose, the provisions of the Constitution as superior law are always directly enforceable and applicable; and the Constitution is essentially the ground norm for the interpretation of the entire legal order.[257]

This character of the Constitution as a supreme norm and the foundation of the legal order is also accompanied by the express prescription that its provisions are obligatory for all branches of government as well as for individuals. The most important consequence of this express consecration of the principle of constitutional supremacy is the establishment of the system of judicial review and particularly the obligation of all judges to assure the integrity of the Constitution (Article 334) (*see supra* paragraph 70; *infra* paragraph 670).

However, the supreme law character of the Constitution implies that it has derogatory power regarding any other norm sanctioned prior to its enactment, and in addition, that any act approved after the enactment of the Constitution that could contradict its provisions is considered null and void.

Finally, the supreme character of the Constitution means that it is accompanied by the principle of rigidity in the sense that the constitutional text is out of the reach of the ordinary legislator and that it cannot be modified by the procedure of formation of the ordinary laws, but only by means of the specific procedures set forth in the Constitution for its revision with popular participation.[258] It also implies that the powers of interpretation assigned to the Constitutional Chamber of the Supreme Tribunal as Constitutional Judge, cannot let to an illegitimate 'mutation' of the sense and meaning of a constitutional provision (*see* paragraphs 713 et seq.).

257. *See* Claudia Nikken, *Consideraciones sobre las fuentes del Derecho Constitucional y la interpretación de la Constitución*, (Caracas, Editorial Jurídica Venezolana, 2018).

258. *See* Allan R. Brewer-Carías, 'La intervención del pueblo en la revisión constitucional en América Latina', in *El derecho público a los 100 números de la Revista de Derecho Público 1980–2005* (Caracas: Editorial Jurídica Venezolana, 2006), 41–52.

§2. PROCEDURE FOR CONSTITUTIONAL REVIEW

126. In effect, the rigidity of the Constitution materialized through the provision of special procedures and institutional channels for constitutional review[259] which implies that the National Assembly through the procedure for enacting ordinary legislation, may in no case modify the Constitution or perform a constitutional review.

The Constitution of 1999 contains three institutional mechanisms for constitutional review, distinguishable according to the importance and magnitude of the changes proposed, which include the Amendment, the Constitutional Reform, and the National Constituent Assembly.[260]

I. Constitutional Amendment

127. The first constitutional review procedure is the 'Constitutional Amendment' which has been established for the purpose of adding or modifying one or more provisions to the Constitution without altering the text's fundamental structures (Article 340).

According to Article 341.1, this amendment procedure can be initiated by a petition signed by 15% of Citizens inscribed in the civil and electoral register; by 30% of the members of the National Assembly; or by the President of the Republic in a decision that must be adopted in the Council of Ministers.

When the initiative stems from the National Assembly, the amendment proposition requires the approval of a majority of its members, and the draft must be debated and approved, following the procedures constitutionally established for the passage of legislation. (Article 341.2). This means that a legislative debate of a proposed amendment only takes place when the amendment procedure is initiated by the National Assembly which, in that case, must approve it. Thus, if an Amendment is proposed by popular initiative or is initiated by the President of the Republic, that proposal is the one to be directly submitted to popular approval by referendum (Article 341.3), without any kind of debate or approval by the National Assembly. In the referendum, at least 25% of registered voters must concur, and in order to approve the proposal, it must be voted for by a simple majority of those voting (Article 73).

---

259. *See* Allan R. Brewer-Carías, 'Los procedimientos de revisión constitucional en Venezuela', in *I Procedimenti di revisione costituzionale nel Diritto Comparato*, ed. Eduardo Rozo Acuña (Coord.) (Urbino, Italia, 1999), 137–181; 'Modelos de revisión constitucional en América Latina', in *Boletín de la Academia de Ciencias Políticas y Sociales*, enero-diciembre 2003, No. 141 (Caracas, 2004), 115–156.

260. Véase Claudia Nikken, 'Breves consideraciones sobre el ejercicio del poder de revisión en Venezuela: a partir de la vigente constitución', in *Revista de Derecho Público,* No. 109 (Caracas: Editorial Jurídica Venezolana, 2007), 27–34; Lolymar Hernández Camargo, 'El Poder Constituyente como principio legitimador de la Constitución', in *El Derecho Público a comienzos del siglo XXI. Estudios homenaje al Profesor Allan R. Brewer-Carías,* vol. I (Madrid: Instituto de Derecho Público, UCV, Civitas Ediciones, 2003), 113–130; José Vicente Haro, 'Sobre los límites materiales de la enmienda y la reforma constitucional', in *Estudios de Derecho Público*, ed. Román Duque Corredor y Jesús María Casal (Coord.), vol. II (Caracas: Universidad Católica Andrés Bello, 2004), 373–420.

Once approved by the people, the President of the Republic is obligated to promulgate Amendments within ten days of their approval (Article 346).

The Constitution requires that Amendments, once approved by referendum, be numbered consecutively, and published as a continuation of the Constitution without altering the original text. However, articles amended are to be annotated with a footnote corresponding to the number and date of their amendments.

Up to 2022, the only Constitutional Amendment to the Constitution was sanctioned and approved by the people in 2009, regarding Articles 160, 162, 174, 192 and 230, providing for the possibility of indefinite re-election of all publicly elected officials.[261] Nonetheless, this 2009 Amendment, because altering one of the fundamental structures of the constitutional text, which is the democratic principle of republican alternance (Article 6), has been considered as being approved violating the Constitution[262] (*see infra* paragraph 721, 724).

II. Constitutional Reforms

128. The second constitutional review procedure established in the 1999 Constitution is the 'Constitutional Reforms', which in Article 342 is designed for partial revisions of the Constitution and for the substitution of one or several provisions but without modifying the structure and fundamental principles of the constitutional text.

The differences between an 'Amendment' and a 'Reform' are thus subtle. The former enables 'the addition or modification of one or several articles of the Constitution, without altering its fundamental structure' (Article 342), while the latter has as its objective, 'the substitution of one or several of its provisions which do not modify the structure and principles of the constitutional text' (Article 340).

From these provisions, it can be said that the 'Amendment' procedure is designed to 'add or modify' articles of the Constitution, while the 'Reform' procedure is designed to 'substitute' articles, but in neither case can the fundamental structure of the Constitution be altered. That is why the 'constitutional reform' proposed and sanctioned in 2007, which was rejected by the people by referendum held in December 2007, was formulated in defraudation of the Constitution (*see infra* paragraphs 265 ff., 651 ff.) because it was seeking to modify essential elements of the State, and even create a new Communal or Popular Power State, through a procedure established for other purposes[263] (*see supra* paragraph 36; *infra* paragraphs 232 et seq.).

Nonetheless, the procedure for the 'Constitutional Reform' is more complicated and requires that a proposed reform be debated and approved by the National Assembly before it can be submitted to a referendum. The initiative of the 'Reform' is assigned to the National Assembly when approved by a Resolution approved by

261. *See Gaceta Oficial* No. 5.908 Extra. Of 19 Feb. 2009.

262. *See* Allan R. Brewer-Carías, *Reforma constitucional y fraude a la Constitución (1999-2009),* (Caracas, Academia de Ciencias Políticas y Sociales, 2009); *Derecho a la democracia y reelección presidencial indefinida. Tres Estudios,* (Buenos Aires, Ediciones Olejnik, 2021).

263. *Ibid.*

a majority of its members; to the President of the Republic in a decision adopted in a Council of Ministers; or to the people through a petition signed by no less than 15% of the registered voters (Article 342). In all these cases, the initiative must be brought before the National Assembly.

129. Once the 'Reform' proposal is filed before the National Assembly, according to Article 343, the draft must be submitted for debate and have three discussions: a first discussion in the period of the Assembly corresponding to the period of the filing of the draft; a second discussion by Titles or by chapters, depending on the draft; and a third discussion, article by article. The Assembly must approve the 'Reform' draft in a term of no more than two years since the draft was filed and accepted. The 'reform' proposal must be considered as approved if voted by two-thirds of the members of the Assembly.

Once the Reform draft is approved, within thirty days, it must be submitted to referendum (Article 344), in which the people are generally required to vote on the Reform in its entirety, that is, as a whole. However, up to one-third of the Reform draft could be submitted to separate vote when one-third of the National Assembly so decides, or if it is requested by the President of the Republic in his initiative of the Reform, or is requested by no less than 5% of registered voters in case of popular initiative.

A 'Constitutional Reform' must be declared approved if the number of affirmative votes exceeds the number of negative votes (Article 345). The President of the Republic is required to promulgate a reform within ten days of its approval. If the President fails to do so according to the provisions of Article 216 of the Constitution, the President of the Assembly must proceed to promulgate it (Article 346).

In the event that a constitutional reform fails to be approved, that is, when rejected by popular vote in the referendum, Article 345 prohibits it from being filed again before the Assembly in the remainder of the constitutional term. Nothing is established in the Constitution regarding the effects of the rejection of 'constitutional amendments', and also, nothing is established regarding the possibility of filing the same rejected 'constitutional reform' proposal, through the procedure of a 'constitutional amendment', as it is now occurring. The case is a matter of interpretation and of determining the intention of the constituent power, which was to establish a limit regarding the possibility of repeatedly asking for the direct expression of the will of the people by referenda. That is, once the people have expressed their popular will through a referendum, it is not possible to ask the people again and again, without limits, on the same matters in the same constitutional term.

For instance, the matter of the continuous presidential re-election in 2007 was proposed through a 'constitutional reform' draft formulated by the President of the Republic in 2007 and was rejected by the people in the Referendum held on December 2007. Nonetheless, in spite of this prohibition, in December 2008, the President of the Republic proposed again to modify the Constitution, using the 'Amendment' seeking his indefinite re-election, although the same proposal was already rejected in his same constitutional term in the Constitutional reform referendum held in December 2007. As above-mentioned, the National Assembly proposed then a constitutional amendment of Articles 160, 162, 174, 192 and 230 of the Constitution, which was approved in the referendum of 14 February 2009, eliminating all the limits established for the re-election of public officials[264] (*see infra* paragraphs 172, 711); which could not be done through an Amendment but only by means of a Constitutional Reform.

III. The National Constituent Assembly

130. The 1999 Constitution, which was a product of a National Constituent Assembly not foreseen nor regulated as an institution for constitutional review by the then-in-force 1961 Constitution, now precisely provides for that institution in cases when the constitutional review proposals seek for 'transforming the State, creating a new legal order, and writing a new Constitution' (Articles 347 et seq.). In these cases, of transforming the State, no constitutional amendment or reform procedures can be used.

131. When establishing the National Constituent Assembly procedure, Article 347 begins by setting forth an essential principle of modern constitutionalism: that the people are the bearers of the 'original constituent power'; so it is in the exercise of that power that the people can convene a National Constituent Assembly with the purpose of transforming the State, creating a new legal order, and drafting a new Constitution. This means that only the people, by means of a referendum, can have the initiative to convene a Constituent Assembly.

This means that in the 1999 Constitution, and contrary to the practice when the 1999 Constituent Assembly was convened, the National Constituent Assembly cannot be convened by the President of the Republic or other public bodies and that the Constituent Assembly cannot be considered in itself as an 'original constituent power', a power that is reserved for the people in an untransferable way. Thus, the people being the only titleholder of the original constituent power, it is for the people to establish the framework of action of the Constituent Assembly. If it is true that in the constitutional provision, no reference is expressly made to the need for a referendum in order to approve the convening of the National Constituent Assembly, it is evident that such a referendum must take place in order for the people to express its will regarding the statute of the National Constituent Assembly, that is, its composition, the system of election of its members, its powers and duration, and its limits.

132. The initiative for convening a referendum in order for the people to convene a National Constituent Assembly is assigned to the President of the Republic

264. The question submitted to referendum and approved by the people was the following: *'Do you approve of the amendment of Articles 160, 162, 174, 192 and 230 of the Constitution of the Republic prepared by initiative of the National Assembly, which extends the political rights of the people in order to allow any citizen in exercise of a public office by popular election to become a candidate to the same office for the constitutionally established term, his or her election depending exclusively from the popular vote?' See* the text in *Gaceta Oficial* No. 5.908 Extra. Of Feb. 19, 2009.

in a decision adopted in the Ministers' Council; to the National Assembly by means of a resolution approved by two-thirds of its members; to two-thirds of the Municipal Councils of the country expressing its votes in open Town Halls (*cabildos abiertos*); or to a petition signed by 15% of registered voters (Article 348).

Once the initiative for convening the Assembly is formulated, the National Electoral Council must convene the referendum in order for the people to convene the Assembly; and once decided by the people, the election of its members must be made. According to Article 349 of the Constitution, once the Constituent Assembly is installed, the constituted powers of the State may in no way impede any of its decisions, which implies that even if it is a decision suspending the constituted powers of government, they cannot obstruct them.

On the one hand, once the new Constitution is approved by the National Constituent Assembly, the President of the Republic cannot object to it and must publish it in the *Gaceta Oficial* (*Official Gazette*). The 1999 Constitution failed to subject the new Constitution to an approbatory referendum, although it is regulated in its Articles 73 and 74, and specifically is established for the approval of constitutional amendments and reforms (Articles 341, 344). On the other hand, the 1999 Constitution itself, after being sanctioned by a National Constituent Assembly, was approved through a referendum on 15 December 1999, in order for it to enter into effect (*see supra* paragraphs 28, 29).

These provisions referring to the National Constituent Assembly were used in an unconstitutional way by President Nicolás Maduro in 2017, when in defraudation of the popular will he directly convened for the election of a National Constituent Assembly, usurping the role of the people.[265] The 'National Constituent Assembly' was eventually elected according to an electoral system contrary to the universal, direct and secret suffrage that is guaranteed by the Constitution, and functioned until the end of 2019, without creating any new State or elaborating any constitutional project, which proved that the only intention for its covenant and election was to supplant the National Assembly elected in December 2015 that was controlled by the opposition. The Constituent Assembly just enacted what were called 'constitutional laws' on different matters that corresponded to the National Assembly, and called in an unconstitutional way, supplanting and usurping the powers of the National Electoral Council, for the anticipated 'reelection' of Nicolás Maduro in May 2018[266] (*see supra* paragraphs 44 et seq.).

265. *See* on this unconstitutional process: Allan R. Brewer-Carías, La inconstitucional convocatoria de una Asamblea Nacional Constituyente en mayo de 2017. Un nuevo fraude a la Cconstitución y a la voluntad popular (Caracas, Editorial Jurídica Venezolana, 2017); Allan R. Brewer-Carías and Carlos García Soto, *Estudios sobre la Asamblea Nacional Constituyente y su inconstitucional convocatoria en 2017* (Bogotá, Caracas, Editorial Temis, Editorial Jurídica Venezolana, 2017).

266. *See* Carlos Ayala Corao and Rafael Chavero Gazdic, *Asamblea Constituyente en Venezuela 2017-2019. El Leviatán de la democracia* (Caracas, Editorial Jurídica Venezolana, 2019).

IV. Limits to the Constitutional Review Powers

133. The 1999 Constitution does not establish in an express way the so-called immutable principles or clauses found in many of the modern constitutions when stating that some provisions cannot ever be changed.[267]

Nonetheless, in an indirect way, it is possible to identify some of those immutable clauses derived from the wording of the constitutional provisions. For instance, when Article 1 of the Constitution proclaims that the Republic is 'irrevocably' free and independent, it means that in no way can the Republic lose its freedom and independence, so no constitutional review can be initiated for such purpose, thus that declaration is an immutable one.

In the same sense, when the same Article 1 of the Constitution declares that independence, freedom, sovereignty, immunity, territorial integrity and national autodetermination are non-renounced rights of the Nation, that is, that those principles cannot be changed in any way, these declarations can be considered as immutable clauses.

Article 5 of the Constitution establishes that sovereignty resides 'untransferably' in the people, which means that that character cannot be changed and that the people in no way can transfer its sovereignty, so no constitutional revision can establish such transfer.

Also, when Article 6 of the Constitution establishes that the government of the Republic and its territorial entities 'is and will always be democratic, participatory, elective, decentralized, alternative, responsible, pluralistic and of revocable mandates', that means that in no way a constitutional review process could change or eliminate any of those characteristics of the government because if they must always be as mentioned, they are immutable. Nonetheless, as already mentioned, the 'altenance' in the democratic government, which is contrary to the indefinite re-election of the President of the Republic, was changed through a Constitutional Amendment in 2009, violating the Constitution (*see infra* paragraph 721).

V. The Changes to the Constitution Through the Illegitimate Mutations of Its Provisions by the Constitutional Judge

134. In addition to the aforementioned regular means for introducing changes in the Constitution, during the past years, the 1999 Constitution has also been changed by means of 'interpretations' issued by the Constitutional Chamber of the Supreme Tribunal of Justice, which have illegitimately mutated the content of its provisions, although without changing its text.[268] It has occurred, in many cases during the past twenty years, for instance, in 2003, when the Constitutional Chamber by interpreting Article 72 of the Constitution changed the repeal referendum of the President of

267. *See* Allan R. Brewer-Carías, 'La reforma constitucional en América Latina y el control de constitucionalidad', en *Reforma de la Constitución y control de constitucionalidad. Congreso Internacional* (Pontificia Universidad Javeriana, Bogotá Colombia, junio 14 al 17 de 2005, Bogotá 2005), 108–159.

268. *See* in general Allan R. Brewer-Carías, *La Constitución de plastilina y vandalismo constitucional. La ilegítima mutación de la Constitución por el Juez Constitucional al servicio del autoritarismo,*

the Republic converting it into a 'ratification' referendum not regulated in the Constitution;[269] in the same year 2003 by interpreting Article 23 of the Constitution, the Constitutional Chamber, to its text, reserved for itself to decide about the direct application of international human rights treaties when they contain more favourable provisions, denying such power to the courts;[270] in 2008, the Constitutional Chamber converted the 'exclusive' power of the States to administer the national highways established in Article 164.10 of the Constitution into a 'concurrent' power altogether with the National Government;[271] and 2009, the Constitutional Chamber ignored the sense of the democratic principle of alternate government established in Article 6, giving it the same sense as 'elective' government, allowing for the indefinite presidential re-election.[272] (*See infra* paragraphs 721 et seq.)

§3. The Sub-national Constitutions

135. According to Article 164 of the 1999 Constitution, the Legislative Councils of the states have the power to enact their own Constitution in order to organize the state branches of government in accordance with what is established in the national Constitution.

This provision follows a traditional constitutional trend regarding the existence of sub-national constitutions sanctioned by each state, as has been the tradition since the 1811 initial Provincial Constitutions (*see supra* paragraph 6). The scope and contents of these states' constitutions, nonetheless, are now completely limited to provide for the organization of the branches of government of the states, which are only two: the legislative branch of government corresponding to the Legislative Councils and the Executive Branch of Government, assigned to the state Governors. There is no judicial power at the state level, and they have no powers to incorporate in their Constitutions other matters like, for instance, constitutional rights, which are of national jurisdiction.

(Caracas, Editorial Jurídica Venezolana, 2022); '¿Reforma constitucional o mutación constitucional?: La experiencia venezolana.' en *Revista de Derecho Público*, No 137 (Caracas, Editorial Jurídica Venezolana, 2014), pp.19–65.

269. Decision No. 2750 of 21 Oct. 2003 (Case: Carlos E. Herrera Mendoza). *See* the comments in Allan R. Brewer-Carías, 'La Sala Constitucional vs. el derecho ciudadano a la revocatoria de mandatos populares: de cómo un referendo revocatorio fue inconstitucionalmente convertido en un 'referendo ratificatorio', in *Crónica sobre la 'In' Justicia Constitucional. La Sala Constitucional y el autoritarismo en Venezuela*, Editorial Jurídica Venezolana, Caracas 2007, 349–78.

270. Decision No. 1492 of 15 Jul. 2003 in *Revista de Derecho Público*, Nos 93–96, (Caracas, Editorial Jurídica Venezolana, Caracas 2003), pp. 136–142.

271. Decision No. 565 of 15 April 2008. *See* the comments in Allan R. Brewer-Carías, 'La Sala Constitucional como poder constituyente: la modificación de la forma federal del estado y del sistema constitucional de división territorial del poder público', in *Revista de Derecho Público*, No. 114, (Caracas, Editorial Jurídica Venezolana, Caracas 2008), pp. 247–262; 'La mutación del Estado federal en Venezuela', in *Revista General de Derecho Público Comparado*, No. 23 (Madrid, Iustel, 2018).

272. Decision No. 53, of 2 Feb. 2009. *See* the comments in Allan R. Brewer-Carías, 'El Juez Constitucional vs. La alternabilidad republicana (La reelección continua e indefinida)', in *Revista de Derecho Público* No. 117, (Caracas, Editorial Jurídica Venezolana, 2009), 205–211.

But even in this limited scope of the sub-national constitutions, the content that can be established in the states' constitutions has been additionally reduced by attributing to the National Assembly thc power to enact a national law on the organization and functioning of one of their main organs, the Legislative Councils (Article 162);[273] and by directly regulating the main aspects of states' executive organization, particularly their Public Administration, which has been the object of various national laws,[274] that are directly applicable to the states' executive branch of government (*see infra* paragraph 334).

Consequently, in practice, if it is true that all the twenty-three states of the Republic have their own Constitutions, the content is very similar, repeating what is already established in the national Constitution or in the laws enacted by the National Assembly. Nothing original is possible to be found in such 'constitutions'.

273. Organic Law on the States Legislative Councils, *Gaceta Oficial* No. 37.282 of 13 Sep. 2001.
274. For Instance, the Organic Law on Public Administration, *Gaceta Oficial* No. 5.890 Extra. of 31 Jul. 2008.

Chapter 2. The Treaties

§1. Incorporation to Internal Law

136. Article 154 of the Constitution set forth that the Treaties entered by the Republic must be approved by the National Assembly before their ratification by the President of the Republic. Thus, international Treaties and conventions must be incorporated into internal law before their ratification by means of their approval by statutes by the National Assembly, which like all statutes, must be published in the *Official Gazette* in order to have an effect (Article 215). This is then the general provision regarding the incorporation of Treaties into internal Law.

The legislative approval of international treaties, conventions or agreements must be made through statutes (Article 156.18) following the general procedure established in the Constitution for the 'formation of laws' (Articles 202 et seq.). After the approval, the ratification of the treaties corresponds to the Executive, and can only refer to the content of the text approved by the National Assembly. Consequently, any change or variation of the approved text in the act of ratification nullifies it.

In the case of approbatory laws of international treaties, the President has the discretion to determine the opportunity in which the said Law must be promulgated and published in the *Official Gazette* (Article 215), according to international conventions and the convenience of the Republic (Article 217).

137. Regarding this general provision on the legislative approval of international treaties, the Constitution establishes a few exceptions where Treaties do not need to be approved by the Legislator in order to be incorporated into internal law. These exceptions refer to those Treaties tending to execute or to improve preexistent obligations of the Republic; those seeking to apply principles expressly recognized by the Republic; those called to execute ordinary international relations acts; and those through which the Executive exercises powers that are expressly given to it by statute.[275]

138. In the process of incorporating Treaties into internal law, the President of the Republic, before ratifying a Treaty and even when the Treaty has been already approved by the National Assembly, is entitled to file a request before the Constitutional Chamber of the Supreme Tribunal for the verification of the constitutionality of the Treaty (Article 336.5) (*see infra* paragraph 690).

139. Treaties, conventions, or other international agreements which can compromise national sovereignty or transfer national powers or competencies to supranational entities, as, for example, in the case of treaties for economic integration,

---

275. *See* Larys Hernández Villalobos, 'Rango o jerarquía de los tratados internacionales en el ordenamiento jurídico de Venezuela (1999)', in *Revista del Tribunal Supremo de Justicia,* No. 3 (Caracas, 2001), 110–131; Boris Bunimov Parra, 'La entrada en vigor de los acuerdos internacionales en Venezuela', in *Libro Homenaje a Antonio Linares* (Caracas: Instituto de Derecho Público. UCV, 1999), 19–26.

may be subject to approbatory referendum (Article 73). The initiative for such referendum can be filled by the President of the Republic in a decision adopted in the Council of Ministers, by the National Assembly in a motion approved by the vote of at least two-thirds of its members, or by popular petition signed by at least 15% of registered voters.

Nonetheless, approbatory laws of international treaties cannot be submitted to referenda intended to abrogate them (Article 74).

§2. Hierarchy

140. The general constitutional consequence of the process of incorporation of international treaties and conventions into internal law by means of statutory approval by the National Assembly is that as a matter of principle treaties have the same rank as statutes in the internal order. Nonetheless, three main exceptions can be identified regarding this hierarchical position of treaties.

The first derives from the general principle established in Article 8 of the Civil Procedure Code referring to matters of private international law regarding which courts are obliged in relation to the specific issue in question to apply first to the international treaties between Venezuela and the respective State.

The second refers to treaties or conventions on human rights, which have a constitutional hierarchy; this being one of the important innovations of the 1999 Constitution on matters of human rights (Article 23) (*see infra* paragraphs 464, 727).[276] This means that treaties, pacts and conventions ratified by Venezuela must be preferred over internal law (*orden interno*) if they have more favourable provisions regarding the enjoyment or exercise of rights. In addition, the same article points out that those international treaties and conventions on human rights are immediately and directly applicable to the courts and any other organ exercising Public Powers.[277] This meant, for instance, that the American Convention of Human Rights ratified by Venezuela in 1977, in addition to its aforementioned constitutional hierarchy in internal law, was a fundamental tool for the international protection of human rights violated, by the State by the Inter-American Court on Human Rights, until Venezuela withdrawal from the Convention in 2012. This governmental decision, considered unconstitutional,[278] fallowed previous judicial decisions issued by the Constitutional Chamber of the Supreme Tribunal of Justice, not only diminishing the mentioned hierarchy but requesting the Government to withdraw from the

276. *See* Carlos Ayala Corao, 'Consecuencias de la jerarquía constitucional de los tratados relativos a los Derechos Humanos' in *La Constitución de 1978 y el Constitucionalismo Iberoamericano*, (Madrid, Centro de Estudios Constitucionales, 2003).

277. *See* Allan R. Brewer-Carías, 'Nuevas reflexiones sobre el papel de los tribunales constitucionales en la consolidación del Estado democrático de derecho: defensa de la Constitución, control del poder y protección de los derechos humanos', in *Dignidad de la persona, Derechos Fundamentales, Justicia Constitucional*, ed. Francisco Fernández Segado (coordinador) (Madrid: Dykinson, 2008), 761–826.

278. *See* Carlos Ayala Corao, 'Unconstitutionality of the Denunciation of the American Convention on Human Rights by Venezuela' in *The Realisation of Human Rights: When Theory Meets Practice. Studies in Honour of Leo Zwaak*, (Cambridge-Antwerp-Portland, Intersentia 2013), p. 497.

Convention.[279] The third exception regarding the hierarchy of treaties refers to the treaties and norms derived from the processes of Latin American and Caribbean integration, in which is set forth that the communitarian law resulting from them must prevail over the internal laws; that is, communitarian treaties and norms have a superior hierarchy regarding statutes (*see supra* paragraph 122).

279. *See* Allan R. Brewer-Carías, 'La ilegitima mutación de la Constitución por el juez constitucional mediante la eliminación del rango supra constitucional de los tratados internacionales sobre derechos humanos, y el desconocimiento en Venezuela de las sentencias de la Corte Interamericana de Derechos Humanos', in *Libro Homenaje al Capítulo Venezolano de la Asociación Mundial de Jóvenes Juristas y Estudiantes de Derecho*: *Recopilación de artículos que desarrollan temas de actualidad jurídica relacionados con el derecho público y el derecho privado* (Caracas: Asociación Mundial de Jóvenes Juristas y Estudiantes de Derecho, 2012).

Chapter 3. The Legislation

141. According to Article 202 of the Constitution, 'law' (statute) on the national level is an act sanctioned by the National Assembly acting as a legislative body through the procedure of laws formation, which imposes the need to have at least two sets of debates regarding the draft (Article 205) (*see infra* paragraph 380).

Laws are 'binding from its publication in the *Official Gazette*' (Article 1, Civil Code), being possible to derogate them 'only by other laws' (Article 7), a principle that is repeated in Article 218 of the Constitution ('Laws are derogated by other laws').

§1. Types of Laws at the National Level

I. Ordinary Laws

142. There are various types of laws in the Constitution, beginning with the ordinary laws (statutes) sanctioned by the National Assembly. Within the laws, the statutes that systematically gather norms concerning a specific subject may be termed 'codes' (Códigos), as is the case, for example, of the Civil, Commercial and Criminal Codes (*see infra* paragraph 162).

II. Organic Laws

143. Article 203 of the Constitution identified one specific type of statute called 'organic laws' (*leyes orgánicas*),[280] distinguishing four categories.

First, those statutes that are expressly termed in the Constitution as organic law, as is the case, for instance, of the Organic Law on Boundaries (*Fronteras*) (Article 15), the Organic Law on Territorial Division (Article 16), the Armed Force Organic Law (Article 41), the Social Security System Organic Law (Article 86), the Land Use Organic Law (*Ordenación del Territorio*) (Article 128), the Municipal Public Power Organic Law (Article 169), the Organic Law on Metropolitan Districts (Articles 171, 172), the Organic Law reserving the State activities, industries and services (Article 302), the Organic Law on the Council for National Defence (Article 323), the Organic Law on Judicial Review (Article 336), the Organic Law on the States of Exception (*Estados de Excepción*) (Article 338), the Organic Law on Asylum and Refugees (Transitory Provision -T.P., 4.2), the Public Defence Organic Law (T.P. 4.5), the Education Organic Law (T.P. 6), the Organic Law on Indigenous Peoples (T.P. 7) or the Labour Organic Law (T.P. 4.3).

---

280. *See* José Peña Solís, 'La nueva concepción de las leyes orgánicas en la Constitución de 1999', in *Revista del Tribunal Supremo de Justicia*, No. 1 (Caracas, 2000), 73–111; Milagros López Betancourt, 'Una aproximación a las Leyes Orgánicas en Venezuela', in *Libro Homenaje a Enrique Tejera París, Temas sobre la Constitución de 1999* (Caracas: Centro de Investigaciones Jurídicas (CEIN), 2001), 109 a 157.

Second, the Constitution qualifies as organic laws those enacted by the National Assembly to organize the various branches of government, as is the case, for instance, of the Public Administration Organic Law (Article 236. 20); the Attorney General Organic Law (Article 247), the Judiciary Organic Law and the Supreme Tribunal of Justice Organic Law (Article 262); the Electoral Power Organic Law (Article 292); the Citizen Power Organic Law, the General Comptroller Office Organic Law, the Public Prosecutor Organic Law, the Peoples' Defender Organic Law (T. P 9); the Municipal Regime Organic Law (Article 169) and the States Legislative Councils Organic Law (Article 162).

Third, also considered as organic laws are those enacted in order to develop the regulation of constitutional rights, which opens an enormous field of matters in the sense that all the statutes enacted to regulate any of the constitutional rights declared in Articles 19–129 must be organic laws.

Fourth, the Constitution also considers as organic laws those enacted for the purpose of serving as a normative framework to other laws, as is the case, for instance, of the Taxation Organic Code which serves as the framework for all the specific tax laws, or the Financial Public Administration Law, that serves as the general framework for all the specific annual budget laws of all the public debts authorizations laws.

144. Except for the first category of organic laws, in all the other cases, the corresponding draft must be admitted by the National Assembly by a vote of two-thirds of the present members before beginning the debate of the project, a majority that also applies in cases of reforms to organic laws (Article 203).

Also, except for the first aforementioned category, the qualification of a law, as an 'organic law' by the National Assembly, must be reviewed regarding the constitutionality of such qualification by the Constitutional Chamber of the Supreme Tribunal of Justice (Article 203). For such purpose, the statutes must be sent to the Constitutional Chamber before their promulgation, and if the Chamber considers that the statute is not an organic law, it will lose this character.

III. Other Laws: Enabling and Cadre Laws

145. According to Article 203 of the Constitution, enabling laws (*leyes habilitantes*) are statutes of legislative delegation, that is, those sanctioned by the National Assembly by a vote of three-fifths of its members, in order to establish the guidelines, the purposes and the framework of the matters that are delegated to the President of the Republic, in order for him to regulate them through decree-laws (decrees with rank and value of laws) during a certain period of time (Articles 203, 236.8).

This possibility for legislative delegation by means of enabling laws can be considered an innovation of the 1999 Constitution, without precedents in modern constitutionalism regarding its scope. It substituted the previous provisions of the 1961 Constitution, which limited the authorization by enabling laws for the President, to adopt extraordinary measures exclusively on economic and financial matters (Article 190.8). In contrast, in the 1999 Constitution, the possibility of legislative delegation has been established in an extended way, without limits regarding the matters that can be regulated by the Executive, which contradicts the general constitutional guarantee of certain matters that must be reserved to the legislator (as a body composed by elected representatives) (*reserva legal*), like the establishment of limits to the exercise of human rights, the approval of taxes (no taxation without representation) and the creation of criminal offences[281] (*see infra* paragraph 466).

146. Regarding the cadre laws (*leyes de bases*), they are established in order to empower the National Assembly to regulate matters of concurrent character between the national and states level that, once enacted by the National Assembly then, can be developed in each state by the corresponding State Legislative Council (Article 165)[282] (*see infra* paragraph 210).

147. It must be mentioned that during the functioning of the fraudulent and unconstitutional National Constituent Assembly between 2017 (*see supra* paragraph 43) and 2020, with the main purpose of supplanting the National Assembly elected in December 2015 that was declared as an institution in contempt by the Constitutional Chamber of the Supreme Tribunal, annulling all its acts (*see supra* paragraphs 40 et seq.); issued what was called 'constituent' or 'constitutional laws' and even 'constitutional decrees', none of which had constitutional basis (*see infra* paragraph 149). Through those acts, the Constituent Assembly 'sanctioned' legislation that according to the Constitution corresponds exclusively to the National Assembly (Article 187.1), for the purpose of enacting new statutes or for reforming previous statutes of the National Assembly.[283]

---

281. *See* Pedro Nikken, 'Constitución venezolana de 1999: La habilitación para dictar decretos ejecutivos con fuerza de ley restrictivos de los derechos humanos y su contradicción con el derecho internacional', *Revista de Derecho Público,* No. 83 (julio-septiembre) (Caracas: Editorial Jurídica Venezolana, 2000), 5–19.
282. *See* José Peña Solís, 'Dos nuevos tipos de leyes en la Constitución de 1999: leyes habilitantes y leyes de bases', in *Revista de la Facultad de Ciencias Jurídicas y Políticas de la UCV,* No. 119 (Caracas, 2000), 79–123.
283. These irregular legislative acts with legislative content with the name as 'constituent' or 'constitutional' laws were the following: Ley Constitucional de la Comisión para la Verdad, la Justicia, la Paz y la Tranquilidad Pública. *Gaceta Oficial* No. 6.323 Extra. of 8 Aug. 2017; Ley Constituyente que crea el conglomerado 'Agrosur'. *Gaceta Oficial* No. 41.272 of 6 Nov. 2017; Ley Constitucional Contra el Odio, por la Convivencia Pacífica y la Tolerancia. *Gaceta Oficial* No. 41.274 ofl 8 Nov. 2017; Ley Constitucional de Precios Acordados. *Gaceta Oficial* No. 6.342 Extra. of 22 Nov. 2017; Ley Constitucional sobre la creación de la Unidad Tributaria Sancionatoria. *Gaceta Oficial.* N 41.305 of 21 Dec. 2017; Ley Constitucional del Régimen Tributario para el Desarrollo Soberano del Arco Minero. *Gaceta Oficial* No. 41.310 of 29 Dec. 2017; Ley Constitucional contra la guerra económica para la racionalidad y uniformidad en la adquisición de bienes, servicios y obras públicas. *Gaceta Oficial* No. 41.318 of 11 Jan. 2018; Ley Constitucional del Comité Local de Abastecimiento y Producción. *Gaceta Oficial* No. 41.330 of 29 Jan. 2018; Ley Constitucional de los Consejos Productivos de Trabajadoras y Trabajadores. *Gaceta Oficial* No. 41.336 of 6 Feb. 2018; Ley Constituyente del Plan de la Patria, Proyecto Nacional Simón Bolívar, Tercer Plan Socialista de Desarrollo Económico y Social de la Nación 2019–2025. *Gaceta Oficial* No. 6.442 Extra. of 3 Apr. 2019; Ley Constitucional que crea el Impuesto a los Grandes Patrimonios. *Gaceta Oficial* No. 41.667 of 3 Jul. 2019; Ley Constitucional de la Fuerza Armada Nacional Bolivariana. *Gaceta Oficial* No. 6.508 Extra. of 30 Jan. 2020; Ley Constitucional Antibloqueo para el Desarrollo Nacional y la Garantía de los Derechos Humanos. *Gaceta Oficial* No. 6.583 Extra. of 12 Oct. 2020; Ley Constitucional que regula la vigencia de los actos emanados de la Asamblea Nacional Constituyente.

IV. Decree-laws

148. The President of the Republic is authorized in the Constitution to enact in three cases decrees-laws, that is, decrees with rank and value of statutes.[284]

First, when the National Assembly approves a legislative delegation through an enabling law authorizing the President to regulate the matters specified in it, through decree-laws, for which purpose the President must conform its legislative acts to the guidelines, the purposes and the framework established in the enabling law, and to the period established for such purpose (*see infra* paragraphs 259, 278, 319). These decree-laws can be the object of an abrogative referendum, as it is expressly set forth in Article 74 of the Constitution, when a popular petition is filed supported by no less than 5% of the registered electors.

Second, when in cases of state of exceptions, that is, in situations that seriously threaten the security of the Nation, its institutions and persons, the President of the Republic considers it necessary to restrict the guarantees of some constitutional rights, in which case, he must establish the rules regarding the exercise of the restricted guarantee (Article 339). In these cases, these decrees, due to the content and object of their regulations referred to as constitutional rights (which can only be regulated by statutes), can be considered as decree-laws (*see infra* paragraphs 30, 479).

The third type of decree-laws refers to those enacted by the President of the Republic regarding the organization of Public Administration. In this respect, Article 236.20 of the Constitution authorizes the President to 'set forth the number, organization and attributions of the Ministries and the organs of National Public Administration, as well as the organization and functioning of the Council of Ministers' (*see infra* paragraph 334). Even though this presidential power is established in the Constitution, its exercise by the Executive, particularly when referred to the creation or suppression of Ministries, and their organization and attributions, always implies the modification of some substantive legislation.

Gaceta Oficial No. 6.604 Extra. of 18 Dec. 2020. Among the 'constituent decrees' with legislative content were the following; Decreto Constituyente mediante el cual se respalda el inicio del nuevo cono monetario a partir del día lunes 20 Aug. 2018 y la supresión de cinco ceros en las denominaciones del Cono Monetario actual, a objeto de brindar mayor fortaleza y estabilidad del Bolívar Soberano, cuyo valor referencial estará anclado al valor del Petro, el cual estará asociado al precio del barril de petróleo venezolano. *Gaceta Oficial* No. 41.452 of 2 Aug. 2018; Decreto Constituyente mediante el cual se establece la derogatoria del régimen cambiario y sus ilícitos. *Gaceta Oficial* No. 41.452 of 2 Aug. 2018; Decreto Constituyente mediante el cual se reforma el Decreto con Rango, Valor y Fuerza de Ley de Impuesto a las Grandes Transacciones Financieras. *Gaceta Oficial* No. 6.396 Extraordinario of 21 Aug. 2018; Decreto Constituyente mediante el cual se Reforma la Ley que establece el Impuesto al Valor Agregado. *Gaceta Oficial* No. 6.396 Extra. of 21 Aug. 2018.

284. *See* Eloisa Avellaneda Sisto, 'El régimen de los Decretos-Leyes, con especial referencia a la Constitución de 1999', in *Estudios de Derecho Administrativo, Libro Homenaje a la UCV*, ed. F. Parra Aranguren y A. Rodríguez G., vol. I (Caracas: Tribunal Supremo de Justicia, 2001), 69 a 106; Allan R. Brewer-Carías, 'El régimen constitucional de los Decretos-Leyes y de los Actos de Gobierno', in *Bases y principios del sistema constitucional venezolano (Ponencias del VII Congreso Venezolano de Derecho Constitucional realizado en San Cristóbal del 21 al 23 de Noviembre de 2001)*, vol. I, 25–74.

V. The Disruption of the Legal Order and the Discretional Power Assigned to the National Executive to Suspend the Application of Statutes (2020)

149. As above-mentioned, one of the most elemental principles of the Venezuelan legal system declared in the Civil Code is that 'the Law is binding from its publication in the *Official Gazette*' (Article 1), being possible to derogate or reform them 'only by other laws' (Article 7). The Executive Power can exercise a veto regarding the publication of the laws and resend it to the National Assembly for its modification (Article 214) (*see* paragraph 308), but cannot reform or suspend the enforcement of the laws.

Nonetheless, all these elemental principles of the rule of law have been disrupted in Venezuela, by means of an unconstitutional law sanctioned, not by the National Assembly, but by the National Constituent Assembly elected in 2017, called the 'Anti-blockade Law for National Development and the Guarantee of Human Rights', for the purpose of obtaining 'additional resources' (Article 18), through the implementation of a 'change' in economic policy consisting of indiscriminately and secretly 'de-estatizing,' denationalizing and privatizing the economy, and conducting new negotiations on public financing, supposedly to meet needs in the country; but all this, totally subverting the legal system. The law declared its provisions to be 'preferentially applicable' to all laws, 'of public order and of general interest', and to be applied by all territorial levels of government and by all persons (Article 2).

This rupture of the legal system can be seen specifically in the following aspects.

First, in the conception of the 'Constitutional Law' as a normative framework of a 'supra-legal' rank, that is, superior to all the organic laws and ordinary laws of the Republic, with respect to which the 'Constitutional Law' is declared as of preferential application (First Transitory Provision), over organic laws and ordinary laws.

Second, in the establishment of an unlimited power assigned to the National Executive to 'disapply' in specific cases, the norms of legal rank that it deems necessary to pursue the purposes of the Law (Article 19), that is, so that it can decide in specific cases that an organic law or any other law does not apply, which undoubtedly implies establishing a legislative delegation without limits to the National Executive, to exercise power to legislate in order to be able to fill the absence of norms or legislative vacuum that will originate the executive decision to 'disapply' those of legal norms.

Third, the establishment also of the same power without limits to the effect that the National Executive 'disapplies' for specific cases, that is, singularly, regulations and other norms of sub-legal rank, whose application it deems counterproductive to comply with the purposes of the Law (Article 19), in violation of the general principle of non-modifiability or singular non-derogability of regulations guaranteed by Article 13 of the Organic Law of Administrative Procedures.

Fourth, the assignment of broad authority to the Executive for the signing of 'international, bilateral or multilateral treaties, agreements and conventions, favoring the integration of free peoples' that must be based 'on pre-existing obligations of the Republic' (Article 10), thereby seeking to obviate the necessary approval of such instruments by law of the National Assembly required by the Constitution (Article 154).

And fifth, the formal and express establishment of a regime of total absence of transparency, since it is foreseen not only to disapply the laws on bidding and public contracting (Articles 21 and 28) but to declare 'secret and reserved' (Article 42) all 'the procedures, acts and registrations carried out on the occasion of the implementation of any of the measures' established in the Law that 'suppose the non-application of norms of legal or sublegal rank'.

The aforementioned amounts to a complete subversion of the legal order of the State, totally incompatible with the most elementary principles of the rule of law, materializing in the formal establishment of the 'inapplicability' of laws, in secret, by the National Executive. In this way, a new term ('non-application') has been invented in the field of the principles of the temporary validity of the law, and that entails an unlimited legislative delegation to the National Executive itself, which is empowered to fill the normative 'vacuum' resulting from the 'non-application' of norms.[285]

§2. Equivalent Legislative Rules at the Regional and Local Governments: The States Laws and the Municipal Ordinances

150. As the Venezuelan State is organized according to a federal form of government, with a system of vertical division of powers, in addition to the legislative powers of the national (federal) level of government, the states and the municipalities also have legislative powers regarding the matters attributed to them in the Constitution.

Regarding the states, Article 162 of the Constitution assigns them the attribution of 'legislate' on matters assigned to the states, as well as to sanction the 'Budget Law of the state.' In this regard, the legislative acts of the Legislative Councils are also called 'laws' (statutes). The Legislative Councils, as aforementioned, are also empowered to sanction the states' constitutions in order to organize the branches of government (Article 164.1) (*see infra* paragraph 208).

At the municipal level, also regarding the matters attributed to the municipalities, Article 175 assigns to the Municipal Councils the 'legislative function', which is exercised through 'Municipal Ordinances' that have always been considered as 'local laws' (*see infra* paragraph 225).

States laws and Municipal Ordinances can be challenged before the Constitutional Chamber of the Supreme Tribunal on the grounds of their unconstitutionality (*see infra* paragraph 684).

285. *See* the comments in Allan R. Brewer-Carías, 'La Ley Antibloqueo: una monstruosidad jurídica para desaplicar, en secreto, la totalidad del ordenamiento jurídico', in *Boletín de la Academia de Ciencias Sociales y Políticas*, No. 161, Julio diciembre 2020, Homenaje al Dr. José Andrés Octavio, Caracas, pp. 1499–1520. https://www.acienpol.org.ve/wp-content/uploads/2021/03/BOLETIN-161-jul-dic-2020.pdf.

§3. HIERARCHY

151. The legislative function in the three levels of government (national, states, municipal) is exercised according to the federal division of power system, and according to the matters assigned to each level. Consequently, in principle, the laws passed at each level are autonomously sanctioned by each legislative body (National Assembly, States Legislative Councils, Municipal Councils) referring only to the matters assigned in the distribution of powers framed in the Constitution (*see infra* paragraphs 214, 221, 225). Any encroachment in the matters reserved to other levels implies usurpation of power, affecting the law as unconstitutional.

152. Due to the centralized form of the Venezuelan federation, almost all matters of public action and policy have been assigned to the national level, so the national laws have general and comprehensive scope and application in all the country. The states scarcely have exclusive matters attributed to their authority, so the states' laws are very few and mainly refer to organizational matters. When the matter is assigned in a concurrent way to the national and state level of government, the states' laws on the matter must be subjected to the national legislation which can also consist of a Cadre Law (Article 165) (*see infra* paragraph 220).

The same occurs at the Municipal level, although in this case, the Constitution assigns more matters in an exclusive way to local governments. Only when matters have been assigned to different levels of government in a concurrent way must the legislation at the local level be subject to national or states' laws.

153. Any conflict between the different legislative entities and any encroachment regarding legislative attributions of the different levels of government can be subjected to judicial review before the Constitutional Chamber of the Supreme Tribunal of Justice, which is empowered to decide conflicts between legal provisions and to declare which must prevail (Article 336.8); as well as to decide constitutional controversies between the different branches of government, not only in the horizontal sense (separation of powers) but in the vertical sense (territorial distribution of powers) (Article 336.9) (*see infra* paragraph 695).

Chapter 4. The Jurisprudence

§1. The General Value of Jurisprudence

154. The general value of jurisprudence derived from judicial decisions is of an auxiliary character, being a very important tool for the correct interpretation and application of laws. Nonetheless, the courts are not subjected to precedents; all the judges are considered sovereign in their decisions, only submitted to the Constitution and the law, not being the judicial decisions a source of law.

This general principle has two exceptions on matters of judicial review (*see infra* paragraphs 670 et seq.): First, on matters of judicial review of constitutionality of legislation and administrative actions when the Constitutional Chamber of the Supreme Tribunal (Article 336) or the courts of the Administrative Contentious Jurisdiction (Judicial Review of Administrative Action Jurisdiction) (Article 259) annul statutes and other State acts, in which cases its annulatory decisions have *erga omnes* effects and are obligatory. This same principle applies to the Chamber of Cassation rulings when reviewing and annulling lower court's judicial decisions (Article 266.8). And second, on matters of constitutional interpretation, when the Constitutional Chamber of the Supreme Tribunal assigns in an express way binding effects to a specific constitutional interpretation it makes on the content or the scope of a constitutional provision or principle (Article 335) (*see infra* paragraph 156).

§2. The Obligatory Character of the Annulatory Decisions of the Constitutional Jurisdiction and of the Contentious Administrative Jurisdictions

155. The Constitutional Chamber of the Supreme Tribunal of Justice, as Constitutional Jurisdiction, exercising powers of judicial review of constitutionality of legislation and of all State acts with the rank of statute or issued in direct application of constitutional provisions (Articles 334, 336), has the task of guaranteeing the supremacy and effectiveness of the constitutional provisions and principles. It is named as the highest and last interpreter of the Constitution, being charged with watching over its uniform interpretation and application (Article 335).

When exercising its powers of judicial review of legislation (Article 336), the decisions of the Constitutional Chamber of the Supreme Tribunal annulling a challenged act on the grounds of its unconstitutionality have general, *erga omnes* effects, thus being of obligatory character for all the courts, the citizens, and public entities (*see infra* paragraph 684).

The Judicial Review of Administrative Action Jurisdiction decisions issued by the Contentious Administrative Jurisdiction courts have the same *erga omnes* effects, when annulling executive regulations and administrative acts (Article 259), being in these cases the jurisprudence obligatory and binding (*see infra* paragraph 706).

In a similar sense, it must be noted that the decisions adopted by the Civil, Criminal and Social Cassation Chambers of the Supreme Tribunal of Justice when hearing a cassation recourse (Article 266.8) have the effect of annulling the judicial decisions submitted for their review, and also have obligatory and binding general effects.

§3. The Binding Effects Assigned to Specific Constitutional Interpretations adopted by the Constitutional Jurisdiction

156. Except when annulling State acts, the Supreme Tribunal decisions (including those issued by the Constitutional Chamber) are not a source of law and carry no more weight than the interpretations of legal scholars and other branches of government unless pursuant to Article 335 of the Constitution, a specific interpretation of the content or scope of a constitutional provision or principle issued by the Constitutional Chamber is explicitly declared in the decision as having 'binding character for the other Chambers of the Supreme Tribunal and all the courts of the Republic'[286] (*see infra* paragraph 681).

This provision regarding the possibility to assign obligatory effects to judicial review rulings on interpretations of the Constitution by the Constitutional Jurisdiction is an innovation introduced in the 1999 Constitution, which explains why the Constitutional Chamber has been emphatic in affirming that 'it is clear that in our legal order, except the doctrine of constitutional interpretation established by this Chamber, the jurisprudence is not a direct source of law'.[287]

Thus, it can be affirmed that the Constitution does not confer a 'binding' character to the phrases, arguments, or reasonings stated within the Constitutional Chamber decisions. On the contrary, an interpretation is only 'binding' pursuant to Article 335 of the Constitution when the Constitutional Chamber expressly states in the text of a decision that it is establishing a 'binding interpretation' (*rule of explicitness*) with general effects, requiring the need for its publication in the *Official Gazette* (rule of publicity).[288] In these cases, a binding interpretation is always related to the *thema decidendum* of the decision and not 'to the *dictum* that refers to marginal,

286. *See* in general, Rubén J. Laguna Navas, *La Sala Constitucional del Tribunal Supremo de Justicia: su rol como máxima y última intérprete de la Constitución* (Caracas: UCV, 2005); Nancy Carolina Granadillo Colmenares, *Sentencias Vinculantes de la Sala Constitucional del tribunal Supremo de Justicia 2000–2007* (Caracas: Paredes Libros, 2008).

287. *See* Supreme Tribunal of Justice, Decision No. 31, 30 Jan. 2009, Case Alejandro Humberto Sosa vs. Decisión Sala de Casación Civil del Tribunal Supremo de Justicia, in *Revista de Derecho Público*, No. 117, (Caracas, Editorial Jurídica Venezolana, 2009), p. 135

288. *See* Allan R. Brewer-Carías, 'La potestad la Jurisdicción Constitucional de interpretar la Constitución con efectos vinculantes' in Jhonny Tupayachi Sotomayor (Coord.), *El Precedente Constitucional Vinculante en el Perú (Análisis, Comentarios y Doctrina Comparada)*, (Lima, Editorial Adrus, 2009), pp. 791–819; 'Los efectos de las sentencias constitucionales en Venezuela', in *Anuario Internacional sobre Justicia Constitucional*, No. 22, (Bogotá, Centro de Estudios Políticos y Constitucionales, 2008), pp. 19, 64.

peripheral, circumstantial or superabundant motivations, which are not binding with *erga omnes* effects, since the latter are only persuasive'.[289]

289. *See* Ramón Escovar León, 'Límites a la interpretación constitucional', *in Revista de Derecho Público,* No. 157–158, (Caracas, Editorial Jurídica Venezolana, 2019, pp. 46–47). *See also*: Hernando Diaz Candia, 'El principio Stare Decisis y el concepto de precedente vinculante a efectos del artículo 335 de la Constitución de la República Bolivariana de Venezuela de 1999', in *Revista de Derecho Constitucional,* No. 8, (Caracas, Edit. Sherwood, 2003), p. 228; Jesús M. Casal H., 'Cosa juzgada y efecto vinculante en la justicia constitucional', in *Revista Derecho Constitucional No. 8, (Caracas, Edit. Sherwood, 2003, pp. 193, 215, 219.*

Chapter 5. The Unwritten Law

§1. Constitutional Principles and Values

157. The 1999 Venezuelan Constitution is one of the Constitutions in the contemporary world, containing not only an impressive number of Articles (350) but also a very rich and numerous declaration of values and principles.

They can be found not only in the Preamble of the Constitution but also in many of its articles, where in a very enumerative and express way, an extensive list of constitutional values and principles are enshrined, as goals intending to guide the State, the Society and the individuals' general conduct. Consequently, in Venezuela, the global values and principles not only derive from the interpretation and application of the Constitution by the courts but from what is set forth in a precise and express way in the text of the Constitution.[290] By means of constitutional judicial decisions, of course, the sense, the scope and the priority character of many of these constitutional principles and values have been defined and enriched; and also, unfortunately, in other cases, they have also been distorted, originating in many cases some constitutional incongruence between what is said in the constitutional text and what is decided in the political practice of government (*see supra* paragraphs 97 et seq.).

In any case, since the Constitution is a text in which the generally shared values of a society are reflected, the declarations of intent contained in it are of indubitable value, both for the State bodies, which must be guided by them, as for the judges, especially the Supreme Tribunal of Justice as its superior judicial guardian.

158. All these constitutional values expressly mentioned in the Constitution, and also those interpreted by the Constitutional Jurisdiction, refer to the State (the Republic, the Nation), its organization (distribution of State powers and branches of government) and functioning (government and Public Administration); to the legal system; to human rights; and to the content and scope of the concept of 'the democratic and social rule of law and justice state' regulated by the Constitution. These values have the same constitutional rank as the express provisions of the Constitution. Consequently, those principles have been an important tool for judicial review of constitutionality exercised by the Constitutional Jurisdiction, to the point that the binding interpretations that can be established in an express way in its rulings by the Constitutional Chamber of the Supreme Tribunal, not only can be referred to the content and scope of the constitutional provisions but also to the 'constitutional principles' (Article 335).

§2. General Principles of Law

159. Article 4 of the Civil Code lays out the basic rules for the interpretation of laws and sets forth that the sense that must be attributed to the law must be the one

290. *See* Allan R. Brewer-Carías, *Principios fundamentales del derecho público* (Caracas: Editorial Jurídica Venezolana, 2005).

that evidently appears from the significance of words, in accordance with their connection and to the intention of the Legislator. When no precise legal provision exists, the provisions regulating similar cases or analogous matters must be taken into account; and if doubts remain, the general principles of law must be applied.

Consequently, the general principles of law are always a source of law for the interpreter, when no express provision exists, and no similar or analogous rules can be applied.

They are also referred to in the Civil Procedure Code, on matters of international private law regarding which the courts must first apply what is established in international treaties between Venezuela and the respective State. When no treaty exists, they must apply what is provided on the matter in the laws of the Republic or what can be deducted from the mind of national legislation, and finally, they must be guided by the principles of law generally accepted (Article 8).

Chapter 6. The Executive Regulations and Administrative Acts

§1. National, States and Municipal Regulations

160. An essential part of the administrative functions is the power assigned to the executive branch of government to enact regulations in order to develop and facilitate the application of statutes. Consequently, in each of the three levels of government: the President of the Republic at the national level (Article 156.10); the Governors at the states level; and the Mayors at the municipal level, have the power to issue regulations referring to the respective national, states or municipal laws.

In addition, the other branches of government have been empowered in the Constitution to issue regulations in order to develop specific statutes, like the National Electoral Council regarding the Electoral Laws (Article 293.1). In other cases, it is in specific statutes that the regulatory powers have been established, like the case of the Comptroller General of the Republic regarding his fiscal control functions according to the Organic Law on the General Comptroller of the Republic (Article 13.1). Regulatory power has also been assigned to the Ministers by the Organic Law on Public Administration,[291] and to specific independent administrative or regulatory authorities by the corresponding statute creating them, like the Superintendence of Banks and Financial Institutions, Superintendence of Insurance, Superintendence on Free Competition Protection, Stock Exchange control Commission. Also, the Supreme Tribunal of Justice has regulatory powers regarding the organization and functioning of the Judiciary (Article 267, Constitution) (*see infra* paragraph 402).

§2. Limits to the Executive Regulatory Powers

161. In all cases, the principal limit to the regulatory powers is those established in Article 156.10 of the Constitution when assigning it to the President of the Republic in the sense that they must always be exercised, regarding statutes, 'without altering its spirit, purpose and reason'.

The consequence of this principle is that regulations are always administrative acts, although of general content, and consequently always subjected to the statutes whose contents always prevail over the regulations. Nonetheless, it is possible for administrative organs to issue 'autonomous regulations', in the sense of regulations that are not intended to specifically develop a particular statute, and are generally referred to organizational matters. In these cases, the limit is always its sub-legal character, and their validity ceases if the matters are later regulated in a statute passed by the National Assembly.

On the other hand, other general limit to the power assigned to the Executive bodies to issue regulations, that is administrative acts of general effects, is the need to follow prior to the enactment of the regulation, a procedure of public consultation

291. *Gaceta Oficial* No. 5.890 Extra. of 31 Jul. 2008.

in order to assure citizens' participation. The Organic Law on Public Administration imposes the nullity of the regulatory executive acts issued without such consultation (Articles 139 and 140).

Regulations, as all administrative acts, are subjected to judicial review by the Judicial Review of Administrative Action Courts (Article 259) (*see infra* paragraph 706).

Chapter 7. Codification, Interpretation and Publication

§1. The Codes

162. As defined in Article 203 of the Constitution, 'codes' are the statutes that systematically gather norms concerning a specific subject, so it is for the National Assembly to sanction codes, that being a competence reserved for the national level of government. No code exists at the states or municipal levels.

The most important Codes are the Civil Code,[292] the Commercial Code,[293] the Criminal Code,[294] the Procedural Codes, Civil Procedure Code,[295] Criminal Organic Procedure Code,[296] and Military Justice Code.[297]

As an organic law, the taxation one has been named Taxation Organic Code,[298] and on Administrative Law matters, the Organic Law on Administrative Procedures[299] has always been considered an important sign of the codification of Administrative Law.

§2. Interpretation

163. The main rule on law interpretation, which applies to all laws, including Codes, as aforementioned, has been set forth in Article 4 of the Civil Code that provides that the sense that must be attributed to the law must be the one that evidently appears from the significance of words, in accordance to their connection and to the intention of the Legislator. When no precise legal provision exists, the provisions regulating similar cases or analogous matters must be taken into account; and if doubts remain, the general principles of law must be applied.

Nonetheless, in addition to the literal sense of the legal provisions, in order to interpret them, according to the doctrine established by the Supreme Tribunal of Justice, summarized in decision No. 895 of the Politico-Administrative Chamber of 30 July 2008, the interpretation of laws must always consider three other elements. Consequently, for the interpretation of laws, the interpreter must take into consideration the following four basic elements: first, the literal, grammatical or philological element, which is the initial point from where must depart any interpretation of laws following the provision of Article 4 of the Civil Code; second, the logical, rational or reasonable element; third, the historical element, in the sense that any legal provision must be inserted within a reality that has its origins and evolution, whose comprehension through its historical paths is important in order to give the

292. *Gaceta Oficial* No. 2.990 Extra. of 26 Jul. 1982.
293. *Gaceta Oficial* No. 475 Extra. of 21 Dec. 1955.
294. *Gaceta Oficial* No. 5.768 Extra. of 13 Apr. 2005.
295. *Gaceta Oficial* No. 3.694 Extra. of 22 Jan. 1986.
296. *Gaceta Oficial* No. 5.930 Extra. of 4 Sep. 2009.
297. *Gaceta Oficial* No. 5.263 Extra. of 17 Sep. 1998.
298. *Gaceta Oficial* No. 37.305 Extra. of 17 Oct. 2001.
299. *Gaceta Oficial* No. 2.818 Extra. of 1 Jul. 1981.

provision an actual sense; and four, the systematic element, or the integral comprehension of law as a social life regulatory system. The Chamber has said, consequently, that any law interpretation must have all four elements, in the sense that there are not four types of interpretation in order to choose one according to the interpreter's choice, but four different operations whose gathering is indispensable for the interpretation of the law, even in the event that one of such elements could have more importance. Consequently, in the interpretative task, it is not possible to rest only on the literal, grammatical or philological element. In addition, there are other relevant elements that the authors have added, like the teleological element, that is, to understand that the law is sanctioned in order to attain certain social goals within the State organization, and the sociological element, which helps to understand the provision from the comprehension of the social, economical, political and cultural reality where the text is going to be applied.[300]

In the same sense, the Constitutional Chamber has also pointed out in a decision of 9 December 2002 that the interpretation of laws has to be made '*in totum*', that is, that the provision must be interpreted within the legal order as a whole.[301] That is, within the whole positive law, because otherwise, it is impossible to get to the bottom of the sense and scope of the legal provision, necessary in order to determine what has been the will of the Legislator.

Regarding matters related to international private law, according to the Civil Procedure Code, the courts on the subject to be decided must first pay attention to what is established in international treaties between Venezuela and the respective State. In the absence of treaties, they must apply what on the matter is provided in the laws of the Republic or what can be deducted from the mind of national legislation. Finally, they must decide according to generally accepted principles of law (Article 8).

§3. Publication and Derogatory Effects

164. In order to have an effect, all statutes and regulations must be published in the *Official Gazette* (*Gaceta Oficial*) (Article 215).

Statutes can be totally or partially reformed, and in the latter case, they must be published in one single text in which the approved modifications must be incorporated.[302]

Statutes, according to Article 218 of the Constitution, can only be abrogated by other statutes or by means of referendum with exceptions established in the Constitution (Article 74). Statutes, however, have derogatory effects regarding previous statutes or regulations.

300. *See* in *Revista de derecho Público*, No. 115 (Caracas: Editorial Jurídica Venezolana, 2008), 468 et seq.
301. *See* File No. 02-2154, Case: *Fiscal General de la República,* quotet in decision No. 2152 of 14 Dec. 2007, in *Revista de Derecho Público*, No. 112 (Caracas: Editorial Jurídica Venezolana, 2007), 446.
302. Official Publications Law, *Gaceta Oficial* No. 20.546 of 22 Jul. 1941.

Part II. Basic Elements of the Representative and Participatory Democratic Political System

165. The 1999 Constitution proclaims that the government of the Republic of Venezuela is and shall always be democratic, participatory, elective, decentralized, alternating, responsible, plural and of revocable mandates (Article 6), establishing, in addition, provisions regarding the need to be subject to accountability (*rendición de cuentas*), particularly of the elected officers, and establishing the possibility for all of them to be subjected to repeal referendums.

In order to establish a democratic government with all such elements, that are defined in the sense of 'rock-like clauses'(*cláusulas pétreas*) in the sense that they must always exist, Article 5 of the Constitution, after setting forth that 'sovereignty resides in a non-transferable way in the people', declares that it can be exercised in two ways: on the one hand, in a 'direct' way by means of referendum and other instruments for direct democracy established in the Constitution; and on the other hand, in an indirect way, 'through suffrage, by the organs that exercise State Powers' (Article 5). These same enunciations are contained in Article 62 of the same Constitution that sets forth the citizens' political right to freely participate in all public affairs, that is, to participate in the formation, execution, and control of public activities in order to achieve their complete collective and individual development, being an obligation of the State and of society to facilitate and create the most favourable conditions for such participation. This political participation, being an essential characteristic of any democracy although not always accomplished, according to the same provision of the Constitution, is exercised in two ways: in a direct way, through instruments of direct democracy, and in an indirect way, through elected representatives, which is one of the essential elements of representative democracy (Article 62).

166. For the purpose of guaranteeing this right to political participation, Article 70 of the Constitution enumerates the following political means for the citizens' rights to participate in the exercise of their sovereignty: on the one hand, regarding *representative democracy*, the direct election of representatives to public office (President of the Republic and representatives to the National Assembly) and the indirect election by the members of the National Assembly of the Magistrates of the Supreme Tribunal of Justice, the members of the National Electoral Council, the Peoples Defendant, the Comptroller General of the Republic and the Prosecutor General of the Republic; and on the other hand, regarding direct democracy, the vote in referenda and in the referendum for the revocation of mandates of elected officers; participation in popular consultations; the legislative or constitutional initiative; participation in open town meeting, and in Citizens' Assemblies whose decisions are binding.

According to these constitutional provisions, the Venezuelan representative and participatory democratic political system is characterized by the following elements: representative democracy and its electoral system; direct democracy instruments and its voting system; plural political parties' regime; alternating system of government and government accountability instruments.

Chapter 1. Representative Democracy

167. Representative democracy, consequently, is one of the basic components of the Democratic System of Venezuela through which citizens exercise their sovereignty by electing representatives to the State organs. It is an indirect means of exercising sovereignty, precisely 'through suffrage, by the organs that exercise State Powers' (Article 5).[303]

But suffrage and periodical, fair and free elections, based on the universal and secret vote expressing the will of the people, do not exhaust representative democracy, which in addition has the other following essential elements: respect for human rights and fundamental liberties; access to power and its exercise with subjection to the rule of law; plural regime of the political parties and organizations; and separation and independence of public powers.

168. Regarding the exercise of sovereignty through representatives by means of elections not only is it the most common element of representative democracy, but it is an irreplaceable one, implying that all the Head Officials of the Executive Branches of Government and the members of Legislative Branches of Government, in all levels of government (*see infra* paragraphs 221, 225, 287) are elected by popular, direct and secret vote. In the national level of government, the President of the Republic is elected for a term of six years by popular, universal, direct and secret vote by all the Citizens registered in the Electoral Registry by a simple majority of votes (Articles 228, 230).

The members or representatives of the National Assembly are also elected for a term of five years (Article 192) by the Citizens registered in the Electoral Registry by popular, universal, direct, and secret vote. In this case, the electoral system applied is a mixed one, combining personalized vote with proportional representation in a number fixed according to a population base of 1.1% of the total population of the country (Article 186) (*see infra* paragraph 363). In addition, three additional national representatives in each State of the Federation must be elected. Also, the indigenous people have the right to elect three national representatives taking into account their traditions and customs (Article 125). Each representative must have a substitute member, also elected in the same process, who is called to act in cases of temporal or absolute absence of the principal (Article 186) (*see infra* paragraph 362).

---

303. *See* Pedro L. Bracho Grand y Miriam Álvarez de Bozo, 'Democracia representativa en la Constitución Nacional de 1999', in *Estudios de Derecho Público: Libro Homenaje a Humberto J. La Roche Rincón,* vol. I (Caracas: Tribunal Supremo de Justicia, 2001), 235–254; and Ricardo Combellas, 'Representación vs. Participación en la Constitución Bolivariana. Análisis de un falso dilema', en *Bases y principios del sistema constitucional venezolano (Ponencias del VII Congreso Venezolano de Derecho Constitucional realizado en San Cristóbal del 21 al 23 de Noviembre de 2001),* vol. II, 383–402; Juan De Stefano, 'El sufragio, el mandato político y su doctrina en la Constitución de 1961 y 1999 y de los Estados Socialistas', in *Tendencias Actuales del Derecho Constitucional. Homenaje a Jesús María Casal Montbrun*, ed. Jesús María Casal, Alfredo Arismendi y Carlos Luis Carrillo Artiles (Coord.), vol. I (Caracas: UCV/Universidad Católica Andrés Bello, 2008), 563–576.

All the other high public officials of the other national Branches of Government (Justices of the Supreme Tribunal of Justice, General Comptroller of the Republic, General Prosecutor of the Republic, Peoples' Defender, and the members of the National Electoral Council) are not elected in direct popular elections, but in an indirect popular election made by the elected representatives to the National Assembly (Articles 265, 279, 296), acting in this case, as an electoral body by the vote of a qualified majority (*see infra* paragraph 304, 415 ff., 442, 445, 455). This indirect election must be made with the active participation of representatives of the various sectors of society that must integrate the Nominating Committees that are the only ones that can nominate the candidates, which must be established for such purposes.[304] Unfortunately, these latter provisions of the Constitution have been distorted by the National Assembly reducing the participation scope of civil society by incorporating in such Committees, representatives of the National Assembly, being transformed, in fact, into common parliamentary commissions controlled by the political party that controls the Assembly(*see infra* paragraph 211). In addition, the election of the high public officials has been made by the Assembly through a simple majority of the votes of the representatives participating in the session, which occurred in 2014, ignoring the qualify majority rule imposed in the Constitution (*see infra* paragraphs 239, 294, 415 ff., 442, 445, 455). In the case of the election of the members of the National Electoral Council, the violation of the Constitution has been even more chocking because since 2004 it has been made by the Constitutional Chamber of the Supreme Tribunal, usurping the functions of the Assembly as electoral body, supposedly supplying the 'omission' of the Assembly derived from the lack of agreement between the representatives (*see infra* paragraph 456).[305]

169. On the state level, the Governors of each of the states are also elected for a term of four years by popular, universal, direct and secret vote of the Citizens registered in the Electoral Registry of the constituency of the respective state by a relative majority of votes (Article 160). The members of the Legislative Councils of each state are elected every four years, in a number of not more than fifteen or less than seven, also by the Citizens registered in the Electoral Registry of the respective state. In this case, the same rules for the election of the representatives to the National Assembly must be followed (Article 162) (*see infra* paragraph 363).

170. On the municipal level, Mayors and members of the Municipal Councils are also elected every four years by popular, universal, direct and secret vote of the

304. *See* Allan R. Brewer-Carías, 'La participación ciudadana en la designación de los titulares de los órganos no electos de los Poderes Públicos en Venezuela y sus vicisitudes políticas', in *Revista Iberoamericana de Derecho Público y Administrativo*, Año 5, No. 5-2005 (San José, Costa Rica, 2005), 76–95.

305. *See* Constitutional Chamber Decisions No. 1864 of 22 Dec. 2014 (available at: http://historico.tsj.gov.ve/decisiones/scon/diciembre/173494-1864-221214-2014-14-1341.HTML); and No. 1865 of 26 Dec. 2014 (available at: http://historico.tsj.gov.ve/decisiones/scon/diciembre/173497-1865-261214-2014-14-1343.HTML). *See* the comments in Allan R. Brewer-Carías, 'El golpe de Estado dado en diciembre de 2014, con la inconstitucional designación de las altas autoridades del Poder Público', *Revista de Derecho Público,* 40 (Caracas: Editorial Jurídica Venezolana, 2014).

majority of Citizens registered in the Electoral Registry of the constituency of the respective municipality (Articles 174, 175) (*see infra* paragraph 222).

171. From the aforementioned, it can be said that according to the Constitution, the general principle is that all public officials that are to occupy positions in public offices representing the people, must always be elected by universal, direct and secret suffrage. The unconstitutional exception to this constitutional rule has been established since 2006 and, in particular, after the rejection of the 2007 Constitutional reform Project,[306] in the 2010 legislative creation of the 'Communal State' framework (*see infra* paragraph 283), in which no popular suffrage is established – in fact is rejected – providing in substitution for the appointment of the members of the Communal Councils and other 'representatives' only through Citizens Assembly duly controlled by the Central Government and the Official Party.[307]

172. The 1999 Constitution initially established that the President of the Republic, the states' Governors and the municipal Mayors could be re-elected only once for the following immediate constitutional term (Articles 160, 174, 230); and that the members of the National Assembly and the members of the States Legislative Councils could be re-elected for two consecutive constitutional terms at a maximum (Article 162, 192). All these limits to re-election of elected officials, established as a consequence of the principle of alternating government according to what is established in Article 6 of the Constitution, were eliminated through a constitutional amendment approved by referendum on 14 February 2009 (*see supra* paragraph 37; *infra* paragraph 258).

---

306. *See* Allan R. Brewer-Carías, Proyectos constitucionales del chavismo: para desmantelar la democracia y establecer un Estado socialista en Venezuela (Del principio al fin: 1999–2019), (Bogotá, Caracas Editorial Temis, Editorial Juridica Venezolana, 2019).

307. *See* Allan R. Brewer-Carías, 'El inicio de la desmunicipalización en Venezuela: La organización del Poder Popular para eliminar la descentralización, la democracia representativa y la participación a nivel local', en *AIDA, Opera Prima de Derecho Administrativo. Revista de la Asociación Internacional de Derecho Administrativo* (Universidad Nacional Autónoma de México, Facultad de Estudios Superiores de Acatlán, Coordinación de Postgrado, Instituto Internacional de Derecho Administrativo 'Agustín Gordillo', Asociación Internacional de Derecho Administrativo, México, 2007), 49–67; Allan R. Brewer-Carías, *Ley de los Consejos Comunales* (Caracas: Editorial Jurídica Venezolana, 2010), 16 et seq.; Antonio Canova González, '¿Extinción de los Municipios? Una propuesta más en el afán de centralizar el poder', in *Erga Omnes. Revista Jurídica de la Sindicatura Municipal de Chacao* (Caracas: Ediciones Sindicatura Municipal de Chacao, No. 1 (julio-diciembre, 2006), 239–252.

Chapter 2. Electoral System

173. For the purpose of guaranteeing representative democracy, the electoral system has been established in the Constitution according to the elected officials.[308] The President of the Republic, the Governors of the states and the Mayors of the municipalities are elected by a simple majority of the voters in universal, direct and secret elections (Articles 160, 174, 228). The constitutional term of the President of the Republic is of six years (Article 230), and those of the Governors of the states and the Mayors (Article 174) are of four years (Articles 160, 174). At the end of their term, the Constitution established that they could be re-elected only once for the subsequent constitutional term, a limit that was eliminated with the constitutional amendment approved by referendum on 14 February 2009 (*see infra* paragraphs 127, 258).

In the case of the representatives to the National Assembly, the Legislative Councils of the states and the Municipal Councils, the electoral system is also based on the universal, direct and secret vote (Article 63). The constitutional term of the National Assembly is of five years (Article 230), and those of the Legislative Councils of the states and the Municipal Councils are of four years (Articles 162, 174).

For the election of the representatives and members of the National Assembly, Legislative Councils and Municipal Councils, the electoral system traditionally applied according to the 1961 Constitution was governed by the d'Hondt proportional representation method. In 1993, the Organic Law on Suffrage and Political Participation,[309] seeking to guarantee more representativeness in the elections, introduced a combination of methods, adding to the proportional representation one a majority elections method in uninominal or plurinominal constituencies that were finally constitutionalized in the 1999 Constitution as a 'personalized proportional representation method' (Article 63).[310] This system, following the trends of the Organic Law on Suffrage and Political Participation of 1993, modified in 1998,[311] was initially regulated in the Electoral Statute approved by the National Constituent Assembly for the 2000 elections,[312] in which it was established that 60% of all representatives had to be elected un uninominal constituencies following the personalized principle; and 40% of them, through the list system, following the proportional representation principle (Article 15). This mixed system imposed the

308. *See* Allan R. Brewer-Carías, 'Reforma electoral en el sistema político de Venezuela', in *Reforma Política y Electoral en América Latina 1978–2007*, ed. Daniel Zovatto y J. Jesús Orozco Henríquez (Coordinadores) (México: Universidad Nacional Autónoma de México-IDEA internacional, 2008), 953–1019.

309. *Gaceta Oficial* No. 5.233 Extra. of 28 May 1998.

310. *See* decision of the Constitutional Chamber of the Supreme Tribunal of Justice, No. 74 of 25 Jan. 2006 in *Revista de Derecho Público*, No. 105 (Caracas: Editorial Jurídica Venezolana, 2006), 122–144.

311. *See Gaceta Oficial* No. 5.233 Extra of 28 May 1998.

312. *See Gaceta Oficial* No. 36.884 of 3 Feb. 2000. *See* Allan R. Brewer-Carías, 'Reforma electoral en el sistema político de Venezuela', in *Reforma Política y Electoral en América Latina 1978–2007*, ed. en Daniel Zovatto y J. Jesús Orozco Henríquez (Coord.) (México: Universidad Nacional Autónoma de México-IDEA internacional, 2008), 953–1019.

need to begin with the adjudication of those elected through the proportional representation method, in order to deduct to the Parties those obtained in the uninominal constituencies, in order to preserve the proportional representation system. This mixed system, nonetheless, was deformed in 2006 by means of an interpretation of the Constitution made by the Constitutional Chamber of the Supreme Tribunal of Justice before the election of the members of the National Assembly in 2006, through which the defrauding method applied by the parties supporting the government name as '*Las Morochas*' was legitimized.[313] The method consisted in allowing the various parties supporting official candidates to enter into agreements in order for some to only file nominations for the uninominal constituencies and others only for the plurinominal constituencies, so being formally 'different' parties (although being part of the same coalition) no deduction of the elected candidates was to be applied.[314] In this way, the system turned out to be, in practice, a preponderant majority system distorting proportional representation. In 2009, a new Organic Law on the Electoral Processes was sanctioned, 'legalizing' this electoral distorting method.[315]

174. Regarding the election of the high official of the other Branches of Government (Judicial, Citizens and Electoral), the Constitution has established a system of popular indirect election, attributed to the National Assembly, not acting as a 'legislative' body but as an electoral body, and only by the vote of a qualified majority of the elected representatives to the National Assembly. This is expressly provided in Articles 265, 279,296 of the Constitution for the election of the Justices of the Supreme Tribunal of Justice, the Prosecutor General, the Comptroller General, the People's Defender and the members of the National Electoral Council; an election that can only be made based on the exclusive proposal of candidates by the corresponding Nominated Committees that in each case are to be integrated exclusively by representatives of the various sectors of society (Articles 270, 279, 295 of the Constitution). This means that citizen participation, since 2000, has unfortunately been distorted by the Legislator, by integrating the Nominating Committees in the successive Organic Laws of the Supreme Tribunal, with a majority of representatives to the National Assembly, instead of representatives of the diverse sectors of civil society.

---

313. Decision No. 74 (Case: *Acción Democrática v. National Electoral Council* and other electoral authorities). *See* in *Revista de Derecho Público*, No. 105 (Caracas: Editorial Jurídica Venezolana, 2006), 122–144.

314. *See* Allan R. Brewer-Carías, 'El juez constitucional vs. El derecho al sufragio mediante la representación proporcional', in *Crónica sobre la 'In'Justicia Constitucional. La Sala Constitucional y el autoritarismo en Venezuela* (Caracas, 2007), 337 et seq.

315. *Gaceta Oficial* No. 5928 Extra. of 12 Aug. 2009. *See* Manuel Rachadell, 'El sistema electoral en la Ley Orgánica de Procesos Electorales', in *Ley Orgánica de los Procesos Electorales*, ed. Juan M. Matheus (Coord.) (Caracas: Editorial Jurídica Venezolana, 2010), 15 et seq.; Juan M. Matheus, 'Representación proporcional de las minorías y Ley Orgánica de Procesos Electorales', *ibid.*, 41 et seq.

Chapter 3. Direct Democracy Institutions and the Referenda Voting System

175. Regarding direct democracy, the 1999 Constitution has also established various mechanisms for its exercise in order to promote direct popular participation in conducting public affairs. In this context, Article 70 of the Constitution, referring to the need for prominent participation of the people, as aforementioned, enumerates as means for direct democracy: the referendums; the popular consultation; the repealing of public mandate; the legislative, constitutional and constituent initiatives; the open town hall meetings *(cabildos abiertos)*, and the Assemblies of Citizens 'whose decisions shall have a binding character'.

§1. Referenda

176. In particular, regarding referenda, the Venezuelan Constitution expressly set forth the following: consultative referendum; repeal referendum for the revocation of mandates; approbatory referendum of statutes and of constitutional revisions and referendum to abrogate statutes.[316] Notwithstanding, during the past twenty-two years only on one occasion a repeal referendum took place.

177. Regarding the consultative referendum, they can be convened for questions regarding matters of pre-eminent national, state or municipal importance. According to Article 71 of the Constitution, at the national level, the initiative for their convening belongs either to the President of the Republic in Council of Ministers; to the National Assembly by means of a Resolution approved by a majority of its members; or to the citizens by means of a petition signed by at least 10% of registered voters. At local levels of government (parish, municipal, states), the consultative referendums can be convened by the Municipal Councils or by the State Legislative Councils on the initiative of two-thirds of their members, respectively; by the Mayor or the State Governor; or by the people through a petition signed by no less than 10% of the registered voters in the specific district or jurisdiction.

178. Regarding revocation or repeal of referendums, they are the consequence of the principle established in the Constitution in the sense that all popular elected public officials are subjected to revocation of their mandate (Article 6).[317] For such

316. *See* Cosimina G. Pellegrino Pacera, 'Una introducción al estudio del referendo como mecanismo de participación ciudadana en la Constitución de 1999', in *El Derecho Público a comienzos del siglo XXI. Estudios homenaje al Profesor Allan R. Brewer-Carías*, vol. I (Madrid: Instituto de Derecho Público, UCV, Civitas Ediciones, 2003), 441–481; Hildegard Rondón de Sansó, 'El referendo en la Constitución de Venezuela de 1999', in *Estudios de Derecho Público*, ed. Román Duque Corredor y Jesús María Casal (Coords), vol. II (Caracas: Universidad Católica Andrés Bello, 2004), 163–212.

317. *See* Carlos Ayala Corao, *El Referendo Revocatorio: 'Una herramienta ciudadana de la democracia'*, (Caracas, Los Libros de El Nacional, 2004); Ricardo Antela, *La revocatoria del mandato (Régimen Jurídico del referéndum revocatorio en Venezuela)* (Caracas: Editorial Jurídica Venezolana, 2011); Carlos Ayala Corao, 'Antecedentes del Referendo Revocatorio', in *Estudios de*

purpose, Article 72 establishes the repeal referendum or referendum of revocation, which can only take place at the mid-point of the term in office. The corresponding petition for a repeal referendum can only be one of popular initiatives that must be signed by at least 20% of the registered voters in the corresponding jurisdiction. In order for a mandate to be repealed or revoked, it is enough that the number of votes for the revocation be equal to or greater than the number that originally elected the official; and the voters must total at least 25% of the registered voters in the corresponding jurisdiction. If the repeal petition is approved, the substitute officer must be elected immediately according to the electoral procedures established in the Constitution and laws (*see infra* paragraph 363). This repeal referendum was distorted in 2004 regarding its application to the President of the Republic[318] and was transformed against the constitutional provision through a constitutional interpretation by the Constitutional Chamber of the Supreme Tribunal into a 'ratifying' referendum (*see infra* paragraph 718).[319]

179. Another referendum established in the Constitution is the approval referendum referred to as Draft statutes which are debated before the National Assembly, which according to Article 73 of the Constitution proceeds when at least two-thirds of the members of the Assembly so decide. In such a case, if the referendum results in the approval of the statute provided that at least 25% of registered voters have concurred, the corresponding bill is to be sanctioned as law. The approbatory referendum can also be proposed by popular initiative (Article 204.7) when the National Assembly fails to take up debate on bills that also were proposed by popular initiative (Article 205).

Also, according to Article 73 of the Constitution, treaties, conventions or other international agreements that can compromise national sovereignty or transfer

---

Derecho Público, ed. Román Duque Corredor y Jesús María Casal (Coord.), vol. II (Caracas: Universidad Católica Andrés Bello, 2004), 213–240.

318. *See* Allan R. Brewer-Carías, 'El secuestro del Poder Electoral y la confiscación del derecho a la participación política mediante el referendo revocatorio presidencial: Venezuela 2000–2004', in *Derecho Constitucional para el Siglo XXI. Actas del Congreso Iberoamericano de Derecho Constitucional*, ed. Juan Pérez Royo, Joaquín Pablo Urías Martínez, Manuel Carrasco Durán, vol. I (Madrid: Thomson-Aranzadi, 2006), 1081–1126; and *Boletín Mexicano de Derecho Comparado*, Instituto de Investigaciones Jurídicas, Universidad Nacional Autónoma de México, No. 112. México, enero-abril 2005 11–73.

319. Decision No. 2750 of 21 Oct. 2003 (Case: *Carlos E. Herrera Mendoza, Interpretación del artículo 72 de la Constitución*), in *Revista de Derecho Público,* Nos 93–96 (Caracas: Editorial Jurídica Venezolana, 2003), 229 et seq. This illegitimate 'mutation' of the Constitution had the precise purpose of avoiding the revocation of the mandate of the President of the Republic (H. Chávez F.) in 2004. He had been elected in August 2000 with 3,757,774 votes, and in the 2004 repeal referendum 3,989,008 votes were cast for the revocation of its mandate, so that from the constitutional point of view the mandate was revoked *ex constitutione*. Nonetheless, because 5,800,629 votes were cast for the 'no revocation', the National Electoral Council, following the Constitutional Chamber interpetation, resolved to 'ratify' the Presidente de la República up to 2007 (*See* in *El Nacional*, Caracas, 28 Aug. 2004, A-1 y A-2). Consequently, in an illegitimate way, a repeal referendum was transformed into a 'ratificatory referendum' or Plebiscite that is not provided in the Constitution. *See* Allan R. Brewer-Carías, 'La Sala Constitucional vs. el derecho ciudadano a la revocatoria de mandatos populares: de cómo un referendo revocatorio fue inconstitucionalmente convertido en un 'referendo ratificatorio', in *Crónica sobre la 'In' Justicia Constitucional. La Sala Constitucional y el autoritarismo en Venezuela* (Caracas: Editorial Jurídica Venezolana, 2007), 349–378.

national powers or competencies to supra-national entities, as is the case of treaties for regional economic integration (*see supra* paragraph 139), may also be subject to approbatory referenda. In this case, the initiative corresponds to the President of the Republic in Council of Ministers, to the National Assembly when approved by a vote of at least two-thirds of its members, or to the popular initiative through a petition signed by at least 15% of registered voters.

180. The Constitution also regulates the referendum for the abrogation of statutes that can be convened regarding all laws, except budgetary laws, tax laws, public debts laws, amnesty laws, human rights laws and those laws approving international treaties (Article 74). The abrogation referendums can be convened on the initiative of at least 10% of registered voters, or on the initiative of the President of the Republic in Council of Ministers. Decrees-laws issued by the President of the Republic (Article 236.8) may also be subjected to abrogation referendum, in which case the initiative to convene it can only be a popular one through a petition signed by at least 5% of registered voters.

In all cases of abrogation referendums, the concurrence of at least 40% of registered voters is necessary to approve the abrogation of a statute or decree-law.

§2. Popular Consultation of Statutes

181. Regarding the popular consultation, in addition to the representatives of the different sectors of society in the Nominating Committees for the elections of High-ranking officials of the Citizen, Judicial and Electoral Branches of Government (*see infra* paragraphs 413 et seq.), in reference to the sanctioning of statutes by the National Assembly, Article 211 of the Constitution imposes on the National Assembly the obligation to always submit draft legislation to public consultation, asking the opinion of Citizens and the organized society. This provision has been distorted by the Constitutional Chamber of the Supreme Tribunal of Justice in Decision No. 203 of 25 March 2014 (*Impugnación del Decreto de la Ley Orgánica de la Administración Pública*), by expressly excluding from the obligatory popular consultation, the statutes approved through decree-law by the President of the Republic resulting from delegate legislation, even though almost all the statutes issued in the country since 1999 have been approved by decree-laws.[320]

Also, according to Article 206, the States must be consulted by the National Assembly, through their Legislative Councils, when legislation regarding them is being considered in the National Assembly. In addition, in all the statutes that have been sanctioned under the 1999 Constitution, a chapter has always been included regarding popular participation by means of consultations on public policies.

320. Available in *Revista de Derecho Público, Revista de Derecho Público,* 137 (Caracas: Editorial Jurídica Venezolana, 2014), 100–103. *See* the comments in Allan R. Brewer-Carías, 'El fin de la llamada 'democracia participativa y protagónica' dispuesto por la Sala Constitucional en fraude a la Constitución, al justificar la emisión de legislación inconsulta en violación al derecho a la participación política', in *ibid.*, 157–164.

182. The Constitution also guarantees popular initiative not only for the introduction of Draft legislation before the National Assembly by means of petitions signed by no less than 0.1% of the registered voters (Article 204.7) but also for the purpose of convening consultative, approbatory and abrogation referenda (*see supra* paragraphs 176 et seq.). Regarding the revocation or repeal referendum, it is an exclusive right of the people to convene them by popular initiative (the Popular initiative, *see supra* paragraph 178).

§3. LOCAL PARTICIPATION

183. The municipalities are conceived in the Constitution as the primary political unit in the national organization (Article 168), thus disposed of as the main institutional channel for political participation in the matters belonging to local life. This principle was ratified in all the municipal organization statutes up to 2010, as was provided in Article 1 of the 2006 Organic Law on the Municipal Public Power.[321] This Law specifically established that the municipalities and the other local entities were the primary areas for citizens' participation in the planning, design, execution, control and evaluation of public policies, imposing on them the duty to create the needed mechanisms in order to guarantee the participation of communities and social groups (Article 7), being obliged to promote them (Article 56). For such purpose, the Organic Law enumerated all the aspects of the citizens' participatory rights (Articles 255, 260), and for such purposes, established that the parishes were to be the information, production and promotion centres for participatory processes, for identifying budgetary priorities, and for the promotion of citizens' participation in public affairs (Article 37).

All these provisions were eliminated in 2010 by incorporating in the Organic Law on Municipal Public Power[322] the unconstitutional framework of the 'Communal State' and the 'Popular Power' (*see infra* paragraphs 232 et seq., 279), depriving the municipalities of their constitutional role of being the primary entities in the national organization of the country, and assigning such character to the Communes and to the Communal Councils (composed by non-elected officials), extinguishing the Parishes as local organizations for political participation composed, as they were, of elected officials.[323]

184. Within the municipal means for political participation, Article 70 of the Constitution specifically refers to the Town Hall Meetings, also regulated in the Municipal Power Organic Law, which can be convened by the Municipal Councils, by the Parish councils and by popular initiative according to what is established in

321. *Gaceta Oficial* No. 38.421 of 21 Apr. 2006. *See* Allan R. Brewer-Carías et al., *Ley Orgánica del Poder Público Municipal* (Caracas: Editorial Jurídica Venezolana, 2006).
322. *Gaceta Oficial* No. 6.015 Extra. 28 Dec. 2010.
323. *Gaceta Oficial* No. 6.015 Extra. of 28 Dec. 2010. *See* Allan R. Brewer-Carías et al., *Leyes Orgánicas del Poder Popular* (Caracas: Editorial Jurídica Venezolana, 2011).

the Municipal Ordinances. The decisions adopted in such Meetings are valid if approved by the majority of the persons present provided that they refer to matters concerning the municipal life.

185. The other direct democracy participative means established in the Constitution are the Citizens Assemblies (Article 70) that were conceived in the Municipal Organic Law as local entities within the municipal framework for participation, with deliberative character, established in order to enforce governance, impulse planning and the decentralization of services and resources, in which all citizens have the right to participate. Their decisions have obligatory character (Article 70, Constitution), provided that they are not contrary to legislation and to the community and State interest. Since 2006 and in particular, with the 2010 reforms on the Popular Power, these *Asambleas de Ciudadanos*, have been attached to the Communal State based on the 'Communes' and the 'Communal Councils', and completely taken from the Municipal Power (*see infra* paragraph 279). In this regard, the specific regulation concerning these Citizens Assemblies was initially established in the 2006 Communal Councils Law[324] where the Citizens' Assemblies were assigned with the duty of creating the Communal Councils at the communal level without any relation with the municipalities, except for the latter to transfer activities or services to the former. However, although being organs of the State, the members of the Communal Councils are not elected by suffrage but only appointed by Assemblies of Citizens, which have been directly controlled by the official political party, and from the institutional and financial point of view, directly dependent on the President of the Republic through a Ministry for the Communes and Citizens Participation[325] (*see infra* paragraph 264). The result of all these reforms has been the complete de-municipalization of the country, and the erasement of the municipalities as the 'primary political entities' in the political organization of the State.[326]

324. *Gaceta Oficial* No. 5.806 Extra. of 10 Apr. 2006.
325. *See* the Communal Councils Law in *Gaceta Oficial* No. 39.335 Extra. of 28 Dec. 2009. *See* Allan R. Brewer-Carías, *Ley Orgánica de los Consejos Comunales* (Caracas: Editorial Jurídica Venezolana, 2009).
326. *See* Allan R. Brewer-Carías, 'El inicio de la desmunicipalización en Venezuela: La organización del Poder Popular para eliminar la descentralización, la democracia representativa y la participación a nivel local', in *AIDA, Opera Prima de Derecho Administrativo. Revista de la Asociación Internacional de Derecho Administrativo* (México: Universidad Nacional Autónoma de México, 2007), 49 a 67.

Chapter 4. The Plural Political Parties Regime

186. A democratic regime cannot exist without political parties and pluralism. That is why, after a short experiment of a dominant party system in the 1940s (1945–1948) (*see supra* paragraph 18), the democratic parties that in 1958 signed the *Pacto de Punto Fijo* after the Democratic Revolution which was initiated that same year against the Military dictatorship (*see supra* paragraphs 20, 24); compromised themselves to establish a competitive and pluralistic multi-party democratic system that functioned up to 1999 (*see supra* paragraphs 21 et seq.).[327]

The democratic period that according to those goals developed in the country during the second half of the twentieth century, was characterized from the beginning as being one with a notorious pre-eminence of the political parties that dominated all aspects of political life, and particularly participation and representation (Party State).[328] It was their crisis and the crisis of their leadership because of the lack of reforms and of updating the functioning of the democratic system that eventually provoked the collapse of the democratic system itself in 1998 (*see supra* paragraphs 24 et seq.). After forty years of controlling political power and having democratized the country, the parties underestimated the need the country had for more means of representation and political participation and failed to open the democratic system through, for instance, political decentralization to allow effective participation. At the end of the twentieth century, the fact was that all of the political ills of the Republic were attributed to the political parties, to the 1958 *Pacto de Punto Fijo* (*see supra* paragraphs 20, 24) and to the Constitution of 1961, and political discussion ignited by the new authoritarian military and populist leadership that took control of the State centred on the anathema against them and on their destruction.

187. The result was that the presidential election of that year and the election of the National Constituent Assembly the next year (1999) were characterized by an anti-party trend that was reflected in the drafting of the new 1999 Constitution, to the point that it can be said that it was conceived as an anti-party instrument, where the expression itself of 'political party' was eliminated from its text, being substituted by the general expression of 'organizations with political purposes' (Article 67).[329] Of course, what in 1998 and in 1999 tended to be ignored were the traditional political parties that up to then had been in control of power.

---

327. *See* Juan Carlos Rey, El sistema de partidos venezolano 1830-1999 (Caracas, Editorial Jurídica Venezolana, 2015).
328. *See* Allan R. Brewer-Carías, *Problemas del Estado de Partidos* (Caracas: Editorial Jurídica Venezolana, 1989).
329. *See* Lolymar Hernández Camargo, 'Los Partidos Políticos en la Constitución de la República Bolivariana de Venezuela de 1999', in *Tendencias Actuales del Derecho Constitucional. Homenaje a Jesús María Casal Montbrun*, ed. Jesús María Casal, Alfredo Arismendi y Carlos Luis Carrillo Artiles (Coord.), vol. I (Caracas: UCV/Universidad Católica Andrés Bello, 2008), 577–590; Roberto V. Pastor; Rubén Martínez Dalmau, 'La configuración de los partidos políticos en la Constitución venezolana', in *Revista de Derecho Constitucional,* No. 4 (enero-julio) (Caracas: Editorial Sherwood, 2001), 375–389; Allan R. Brewer-Carías, 'Regulación jurídica de los partidos políticos en Venezuela', in *Regulación jurídica de los partidos políticos en América Latina*, ed. Daniel Zovatto (Coordinador) (México: Universidad Nacional Autónoma de México, International IDEA, 2006), 893–937.

188. The constitution-making process of 1999 and the sanctioning of the new Constitution unfolded in this context and gave way to new political parties mainly constituted for electoral purposes and from the government, crushing the old and then marginalized political parties which abstained from participating in that process. During the subsequent years, these new political parties continued to act supportive of the new government and its President, and eventually resulted in being more centralized than the traditional ones, with internal governing centralized structures linked to the President of the Republic. The final result of this process was the presidential initiative, in 2006, to promote the constitution of a single United Socialist Party, using the State structures and services, which the President of the Republic presides, intending to unite in it all the various political parties that have supported his tenure. The total unification failed because the Communist Party refused to disappear, which did not prevent the official United Socialist Party from declaring itself in 2010 as a 'Marxist' party following the 'Bolivarian doctrine'.[330]

This official United Socialist Party was in charge of supporting the presidential Constitutional Reform Draft submitted to a referendum in 2007, which nonetheless was rejected by popular vote, and was also the supporting instrument of the Government candidates to the regional and municipal elections in November 2008, in which the Government's candidates lost the elections in the most important and populated states and municipalities of the country where opposition candidates to Governors and Mayors were elected.

In any case, the result of the two decades of the political life under the 1999 Constitution, has been to increase partisanship and 'party-autocracy', particularly regarding the official party that has been embodied in the State structures, in a way never before seen.

189. However, regarding the 1999 Constitution provisions related to political organizations, the traditional lack of internal democracy within the parties with their traditional pattern of leaders in perpetuity, led to a provision according to which not only the members of governing boards have to be elected by the members of each party but also choosing party candidates for elections to representative offices must also be made through democratic internal elections (Article 67). To this end, the Constitution imposed the obligation that the National Electoral Council must organize such internal elections (Article 293.6), which in practice, due to the lack of statutory development of the constitutional provisions has not occurred during the first decade of the Constitution.

190. In addition, also as a reaction against the problems stemming from the public funding of political parties that was regulated under the 1998 Organic Law of Suffrage and Political Participation,[331] which led to cornering and monopolizing of those funds by the traditionally dominant parties, the drafters of the new 1999 Constitution simply prohibited public funding of organizations with political purposes and established new controls for their private financing (Article 67). This was a

330. *See* 'Declaration of Principles' of the PSUV (23 Apr. 2010), available at http://psuv.org.ve/files/tcdocumentos/Declaracion-de-principios-PSUV.pdf.

331. *Gaceta Oficial* No. 5.233 Extra. of 28 May 1998.

regression in addressing what is a constant problem in the democratic world: the possibility for public funding of political parties in order to avoid irregular and illegitimate funding, particularly of governing parties.[332] Nonetheless, in a 2008 decision of the Constitutional Chamber of the Supreme Tribunal interpreting Article 67 of the Constitution, the Chamber has mutated the Constitution, concluding in a way contrary to the constitutional provision, ruling that what the Article intended was to prohibit the public financing only regarding the 'internal activities' of the parties, and not their electoral activities, which consequently since 2008 has then been accepted.[333]

However, Article 67 of the Constitution refers to a statute with the task of regulating the scope of private contributions to and finances of 'organizations with political purposes', including mechanisms to oversee the origins and management of these funds. This statute must regulate political and election campaigns, overseeing their duration and spending limits, and inclining them towards democratization. These matters previously regulated in the 1998 Organic Law of Suffrage and Political Participation, since 2009, are regulated in the Organic Law on Electoral Processes.[334]

191. In the same trend of reacting against political parties, the Constitution also established the principle that the members of the National Assembly are representatives of the whole of the people and 'are not to be subject to mandates or instructions other than their own conscience' (Article 200), seeking to eliminate parliamentary party groups. Nonetheless, in practice, the parliamentary factions have only changed their names and since 2000 have been called 'opinion groups'. In any case, and particularly regarding the governing party, its board, presided by the President of the Republic itself, has had more centralized control over the representatives to the National Assembly than the traditional parties before 1999.

The result of all these provisions, constitutional distortions and absence of legislation has been that in political practice, under the new Constitution, the parties have a greater presence than they ever had, to the point that, as aforementioned, since 1999, the President of the Republic is the President of the governing Party, which since 2007 has been the Venezuelan Unique Socialist Party, and almost all the Ministers are also members of the party's National Coordination Board. As never before, the symbiosis between the governing political party and the State and its Public Administration has been organically sealed in Venezuela, opening lines of communication and financial channels that could not have been seen in the golden

332. *See* Juan Carlos Rey y otros, *El financiamiento de los partidos políticos y la democracia en Venezuela* (Caracas, 1981); Allan R. Brewer-Carías, 'Consideraciones sobre el financiamiento de los partidos políticos en Venezuela', in *Financiamiento y democratización interna de partidos políticos. Memora del IV Curso Anual Interamaricano de Elecciones* (San José, Costa Rica, 1991), 121 a 139.

333. Decision of the Constitutional Chamber of the Supreme Tribunal of Justice, No. 780, of 8 May 2008 (Interpretaton of Art. 67 of the Constitucion), in *Revista de Derecho Público*, No. 114 (Caracas: Editorial Jurídica Venezolana, 2008), 126 et seq. *See* Allan R. Brewer-Carías, 'El juez constitucional como constituyente: el caso del financiamiento de las campañas electorales de los partidos políticos en Venezuela', in *Revista de Derecho Público*, No. 117 (Caracas, 2009, 195–203).

334. *See* in *Gaceta Oficial* No. 5.928 Extra. of 12 Aug. 2009.

age of 'party-autocracy' of the 1980s. The result has been that the same 'Party State' has continued, with the same vices of patronage system, and the same control by officials sitting in governing boards at the helm of the parties who have not been chosen in free and democratic internal elections.

192. Finally, it should be emphasized that the Constitution conferred to one of the national branches of government, the Public Electoral Power through the National Electoral Council, the duty not only to organize all electoral processes but also to 'organize elections in the organizations with political purposes' (Article 293.6), establishing an intolerable principle of State intervention in the internal functioning of political parties (*see infra* paragraph 454). This State intervention has increased due to the role assumed by the Constitutional Chamber of the Supreme Tribunal, acting as a tool of the authoritarian government, controlling in 2012 the political parties usurping the National Electoral Council,[335] limiting in 2015, the autonomy of the political parties,[336] and even dismissing in 2020 the Board of Directors of the main opposition parties and appointing in substitution persons related to the government.[337]

335. *See* Allan R. Brewer-Carías, 'El juez constitucional usurpando, de oficio, funciones del Poder Electoral en materia de control de partidos políticos y de respaldo de candidaturas presidenciales', en *Revista de Derecho Público,* No. 132 (Caracas, Editorial Jurídica Venezolana, 2012), pp. 195–200.

336. *See* Allan R. Brewer-Carías, 'Un nuevo golpe a la democracia: La confiscación de la autonomía de los partidos políticos decretada por el Juez Constitucional', en *Revista de Derecho Público*, No. 143–144, (Caracas, Editorial Jurídica Venezolana, 2015), pp. 460–467.

337. *See* Allan R. Brewer-Carías, 'Algunas consecuencias de la ilegitimidad e inconstitucionalidad de las pretendidas elecciones parlamentarias de diciembre de 2020', in *Revista de Derecho Público*, No. 163–164, (Caracas, Editorial Jurídica Venezolana. 2020), pp. 439–452.

Chapter 5. Institutions for Governmental Accountability

193. As aforementioned, the 1999 Constitution, in addition to qualifying the government of the Republic as democratic, participatory, elective, decentralized, alternating, responsible, plural and of revocable mandates (Article 6), has established that the officials are subject to accountability (*rendición de cuentas*), which in particular applies to elected officers, which can be subjected to repeal referendums.

Regarding the President of the Republic, the Constitution imposes on him the duty to formulate before the National Assembly in ordinary sessions of the National Assembly, each year during the first ten days of its instalment, a State of the Republic message giving an account of the political, economic, social and administrative aspect of his actions during the previous year (Article 237). Regarding the Governors of states, they must give an account of their actions, not before the Legislative Councils, but only before the Comptroller General of each state, having only to formulate before the Councils a report (Article 161). Regarding the representatives to the National Assembly, the Constitution imposes on them the duty to give an annual account of their actions to their electors, being subjected to a repeal referendum (Article 197).

194. Within the institutions of accountability, the most distinguishing feature of the Venezuelan constitutional system is the express establishment of the repeal referendum as an institution of direct democracy (*see supra* paragraph 178) referred to all elective officials, in the sense that the mandates of all elected officers are essentially revocable (Article 72). In this regard, the popular revocation of mandates is one of the means for direct political participation of the people in the exercise of its sovereignty (Article 70). The revocation of mandates, consequently, can only take place by means of the revocation referendum, which according to Article 72 of the Constitution must be made according to the following rules: First, the repeal referendum can only be convened once half of the term of the elected officer has been elapsed. Second, the request for convening a repeal referendum can only be made by popular initiative, signed by no less than 25% of the registered electors in the corresponding constituency and filed before the National Electoral Council (Article 293.5). There cannot be more than one request for repeal referendum during the same constitutional term of the elected official. Third, in the convened repeal referendum, a number equal to or superior to the equivalent to the 25% of the registered electors must concur as voting persons. Fourth, in order for a repeal of a mandate to be approved, it is sufficient that a number of voters equal or superior to those that have elected the officer must have voted in the referendum for the revocation of the mandate. In this case, the mandate of the officer must be considered revoked, and a new election must take place immediately in order to fill the absolute absence according to the Constitution (Articles 72, 233).

195. Regarding the President of the Republic, since the revocation of his mandate has the effect of an absolute absence, in case a revocation occurs, his replacement must be done as follows: if the revocation takes place during the first four years of his mandate, a new election must be made in order for the newly elected to complete the revoked President's term. If the revocation takes place during the last two years of the presidential term, the Executive Vice President must assume the position up to the end of the term (Article 233).

However, the Constitution only provided for the effects of the mandate revocation regarding the revoked official in the cases of the representatives to the National Assembly, in which case, the revoked representatives cannot seek a new election in the next constitutional term (Article 198). Nothing in this regard was established regarding the mandate revoking the other public elected officers.

196. On these matters of repeal referendums, the only experience the country had during the first decade of the 1999 Constitution was the repeal referendum of the President of the Republic (who was elected in 2000 by 3,757,774 votes), convened in 2004 by popular initiative signed by more than three and a half million signatures, which was held in August 2004.[338] In it, 3,989,008 voters voted *YES* for the repeal of its mandate, that is, a number of votes superior to the ones that elected him in 2000. The consequence of that voting result, according to express provision of the Constitution, was to consider the mandate of the President revoked and to call for a new election. Nonetheless, the National Electoral Council, following a phrase in a Constitutional Chamber of the Supreme Tribunal decision, converted the repeal referendum of the President into a 'ratification referendum'[339] that does not exist in the Constitution just because a superior number of voters cast a *NO* vote, a condition or situation not established in the Constitution (*see infra* paragraph 718).

338. *See* Allan R. Brewer-Carías, 'El secuestro del Poder Electoral y la confiscación del derecho a la participación política mediante el referendo revocatorio presidencial: Venezuela 2000–2004', in *Revista Jurídica del Perú*, Año LIV No. 55 (Lima, March–April 2004), 353–396; 'El secuestro del Poder Electoral y de la Sala Electoral del Tribunal Supremo y la confiscación del derecho a la participación política mediante el referendo revocatorio presidencial: Venezuela: 2000–2004', in *Revista Costarricense de Derecho Constitucional*, vol. V (Instituto Costarricense de Derecho Constitucional, Editorial Investigaciones Jurídicas S.A., San José, 2004), 167–312; 'El secuestro del poder electoral y la confiscación del derecho a la participación política mediante el referendo revocatorio presidencial: Venezuela 2000–2004', *Stvdi Vrbinati*, Rivista tgrimestrale di Scienze Giuridiche, Politiche ed Economiche, Year LXXI –2003/04 Nuova Serie A– N. 55,3, Università degli studi di Urbino, Urbino, 2004, 379–436; 'El secuestro del Poder Electoral y la confiscación del derecho a la participación política mediante el referendo revocatorio presidencial: Venezuela 2000–2004', in *Boletín Mexicano de Derecho Comparado* (Instituto de Investigaciones Jurídicas, Universidad Nacional Autónoma de México, No. 112. México, January–April 2005), 11–73.

339. *See* Allan R. Brewer-Carías, 'La Sala Constitucional vs. el derecho ciudadano a la revocatoria de mandatos populares: de cómo un referendo revocatorio fue inconstitucionalmente convertido en un 'referendo ratificatorio', in *Crónica sobre la 'in' justicia constitucional. La Sala Constitucional y el autoritarismo en Venezuela*, ed. Allan R. Brewer-Carías (Caracas: Colección Instituto de Derecho Público, UCV, No. 2, 2007), 349–378.

Part III. The Federation and the Territorial Distribution of State Powers

197. The Venezuelan State has always been organized as a Federation. The federal form of Government was adopted in 1811 (*see supra* paragraph 2) when an elected General Congress adopted on 21 December 1811, the first Constitution of any Latin American country, the '*Federal Constitution for the States of Venezuela*', which declared the former colonial provinces as sovereign States, all of which 1810–1811 had declared independence from Spain and adopted their own provincial constitutions or forms of government. By means of this 1811 Constitution, the country adopted a federal form of government, following the influence of the United States' Constitution, at a time when the Federation was the only new constitutional instrument recently invented, different to the centralized monarchical States. That invention was followed by the Venezuelan framers of the new State in order to unite the former Spanish Colonial Provinces that formed the Venezuelan State, which had never been previously united. In those territories, there were no Viceroyalties or *Audiencias* (until 1786), and a General Captaincy exclusively for military purposes integrating the Provinces was only established in 1777. Thus, it can be said that Venezuela was the second country in constitutional history to adopt federalism.[340]

198. The federation was later reaffirmed in the 1864 Constitution, organizing the Republic as the United States of Venezuela (*see supra* paragraph 12). Even though this latter denomination was eliminated in the 1953 Constitution, the federal form of the State was kept in the following 1961 and 1999 Constitutions, in which the national Territory is divided into twenty-three states, a Capital District exists, Federal Dependencies and Federal Territories (Article 16).

199. But in practice, with all this territorial division and the State named in the Constitution as a 'Federal Decentralized State' (Article 4), federalism in Venezuela reveals a very contradictory form of government. In effect, a Federation is a politically decentralized State organization based on the distribution of State power in two or three levels of territorial political entities functioning with some sort of autonomy. Nonetheless, in Venezuela, with a Federation organized into three levels of government (national, states and municipal), the competencies of the states and

340. After the North American independence (1776) and Federation (1777), the first Latin American Country to declare independence and adopt a Constitution was Venezuela in 1811, adopting the federal form of State.

municipal levels are scarce, and their autonomy is very weak, lacking effective public policies and even substantive sub-national constitutions. Consequently, in contrast to many Federations, what has been established in Venezuela in a very contradictory way is a Centralized Federation. Nonetheless, this situation has not always been like it is now. The process of centralization really began and developed during the twentieth century (*see supra* paragraph 67), being particularly more accentuated precisely during the first decade after the approval of the 1999 Constitution.[341]

341. *See* Allan R. Brewer-Carías, 'El 'Estado Federal descentralizado' y la centralización de la Federación en Venezuela. Situación y Perspectiva de una contradicción constitucional', in *Revista de Estudios de la Administración Local (REAL)*, 292–293, mayo-diciembre 2003 (Madrid, 2003), 11–43; 'La descentralización política en la Constitución de 1999: Federalismo y Municipalismo (una reforma insuficiente y regresiva)' in *Boletín de la Academia de Ciencias Políticas y Sociales*, No. 138, Año LXVIII, enero-diciembre 2001 (Caracas, 2002), 313–359, and in *Provincia. Revista Venezolana de Estudios Territoriales*, No. 7, julio-diciembre 2001, II Etapa, Centro Iberoamericano de Estudios Provinciales y Locales (CIEPROL) (Mérida: Universidad de los Andes, 2001), 7–92.

Chapter 1. The Centralization Process of the Federation

200. In effect, the centralization process of the Federation began with the instalment of the authoritarian government resulting from the 1899 Liberal Restorative Revolution, and particularly under the almost three decades of Juan Vicente Gómez dictatorship, spanning the first half of the twentieth century. During these years, no democratic institutions were developed (*see supra* paragraph 16). So it was after the endless civil conflict that marked the history of Venezuela during the nineteenth century that the federal form of government began to be limited. The conflict stemmed from the permanent struggles between the regional *caudillos* and the weak central power that had been formed, giving rise to the centralizing tendencies derived from the consolidation of the Nation State, a process that was particularly reinforced during the first half of the twentieth century.

During these decades, the autocratic regimes of the country, aided by the income derived from the new exploitation of oil by the national State (oil and the subsoil always has been the public property of the State), contributed to the consolidation of the Nation State in all aspects, based on the creation of a national army, a centralized public administration, a central taxation system, and national legislation. These centralizing tendencies almost provoked the disappearance of the Federation, the territorial distribution of power, and the effective autonomy of the twenty-three states and of the Federal District.

201. The transition from autocracy to democracy began with the death of Gómez, and later, between 1945 and 1958, when a democratic regime, in accordance with the democratic Constitution of 1961, was progressively developed in which the Federal form of the State was kept, but with a highly centralized national organization. This democratic Constitution was the longest Constitution in force in all of Venezuelan history, assuring the dominance of a very centralized political party system. During its forty years of functioning, this democratic centralized political party system, without doubt, restrained the development of effective federal institutions. Nonetheless, due to the democratization process of the country and according to express constitutional provisions, a political decentralization process was forced to be applied in order to politically decentralize the federation with the transfer of powers and services from the national level of government to the state level. The process began in 1989 when the party system crisis exploded and was forced by the democratic pressure exercised against the political parties, all of which were in the middle of a severe leadership crisis. One of the most important reforms then adopted was the provision of the direct election of the states' Governors which, until that year, were just public officials appointed by the President of the Republic.[342] In December 1989, for the first time since the nineteenth century,

342. *See* Allan R. Brewer-Carías, 'Problemas de la Federación centralizada (A propósito de la elección directa de Gobernadores)', *IV Congreso Iberoamericano de Derecho Constitucional* (México: Universidad Nacional Autónoma de México, 1992), 85–131.

states' Governors were elected by universal, direct and secret suffrage,[343] and regional political life began to play an important role in the country, initializing the increasing appearance of regional and local political leaders, many of whom were from outside the traditional political parties.

Nonetheless, after important efforts in 1993, the process to politically decentralize the federation was later abandoned, mainly due to the crisis of the centralized party system, and the consequential political void it produced in the country.

202. Ultimately, it was this crisis in the centralized party system that gave rise to the covenant of a National Constituent Assembly not regulated in the 1961 Constitution, resulting in the sanctioning of a new Constitution, the 1999 Constitution of the 'Bolivarian Republic of Venezuela' approved by referendum (15 December 1999). This new Constitution, if it is true that it provoked a radical change in the political players nationwide, also started the reversal of the decentralizing political efforts that were being made. The new Constitution continued with the same centralizing foundation embodied in the previous Constitution and, in some cases, centralizing even more aspects. For instance, although defining the decentralization process as a 'national policy devoted to strengthened democracy' (Article 158), in contrast, the national public policy executed during the past decade can be characterized as a progressive centralization of government, without any real development of local and regional authorities.

Consequently, in Venezuela, federalism has been postponed and democracy has been progressively weakened; and the Constitution covers with a democratic veil an authoritarian regime, regulating a very centralized system of government where all powers of the State can be concentrated, as they now are. The Constitution has excellent declarations, including the one referring to the 'Decentralized Federal State', the enumeration of human rights, and the 'penta separation' of State branches of government. However, each of these declarations is contradicted by other regulations in the same Constitution, which allow a contrary result.

343. Election and Remotion of States' Governors Law, *Gaceta Oficial* No. 4.086 Extra. of 14 Apr. 1989. *See* the comments in Allan R. Brewer-Carías, 'Los problemas de la federación centralizada en Venezuela', in *Revista Ius et Praxis* (Universidad de Lima, No. 12, 1988), 49 a 96; and 'Bases legislativas para la descentralización política de la federación centralizada (1990: El inicio de una reforma', in *Leyes y reglamentos para la descentrlización política de la Federación*, ed. Allan R. Brewer-Carías et al. (Caracas: Editorial Jurídica Venezolana, 1994), 7–53.

Chapter 2. The Contradictory 'Decentralized Federation' in the 1999 Constitution

§1. Constitutional Provisions Relating to Federalism in the 1999 Constitution

203. A Federation, above all, is a form of government in which public power is territorially distributed among various levels of government each of them with autonomous democratic political institutions. That is why in principle, federalism and political decentralization are intimately related concepts. Specifically, decentralization is the most effective instrument not only for the guaranteeing of civil and social rights, but to allow effective participation of the citizens in the political process. In this context, the relation between the local government and the population is essential. That is why all consolidated democracies in the world today are embodied in clearly decentralized forms of governments, such as Federations, or like the new Regional states, as is the case of countries like Spain, Italy and France. That is why it can be said that the strong centralizing tendencies developing in Venezuela in recent years are contrary to democratic governance and political participation.

204. According to Article 4 of the 1999 Constitution, the Republic of Venezuela is formally defined 'as a decentralized Federal State under the terms set out in the Constitution' governed by the principles of 'territorial integrity, solidarity, concurrence and co-responsibility'. Nonetheless, 'the terms set out in the Constitution', are without a doubt centralizing, and Venezuela continues to be a contradictory 'Centralized Federation'.[344]

Article 136 of the 1999 Constitution states that 'public power is distributed among the municipal, state and national entities', establishing a Federation with three levels of political governments and autonomy: *a national level* exercised by the Republic (federal level); the *States level*, exercised by the twenty-three states and a Capital District; and the *municipal level,* exercised by the 338 existing municipalities. On each of these three levels, the Constitution requires 'democratic, participatory, elected, decentralized, alternating, responsible, plural and with revocable mandates' governments (Article 6). Regarding the Capital District, it has substituted the former Federal District which was established in 1863, with the elimination of traditional federal interventions that existed regarding the authorities of the latter.

205. The organization of the political institutions at each territorial level is formally guided by the principle of the organic separation of powers, but with different

344. *See* Allan R. Brewer-Carías, *Federalismo y Municipalismo en la Constitución de 1999* (Caracas: Universidad Católica del Táchira-Editorial Jurídica Venezolana, 2001); 'Centralized Federalism in Venezuela', in *Duquesne Law Review*, vol. 43, No. 4, summer 2005. Duquesne University, Pittsburgh, Pennsylvania, 2005, 629–643. *See also* Allan R. Brewer-Carias & Jan Kleinheisterkamp, 'Venezuela: The End of Federalism?', in *Federalism and Legal Unification: A Comparative Empirical Investigation of Twenty Systems,* ed. Daniel Halberstam & Mathias Reimann (London: Springer, 2014), 523–543.

scopes. On the *national level*, with a presidential system of government, the national public power is separated among five branches of government, including: the 'Legislative, Executive, Judicial, Citizen and Electoral' (Article 136). Thus, the 1999 Constitution has surpassed the classic tripartite division of power by adding to the traditional Legislative, Executive and Judicial branches, the Citizen branch, which includes the Public Prosecutor Office, the General Comptrollership Office, and the People's Rights Defender Office, as well as an Electoral branch of government-controlled by the National Electoral Council (*see infra* paragraphs 453 et seq.).

The new Citizen and Electoral branches, as well as the Judiciary, are reserved only for the national or federal level of government. Therefore, Venezuela does not have a Judiciary at the state level. In fact, since 1945, the Judicial branch has been reserved to the national level of government, basically due to the national character of all major legislation and Codes (Civil, Commercial, Criminal, Labour and Procedural Codes) (*see supra* paragraphs 142, 162). Consequently, since Courts are national (federal), there is no room for state constitution regulations on these matters. Regarding judicial review, the Constitutional Chamber of the Supreme Tribunal of Justice is the constitutional organ with the power to review and annul with *erga omnes* effects (Article 336) all laws (national, state and municipal) including state constitutions when contrary to the national constitution (*see infra* paragraphs 684 et seq.), so there are no state courts or judicial organization.

206. Pertaining to the Legislative branch, it must be noted that the Constitution of 1999 established a one-chamber National Assembly, thus ending the country's federalist tradition of bicameralism by eliminating the Senate. As a result, Venezuela has also become a rare federal State without a federal chamber or Senate where the states, through their representatives, can be equal in the sense of equal vote. In the National Assembly, there are no representatives of the states, and its members are global representatives of the citizens and of all the states collectively. Theoretically, these global representatives are not subject to mandates or instructions, but only subject to the 'dictates of their conscience' (Article 201). This has effectively eliminated all vestiges of territorial representation.

207. Regarding the states' branch of government, the 1999 Constitution established that each state has a Governor who must be elected by a universal, direct and secret vote (Article 160). Each state must also have a Legislative Council comprised of representatives elected according to the principle of proportional representation (Article 162). According to the Constitution, it is the responsibility of each state's Legislative Council to enact their own Constitution in order 'to organize their branches of government' along the guidelines of the national Constitution, which in principle guarantees the autonomy of the states (Article 159).

§2. Limits to the Contents of the Sub-national Constitutions

208. Consequently, each state has constitutional power to enact its own sub-national constitution in order to organize the state's Legislative and Executive branches of government and to regulate the state's own organ for audit control. But in spite of these regulations on the organization and functioning of the state branches of government, the scope of states' powers has also been seriously limited by the 1999 Constitution, particularly due to the fact that for the first time in federal history, the Constitution refers to a national legislation for the establishment of the general regulation on this matter.

209. In effect, and in relation to the states' Legislative branch of government, the 1999 Constitution states that the organization and functioning of the states' Legislative Councils must be regulated by a *national statute* (Article 162), a manifestation of centralism never before envisioned, according to which the National Legislative Power has the power to enact legislation in order to determine the organization and functioning of all of the state legislatures.

According to this power, the National Assembly has sanctioned an *Organic Law for the State Legislative Councils* (2001)[345] in which detailed regulations are established regarding their organization and functioning, and in addition, even without constitutional authorization, regarding the statutes and attributions of the Legislative Council members, as well as regarding the general rules for the exercise of the legislative functions, or the law enacting procedure itself. With this national regulation, the effective contents of the state constitutions regarding their Legislative branch have been voided, and are limited to repeating what is established in the said national organic law or statute.

210. Additionally, the possibility of organizing the executive branch of government of each state was also limited by the 1999 Constitution, which established the basic rules concerning the Governors as head of the executive branch. The Constitution has additional regulations referring to the public administration (national, states and municipal), public employees (civil service), and the administrative procedures and public contracts in all of the three levels of government. All of these rules have also been developed in two 2001 national *Organic Laws on Public Administration*[346] *and on Civil Service.*[347] Therefore, state constitutions have also been voided of real content in these matters, have limited scope, and their norms tend to just repeat what has been established in the national organic laws or statutes.

211. Finally, regarding other state organs, in 2001, the National Assembly also sanctioned a *Law on the appointment of the States' Controller,*[348] limiting the powers of the State Legislative Councils on the matter without constitutional authorization.[349] In addition, the national intervention regarding the various state constitutions and their respective regulations in relation to their own state organizations has been completed by the Constitutional Chamber of the Supreme Tribunal

345. *Gaceta Oficial* No. 37.282 Extra. of 13 Sep. 2001.
346. *Gaceta Oficial* No. 6.147 Extra. of 17 Nov. 2014.
347. *Gaceta Oficial* No. 37.522 Extra. of 6 Sep. 2002.
348. *Gaceta Oficial* No. 37.304 Extra. of 16 Oct. 2001.
349. This Law was specifically abrogated by Law published in *Gaceta Oficial* No. 39.217 of 9 Jul. 2009, and a specific Regulation on the matter was issued by the Comproller General of the Republic.

of Justice. Specifically, the Constitutional Chamber of the Supreme Tribunal of Justice's rulings during the past years (2001–2002) included the annulment of the articles of three state constitutions creating an Office of the Peoples' Defender, on the grounds that citizens' rights are a matter reserved to the national (federal) level of government.[350]

212. As mentioned, the National Constitution establishes three levels of territorial autonomy and regulates the distribution of state powers, directly regulating the local or municipal government in an extensive manner. Therefore, the states' constitutions and legislations can regulate municipal or local government only according to what is established in the national Constitution, and in the *National Organic Law on Municipal Power*,[351] which leaves very little room for the state regulation.

Thus, without any possibility for the state legislatures to regulate anything related to civil, economic, social, cultural, environmental or political rights, and with the limited powers to regulate their own branches of government, as well as other state organizations, including the General Comptroller and Peoples' Defender, very little scope has been left for the contents of sub-national constitutions.[352]

§3. The Constitutional System of Distribution of Powers within the National, State and Municipal Levels of Government

213. Federalism is based on an effective distribution of powers within the various levels of government, and in Venezuela, between the national, state and municipal levels. Accordingly, the National Constitution enumerates the competencies attributed in an exclusive way to the national (Article 156), state (Article 154), and municipal (Article 178) levels of government, but in fact, under these regulations, these exclusive matters are almost all reserved for the national level of government, an important portion attributed to the municipalities, and very few of the exclusive matters are attributed to the states.[353]

---

350. *See* decisions No. 1182 of 11 Oct. 2000, No. 1395 of 7 Aug. 2001 and No. 111 of 12 Feb. 2004 (States of Mérida, Aragua and Lara), in *Revista de Derecho Público*, No. 84 (Caracas: Editorial Jurídica Venezolana, 2000), 177 et seq.; and in *Revista de Derecho Público* Nos 85–88 (Caracas: Editorial Jurídica Venezuela, 2001).

351. *Gaceta Oficial* No. 6.015 Extra. of 28 Dec. 2010.

352. *See* Michael Penfold-Becerra, 'Federalism and Institutional Change in Venezuela', in *Federalism and Democracy in Latin America*, ed. Edward L. Gibson (Baltimore, 2004) 197–225; Rafael J. Chavero Gazdik, 'La forma de Estado prevista en la Constitución de 1999 (¿Un canto de sirenas?)', in *Revista de Derecho Público*, No. 81 (Caracas: Editorial Jurídica Venezolana, 2000), 29–39; José Peña Solís, 'Aproximación al proceso de descentralización delineado en la Constitución de 1999', in *Estudios de Derecho Público: Libro Homenaje a Humberto J. La Roche Rincón*, vol. II. (Caracas: Tribunal Supremo de Justicia, 2001), 217–282.

353. *See* Gustavo J. Linares Benzo, 'El sistema venezolano de repartición de competencias', in *El Derecho Público a comienzos del siglo XXI. Estudios homenaje al Profesor Allan R. Brewer-Carías*, vol. I (Madrid: Instituto de Derecho Público, UCV, Civitas Ediciones, 2003), 702–713; Manuel Rachadell, 'La distribución del poder tributario entre los diversos niveles del Poder Público según la Constitución de 1999', in *Revista de Derecho Administrativo*, No. 8 (enero-abril) (Caracas: Editorial Sherwood, 2000), 179–205; and Allan R. Brewer Carías, 'Consideraciones sobre el régimen de distribución de Competencias del Poder Público en la Constitución de 1999', in *Estudios de*

214. According to Article 156, the National Power has exclusive competencies in the following matters: international relations; security and defence; nationality and alien status; national police; economic regulations; mining and oil industries; national policies and regulations on education, health, the environment, land use, transportation, industrial, and agricultural production; post, and telecommunications; and legislation concerning constitutional rights; civil law, commercial law, criminal law, the penal system, procedural law and private international law; electoral law; expropriations for the sake of public or social interests; public credit; intellectual, artistic, and industrial property; cultural and archaeological treasures; agriculture; immigration and colonization; indigenous people and the territories occupied by them; labour and social security and welfare; veterinary and phytosanitary hygiene; notaries and public registers; banks and insurances; lotteries, horse racing, and bets in general; and the organization and functioning of the organs of the central authority and the other organs and institutions of the State. The administration of justice, as mentioned, also falls within the exclusive jurisdiction of the national government (Article 156.31).

Article 156.32 of the Constitution also specifies that the national level of government also has legislative attributions on all matter of 'national competence', which explicitly attributes to the National Assembly power to legislate regarding the following matters: armed forces and civil protection; monetary policies; the coordination and harmonization of the different taxation authorities; the definition of principles, parameters, and restrictions, and in particular the types of tributes or rates of the taxes of the states and municipalities; as well as the creation of special funds that assure the inter-territorial solidarity; foreign commerce and customs; mining and natural energy resources like hydrocarbon, fallow and waste land; and the conservation, development and exploitation of the woods, grounds, waters, and other natural resources of the country; standards of measurement and quality control; the establishment, coordination, and unification of technical norms and procedures for construction, architecture, and urbanism, as well as the legislation on urbanism; public health, housing, food safety, environment, water, tourism, and the territorial organization; navigation and air transport, ground transport, maritime and inland waterway transport; post and telecommunication services and radio frequencies; public utilities such as electricity, potable water, and gas. Furthermore, the Constitution attributes to the national power the powers to conclude, approve and ratify international treaties (Article 154); and legislate on antitrust and the abuse of market power (Articles 113 and 114).

215. Regarding local governments, Article 178 assigns the municipalities power to govern and administrate the matters attributed to them in the Constitution and the national laws with respect to local life, and within them, the ones related to urban

---

Derecho Administrativo: Libro Homenaje a la Universidad Central de Venezuela, vol. I (Caracas: Imprenta Nacional, 2001), 107–138, and 'La distribución territorial de competencias en la Federación venezolana', in *Revista de Estudios de la Administración Local, Homenaje a Sebastián Martín Retortillo,* No. 291, enero-abril 2003 (Madrid: Instituto Nacional de Administración Pública, 2003), 163–200; and 'Consideraciones sobre el régimen constitucional de la organización y funcionamiento de los Poderes Públicos', in *Revista Derecho y Sociedad de la Universidad Monteávila,* No. 2 (abril) (Caracas, 2001), 135–150.

land use, historic monuments, social housing, local tourism, public space for recreation, construction, urban roads and transport, public entertainment, local environmental protection and hygiene, advertising regulations, urban utilities, electricity, water supply, garbage collection and disposal, basic health and education services, municipal police, funerals services, child care and other community matters. Only the matters related to local public events and funerals can be regarded as exclusive powers of the municipalities, and the rest are concurrent with the national government. Nonetheless, these matters can always be regulated by national legislation, as the municipal autonomy is essentially limited (Article 168).

216. Regarding state competencies, the National Constitution fails to enumerate substantive matters within exclusive state jurisdiction, and only assigns as matters corresponding to them, generally in a concurrent way, the municipal organizations, the non-metallic mineral exploitation, the police, the state roads, the administration of national roads, and the commercial airports and ports (Article 164). Nonetheless, for instance, in the Constitution, the possibility for the state legislature to regulate its own local government is also very limited, being subjected to what is established in the national Organic Municipal Law.

According to the Constitution, State Legislative Councils can enact legislation on matters that are in the states' scope of powers (Article 162). However, these powers are referred to as concurrent matters, and according to the National Constitution, their exercise depends on the previous enactment of national statutes and regulations (framework laws) (*see supra* paragraphs 125). As a result, the legislative powers of the states are also very limited, and in any event, the resulting states' legislation on concurrent matters must always adhere to the principles of 'interdependence, coordination, cooperation, co-responsibility and subsidiary' (Article 165).

217. However, regarding residual competencies, the principle of favouring the states as in all federations, although being a constitutional tradition in Venezuela, in the 1999 Constitution has also been limited by expressly assigning the national level of government a parallel and prevalent residual taxation power in matters not expressly attributed to the states or municipalities (Article 156.12). Furthermore, Article 156.33 provides for the jurisdiction of the national power 'in all other matters that correspond to it due to their nature or kind', establishing an implicit powers clause in favour of the federal government[354] that has been strengthened by the Constitutional Chamber jurisprudence.[355] In summary, the general residual power allocated to the states is a rather theoretical one, and in practice, in case of doubt, the presumption in favour of federal powers will virtually always prevail.

354. *See* C. Ayala Corao, 'Naturaleza y Alcance de la Descentralización Estadal', in *Leyes y reglamentos para la Descentralización Política de la Federación* 94, ed. Allan R. Brewer-Carías et al. (Caracas, 1990), referring to the *Exposición de Motivos* of the 1961 Constitution.

355. *See* decision of the Constitutional Chamber of the Supreme Tribunal of 15 Apr. 2008, in *Revista de Derecho Público*, No. 114 (Caracas: Editorial Jurídica Venezolana, 2008), 164.

218. Another aspect that must be mentioned regarding the distribution of competencies between the national and state levels is the provision in the 1999 Constitution, following the same provision of the 1961 Constitution, allowing the possibility of decentralizing competencies via their transfer from the national level to the states.[356] This process was regulated in the 1989 Law on Delimitation, Transfer and Decentralization Competencies between public entities, and even though important efforts for decentralization were made between 1990 and 1994 in order to revert the centralizing tendencies,[357] the process, unfortunately, was later abandoned. Since 2003, the transfers of competencies that were made, including health services, started the reversion process, which was completed in 2008,[358] in particular with the reform of the aforementioned 1989 Decentralization Law, sanctioned by the National Assembly on 17 March 2009, reverting to the national level the 'exclusive' competence of the states for the management and making use of national highways, bridges and commercial ports located in the states, established in Article 164.10 of the Constitution.[359] This reform was also proposed by the President of the Republic in the rejected 2007 Constitutional Reform.

356. *See* José Peña Solís, 'Aproximación al proceso de descentralización delineado en la Constitución de 1999', in *Estudios de Derecho Público: Libro Homenaje a Humberto J. La Roche Rincón*, vol. II (Caracas: Tribunal Supremo de Justicia, 2001), 217–282.
357. *See* Allan R. Brewer-Carías et al., *Leyes y reglamentos para la Descentralización Política de la Federación* (Caraca: Editorial Jurídica Venezolana, 1990); *Informe sobre la descentralización en Venezuela 1993. Informe del Ministro de Estado para la Descentralización* (Caracas, 1994).
358. *See* Decree No. 6.543, on the renationalization of the Health Care services in Miranda State, *Gaceta Oficial* No. 39.072 of 3 Dec. 2008.
359. *Gaceta Oficial* No. 39.140 of 17 Mar. 2009. For the purpose of this reform, the Constitutional Chamber previously issued Decision No. 565 of 15 Apr. 2008 'interpreted' the Constitution changing the character of such 'exclusive' competency into a 'concurrent' one. *See* in www.tsj.gov.ve/decisiones/scon/Abril/565-150408-07-1108.htm. *See* Allan R. Brewer-Carías, 'La Sala Constitucional como poder constituyente: la modificación de la forma federal del estado y del sistema constitucional de división territorial del poder público', in *Revista de Derecho Público*, No. 114 (April–June 2008) (Caracas: Editorial Jurídica Venezolana, 2008), 247–262.

Chapter 3. The Organization of Public Power in the Territory

§1. The States

I. The Limited States Autonomy

219. The territorial distribution of state power within the framework of a federation implies a decentralized structure of political entities that must be essentially autonomous. For this reason, Article 159 of the Constitution establishes that the twenty-three states (*see supra* paragraph 114) are 'politically autonomous and equal' entities with full legal personality. The states are required to uphold the independence, sovereignty and integrity, as well as the Constitution and laws of the Republic, and to ensure that these are obeyed within their territory.

This states' autonomy is, of course, political (in the election of its authorities), organizational (in drafting of their own Constitutions), administrative (in the investment of their revenue), legal (in the non-reviewing of state actions except through the courts of law) and taxing (in the creation of state taxes); aspects that in principle must not be regulated by national legislation, but only in the national Constitution.

220. Nonetheless, as aforementioned, state autonomy is limited in the Constitution corresponding, for instance, to a national statute to establish the organic and functional regime of states' Legislative Councils (Article 162), which should be the exclusive competence of states, and be regulated according to the state drafted Constitutions (Article 164.1).

Similar limitations are established by the 1999 Constitution with respect to the exercise of other states' competencies. For example, in the area of taxation, not only has the Constitution left the matter to future *national* legislation, but it has also definitively established that it is to be the National Power that will coordinate state and municipal taxing authority (Article 156.13).

In regards to concurrent powers between state and national governments, these, according to the Constitution of 1999, are to be exercised by the states only in conformity to 'framework laws' *(leyes de base)* pre-enacted on the national level (Article 165). In some cases, as in the area of police, the functioning of state police may only be exercised in accordance with applicable national legislation (Article 164, Order 6).

II. The States' Executive and Legislative Powers

221. According to Article 160, the government and administration of each state is the responsibility of a Governor who is elected for a term of four years by a majority of the voters. According to the Constitution, the Governor could be re-elected for a consecutive second term, a limit that was eliminated with the constitutional amendment approved by referendum on 14 February 2009 (*see supra* paragraph 37).

Legislative powers are exercised in each state by a Legislative Council constituted by no more than fifteen and no less than seven members who proportionally represent the population of the states as well as municipalities (Article 162).

As mentioned, the Constitution undermines the autonomy of the states by attributing to the National Assembly the power to establish the organization and functions of states' Legislative Councils (Article 162) when this ought to correspond to state constitutions drafted by State Legislative Councils under Article 164. In all events, with respect to competency, State Legislative Councils have been attributed the powers to legislate on matters within state competence, to approve the state budget, and exercise the other powers conferred to the states by the Constitution and the statutes (Article 162).

§2. The Municipalities

I. The Municipal Autonomy

222. According to Article 168 of the Constitution, municipalities are the primary political units in the organization of the nation, having legal personality and autonomy within constitutional and legal limits. Municipal organization is to be, in all events, democratic and possess the characteristics of local government (Article 169).[360]

Municipal autonomy entails the following under Article 168: the election of municipal authorities; the administration and governance of matters falling within municipal jurisdiction; and the creation, collection, and investment of municipal taxes. In addition, except through designated courts of law, municipal actions may not be impugned or otherwise reviewed on the national and state levels.[361] The organizational regime of municipalities and other local entities is to be governed by the legislation enacted according to the principles laid down in the Constitution, by national organic legislation, and by-laws sanctioned by the State Legislative Councils (Article 169).

As aforementioned, Article 168 of the Constitution establishes the principle of participation providing that actions carried out by municipalities within their jurisdiction are to be undertaken while incorporating citizens' participation in the definition, execution, regulation and evaluation of the results of public business, according to law, in an adequate, effective and opportune manner.

223. One of the most important problems of the system of municipal government in Venezuela has been the excessive uniformity in the organization of municipal governments, provoking the almost inapplicability of the Organic Law of

360. *See* Argenis Urdaneta, 'El Poder Público Municipal en el Estado federal descentralizado', in *El Derecho Público a comienzos del siglo XXI. Estudios homenaje al Profesor Allan R. Brewer-Carías,* vol. I (Madrid: Instituto de Derecho Público, UCV, Civitas Ediciones, 2003), 731–744.

361. *See* José L. Villegas Moreno, 'La autonomía local y su configuración en la Constitución venezolana de 1999', in *El Derecho Público a comienzos del siglo XXI. Estudios homenaje al Profesor Allan R. Brewer-Carías,* vol. I (Madrid: Instituto de Derecho Público, UCV, Civitas Ediciones, 2003), 715–729.

Municipal Power[362] particularly in many small municipal entities. To avoid this situation, Article 169 of the Constitution establishes the principle that the legislation passed to develop and apply constitutional principles regarding municipalities and other local entities must create diverse organizational regimes for their administration and government, taking into account such local factors as population, economic development, capacity for generating revenue, geographic situation and other historic and cultural factors that may have relevance to government. In particular, such legislation is to establish options for the organization of local government and administration suitable to municipalities containing indigenous populations. Unfortunately, none of these aspects has been regulated in the Organic Law.

224. However, it must be pointed out that municipalities, according to Article 168 of the Constitution, are the 'primary political unit of the national organization', and the basis for political participation. Nonetheless, this has been virtually rendered moot by the creation, since 2006, of the parallel structure of the Communal Councils,[363] which are designated by local 'assemblies of the Citizens' (Article 70), which can be formed by interested citizens. These Assemblies, since 2010, have been organized as one of the main organizations of the 'Communal State' for the exercise of the 'Popular Power' that has been established by passing the Constitution[364] (*see infra* paragraphs 263, 267 et seq.) having jurisdiction to 'approve the rules of the communal living of the community' (Article 6.1). The 'Community' is defined as 'the social conglomerate of families and citizens which live in a specific geographic area, which share a common history and interests, which know each other and have relations with each other, use the same public utilities and share similar economic, social, urban and other necessities and potentials' (Article 4.1). Although these structures are supposed to allow self-governance of local communities, this is contradicted due to the high degree of centralization set forth by their organization being directly coordinated, supervised and financed by the National Executive through a Ministry of the Communes and Citizens Participation, without the participation of the states or the municipalities. In addition, the Communal Councils have been created outside the municipal organization of the country.

---

362. *Gaceta Oficial* No. 6.015 Extra. 28 Dec. 2010. On the previous 2006 Law (*Gaceta Oficial* No. 38.421 of 21 Apr. 2006), *see* Allan R. Brewer-Carías et al., *Ley Orgánica del Poder Público Municipal* (Caracas: Editorial Jurídica venezolana, 2006).

363. *Gaceta Oficial* No. 5.806 Extra. of 10 Apr. 2006. *See* Allan R. Brewer-Carías, 'El inicio de la desmunicipalización en Venezuela: La organización del Poder Popular para eliminar la descentralización, la democracia representativa y la participación a nivel local', in *Revista de la Asociación Internacional de Derecho Administrativo* (Mexico, 2007), 49–67.

364. Organic Law on the Communal Councils in *Gaceta Oficial* No. 39.335 of 28 Dec. 2009. *See* Allan R. Brewer-Carías et al., *Ley Orgánica de los Consejos Comunales* (Caracas:Editorial Jurídica venezolana, 2010). *See* also Organic Law on the Popular Power, in *Oficial* No. 6.011 Extra. of 21 Dec. 2010. *See* Allan R. Brewer-Carías et al., *Leyes Orgánicas sobre el Poder Popular y el Estado Comunal* (Caracas: Editorial Jurídica Venezolana, 2011).

II. The Municipal Executive and Legislative Powers

225. Municipal government and administration correspond to the Mayors, who, according to the terms of the Civil Code (Articles 446 et seq.), are the primary civil authority (Article 174). The Mayors are elected for a term of four years, by a majority of those who vote in an election, and the Constitution established that they could be re-elected for a single second consecutive term, a limit that was eliminated with the constitutional amendment approved by referendum on 14 February 2009 (*see supra* paragraphs 64, 172).

Article 175 of the Constitution confers the legislative functions of municipalities to the Municipal Councils composed of members elected by universal, secret and direct suffrage in a number, and according to conditions, established in the national legislation based on the system of proportional representation and personalized vote (*see supra* paragraph 168). These Municipal Councils are empowered to enact Municipal Ordinances that are 'local laws' related to the matters assigned to the municipalities.

§3. The Capital District and the Metropolitan Municipal Government of Caracas

226. According to Article 16 of the Constitution, in addition to the twenty-three states, the national territory has also a Capital District and Federal Dependencies that are the Venezuelan Islands in the Caribbean Sea. Since 1992 there have been no Federal Territories.

The Capital District was established in the 1999 Constitution in substitution of the Federal District that existed since 1863 with a very dependent configuration regarding the President of the Republic, who used to be the highest authority in the District. He exercised his powers through an appointed Governor (Article 190.17, 1961 Constitution). With the 1999 Constitution, the Capital District was conceived as an additional political entity in the territory, independent from the National Executive that needed to have a democratic government of its own. Nonetheless, and in spite of such new democratic configuration, the National Assembly passed on April 2009 a Special Law on the Organization and regime of the Capital District,[365] establishing just an administrative entity dependent upon the national level of government, so the Chief Executive of the Capital District is freely appointed and dismissed by the President of the Republic, and the legislative functions in the District correspond to the National Assembly (Article 7). In the rejected 2007 Constitutional Reform, the President of the Republic proposed this same configuration of the Capital District with the patterns of the former Federal District established in 1863.

227. The municipal government in the territory of the Capital District, where part of the City of Caracas as the Capital of the Republic is located, was organized

365. *Gaceta Oficial* No. 39.156 of 13 Apr. 2009. *See* Allan R. Brewer-Carías et al., *Leyes sobre el Distrito Capital y el Área Metropolitána de Caracas* (Caracas: Editorial Jurídica Venezolana, 2009).

in the Constitution with two levels of local government organization: at the metropolitan level, the Metropolitan Government of Caracas (Article 18), with a Head Mayor (*Alcalde Mayor*) and a Metropolitan Council, both elected by popular vote; and at the municipal level, with their corresponding Mayors and Municipal Councils in the various municipalities of the city (*Libertador, Baruta, Chacao, Sucre, El Hatillo*) elected by the people. This metropolitan organization was established according to the Special Law on the Metropolitan District Regime sanctioned by the National Constituent Assembly in March 2000.[366]

228. All this constitutional organization of the Metropolitan Government in Caracas was eliminated in an unconstitutional way, by means of a 'constituent decree' enacted by the fraudulent and unconstitutionally elected National Constituent Assembly of 2017 (*see supra* paragraphs 39–43).[367] According to such 'decree', the Mayor of Caracas, in a contrary way to what is provided in the Constitution, is appointed by the President of the Republic, going back the regime to the one existing until 1999 when the Federal District was the territorial organization of the Capital of the Republic, and the President appointed its Governor.

366. *Gaceta Oficial* No. 36.906 of 8 Mar. 2000. *See* Manuel Rachadell, '¿Distrito Capital o Distrito Metropolitano?', in *El Derecho Público a comienzos del siglo XXI. Estudios en homenaje al Profesor Allan R. Brewer-Carías,* vol. III (Madrid: Instituto de Derecho Público, UCV, Civitas Ediciones, 2003), 3271 a 3311; Alfredo De Stefano Pérez, 'Aproximación al estudio del Distrito Metropolitano de Caracas', in *Temas de Derecho Administrativo: Libro Homenaje a Gonzalo Pérez Luciani,* vol. II (Caracas:Editorial Torino, 2002), 553–592; Allan R. Brewer-Carías, 'Consideraciones sobre el régimen constitucional del Distrito Capital y del sistema de gobierno municipal de Caracas', in *Revista de Derecho Público*, No. 82 (abril-junio) (Caracas: Editorial Jurídica Venezolana, 2000), 5–17; and in *Revista Iberoamericana de Administración Pública (RIAP),* Ministerio de Administraciones Públicas, No. 5, julio-diciembre 2000 (Madrid: 2000), 17–39.

367. *See* 'Decreto Constituyente mediante el cual se suprime y ordena la liquidación de la Alcaldía Metropolitana, el Cabildo Metropolitano y la Contraloría Metropolitana, todas éstas del Área Metropolitana de Caracas y del Distrito del Alto Apure, sus órganos y entes adscritos, a partir de la publicación del presente Decreto Constituyente en la Gaceta Oficial de la República Bolivariana de Venezuela.' *Gaceta Oficial* No. 41.308 of 27 Dec. 2017.

Chapter 4. The Financing System of the Federation

229. Regarding the financing of the federation, virtually everything in the 1999 Constitution concerning the taxation system is more centralized than in the previous 1961 Constitution, and the powers of the states in tax matters are essentially eliminated.

The National Constitution lists the national government competencies with respect to basic taxes, including income tax, inheritance and donation taxes; taxes on capital and production; value-added tax (VAT); taxes on hydrocarbon resources and mines; taxes on the import and export of goods and services; taxes on the consumption of liquor, alcohol, cigarettes and tobacco (Article 156.12). The National Constitution also expressly allocates local taxation powers to the municipalities including property, commercial and industrial activities taxes (Article 179). The National Constitution gives the national government residual competencies in tax matters (Article 156.12).

In contrast, the Constitution does not grant the states competencies in matters of taxation, except with respect to official stationery and revenue stamps (Article 164.7). Thus, the states can only collect taxes when the National Assembly expressly transfers the power to them by a statute, which contains specific taxation powers (Article 167.5). No such statute has yet been approved (*see infra* paragraph 640).

230. Lacking their own resources from taxation, state financing is accomplished by the transfer of national financial resources through three different channels, which are all politically controlled by the national government. The first channel is by means of the 'Constitutional Contribution' (*Situado Constitucional*) which is an annual amount established in the National Budget Law (*see infra* paragraph 646) equivalent to a minimum of 15% and a maximum of 20% of total ordinary national income, estimated annually (Article 167.4), which must be distributed among the states according to their population. The second channel is through a nationally established system of special economic allotments for the benefit of those states in the territories in which mining and hydrocarbon projects are being developed. The benefits that accompany this statute have also been extended to include other non-mining states (Article 156.16).[368] The third channel of financing for states and municipalities also comes from national funds. The most important source was the Intergovernmental Fund for Decentralization, created by statute in 1993[369] as a consequence of the national regulation of VAT, which was to be substituted by an Interstate Compensation Fund established in the National Constitution (Article 167.6),

368. *See* Law on Special Economic Allotments derived from Mines and Hydrocarbons to the States and the Metropolitan District of Caracas, *Gaceta Oficial* No. 37086 of 27 Nov. 2000; substituted by the Law on Special Economic Allotments derived from Mines and Hydrocarbons, *Gaceta Oficial* No. 5991 Extra. of 29 Jul. 2010. *See* Adriana Vigilanza García, *La Federación descentralizada. Mitos y realidades en el reparto de tributos y otros ingresos entre los entes políticos territoriales de Venezuela* (Caracas, 2010).

369. *See* in *Gaceta Oficial* No. 5.805 Extra. of 22 Mar. 2006.

and that was created in 2010, in the Law establishing the Federal Council of Government.[370] This Council was conceived in the 1999 Constitution as an intergovernmental entity for the purpose of planning and coordinating the policies and actions for the development of the decentralization process and transfer of powers from the central government to the component states and municipalities. It is headed by the Vice President of the Republic and integrated by Ministers, Governors of the component states and one Mayor from each component state, as well as representatives of the civil society (Article 185). Nonetheless, in the 2010 Law, such entity has only been organized as an instrument controlled by the Central Government, designed to reinforce the centralization process through a central planning system.

However, following a long tradition, the states and municipalities cannot borrow nor have public debt due to the requirement of a special national statute to approve state borrowing.

231. As it can be deduced from what has been said, the declaration of Article 4 of the 1999 Constitution regarding the 'Federal Decentralized' form of the Venezuelan government is mere wording, being a formula that is contradicted by all the other regulations regarding the federalism contained in the Constitution, which, on the contrary, shows that the Federation in Venezuela is a very Centralized Federation. This situation, of course, affects the democratic regime and governance deeply.

Federalism and decentralization in the contemporary world are matters of democracy. There are no decentralized autocracies, and there have never been decentralized authoritarian governments, only democracies can be decentralized. Autocracies and authoritarian governments have been, and will remain, centralized. Thus, the reality of the political situation in Venezuela is that democracy is very weak. Although democracy is based on elections, it cannot be consolidated without a real separation of powers, and without the real possibility of political participation due to the lack of decentralization.

370. *See* in *Gaceta Oficial* No. 5.963 Extra. of 22 Feb. 2010. *See* Manuel Rachadell, 'El Consejo Federal de Gobierno y el Fondo de Compensación', in *Revista de Derecho del Tribunal Supremo de Justicia,* No. 7 (Caracas, 2002), 417 a 457; Emilio Spósito Contreras, 'Reflexiones sobre el Consejo Federal de Gobierno como máxima instancia de Participación administrativa', in *Temas de derecho administrativo, Libro Homenaje a Gonzalo Pérez Luciani,* vol. II, Tribunal Supremo de Justicia, Colección Libros Homenaje, No. 7 (Caracas, 2002), 827 a 863; José V. Haro, 'Aproximación a la noción del Consejo Federal de Gobierno previsto en la Constitución de 1999', in *Revista de Derecho Constitucional,* No. 7 (enero-junio) (Caracas: Editorial Sherwood, 2003), 161–166.

Chapter 5. The Parallel Organization of the 'Communal State', Affecting the Federal Distribution of State Powers

232. After the 2007 Constitutional Reform was rejected by the people that same year, the Government that had made approved by the National Assembly the previous year in 2006 a Law of the Communal Councils,[371] proceeded to make it approved by the same National Assembly on 21 December 2010 a group of Organic Laws for the implementation, in contempt of the will of the people, of one of the key proposals of the rejected constitutional reform of 2007 which was the creation of the 'Communal State' or 'State of Popular Power'. Those Organic laws were the laws on the Popular Power; of the Communes; the Communal Economic System; the Public and Communal Planning; and the Social Comptrollership.[372] Furthermore, in the same framework of organizing the Communal State, based on the Popular Power, the reform of the Organic Law of Municipal Public Power and the Public Policy Planning and Coordination of the State Councils,[373] and the Local Council Public Planning Laws stand out. The National Assembly also passed an enabling Law authorizing the President, through delegated legislation, to enact laws on all imaginable subjects, including laws of organic nature, emptying the new National Assembly of matters on which to legislate for a period of eighteen months until 2012.

233. The general defining framework of the Socialist State imposed on Venezuelans through such unconstitutional legislation, and for which nobody had voted, was supposedly based on the exercise of the sovereignty of the people but exclusively in a 'direct' manner through the exercise of the Popular Power and the establishment of a Communal State, in parallel to the Federal State.[374] This is contained in the Organic Law for Popular Power, which is to be applied to everyone and everything as an essential part of the new 'socialist principle of legality' in the creation, implementation and control of public management.

234. The main purpose of these laws was the organization of the 'Communal State' which has the commune as its fundamental unit, seeking to unconstitutionally supplant the municipalities as the 'primary political units of the national organization' (Article 168 of the Constitution), through whose organization the Popular Power is exercised, and which is manifested in the exercise of popular sovereignty although not through representatives. It is therefore a political system in which representative democracy is ignored, openly violating the Constitution.

The Socialist State or Communal State sought to be established through these laws, in parallel to the Constitutional Federal State, is supposedly based on Article

371. Communal Councils Law, *Gaceta Oficial,* Extra. 5.806, of 10 Apr. 2006. This statute was replaced by Organic Law on the Communal Councils. *See Gaceta Oficial* No. 39.335 of 28 Dec. 2009.

372. *See* the text of all these Laws in *Gaceta Oficial* No. 6.011 Extra. 21 Dec. 2010. *See* on all these organic laws, Allan R. Brewer-Carías et al., *Leyes Orgánicas sobre el Poder Popular y el Estado Comunal* (Caracas: Editorial Jurídica Venezolana, 2011), 361 et seq.

373. *See Gaceta Oficial* No. 6.015 Extra. of 28 Dec. 2010.

374. *See* Rafael Badell Madrid, *Del Estado Federal al Estado Comunal*, (Caracas, Academia de Ciencias Políticas y Sociales, 2021).

5 of the Constitution, that provides that 'Sovereignty resides untransferably in the people, who exercise it directly as provided in this Constitution and the Law, and indirectly, by suffrage, through the organs exercising Public Power', but by-passing the basic rule of the Constitutional State structure grounded on the concept of representative democracy, that is, the exercise of sovereignty indirectly through the vote. The Communal State is now structured based only on the supposedly direct exercise of sovereignty[375] through the Communes, 'with an economic model of social property and endogenous sustainable development that allows reaching the supreme social happiness of the Venezuelan people in a socialist society' (Article 8.8),[376] called the 'Communal Economic System' (*see infra* paragraph 664).

235. What is being sought is to establish a Socialist or Communal State alongside the Federal Constitutional State: the first one based on the direct exercise of sovereignty by the people; and the second, also based on the indirect exercise of sovereignty by the people through elected representatives by universal suffrage; in a system in which the former will gradually strangle and empty competencies from the second. All of this is unconstitutional, particularly because in the structure of the Communal State that is established, in the end, the exercise of sovereignty is factually indirect, through supposed 'representatives' that are not popularly elected through universal and direct suffrage, but 'elected' in Citizens' Assemblies. They are the ones called to exercise Popular Power in the name of the people, with the name of 'spokespersons', but that, as already mentioned, are not elected by the people through universal, secret and direct suffrage.

This system that is being structured, directly controlled by a Ministry from the National Executive Branch of Government, far from being an instrument of participation and decentralization – a concept that is indissolubly linked to political autonomy – is a centralized and tightly controlled system of the communities by the central power, in which the members of the communal councils, the communes and all organizations of the Popular Power are not elected but 'appointed' through a show of hands by assemblies controlled by the official party and the executive branch.

236. This Communal State system, parallel to the Federal Constitutional State, is structured on a unique concept which is socialism so that anyone who is not a socialist is automatically discriminated. It is not possible, therefore, under the

---

375. This has even been 'legitimized' by the Supreme Tribunal Constitutional Chamber's decisions analysing the organic character of the laws, such as the one issued in connection with the Organic Law of Municipalities. *See* Decision No. 1.330, Case: Organic Character of the Law of the Communes 12/17/2010, in www.tsj.gov.ve/decisiones/scon/Diciembre/1330-171210-2010-10-1436.html.

376. The Organic Law of Municipalities, however, defines the Communal State as follows:

> Form of sociopolitical organization, based on the democratic and social state of law and justice established *in* the Constitution of the Republic, whose power is exercised directly by the people through communal self governments, with an economic model of social property and endogenous and sustainable development that achieves the supreme social happiness of the Venezuelan people in a socialist society. Forming the basic unit of the Communal State is the commune' (Art. 4.10).

framework of these laws to reconcile pluralism and the principle of non-discrimination on the grounds of 'political opinion' guaranteed by the Constitution, with the provisions of these Laws pursuing the opposite, that is, the establishment of a Communal State whose bodies can only act on the basis of socialism and in which any citizen who has another opinion is excluded. That is, through these Organic Laws, the defining framework of a new model of a State parallel and different from the Constitutional State has been established called the Communal State based exclusively on Socialism as the political doctrine and practice.

In this regard, Article 5 of the Organic Law on the Popular Power states, in addition, that 'people's organization and participation in exercising its sovereignty is based on Simon Bolivar the Liberator's doctrine, and is based on socialist principles and values',[377] – a link that, as aforementioned, is untenable – matching the organization of the Communal State (established in parallel to the Constitutional State) with the socialist political ideology.

Article 7 of the same Organic Law on the Popular Power defines the purpose of the Popular Power, to strengthen 'the organization of the people in order to consolidate the revolutionary democracy and build the bases of a socialist society, democratic, of law and justice', and to 'establish the bases that allow organized communities to exercise social comptrollership to ensure that the investment of public resources is efficiently performed for the collective benefit; and monitor that the activities of the private sector with social impact develop within legal rules that protect users and consumers'. This, of course, is a well-known procedure established in other authoritarian regimes in order to construct a general system of social espionage to be developed among people in order to institutionalize the denunciation and persecution of any deviation regarding the socialist framework imposed on the citizenship.[378]

According to the Law of the Communes,[379] these communes are conceived as a 'local entity' or 'socialist space' of the Communal State, where citizens exercise the 'Popular Power' (Article 1). Nonetheless, according to the Constitution, this expression of 'local entity' can only be applied to local political entities of the Constitutional State with self-governments composed of elected representatives by universal, direct and secret ballot (Article 169), so there can be no 'local entities' directed by persons that are not elected by the people but appointed by other bodies. On the contrary, the origin of the so-called governments of the communes, this legislation on Popular Power and its organizations, according to its text, is not guaranteed through democratic representative election by universal, direct and secret suffrage, thus being an unconstitutional conception.

---

377. The same expression was used in the Organic Law of the Communes with respect to their constitution, shaping and functioning (Art. 2), in the Communal Council's Law (Art. 1) and in the Organic Law of Social Comptrollership (Art. 6).

378. *See* Luis A. Herrera Orellana, 'La Ley Orgánica de Contraloría Social: Funcionalización de la participación e instauración de la desconfianza ciudadana', in Allan R. Brewer-Carías et al., *Leyes Orgánicas sobre el Poder Popular y el Estado Comunal* (Caracas: Editorial Jurídica Venezolana, 2011), 361 et seq.

379. *See Gaceta Oficial* No. 6.011 Extra. Of 21 Dec. 2010.

237. This Communal State, regulated on the fringes of the Constitution,[380] as mentioned, has been established as a 'Parallel State' to the Constitutional Federal State, but with provisions that, if implemented, will enable the Communal State to drown the Constitutional State, for which purpose the Law has provided that all organs of the Constitutional State that exercise Public Power is subjected to the mandates of the organizations of Popular Power, establishing a new principle of government, so-called in the Law, the principle of 'govern obeying', no other than obeying the wishes of the central government.[381]

As the Popular Power organizations have no political autonomy, since their 'spokespersons' are not democratically elected by universal, direct and secret ballot, but appointed by citizen Assemblies politically controlled and operated by the governing party and the National Executive who controls and guides all the organizational process of the Communal State in the sphere of socialist ideology, there is no way there can be a spokesperson who is not a socialist.

Consequently, this 'govern obeying' principle is a limitation to the political autonomy of the elected bodies of the Constitutional State such as the National Assembly, Governors and Legislative Councils of states and Mayors and Municipal Councils, upon whom ultimately is imposed an obligation to obey any provision made by the National Government and the ruling party, framed exclusively in the socialist sphere as a political doctrine.

Therefore, in the unconstitutional framework of these Popular Power Laws, the popular will expressed in the election of representatives of the Federal Constitutional State bodies has no value whatsoever, and the people have been confiscated of their sovereignty by transferring it to assemblies that do not represent them.

238. With this Organic Law of Popular Power framework, there is no doubt about the political decision taken on 21 December 2010 by the completely delegitimized National Assembly that was elected in 2005, and that no longer represented the majority of the popular will as it was expressed in the 26 September 2010 legislative election, against the President of the Republic, the National Assembly itself and socialist policies they have developed. These policies were aimed at imposing on Venezuelans, against popular will and defrauding the Constitution, a Socialist State model, called 'the Communal State' and conceived as a Socialist State, in order to supposedly exercise Popular Power directly by the people, as an alleged form of direct exercise of sovereignty, which is not true because it is exercised through 'spokespersons' who supposedly 'represent' them but without being elected in universal, direct and secret suffrage.

---

380. *See* Allan R. Brewer-Carías, 'The Process of "Deconstitutionalization" of the Venezuelan Constitutional State, as the Most Important Current Constitutional Issue in Venezuela', *Duquesne Law Review*, Volume 51, Number 2, Spring 2013, (Pittsburgh, Duquesne University, 2013), pp. 349–386.

381. Article 24 of the Law establishes the following principle: 'Proceedings of the bodies and entities of Public Power. All organs, entities and agencies of Public Power will govern their actions by the principle of "govern obeying", in relation to the mandates of the people and organizations of Popular Power, according to the provisions in the Constitution of the Republic and the laws.'

By regulating this Communal State of the Popular Power through ordinary legislation, in addition to defrauding the Constitution, a technique that has been consistently applied by the authoritarian regime in Venezuela since 1999 to impose its decisions outside of the Venezuelan Constitution,[382] it now adds fraud to the popular will by imposing on Venezuelans through organic laws a State model for which nobody has voted.

The new State framework radically and unconstitutionally changes the text of the 1999 Constitution, which has not been reformed as the regime had wished in 2007, and is in open contradiction to the popular rejection that the majority expressed in the attempt the regime developed to reform the Constitution in the referendum of 2 December 2007, even in violation of the Constitution, and the popular rejection that the majority of the people expressed regarding the socialist policies of the President to the Republic and his National Assembly on the occasion of the parliamentary elections of 26 September 2010.

What is clear about all this is that there are no masks to deceive anyone, or by reason of which someone pretends to be deceived or fooled about what essentially the 'Bolivarian revolution' is; nothing else but a communist Marxist revolution, carried out deliberately by misusing and defrauding constitutional institutions.

---

382. *See* Allan R. Brewer-Carías, *Reforma constitucional y fraude a la Constitución (1999–2009)* (Caracas: Academia de Ciencias Políticas y Sociales, 2009); *Dismantling Democracy. The Chávez Authoritarian Experiment* (New York: Cambridge University Press, 2010); *Estado totalitario y desprecio a la ley. La desconstitucionalización, desjuridificación, desjudicialización y desdemocratización de Venezuela,* Fundación de Derecho Público, Editorial Jurídica Venezolana, 2014, p. 532; segunda edición, (Con prólogo de José Ignacio Hernández), Caracas 2015.

Part IV. The Constitutional System of Separation of Powers

Chapter 1. The Principle of Separation of Powers

§1. The Venezuelan Constitutional Tradition

239. The principle of separation of powers, following the provisions of the Constitution of Virginia of 1776 (section 3.1), and of the French Declaration of Rights of Man and Citizens of 1789 (Article 16), was incorporated in the first modern Constitution adopted in all Latin America, which as aforementioned, was the 1811 Federal Constitution of the States of Venezuela, setting forth in its Preamble that:

> The exercise of authority conferred upon the Confederation could never be reunited in its respective functions. The Supreme Power must be divided in the Legislative, the Executive and the Judicial, and conferred to different bodies independent between them and regarding their respective powers.

To this proposition, Article 189 of the Constitution added that:

> The three essential Departments of government, that is, the legislative, the Executive and the Judicial, must always be kept separated and independent one from the other according to the nature of a free government, which is convenient in the connection chain that unites all the fabric of the Constitution in an indissoluble way of Friendship and Union.

Consequently, since the beginning of modern constitutionalism, the principle of separation of constitutional power was also adopted in Venezuela, in particular, according to the trends of the presidential system of government within a check and balance conception, granting the Judiciary specific powers of judicial review. The latter, according to the objective guarantee of the Constitution established in Article 227 of the same 1811 Constitution, in the sense that 'The laws sanctioned against the Constitution will have no value except when fulfilling the conditions for a just and legitimate revision and sanction [of the Constitution]'; and in Article 199, in the sense that any law sanctioned by the federal legislature or by the provinces contrary to the fundamental rights enumerated in the Constitution 'will be absolutely null and void'.

240. Since 1811, all the Constitutions in Venezuelan history have established and guaranteed the principle of separation of powers, particularly between the three classical Legislative, Executive and Judicial Branches of Government (powers) in a system of checks and balances, and always giving the Judiciary, judicial review power. For such purpose, the independence and autonomy of the branches of government have been the most important aspects regulated in the Constitutions, particularly during democratic regimes, due to the fact that the principle of separation of powers in contemporary constitutionalism has become one of the basic conditions for its existence, and for the possibility of guaranteeing the enjoyment and protection of fundamental rights. On the contrary, without separation of powers, and without autonomy and independence between the branches of government, no democratic regime can be developed, and no guarantee of fundamental rights can exist.

§2. Separation of Powers and Democracy

241. In effect, the essential components of democracy are much more than the sole popular or circumstantial election of government officials, as since 2001, been formally recognized in the Inter-American Democratic Charter *(Carta Democratica Interamericana)* adopted by the OAS,[383] after so many anti-democratic, militarist and authoritarian regimes disguised as democratic because of their electoral origin that Latin American countries have suffered.

The Charter, in effect, enumerates among the *essential elements of the representative democracy,* in addition to having periodic, fair and free elections based on the universal and secret vote as an expression of the will of the people, the following: respect for human rights and fundamental liberties; access to power and its exercise with subjection to the rule of law; plural regime of the political parties and organizations; and what is the most important of all, '*separation and independence of public powers*' (Article 3), that is, the possibility of controlling the different branches of government. The *Inter-American Charter*, in addition, also defined the following *fundamental components of the democracy*: transparency of governmental activities; integrity; responsibility of governments in the public management; respect of social rights and freedom of speech and press; constitutional subordination of all institutions of the State to the legally constituted civil authority; and respect to the rule of law of all the entities and sectors of society.

The principle of separation and independence of powers is so important, as one of the 'essential elements of democracy', that it is the one that can allow all the other 'fundamental components of democracy' to be politically possible. To be precise, democracy, as a political regime, can only function in a constitutional rule of

383. *See* on the Inter-American Democratic Charter, in Allan R. Brewer-Carías, *La crisis de la democracia venezolana. La Carta Democrática Interamericana y los sucesos de abril de 2002* (Caracas: Ediciones El Nacional, 2002), 137 et seq.; Asdrúbal Aguiar, *El Derecho a la Democracia* (Caracas: Editorial Jurídica Venezolana, 2008); Allan R. Brewer-Carías, *Sobre la democracia* (New York/ Caracas. Editorial Jurídica Venezolana, 2919).

law system where the control of power exists; that is, check and balance based on the separation of powers with their independence and autonomy guaranteed, so that power can be stopped by power itself.

242. Consequently, without separation of powers and the possibility of control of power, any of the other essential factors of democracy cannot be guaranteed because only by controlling Power, can free and fair elections and political pluralism exist; only by controlling Power, can effective democratic participation be possible, and effective transparency in the exercise of government be assured; only by controlling Power can there be a government submitted to the Constitution and the laws, that is, the rule of law; only by controlling Power can there be an effective access to justice functioning with autonomy and independence; and only by controlling Power can there be a true and effective guarantee for the respect of human rights.[384]

243. The constitutional situation in Venezuela since the constitution-making process that took place in 1999, which resulted in the complete take-over of all powers of the State and the sanctioning of the current 1999 Constitution, in spite of its provisions, unfortunately has been of a very weak democracy, precisely because of the progressive demolishing of the principle of separation of powers.[385] In it, a process of concentration of powers has taken place, first with the 1999 constitution-making process itself, which intervened in all branches of government before sanctioning the new constitution (*see supra* paragraph 25), and after, due to some provisions of the 1999 Constitution, which weakened the effective independence and autonomy of the branches of government.

---

384. *See* Allan R. Brewer-Carías, 'Democracia: sus elementos y componentes esenciales y el control del poder', in *Grandes temas para un observatorio electoral ciudadano, vol. I, Democracia: retos y fundamentos*, ed. Nuria González Martín (Compiladora) (México: Instituto Electoral del Distrito Federal, 2007), 171–220.

385. *See* Allan R. Brewer-Carías, 'El principio de la separación de poderes como elemento esencial de la democracia y de la libertad, y su demolición en Venezuela mediante la sujeción política del Tribunal Supremo de Justicia', *Revista Iberoamericana de Derecho Administrativo, Homenaje a Luciano Parejo Alfonso,* 12 (San Jos', Costa Rica, Asociación e Instituto Iberoamericano de Derecho Administrativo Prof. Jesús González Pérez, 2012), 31–43.

Chapter 2. Concentration of Powers and Authoritarianism in Defraudation of the Constitution

244. The result has been that in 2023, Venezuela still has an authoritarian government which is not the result of a classical Latin American military *coup d'état*, but of a systematic process of destruction and dismantling of all the basic principles of democracy and of the Constitution.[386] This process, as aforementioned, began with the 1998 election of Hugo Chávez Frías as President of the Republic, a position he held until his death in 2012, having been the President with the longest continued tenure in all the Venezuelan constitutional history. He was succeeded in a very unconstitutional way by the then Executive Vice President Nicolas Maduro, who immediately was elected to the Presidency of the Republic in 2013,[387] and re-elected in 2018 in an election that was declared inexistent, and null and void, by the National Assembly.[388]

245. The 1999 Constitution, if it is read in a vacuum, ignoring the political reality of the country, can mislead any elector. As aforementioned, it is the only Constitution in the contemporary world that has established, not only a tripartite separation of powers between the traditional Legislative, Executive and Judicial Branches of Government, but a *penta* separation of powers, adding to the latter two more branches of government: the Electoral Power, attributed to the National Electoral Council, in charge of the organization and conduct of the elections; and the Citizen Power, attributed to three different State entities: the General Prosecutor Office (Public Prosecutor) (*Fiscalía General de la República*), the General Comptroller Office (*Contraloría General de la República*), and the Peoples' Defender (*Defensor del Pueblo*) (Article 136) (*see infra* paragraphs 438 et seq.).[389] This

---

386. *See* Allan R. Brewer-Carías, *Dismantling Democracy. The Chávez Authoritarian Experiment* (New York: Cambridge University Press, 2010); *Authoritarian Government v. The Rule of Law. Lectures and Essays (1999-2014) on the Venezuelan Authoritarian Regime Established in Contempt of the Constitution*, (Caracas, Editorial Jurídica Venezolana, 2014); *La ruina de la democracia. Algunas consecuencias.* Venezuela 2015, (Caracas, Editorial Jurídica Venezolana, 2015); *The Collapse of the Rule of Law and the Struggle for Democracy in Venezuela. Lectures and Essays (2015–2020)*, (Miami, Miami Dade College, 2020).

387. *See* Asdrúbal Aguiar (Compilador), *El Golpe de Enero en Venezuela (Documentos y testimonios para la historia)*, (Caracas, Editorial Jurídica Venezolana, 2013); Allan R. Brewer-Carías, 'El juez constitucional y la demolición del principio democrático de gobierno. O de cómo la Jurisdicción Constitucional en Venezuela impuso arbitrariamente a los ciudadanos, al inicio del período constitucional 2013-2019, un gobierno sin legitimidad democrática, sin siquiera ejercer actividad probatoria alguna, violentando abiertamente la Constitución', in *Revista de Derecho Público,* No. 133 (Caracas, Editorial Jurídica Venezolana, 2013), pp. 179–212.

388. *See* Allan R. Brewer-Carías, 'Reflexiones sobre la dictadura en Venezuela, después de la fraudulenta "reelección" presidencial de mayo de 2018', in *Revista de Derecho Público*, Nos 153–154, (Caracas, Editorial Jurídica Venezolana, 2018), pp. 177–216

389. *See* Cecilia Sosa Gómez, 'La organización política del Estado venezolano: El Poder Público Nacional', in *Revista de Derecho Público,* No. 82 (abril-junio) (Caracas: Editorial Jurídica Venezolana, 2000), 71–83; C. Kiriadis Iongui, 'Notas sobre la estructura orgánica del Estado venezolano en la Constitución de 1999', in *Temas de Derecho Administrativo: Libro Homenaje a Gonzalo Pérez Luciani,* vol. I (Caracas: Editorial Torino, 2002), 1031–1082.

penta separation of powers, in any case, was the culmination of a previous constitutional process and tendency initiated in the 1961 Constitution that consolidated the existence of State organs with constitutional rank not dependent on the classical powers, as was, for instance, the case of the Public Prosecutor Office, the Council of the Judiciary, and the Comptroller General Office.

But as mentioned, in spite of this *penta* division of powers, the fact is that the autonomy and independence of the branches of government are not completely and consistently assured in the Constitution, its application leading, on the contrary, to a concentration of State powers in the National Assembly, and through it, in the Executive Power.

§1. The Constitutional Supremacy of the National Assembly

246. In effect, in any system of separation of powers, even with five separate branches of government (Legislative, Executive, Judicial, Citizen and Electoral), in order for such separation to become effective, the independence and autonomy among them have to be assured in order to allow check and balance, that is, the limitation and control of power by power itself. This was the aspect that was not designed as such in the 1999 Constitution, and notwithstanding the aforementioned *penta* separation of powers, an absurd distortion of the principle was introduced by giving the National Assembly the authority not only to elect but to dismiss the Magistrates of the Supreme Tribunal of Justice, the Prosecutor General, the General Comptroller, the People's Defender and the Members of the National Electoral Council (Articles 265, 279 and 296); and in some cases, even by simple majority of votes. This latter solution was even proposed to be formally introduced in the rejected 2007 Constitutional reform proposals, seeking to eliminate the guarantee of the qualified majority of the members for the approval of the National Assembly for such dismissals.

247. It is simply impossible to understand how the autonomy and independence of separate powers can function and how they can exercise mutual control when the tenure of the Head Officials of the Branches of Government (except the President of the Republic) depends on the political will of one of the branches of government, that is, the National Assembly. The sole fact of the possibility for the National Assembly to dismiss the head of the other branches makes futile the formal consecration of the autonomy and independence of powers since the High officials of the State are aware that they can be removed from office at any time precisely if they effectively act with independence.[390]

---

390. *See* 'Democracia y control del poder', in Allan R. Brewer-Carías, *Constitución, democracia y control de poder* (Mérida: Centro Iberoamericano de Estudios Provinciales y Locales. Universidad de Los Andes, 2004); and 'Los problemas del control del poder y el autoritarismo en Venezuela', in *El control del poder. Homenaje a Diego Valadés,* Instituto de Investigaciones Jurídicas, ed. Peter Häberle and Diego García Belaúnde (Coords.), vol. I (México: Universidad Nacional Autónoma de México, 2011), 159–188.

Unfortunately, this has happened in Venezuela during the past two decades, so when there have been minimal signs of autonomy from some holders of State institutions who have dared to adopt their own decisions distancing themselves from the Executive will, they have been dismissed, and when the National Assembly passed to be controlled by the opposition after 2016 it was completely crushed through decisions of the Constitutional Chamber of the Supreme Tribunal.[391] Regarding the former, it occurred, for instance, in 2001 with the People's Defender and with the Prosecutor General of the Republic, originally appointed in 1999 by the Constituent National Assembly, who were separated from their positions[392] for failing to follow the dictates of the Executive Power; and this also happened with some Judges of the Supreme Tribunal who dared to vote on decisions that could question the Executive action, who were immediately subjected to investigation and some of them were removed or duly 'retired' from their positions.[393] However, since 2004, the members of the National Electoral Council have been appointed by the Constitutional Chamber of the Supreme Tribunal, usurping the functions of the National Assembly, in order to prevent any democratic 'deviation'.[394]

248. The consequence resulting from this factual 'dependency' of the State organs regarding the National Assembly has been the total absence of fiscal or audit control regarding all the State entities. The General Comptroller Office has ignored the results of the huge and undisciplined disposal of the oil wealth that has occurred in Venezuela, not always in accordance with budget discipline rules. But on the contrary, the most important decisions taken by the Comptroller General were those directed to disqualify many opposition candidates from the November 2008 regional and municipal elections, based on 'administrative irregularities', although the Constitution establishes that the constitutional right to run for office can only be

---

391. *See* Allan R. Brewer-Carías, *La dictadura judicial y la perversión del Estado de derecho. El juez constitucional y la destrucción de la democracia en Venezuela* (Madrid, Ediciones El Cronista, Editorial IUSTEL, 2017).
392. In the case of the General Prosecutor of the Republic, appointed in December of 1999, he thought he could initiate a criminal impeachment proceeding against the then Minister of the Interior; and in the case of the People's Defendant, also appointed in December of 1999 she also thought that she could challenge the Special Law of the 2001 National Assembly on appointment of Judges of the Supreme Tribunal without complying with the constitutional requirements. They were both duly dismissed in 2001.
393. It was the case of the First Vice President of the Supreme Tribunal of Justice, who delivered a decision of the Supreme Tribunal dated 14 Aug. 2002 regarding a criminal process against the generals who acted on 12 Apr. 2002, when the President of the Republic resigned to his position, declaring that there were no grounds to judge them due to the fact that in said occasion no military coup took place; and that of the President and two more members of the Electoral Chamber of the Supreme Tribunal who undersigned Decision No. 24 of 15 Mar. 2004 (Case: *Julio Borges, Cesar Perez Vivas, Henry Ramos Allup, Jorge Sucre Castillo, Ramón Jose Medina and Gerardo Blyde v. the National Electoral Council*), that suspended the effects of Resolution No. 040302-131, dated 2 Mar. 2004 of the National Electoral Council which, in that moment, stopped the realization of the presidential recall referendum.
394. *See* Alan R. Brewer-Carías, 'El secuestro del Poder Electoral y la confiscación del derecho a la participación política mediante el referendo revocatorio presidencial: Venezuela 2000-2004', in *Boletín Mexicano de Derecho Comparado,* No. 112 (Mexico, Universidad Nacional Autónoma de México, 2005), pp. 11–73.

suspended when a judicial criminal decision is adopted (Articles 39, 42);[395] which the Constitutional Chamber of the Supreme Tribunal has upheld in defraudation of the Constitution.[396]

Regarding the People's Defender, it has been perceived more as a defender of State powers than of the people's rights, even if the Venezuelan State has never before been denounced so many times as has happened during the past two decades before the Inter-American Commission on Human Rights. Finally, the Public Prosecutor has been characterized by using its powers to prosecute using, in an indiscriminate way, the controlled Judiciary as a tool to persecute any political dissidence.

§2. The Defraudation of Political Participation in the Election of High Governmental Officers

249. But the process of concentration of powers that Venezuela has experienced during the past decade has also been the result of a process of defraudation of the Constitution, particularly ignoring the limits the 1999 Constitution established to reduce the former complete discretional power of the National Assembly in the process of the indirect election of the non-popularly direct elected Heads of the different branches of government, which before the drafting of the Constitution had been highly criticized.[397]

In effect, independently of the constitutional provisions regarding the possible dismissal by the National Assembly of the Heads of the Citizens, Judicial and Electoral Branches of Government, and its distortions, one of the mechanisms established in the 1999 Constitution in order to assure their independence was the establishment of an indirect electoral system by the National Assembly, acting in

395. In October 2008, the European Parliament approved a Resolution asking the Venezuelan government to end with these practices (political incapacitation in order to impede the presence of opposition leaders in the regional and local elections) and to promote a more global democracy with complete respect of the principles established in the 1999 Constitution. *See* http:// venezuelanoticia.com/ archives/8298. *See* Allan R. Brewer-Carías, 'El derecho político de los ciudadanos a ser electos para cargos de representación popular y el alcance de su exclusión judicial en un régimen democrático (O de cómo la Contraloría General de la República de Venezuela incurre en inconstitucionalidad e inconvencionalidad al imponer sanciones administrativas de inhabilitación política a los ciudadanos)', en *Libro homenaje a Francisco Cumplido* (Santiago de Chile: Asociación Chilena de Derecho Constitucional, 2011).

396. Teodoro Petkoff has pointed out that with this decision 'the authoritarian and autocratic government of Hugo Chávez has clearly shown its true colors in this episode', explaining that 'The political rights to run for office is only lost when a candidate has received a judicial sentence that has been upheld in a higher court. The recent sentence by the Venezuelan Supreme Court, upholding the disqualifications, as well as the constitutionality of Art. 105 [of the Organic Law of the Comptroller General Office], constitute a defraudation of the Constitution and the way in which the decision was handed down was an obvious accommodation to the president's desire to eliminate four significant opposition candidates from the electoral field' *See* Teodoro Petkoff, 'Election and Political Power. Challenges for the Opposition', in *Revista. Harvard Review of Latin America* (Harvard University:David Rockefeller Centre for Latin American Studies, Fall 2008), 11.

397. Véase Allan R. Brewer-Carías, *Los problemas del estado de partidos* (Caracas: Editorial Jurídica Venezolana, 1988).

this case as an electoral body with the vote of a majority of two-thirds of its members, limited by the necessary participation of special collective bodies called Nominating Committees that must be integrated with representatives of the different sectors of society (Articles 264, 279, 295). Those Nominating Committees are in charge of selecting and nominating the candidates, guaranteeing the political participation of the Citizens in the process.

Consequently, the indirect election of the Justices of the Supreme Tribunal, of the Members of the National Electoral Council, of the Prosecutor General of the Republic, of the People's Defender and of the Comptroller General of the Republic can only be made by the National Assembly among the candidates proposed by the corresponding 'Nominating Committees', which are the ones in charge of selecting and nominating the candidates before the Assembly. These constitutional provisions, as mentioned, were designed in order to limit the discretional power the political, legislative organ traditionally had to elect those high officials through political party agreements, by assuring political Citizenship participation.[398]

250. Unfortunately, these exceptional constitutional provisions have not been applied, due to the fact that the National Assembly during the past years, also defrauding the Constitution, has deliberately 'transformed' the said Committees into simple 'parliamentary Commissions' reducing the civil society's right to political participation. The Assembly, in all the statutes sanctioned regarding such Committees and the election process, has established the composition of all the Nominating Committees with a majority of parliamentary representatives (who by definition cannot be representatives of the 'civil society'), although providing, in addition, for the incorporation of some other members chosen by the National Assembly itself from strategically selected 'non-governmental organizations'.[399]

The result has been the complete political control of the Nominating Committees, and the persistence of the discretional political and partisan way of electing the official heads of the non-directly elected branches of government, which the provisions of the 1999 Constitution intended to limit, by a National Assembly that since 2000 has been completely controlled by the Executive. In addition, the indirect electoral process was completely distorted in December of 2014, by the election of the

398. *See* Allan R. Brewer-Carías, 'La participación ciudadana en la designación de los titulares de los órganos no electos de los Poderes Públicos en Venezuela y sus vicisitudes políticas', in *Revista Iberoamericana de Derecho Publico y Administrativo,* Año 5, No. 5-2005 (San Jose, Costa Rica, 2005), 76–95.

399. *See* regarding the distortion of the 'Judicial Nominating Committee' in Allan R. Brewer-Carías, *Ley Orgánica del Tribunal Supremo de Justicia* (Caracas: Editorial Jurídica Venezolana, 2004); the distortion on the 'Citizen Power Nominating Committee' in Allan R. Brewer-Carías et al., *Ley Orgánica del Poder Ciudadano* (Caracas: Editorial Jurídica Venezolana, 2005); and in 'Sobre el nombramiento irregular por la Asamblea Nacional de los titulares de los órganos del poder ciudadano en 2007', in Revista *de Derecho Público*, No. 113 (Caracas: Editorial Jurídica Venezolana, 2008), 85–88; and the distortion on the Electoral Nominating Committee in Allan R. Brewer-Carías, *Crónica sobre la 'in' justicia constitucional. La Sala Constitucional y el autoritarismo en Venezuela*, No. 2 (Caracas: Colección Instituto de Derecho Público, Universidad Central de Venezuela, 2007), 197–230.

aforementioned head of the branches of government by the National Assembly, acting as a simple legislative body and not as the electoral body established in the Constitution, applying a simple majority of votes instead of the qualified majority set forth in the Constitution; which was accepted unconstitutionally by the Constitutional Chamber.[400]

This practice even pretended to be constitutionalized through the rejected Constitutional Reform of 2007 with the proposal to formally establish exclusively parliamentary Nomination Committees, instead of being composed of representatives of the various sectors of civil society.

§3. The Catastrophic Dependence and Subjection of the Judiciary

251. The effects of the dependency of the branches of government subjected to the Legislative Power and through it to the Executive have been particularly catastrophic regarding the Judiciary, which after being initially intervened by the Constituent National Assembly in 1999 (*see supra* paragraph 31), continued to be intervened with the unfortunate consent of the Supreme Tribunal of Justice itself. In this matter, in the past two decades, the country has witnessed a permanent and systematic demolition process of the autonomy and independence of the judicial power[401] aggravated by the fact that according to the 1999 Constitution, the Supreme Tribunal that is completely controlled by the Executive is in charge of administering all the Venezuelan judicial system, particularly, by appointing and dismissing judges[402] (*see infra* paragraphs 402 et seq.).

252. The process began with the appointment, in 1999, of new Magistrates of the Supreme Tribunal of Justice without complying with the constitutional

400. *See* Constitutional Chamber Decisions No. 1864 of 22 Dec. 2014 (available at: http://historico.tsj.gov.ve/decisiones/scon/diciembre/173494-1864-221214-2014-14-1341.HTML); and No. 1865 of 26 Dec. 2014 (available at: http://historico.tsj.gov.ve/decisiones/scon/diciembre/173497-1865-261214-2014-14-1343.HTML). *See* the comments in Allan R. Brewer-Carías, 'El golpe de Estado dado en diciembre de 2014, con la inconstitucional designación de las altas autoridades del Poder Público', *Revista de Derecho Público,* 40 (Caracas: Editorial Jurídica Venezolana, 2014).

401. *See* Allan R. Brewer-Carías, *La demolición de la independencia y autonomía del Poder Judicial en Venezuela 1999–2021,* (Caracas, Editorial Jurídica Venezolana, 2021); 'Dismantling the Rule of Law by politically controlling the Judiciary in Venezuela and its harmful projection on the Inter-American judicial system for the protection of human rights', in *European Review of Public Law/ Revue Européenne de Droit Public*, vol. 33, No 3, (European Public Law Organization, 2021), pp. 877–918

402. *See* Rafael J. Chavero Gazdik, *La Justicia Revolucionaria. Una década de reestructuración (o involución) Judicial en Venezuela* (Caracas: Editorial Aequitas, 2011); Laura Louza Scognamiglio, *La revolución judicial en Venezuela* (Caracas: FUNEDA, 2011); Allan R. Brewer-Carías, 'La progresiva y sistemática demolición de la autonomía e independencia del Poder Judicial en Venezuela (1999–2004)', in *XXX Jornadas J.M. Dominguez Escovar, Estado de derecho, Administración de justicia y derechos humanos* (Barquisimeto: Instituto de Estudios Jurídicos del Estado Lara, 2005), 33–174; and 'La justicia sometida al poder (La ausencia de independencia y autonomía de los jueces en Venezuela por la interminable emergencia del Poder Judicial (1999–2006)' in *Cuestiones Internacionales. Anuario Jurídico Villanueva 2007* (Madrid: Centro Universitario Villanueva, Marcial Pons, 2007), 25–57.

conditions, made by the National Constituent Assembly itself, by means of a Constitutional Transitory regime sanctioned after the Constitution was approved by referendum (*see supra* paragraph 29). From there on, the intervention process of the Judiciary continued up to the point that the President of the Republic politically controlled the Supreme Tribunal of Justice and, through it, the complete Venezuelan judicial system.

253. For that purpose, the constitutional conditions needed to be elected Magistrate of the Supreme Tribunal and the procedures for their nomination with the participation of representatives of the different sectors of civil society were violated since the beginning. First, as aforementioned, in 1999, the National Constituent Assembly itself once it dismissed the previous Justices, appointing new ones without receiving any nominations from any Nominating Committee, and many of them without compliance with the conditions set forth in the Constitution to be Magistrate. Second, in 2000, the newly elected National Assembly by sanctioning a Special Law in order to elect the Magistrates, in a transitory way, without compliance with those constitutional conditions.[403] Third, in 2004, again by the National Assembly by sanctioning the Organic Law of the Supreme Tribunal of Justice, increasing the number of Justices from twenty to thirty-two, and distorting the constitutional conditions for their election and dismissal, allowing the government to assume absolute control of the Supreme Tribunal, and in particular, of its Constitutional Chamber.[404] Fourth, in 2010, once more, the National Assembly reformed the Organic Law of the Supreme Tribunal of Justice, first in a regular way,[405] and subsequently in an irregular manner,[406] in order to pack the Tribunal with new government-controlled members. Fifth, in 2014, the election of the Magistrates by the National Assembly, by simple majority of votes, distorting the character of the election as an indirect popular election by the Assembly acting as an electoral body, with the vote of the two third of its members.[407] Finally, in 2022, the re-election of Magistrates violating the constitutional prohibition of re-election and the maximum constitutional tenure of twelve years.[408]

---

403. For this reason, in its 2003 *Report on Venezuela,* the Inter-American Commission on Human Rights, observed that the election of Judges of the Supreme Court of Justice did not apply to the Constitution, so that 'the constitutional reforms introduced in the form of the election of these authorities established as guaranties of independence and impartiality were not used in this case'. *See* Inter-American Commission of Human Rights, 2003 *Report on Venezuela*; para. 186.

404. *Gaceta Oficial* No. 37.942 of 20 May 2004. *See* the comments in Allan R. Brewer-Carías, *Ley Orgánica del Tribunal Supremo de Justicia* (Caracas: Editorial Jurídica Venezolana, 2004).

405. *Gaceta Oficial* No. 39.483 of 9 Aug. 2010 and No. 39.522 of 1 Oct. 2010. *See* the comments in Allan R. Brewer-Carías & Víctor Hernández Mendible, *Ley Orgánica del Tribunal Supremo de Justicia* (Caracas: Editorial Jurídica Venezolana, 2010).

406. *See* the comments Víctor Hernández Mendible, 'Sobre la nueva reimpresión por "supuestos errores" materiales de la Ley Orgánica del Tribunal Supremo, octubre 2010', and Antonio Silva Aranguren, 'Tras el rastro del engaño, en la web de la Asamblea Nacional', in *Revista de Derecho Público*, No. 124 (Caracas: Editorial Jurídica Venezolana, 2010), 10–113.

407. *See* Allan R. Brewer-Carías, 'El golpe de Estado dado en diciembre de 2014, con la inconstitucional designación de las altas autoridades del Poder Público', *Revista de Derecho Público,* 40 (Caracas: Editorial Jurídica Venezolana, 2014).

408. *See* Allan R. Brewer-Carías, 'Sobre los once (11) vicios de inconstitucionalidad de las sentencias de la Sala Constitucional que declararon la "constitucionalidad" de la reforma de la Ley Orgánica

254. After the 2004 reform of the Organic Law of the Supreme Tribunal, the process of selection of new Justices has been openly subjected to the President of the Republic's will, as was publicly admitted by the President of the Parliamentary Commission in charge of selecting the candidates for Magistrates of the Supreme Tribunal Court of Justice, who later was appointed Minister of the Interior and Justice. On December 2004, he said the following:

> 'Although we, the representatives, have the authority for this selection, the President of the Republic was consulted and his opinion was very much taken into consideration.' He added: 'Let's be clear, we are not going to score auto-goals. In the list, there were people from the opposition who comply with all the requirements. The opposition could have used them in order to reach an agreement during the last sessions, but they did not want to. We are not going to do it for them. There is no one in the group of postulates that could act against us.'[409]

This configuration of the Supreme Tribunal, as highly politicized and subjected to the will of the President of the Republic was reinforced, since in 2010,[410] eliminating all autonomy of the Judicial Power and even the basic principle of the separation of power, as the cornerstone of the rule of law and the base of all democratic institutions.

255. However, as aforementioned, according to Article 265 of the 1999 Constitution, the Magistrates can be dismissed by the vote of a qualified majority of the National Assembly, when grave faults are committed, following a prior qualification by the Citizen Power (*see infra* paragraph 422). This qualified two-thirds majority was established to avoid leaving the existence of the heads of the judiciary in the hands of a simple majority of legislators. Unfortunately, this provision was also distorted by the 2004 Organic Law of the Supreme Tribunal of Justice, in which it was established in an unconstitutional way that the Magistrates could be dismissed by simple majority when the 'administrative act of their appointment' is revoked (Article 23.4). This distortion, contrary to the independence of the Judiciary, although eliminated in the reform of the Law in 2010, also pretended to be constitutionalized with the rejected 2007 Constitutional reform, which proposed to

---

del Tribunal Supremo de Justicia. (Comentarios a las sentencias No. 81 y 83 de 15 y 21 de marzo de 2022),' in *Boletín de la Academia de Ciencias Políticas y Sociales*, *Homenaje a José Guillermo Andueza*, No. 168, (Caracas 2022), pp. 335–368.

409. *See* in *El Nacional* (Caracas, 13 Dec. 2004). That is why the Inter-American Commission on Human Rights suggested in its Report to the General Assembly of the OAS corresponding to 2004 that 'these regulations of the Organic Law of the Supreme Court of Justice would have made possible the manipulation, by the Executive Power, of the election process of judges that took place during 2004'. *See* Inter-American Commission on Human Rights, 2004 *Report on Venezuela*; para. 180.

410. *See* Hildegard Rondón de Sansó, '*Obiter Dicta*. En torno a una elección', in *La Voce d'Italia* (Caracas, 14 Dec. 2010).

establish that the Magistrates of the Supreme Tribunal could be dismissed in case of grave faults, but just by the vote of the majority of the members of the National Assembly.

256. The consequence of this political subjection is that all the principles tending to assure the independence of judges at any level of the Judiciary have been postponed. In particular, the Constitution establishes that all judges must be selected by public competition for the tenure; and that the dismissal of judges can only be made through disciplinary trials carried out by disciplinary judges (Articles 254 and 267). Unfortunately, none of these provisions has been implemented, and on the contrary, since 1999, the Venezuelan Judiciary has been composed of temporal and provisional judges,[411] lacking stability and being subjected to the political manipulation, altering the people's right to an adequate administration of justice. Also regarding the disciplinary jurisdiction of the judges, it was only in 2010[412] that it was established. Until then, with the authorization of the Supreme Tribunal, a 'transitory' Reorganization Commission of the Judicial Power created since 1999, continued to function, removing judges without due process[413] (*see infra* paragraph 424).

The worst of this irregular situation is that since 2006 the problem of the provisional status of judges has been 'regularized' through a 'Special Programme for the Regularization of Tenures', addressed to accidental, temporary or provisional judges, by-passing the entrance system constitutionally established by means of public competitive exams (Article 255), by consolidating the effects of the provisional appointments and their consequent power dependency.

§4. The Factual Political Supremacy of the Executive and the Absence of Checks and Balances

257. But if the supremacy of the National Assembly over the Judicial, Citizen and Electoral Powers is the most characteristic sign of the implementation of the Constitution of 1999 during the past two decades, the distortion of the separation of

---

411. The Inter-American Commission on Human Rights said: 'The Commission has been informed that only 250 judges have been appointed by opposition concurrence according to the constitutional text. From a total of 1772 positions of judges in Venezuela, the Supreme Court of Justice reports that only 183 are holders, 1331 are provisional and 258 are temporary', *Informe sobre la Situación de los Derechos Humanos en Venezuela*; OAS/Ser.L/V/II.118. d.C. 4rev. 2; 29 Dec. 2003; para. 11. The same Commission also said that 'an aspect linked to the autonomy and independence of the Judicial Power is that of the provisional character of the judges in the judicial system of Venezuela. Today, the information provided by the different sources indicates that more than 80% of Venezuelan judges are "provisional"'. *Ibid.*, para. 161.

412. The Law on the Ethics Code of the Venezuelan Judges *Gaceta Oficial* No. 39.494 of 24 Aug. 2010, created the expected Disciplinary Judicial Jurisdiction. In 2011 the corresponding tribunal was appointed.

413. *See* Allan R. Brewer-Carías, 'La justicia sometida al poder y la interminable emergencia del poder judicial (1999–2006)', *in Derecho y democracia. Cuadernos Universitarios,* No. 11 (Caracas: Órgano de Divulgación Académica, Vicerrectorado Académico, Universidad Metropolitana, Año II, septiembre 2007), 122–138.

powers principle transformed into a power concentration system, also derives from the supremacy that, from a political party's point of view, the Executive Power has over the National Assembly.

258. In the Constitution of 1999, the presidential system has been reinforced, among other factors, because of the extension to six years of the presidential term; the authorization of the immediate re-election for an immediate following period of the President of the Republic (Article 203), and the maintaining of it in election by simple majority (Article 228) (*see infra* paragraph 287). In the rejected Constitutional Reform of 2007, the term of the President was even proposed to be extended up to seven years, and the indefinite re-election of the President of the Republic was one of the main proposals contained in it. In 2008, again, and by passing the prohibition established in the Constitution to propose again within the same constitutional term a reform already rejected by the people, the National Assembly approved the proposal for a 'constitutional amendment' allowing the indefinite and continuous re-election of all elected public officials, that was submitted to referendum and approved by the people in February 2009 (*see supra* paragraphs 64, 221).

With this presidential model, to which the possibility of the dissolution of the National Assembly by the President of the Republic is added, although in exceptional cases (Articles 236.22 and 240), the presidential system has been reinforced. No check and balance possibility exists, for instance, from the Senate, which was eliminated in 1999.[414]

259. Also, the presidential system has been reinforced with other reforms, like the provision for legislative delegation to authorize the President of the Republic by means of 'delegating statutes' (enabling laws), to issue decree-laws and not only in economic and financial matters (Article 203). According to this provision, the fact is that the fundamental legislation of the country sanctioned during the past decade has been contained in these decree-laws, which have been approved without assuring the mandatory constitutional provision for public hearings, established in the Constitution (Article 211) to take place before the sanctioning of all statutes (*see supra* paragraph 181).

260. In order to enforce this constitutional right of the Citizens to participation (*see infra* paragraph 184), the Constitution specifically set forth that the National Assembly is compelled to submit draft legislation to public consultation, asking the opinion of Citizens and the organized society (Article 211). This is the concrete way by which the Constitution tends to assure the exercise of the political participation right in the process of drafting legislation. This constitutional obligation, of course, must also be accomplished by the President of the Republic when a legislative delegation takes place. But nonetheless, in 2007, 2008, 2011 and 2014, the President

414. *See* María M. Matheus Inciarte y María Elena Romero Ríos, 'Estado Federal y unicameralidad en el nuevo orden constitucional de la República Bolivariana de Venezuela', in *Estudios de Derecho Público: Libro Homenaje a Humberto J. La Roche Rincón,* vol. I (Caracas: Tribunal Supremo de Justicia, 2001), 637–676.

of the Republic, following the same steps adopted in 2001,[415] has extensively legislated without any public hearing or consultation. In this way, in defraudation of the Constitution, by means of legislative delegation, the President has enacted decree-laws without complying with the obligatory public hearings, violating the Citizens' right to political participation (*see infra* paragraph 101).

415. *See* the comments in Allan R. Brewer-Carías, 'Apreciación general sobre los vicios de inconstitucionalidad que afectan los Decretos Leyes Habilitados' in *Ley Habilitante del 13-11-2000 y sus Decretos Leyes* (Caracas: Academia de Ciencias Políticas y Sociales, 2002), 63–103.

Chapter 3. The Rupture of the Rule of Law, the Rejected 2007 Constitutional Reform and Its Illegitimate Implementation

261. As it can be deducted from the aforementioned, in order for a democratic rule of law State to exist, the declarations contained in constitutional texts on separation of power are not enough, an effective check and balance system between the State powers being indispensable. This is the only way to assure the enforcement of the rule of law and democracy, and the effective enjoyment of human rights.

And checks and balances and control of State Powers in a democratic rule of law State can only be achieved by dividing, separating and distributing Public Power, either horizontally by means of the guarantee of the autonomy and independence of the different branches of government to avoid the concentration of power; or vertically, by means of its distribution or spreading in the territory, creating autonomous political entities with representatives elected by votes to avoid its centralization. The concentrations of power, as well as its centralization, then, are essentially anti-democratic State structures.

262. It is precisely there where the problems of the formally declared rule of law and of democracy in Venezuela begin, due to the fact that its deformation lies in the same constitutional text of 1999, whose institutional framework unfortunately was established to encourage authoritarianism, affecting the possibility of controlling power. This has permitted the centralization of power, provoking the dismantling process of federalism and municipalism (*see supra* paragraph 198) and twisting the possibility of the effective political participation in spite of the direct democracy mechanisms established.

This process of centralization of powers was also proposed to be constitutionalized in 2007 by means of a Constitutional Reform draft submitted by the late President Hugo Chávez, and sanctioned by the National Assembly, in which the intention was to transform the Democratic Rule of Law and Decentralized Social State established in the 1999 Constitution, into a Socialist, Centralized, Repressive and Militaristic State, grounded in a so-called Bolivarian doctrine, which was identified with 'XXI Century Socialism', and an economic system of State capitalism (*see supra* paragraphs 35, 53).

§1. The Sense and Objectives of the Reform Proposals

263. In effect, in order to formally consolidate in the Constitution an authoritarian government and a socialist, centralized and communal State, the President of the Republic proposed to the National Assembly in 2007 the sanctioning of a Constitutional Reform[416] based on the configuration of a so-called State of the Popular

416. *See* Allan R. Brewer-Carías, *Hacia la Consolidación de un Estado Socialista, Centralizado, Policial y Militarista. Comentarios sobre el sentido y alcance de las propuestas de reforma constitucional 2007,* Colección Textos Legislativos, No. 42 (Caracas: Editorial Jurídica Venezolana, 2007).

Power or Communal State. As aforementioned, nevertheless, once it was put to popular vote, it was rejected by the people on 2 December 2007.

That constitutional reform was intended to transform the most essential and fundamental aspects of the State,[417] making it one of the most important reform proposals in all of Venezuelan constitutional history. With it, the decentralized, democratic, pluralistic and social State built and consolidated since the Second World War would have been radically changed to create a socialist, centralized, repressive and militaristic State grounded in a so-called Bolivarian doctrine, which at the time was identified with 'twenty-first-century socialism' and a socialist economic system of State capitalism. This reform was sanctioned evading the procedure established in the Constitution for such fundamental change, which imposes the convening of a Constituent Assembly. The reform defrauded the Constitution[418] as one more step of the 'permanent *coup d'état*' that since 1999 has occurred in Venezuela.[419]

The most important consequence of this draft reform from the citizens' perspective was that, with it, an official State ideology and doctrine was to be formally established in Venezuela, which was the socialist and supposedly 'Bolivarian' doctrine, implying if approved by the people, the duty for all citizens to actively contribute to its implementation, eliminating any vestige of political pluralism, and allowing for the formal criminalization of any dissidence regarding the unique and official way of thinking.

264. Guidelines for the proposed reforms emerged from various discussions and speeches of the President. These pointed to, on the one hand, the formation of a State of 'popular power' or of 'communal power', or a 'communal state' (*Estado del poder popular o del poder communal, o Estado comunal*) built on the communal councils (*consejos comunales*) as primary political units or social organizations. The communal councils, whose members are not elected by means of universal, direct and secret suffrage, in a way contrary to the democratic principles established in the Constitution, had already been created by statute in 2006,[420] parallel to the municipal entities, supposedly to channel citizen participation in public affairs.

---

417. *See* Rogelio Pérez Perdomo, 'La Constitución de papel y su reforma', in *Revista de Derecho Público* 112 *(Estudios sobre la reforma constitucional)* (Caracas: Editorial Jurídica Venezolana, 2007), 14; Alfredo Arismendi, 'Utopía Constitucional', in *ibid.*, 31; Manuel Rachadell, 'El personalismo político en el Siglo XXI', in *ibid.*, 66; Allan R. Brewer-Carías, 'El sello socialista que se pretendía imponer al Estado', in *ibid.*, 71–75; Alfredo Morles Hernández, 'El nuevo modelo económico para el Socialismo del Siglo XXI', in *ibid.*, 233–236.

418. *See* Gerardo Fernández, 'Aspectos esenciales de la modificación constitucional propuesta por el Presidente de la República. La modificación constitucional en fraude a la democracia', in *Revista de Derecho Público* 112 *(Estudios sobre la reforma constitucional)* (Caracas: Editorial Jurídica Venezolana, 2007), 21–25; Fortunato González, 'Constitución histórica y poder constituyente', in *ibid.*, 33–36; Lolymar Herández Camargo, 'Los límites del cambio constitucional como garantía de pervivencia del Estado de derecho', in *ibid.*, 37–45; Claudia Nikken, 'La soberanía popular y el trámite de la refroma constitucional promovida por iniciativa presidencial el 15 de agosto de 2007', in *ibid.*, 51–58.

419. *See* José Amando Mejía Betancourt, 'La ruptura del hilo constitucional', in *ibid.*, 47. The term was first used by Francois Mitterand, *Le coup d'État permanent*, Éditions 10/18 (Paris, 1993).

420. Communal Councils Law, *Gaceta Oficial,* Extra. 5.806, of 10 Apr. 2006. This statute was replaced by Organic Law on the Communal Councils. *See Gaceta Oficial* No. 39.335 of 28 Dec. 2009.

However, since their creation, they have operated within a system of centralized management by the national executive power and without any political or territorial autonomy.[421]

On the other hand, the guidelines for reform also referred to the structuring of a Socialist State and the substitution of the existing system of economic freedom and mixed economy with a State and collectivist socialist economic system subject to centralized planning, which minimizes the role of individuals and eliminates any vestige of economic liberties or private property as constitutional rights.

265. In accordance with these orientations, the 2007 rejected reform intended to radically transform the State by creating a completely new juridical order. A change of that nature, according to Article 347 of the 1999 Constitution, required the convening and election of a Constituent Assembly and could not be undertaken by means of mere constitutional reform procedures. This procedure for constitutional reform is applicable only to 'a partial revision of the Constitution and a substitution of one or several of its norms without modifying the structure and fundamental principles of the Constitutional text' (*see supra* paragraph 97). In such a case, the limited constitutional change is achieved through debate and sanctioning in the National Assembly, followed by approval in popular referendum.

266. Nonetheless, despite these constitutional provisions, with the rejected reform proposals, a political tactic that has been a common denominator in the actions of the authoritarian regime since 1999 was repeated: acting fraudulently with respect to the Constitution. As was ruled in other matters by the Constitutional Chamber of the Supreme Tribunal of Justice in a Decision No. 74 of 25 January 2006, a defraudation of the Constitution (*fraude a la Constitución*) occurs when democratic principles are destroyed 'through the process of making changes within existing institutions while appearing to respect constitutional procedures and forms'. The Chamber also ruled that a 'falsification of the Constitution' (*falseamiento de la Constitución*) occurs when 'constitutional norms are given an interpretation and a sense different from those that they really possess: this is in reality an informal modification of the Constitution itself'.[422] The Chamber concluded by affirming that 'A Constitutional reform not subject to any type of limitations would constitute a defraudation of the constitution.'[423] This is to say, a defraudation of the Constitution occurs when the existing institutions are used in a manner that appears to adhere to constitutional forms and procedures in order to proceed, as the

421. *See* Allan R. Brewer-Carías, 'El inicio de la desmunicipalización en Venezuela: La organización del poder popular para eliminar la descentralización, la democracia representativa y la participación a nivel local', in *AIDA, Revista de la Asociación Internacional de Derecho Administrativo* (Mexico City: Universidad Nacional Autónoma de México, Asociación Internacional de Derecho Administrativo, 2007), 49–67.

422. *See* Allan R. Brewer-Carías and Humberto Romero Muci (Coordinadores), *El Falseamiento del Estado de derecho* (Caracas, Academia de Ciencias Políticas y Sociales, 2021).

423. *See* in *Revista de Derecho Público,* No. 105 (Caracas: Editorial Jurídica Venezolana, 2006), 76 et seq.

Supreme Tribunal warned, 'towards the creation of a new political regimen, a new constitutional order, without altering the established legal system'.[424]

That is, existing institutions were used in a manner that appeared to adhere to constitutional form and procedure to proceed, as the Supreme Tribunal had warned, 'towards the creation of a new political regime, a new constitutional order, without altering the established legal system'.[425] This occurred in February 1999 in the convening of a consultative referendum on whether to convene a Constituent Assembly when that institution was not prefigured in the then-existing Constitution of 1961[426] (*see supra* paragraph 25). It occurred with the December 1999 Decree on the Transitory Regime of the Public Powers, with respect to the 1999 Constitution, which was never the subject of an approbatory referendum[427] (*see supra* paragraph 28). It occurred in 2017 with the unconstitutional convening of a National Constituent Assembly violating the right of the people.[428] It has continued to occur in the past two decades with the progressive destruction of democracy through the exercise of power, eliminating all effective separation of powers, and the sequestering of successive public rights and liberties, all supposedly based on legal and constitutional provisions.[429]

In this instance, once again, constitutional provisions were fraudulently used for ends other than those for which they were established; they were used to radically transform the State, thus disrupting the civil order of the social-democratic State to convert the State into a socialist, centralized, repressive and militarist State in which representative democracy, republican alternation in office and the concept of decentralized power would have disappeared, with all power instead concentrated in the decisions of the head of State.[430]

---

424. *Ibid.*
425. *See* the decision of the Constitutional Chamber of the Supreme Tribunal of Justice No. 74 (25 Jan. 2006), in *Revista de Derecho Público* 105 (Caracas: Editorial Jurídica Venezolana, 2006), 76 et seq.
426. *See* Allan R. Brewer-Carías, *Asamblea constituyente y ordenamiento constitucional* (Caracas: Academia de Ciencias Políticas y Sociales, 1999).
427. *See* Allan R. Brewer-Carías, *Golpe de estado y proceso constituyente en Venezuela* (Mexico City: Universidad Nacional Autónoma de México, 2002).
428. Allan R. Brewer-Carías, *Usurpación constituyente. 1999, 2017. La historia se repite: una vez como farsa y la otra como tragedia,* (New York, Caracas, Editorial Jurídica Venezolana International, 2018).
429. *See* Allan R. Brewer-Carías, 'Constitution-Making Process in Defraudation of the Constitution and Authoritarian Government in Defraudation of Democracy: The Recent Venezuelan Experience', paper presented at the *VII International Congress of Constitutional Law*, Athens, June 2007. *See also* Allan R. Brewer-Carías, 'El autoritarismo establecido en fraude a la Constitución y a la democracia y su formalización en Venezuela mediante la reforma constitucional. (De cómo en un país democrático se ha utilizado el sistema eleccionario para minar la democracia y establecer un régimen autoritario de supuesta "dictadura de la democracia" que se pretende regularizar mediante la reforma constitucional)', in *Temas constitucionales. Planteamientos ante una reforma* (Caracas: Fundación de Estudios de Derecho Administrativo, 2007), 13–74.
430. As is constitutionally proscribed, and as the Constitutional Chamber of the Supreme Tribunal of Justice summarized in Decision No. 74 (25 Jan. 2006), a symbolic case, it occurred 'with the fraudulent use of powers conferred by martial law in Germany under the *Weimar* Constitution, forcing the Parliament to concede to the fascist leaders, on the basis of terms of doubtful legitimacy, plenary constituent powers by conferring an unlimited legislative power'. *See* the Constitutional

This was constitutionally proscribed, and as the Constitutional Chamber of the Supreme Tribunal of Justice summarized it, in its aforementioned Decision No. 74 of 25 January 2006, referring to a symbolic case, it occurred 'with the fraudulent use of powers conferred by martial law in Germany under the *Weimar* Constitution, forcing the Parliament to concede to the fascist leaders, on the basis of terms of doubtful legitimacy, plenary constituent powers by conferring an unlimited legislative power'.[431] Nonetheless, in the case of the constitutional reform of 2007, the Supreme Tribunal deliberately refused to take any decision on judicial review regarding the unconstitutional procedure that was followed by the President of the Republic, the National Assembly and the National Electoral Council.[432]

267. In the case of the 2007 reforms, the various acts adopted (the presidential initiative, the sanction by the National Assembly, the convening of referendum by the National Electoral Council) were all challenged through judicial review actions of unconstitutionality and actions of *amparo* and, in all cases, the Supreme Tribunal, completely controlled by the Government, diligently declared all as inadmissible.[433]

Nonetheless, the fraud on the Constitution was initially evidenced in the proposals elaborated by the President's Council for Constitutional Reform that began to circulate in June 2007, despite the President's ordered 'pact of confidentiality',[434] and which were later given concrete form in the first draft constitutional reforms, which the President presented to the National Assembly on 15 August 2007,[435] proposing a radical transformation of the State to create a new juridical order.[436]

Chamber of the Supreme Tribunal of Justice, Decision No. 74 (25 Jan. 2006) in *Revista de Derecho Público* 105 (Caracas: Editorial Jurídica Venezolana, 2006), 76 et seq.

431. *See* in *Revista de Derecho Público,* No. 105 (Caracas: Editorial Jurídica Venezolana, 2006), 76 et seq.
432. *See* Allan R. Brewer-Carías, 'El juez constitucional vs. la supremacía constitucional. O de cómo la Jurisdicción Constitucional en Venezuela renunció a controlar la constitucionalidad del procedimiento seguido para la "reforma constitucional" sancionada por la Asamblea Nacional el 2 de noviembre de 2007, antes de que fuera rechazada por el pueblo en el referendo del 2 de diciembre de 2007', in *Revista de Derecho Público*, No. 112 (Caracas: Editorial Jurídica venezolana, 2007), 661 et seq.
433. On these decisions, *see* Allan R. Brewer-Carías, 'El juez constitucional vs. la supremacía constitucional. O de cómo la jurisdicción constitucional en Venezuela renunció a controlar la constitucionalidad del procedimiento seguido para la "reforma constitucional" sancionada por la Asamblea Nacional el 2 de noviembre de 2007, antes de que fuera rechazada por el pueblo en el referendo del 2 de diciembre de 2007', in *Revista de Derecho Público* 112 *(Estudios sobre la reforma constitucional)* (Caracas: Editorial Jurídica Venezolana, 2007), 661–694.
434. The document circulated in June 2007 under the title *Consejo Presidencial para la Reforma de la Constitución de la República Bolivariana de Venezuela, 'Modificaciones Propuestas'.* The complete text was published as *Proyecto de reforma constitucional. Versión atribuida al Consejo Presidencial para la reforma de la Constitución de la República Bolivariana de Venezuela* (Caracas: Editorial Atenea, 2007), 146.
435. The full text was published as *Proyecto de Reforma Constitucional. Elaborado por el ciudadano Presidente de la República Bolivariana de Venezuela, Hugo Chávez Frías* (Caracas: Editorial Atenea, 2007).
436. In this sense, the director of the National Electoral Council, Vicente Díaz, stated on 16 Jul. 2007, 'The presidential proposal to reform the constitutional text modifies fundamental provisions and for that reason it would be necessary to convene a National Assembly to approve them.' This council

Finally, the defrauding of the Constitution was consummated in November 2007 with the National Assembly's sanctioning of the reform,[437] in which.

268. *First*, the State was to be converted into a centralized State of concentrated power under the illusory guise of a popular power, implying definitive elimination of the federal form of the State,[438] rendering political participation impossible, and degrading representative democracy. For such purpose, the reform established a new 'popular power' (*poder popular*) (Article 16), composed of communities (*comunidades*), each of which 'shall constitute a basic and indivisible spatial nucleus of the Venezuelan Socialist State, where ordinary citizens will have the power to construct their own geography and their own history'; which were to be grouped into communes (*comunas*).[439] The main aspect of these reforms was that they provided that the popular power 'is expressed through the constitution of communities, communes, and the self-government of the cities, by means of the communal councils, workers' councils, peasant councils, student councils, and other entities established by law'. However, although 'the people' (*el pueblo*) were designated as the 'depositary of sovereignty', to be 'exercised directly through the popular power', it was expressly stated that the popular power 'does not arise from suffrage or from any election, but arises from the condition of the organized human groups that form the base of the population'. Consequently, representative democracy at the local level and territorial political autonomy was to disappear, substituted with a supposed participatory and protagonist democracy that would, in fact, be controlled by the President and that proscribed any form of political decentralization and territorial

member was consulted on this matter on Unión Radio, 16 Aug. 2007, at www.unionradio.com.ve/Noticias/No-ticia.aspx?noticiaid=212503. The initiation of the reform process in the National Assembly could have been challenged before the Constitutional Chamber of the Supreme Tribunal on the basis of unconstitutionality. Nonetheless, the president of the Constitutional Chamber – who was also a member of the Presidential Council for the Reform of the Constitution – made clear that 'no legal action related to modifications of the constitutional text would be heard until such modifications had been approved by citizens in referendum', adding that 'any action must be presented after a referendum, when the constitutional reform has become a norm, since we cannot interpret an attempted norm. Once a draft reform has become a norm we can enter into interpretations of it and hear nullification actions'. *See* Juan Francisco Alonso, *El Universal* (Caracas, 18 Aug. 2007).

437. On the reform proposals, *see* Allan R. Brewer-Carías, *Hacia la consolidación de un estado socialista, centralizado, policial y militarista. Comentarios sobre el sentido y alcance de las propuestas de reforma constitucional 2007,* Colección Textos Legislativos No. 42 (Caracas: Editorial Jurídica Venezolana, 2007); *La reforma constitucional de 2007 (Comentarios al proyecto inconstitucionalmente sancionado por la Asamblea Nacional el 2 de noviembre de 2007)*, Colección Textos Legislativos No. 43 (Caracas: Editorial Jurídica Venezolana, 2007). *See also* all the articles published in *Revista de Derecho Público* 112 *(Estudios sobre la reforma constitucional)* (Caracas: Editorial Jurídica Venezolana, 2007).

438. *See* Manuel Rachadell, 'El personalismo político en el Siglo XXI', in *Revista de Derecho Público* 112 *(Estudios sobre la reforma constitucional)* (Caracas: Editorial Jurídica Venezolana, 2007), 67; Ana Elvira Araujo, 'Proyecto de reforma constitucional (agosto a noviembre 2007). Principios fundamentales y descentralización política', in *ibid.*, 77–81; José Luis Villegas, 'Impacto de la reforma constitucional sobre las entidades locales', in *ibid.*, 119–123.

439. The communes were created in the statute on the Federal Council of Government. *See* Organic Law on the Federal Council of Government, *Gaceta Oficial* No. 5.963 Extra. of 22 Feb. 2010.

autonomy.[440] Even anticipating the constitutional reform proposal, perhaps being sure of its approval, in 2006, the Law on the Councils of the Popular Power (*Consejos del Poder Popular*) was sanctioned.[441] In the same trend of such Law, the reforms proposals conceived 'the communes and communities' (*comunas y comunidades*) as 'the basic and indivisible spatial nucleus of the Venezuelan Socialist State' (Article 15), adding that the only objective of the constitutional provision for political participation, was 'for the construction of socialism', requiring that all citizens' political associations be devoted 'to develop the values of mutual cooperation and socialist solidarity' (Article 70) (*see supra* paragraphs 232 et seq.).

269. Second, the State was to be converted into a Socialist State, being obligated to 'promote people's participation as a national policy, devolving its power and creating the best conditions for the construction of a Socialist democracy' (Article 158), thus establishing a political official doctrine of socialist character – Bolivarian doctrine. The consequence of this would be that any thoughts different from the official one were to be rejected, as the official political doctrine was incorporated into the Constitution itself, establishing a constitutional duty for all citizens to ensure its compliance, imposing the teaching in the schools of the '*ideario bolivariano*' (Bolivarian ideology), and stating that the primary investment of the State in education was to be done 'according to the humanistic principles of the Bolivarian socialism'. As a consequence, the basis for criminalizing all dissidence was formally established.

270. Third, the economic system was to be converted into a State-owned, socialist, centralized economy by means of eliminating economic liberty and private initiative as constitutional rights, as well as the constitutional right to private property (*see infra* paragraphs 619 ff.), colliding with the ideas of liberty and solidarity proclaimed in the 1999 Constitution and established a State that substitutes itself for society and private economic initiative.

271. Fourth, the State was to be converted into a repressive (police) State, given the regressive character of the regulations established in the reform regarding

---

440. This fundamental change, as the President stated on 15 Aug. 2007, constituted the development of what we understand by decentralization because the Fourth Republic concept of decentralization is very different from the concept we must work with. For this reason, we have here stated 'the protagonist participation of the people, transferring power to them, and creating the best conditions for the construction of social democracy'. *See Discurso de orden pronunciado por el ciudadano Comandante Hugo Chávez Frías*, *supra*, 50.

441. *See* Giancarlo Henríquez Maionica, 'Los Consejos Comunales (una breve aproximación a su realidad y a su proyección ante la propuesta presidencial de reforma constitucional)', in *Revista de Derecho Público* 112 *(Estudios sobre la reforma constitucional)* (Caracas: Editorial Jurídica Venezolana, 2007), 89–99; Allan R. Brewer-Carías, 'El inicio de la desmunicipalización en Venezuela: La organización del poder popular para eliminar la descentralización, la democracia representativa y la participación a nivel local', in *AIDA, Opera Prima de Derecho Administrativo. Revista de la Asociación Internacional de Derecho Administrativo* (Mexico City: Universidad Nacional Autónoma de México, Asociación Internacional de Derecho Administrativo, 2007), 49–67. The 2006 law was replaced by Organic Law on Communal Councils, *Gaceta Oficial* No. 39.335 of 28 Dec. 2009. *See* the comments on this Law in Allan R. Brewer-Carías, *Ley Orgánica de los Consejos Comunales* (Caracas: Editorial Jurídica Venezolana, 2010).

human rights, particularly civil rights, and the expansion of the President's emergency powers, under which he was authorized to indefinitely suspend constitutional rights.

272. *Fifth*, and finally, the State was to be converted into a militarist State, on the basis of the role assigned to the 'Bolivarian Armed Force' (*Fuerza Armada Bolivariana*), which was configured to function wholly under the President, and the creation of the new 'Bolivarian National Militia' (*Milicia Nacional Bolivariana*). All were to act 'by means of the study, planning and execution of Bolivarian military doctrine' – that is, according to socialist doctrine. All the reforms implied the radical transformation of the Venezuelan political system; sought to establish a centralized socialist, repressive and militaristic State of popular power; and departed fundamentally from the concept of a civil social-democratic State under the rule of law and justice based on a mixed economy.

273. The motives for the reforms were all very explicitly expressed by the President of the Republic in 2007, beginning with his speech of presentation of the draft reforms before the National Assembly, in which he said that the reforms' main objective was 'the construction of a Bolivarian and socialist Venezuela' – that is, to sow 'socialism in the political and economic realms'.[442] He clearly expressed that in his presidential campaign in 1999, he did not propose such thing as 'projecting the road of socialism' to be incorporated in the Constitution, but conversely, in 2006, as a candidate for re-election, he said: 'Let us go to Socialism', deducting from that that 'everyone who voted for [re-electing] candidate Chávez then, voted to go to socialism'.[443]

This was then the motivation for the drafting of the constitutional reforms in 2007, aiming to construct 'Bolivarian Socialism, Venezuelan Socialism, our Socialism, and our socialist model', having 'the community' (*la comunidad*), a 'basic and indivisible nucleus', and considering that 'real democracy is only possible in socialism'. However, the democracy referred to was not at all a representative democracy because it was 'not born of suffrage or from any election, but rather is born from the condition of organized human groups as the base of the population'.[444]

The President in that speech summarized the aims of his reform proposals explaining that on the political ground, the purpose was to 'deepen popular Bolivarian democracy', and on the economic ground, to 'create better conditions to sow and construct a socialist productive economic model', which he considered 'our

442. *See Discurso de orden pronunciado por el ciudadano Comandante Hugo Chávez Frías, Presidente Constitucional de la República Bolivariana de Venezuela en la conmemoración del ducentécimo segundo aniversario del juramento del Libertador Simón Bolívar en el Monte Sacro y el tercer aniversario del referendo aprobatorio de su mandato constitucional*, special session, 15 Aug. 2007, Asamblea Nacional, División de Servicio y Atención legislativa, Sección de Edición (Caracas, 2007), 4, 33.

443. *Ibid.*, 4. That is, it sought to impose the wishes of only 46% of registered voters who voted to re-elect the President on the remaining 56% of registered voters who did not vote for presidential re-election. According to official statistics from the National Electoral Council, of 15,784,777 registered voters, only 7,309,080 voted to re-elect the President.

444. *See Discurso de orden pronunciado por el ciudadano Comandante Hugo Chávez Frías, supra*, 32, 34, 35.

model'. That is, 'in the political field: socialist democracy; on the economic, the productive socialist model; in the field of public administration, incorporate new forms in order to lighten the load, to leave behind bureaucracy, corruption, and administrative inefficiency, which are heavy burdens of the past still upon us like weights, in the political, economic and social areas'.[445]

274. All his proposals to construct socialism were linked by the President to Simón Bolívar's 1819 Constitution of Angostura, which he considered 'perfectly applicable to a socialist project' in the sense of considering that it was possible to 'take the original Bolivarian ideology as a basic element of a socialist project'.[446] Of course, this assertion has no serious foundations: it is enough to read Bolívar's 1819 Angostura discourse on presenting the draft constitution to realize that it has nothing to do with a 'socialist project' of any kind.[447]

The rejected constitutional reform, without doubt, would have altered the basic foundations of the State.[448] This is true particularly with respect to the proposals on the constitutional amplification of the Bolivarian doctrine; the substitution of the democratic, social State with the Socialist State; the elimination of decentralization as a policy of the State designed to develop public political participation; and the elimination of economic freedom and the right to property.[449]

All these constitutional reforms, approved by the National Assembly defrauding the Constitution, as aforementioned, were submitted to popular vote and were all rejected by the people in the referendum that took place on 2 December 2007.[450]

---

445. *Ibid.*, 74.
446. *Ibid.*, 42. Only one month before the President's speech on the proposed constitutional reforms, the former minister of defence, General in Chief Raúl Baduel, who was in office until 18 Jul. 2007, stated on leaving the Ministry of Popular Power for the Defence that the President's call to 'construct socialism for the twenty-first century, implied a necessary, pressing and urgent need to formalize a model of Socialism that is theoretically its own, autochthonous, in accord with our historical, social, political and cultural context'. He added, 'Until this moment, this theoretical model does not exist and has not been formulated.' It is hard to imagine that it could have been formulated just one month later.
447. *See* Simón Bolívar, *Escritos fundamentales* (Caracas, 1982). *See also* Pedro Grases (ed.), *El Libertador y la Constitución de Angostura de 1819* (Caracas, 1969); José Rodríguez Iturbe (ed.), *Actas del Congreso de Angostura* (Caracas, 1969). The contrary at least would have been noticed by Karl Mark who, on the contrary, in 1857 wrote a very critical entry regarding Bolivar, without discovering any socialist trends in his life, for the *The New American Cyclopaedia*, vol. III (1858), on 'Bolivar y Ponte, Simón.' Available at www.marxists.org/archive/marx/works/1858/01/bolivar.htm.
448. *See* Eugenio Hernández Bretón, 'Cuando no hay miedo (ante la Reforma Constitucional)', in *Revista de Derecho Público* 112 *(Estudios sobre la reforma constitucional)* (Caracas: Editorial Jurídica Venezolana, 2007), 17–20; Manuel Rachadell, 'El personalismo político en el Siglo XXI', in *ibid.*, 65–70.
449. *See* on these reforms, Allan R. Brewer-Carías, *Dismantling Democracy. The Chávez Authoritarian Experiment* (Cambridge University Press, 2010).
450. *See* Allan R. Brewer-Carías, 'La proyectada reforma constitucional de 2007, rechazada por el poder constituyente originario', in *Anuario de Derecho Público 2007,* Año 1 (Caracas: Instituto de Estudios de Derecho Público de la Universidad Monteávila, 2008), 17–65. According to information from the National Electoral Council on 2 Dec. 2007, of 16,109,664 registered voters, only 9,002,439 voted (44.11% abstention); of voters, 4,504,354 rejected the proposal (50.70%). This means that there were only 4,379,392 votes to approve the proposal (49.29%), so only 28% of registered voters voted for the approval.

§2. The Irregular and Illegitimate Implementation in 2008 of the Rejected Reform Proposals Through Ordinary Legislation

275. In spite of which the popular rejection of the 2007 constitutional reform was a very important step back to the authoritarian government of President Chávez, in 2008, he announced his intention to seek the imposition of the rejected constitutional reform, again, in defraudation of the Constitution. First, in January 2008, he suggested that in order to assure the possibility for his indefinite re-election, he was willing to propose a repeal referendum of himself, seeking to convert the eventual rejection of such referendum into a plebiscite for his re-election;[451] and second, as mentioned in December 2008, he formally asked the National Assembly to approve a constitutional amendment in order to establish the possibility of the indefinite re-election of the President of the Republic which was submitted and approved by referendum on 14 February 2009 (*see supra* paragraph 37), in spite of the constitutional prohibition to ask the people to vote about the same constitutional reform already rejected by popular vote (*see supra* paragraph 127).

276. It must also be noted that during the months before the Constitutional Reform was submitted to the National Assembly, during July and August 2007, the President of the Republic, exercising the powers to legislate by decree that were delegated to him by his completely controlled National Assembly in January 2007,[452] sanctioned twenty-six very important new Statutes with the intention of beginning with the implementation, beforehand and in a fraudulent way, with the constitutional reform proposals that eventually were rejected by the people in the 2007 December referendum.[453] Unfortunately, even though all were unconstitutional, those decree-laws were enacted and applied without any possibility of control or judicial review. The President was sure that no Constitutional Chamber judicial review decision was to be issued, being such Chamber is a wholly controlled entity that has proved to be his most effective tool for the consolidation of his authoritarian government. This dependence on the Supreme Tribunal regarding the President

451. *See El Universal*, Caracas 27 Jan. 2008.
452. *See* the January Enabling Law of January 2007, in *Gaceta Oficial,* 38.617 of 1 Feb. 2007.
453. Regarding these 2008 Decree Laws, *see Revista de Derecho Público,* No. 115, *Estudios sobre los Decretos leyes Julio-Agosto*, 2008 (Caracas: Editorial Jurídica Venezolana, 2008). Referring to these Decree Laws, Teodoro Petkoff has pointed out that: 'In *absolute contradiction* to the results of the 2 Dec. 2007 referendum in which voters rejected constitutional reforms, in several of the laws promulgated the president presents several of the aspects of the rejected reforms almost in the same terms. The proposition of changing the name of the Venezuelan Armed Forces to create the Bolivarian National Militia was contained in the proposed reforms; the power given to the President to appoint national government officials over the Governors and Mayors to, obviously, weaken those offices and to eliminate the last vestiges of counterweight to the executive in general and the presidency in particular, was also contained in the reforms; the recentralization of the national executive branch of powers that today belong to the states and decentralized autonomous institutes was also part of the reforms: the enlargement of government powers to intervene in economic affairs was also contained in the reform. To ignore the popular decision about the 2007 proposal to reform the constitution in conformity with the will and designs of an autocrat, without heed to legal or constitutional norms, is, *stricto sensu*, a tyrannic act.' *See* Teodoro Petkoff, 'Election and Political Power. Challenges for the Opposition', in *Revista. Harvard Review of Latin America* (Harvard University: David Rockefeller Centre for Latin American Studies, Fall 2008), 12.

of the Republic was admitted by himself in 2007, when he publicly complained about the fact that the Supreme Tribunal had issued an important ruling in which it 'modified' the Income Tax Law, without previously consulting the 'leader of the Revolution'.[454]

277. All this situation is the only explanation a constitutional lawyer can find to understand why a Head of State of our times, as was the case of President Chávez in Venezuela, can say, challenging his opponents in a political rally held on 28 August 2008, 'I am the Law' and 'I am the State.'[455] Anyway, this was not the first time that the President of the Republic used this expression. In 2001, when he approved more than forty-eight decree-laws, also via delegate legislation, he also said, although in a different way: 'The law is me. The State is me.'[456] This phrase, which although attributed to Louis XIV was never delivered by him,[457] expressed by a Head of State of our times, is enough to realize and understand the tragic institutional situation of Venezuela in the period 1999–2009, precisely characterized by a complete absence of separation of powers and consequently, of a democratic government.[458]

---

454. The case was a very polemic and discussed one, decided by the Constitutional Chamber of the Supreme Tribunal in decision No. 301 of 27 Feb. 2007, regarding which the President of the Republic said: 'Many cases arrive when the Revolutionary Government wants to take a decision against something that for instance, deals with or has to pass through judicial decisions, and then they begin to move themselves in contrary sense in the shadow, and in many cases they attain to neutralize the decisions of the Revolution yon by means of a judge, or a court, and even through the own Supreme Tribunal of Justice, behind the *backs of the Leader of the Revolution,* acting from inside, against the Revolution. This is, I insist, treason to the people, treason to the Revolution.' (emphasis added). *Discurso en el Primer Evento con propulsores del Partido Socialista Unido de Venezuela desde el teatro Teresa Carreño, 24 marzo 2007.*

455. He said: 'I warn you, group of Stateless, putrid opposition. Whatever you do, the 26 Laws will go ahead! And the other 16 Laws,... also. And if you go out in the streets, like on 11 Apr. (2002) ... we will sweep you in the streets, in the barracks, in the universities. I will close the golpista media; I will have no compassion whatsoever ... This Revolution came to stay, forever! You can continue talking stupidities ... I am going to intervene all communications and I will close all the enterprises I consider that are of public usefulness or of social interest! Out [of the country] Contractors and Forth Republic corrupt people! *I am the Law ... I am the State*' (*Yo soy la Ley ..., Yo soy el Estado!!*). *See* in Gustavo Coronel, *Las Armas de Coronel*, 15 de octubre de 2008: http://lasarmasdecoronel.blogspot.com/2008/10/yo-soy-la-leyyo-soy-el-estado.html.

456. 'La ley soy yo. El Estado soy yo'. *See* in *El Universal* (Caracas, 12 Apr. 2001), 1, 1 and 2, 1.

457. This famous phrase was attributed to Louis XIV, when in 1661 he decided to govern alone after the death of Cardinal Mazarin, but was never pronounced by him. *See* Yves Giuchet, *Histoire Constitutionnelle Française (1789–1958)*, ed. Erasme (Paris, 1990), 8.

458. This situation was summarized by Teodoro Petkoff, editor and founder of *Tal Cual*, one of the important newspapers in Caracas, as follows: 'Chavez controls all the political powers. More than 90% of the Parliament obey his commands; the Venezuelan Supreme Court, whose number were raised from 20 to 32 by the parliament to ensure an overwhelming officialist majority, has become an extension of the legal office of the Presidency ... The Prosecutor General's Office, the Comptroller's Office and the Public Defender are all offices held by 'yes persons', absolutely obedient to the orders of the autocrat. In the National Electoral Council, four of five members are identified with the government. The Venezuelan Armed Forces are tightly controlled by Chávez. Therefore, from a conceptual point of view, the Venezuelan political system is autocratic. All political power is concentrated in the hands of the President. There is no real separation of Powers.' *See* Teodoro

278. This legislative delegation was sanctioned by the National Assembly parallel to the announcement by the President at the beginning of the 2007 constitutional reform process. As aforementioned, perhaps assuming that the presidential constitutional reform proposal was to be approved by the people, the President began implementing it through the enabling law (delegate legislation) sanctioned in 2007 that was later also used fraudulently to implement the rejected reforms,[459] particularly in economic and social matters, in order to structure a socialist centralized State.[460] This process, however, was developed in absolute secrecy with no public consultation and participation in violation of Article 210 of the Constitution.[461]

279. Regarding the 2007 rejected constitutional reforms related to eliminating local-level representative democracy, as aforementioned, the same began to be implemented in 2006, even before its formal proposal, with the sanctioning of the Communal Councils Law, which created them as social units and organizations not directed by popularly elected officials, without any sort of territorial autonomy, supposedly devoted to channelling citizens' participation but in a centralized conducted system from the apex of the national executive.[462] This Law was later reformed and elevated to organic law rank in 2009.[463]

A primary purpose of the 2007 constitutional reforms was to complete the dismantling of the federal form of the State by centralizing power attributions of the States, creating administrative entities to be established and directed by the national executive, attributing powers to the President to interfere in regional and local

---

Petkoff, 'Election and Political Power. Challenges for the Opposition', in *ReVista. Harvard Review of Latin America* (Harvard University: David Rockefeller Centre for Latin American Studies, Fall 2008), 12.

459. *See* Lolymar Hernández Camargo, 'Límites del poder ejecutivo en el ejercicio de la habilitación legislativa: Imposibilidad de establecer el contenido de la reforma constitucional rechazada vía habilitación legislativa', in *Revista de Derecho Público* 115 *(Estudios sobre los Decretos Leyes)* (Caracas: Editorial Jurídica Venezolana, 2008), 51 et seq.; Jorge Kiriakidis, 'Breves reflexiones en torno a los 26 Decretos-Ley de julio-agosto de 2008, y la consulta popular refrendaría de diciembre de 2007', in *ibid.*, 57 et seq.; José Vicente Haro García, 'Los recientes intentos de reforma constitucional o de cómo se está tratando de establecer una dictadura socialista con apariencia de legalidad (A propósito del proyecto de reforma constitucional de 2007 y los 26 decretos leyes del 31 de julio de 2008 que tratan de imponerla)', in *ibid.*, 63 et seq.

460. *See* Ana Cristina Nuñez Machado, 'Los 26 nuevos Decretos-Leyes y los principios que regulan la intervención del Estado en la actividad económica de los particulares', in *ibid.*, 215–220.

461. *See* Aurilivi Linares Martínez, 'Notas sobre el uso del poder de legislar por decreto por parte del Presidente venezolano', in *ibid.*, 79–89; Carlos Luis Carrillo Artiles, 'La paradójica situación de los Decretos Leyes Orgánicos frente a la Ingeniería Constitucional de 1999', in *ibid.*, 93–100; Freddy J. Orlando S., 'El "paquetazo", un conjunto de leyes que conculcan derechos y amparan injusticias', in *ibid.*, 101–104.

462. Ley Orgánica de los Consejos Comunales, *Gazeta Oficial* No. 39.335, 28 Dec. 2009. *See* Juan M. Raffali A., 'Límites constitucionales de la Contraloría Social Popular', in *Revista de Derecho Público*, 115 *(Estudios sobre los Decretos Leyes)* (Caracas: Editorial Jurídica Venezolana, 2008), 133–147.

463. *See Gaceta Oficial* No. 39.335 of 12 Dec. 2009. *See* Decision No. 1.676 12 Mar. 2009 Constitutional Chamber, Supreme Tribunal of Justice about the constitutionality of the organic character of the Communal Councils Organic Law, in www.tsj.gov.ve/decisiones/scon/diciembre/1676-31209-2009-09-1369.html. *See* Allan R. Brewer-Carías, *Ley Orgánica de los Consejos Comunales* (Caracas: Editorial Jurídica Venezolana, 2010).

affairs, and voiding state and municipal competency by means of compulsory transfer of that competency to communal councils.[464] The implementation of the rejected constitutional reforms regarding the organization of the 'Popular Power' based on the strengthening of the communes and communal councils was completed with the approval in 2010 of the Law on the Federal Council of Government.[465]

To implement these reforms, not only the last mentioned aspect was achieved, forcing the states and municipalities to transfer their attributions to local institutions controlled by the central power (communal councils), but also by means of Decree-Law No. 6217 of 15 July 2008, on the Organic Law of Public Administration[466] that began to be directly applicable to the states' and municipalities' Public Administrations, the national executive has implemented the principle of centralized planning, subjecting regional and local authorities to the Central Planning Commission. This Organic Law also assigns to the President, as proposed in the 2007 reforms, the power to appoint regional authorities with powers to plan, execute, follow up on and control land use and territorial development policies, thus subjecting all programmes and projects to central planning approval.

280. Regarding the vertical distribution of State attributions between the national level and the states, one of the general purposes of the rejected 2007 constitutional reform was to change the federal form of the State and the territorial distribution of the competencies established in Articles 156 and 164 of the Constitution, thus centralizing the State even more by concentrating almost all competencies of the public power at the national level. Particularly, 'nationalizing' the competency set forth in Article 164.10 of the Constitution, which attributed to the State's exclusive jurisdiction on the conservation, administration and use of national highways, roads, ports and airports.[467] Despite the rejection of the constitutional reforms in the December 2007 referendum in order to change such provision, the Constitutional Chamber of the Supreme Tribunal, in Decision No. 565 (15 April

464. *See* Manuel Rachadell, '*La centralización del poder en el Estado federal descentralizado*', in *Revista de Derecho Público*, 115 *(Estudios sobre los Decretos Leyes)* (Caracas: Editorial Jurídica Venezolana, 2008), 111–131.

465. *See* Organic Law on the Federal Council of Government, *Gaceta Oficial* No. 5.963 Extra. of 22 Feb. 2010.

466. *Gaceta Oficial* No. 5.890, Extra. of 31 Jul. 2008. *See* Allan R. Brewer-Carías, 'El sentido de la reforma de la Ley Orgánica de la Administración Pública', in *Revista de Derecho Público* 115 *(Estudios sobre los Decretos Leyes)* (Caracas: Editorial Jurídica Venezolana, 2008), 155–161; Cosimina G. Pellegrino Pacera, 'La reedición de la propuesta constitucional de 2007 en el Decreto No. 6.217, con Rango, Valor y Fuerza de Ley Orgánica de la Administración Pública', in *ibid.*, 163–68; Jesús Caballero Ortíz, 'Algunos comentarios sobre la descentralización funcional en la nueva Ley Orgánica de la Administración Pública', in *ibid.* 169–174; Alberto Blanco-Uribe Quintero. 'Afrenta a la Debida Dignidad frente a la Administración Pública. Los Decretos 6.217 y 6.265', in *ibid.*, 175–179. The Organic Law has been reformed in 2014. *See Gaceta Oficial* No. 6.147, Extra. of 17 Dec. 2014.

467. *See* Allan R. Brewer-Carías, *Hacia la consolidación de un estado socialista, centralizado, policial y militarista. Comentarios sobre el sentido y alcance de las propuestas de reforma constitucional 2007* (Caracas: Editorial Jurídica Venezolana, 2007), 41 et seq.; and *La Reforma Constitucional de 2007 (Comentarios al proyecto inconstitucionalmente sancionado por la Asamblea Nacional el 2 de noviembre de 2007)* (Caracas: Editorial Jurídica Venezolana, 2007), 72 et seq.

2008),[468] issued an abstract constitutional interpretation at the request of the Attorney General of the Republic, modified the content of the constitutional provision, arguing that the 'exclusive' attribution 'was not exclusive' but 'concurrent' – meaning that the national government could also exercise that competency interfering with the states' powers. With that interpretation, the Chamber illegitimately modified the Constitution, usurping popular sovereignty, and changed the federal form of the State by misrepresenting the territorial distribution system of powers between the national power and the states.[469] The Chamber, consequently, urged the National Assembly to issue legislation against the provisions of the 1999 Constitution, which was effectively accomplished in May 2009 by reforming the Organic Law on Decentralization, Delimitation, and Transfer of Public Attributions,[470] eliminating the aforementioned exclusive attribution of the states.[471]

281. The rejected 2007 constitutional reforms also sought to eliminate the Capital District that the 1999 Constitution had created as a political entity in substitution of the former Federal District, which was dependent on the national level of government. Notwithstanding popular rejection of the 2007 reform proposals, in April 2009, such reform was unconstitutionally implemented by the National Assembly, defrauding once more the Constitution by sanctioning the Special Law on the Organization and Regime of the Capital District.[472] In it, instead of organizing a democratic political entity to govern the capital district, in Caracas, the Capital of the Republic, the law established an organization completely dependent on the national level of government in the same territorial jurisdiction that 'used to be one of the extinct Federal District'. According to this law, the capital district, contrary to what is provided for in the Constitution, has no elected authorities of government and is governed by the national level by means of a 'special regime' consisting of the exercise of the legislative function by the National Assembly itself and a chief of government as the executive branch (Article 3) appointed by the President. This means that through a national statute, in the same territory of Caracas, a new national structure has been unconstitutionally imposed.

282. Finally, although the 2007 constitutional proposed reforms regarding the military and the Armed Force that sought to transform them into the Bolivarian Armed Force organized for the purpose of reinforcing socialism were rejected in the

468. *See* Decision No. 565 of the Constitutional Chamber (15 Apr. 2008) (Case: *Procurador General de la república, Interpretación del artículo 164.10 de la Constitución)*, available at www.tsj.gov.ve/decisio-nes/scon/Abril/565-150408-07-1108.htm.
469. *Ibid*
470. *Gaceta Oficial* No. 39.140 of 17 Mar. 2009.
471. *See* Allan R. Brewer-Carías, 'La Sala Constitucional como poder constituyente: La modificación de la forma federal del estado y del sistema constitucional de división territorial del poder público', in *Revista de Derecho Público* 114 (Caracas: Editorial Jurídica Venezolana, 2008), 247–262; Manuel Rachadell, '*La centralización del poder en el Estado federal descentralizado*', in *Revista de Derecho Público*, No. 115 (Estudios sobre los Decretos Leyes) (Caracas: Editorial Jurídica Venezolana, 2008), 120.
472. *Gaceta Oficial* No. 39.156 of 13 Apr. 2009. *See* the comments on this Law in Allan R. Brewer-Carías et al., *Leyes sobre el Distrito Capital y el Área Metropolitana de Caracas* (Caracas: Editorial Jurídica Venezolana, 2009).

December 2007 referendum, the radical changes it contained have been implemented by the President, also usurping the constituent power, by means of a Decree-Law reforming the Organic Law on the Armed Force,[473] creating the 'Bolivarian National Armed Force' subjected to a 'military Bolivarian Doctrine', and creating in it the 'National Bolivarian Militia' – all of this according to what was proposed and rejected by the people in the 2007 Constitutional Reform.[474]

§3. The Unconstitutional Implementation in 2010–2011 of the Rejected Reform Proposals Through Organic Laws

283. On 26 September 2010, a parliamentary election was held in the country, the result of which being that the opposition to the government won the popular vote, although not the majority of seats in the National Assembly, due to distorting electoral regulations. This result meant, in fact, that the majority of popular vote expressed was against the proposals debated in the electoral campaign for the establishment of a Socialist State in Venezuela, a matter that the President and the governmental majority of the National Assembly, with a massive campaign for their candidates, posed as a 'plebiscite' on the President, his performance and his socialist policies.

284. In disdain of the popular will expressed ratifying the previous rejection by the people of the reforms in the 2007 referendum, the President and his party, having lost the absolute control they used to have since 2005 over the National Assembly before the newly elected deputies to the Assembly could have taken possession of office in January 2011, in December 2010 forced the National Assembly to proceed to sanction a set of organic laws on the popular power through which they have finished defining the legislative framework for a new State. In this way, by-passing the Constitution and in parallel to the Constitutional State, the National Assembly regulated a socialist, centralized, military and police State, called the 'Communal State' of the 'Popular Power' in spite of having been already rejected by the people in 2007 (*see supra* paragraphs 232 et seq.).

473. Decree La w No. 6.239, on the Organic Law of the National Bolivarian Armed Force, in *Gaceta Oficial* No. 5.933, Extra. of 21 Oct. 2009.

474. *See* Alfredo Arismendi A., 'Fuerza Armada Nacional: Antecedentes, evolución y régimen actual', in *Revista de Derecho Público*, No. 115 (Estudios sobre los Decretos Leyes) (Caracas: Editorial Jurídica Venezolana, 2008), 187–206; Jesús María Alvarado Andrade, 'La nueva Fuerza Armada Bolivariana (Comentarios a raíz del Decreto No. 6.239, con rango, valor y fuerza de Ley Orgánica de la Fuerza Armada Nacional Bolivariana)', in *ibid.*, 207–214.

Part V. The Government

285. Within the presidential system of government[475] (*see supra* paragraph 64), according to Article 255 of the Constitution, the Executive Power is exercised by the President of the Republic, the Executive Vice President, the Ministers, and the other officials as determined by the Constitution and by statutes.

475. *See* in general, Donato Lupidii, 'El sistema presidencial y la Constitución venezolana de 1999', en *El Derecho Público a comienzos del siglo XXI. Estudios homenaje al Profesor Allan R. Brewer-Carías,* vol. I (Madrid: Instituto de Derecho Público, UCV, Civitas Ediciones, 2003), 819–835; Miguel A. Gómez Ortiz, 'El régimen presidencial en Venezuela', en *Bases y principios del sistema constitucional venezolano (Ponencias del VII Congreso Venezolano de Derecho Constitucional realizado en San Cristóbal del 21 al 23 de Noviembre de 2001),* vol. II, 299–336; José Peña Solis, 'Notas sobre los Sistemas de Gobierno parlamentario y Presidencial. Breve Referencia al Sistema Venezolano', en *Tendencias Actuales del Derecho Constitucional. Homenaje a Jesús María Casal Montbrun,* vol. I, ed. Jesús María Casal, Alfredo Arismendi y Carlos Luis Carrillo Artiles (Coord.) (Caracas: Universidad Central de Venezuela/Universidad Católica Andrés Bello, 2008), 405–430; Alfredo Arismendi, 'La Separación de Poderes y el Sistema Presidencial', en *Tendencias Actuales del Derecho Constitucional. Homenaje a Jesús María Casal Montbrun*, ed. Jesús María Casal, Alfredo Arismendi y Carlos Luis Carrillo Artiles (Coord.), vol. I (Caracas: Universidad Central de Venezuela/Universidad Católica Andrés Bello, 2008), 465–484.

Chapter 1. The National Executive

§1. The President of the Republic

I. Head of State and of the Government

286. Article 226 of the Constitution provides that the President of the Republic is both the Chief of State, and the Chief of the National Executive branch, and in which capacity he directs the government.

The President of the Republic is elected through direct, secret and universal suffrage, by relative majority of votes (Article 228). To be elected President, the candidate must be Venezuelan by birth, possess no other nationality, be older than 30 years of age, and not be convicted of a crime (Article 227). Those that on the day of the nomination for President or on any date between that date and the day of the election, are or have been acting as Executive Vice President, Governor of a state or municipal Mayor, may not lawfully be elected to the Presidency of the Republic (Article 229).

287. The President's constitutional term is of six years. For the first time since the nineteenth century, after forbidding presidential re-elections, the 1999 Constitution provided that the President could be re-elected for a consecutive term, although only once (Article 230). This limit was eliminated in 2009, first by means of a constitutional interpretation on the alternating principle of government,[476] and second, through a constitutional amendment approved by referendum on 14 February 2009 (*see supra* paragraph 648). President Hugo Chávez Frias, after being elected in 1998 and subsequently in 2000 once the new Constitution was approved, was re-elected in 2006. In 2007 he proposed a Constitutional Reform Draft seeking the establishment in the Constitution of the possibility for the indefinite re-election of the President of the Republic, which was rejected by the people in the referendum held on December 2007. Nonetheless, as aforementioned, in January 2008, he announced that he was going to seek a constitutional amendment, and in December 2008, after important defeats in the regional and municipal elections, he asked the National Assembly to approve a constitutional amendment draft on the same matter of indefinite presidential election, which was approved by referendum on February 2009. Chavez was re-elected in the October 2012 elections for the period 2013–2019, but got severely ill in December 2012, being hospitalized in La Habana, Cuba, and since 9 December 2012, was not seen in public any more. He failed to take the oath in January 2013, and through an unconstitutional 'interpretation' of the Constitution, the Executive Vice-President Nicolás Maduro was allowed to 'continue' his mandate until he announced the death of Chavez on the 5 March 2013. Subsequently, the Supreme Tribunal allowed the Vice President in charge of the Presidency to be a candidate in the subsequent election that took place in the same month of March 2013. In it, Nicolás Maduro was elected for the period 2013–2019,

476. *See* Allan R. Brewer-Carías, 'El Juez Constitucional vs. La alternabilidad republicana (La reelección continua e indefinida)', in *Revista de Derecho Público*, No. 117 (Caracas, 2009), 205–211.

and in an anticipated election that took place in May 2018, unconstitutionally convened by the National Constituent Assembly elected in 2017, was re-elected for the period 2019–2025, an election that was declared null and void and as inexistent by the National Assembly (*see supra* paragraphs 44 et seq.).[477]

288. It must also be mentioned that the Constitution has established the possibility for the Supreme Tribunal of Justice to decide 'the removal from office of the President of the Republic' (Article 233) without any other significant specific delineation or definition of the conditions for exercising that power.

II. The Absences of the President of the Republic and Its Substitutions

289. The Constitution distinguishes two kinds of absences of the President from his tenure: absolute and temporal, and the ways to replace him.

According to Article 233, the absolute absence of the President of the Republic is produced in cases of death; resignation; dismissal by the Supreme Tribunal; physical or mental incapacity certified by a medical panel appointed by the Supreme Tribunal with the approval of the National Assembly; the abandonment of the office declared by the National Assembly, and the repeal of his mandate by referendum.

In such cases, if the absolute absence is produced before his inauguration, a new universal, direct and secret election must be convened within the following thirty days. In this case, in the meantime, the President of the National Assembly must take charge of the Presidency of the Republic. If the absolute absence takes place within the first four years of the constitutional term, a new universal and direct election must be convened within the following thirty days. In this case, in the meantime, the Executive Vice President must take charge of the Presidency of the Republic. In all these situations, the new President must finish the constitutional term of the absent President.

If the absolute absence is produced during the last two years of the constitutional term of the President, the Executive Vice President must assume the Presidency of the Republic up to the end of the term.

290. Regarding the temporary absences of the President, such as for instances when travelling abroad, Article 234 establishes that in such cases, he must be replaced by the Executive Vice President for up to ninety days, which can be extended by the National Assembly for another ninety days. If the temporary absence exceeds the latter ninety days, the National Assembly can decide by a majority vote of its members to consider it as an absolute absence of the President.

Regarding the travels of the President outside the national territory, only trips abroad for more than five days require the authorization of the National Assembly (Article 235).

477. *See* the comments on all the incidences and decisions issued in this process in Asdrúbal Aguiar (Compilador), *El Golpe de Enero en Venezuela (Documentos y testimonios para la historia)*, (Caracas, Editorial Jurídica Venezolana, 2013).

All these constitutional provisions were openly violated during the last years of Chávez, who was submitted to intermittent medical treatment in La Habana, Cuba, until his death in December 2012, but without the government even considering that a temporal absence occurred.[478] Not to mention the absolute absence situation produced by the death of President Chavez and the unconstitutional succession in the Presidency decree by the Constitutional Chamber of the Supreme Tribunal in January 2013.[479]

§2. The Executive Vice President

291. One of the innovations in the Constitution of 1999 was the creation of the office of the Executive Vice President, which is a non-elected organ appointed by the President and directly tied to his office, which has the power to freely appoint or dismiss him. The Executive Vice President must meet the same qualifications for the office as the President and must have no blood or marriage relation with the President.

The Executive Vice President is thus an immediate collaborator of the President in his capacity as Chief Executive (Article 238). Consequently, its creation in the Constitution does not alter the nature of the presidential system of government.[480] Its main attributions are the following (Article 239): to collaborate with the President in the direction of Government action; coordinate National Public Administration according to the President's instructions; propose to the President the appointment and dismissal of Ministers; preside over the Council of Ministers, with prior authorization of the President (Article 242); coordinate the relations of the National Executive with the National Assembly; and fill the temporal absences of the President (Article 234).

292. As mentioned, the Executive Vice President is appointed and dismissed by the President of the Republic. Nonetheless, according to Article 240 of the Constitution, a motion to censure the Vice President, arising from a vote of at least three-fifths of the members of the National Assembly, will result in his removal from office. In such a case, the Executive Vice President may not occupy that office or that of a Minister for the remainder of the President's term in office. However, three

478. *See* Allan R. Brewer-Carías, 'La extraña situación constitucional respecto del funcionamiento del gobierno en Venezuela, durante la falta temporal del Presidente de la República, por su ausencia del territorio nacional entre el 5 de junio y el 4 de julio de 2011', *Revista de Derecho Público*, 126 (Caracas: Editorial Jurídica Venezolana, 2011, 59–75; 'Comentario sobre la bizarra situación constitucional y administrativa derivada de la ausencia temporal del Presidente de la República entre el 17 y 24 de julio de 2011 por encontrarse en tratamiento médico en La Habana, Cuba', *Revista de Derecho Público* 127 (Caracas: Editorial Jurídica Venezolana 2011), 47–54.

479. *See* Allan R. Brewer-Carías, 'Crónicas Constitucionales sobre el régimen constitucional en Venezuela con motivo de la ausencia del territorio nacional del Presidente (re-electo) de la República, a partir del 9 de diciembre de 2012 (Crónicas I-IX: 29-1-2012 / 12-1-2013)', *Revista digital Elementos de juicio. Temas Constitucionales* (Bogotá, José Gregorio Galindo Publicaciones y medios, 2013), 99–165.

480. *See* Carlos Ayala Corao, *El Régimen Presidencial en América Latina y los planteamientos para su Reforma* (Caracas, 1992).

removals of Executive Vice Presidents due to a legislative motion to censure approved during the same constitutional term of the Legislature, authorizes the President of the Republic to dissolve the National Assembly.

This is the only situation in which the President is entitled to dissolve the National Assembly, such a situation being difficult to conceive unless the Assembly itself 'provoked' its own dissolution by voting to approve a third motion to censure. In such case, the Executive Decree dissolving the Assembly implies the need to convene new elections for the National Assembly that must take place within sixty days of its dissolution. In no case can the Assembly be dissolved during the last year of its constitutional term.

§3. THE MINISTERS

293. The Ministers' offices are also directly linked to the President of the Republic, being directly under his control. The Ministers, sitting together with the President and the Executive Vice President, constitute the Council of Ministers (Article 242).

The Ministers are usually the head of the Ministries, which are the most important executive organs of the Government. They are freely appointed and dismissed by the President (Article 236.3). Nonetheless, Article 246 of the Constitution establishes the possibility for the National Assembly to approve motions to censure the Minister, and when the motion arises from a vote of not less than three-fifths of the members present in the National Assembly, the decision will result in the Minister's removal. The Minister may not then occupy any other office of Minister or of Executive Vice President for the remainder of the Presidential term.

294. The number, organization and functions of the Ministries are established by the President of the Republic, by Executive Decree (Article 236.20) according to the general provisions established in the Organic Law of Public Administration.[481] In accordance with Article 243 of the Constitution, the President of the Republic may also name Ministers of State, who, in addition to forming part of the Council of Ministers and without a Ministerial Office, assist the President and Vice President in certain functions.

295. The Ministers have the right to speak before the National Assembly (Article 211), and they can take part in its debates, although without a vote (Article 245). However, the National Assembly can convoke the Ministers to its sessions, with the Assembly having the right to question them. The Ministers, as well as any public official, are also obliged to appear before the Assembly and to give them all the information and documents it requires for its legislative and control functions (Article 223). The National Assembly has the power to declare political responsibility of the Ministers and can ask the Citizen Power to prosecute them. As already mentioned, the Assembly can also approve motions of censure of the Ministers (Article 246).

481. *Gaceta Oficial* No. 6.47 Extra. of 17 Nov. 2014.

Finally, the Ministers must deliver before the National Assembly, within the first sixty days of each year, a motivated sufficient memoir referring to their activities in the previous year (Article 224).

§4. The Council of Ministers

296. As indicated, when sitting together with the President and the Executive Vice President, the Ministers constitute the Council of Ministers (Article 242). According to Article 236 of the Constitution, the President of the Republic, sitting in Ministers' Council, is required to exercise a set of functions designated in sections 7, 8, 9, 10, 12, 13, 14, 18, 20, 21, 22 of that article, as well as those imposed by statutes. Within these attributions that the President must always exercise in Council of Ministers are the following: declaration of states of exception and the suspension of constitutional guarantees; issuing of decrees-laws according to the legislative delegation made by the National Assembly; convening of the National Assembly to extraordinary sessions; issuing of regulations to statutes; approval of the National Plan for Development; the fixation of the number and organization of the Ministries; ordering the dissolution of the National Assembly, and convening referendums.

The Council of Ministers is presided over by the President of the Republic, although the President may authorize the Executive Vice President to preside when unable to attend. In all events, decisions of the Ministers' Council must always be ratified by the President.

§5. Other Constitutional Executive Organs

297. The Attorney General of the Republic is also an Executive organ of the Government and is required to attend the Council of Ministers but only with the right to speak, without the vote (Article 250). It is defined in the Constitution as an organ of the National Executive Branch that assists defends and represents the interests of the Republic in judicial and non-judicial matters (Article 247). In particular, the Constitution requires the advice of the Attorney General with respect to the approval of contracts of national public interest to be signed by the executive (Article 247).

298. One of the innovations of the Constitution of 1999 was the creation of the Council of State as a superior advisory organ of the Government and of the National Public Administration (Article 251). The Council of State is formally charged with making policy recommendations regarding matters of national interest that the President of the Republic recognizes as being of special importance, requiring the Council's point of view.

The Council of State's specific functions and attributes must be determined by law, which up to 2011, had not been sanctioned. Anyway, regarding the constitutional provisions, the Executive Vice President must preside over the Council of

State, which must be integrated, in addition, to five individuals named by the President of the Republic, a representative designated by the National Assembly, a representative designated by the Supreme Tribunal of Justice, and a Governor collectively designated by the chief executives of the states (Article 252). In practice, during the first decade of the 1999 Constitution, the Council of State has not been integrated and has not functioned.

299. Another innovation in the 1999 Constitution was the creation of the Federal Council of Government in charge of planning and coordinating the policies and actions for the process of decentralization and transfer of competencies from the national level of government to the states and municipalities. As aforementioned, this Council is presided over by the Executive Vice President, and integrated by the Ministers, the state Governors, one municipal Mayor from each state and representatives of the organized society; and is in charge of managing the Inter-territorial Compensatory Fund (Article 185), in order to finance the public investments to promote the equitable development of the regions, the cooperation and complementation of development policies and initiatives of the public territorial entities.[482]

In 2010 the Organic Law on the Federal Council of Government was approved, following the centralistic character of the Government developed during the first decade of the Constitution (*see supra* paragraph 67), creating the Inter-territorial Compensatory Fund in substitution of the former Intergovernmental Fund on Decentralization established in 1993.[483]

300. Finally, Article 323 of the Constitution has also created the Council of Nation's Defence, presided over by the President of the Republic, as the country's highest authority for defence planning, advice and consultation regarding all public entities (Public Powers) on all matters related to the defence and security of the Nation's sovereignty, territorial integrity and strategic thinking (*see infra* paragraphs 355 et seq.).

482. *See* Manuel Rachadell, 'El Consejo Federal de Gobierno y el Fondo de Compensación', in *Revista de derecho del Tribunal Supremo de Justicia,* No. 7 (Caracas, 2002), 417 a 457; Emilio Spósito Contreras, 'Reflexiones sobre el Consejo Federal de Gobierno como máxima instancia de Participación administrativa', in *Temas de derecho administrativo, Libro Homenaje a Gonzalo Pérez Luciani* II, no. 7 (Caracas: Tribunal Supremo de Justicia, Colección Libros Homenaje, 2002), 827 a 863,; and José V. Haro, 'Aproximación a la noción del Consejo Federal de Gobierno prrevisto en la Constitución de 1999', in *Revista de Derecho Constitucional,* No. 7 (enero-junio) (Caracas: Editorial Sherwood, 2003), 161–166.

483. *See* in *Gaceta Oficial* No. 5.963 Extra. of 22 Feb. 2010.

Chapter 2. Constitutional Powers of the National Executive

301. The President of the Republic is at the same time the Head of the State and the Head of Government and of Public Administration, and as such, directs the Government's actions (Article 226). Thus, the two basic functions of the National Executive are political and administrative, being subjected in both cases to the control of the National Assembly.

§1. The Political Functions of Government in the Constitution and the Parliamentary Control

302. As aforementioned, the President of the Republic directs the Government's actions (Articles 226; 236.2), and for such purpose, the Constitution directly assigns him a series of political attributions. Among these, for instance, are the direction of foreign relations, the convening of extraordinary sessions of the National Assembly, and the declaration of states of exception, or the restriction of constitutional guarantees, in the latter case according to the corresponding Organic Law (Article 338).

In all these cases of political acts enumerated in Article 236 of the Constitution, the Executive decisions must be counter-signed by the Vice President and by the corresponding Ministers, except the acts of the appointment of the Vice President and of the Ministers, and the decrees of pardon.

303. In these matters, the National Assembly 'exercises its control functions over the Government' (Article 187.3), according to which it can approve motions to censure the Vice President and the Ministers, which can lead to their removal when approved by three-fifths of the representatives (Articles 187.10; 240). As already mentioned, the National Assembly must also decide certain cases of absolute absence of the President because of physical or mental incapacity or abandonment of the office, or the conversion of a temporal absence into an absolute one (Articles 233, 234) (*see supra* paragraph 289). The National Assembly can also authorize criminal processes against the President (Article 266.2) and must always review the Decrees of State of Exception (Articles 338, 339).

304. The National Assembly also has important attributions in political matters like the indirect election, as an electoral body representing the people, of the Magistrates of the Supreme Tribunal of Justice and the High officials of the Citizen and Electoral Branches of Government (Prosecutor General, Peoples' Defender, Comptroller General, and Members of the National Electoral Council), and their removal or dismissal (Articles 265, 279, 296) (*see infra* paragraphs 415 et seq., 438 et seq.).

I. The Direction of Foreign Relations

305. The President of the Republic has within his attributions 'to direct the foreign relations of the Republic and to sign and ratify international treaties, covenants and agreements' (Article 236.4). Regarding the latter, they must be approved by special statute (Article 187.18), before their ratification by the President, except when they execute or perfect pre-existent obligations of the Republic; they apply principles expressly recognized by it; they execute international relations ordinary acts; or they exercise attributions expressly assigned by statute to the President (Article 154) (*see supra* paragraphs 136 et seq.).

However, as mentioned before, the National Assembly must authorize the President's trips abroad when they exceed more than five days (Article 187.17).

II. The Executive Initiatives on Matters of Constitutional Review and of Referendum

306. The President of the Republic in Council of Ministers has the initiative to propose amendments (Article 341) and reforms (Article 342) to the Constitution, as well as to convene a National Constituent Assembly for major constitutional changes to it (Article 348). The National Assembly also has initiative rights regarding constitutional review (Articles 341, 342, 348), and in the case of constitutional reforms, the draft must always be debated before it (Article 343) (*see supra* paragraph 128).

The President of the Republic, also in Council of Ministers (Article 236.22), has the initiative to submit to consultative referendum matters he considers as of special national interest (Article 71); to submit to approbatory referendum, international treaties, covenants or agreements that could compromise the national sovereignty or that could imply the transfer of State attributions to supra-national organs (Article 73); and to submit statutes to total or partial abrogate referendum (Article 74). However, the National Assembly has the initiative for the approbatory referendums of statutes (Article 73).

III. The Military Powers of the President of the Republic

307. According to Article 236 of the Constitution, the President of the Republic, in his position of Commander in Chief, has the attribution of directing the National Armed Force to exercise the supreme authority upon it and to fix its contingent (Article 236.5). In such position, the President exercises the supreme command of the National Armed Force, and has the power to promote its officers from the rank of colonel or navy captain and to appoint them for their corresponding positions (Article 236.6). In case of use of military missions abroad, or in case of foreign military missions in the country, the National Assembly must always give the corresponding authorization (Article 187.11).

IV. Executive Powers Regarding the National Assembly

308. The President of the Republic has legislative initiative and can send to the National Assembly Draft statutes for its discussion (Article 304.1). He also has, in

Council of Ministers, the power to convene the National Assembly to extraordinary sessions, and to dissolve the Assembly in case of its approval of three motions of censure against the Executive Vice President (Articles 236.21; 240) (*see infra* paragraph 292). The President of the Republic can personally or through the Executive Vice President, direct reports or special messages to the National Assembly (Article 236.17).

V. Executive Powers in Situations of Exception

309. Chapter II of the Constitution, titled 'Protection of the Constitution', regulates cases of exceptional circumstances provoking 'situation of exception' that can seriously threaten the security of the Nation, and of its institutions and persons, in which the adoption of special political-constitutional measures to confront them is necessary.

Article 337 of the Constitution defines these 'states of exception'[484] as the circumstances affecting the social, economic, political or natural order regarding which ordinary powers of government are considered insufficient to confront, as well as those gravely affecting the security of the Nation, and its institutions and Citizens. These are exceptional circumstances whose characteristics exceed the possibility of being attended to by the State through the institutional mechanisms established for normal situations. In these cases, the President of the Republic, in Council of Ministers, can decree the state of exceptions and also restrict some constitutional guarantees (Article 236.7).

310. According to the Organic Law on the States of Exception, which was sanctioned according to Article 338 of the Constitution,[485] the following states of exception can be decreed: The 'state of alarm' can be decreed in cases of 'catastrophes, public calamities or similar events' exposing the Nation or its Citizens to serious danger. This state of exception is to have a duration of thirty days, which may be extended for an additional period of equal length. The 'state of economic emergency' that can be decreed when 'extraordinary economic circumstances arise' that 'gravely affect the Nation's economic life'. The permitted duration of this exceptional situation is sixty days, a term that may again be extended for an equal period. The 'state of interior or exterior commotion' that can be decreed in cases of 'interior or exterior conflict that seriously endangers the security of the Nation, its Citizens or institutions'. Here, the state of exception can last up to ninety days and may be extended for an equal period.

---

484. *See* in general Jesús M. Casal H., 'Los estados de excepción en la Constitución de 1999', in *Revista de Derecho Constitucional,* No. 1 (septiembre-diciembre) (Caracas: Editorial Sherwood, 1999), 45–54; Salvador Leal W., 'Los estados de excepción en la Constitución', in *Revista del Tribunal Supremo de Justicia*, No. 8 (Caracas, 2003), 335–359; María de los Ángeles Delfino, 'El desarrollo de los Estados de Excepción en las Constituciones de América Latina', in *Constitución y Constitucionalismo Hoy* (Caracas: Editorial Ex Libris, 2000), 507–532.

485. *See* the Organic Law on States of Exception, *Gaceta Oficial* No. 37.261 of 15 Aug. 2001.

311. In the above exceptional circumstances, the President of the Republic, sitting in Council of Ministers, is the one that has the prerogative and responsibility to decree these States of Exception (Article 337). Article 339 of the Constitution requires that within eight days of being issued, the decree must be sent for consideration and approval by the National Assembly or to its Delegated Commission, and to the Constitutional Chamber of the Supreme Tribunal of Justice which must decide whether the decree is constitutional (Article 336.6)) (*see infra* paragraph 687). The decree must be in compliance with the requirements, principles and guarantees of the International Covenant on Civil and Political Rights[486] and the American Convention on Human Rights.[487]

The President of the Republic may also request the National Assembly to extend the duration of a decree for a term equal to its original constitutional one. The decree may be revoked by the National Executive, the National Assembly or its Delegated Commission before the completion of the decree's term should the causes that motivated its declaration cease. In all cases, however, the National Assembly must approve any extension of the duration of a decree (Article 338).

312. In addition, when a state of exception is decreed, the President of the Republic, sitting in Council of Ministers, is authorized in the Constitution to temporarily restrict constitutional guarantees, with the exception of those referring to the right to life, the right against *incomunicado* detentions and torture, the right to due process of law, the right to information, and those considered untouchable (intangibles) human rights (Article 377). In the latter category can be identified those human rights provided in the International Covenant on Civil and Political Rights (Article 4), and in the American Convention on Human Rights (Article 27), like the guarantee of equality before the law and non-discrimination; the guarantee against being imprisoned for contract obligations; the guarantee against retroactive or ex post facto laws; the right to individual personality; religious liberty; the guarantee to be free of slavery or involuntary servitude; the right to the physical integrity of the person; the principle of legality; the protection of the family; the rights of children; the guarantee against arbitrary deprivation of nationality and the political rights to suffrage, and the guarantee of public access in government affairs.

The consequence of these provisions is that, *in the first place*, the Constitution has here eliminated the possibility of 'suspending' individual constitutional rights or guarantees, which on the contrary, was authorized by the Constitution of 1961 (Articles 241; 190.6), contributing to innumerable institutional abuses. By contrast, in the 1999 Constitution, the President is left with only the power to 'restrict' (Article 236.7) constitutional guarantees. In the second place, the Constitution now expressly requires that an Executive Decree declaring a state of emergency that 'restricts' a constitutional guarantee must 'regulate the exercise of the right whose guarantee is restricted' (Article 339). Thus, it is no longer constitutionally possible for the President to simply 'restrict' a constitutional guarantee, but it is now indispensable that the text of the decree itself expressly sets forth the specific normative regulation and concrete limitations of the exercise of the right.

486. International Covenant on Civil and Political Rights of 16 Dec. 1966.
487. American Convention on Human Rights, San José, Costa Rica, of 22 Nov. 1969.

313. Finally, it must be mentioned that the declaration of a state of exception cannot in any event interrupt the functioning of the branches of governments and other organs of the State (Article 339). Moreover, the declaration of a state of emergency does not alter the liability of the President of the Republic, those of the Executive Vice President, or of the Ministers, in conformity with the Constitution and laws (Article 232).[488]

VI. Executive Pardon Powers

314. The President of the Republic has the power to give pardons (*indultos*) (Article 236.19), although the National Assembly is the one empowered to decree amnesties (Article 187.5).

VII. The Legislation Veto Powers of the President of the Republic

315. The President of the Republic must promulgate all statutes sanctioned by the National Assembly within ten days of having received the statute's approval (Article 214), and legislation is considered promulgated and producing effects once published in the *Gaceta Oficial de la República* (Article 215) with the corresponding order that it be put into effect.

The President may, however, within the ten-day period, in a decision adopted in Council of Ministers, and on the basis of a reasoned exposition, request that the National Assembly modify some aspect of the legislation or reverse the approval of all or a part of it.

The National Assembly must decide on the President's proposal through a vote by an absolute majority of representatives present, and must then send the statute for promulgation. The President must then promulgate the law within five days of receiving it and may not propose new changes.

316. However, when the President of the Republic considers that a statute or certain of its articles are unconstitutional, he must request a declaration on the matter from the Constitutional Chamber of the Supreme Tribunal of Justice during the ten-day period in which the law must be promulgated or returned to the Assembly (*see infra* paragraph 692). The Constitutional Chamber must then issue its decision within fifteen days of receiving the communication from the President. If the Tribunal denies the unconstitutionality of the law or fails to decide within the allotted time period, the President must promulgate the law within five days (Article 214).

317. If the President of the Republic fails to promulgate statutes according to the above-mentioned rules, the President and the two Vice Presidents of the National

488. The first declaration of a 'state of Emergency' adopted according to the 1999 Constitucion, was issued referred to some Municipalities of state of Táchira in the Venezuelan border, on matters of Economic Emergency, *See* Decree-Law No. 1.950 of 21 Aug. 2015 *Gaceta Oficial* No. 6.194 of 21 Aug. 2001.

Assembly must proceed to promulgate the statute as indicated, without prejudice to the responsibility incurred by the President of the Republic for his omission (Article 216).

318. In the case of statutes approving international treaties, agreements or conventions, they may be promulgated at the moment determined at the discretion of the National Executive, according to international custom and the national interest (Article 217).

VIII. Delegate Legislation

319. As aforementioned, the President of the Republic can be authorized by the National Assembly, by means of an 'enabling law' approved by the vote of three-fifths of its members, to enact legislation by means of delegate legislation. In these cases, the enabling law must fix the guidelines, purpose and framework of the matters that are delegated to the President's legislative powers, and the term for the issuing of the corresponding decrees-laws (Articles 203; 236.8) (*see supra* paragraphs 65, 148, 278).

§2. The Administrative Functions of Government in the Constitution and the Parliamentary Control

I. The President of the Republic as Head of Public Administration

320. According to Article 236.11 of the Constitution, the President is the head of the Public Administration, which he administers. In all his acts in these matters, the Ministers must always countersign the corresponding executive acts. In particular, the President is empowered in Article 236.20 of the Constitution to determine the numbers, competencies and organization of the Ministries and other organs of Public Administration.

In all these administrative matters, the National Assembly also exercises its control over Public Administration (Article 187.3), being competent to discuss and approve the national budget and all public debt statutes (Articles 187.6, 314, 317).

321. In his position of Head of Public Administration, Article 236 of the Constitution assigns the President with the following attributions: to appoint and dismiss the Executive Vice President and the Ministers (Article 236.3); to appoint, after parliamentary approval, the Attorney General of the Republic as well as the ambassadors and head of permanent diplomatic missions (Articles 236.15, 187.14); and in general, to appoint all other public officials when attributed in the Constitution by statutes (Article 236.16).

322. On matters of public contracts, the same Article 236 of the Constitution assigns the President of the Republic in Council of Ministers, the power to negotiate public national debt (Article 236.12); and to sign national interest contracts according to the Constitution (Article 236.14). For the signing of these contracts, the National Assembly must approve them only when it is expressly required by a statute (Article 150), except in cases of contracts to be signed with foreign States or official foreign entities, or enterprises not domiciled in the country, in which cases the parliamentary approval is necessary (Article 187.9). Also, parliamentary authorization is required in cases of public contracts selling public immoveable property (Article 187.12).

II. The Formulation of the National Development Plan

323. Article 236.18 of the Constitution assigns the President of the Republic in Council of Ministers the attribution to formulate the National Development Plan and direct its execution. The National Assembly must approve the general guidelines of the economic and social development plan, which the National Executive must file before the Assembly within the first trimester of the first year of the constitutional term (Article 236.18).

III. The Regulatory Powers of the President of the Republic

324. According to Article 236.10 of the Constitution, the President of the Republic in Council of Ministers has extensive powers to issue regulations to totally or partially develop statutory provisions, 'without altering the spirit, purpose and ratio' of the statute (*see supra* paragraph 158).

§3. Liabilities

325. The President of the Republic is responsible for his acts and for the accomplishment of his duties. He is specifically obliged to seek for the guarantee of the Citizens' rights and liberties, as well as for the independence, integrity, sovereignty of the territory and the defence of the Republic (Article 232). The declaration of states of exception does not modify the liability principles regarding the President, or the Executive Vice President and the Ministers (Article 232).

326. However, the Executive Vice President and the Ministers are also individually, civilly, criminally and administratively responsible for their actions (Articles 241, 244). They are also politically responsible before the President of the Republic, as head of Government, and before the National Assembly that can censure them.

327. According to Article 242 of the Constitution, the Executive Vice President and all the Ministers that have concurred in a decision of the Council of Ministers are jointly liable for their decisions. Only those that have formally expressed a dissenting or negative vote are excluded from this liability. The President of the Republic is, of course, also subject to joint liability for the Council's decisions, when he presides over it.

Chapter 3. Public Administration

§1. The Constitutional Principles Related to Public Administration and Administrative Activities

328. In the 1999 Constitution, it can be said that a complete process of constitutionalizing administrative law occurred having incorporated in the text of the Constitution all the basic foundations of administrative law.[489] In this regard, the title referred to the 'Public Power', the 1999 Constitution included a section related to 'Public Administration',[490] whose provisions have been developed by the Organic Law on Public Administration of 2001, reformed in 2008 and 2014.[491] These provisions are applicable to all the organs and entities of all branches of government exercising administrative functions, and not only of the executive branch, and to the national, states and municipal public administrations.[492]

The Constitution sets forth a series of principles related to Public Administration, and within them, those that are common to all of the organs of the branches of government: principle of legality, principle of liability of the State and of its officials, and principle of finality.

329. The *first* principle related to Public Administration and to all State organs is the principle of legality enunciated in Article 137 of the Constitution when establishing that 'The Constitution and the law would define the attributions of the organs exercising Public Power, to which they must subject all the activities they perform.' This provision imposes the necessary submission of Public Administration to the law, being the consequence of it, that all administrative activities contrary to it can be reviewed by the Constitutional Jurisdiction (Article 334) and by the Administrative Jurisdiction (Article 259), whose courts have the power to annul illegal acts (*see infra* paragraphs 683, 706).

The principle of legality is also declared in the Constitution as one of the foundations of Public Administration, defined as the 'complete subjection to the law'

489. *See* Allan R. Brewer-Carías, *El derecho administrativo en la Constitución*, (Caracas Editorial Jurídica Venezolana, 2022); 'Algunos aspectos de proceso de constitucionalización del derecho administrativo en la Constitución de 1999', in *Los requisitos y vicios de los actos administrativos. V Jornadas Internacionales de Derecho Administrativo Allan Randolph Brewer-Carías, Caracas 1996,* (Caracas, Fundación Estudios de Derecho Administrativo, 2000), pp. 23–37.

490. *See* Antonieta Garrido de Cárdenas, 'La Administración Pública Nacional y su organización administrativa en la Constitución de 1999', in *Estudios de Derecho Administrativo: Libro Homenaje a la Universidad Central de Venezuela,* vol. I (Caracas: Imprenta Nacional, 2001), 427–471.

491. *See Gaceta Oficial* No. 6.147 Extra. of 17 Nov. 2014. The 2008 Law was published in *Gaceta Oficial* No. 5.890 Extra. of 31 Jul. 2008. Allan R. Brewer-Carías & Rafael Chavero Gazdik y Jesús María Alvarado Andrade, *Ley Orgánica de la Administración Pública, Decreto Ley* No. *4317 de 15 Jul. 2008* (Caracas: Editorial Jurídica Venezolana, 2009); Gustavo Briceño Vivas, 'Principios constitucionales que rigen la Administración en la nueva Ley Orgánica de la Administración Pública', in *Temas de derecho administrativo, Libro Homenaje a Gonzalo Pérez Luciani* vol. I, No. 7 (Caracas: Tribunal Supremo de Justicia, Colección Libros Homenaje, 2002), 351 a 372.

492. *See* Allan R. Brewer-Carías, *Principios del Régimen Jurídico de la Organización Administrativa Venezolana* (Caracas, 1994), 11 y 53.

(Article 141), being one of the basic missions of the organs of the Citizen Power, to assure 'the complete subjection of the administrative activities of the State to the law' (Article 274).

330. The *second* general principle of Public administration is the principle of State liability, incorporated in an express way in the 1999 Constitution (Article 140), setting forth that 'The State is liable for the damages suffered by individuals in their goods and rights, provided that the injury be imputable to the functioning of Public Administration', being possible to comprise in the expression 'functioning of Public Administration', its normal or abnormal functioning.[493] Although doubts can result from the wording of the article regarding the liability of the State caused by legislative actions that nonetheless are derived from the general principles of public law,[494] regarding the liability caused by judicial acts, it is clarified by the express provisions of Articles 49.8 and 255 of the Constitution, in which it is established, in addition, the State liability caused because of 'judicial errors or delay'.[495]

331. The *third* general constitutional principle regarding Public Administration is the principle of liability of public officials in the exercise of public functions established in Article 139 of the Constitution, based on the 'abuse or deviation of powers or the violation of the Constitution or of the law'. In addition, Article 25 of the Constitution, following a long constitutional tradition, expressly establishes the specific civil, criminal and administrative liability of any public officials when issuing or executing acts violating human rights guarantees in the Constitution and the statutes, any excuse due to superior orders not being acceptable.

332. The *fourth* principle of Public Administration incorporated in the 1999 Constitution is the principle of finality (Article 141), emphasizing that 'Public

493. *See* Jesús Caballero Ortiz, 'Consideraciones fundamentales sobre la responsabilidad administrativa en Francia y en España y su recepción en la Constitución venezolana de 1999', in *Estudios de Derecho Público: Libro Homenaje a Humberto J. La Roche Rincón,* vol. II (Caracas: Tribunal Supremo de Justicia, 2001), 255–271; Luis A. Ortiz-Álvarez, 'La responsabilidad patrimonial del Estado y de los funcionarios públicos en la Constitución de 1999', in *Estudios de Derecho Administrativo: Libro Homenaje a la Universidad Central de Venezuela,* vol. II (Caracas: Imprenta Nacional, 2001), 149–208, and in *Revista de Derecho Constitucional*, No. 1 (septiembre-diciembre) (Caracas: Editorial Sherwood, 1999), 267–312; María E. Soto, 'Régimen constitucional de la responsabilidad extracontractual de la Administración Pública', in *Revista LEX NOVA del Colegio de Abogados del Estado Zulia,* No. 239 (Maracaibo, 2001), 49–72; Ana C. Núñez Machado, 'La nueva Constitución y la responsabilidad patrimonial del Estado', in *Comentarios a la Constitución de la República Bolivariana de Venezuela* (Caracas: Vadell Hermanos Editores, 2000), 35–64; and 'Reflexiones sobre la interpretación constitucional y el artículo 140 de la Constitución sobre responsabilidad patrimonial del Estado', in *Revista de Derecho Administrativo,* No. 15 (mayo-diciembre) (Caracas: Editorial Sherwood, 2002), 207–222.

494. *See* Carlos A. Urdaneta Sandoval, 'El Estado venezolano y el fundamento de su responsabilidad patrimonial extracontractual por el ejercicio de la función legislativa a la luz de la Constitución de 1999', in *Revista de Derecho Constitucional,* No. 5 (julio-diciembre) (Caracas: Editorial Sherwood, 2001), 247–301.

495. *See* Abdón Sánchez Noguera, 'La responsabilidad del Estado por el ejercicio de la función jurisdiccional en la Constitución venezolana de 1999', in *Revista Tachirense de Derecho,* No. 12 (enero-diciembre) (San Cristóbal: Universidad Católica del Táchira, 2000), 55–74.

Administration is at the service of Citizens', and as an organ of the State, it must also 'guaranty the inalienable, indivisible and interdependent enjoyment and exercise of human rights to all persons, according to the principle of progressiveness and without discrimination'.

333. And *fifth*, Article 141 of the Constitution also enumerates in an express way the general principles concerning administrative activities, providing that all activities of Public Administration are founded in the principles of 'honesty, participation, celerity, efficacy, efficiency, transparency, accountability and liability in the exercise of public functions, with complete subjection to the law'.

All these principles have been developed in the Organic Law on Public Administration (Article 12), adding to them, the principles of economy, simplicity, objectivity, impartiality, good faith and confidence (Article 12), and in the Administrative Procedure Organic Law.[496]

§2. Constitutional Provisions Related to the Organization of Public Administration: Centralized and Decentralized Public Administration

334. The Constitution establishes the basic principles for the organization of Public Administration, distinguishing between the Central Public Administration and Decentralized Public Administration.

Regarding Central Public Administration, it is conformed by the Executive organs of the State in each of the three levels of government, according to the federal form of the State: at the national level, the President of the Republic is the head of National Public Administration; at the states level, the Governors of the states are the head of their states' Public Administrations (Article 160); and at the municipal level, the Mayors are the Heads of the Municipal Public Administrations (Article 174).

Regarding the Central National Public Administration, as aforementioned, it is basically organized around the Ministries, being the President of the Republic as the competent organ, following the general principles established in the Organic Law on Public Administration, to determine their number, attributions and organization as well as of the other entities of Central Public Administration (Article 236.20).[497]

335. Regarding the National Decentralized Public Administration, the Constitution basically refers to the creation of autonomous institutions (public corporations), which is a power reserved to statutes (Article 142), and such institutions are

496. *Gaceta Oficial* No. 2818 Extra. of 7 Jul. 1981. *See* Allan R. Brewer-Carías et al., *Ley Orgánica de Procedimientos Administrativos,* 13 edición (Caracas: Editorial Jurídica Venezolana, 2006), 175 y ss.

497. *See* Decree No. 1.612, *Gaceta Oficial* No. 6.173 Extra. Of 18 Feb. 2015. *See* on this matter: Daniel Leza Betz, 'La organización y funcionamiento de la administración pública nacional y las nuevas competencias normativas del Presidente de la República previstas en la Constitución de 1999. Al traste con la reserva legal formal ordinaria en el Derecho Constitucional venezolano', in *Revista de Derecho Público,* No. 82 (abril-junio) (Caracas: Editorial Jurídica Venezolana, 2000), 18–55.

always subjected to State control. Other forms of administrative functional decentralization, like public enterprises or public foundations, are regulated in the Organic Law on Public Administration. Petróleos de Venezuela S.A., the State-owned oil company, is also regulated in Article 302 of the Constitution as a decentralized nationalized entity.

Regarding independent Regulatory Administrations, they are all regulated by statutes (Banking Superintendence, Insurance Superintendence, Free Competition Superintendence, Stock Exchange Commission). The Central Bank of Venezuela is also regulated as a special autonomous decentralized entity in the Constitution (Article 320).

§3. Constitutional Principles Regarding Administrative Information

336. Finally, Article 143 of the Constitution is also innovative regarding Citizens' Rights to be informed and to have access to administrative information. In the first place, it provides for the right of Citizens to be promptly and truly informed by Public Administration regarding the situation of the procedures in which they have direct interest, and to know about the definitive resolutions therein adopted, to be notified of administrative acts and to be informed on the courses of the administrative procedure.

The constitutional article also establishes that for the individual right, everybody has to have access to administrative archives and registries, without prejudice of the acceptable limits imposed in a democratic society related to the national or foreign security, criminal investigation, the intimacy of private life, all according to the statutes regulating the matter of secret or confidential documents classification. The same article provides for the principle of prohibition of any previous censorship referring to public officials regarding the information they could give referring to matters under their responsibility.[498]

The Constitutional Chamber of the Supreme Tribunal in 2010, through constitutional interpretation, restricted the scope of this right to have access to administrative information, denying the request made by a non-governmental organization regarding the salary of the Comptroller General of the Republic, arguing that on the matter the privacy of the economic rights of the latter prevailed.[499]

---

498. *See* Orlando Cárdenas Perdomo, 'El derecho de acceso a los archivos y registros administrativos en la Constitución de 1999', in *Estudios de Derecho Administrativo: Libro Homenaje a la Universidad Central de Venezuela,* vol. I (Caracas: Imprenta Nacional, 2001), 177–217; Manuel Rodríguez Costa, 'Derecho de acceso a los archivos y registros de la Administración Pública', in *El Derecho Público a comienzos del siglo XXI. Estudios homenaje al Profesor Allan R. Brewer-Carías,* vol. II (Madrid: Instituto de Derecho Público, UCV, Civitas Ediciones, 2003), 1483–1505; Javier T. Sánchez Rodríguez, 'La libertad de acceso a la información en materia del medio ambiente', in *Revista de derecho del Tribunal Supremo de Justicia,* No. 7 (Caracas, 2002), 459 a 495.

499. *See* Allan R. Brewer-Carías, 'De la Casa de Cristal a la Barraca de Hierro: el Juez Constitucional vs. El derecho de acceso a la información administrativa', in *Revista de Derecho Público*, No. 123 (julio-septiembre 2010) (Caracas: Editorial Jurídica Venezolana, 2010), 197–206.5.

§4. Constitutional Principles Regarding Civil Service

337. In the 1999 Constitution, also in an innovative way, the general principles of the organization of civil service are established (Articles 144 et seq.), which have been developed by the Statute on the Civil Service.[500] In the first place, Article 145 establishes the general principle that all public officials are at the State service, and that they cannot serve any political group, also providing that their appointment and dismissal cannot be determined by political affiliation or orientation. Unfortunately, this constitutional principle has not been respected, due to the authoritarian government that has developed during the last decade (2000–2011) in the country, characterized by political discrimination in Public Administration regarding those citizens that signed petitions for presidential repeal referendums in 2003–2004 (*see supra* paragraph 143), the absence of pluralism, and the interrelation between the official party and Public Administration) (*see supra* paragraphs 195, 196).

338. In the second place, the Constitution distinguishes between two sorts of public officials: those following career positions and those in positions of free appointment and dismissals (Article 146), establishing in an express way that all career positions in the Public Administration must always be filed through public competition (*concurso público*), based on honesty, competence and efficiency considerations. Also, the promotions must be subjected to scientific methods based on a merit system, and the transfer, suspension and dismissals must be decided according to their performance. Unfortunately, due to the strict political control of all the bureaucracy, neither of these constitutional provisions factually are in force.

339. In third place, the Constitution also establishes the general principle of discipline in public spending regarding the provisions of public official positions, in the sense that being remunerated, they can only be provided when there are enough budget provisions for funds (Article 147). The scale of remunerations for public officials must be established by statute, and the National Assembly has been empowered to establish limits for municipal, states and national public officers (Article 229). The regime for pensions and retirements is also attributed in the Constitution to be established by the National Assembly.[501]

340. In addition, other constitutional provisions are established regarding public officers. For instance, the principle of incompatibility to occupy more than one remunerated position (Article 148), except in cases of academic, transitory, assistant or teaching positions. In any case of acceptance of a new position, it implies

500. *Gaceta Oficial* No. 37.522 of 6 Sep. 2002. *See* Jesús Caballero Ortíz, 'Bases constitucionales del derecho de la función pública', in *Revista de Derecho Constitucional,* No. 5, julio-diciembre-2001 (Caracas: Editorial Sherwood, 2002), 21 a 46; Antonio de Pedro Fernández, 'Algunas consideraciones sobre la función pública en la Constitución de la República Bolivariana de Venezuela', in *Estudios de Derecho Administrativo: Libro Homenaje a la Universidad Central de Venezuela,* vol. I (Caracas: Imprenta Nacional, 2001), 307–342.

501. Law on the Remuneration, Pensions and Retrat of High Public Officials of Public Power, *Gaceta Oficial* No. 39.592 of 12 Jan. 2011.

the renunciation of the first, except in cases of deputies, up to the definitive replacement of the principal. In addition, the Constitution provides that a public officer cannot benefit from more than one pension (Article 148).

The Constitution also establishes the prohibition for public officers to sign contracts with the municipalities, the states, the Republic and with any other public law or State-owned entity (Article 145).

§5. Constitutional Principles Regarding Public Contracts

I. The Public Interest Contracts

341. Public contracts are regulated in the 1999 Constitution, following a previous constitutional tradition, with the expression of 'public interest contracts' (Articles 150,151, 187.9, 236, 247), having completed the traditional constitutionalization of public contracts regime,[502] also regulating some inter-administrative public contracts, that is, those signed between public entities.[503] The expression 'administrative contracts' is not used in the Constitution or in the legal system.[504]

342. In particular, Articles 150 and 151 of the Constitution refer to public interests contracts by providing, first, the scope of the powers of the National Assembly to control the Government and Public Administration on matters of 'public interest contracts'; and second, certain limits regarding the clauses that can be included in such contracts; being the notion 'public interest contracts' used in a broad sense, comprising all public contracts entered into by public organs and entities at the three territorial levels of the State.

As the Venezuelan State is organized as a federal one (Article 4) as it has been analyzed (*see supra* paragraphs 203 et seq.), there are three levels of autonomous governments (National, State, and Municipal) (Article 136), being possible for the organs and entities in each of such levels to enter into public contracts, which under Article 150 of the Constitution are classified in three subcategories: *national* public

502. *See* Allan R. Brewer-Carías, 'Algunos aspectos del proceso de constitucionalización del Derecho administrativo en Venezuela', in *V Jornadas internacionales de Derecho Administrativo Allan Randolph Brewer Carías, Los requisitos y vicios de los actos administrativos* (Caracas: FUNEDA 2000), 21 a 37.

503. This is the case of the intergovernmental contracts entered by the Republic and the states or between the states, or entered by the states and the municipalities, particularly as consequence of the process of transfer of competencies, derived from the decentralization process (Art. 170). For instance, as was initially established in the Organic Law on Decentralization, Delimitation and Transfer of attributions among public entities. (*Gaceta Oficial* No. 37.753 of 14 Aug. 2003 (Art. 165). and for contracts that can be signed by the municipalities (mancomunidades) in order to develop activities together (Art. 170). The Constitution also has provisions regarding contracts signed between the states and the municipalities with the organized community for the transfer of services to them (Article 184).

504. The legal regime on public contracts was established in the Public Contracting Law of 2010 (*Gaceta Oficial*, No. 39.503 of 6 Sep. 2010), reformed in 2014 (*Gaceta Oficial*, No. 6.154 Extra. of 19 Nov. 2014). *See* Allan R. Brewer-Carías et al., *Ley de Contrataciones Públicas* (Caracas: Editorial Jurídica Venezolana, 2011).

interest contracts, *state* public interest contracts and *municipal* public interest contracts; depending on whether they are entered into, respectively, by an organ of the Central Public Administration of each of the territorial entities of the State (Republic, States, Municipalities) or by a decentralized entity (autonomous institutions, state-owned enterprises) of the Public Administration of the said three territorial levels of the State.

Notwithstanding the inclusion of all the aforementioned provisions in the Constitution of 1999, in its text, no express definition of the concept of public interest contracts was included, establishing only a 'generic' concept of 'public interest contracts' and its 'species': 'national public interest contracts', 'state public interest contracts' and 'municipal public interest contracts', that is, public contracts that are entered into by the public entities that conform to the Public Administration in the three levels of government.

343. Specifically, regarding the national level of government, the intention of the provisions included in said Articles 150 and 151 of the Constitution, was to comprise the notion of 'national public interest contracts', not only those entered by the Republic through any of her national government agency or organs (Central Administration) but also by any other national public decentralized entity like a public corporation or a state-owned enterprise, which are the more common and important of public contracts. In other words, the Public Administration in Venezuela is not only the Central Administrations in the three levels of government (Republic, States and Municipalities), but it encompasses all the universe of public entities that constitutes the public sector in each level of government, including state-owned enterprises. At the national level, according to the Public Administration Organic Law,[505] it is constituted not only by the Central Public Administration, that is, the organs of the National Executive like the Ministries but also by the Decentralized Public Administration, composed of the Public Corporations (*institutos autónomos*) created by statute and the state-owned enterprises, incorporated according to commercial law provisions[506] (*see supra* paragraph 324).

344. The Constitution also establishes some prohibitions regarding public contracts, for instance, on territorial matters, due to the constitutional principle that 'the national territory could never be ceded, trespassed, leased or in any way sold, even temporally or partially to Foreign States or international law entities' (Article 13). The only constitutional exception in this regard refers to the land needed for foreign embassies (Article 13)

These prohibitions also refer to all the cases of public domain declared in the Constitution, regarding which the State cannot sign any contracts that could signify the loss of such character. It occurs with the subsoil, mines and hydrocarbons (Article 12); with the maritime coast (Article 12); with all waters (Article 304); with

505. *See Gaceta Oficial* No. 6.147 Extra. of 17 Nov. 2014.
506. On the notion of public interest contracts *see* Allan R. Brewer-Carías, 'Constitutional regime Applicable to Public National Interest Contracts and Parliamentary Control', in José Ignacio Hernández G. and Allan R. Brewer-Carías, *The Defense of the Rights and Interests of the Venezuelan State by the Interim Government before Foreign Courts. 2019–2020,* (Caracas, New York, Editorial Jurídica Venezolana International, 2021), pp. 275–376.

war weapons (Article 324); and with the shares of Petróleos de Venezuela S.A., the State-owned oil company (Article 303). Nonetheless, regarding natural resources and their exploitation, the Constitution establishes the possibility for the State to subscribe to temporal concession contracts with private parties (Article 113), with the express prohibition to sign for mines concessions for an indefinite term (Article 156.16).

Regarding private law immoveable property of public entities, some of those lands also have a constitutional prohibition to be sold, as is the case of national land located on islands (Article 13) and municipal lands in urban areas that can only be sold for urban development (Article 181).

The same restriction regarding public contracts exists in all the cases in which the State has reserved by statute some services, exploitations or industries for national interest motives (Article 302), as is the case of the oil industry, the iron mining industry, and the natural gas industry all nationalized since 1975.[507] This implies, for instance, regarding the oil industry, that since the sanctioning of the 2001 Organic Law on Hydrocarbons,[508] the only way in which private companies can participate in the exploitation of the oil industry is through their participation in mixed public enterprises, with State-owned majority of shares (*see infra* paragraph 661).

II. Obligatory Constitutional Clauses in Public Interest Contracts

345. Following the trends of the 1961 Constitution, the 1999 Constitution has also established in its norms, a series of contractual clauses that must always be incorporated in all public contracts, particularly, the jurisdiction immunity clause, the 'Calvo' clause, and the environmental protection clause.

A. The Jurisdiction Immunity Clause

346. Article 151 of the Constitution establishes that in all public interest contracts if it were not unsuitable according to their nature, a clause must be considered as incorporated even if not expressly provided, according to which all doubts and controversies that could arise from such contracts and that could not be amicably resolved by the contracting parties, must be decided by the competent courts of the Republic according to its laws.

It is, thus, an obligatory constitutional clause that follows the relative jurisdiction immunity system,[509] according to which, for example, in contracts with commercial

507. Organic Law reserving the State the Industry and Commerce of Hydrocarbon, Gaceta Oficial No. 35.754 of 17 Jul. 1975. *See Régimen jurídico de las Nacionalizaciones en Venezuela, Homenaje del Instituto de Derecho Público al Profesor Antonio Moles Caubet, Archivo de Derecho Público y Ciencias de la Administración*, vol. VIII (1972–1979) (Caracas: Instituto de Derecho Público, Universidad Central de Venezuela, 1981).

508. The Law was reformed in 2006. Gaceta Oficial No. 38.493 of 4 Aug. 2006.

509. *See* Allan R. Brewer-Carías, *Debate Constituyente (Aporte a la Asamblea Nacional Constituyente)*, vol. II (Caracas: Fundación de Derecho Público, 1999), 175 a 177; 'Comentarios sobre la doctrina

purposes, like, for example, those that had the purpose of exploiting hydrocarbons (*ius gestionis*),[510] the Venezuelan State can accept to submit contractual controversies to be resolved by arbitration and even subjected to foreign law.[511] In the latter case, of course, foreign law can only be applied to the performance of the contract but not to the conditions of validity of the contracts, for instance, regarding the power or competence of the public entity to contracting, which being a matter of public policy (*orden público*) can only be subjected to Venezuelan public law.

B. The 'Calvo' Clause

347. The second obligatory clause that is considered incorporated in all public interest contracts according to the Constitution is the so-called Calvo Clause which implies that their execution in any case can originate foreign claims by the States on behalf of its citizens or nationals (Article 151).[512] The origin of this clause is to be found in the 1893 Constitution as a consequence of the international diplomatic claims the European countries initiated by force against Venezuela as a consequence of contracts signed by the country with foreign citizens. Its conception was the work of Carlos Calvo in his book *Tratado de Derecho Internacional*, initially edited in 1868, after studying the Franco–British intervention in Rio de la Plata and the French intervention in Mexico.[513] This Calvo clause also helped the adoption of the so-called *Drago Doctrine* conceived in 1902 by the then Argentinean Minister of Foreign Relations, Luis María Drago, who, regarding the threats of using force made by Germany, Great Britain and Italy against Venezuela, formulated its thesis condemning the compulsory collection of public debts by the States.[514]

---

del acto de gobierno, del acto político, del acto de Estado y de las cuestiones políticas como motivo de inmunidad jurisdiccional de los Estados en sus Tribunales nacionales', in *Revista de Derecho Público*, No. 26 (Caracas: Editorial Jurídica Venezolana, abril-junio 1986), 65–68.

510. *See* Allan R. Brewer-Carías, 'La progresiva aceptación del arbitraje en el derecho público', in Revista *Principia 5-2021,* (Caracas, Universidad Monteávila, 2021).

511. *See* Tatiana Bogdanowsky de Maekelt, 'Inmunidad de Jurisdicción de los Estados', in *Libro Homenaje a José Melich Orsini,* vol. 1 (Caracas, 1982), 213 et seq.; Allan R. Brewer-Carías, *Contratos Administrativos*, Colección Estudios Jurídicos No. 44 (Caracas: Editorial Jurídica Venezolana, 1992), 262–265; Allan R. Brewer-Carías, 'Principios especiales y estipulaciones obligatorias en la contratación administrativa', in *El Derecho Administrativo en Latinoamérica*, vol. II (Bogotá: Ediciones Rosaristas, Colegio Mayor Nuestra Señora del Rosario, 1986), 345–378; Allan R. Brewer-Carías, 'Algunos comentarios a la Ley de Promoción y Protección de Inversiones: contratos públicos y jurisdicción' in *Arbitraje comercial interno e internacional. Reflexiones teóricas y experiencias prácticas* (Caracas: Academia de Ciencias Políticas y Sociales, 2005), 279–288; 'El arbitraje y los contratos de interés nacional' in *Seminario sobre la Ley de Arbitraje Comercial,* No. 13 (Caracas: Biblioteca de la Academia de Ciencias Políticas y Sociales, Serie Eventos, 1999), 169–204.

512. *See* Allan R. Brewer-Carías', Algunos aspectos de la inmunidad jurisdiccional de los Estados y la cuestión de los actos de Estado (*act of state*) en la jurisprudencia norteamericana' in *Revista de Derecho Público*, No. 24 (Caracas: Editorial Jurídica Venezolana, octubre-diciembre 1985), 29–42.

513. *See* Carlos Calvo, *Tratado de Derecho Internacional,* vol. I, para. 205, *supra,* by L.A. Podestá Costa, *Derecho Internacional Público,* vol. I (Buenos Aires, 1955), 445–446.

514. *See* Victorino Jiménez y Núñez, *La Doctrina Drago y la Política Internacional* (Madrid, 1927).

C. The Environmental Protection Clause

348. Article 129 of the Constitution also imposes the obligation for Public Administration to include an environment protection clause in any national public contract whose execution could affect natural resources,[515] providing for the obligation of the private party to the contract to preserve the ecological equilibrium, allow the access and transfer of environmental protection technology, and restore the environment to its natural state if altered.

III. The Parliamentary Approval of Public Interest Contracts

349. The constitutional system of Venezuela has traditionally provided for the intervention of the Legislature regarding the approval or authorization of public interest contracts. The 1961 Constitution provided for a legislative approval in a general way, as a condition for the validity of national public interest contracts, except for contracts that were normal in the development of public administration (Article 126). This coalification originated many discussions and interpretations about when a public contract was or was not related to the 'normal development of the public administration', to determine if they were or were not to be submitted to the approval of the former Congress.[516]

350. This provision was expressly and radically changed in Article 150 of the 1999 Constitution,[517] changing its sense,[518] by providing that 'The execution of national public interest contracts shall require the approval of the National Assembly in those cases in which such requirement is determined by law'; adding that public interest contracts entered into with 'foreign States or official entities, or with

515. *See* Alberto Blanco-Uribe Quintero, 'La tutela ambiental como derecho-deber del Constituyente. Base constitucional y principios rectores del derecho ambiental', in *Revista de Derecho Constitucional,* No. 6 (enero-diciembre) (Caracas: Editorial Sherwood, 2002), 31–64.

516. *See* among many other works regarding the discussions on the traditional notion of 'national public interest contracts': Eloy Lares Martínez, 'Contratos de interés nacional', in *Libro Homenaje al Profesor Antonio Moles Caubet*, Tomo I, Caracas, UCV, 1981, p. 117; José Melich Orsini, 'La Noción de contrato de interés público', in Revista de Derecho Público No. 7, Caracas, 1981, p. 61; Allan R. Brewer-Carías, 'Los contratos de interés público nacional y su aprobación legislativa' in *Revista de Derecho Público*, No. 11, Caracas, 1982, pp. 40–54; Gonzalo Pérez Luciani, 'Contratos de interés nacional, contratos de interés público y contratos de empréstito público', in *Libro Homenaje al Doctor Eloy Lares Martínez*, Tomo I, Caracas, 1984, p. 103; and Jesús Caballero Ortiz, 'Los contratos administrativos, los contratos de interés público y los contratos de interés nacional en la Constitución de 1999', in *Estudios de Derecho Administrativo: Libro Homenaje a la Universidad Central de Venezuela*, vol. I, Imprenta Nacional, Caracas, 2001, pp. 139–154.

517. *See* this author proposed to include this provision of Article 150 in the Constitution in 'Régimen General del Poder Público y las competencias del Poder Público Nacional', in Allan R. Brewer-Carías, *Debate Constituyente (Aportes a la Asamblea Nacional Constituyente)*, Tomo II (9 septiembre–17 octubre 1999), Fundación de Derecho Público, Editorial Jurídica Venezolana, Caracas 1999, pp. 175–177.

518. Such Article 126 provided the following: 'Article 126. Without the approval of Congress, no contract of national interest may be entered into, except as necessary for the normal conduct of the Public Administration or as permitted by law.'

companies not domiciled in Venezuela', or transferred to any of them must also be approved by the National Assembly. Article 187.9 reiterates this later parliamentary intervention by providing for a parliamentary 'authorization.'

351. In sum, the 1999 Constitution distinguishes two basic regimes related to the intervention of the legislative branch on matters of 'public interest contracts':

First, ratifies the principle that 'public interest contracts', when entered into by public entities with 'States or official foreign entities or with companies not domiciled in Venezuela' have always to be previously authorized by the National Assembly. Consequence, for a foreign company to enter into a public interest contract with a public entity in Venezuela without parliamentary intervention, it has to be domiciled in Venezuela.[519]

Consequently, if the foreign company is not domiciled in the country, as it was ruled by the Constitutional Chamber of the Supreme Tribunal of Venezuela in Decision No. 2241 of 24 September 2002 (*Andres Velázquez et al*, case), whereas Article 80 of the Organic Law on Financial Administration of the Public Sector was annulled, 'the application of the system of prior control or authorization for procurement by the National Assembly is *inescapable*'.[520]

If the authorization of the National Assembly is not obtained when constitutionally required, there can be no valid consent and thus no contract can be formed. That is, a public interest contract executed without the required National Assembly authorization is invalid and null and void *ab initio*.[521] Such a contract is illegal in the sense that it was signed in violation of the Venezuelan Constitution. Not only is such a contract entirely unenforceable, but it cannot be subsequently validated because it never came into existence in the first place due to a lack of valid consent.[522]

Second, establishes the rule that the submission of public 'national public interest contracts' to the approval or authorization of the National Assembly is necessary

---

519. 'Companies domiciled in Venezuela' are the national companies incorporated in the country, and also the companies incorporated outside Venezuela, but that have met the requirements set forth in the Commercial Code to be domiciled or to have register a branch in Venezuela (Art. 354).
520. In Decision No. 2241 of 24 Sep. 2002, the Constitutional Chamber of the Supreme Tribunal partially annulled Article 80 of the Financial Management of the Public Sector Organic Law because this article did 'not enshrin[e] the constitutional obligation of the National Executive to require the authorization of the National Assembly for the conclusion of contracts of national public interest, in the context of public credit transactions, when such contracts are concluded with States, foreign official entities or companies not domiciled in Venezuela'. *See* Tribunal Supremo de Justicia, Sala Constitucional, Decision No. 2241 Case: Andrés Velásquez y otros, nulidad parcial artículo 80 de la Ley Orgánica de Administración Financiera del sector Público). Available at http://historico.tsj.gob.ve/decisiones/scon/septiembre/ 2241-240902-00-2874%20.HTM
521. *See* Allan R. Brewer-Carías, 'La formación de la voluntad de la Administra-ción Pública Nacional en los contratos administrativos', in *Revista de la Facultad de Derecho*, No. 28, Universidad Central de Venezuela, Caracas 1964, pp. 81–82. Available at: http://allanbrewercarias. net/Content/ 449 725 d9-f1cb-474b-8ab2-41efb849fea8/Content/II.4.13.pdf.
522. *See* Allan R. Brewer-Carías, 'Constitutional Regime applicable to Public National Interest Contracts and Parliamentary Control' in José Ignacio Hernández and Allan R. Brewer-Carías, *The defense of the Rights and Interests of the Venezuelan State by the Interim Government Before Foreign Courts*, and their International Recognition 2019–2020, (New York, Editorial Jurídica Venezolana International, 2021), p. 356.

only when a statute so expressly provided, granting the Assembly the power to establish in said statute the exceptions to its own regulations. This means that under this first provision of Article 150 of the 1999 Constitution, and regarding the national public interest contracts, it only requires such approval when a statute so expressly determines.

It is pursuant to this constitutional provision that many statutes have provided for the National Assembly's control over national public interest contracts. It is the case, for instance, of Article 33 of the Hydrocarbon Organic Law on national public interest contracts of association for the 'establishment of joint ventures and the conditions governing the realization of primary [hydrocarbon] activities', establishing that they are subjected to 'the prior approval of the National Assembly'[523] (*see supra* paragraph 349).

If the approval of the National Assembly is not obtained when constitutionally required, the contract cannot be executed and cannot produce effects, that is, it cannot be enforceable.

However, it must be mentioned that a prior authorization of the National Assembly, according to Articles 150 and 312 of the Constitution, has also been traditionally required in Venezuela for national public interest contracts of public debt, being the matter regulated in the Financial Management of the Public Sector Organic Law.[524]

IV. Principles Related to the State's Contractual Liabilities

352. In parallel to the provision of the general regime of State liability (Article 140) (*see supra* paragraph 325), the 1999 Constitution also establishes the general basis and conditions for the contractual liability of the State, providing that it will only recognize as contracted obligations those entered by legitimate organs of the State; a constitutional provision that had its origin in the nineteenth century when the State was sued because of damages caused in civil wars by rebels who claimed to be acting as the legitimate government.

In any case, the legitimacy of contracting obligations is related to the competency of the respective public officer to sign the contract, for which purpose the Constitution assigns, for instance, the President of the Republic power to enter into national public contracts (Article 236.14) and to negotiate national public debt (Article 236.12); powers that of course are not exclusive, because such attributions can and are assigned to the corresponding Ministries as its direct organs (Article 242).

However, the Constitution imposes some budget restrictions in the execution of contracts by providing that no spending can be made if not established in the budget's annual statute (Article 314).

523. *See Gaceta Oficial* No. 38.493 of 4 Aug. 2006.
524. *See Gaceta Oficial* No. 6210 Extra. of 30 Dec. 2015.

§6. PREROGATIVES OF THE ADMINISTRATION

353. The Constitution does not provide for prerogative or privilege of the Republic regarding other legal persons, having then the same rights and obligation as them in their legal relations, which as aforementioned, is particularly important on matters of State responsibility and liability (*see supra* paragraph 325).

Nonetheless, on procedural matters regarding the position of public entities in judicial processes, the Organic Law of the Attorney General,[525] provide specific procedural prerogatives for public entities, related to the time set for them to be considered notified or summoned, the effects of their failure to appear in court to answer a claim, the exception established for public entities not to impose any bail of guarantee for procedural purposes, or the privilege for public property not to be the object of procedural preventive or executive seizure measures.

525. *Gaceta Oficial* No. 5.892 Extra. of 31 Jul. 2008.

Chapter 4. The Military and the National Security System

354. The 1999 Constitution made substantial departures from the provisions of the 1961 Constitution regarding the National Security and Defence system and the Military. The latter Constitution contained only three provisions on the subject: Article 133, establishing restrictions regarding the possession of arms; Article 131, prohibiting the simultaneous exercise of civilian and military authority by any public official other than the President of the Republic as Commander in Chief of the Armed Forces; and, Article 132, referring to the general regulation of the Armed Forces.

355. In the 1999 Constitution, on the contrary, a marked militarist shape was given to the State, with board provisions regarding not only the Military but the security and defence system, without precedent in Venezuelan constitutionalism.

Article 322 of the Constitution of 1999 begins by stating that the security of the nation falls within the essential competence and responsibility of the State, founded upon the State's 'integral development'; the defence of the State being the responsibility of Venezuelans, and of all natural and legal persons, whether of public or private law, founded within the geographic territory of the State.

In addition, Article 326 sets forth the general principles of National Security declaring that its preservation in 'economic, social, political, cultural, geographic, environmental and military areas', mutually corresponds (co-responsibility) to the State and to Civil Society, in order to fulfil the principles of 'independence, democracy, equality, peace, liberty, justice, solidarity, promotion and conservation of the environment, the affirmation of human rights, and, the progressive satisfaction of the individual and collective needs of Venezuelans on the basis of sustainable and productive development fully covering the national community'. All of these principles are also those enumerated in the opening Articles 1, 2, and 3 of the Constitution of 1999. For the purposes of implementing these principles of national security in the country's territorial border regions, Article 327 provides for the establishment of a special regime.

356. Also for such purposes, the Constitution created a new council, the 'National Council of Defense' (Article 323), as the nation's highest authority for defence planning, advice and consultation to the State (Public Powers) on all matters related to the defence and security of the Nation's sovereignty, territorial integrity and strategic thinking. This Council is presided over by the President of the Republic and integrated by the Executive Vice President, the President of the National Assembly, the President of Supreme Tribunal of Justice, the President of the Moral Republican Council (Citizen Branch of government, Article 237), the Ministers of the defence sectors: interior security, foreign relations and planning, and others whose participation is considered pertinent.

357. According to the Constitution, the traditional National Armed Forces (which is comprised of the Army, the Navy, the Air Force and the National Guard) have become integrated into a single institution, named the 'National Armed Force', which nonetheless, according to Article 328, is comprised of the Army, the Navy, the Air Force and the National Guard, each working within its area of competence to fulfil its mission, and with its own system of social security, as established by its respective organic legislation.

It must be mentioned that in the 2007 constitutional reform project that was rejected by popular referendum, the proposal of the President of the Republic was to change the name of the National Armed Force to the 'Bolivarian Armed Force', to create a 'Bolivarian Military Doctrine'; to create the 'Bolivarian Popular Militia', as a new component of the Armed Force, and to eliminate the character of the Armed Force as an 'essential professional institution, without political militancy', converting it into 'an essentially patriotic, popular and anti-imperialist corp'. As mentioned, the people, through referendum rejected all such Constitutional Reforms, but nonetheless, the President of the Republic approved them all, six months after the popular rejection, in July 2008, through delegate legislation.[526]

358. According to Article 329, the Army, Navy, Air Force and National Guard each has essential responsibilities for planning, execution and control of military operations necessary to ensure the defence of the Nation. The National Guard, however, only has a cooperative role in these functions and basic responsibility to carry out operations necessary for the maintenance of internal order in the country. The Constitution also establishes that the National Armed Force can carry out police administrative activities and criminal investigations as authorized by law.

359. Article 328 defines the character of the Armed Forces as an essentially professional institution, without a militant political function, organized by the State to guarantee the independence and sovereignty of the Nation, and to ensure the integrity of the Nation's geographic space by means of military defence and cooperation in the maintenance of internal order, as well as active participation in national development. According to the wording of this article, in order to fulfil these functions, the Armed Force is at the exclusive service of the Nation and in no case may be at the service of any particular person or political partiality. The foundations of the Armed Forces are discipline, obedience and subordination.

Nonetheless, the 1999 Constitution failed to provide for the 'apolitical and non-deliberative' character of the Armed Force that was established in Article 132 of the 1961 Constitution; and it has no provision establishing the essential obligation of the Armed Force to ensure 'the stability of the democratic institutions' and to 'respect the Constitution and laws, the adherence which is above any other obligation', as was declared in Article 132 of the 1961 Constitution. What the 1999 Constitution was innovative in these matters was in giving the military the right to vote (Article 325).

---

526. *See* Organic Law on the Bolivarian Armed Force, *Gaceta Oficial* No. 5.891 Extra. of 31 Jul. 2008. *See* Jesús María Alvarado Andrade, 'La nueva Fuerza Armada Bolivariana (comentarios a raíz del Decreto No. 6.239, con rango, valor y fuerza de Ley Orgánica de la Fuerza Armada Nacional Bolivariana)', en *Revista de Derecho Público,* No. 115 *(Estudios sobre los Decretos Leyes 2008)* (Caracas: Editorial Jurídica Venezolana, 2008), 205 ss.; Alfredo Arismendi, 'Fuerza Armada Nacional: Antecedentes, evolución y régimen actual', en *Revista de Derecho Público,* No. 115 *(Estudios sobre los Decretos Leyes 2008)* (Caracas: Editorial Jurídica Venezolana, 2008), 187–206.

In addition, the Constitution established the general regime applicable to military promotions, providing that they are to be based on merit, seniority and the availability of vacancies, and are the exclusive competence of the National Armed Forces (Article 331). Consequently, the traditional intervention of the Legislature to approve the promotions of high-ranking military officials (Article 150.5, 1961 Constitution) was eliminated.

360. All these constitutional provisions conform to a normative framework with clear marks of a militarist structure, which when combined with the centralization tendency of State Power and the concentration of State Power in the President of the Republic by his control over the National Assembly, the result is a system that unfortunately has led to authoritarianism. In particular, in the 1999 Constitution's provisions on military matters, the idea of the subjection or subordination of military authority to civilian authority has disappeared; and instead, what has been consecrated is a greater autonomy of the National Armed Force, whose four branches (and since 2008, five branches) have been unified into one institution with the possibility of intervention in civilian functions. This militaristic tendency is evidenced by the following constitutional rules, as already indicated: *first,* the elimination of the traditional prohibition that military and civilian authority be exercised simultaneously, as was established by the Article 131 of the 1961 Constitution; *second*, the elimination of control by the National Assembly of military promotions in the top brass, as provided in Article 331 of the 1961 Constitution and throughout the country's traditional constitutionalism; *third*, the elimination of the constitutionally 'non-deliberative and apolitical' character of the military institution, as established in Article 132 of the 1961 Constitution, which has opened the way for the Armed Force, as a military institution, to deliberate politically, intervene, and give its opinion on matters under resolution within the civil organs of the State; *fourth,* the elimination of the obligation of the Armed Force to ensure the stability of democratic institutions required by Article 132 of the 1961 Constitution; *fifth,* the elimination of the obligation of the Armed Force to respect the Constitution and laws 'the adherence to which will always be above any other obligation' as was set forth in Article 132 of the 1961 Constitution; *sixth,* the express right of suffrage granted to members of the military in Article 330 of the 1999 Constitution, which in many cases has been politically incompatible with the principle of obedience; *seventh,* the submission of authority over the use of all weapons, for war or otherwise, to the Armed Force, while removing this authority from the civil Administration of the State (Article 324); *eighth,* the general attribution of police administrative functions to the Armed Force (Article 329); *ninth,* the establishment of procedural privilege for generals and admirals in the sense that in order for them to be tried, the Supreme Tribunal of Justice must declare in advance of trial whether or not the proceeding has merit (Article 266.3); and *tenth*, the adoption in the Constitution of the concept of the 'doctrine of national security', as a global, totalistic and omni-comprehensive doctrine in the sense that everything that happens in the State and in the Nation concerns the security of the State, including economic and social development (Article 326); with the duty for the Armed Force to have an 'active participation in national development' (Article 328). All these provisions set forth a picture of militarism, unique in Venezuelan constitutional history, not even found in former military regimes.

Part VI. The Legislature

Chapter 1. The National Assembly

§1. The Unicameral Parliamentary System

361. In 1999, and contrary to the previous 200 years of parliamentary bicameral tradition, the new Constitution eliminated the Senate and established a National Assembly following the unicameral parliamentary trend, exercising the National Legislative Power.[527] The consequence being that although the State is configured as a federation, no federal chamber exists representing the states in which they could really be equals, in the sense of having an equal vote. Consequently, the clause contained in Article 159 of the Constitution points out that states of the federation are *equal* political entities cannot effectively materialize. However, in spite of this wording, from the point of view of their territory, population and economic and social development, the states are very different.

362. According to Article 186 of the Constitution, the National Assembly is composed of representatives (*diputados*) elected within each state and the Capital District (the former Federal District) by universal, direct and secret vote according to a mixed system combining personalized nomination and proportional representation scrutiny. The number of representatives is based on national population, calculating one representative per 1.1% of the total population of the country. Each representative must have a substitute member, also elected in the same process, who is called to act in cases of temporal or absolute absence of the principal (Article 186).

Each of the twenty-three states and the Capital District, in addition, has the right to elect three additional representatives to the National Assembly. The indigenous people's communities in the Republic have the right to elect three representatives according to the prescriptions of the electoral law, observing their traditions and customs (Article 125) (*see infra* paragraph 568). In all cases, each representative must have an alternate representative also elected through the same process.

527. *See* Allan R. Brewer-Carías, *Debate Constituyente (Aportes a la Asamblea Nacional Constituyente),* vol. III (18 octubre-30 noviembre 1999) (Caracas: Fundación de Derecho Público-Editorial Jurídica Venezolana, 1999), 196–198; María M. Matheus Inciarte y María Elena Romero Ríos, 'Estado Federal y unicameralidad en el nuevo orden constitucional de la República Bolivariana de Venezuela', in *Estudios de Derecho Público: Libro Homenaje a Humberto J. La Roche Rincón,* vol. I (Caracas: Tribunal Supremo de Justicia, 2001), 637–676.

The constitutional term of office for representatives is five years, according to Article 193, with the possibility of consecutive re-election for a maximum of two additional terms. Nonetheless, this limit was eliminated through a constitutional amendment approved by referendum on February 2009, providing for the possibility of the continuous election of the representatives (*see infra* paragraphs 66, 721). However, the President of the Republic has, in Council of Ministers, the power to dissolve the Assembly in case of its approval of three motions of censure against the Executive Vice President (Articles 236.21, 240).

§2. The Representatives

I. Eligibility Conditions

363. Article 188 of the Constitution establishes the following conditions of eligibility for the representatives to the National Assembly: to be a Venezuelan citizen, and in case of naturalized citizens, with fifteen years of residence in the Venezuelan territory; to be at least 21 years of age; and to have resided for at least four consecutive years in the territory of the state where the election will take place.

In addition, Article 189 establishes the cases of ineligibility for representatives, excluding the President of the Republic, the Executive Vice President, the Ministries, the Secretary of the President Office, the Presidents of Public Corporations and public enterprises, the Governors and Secretaries of government of the states from the possibility of running for such position up to three months after their separation from office. Also, all the national, states or municipal public officers, as well as those serving in public corporations of public enterprises, cannot be elected representatives if the election takes place in their respective jurisdictions, except in cases of provisional, health, teaching or academic positions. Other situations of ineligibility can also be established by statutes.

II. Tenure, Incompatibilities, Accountability and Revocation of Mandate

364. The tenure of the representatives, as provided in Article 197 of the Constitution, is a full-time job that must be accomplished for the benefit of the people. That is why the same article imposes upon them the duty to maintain permanent relations with their electors, paying attention to their opinions and informing them of their accomplishments and of the work of the Assembly (Article 197).

In addition, representatives must annually inform their electors about their activities[528] and can be subjected to repeal referendum (Article 72). In such cases, the representative whose mandate is repealed cannot be re-elected as representative for the next term (Article 198). Except in case of repeal referendum expressing the will of the people, the democratic principle means that in no other way, except for criminal

528. *See* María E. León Álvarez, 'La rendición de cuentas en la gestión de los asuntos públicos en el nuevo orden constitucional venezolano', in *Revista de Derecho Público,* No. 84 (octubre-diciembre) (Caracas: Editorial Jurídica Venezolana, 2000), 70–81.

reasons, the representatives can be removed. Nonetheless, in 2014, the Supreme Tribunal, in an unconstitutional way, decided to revoke the mandate of one representative, based on exclusively political reasons.[529]

365. However, the Constitution forbids the representatives the possibility of being owners, administrators or directors of enterprises that have entered into contracts with public entities, and cannot develop private activities with lucrative interests. On matters that are discussed before the Assembly, in which economic interest conflicts could exist, the involved representative must abstain from participating (Article 190).

366. Regarding public sector activities, the representatives cannot accept or exercise public offices without losing their tenure, except in cases of teaching, academic, provisional or health activities, provided that they do not imply a full-time job (Article 191). Consequently, with the 1999 Constitution, the possibility for the representatives to be appointed Ministers in the executive without losing their legislative tenure, as established by the 1961 Constitution (Article 141), was expressly eliminated.

III. Liability and Immunity

367. The members of the National Assembly represent the people as a whole and also represent the states where they were elected. In their legislative activities, they are not bound to the instructions of any other than their own conscience, their vote being a personal one (Article 201). This provision is another of the series established in the Constitution, based on the anti-partisan spirit inspiring it, for the purpose of supposedly protecting the votes in the Assembly against the formation of partisan and other parliamentary factions (*see supra* paragraph 33). Nonetheless, the fact is that never before has the country witnessed an official party controlling its representatives in the Legislature in a stricter way than the way experienced during the years of enforcement of the 1999 Constitution (1999–2011).

368. Regarding responsibility, representatives of the National Assembly are not liable for their votes and opinions are given in the exercise of their functions. They are only responsible before their electors and before the National Assembly according to the Constitution and the Assembly's internal regulations (Article 199).

369. On criminal matters, during their tenure, representatives have immunity from their inauguration up to the end of their tenure or their resignation (Article 200); and all public officers that violate parliamentary immunity, are criminally

529. *See* Decision No. 207 de 31 de marzo de 2014, available at en http://www.tsj.gov.ve/decisiones/scon/marzo/162546-207-31314-2014-14-0286.HTML Also published in *Gaceta Oficial* No. 40385 of 2 Apr. 2014. *See* the comments in Allan R. Brewer-Carías, 'La revocación del mandato popular de una diputada a la Asamblea Nacional por la Sala Constitucional del Tribunal Supremo de oficio, sin juicio ni proceso alguno (El caso de la Diputada María Corina Machado)', *Revista de Derecho Público,* 137 (Caracas: Editorial Jurídica Venezolana, 2014), 165–189.

liable and must be punished accordingly. Only in cases of flagrant crime committed by a representative can the corresponding authority put him in custody in his residence and must immediately inform the facts to the Supreme Tribunal of Justice, which is the competent court to order, with the authorization of the National Assembly, their detention and to continue their judicial prosecution.

§3. Organization and Commissions

370. The National Assembly has a Board of Directors integrated by its President and two Vice Presidents elected within the representatives, and a Secretary and a Deputy Secretary designated from outside the members of the Assembly, all appointed for a one-year term (Article 194). The President and the two Vice Presidents of the Assembly must be Venezuelan by birth and without other nationalities (Article 41).

371. The Assembly has ordinary and special Permanent Commissions. The latter can be created in the various activities sectors, by the favourable vote of two-thirds of the representatives, composed of no more than fifteen representatives each. The Assembly can also create temporal commissions for the investigation or study of determined matters (Article 193).

§4. Sessions of the National Assembly and Its Delegate Commission

372. The Assembly has two periods of ordinary sessions, from January to August and from September to December. The first session must begin without any previous notification on 5 January of each year or the following immediate and possible day enduring up to 15 August, and the second, on 15 September or the following immediate and possible day enduring up to 15 December (Article 219). The National Assembly can also have extraordinary sessions in order to consider the matters expressed in the convening and the related ones. It can also consider those matters declared urgent by its members (Article 220).

373. The conditions for the instalment of the Assembly and for its sessions, as well as for the functioning of its Commissions, must be established in the internal parliamentary regulation, except the quorum conditions that are provided in the Constitution establishing that in all cases it cannot be less than the absolute majority of the representatives composing the Assembly (Article 221).

374. During the periods when the National Assembly is not in session (15 December–5 January, and 15 August–15 September), a Delegate Commission must function, integrated by the President, the Vice Presidents and the Presidents of the Permanent Commissions (Article 195). This Commission, which exists in almost all Latin American countries, has the following attributions: to convene the National Assembly for extraordinary sessions, when needed; authorize the trips of the President abroad; authorize the National Executive to decree additional credits to the budget; designate temporal Commissions of the Assembly; exercise the investigative functions of the Assembly; and authorize the National Executive, by a vote of two-thirds of the representatives, create, modify and suspend public services in cases of confirmed urgency (Article 196).

§5. The Attributions of the National Assembly

375. The National Assembly, as the Legislature, has the power to legislate on matters of national character (Article 187.1) (*see supra* paragraph 214) and, in particular, to discuss and approve the Budget Law and all taxation and public debt laws (Articles 187.6; 314, 317, 312); and to sanctioned laws for the approval of international treaties and conventions (Articles 187.19; 154).

In addition to these legislative functions, according to Article 187, the Assembly has another series of powers on constitutional, political and administrative matters that gives it, its pre-eminent character in the political system of separation of powers (*see supra* paragraph 246).

376. On constitutional matters, the Assembly can propose amendments and reforms to the Constitution and must discuss and approve all constitutional reforms drafts (Articles 341, 343, 344) (*see supra* 128). Also, on constitutional matters, the National Assembly have the constitutional character of being an electoral body in order to elect, in an indirect way representation of the people, by a qualified majority of two-thirds of its members, the High Officials Head of the Citizen's, Electoral and Judicial Branches of Government (Articles 264, 279, 296) (*see* paragraphs *supra* 168, 239, 304; *infra* 415 ff., 442, 435, 455).

377. On political matters, the Assembly is empowered to decree amnesties (Article 187.5); to approve censure votes to the Executive Vice President and to the Ministers (Article 187.10); authorize the use of Venezuelan military missions abroad and foreign military missions in the country (Article 187.11); watch over the interests and autonomy of the states of the federation (Article 187.16); authorize the trips abroad of the President of the Republic for more than five days (Article 235); decide cases of absolute and temporal absence of the President (Articles 233, 234) (*see supra* paragraph 289); authorize the criminal processing of the President of the Republic (Article 266.2); and debate on the Decrees of States of Exception (Articles 338, 339) (*see supra* paragraph 311).

Also, on political matters, the Assembly is empowered to elect and remove the head of the Judicial, Citizen and Electoral Branches of Government (*see infra* paragraph 444), that is, to elect and remove from office the Magistrates of the Supreme Tribunal of Justice (Article 265), the Comptroller General of the Republic, the Prosecutor General of the Republic, the Peoples' Defender (Article 279), and the members of the National Electoral Council (Article 296). These are powers that give preeminence to the Legislature, which, as aforementioned, basically contradict the principle of the independence of the Judicial, Citizen and Electoral Powers, respectively (*see supra* paragraph 236).

378. On administrative matters, the Assembly must authorize the appointment of the Attorney General of the Republic (*see supra* paragraph 297) and the Head of diplomatic missions (Article 187.14); and, most importantly, exercise control powers regarding the Government and the National Public Administration (Article 187.3), being competent to authorize additional credits to the budget (Article 187.7); approve the general guidelines of the Economic and Social Development Plan formulated by the President of the Republic within the first year of each constitutional term (Articles 187.8, 236.18); authorize the National Executive to sign national public interest contracts when required by statute, and in any case, public interest contracts when signed with foreign State or foreign public entities with enterprises non-domiciled in Venezuela (Articles 187.9, 150); and authorize the national executive to sell immovable State properties (Article 187.12) (*see supra* paragraph 349).

379. On internal parliamentary matters, the National Assembly has its own powers to organize and promote citizens' participation in legislative matters (Article 187.4); to approve its own internal regulations, organize its own internal security services, establish and execute its own budget, and regulate its own civil service[530] (Articles 187.19, 21, 22). The Assembly is also empowered to qualify its own members and to receive their resignations (Article 187.20).

530. Estatute of National Assembly Public empoyees, *Gaceta Oficial* No. 37.598 of 26 Dec. 2002.

Chapter 2. Legislative Procedure

380. The initiative to introduce draft legislation (Codes, Organic Laws, ordinary laws) (*see supra* paragraphs 140 et seq.) before the National Assembly was expanded in Article 204 of the 1999 Constitution, conferring that power to: the National Executive, the Commissions of the National Assembly; three or more members of the National Assembly; the Supreme Tribunal of Justice in the case of legislation relating to the Judiciary and to procedural matters; the Citizen Power with respect to legislation relating to the Comptroller General, the Prosecutor General or the Peoples Defender; the Electoral Power in electoral matters; the State Legislative Councils in matters relating to the states; and the citizens by means of a petition supported by no less than 0.1% of the registered voters. In this latter case, the debate in the Assembly must begin no later than in the legislative session following the session in which the proposed legislation was introduced. If the debate does not begin within this time, the popular proposed legislation must be submitted to an approbatory referendum (Article 205) (*see supra* paragraph 174).

381. All draft legislation in order to acquire the status of a statute must be submitted to two discussions (Article 205), on different days, according to the rules established in the Assembly's internal regulation. Once the draft is approved, the President of the Assembly must declare the statute sanctioned (Article 207).

The first discussion, according to Article 208, must refer to the motives of the proposed legislation and its purpose, scope and viability, in order to determine its pertinence. In addition, a global discussion on its articles must take place. Once approved in the first discussion, the draft must be sent directly to the Commission related to its content, in order for it to study the draft and prepare a report that must be completed within a period of thirty days.

The second discussion must be held once the Commission's Report is received by the Assembly. In this case, discussion then must be made article by article. If the draft is approved without modification, the statute will be sanctioned. If modifications are introduced, the draft must be returned to the corresponding Commission, which must prepare a new report. This report must be read in a plenary session of the Assembly, which must decide by a majority of votes. If approved, the President of the Assembly must declare the statute sanctioned.

382. In order to allow people's participation, the 1999 Constitution establishes the obligation for the National Assembly or its Commissions during the debate of the legislative draft, to consult with other entities of government, with the citizens, and with organizations of society in order to hear their point of view with respect to such legislation (Article 211). Also, according to Article 206, the states must be consulted by the National Assembly, through their Legislative Councils, when legislation regarding them is being considered in the Assembly. Nonetheless, all these provisions regarding popular participation have been bypassed in cases of legislative delegations to the Executive, and decree-laws have been enacted without any sort of consultation, as happened from 2000 to 2014, a period in which the most important legislation of the country was enacted through decree-laws (*see supra* paragraphs 148, 309).

383. During the discussions of the drafts' legislation, and according to the regulations established by the National Assembly, the Ministers of the Executive branch have the right to express their views in the legislative debate (*see supra* paragraph 285), as do the Magistrates of the Supreme Tribunal of Justice, the representatives of the Citizen Power; the members of the Electoral Power; the states, through a representative designated by the Legislative Council of each, and representatives of social organizations (Article 211).

384. Once a statute is sanctioned by the National Assembly, it must be promulgated by the President of the Republic within ten days of having received it from the National Assembly (Article 214). Legislation is considered promulgated once published in the *Official Gazette* of the Republic (Article 215) with the corresponding presidential order that it be put into effect. The President may, however, within the said period, in a decision taken in Council of Ministers, and on the basis of a reasoned report, request the National Assembly to modify some aspect of the sanctioned legislation or reverse its approval of all or a part of it (presidential veto).

The National Assembly must decide on the President's arguments by absolute majority of members present and must send the law for promulgation. In these cases, the President must promulgate the law within five days of receiving it, without proposing new changes.

385. However, when the President of the Republic considers that legislation or certain articles of a statute are unconstitutional, during the ten-day period in which the law must be promulgated, he can request the matter to be reviewed by the Constitutional Chamber of the Supreme Tribunal of Justice. This is one of the *a priori* judicial review means provided in the Constitution (*see infra* paragraph 692). The Constitutional Chamber must decide within fifteen days of receiving the request from the President.

If the Tribunal denies the presidential unconstitutionality argument or fails to decide within the allotted time period, the President must promulgate the law within five days.

386. If the President of the Republic fails to promulgate a statute according to all these rules, the President and the two Vice Presidents of the National Assembly must proceed to promulgate the law as indicated, without prejudice of the President of the Republic's liability for his omission (Article 216).

Only legislation approving international treaties, accords or conventions may be promulgated at the opportune time determined within the discretion of the National Executive, according to international custom and the national interest (Article 217).

Chapter 3. Political and Administrative Legislative Control Procedures

387. As set forth in Article 222 of the Constitution, the National Assembly may exercise its powers of control in political and administrative matters through the questioning (*interpelación*) procedure, in which a Minister or other official is summoned to the Assembly to answer specific questions with respect to his actions. In addition, the Assembly and its Commissions can also make investigations or inquiries (Article 223).

388. In exercising parliamentary control, the Assembly can declare the political responsibility of government officials[531] and request the Citizen Power to initiate the necessary legal actions to enforce such responsibility.

All public officials are obligated, subjected to sanctions, to appear before the Assembly's Commissions, and to furnish them with any information and documentation they may require to fulfil their functions. This obligation is also imposed upon private individuals, but cannot refer to those matters protected by constitutional guarantees.[532]

In no case could the exercise of the Assembly's investigatory power affect the powers of the other branches of government. Nonetheless, judges are required to provide evidence to the Assembly and its Committees when ordered to do so (Article 224).

Nonetheless, all these constitutional provisions regarding legislative, political and administrative control over the National Executive were completely neutralized by the Constitutional Chamber of the Supreme Tribunal during 2016 and 2019, through multiple judicial review decisions that in fact and factually eliminated all the National Assembly powers of control.[533]

531. On this subject, *see* Allan R Brewer-Carías 'Aspectos del control político sobre la Administración Pública', in *Revista de Control Fiscal,* 101 (Caracas: Contraloría General de la República, 1981), 107–130.

532. *See* Allan R. Brewer-Carías, 'Los poderes de investigación de los cuerpos legislativos y sus limitaciones, con particular referencia a los asuntos secretos', in *Revista de Derecho Público,* 10 (Caracas: Edirorial Jurídica Venezolana 1982), 25–42.

533. *See* the comments on all the decisions in Allan R. Brewer-Carías, *La dictadura judicial y la perversión del Estado de derecho. El Juez Constitucional y la destrucción de la democracia en Venezuela* (Madrid, Editorial IUSTEL, Madrid 2017); and *Consolidación de la tiranía judicial. El Juez Constitucional controlado por el Poder Ejecutivo, asumiendo el poder absoluto*, (Caracas, New York, Editorial Jurídica Venezolana International, 2017).

Part VII. The Judiciary

Chapter 1. General Constitutional Regime Referred to the Judiciary

§1. Justice and the Judicial System

I. Justice and the Components of the Judicial System

389. The power to render or administer justice according to Article 253 of the Constitution emanates from the citizenry and is imparted in the name of the Republic and by the authority of the law. For such purposes, Article 26 of the Constitution provides that the State must guarantee a 'cost-free, accessible, impartial, adequate, transparent, autonomous, independent, accountable, equitable, and expeditious justice, without undue or dilatory delay, formalism, or unnecessary replication of procedures'.[534]

The system of justice, according to the same Article 253 of the Constitution, is composed not only by the organs of the Judicial Branch (Supreme Tribunal of Justice and all the other courts established by law) but by the offices of the Prosecutor General, the Peoples' Defender, the criminal investigatory organs, the penitentiary system, the alternative means of justice, the citizens who participate in the administration of justice as provided in the law and the attorneys authorized to practice law.[535]

II. Independence and Autonomy of the Judicial Branch

390. The principle of the independence of the Judicial Power is set forth expressly in Article 254 of the Constitution, which, in addition, establishes its

534. *See* Gustavo Urdaneta Troconis, 'El Poder Judicial en la Constitución de 1999', in *Estudios de Derecho Administrativo: Libro Homenaje a la Universidad Central de Venezuela,* vol. I (Caracas: Imprenta Nacional, 2001), 521–564.

535. *See* the Law on the Judicial System, *Gaceta Oficial* No. 39.276 of 1 Oct. 2009. *See* in general Gustavo Urdaneta Troconis, 'El Poder Judicial en la Constitución de 1999', en *Estudios de Derecho Administrativo: Libro Homenaje a la Universidad Central de Venezuela,* vol. I (Caracas: Imprenta Nacional, 2001), 521–564; Román J. Duque Corredor, 'El sistema de Justicia', en *Tendencias Actuales del Derecho Constitucional. Homenaje a Jesús María Casal Montbrun*, ed. Jesús María Casal, Alfredo Arismendi y Carlos Luis Carrillo Artiles (Coord.), vol. II (Caracas: Universidad Central de Venezuela/Universidad Católica Andrés Bello, 2008), 87–112.

financial autonomy,[536] and assigns 'functional, financial, and administrative autonomy' to the Supreme Tribunal. As mentioned, unfortunately, the independence and autonomy of the Judiciary in general have been neutralized due to the Executive political control over the National Assembly and the Supreme Tribunal (*see supra* paragraphs 241 et seq., 244; *infra*, 423 ff., 428).

In any case, the Constitution provides that within the National general annual budget, an appropriation of at least 2% of the ordinary national budget is established for the judiciary, a percentage amount that cannot be changed without prior approval by the National Assembly.

Article 26 of the Constitution guarantees 'cost-free justice'; consequently, the Constitution denies the Judiciary the power to establish court costs or fees, or to require payment for services (Article 254).

391. With the purpose of guaranteeing the impartiality and independence of judges in the exercise of their duties, Article 256 of the Constitution requires that magistrates, judges and prosecutors of the Public Prosecutor and the Public Defenders' offices may not, from the time of entering their respective jobs until they step down, engage in partisan political activity other than voting. This includes political party activism, union, guild and similar activities. Magistrates, judges and prosecutors are also prohibited from engaging in private or business activities that are incompatible with their judicial functions, on their own behalf or on behalf of others, and they may not undertake any other public functions other than educational activities.

Judges are prohibited from associating with one another (Article 256), which is a limit regarding the constitutional right of association set forth in Article 52 of the Constitution.

III. Judicial Process as the Instrument for Justice

392. According to Article 257 of the Constitution, the fundamental instrument for the realization of justice is the judicial process, regarding which the procedural laws must establish simplified, uniform and effective procedures, and adopt brief, public and oral proceedings, through which in no case justice should be sacrificed based on the omission of non-essential formalities. These provisions are complemented by Article 26 of the Constitution that sets forth that the State must guarantee expeditious justice without undue delay, formalisms or useless procedural repositions. In addition, being the alternative means of justice part of the judicial system (Article 253), Article 258 of the Constitution imposes on the Legislator the duty to promote arbitration, conciliation, mediation and other alternative means for conflict resolution.

---

536. *See* Juan Rafael Perdomo, 'Independencia y competencia del Poder Judicial', in *Revista de derecho del Tribunal Supremo de Justicia,* No. 8 (Caracas, 2003), 483 a 518.

IV. Judicial Liability

393. According to Article 255 of the Constitution, judges are personally responsible for unjustified errors, delays or omissions, for substantial failures to observe procedural requirements, for abuse of or refusal to apply the law (*denegación*), for bias, for the crime of graft (*cohecho*) and for criminally negligent or intentional injustice (*prevaricación*) effectuated in the course of performing their judicial functions.

§2. Judicial Jurisdictions in the Constitution

394. In addition to the basic civil, commercial, labour, agrarian and criminal Jurisdictions established in the legal order to fulfil the realization of justice through the judicial processes, the 1999 Constitution has specifically included express provisions regarding jurisdictions in constitutional matters (Article 334), matters related to discipline in the judiciary (Article 267), judicial review of administrative actions matters (Article 259), electoral matters (Article 297), criminal military matters (Article 261), justices of the peace (Article 258), and justice within the Indigenous Peoples (Article 260).[537]

395. In particular, Article 334 of the Constitution has created the Constitutional Chamber of the Supreme Tribunal of Justice with the exclusive power to exercise jurisdiction on constitutional matters (Constitutional Jurisdiction), including the power to declare the nullity of legislation or other acts of State organs issued in direct and immediate execution of the Constitution or that have the same rank of Statutes (Article 334) (*see infra* paragraph 693). This Jurisdiction is regulated in the Organic Law of the Supreme Tribunal[538] (*see supra* paragraphs 409, 670).

396. Concerning the Judicial Review of Administrative Action Jurisdiction, Article 259 of the Constitution attributed it to the Supreme Tribunal of Justice and to all the other courts established by law, assigning them the power to annul general and individual administrative acts contrary to the legal order, including those issued with abuse of public power (*desviación de poder*). These courts are also competent to condemn the State to pay sums of money, and repair injuries or damages caused by the Administration, hear claims concerning the rendering of public services, and rule as necessary to re-establish subjective legal rights affected by administrative acts. This Jurisdiction is regulated in the 2010 Organic Law on the Contentious Administrative Jurisdiction[539] (*see infra* paragraph 706).

537. *See* María E. León Álvarez, 'El sistema de justicia en la Constitución de Venezuela de 1999. Estudio crítico acerca de la jurisdicción especial indígena', in *Revista del Tribunal Supremo de Justicia*, No. 4 (Caracas, 2002), 369–377.
538. *See* in *Gaceta Oficial* No. 39.522 of 1 Oct. 2010. Last reform: in *Gaceta Oficial* No. 6.684 Extra. of 19 Jan. 2022.
539. Véase en *G. O.* No. 39.451 de 22 Jun. 2010. *See* Allan R. Brewer-Carías y Víctor Hernández Mendible, *Ley de la Jurisdicción Contencioso Administrativa* (Caracas: Editorial Jurídica venezolana, 2011); María L. Acuña López, 'Algunas notas relacionadas con los principios constitucionales que

In addition, on contentious administrative matters, Article 297 of the Constitution has established a specific Jurisdiction on electoral matters attributed to the Electoral Chamber of the Supreme Tribunal and all the other courts determined by law[540] (*see infra* paragraph 706).

397. Regarding the disciplinary regime of the judges, Article 276 of the Constitution establishes the Judicial Disciplinary Jurisdiction, which implies the need to create disciplinary tribunals to judge the judges. It was only in 2010 when the Disciplinary Jurisdiction was created, with judges appointed by the National Assembly in 2011, conforming to a Court with competence on this matter[541] (*see infra* paragraph 408).

398. Article 261 of the Constitution establishes the rules for a criminal military jurisdiction as an integral part of the Judicial Branch, whose judges are to be selected competitively. Its sphere of competence, organization and forms of functioning is governed by the accusatory (adversarial) system of criminal procedure, as provided in the Organic Code of Military Justice.[542] In all events, the Constitution expressly provides that ordinary civil crimes, human rights violations, and crimes against humanity by military personnel are to be adjudicated in the ordinary courts, while the competence of military tribunals is limited to military crimes.

399. Following the orientation of the Organic Law of Justice of the Peace,[543] Article 258 refers to the election of the Judges of the Peace by universal, direct and secret vote, being the only elected judges in the country (Article 261).

400. Article 260 of the Constitution also authorizes the legitimate authorities of indigenous peoples to apply their own jurisdiction, laws and procedure based upon their ancestral traditions within their territory and with effect only with respect to their members. Indigenous law must not, however, be in violation of the Constitution or laws of the country and the means of coordination of this special jurisdiction with the national legal system is to be established by national law.[544]

---

regulan el sistema de justicia venezolano y su alcance en la jurisdicción contencioso-administrativa', en *Estudios de Derecho Administrativo: Libro Homenaje a la Universidad Central de Venezuela,* vol. I (Caracas: Imprenta Nacional, 2001), 521–564.

540. *See* Miguel A. Torrealba Sánchez, 'Notas sobre la jurisdicción contencioso electoral en la Constitución de 1999', in *Revista de Derecho Administrativo,* No. 12 (mayo-agosto) (Caracas: Editorial Sherwood, 2001), 165–192. The Electoral Jurisdiction is regulated in the Organic Law of the Supreme Tribunal of Justice, *Gaceta Oficial* No. 39.522 of 1 Oct. 2010. Last reform: in *Gaceta Oficial* No. 6.684 Extra. of 19 Jan. 2022.

541. *See* the Law in the Ethics Code of the Venezuelan Judge, *Gaceta Oficial* No. 39.494 of 24 Aug. 2010. This Code expressly abrogated the regulation concerning the Commission on the Functioning of the Judiciary established in 1999. The members of the Disciplinary Judicial Court were appointed by the Nacional Assembly in June 2011, *Gaceta Oficial* No. 39.693 of 10 Jun. 2011. The Court was organized on 28 Jun. 2011, *Gaceta Oficial* No. 39.704 of 29 Jun. 2011.

542. *Gaceta Oficial* Extra. No. 5.263 of 17 Sep. 1998.

543. *Gaceta Oficial* Extra. No. 4.817 of 21 Dec. 1994.

544. *See* María E. León Álvarez, 'El sistema de justicia en la Constitución de Venezuela de 1999. Estudio crítico acerca de la jurisdicción especial indígena', en *Revista del Tribunal Supremo de Justicia,* No. 4 (Caracas, 2002), 369–377.

401. All the other jurisdictions within the Judiciary are established by statute, as is the case of the Civil and Commercial Jurisdiction, the Criminal Jurisdiction, the Labour Jurisdiction, the Juvenile Jurisdiction, and the Agrarian Jurisdiction.[545]

§3. Governance and Administration of the Judicial Branch

402. One of the innovations of the 1999 Constitution was to confer to the Supreme Tribunal of Justice 'the Governance and Administration of the Judicial Branch', while eliminating the former Council of the Judiciary (*Consejo de la Judicatura*) which exercised these functions under Article 217 of the Constitution of 1961, as one of the organs with functional autonomy separate and independent from all the branches of government, including the former Supreme Court of Justice.

Consequently, since 2000, as provided in Article 267 of the Constitution, the Supreme Tribunal of Justice has been charged with the direction, governance and administration of the Judicial Branch,[546] including inspection and oversight of the courts of the Republic as well as the offices of the Public Defenders. For such purposes, the Supreme Tribunal is in charge of drafting and putting into effect its own budget and the budget of the Judicial Branch in general, according to principles set out in Article 254; and was in charge of appointing the Inspector General of Courts and the Director of the National Judiciary School, until January 2022 when a reform of the Orgánic on the Supreme Tribunal[547] unconstitutionally assigned such appointments to the National Assembly, which was accepted by the Constitutional Chamber of the Supreme Tribunal.[548]

403. In order to perform these functions, the plenary Supreme Tribunal of Justice has created an Executive Directorate of the Judiciary (*Dirección Ejecutiva de la Magistratura*) with regional offices. Judicial circuits are to be established and organized by statute, as is the creation of jurisdictions of tribunals and regional courts in order to promote administrative and jurisdictional decentralization of the Judicial Power (Article 269).

545. Organic Law on the Judiciary, *Gaceta Oficial* Extra. No. 5.262 11 Sep. 1998.
546. *See* the Organic Law of the Supreme Tribunal of Justice *Gaceta Oficial* No. 39.522 of 1 Oct. 2010. Last reform: in *Gaceta Oficial* No. 6.684 Extra. of 19 Jan. 2022, *See* Allan R. Brewer-Carías and Víctor Hernández Mendible, *Ley Orgánica del Tribunal Supremo de Justicia 2010* (Caracas: Editorial Jurídica Venezolana, 2010); Laura Louza, 'El Tribunal Supremo de Justicia en la Constitución de la República Bolivariana de Venezuela', en *Revista del Tribunal Supremo de Justicia,* No. 4 (Caracas, 2002), 379–437; Nélida Peña Colmenares, 'El Tribunal Supremo de Justicia como órgano de dirección, gobierno, administración, inspección y vigilancia del Poder Judicial venezolano', in *Revista de derecho del Tribunal Supremo de Justicia,* No. 8 (Caracas, 2003), 391 a 434; and Olga Dos Santos, 'Comisión Judicial del Tribunal Supremo de Justicia', in *Revista de derecho del Tribunal Supremo de Justicia*, No. 6 (Caracas, 2002), 373 a 378.
547. *See* in *Gaceta Oficial* No. 6.684 Extra. of 19 Jan. 2022.
548. *See* Allan R. Brewer-Carías, 'Sobre los once (11) vicios de inconstitucionalidad de las sentencias de la Sala Constitucional que declararon la "constitucionalidad" de la reforma de la Ley Orgánica del Tribunal Supremo de Justicia. (Comentarios a las sentencias No 81 y 83 de 15 y 21 de marzo de 2022)', in *Boletín de la Academia de Ciencias Políticas y Sociales, Homenaje a José Guillermo Andueza,* No. 168, Caracas, 2022) pp. 335–368.

404. As mentioned, jurisdiction for judicial discipline is to be carried out by disciplinary tribunals as determined by law (Article 267), which, as has been previously mentioned, was eventually established in 2010–2011 after the sanctioning of the Code of Ethics of the Venezuelan Judge. Disciplinary proceedings must be public, oral and brief, in conformity with due process of law.

§4. Regimen Governing the Judicial Career and the Stability of Judges

405. The basic constitutional provision in order to guarantee the independence and autonomy of courts and judges is established in Article 255, which provides for a specific mechanism to assure the independent appointment of judges and to guarantee their stability.

406. In this regard, the judicial tenure is considered a judicial career, in which the admission as well as the promotion of judges within it must be the result of a public competition or examinations to assure the excellence and adequacy of qualifications of the participants, who are to be chosen by panels from the judicial circuits (Article 255). The naming and swearing-in of judges are to be done by the Supreme Tribunal of Justice, and the citizens' participation in the selection procedure and designation of judges are to be guaranteed by law. Unfortunately, up to 2011, all these provisions have not been applicable because of a lack of legislation implementing them.

407. The Constitution also creates a Judicial Nominations Committee (Article 270) as an organ for the assistance of the Judicial Branch in selecting not only the Magistrates for the Supreme Tribunal of Justice (Article 264) (*see supra* paragraphs 239 et seq.) but also to assist judicial colleges in selecting judges for the courts including those of the jurisdiction in Judicial Discipline. This Judicial Nominations Committee is to be composed of representatives from different sectors of society, as determined by law. The law is required to promote the professional development of judges, to which end universities are to collaborate with the judiciary by developing training in judicial specialization in law school curricula.

As aforementioned, none of these provisions has been implemented, and on the contrary, since 1999, the Venezuelan Judiciary has been almost completely composed by temporal and provisional judges,[549] lacking stability and being subjected to political manipulation, altering the people's right to an adequate administration of justice.

549. The Inter-American Commission on Human Rights said: 'The Commission has been informed that only 250 judges have been appointed by opposition concurrence according to the constitutional text. From a total of 1772 positions of judges in Venezuela, the Supreme Court of Justice reports that only 183 are holders, 1331 are provisional and 258 are temporary', *Informe sobre la Situación de los Derechos Humanos en Venezuela*; OAS/Ser.L/V/II.118. d.C. 4rev. 2; 29 Dec. 2003; para. 11. The same Commission also said that 'an aspect linked to the autonomy and independence of the

408. However, in order to guarantee the stability of judges according to the express provision of the Constitution, they can only be removed or suspended from office through judicial procedures or trails expressly established by statutes, led by Judicial Disciplinary Judges (Article 255). Nonetheless, up to 2011, because of the lack of implementing the Disciplinary Jurisdiction, judges were removed without due process guarantees by a 'transitory' Reorganization Commission of the Judicial Power in charge of the disciplinary procedures, that if it is true that it was eliminated in June 2011 (*see infra* paragraph 424), it was substituted by courts but whose judges are appointed by the political organ of the State, the National Assembly, instead of by the Supreme Tribunal of Justice.

Judicial Power is that of the provisional character of the judges in the judicial system of Venezuela. Today, the information provided by the different sources indicates that more than 80% of Venezuelan judges are "provisional"'. *Ibid.*, para. 161.

Chapter 2. The Supreme Tribunal of Justice

§1. Composition

409. The Constitution of 1999 created the Supreme Tribunal of Justice in substitution of the former Supreme Court of Justice established in the 1961 Constitution. The Supreme Tribunal is composed of six Chambers: Constitutional, Politico-Administrative, Electoral, Civil Cassation, Criminal Cassation and Social Chambers. The Supreme Tribunal can also seat and function in Plenary Session (*Sala Plena*).[550]

The Constitution did not expressly provide for the number of Justices integrating the Supreme Tribunal of Justice or each of its Chambers, a matter that was left to the provisions of the Organic Law of the Supreme Tribunal which was first sanctioned in 2004 (*see supra* paragraph 241). Initially, the Supreme Tribunal was composed in 1999 of twenty Magistrates, a number that was increased to thirty-two Magistrates in 2004, and reduced again in the Organic Law reform of January 2022 to twenty Magistrates.[551]

§2. Jurisdiction

410. According to the express provision of Article 266 of the Constitution, the Supreme Tribunal of Justice exercises in an exclusive way the Constitutional Jurisdiction (Article 334) (*see infra* paragraph 670); it is the highest court within the Administrative Jurisdiction (judicial review of administrative actions (Article 295) (*see infra* paragraph 705); and exercises the Electoral Jurisdiction (judicial review of electoral acts, Article 297). The Tribunal also has competence to decide conflicts between superior courts of justice; has the exclusive power to interpret statutes by means of recourses of interpretation (*see infra* paragraph 706); decides in an exclusive way recourses of cassation; has competence to declare that there are merits for the prosecution of High officials of the State; has attributions to decide on the dismissal of the President of the Republic (A233), and to express its opinion on the dismissal of the Comptroller General, the Prosecutor General, the Peoples' Defender and the members of the National Electoral Council (Articles 296, 297).

411. In addition, the Constitution establishes some provisions related to attributions of the Constitutional, Politico-Administrative and Electoral Chambers, as well as of the Social Chamber particularly in agrarian, labour and juvenile matters (Article 262). According to these provisions, the Supreme Tribunal of Justice exercises jurisdiction on constitutional matters (judicial review) exclusively through its

550. *See* Laura Louza, 'El Tribunal Supremo de Justicia en la Constitución de la República Bolivariana de Venezuela', in *Revista del Tribunal Supremo de Justicia,* No. 4 (Caracas, 2002), 379–437.
551. *Gaceta Oficial* No. 37.942 of 20 May 2004. *See* Allan R. Brewer-Carías, *Ley Orgánica del Tribunal Supremo de Justicia. Procesos y procedimientos constitucionales y contencioso-administrativos* (Caracas, 2004). The Law was reformed in 2010, *Gaceta Oficial* No. 39.522 of 1 Oct. 2010, and in January 2022, *Gaceta Oficial* No. 6.684 Extra. of 19 Jan. 2022.

Constitutional Chamber (Article 334); through the Politico-Administrative Chamber which is the highest judicial court on judicial review of administrative action proceedings (contentious administrative jurisdiction) (Article 259); and through the Social and Cassation Chambers which hears cases in cassation. The Supreme Tribunal, through the two first Chambers, is also competent to decide constitutional and administrative conflicts between territorial entities; and through all the Chambers decide recourses of interpretation regarding the content and scope of statutes. In Plenary Session, the Supreme Tribunal is in charge of deciding whether there are or not grounds to prosecute high government officials (Article 266).

412. In addition to its jurisdictional attributions, as aforementioned, the Supreme Tribunal of Justice, according to the Constitution of 1999, is in charge of the 'governance and administration of the Judiciary' (Article 267), through the Executive Board of the Judiciary (*see supra* paragraph 402).

§3. Status of the Supreme Tribunal Magistrates

I. Conditions to be Magistrate of the Supreme Tribunal Justice

413. Article 263 of the Constitution is very precise in establishing in detail the conditions for being elected Magistrate to the Supreme Tribunal of Justice, leaving the procedures for election of Magistrates on the Tribunal to be determined by law (Article 264).

The conditions to be Magistrate are the following: to be a Venezuelan national by birth, without any other nationality (Article 41); a citizen of recognized honourability; a recognized jurist, with professional practice of at least fifteen years, having university postgraduate degree; or with university teaching career of at least fifteen years; or with judicial positions in courts of appeal in jurisdictions related with the attributions of the corresponding Chamber, for at least fifteen years; and having recognized prestige in his functions.

414. These strict conditions to be Magistrates of the Supreme Tribunal were bypassed in 1999, when the first provisional 'election' of Magistrates was made by the Constituent Assembly (*see supra* paragraph 241), and again in 2000 when the then newly elected National Assembly also made election of Magistrates without sanctioning the Organic Law of the Tribunal, and without complying with the constitutional conditions, in execution of a Special Law sanctioned specifically for such election purposes.[552]

This statute was challenged for judicial review by means of an action of unconstitutionality filed by the then Peoples' Defender, that has never been decided. Nonetheless, when deciding on the admissibility of the action, and particularly of a

552. *Gaceta Oficial* No. 37.077 of 14 Nov. 2000. *See* Carlos Luis Carrillo Artiles, 'El desplazamiento del principio de supremacía constitucional por la vigencia de los interregnos temporales', *Revista de Derecho Constitucional,* No. 3 (Caracas, 2000), 86 y ss.

petition for protection of constitutional rights (*amparo*),[553] the Constitutional Chamber explained that since 2000 two constitutional regimes were in effect: the one established in the 1999 Constitution and the one established in the Transitory Constitutional Regime Decree of the same year 1999 (*see supra* paragraph 30), decided to ask the Peoples' Defender to clarify its petition, although incidentally ruling that the conditions established in the Constitution to be magistrate were not applicable to themselves, those that were deciding the case, because they were not to be elected but to be ratified (*see infra* paragraph 416).

II. The Nomination and Election Procedure

415. The Constitution attributed the election of Magistrates for a single term of twelve years to the National Assembly (Article 264), specifically limiting the discretionary power that the former Congress had in this regard. For such purpose, the Constitution provides that the Assembly can only elect magistrates that are nominated by a specific Judicial Nominations Committee, which is the organ to receive the nominations presented whether by own initiative of the candidate or by organizations related to the judicial activities. This Judicial Nominations Committee, according to express constitutional provision, is to be integrated only by 'representatives of the different sectors of society' (Article 270).

According to the same Article 264 of the Constitution, for the purpose of proposing candidates before the National Assembly, the Committee, having heard the opinion of the community, must pre-select a group of nominees that must be presented before the Citizen Power (Prosecutor General, Comptroller General, Peoples' Defender), which must make a second pre-selection of nominees that is the one to be submitted to the National Assembly. Finally, the Constitution also provides for the rights of any Citizens to file well-founded objections to any of the nominees before the Judicial Nominations Committee or before the National Assembly. As mentioned, the main purpose of this constitutional procedure was to limit the discretional power the former Congress had in the election of Magistrates to the Supreme Court, based on political agreements and without any sort of citizen or society control.

416. But as aforementioned, ignoring all these provisions, and of course, without the previous sanctioning of the Supreme Tribunal Organic Law, the 1999 National Constituent Assembly, in a 'Decree on the Regimen for the Transition of Public Powers', issued on 22 December 1999, one week after the Constitution was already approved by popular vote (15 December 1999) (*see supra* paragraph 30), dismissed the then-existing fifteen Justices of the former Supreme Court of Justice that were still in their tenure. It appointed in substitution twenty new Justices for the new Supreme Tribunal of Justice, although in a transitory way. In the absence of

553. Decision of 12 Dec. 2000, in *Revista de Derecho Público*, No. 84 (octubre-diciembre) (Caracas: Editorial Jurídica Venezolana, 2000), 108 y ss. *See* Allan R. Brewer-Carías, *Golpe de Estado y Proceso Constituyente en Venezuela* (México: UNAM, 2002), 395 y ss.

constitutional or legal provisions regarding the number of Magistrates, the Constituent Assembly provided for the appointment of three Justices for each of the five: Political-Administrative, Electoral, Civil Cassation, Criminal Cassation and Social Chambers, and five Justices for the Constitutional Chamber. These appointments, as mentioned, had no constitutional or legal basis due to the fact that the Constitution or the Law did not specify the number of Justices in each Chamber of the Supreme Tribunal. In addition, the National Constituent Assembly had no power to enact constitutional provisions without popular approval by referendum, and the Constitutional Transitory Constitutional Regime Decree was enacted after the Constitution approbatory referendum of 15 December 1999, thus without popular approval. The appointments made on December 1999, however, were made by the Constituent Assembly without complying with the provisions regarding the ineludibly need for a Judicial Nomination Committee integrated by representatives of the different sectors of the society, to select and propose the candidates in order to guarantee the Citizens' participation.[554]

417. After the election of the new National Assembly in 2000 and according to the provisions of the new Constitution, it was supposed to enact the Organic Law of the Supreme Tribunal of Justice in order to determine the number of Magistrates of each of its Chambers, and to provide for the integration, organization and functioning of the Judicial Nominating Committee so as to elect in a definitive way the Justices of the Supreme Tribunal. But the Assembly, as aforementioned, instead of passing such Organic Law, on 14 November 2000 sanctioned a 'Special Law for the ratification or election of the High Officials of the Citizen Power and of the Magistrates of the Supreme Tribunal of Justice for the first constitutional term',[555] creating a Parliamentary Commission integrated by a majority of representatives as 'Nominating Committee' to select the Magistrates, by-passing the constitutional provision and imposing the need to create and regulate the Judicial Nominating Committee integrated exclusively with representatives of different sectors of society. The Assembly, in fact, appointed 'a Commission integrated by fifteen deputies, that shall act as the Committee for the Evaluation of Nominations' (Article 3), that was to select 'a list of twelve representatives of the different sectors of the society by means of mechanisms of consultation', and present the list to the National Assembly so that it may choose, by an absolute majority, six persons to sit on the Commission (Article 4).

418. The Peoples' Defender at the time (who had been provisionally appointed in December 1999) filed an action of unconstitutionality with an *amparo* petition against this Special Law, in order to protect the rights of political participation,[556] a process that the Supreme Tribunal has never decided. The response to that sign of

554. *See* Allan R. Brewer-Carías, 'La participación ciudadana en la designación de los titulares de los órganos no electos de los Poderes Públicos en Venezuela y sus vicisitudes políticas', in *Revista Iberoamericana de Derecho Publico y Administrativo*. Year 5. No. 5-2005 (San Jose, Costa Rica, 2005), 76–95.
555. *Gaceta Oficial* No. 37.077 of 14 Nov. 2000.
556. *See*, *El Universal*, Caracas 13 Dec. 2000, 1–2.

independence was the Legislator's decision not to ratify the titleholder of that position, and in a preliminary ruling in the case, the Constitutional Chamber deciding the *amparo* petition ruled that the eligibility conditions for the election of the Magistrates of the Tribunal set forth in a very precise way in Article 263 of the Constitution, were not applicable to those Magistrates sitting in the Supreme Tribunal that was precisely deciding the matter. The Magistrates considered that according to the Special Law they could be 'ratified' in their positions by the National Assembly even without compliance with the constitutional conditions to be Magistrates, arguing that the 'ratification' was a concept not foreseen in the Constitution (that only provided for the nomination). Therefore, Article 263 was to be applied only to *ex novo* elections of Magistrates but not to those that were already in the position that were going to be 'ratified'.[557] In this way, the Constitutional Chamber simply decided that the Constitution was inapplicable precisely with respect to its own Magistrates and particularly to those of the Constitutional Chamber that were the deciding judges in this case itself. The Magistrates eventually decided in their own case.[558]

419. The result of this process was that civil society was marginalized, and the Magistrates, as well as the High officials of the Citizen Power and of the Electoral Power were elected by the National Assembly in a discretionary way, as before, even without complying in all cases with the constitutional conditions required to be a magistrate. Through the Special Law the political control of the Branches of government was consolidated,[559] a situation that has persisted, particularly regarding the election of the Magistrates of the Supreme Tribunal.

---

557. The Tribunal ruled:

> 'The consequence of the Regimen for the Transition of the Public Powers – of constitutional rank as this Chamber has pointed out – is that the concept of ratification is applied only to Magistrates of the Supreme Tribunal of Justice, since the concept is not foreseen by the Constitution itself. Because of this, the phrase in *Art. 21 of the Regimen for the Transition of Public Powers* that states that definitive ratifications or appointments *shall be done according to the Constitution,* is inapplicable, since as this Chamber stated out previously, the current Constitution did not provide for ratification of Magistrates to the Supreme Tribunal of Justice.'

See decision of 12 Dec. 2000 in *Revista de Derecho Público*, No. 84 (Caracas: Editorial Jurídica Venezolana, 2000), 108 et seq.

558. That is why the Peoples' Defendant announced that she was going to ask for the inhibition of the Magistrates of the Constitutional Chamber in the case. *See El Universal* (Caracas, 16 Dec. 2000), 1–4.

559. This constitutional problem was pointed out by the Secretary General of the OAS, in its Report to the General Assembly of 18 Apr. 2002, and was highlighted with emphasis by the Inter-American Commission of Human Rights in a press Communiqué No. 23/02 of 10 May 2002, which referred to the questioning it has received 'related to the legitimacy of the process of selecting of the Highest Titleholders of the Judiciary..., [by means of] proceedings not stipulated in the Venezuelan Constitution. The received information pointed out that those officials were not nominated by the Committees provided in the Constitution but instead based on a statute sanctioned by the National Assembly after the approval of the Constitution...' (No. 7). The matter was more precisely referred to by the same Inter-American Commission in the Preliminary Remarks of 10 May 2002, in which it said that: 'The constitutional reforms established regarding the way to appoint those authorities

420. The subsequent step in this regard was made in 2004, with the enactment of the Organic Law of the Supreme Tribunal of Justice, in which the Judicial Nominating Committee was regulated, but instead of being integrated by representatives of the different sectors of society as imposed by the Constitution, it was established that it was to be integrated by' eleven members, from which five must be elected from the National Assembly, and the other six from the other sectors of society elected in a public proceeding' (Article 13.2). In practice, this Committee has been a Parliamentary Commission with additional non-parliamentary members that function within the Assembly (Article 13).

421. The 2004 Organic Law, in addition, for the first time since the approval of the Constitution (1999), established the number of the Magistrates of the Chambers of the Supreme Tribunal, extending it to a total of thirty-two Justices, whose nomination by the new Nominating Committee was completely controlled by the government. This was publicly announced by the President of the Parliamentary Nominating Commission in charge of selecting the candidates for Magistrates of the Supreme Tribunal Court of Justice (who a few months later was appointed Minister of the Interior and Justice), when he publicly declared on December 2004 that none of the elected Magistrates was to decide against the government interests.[560]

The last expression of this executive control on the Judiciary occurred in 2010, after an illegitimate 'reform' of Organic Law of the Supreme Tribunal of Justice, by means of its 'reprinting' due to a supposed printing (material) error,[561] allowing the election of new Magistrates of the Tribunal before the new National Assembly elected in September 2010 convened in January 2011.[562]

---

were not used in this case. Those provisions precisely seek to limit the undue interventions, assuring more independenence and impartiality, allowing diverse society opinions to be heard in the election of such high authorities' (No. 26).

560. This is what the representative said: 'Although we, the representatives, have the authority for this selection, the President of the Republic was consulted and his opinion was very much taken into consideration.' He added: 'Let's be clear, we are not going to score auto-goals. In the list, there were people from the opposition who comply with all the requirements. The opposition could have used them in order to reach an agreement during the last sessions, be they did not want to. We are not going to do it for them. There is no one in the group of postulates that could act against us ... .' *See* in *El Nacional* (Caracas, 13 Dec. 2004). That is why the Inter-American Commission on Human Rights suggested in its Report to the General Assembly of the OAS corresponding to 2004 that 'these regulations of the Organic Law of the Supreme Court of Justice would have made possible the manipulation, by the Executive Power, of the election process of judges that took place during 2004'. *See* Inter-American Commission on Human Rights, 2004 *Report on Venezuela*; para. 180.

561. *See* the comments of Víctor Hernández Mendible, 'Sobre la nueva reimpresión por "supuestos errores" materiales de la Ley Orgánica del Tribunal Supremo, octubre de 2010', y Antonio Silva Aranguren, 'Tras el rastro del engaño, en la web de la Asamblea Nacional', in *Revista de Derecho Público*, No. 124 (Caracas: Editorial Jurídica Venezolana, 2010), 110–113.

562. A former member of the Supreme Court of Justice, regarding such reform, said that 'the Nomination Judicial Committee was unconstitutionally converted into an appendix of the Legislative Power'. *See* Hildegard Rondón de Sansó, '*Obiter Dicta*. En torno a una elección', in *La Voce d'Italia* (Caracas, 14 Dec. 2010).

III. The Removal and Dismissal of the Magistrates

422. However, according to Article 265 of the Constitution, the Magistrates of the Supreme Tribunal of Justice although elected for a twelve years tenure, can be dismissed by the National Assembly by a vote of two-thirds of its members following a hearing in cases of serious or major offences as determined by the Citizen Power. This sole possibility for the Legislative Power to dismiss the Head of the Judiciary contradicts the principle of separation of powers and the independence of the Judiciary.[563] Nonetheless, the qualified two-thirds majority vote was established to avoid leaving the existence of the Heads of the Judiciary in the hands of a simple majority of legislators.

For such purpose, Article 12.1 of the 2004 Organic Law of the Supreme Tribunal of Justice defines as grave faults of a magistrate, among others, not to be impartial or independent in the exercise of his functions; to have political activism on party or trade-union matters; to exercise private activities or activities incompatible with their functions; not to accomplish their functions of being manifestly negligent of it; to publicly act against the respectability of the Judiciary and its organs; to endanger the credibility and impartiality of their position, compromising the dignity of the office; to act with abuse or excess of power; or to commit grave and inexcusable errors, prevarication or denials of justice.

But the 2004 Organic Law of the Supreme Tribunal, in an evident fraud to the Constitution, established another way to dismiss Magistrates of the Supreme Court, by-passing the qualified majority required in the Constitution, by adding the possibility for the National Assembly to approve by just a simple majority of votes, to 'annul the administrative act of appointment of the Magistrate', in cases of them have given false information when nominated; of public attitude that could harm the prestige of the Supreme Tribunal, its Chambers and Magistrates; and of actions against the functioning of the Tribunal (Article 234). Although the National Assembly used this power to dismiss Magistrates after deciding on some particular sensible questions not according to the government's willingness,[564] such provision was eliminated in the 2010 reform of the Organic Law of the Supreme Tribunal.

563. *See* Allan R. Brewer-Carías, *Separation of Powers and Authoritarian Government in Venezuela*, Lecture given in the Seminar on Separation of Powers in the Americas and Beyond, Duquesne University, School of Law, Pittsburgh, 7 and 8 Nov. 2008, in www.allanbrewercarías.com (I,1,982,2 008); 'La justicia sometida al poder y la interminable emergencia del poder judicial (1999–2006)', in *Derecho y democracia. Cuadernos Universitarios*, Órgano de Divulgación Académica, Vicerrectorado Académico (Caracas: Universidad Metropolitana, Año II, No. 11, septiembre 2007), 122–138.

564. It was the case of the Vice President of the Supreme Tribunal of Justice, who delivered the decision of the Supreme Tribunal of 14 Aug. 2002 regarding the criminal process against the generals who acted on 12 Apr. 2002, declaring that there were no grounds to judge them due to the fact that in said occasion no military coup took place; and that of Alberto Martini Urdaneta, President of the Electoral Court, and Rafael Hernandez and Orlando Gravina, Judges of the same Court who undersigned Decision No. 24 of 15 Mar. 2004 (Case: *Julio Borges, Cesar Perez Vivas, Henry Ramos Allup, Jorge Sucre Castillo, Ramón Jose Medina and Gerardo Blyde v. the National Electoral Council*), that suspended the effects of Resolution No. 040302-131, dated 2 Mar. 2004 of the National Electoral Council which, in that moment, stopped the realization of the presidential recall referendum.

Chapter 3. The Dependence of the Judiciary and Factual Absence of Judicial Autonomy and Independence

423. The progressive process of centralization and concentration of powers (*see supra* paragraphs 234 ff.) developed in Venezuela since 1999, by means of a continuous, persistent, and deliberate process of demolishing the rule of law institutions[565] and of destroying democracy in a way never before experienced in all the constitutional history of the country,[566] has led to the configuration of a highly politicized Supreme Tribunal, subjected to the will of the President of the Republic; which was reinforced with the election of Magistrates in 2010,[567] in 2014 and in 2022, eliminating all autonomy of the Judicial Power and even the basic principle of the separation of powers, as the cornerstone of the Rule of Law and the base of all democratic institutions.[568]

§1. The Judiciary Packed by Temporal and Provisional Judges and the Use of the Judiciary for Political Persecution

424. It has been through the Supreme Tribunal, which oversees governing and administering the Judiciary, that the political control over all judges has been assured, reinforced by means of the survival until 2011, of the 1999 'provisional' Commission on the Functioning and Restructuring of the Judicial System, which

565. *See* in *general*, Allan R. Brewer-Carías, 'La progresiva y sistemática demolición de la autonomía e independencia del Poder Judicial en Venezuela (1999–2004)', *XXX Jornadas J.M Dominguez Escovar, Estado de Derecho, Administración de Justicia y Derechos Humanos* (Barquisimeto, Instituto de Estudios Jurídicos del Estado Lara, 2005), 33–174; Allan R. Brewer-Carías, 'El constitucionalismo y la emergencia en Venezuela: entre la emergencia formal y la emergencia anormal del Poder Judicial', in Allan R. Brewer-Carías, 2007. *Estudios Sobre el Estado Constitucional (2005–2006)* (Caracas: Editorial Jurídica Venezolana, 2007), 245–269; and Allan R. Brewer-Carías 2007. 'La justicia sometida al poder. La ausencia de independencia y autonomía de los jueces en Venezuela por la interminable emergencia del Poder Judicial (1999–2006)', *Cuestiones Internacionales. Anuario Jurídico Villanueva (*Centro Universitario Villanueva, Madrid: Marcial Pons, 20070, 25–57. *See also* Allan R. Brewer-Carías, 2008. *Historia Constitucional de Venezuela*, vol. II (Caracas: Editorial Alfa, 402–454).

566. *See*, in general, Allan R. Brewer-Carías, 2007. El autoritarismo establecido en fraude a la Constitución y a la democracia y su formalización en 'Venezuela mediante la reforma constitucional. (De cómo en un país democrático se ha utilizado el sistema eleccionario para minar la democracia y establecer un régimen autoritario de supuesta "dictadura de la democracia" que se pretende regularizar mediante la reforma constitucional)', *Temas constitucionales. Planteamientos ante una Reforma,* Fundación de Estudios de Derecho Administrativo, Caracas FUNEDA, 13–74; and Allan R. Brewer-Carías, 'La demolición del Estado de Derecho en Venezuela Reforma Constitucional y fraude a la Constitución (1999–2009),'in *El Cronista del Estado Social y Democrático de Derecho*, No. 6, (Madrid, Editorial Iustel, 2009), 52–61.

567. *See* Hildegard Rondón de Sansó, 2010. *Obiter Dicta*. En torno a una elección, *La Voce d'Italia*, Caracas 14 Dec. 2010.

568. *See* in general Allan R. Brewer-Carías, 'Dismantling the Rule of Law by politically controlling the Judiciary in Venezuela and its harmful projection on the Inter-American judicial system for the protection of human rights', *European Review of Public Law/Revue Européenne de Droit Public*, vol. 33, No. 3, autumn/automne 2021 pp/ 877-918; and *La demolición de la independencia y autonomía del Poder Judicial en Venezuela 1999–2021*, (Caracas, Editorial Jurídica Venezolana, 2021).

was legitimized by the same Tribunal, making completely inapplicable the 1999 constitutional provisions seeking to guarantee the independence and autonomy of judges.

In effect, as aforementioned (*see supra* paragraph 406), according to the text of the 1999 Constitution, judges can only enter the judicial career by means of public competition that must be organized with citizens' participation. Nonetheless, this provision has not yet been implemented, being the judiciary is almost exclusively made up of temporary and provisional judges, without any stability. Regarding this situation, for instance, since 2003, the Inter-American Commission on Human Rights repeatedly expressed concern about the fact that provisional judges are susceptible to political manipulation, which alters the people's right to access justice, reporting cases of dismissals and substitutions of judges in retaliation for decisions contrary to the government's position.[569] In its *2008 Annual Report*, the Commission again verified the provisional character of the judiciary as an 'endemic problem' because the appointment of judges was made without applying constitutional provisions on the matter –thus exposing judges to discretionary dismissal– which highlights the 'permanent state of urgency' in which those appointments have been made.[570]

425. Contrary to these facts, according to the words of the Constitution, in order to guarantee the independence of the Judiciary, judges can be dismissed from their tenure only through disciplinary processes, conducted by disciplinary courts and judges of a Disciplinary Judicial Jurisdiction. Nonetheless, as aforementioned, that jurisdiction was only created in 2011, corresponding to that year the disciplinary judicial functions to the already mentioned transitory Commission,[571] which, as reported by the same Inter-American Commission in its *2009 Annual Report:*

> in addition to being a special, temporary entity, does not afford due guarantees for ensuring the independence of its decisions,[572] since its members may also be appointed or removed at the sole discretion of the Constitutional Chamber of the Supreme Tribunal of Justice, without previously establishing either the grounds or the procedure for such formalities.[573]

The Commission then 'cleansed' the Judiciary of judges not in line with the authoritarian regime, removing judges in a discretionary way when they have issued

569. *See Informe sobre la Situación de Derechos Humanos en Venezuela*; OAS/Ser.L/V/II.118. doc.4rev.2; 29 Dec. 2003, paras 161, 174, available at http://www.cidh.oas.org/coun-tryrep/Venezuela2003eng/toc.htm.
570. *See Annual Report 2008* (OEA/Ser.L/V/II.134. Doc. 5 rev. 1. 25 febrero 2009), para. 39.
571. The Politico Administrative Chamber of the Supreme Tribunal has decided that the dismiss of temporal judges is a discretionary power of the Commission on the Functioning and Reorganization of the Judiciary, which adopts its decision without following any administrative procedure rules or due process rules. *See* Decision No. 00463-2007 of 20 Mar. 2007; Decision No. 00673-2008 of 24 Apr. 2008 (cited in Decision No. 1.939 of 18 Dec. 2008, 42). The Chamber has adopted the same position in Decision No. 2414 of 20 Dec. 2007 and Decision No. 280 of 23 Feb. 2007.
572. *See* Decisión No. 1.939 of 18 Dec. 2008 (Caso: *Gustavo Álvarez Arias et al.*)
573. Véase *Annual Report 2009*, Par. 481, en http://www.cidh.org/annualrep/2009eng/Chap. IV.f.eng-.htm.

decisions not within the complacency of the government.[574] This led the Inter-American Commission on Human Rights, to observe in its *2009 Annual Report*, that 'in Venezuela, judges and prosecutors do not enjoy the guaranteed tenure necessary to ensure their independence'.[575]

426. One of the leading cases showing this situation took place in 2003 when a High Contentious Administrative Court ruled against the government in a politically charged case regarding the hiring of foreign physicians (not licensed in Venezuela) for medical social programs. In response to a provisional judicial measure suspending the hiring procedures, due to discrimination allegations made by the Council of Physicians of Caracas,[576] the government after declaring that the decision was not going to be accepted,[577] seized the Court using secret police officers and dismissed its judges after being offended by the President of the Republic.[578] The case was brought before the Inter-American Court of Human Rights and after it ruled in 2008 that the dismissal effectively violated the American Convention on Human Rights,[579] the Constitutional Chamber of the Supreme Tribunal response to the Inter-American Court ruling, at the request of the government, was that the decision of the Inter-American Court could not be enforced in Venezuela,[580] showing the subordination of the Venezuelan judiciary to the policies, wishes, and dictates of the President.

427. In December 2009, another astonishing case was the detention of a criminal judge for having ordered, based on a previous recommendation of the UN Working Group on Arbitrary Detention, the release of an individual in order for him to face criminal trial while in freedom, as guaranteed in the Constitution. On the same day of the decision, the President of the Republic publicly asked for the judge to be incarcerated asking to apply her a thirty-year prison term, which is the maximum

574. Decision No. 1.939 (18 Dec. 2008) (Case: *Abogados Gustavo Álvarez Arias y otros*), in which the Constitutonal Chamber declared the non-enforceability of the decision of the Inter-American Court of Human Rights of 5 Aug. 2008, Case: *Apitz Barbera y otros ('Corte Primera de lo Contencioso Administrativo') v. Venezuela* Serie C, No. 182.
575. *See Informe Anual de 2009*, para. 480, available at http://www.cidh.oas.org/annual-rep/2009eng/Chap.IV.f.eng.htm.
576. *See* Decision of 21 Aug. 2003, in *Revista de Derecho Público*, Nos 93–96 (Caracas: Editorial Jurídica Venezolana, 2003), 445 ff. *See* the comments in Claudia Nikken, 'El caso "Barrio Adentro": La Corte Primera de lo Contencioso Administrativo ante la Sala Constitucional del Tribunal Supremo de Justicia o el avocamiento como medio de amparo de derechos e intereses colectivos y difusos', *Revista de Derecho Público*, Nos 93–96 (Caracas: Editorial Jurídica Venezolana, 2003), 5 ff.
577. The President of the Republic said: '*Váyanse con su decisión no sé para donde, la cumplirán ustedes en su casa si quieren ...*' (You can go with your decision, I don't know where; you will enforce it in your house if you want ...). *See El Universal*, Caracas, 25 Aug. 2003 and *El Universal*, Caracas, 28 Aug. 2003.
578. *See* in *El Nacional*, Caracas 5 Nov. 2004, A2.
579. *See* Inter-American Court of Human Rights, case: *Apitz Barbera et al. (Corte Primera de lo Contencioso Administrativo) v. Venezuela*, Decision of 5 Aug. 2008, available at www.corteidh.or.cr. *See also*, *El Universal*, Caracas, 16 Oct. 2003; and *El Universal*, Caracas, 22 Sep. 2003.
580. Supreme Tribunal of Justice, Constitutional Chamber, Decision No. 1.939 of 18 Dec. 2008 (Case: *Abogados Gustavo Álvarez Arias et al.*) (Exp. No. 08-1572), available at http://www.tsj.gov.ve/decisiones/scon/Diciembre/1939-181208-2008-08-1572.html.

punishment in Venezuelan law for horrendous or grave crimes. The fact is that the judge remained in for years detention without trial. The UN Working Group described these facts as 'a blow by President Hugo Chávez to the independence of judges and lawyers in the country', demanding 'the immediate release of the judge', concluding that 'reprisals for exercising their constitutionally guaranteed functions and creating a climate of fear among the judiciary and lawyers' profession, serve no purpose except to undermine the rule of law and obstruct justice'.[581]

428. The fact is that in Venezuela, no judge can adopt any decision that could affect the government policies, or the President's wishes, the state's interest, or public servants' will, without previous authorization from the same government.[582] That is why the Inter-American Commission on Human Rights, after describing in its *2009 Annual Report* 'how large numbers of judges have been removed, or their appointments voided, without the applicable administrative proceedings', noted 'with concern that in some cases, judges were removed almost immediately after adopting judicial decisions in cases with a major political impact', concluding that 'The lack of judicial independence and autonomy vis-à-vis political power is, in the Commission's opinion, one of the weakest points in Venezuelan democracy.'[583]

429. In this context of political subjection, the Constitutional Chamber of the Supreme Tribunal, since 2000, far from acting as the guardian of the Constitution, has been the main tool of the authoritarian government for the illegitimate mutation of the Constitution, by means of unconstitutional constitutional interpretations,[584] not only regarding its own powers of judicial review, which have been enlarged but also regarding substantive matters. The Supreme Tribunal has distorted the Constitution through illegitimate and fraudulent 'constitutional mutations' in the sense of changing the meaning of its provisions without changing its wording. And all this, of course, without any possibility of being controlled,[585] so the eternal question arising from the uncontrolled power – *Quis custodiet ipsos custodes?* – in Venezuela also remains unanswered.

---

581. Case María Lourdes Afiuni Mora. *See* the text of the UN Working Group in http://www.unog.ch/unog/website/ news_media.nsf/%28httpNewsByYear_en%29/93687E8429BD53A1C125768E005 29DB6?OpenDocument&cntxt=B35C3&cookielang=fr. In 14 Oct. 2010, the same Working Group asked the Venezuelan Government to subject the Judge to a trail ruled by the due process guaranties and in freedom. *See in El Universal*, 14 Oct. 2010, available at http://www.eluniversal.com/2010/10/14/pol_ava_instancia-de-la-onu_14A4608051.shtml.
582. *See* Antonio Canova González, *La realidad del contencioso administrativo venezolano (Un llamado de atención frente a las desoladoras estadísticas de la Sala Político Administrativa en 2007 y primer semestre de 2008)* (Caracas: FUNEDA, 2008) p. 14.
583. *See* in ICHR, *Annual Report 2009*, para. 483, available at http://www.cidh.oas.org/-annualrep/2009eng/Chap.IV.f.eng.htm.
584. *See* Allan R. Brewer-Carías, *Crónica sobre la 'In' Justicia Constitucional. La Sala Constitucional y el autoritarismo en Venezuela* (Caracas: Editorial Jurídica Venezolana, 2007).
585. *See* Allan R. Brewer-Carías, *Quis Custodiet ipsos Custodes*: De la interpretación constitucional a la inconstitucionalidad de la interpretación, *VIII Congreso Nacional de Derecho Constitucional* (Arequipa: Fondo Editorial Colegio de Abogados de Arequipa, 2005), 463–489; and Allan R. Brewer-Carías, *Crónica de la 'In'Justicia constitucional: La Sala constitucional y el autoritarismo en Venezuela* (Caracas: Editorial Jurídica Venezolana, 2007), 11–44 and 47–79.

430. However, some fundamental rights essential for a democracy to function, like the freedom of expression, contrary to the principle of progressiveness established in the Constitution, it has been the Supreme Tribunal of Justice the State organ in charge of limiting its scope. First, in 2000, it was the Political-Administrative Chamber of the Supreme Tribunal that ordered the media not to transmit certain information, eventually admitting limits to be imposed on the media, regardless of the general prohibition of censorship established in the Constitution.

The following year, in 2001, it was the Constitutional Chamber of the Supreme Tribunal, the one that distorted the Constitution when dismissing an *amparo* action filed against the President of the Republic by a citizen and a non-governmental organization asking for the exercise of their right to response against the attacks made by the President in his weekly TV programme. The Constitutional Chamber reduced the scope of freedom of information, eliminating the right to response and rectification regarding opinions in the media when they are expressed by the president in a regularly televised programme. In addition, the tribunal excluded journalists and all those persons that have a regular programme on the radio or a newspaper column, from the right to rectification and response.[586]

In addition, in 2003, the Constitutional Chamber dismissed an action of unconstitutionality filed against a few articles of the Criminal Code that limit the right to formulate criticism against public officials, considering that such provisions could not be deemed as limiting the freedom of expression, contradicting a well-established doctrine on the contrary ruled by the Inter-American Courts on Human Rights. The Constitutional Chamber also decided in contradiction with the constitutional prohibition of censorship, that through a statute, it was possible to prevent the diffusion of information when it could be considered contrary to other provisions of the Constitution.[587]

Regarding other cases in which the Judiciary has been used for political persecution, they are referred to as the exercise of freedom of expression, concluding in the shutdown of TV stations that had a line of political opposition regarding the government and the persecution of their main shareholders. One leading case was the *Radio Caracas Televisión (RCTV)* case, which referred to a TV station that, in 2007, was the most important television station in the country, critical of the administration of President Hugo Chavez. In that case, it was the Supreme Tribunal in 2007, the State organ, that materialized the State intervention in order to terminate authorizations and licenses of the TV station, whose assets were confiscated and its equipment assigned to a state-owned enterprise through an illegitimate Supreme Tribunal

586. *See* Allan R. Brewer-Carías, 'La libertad de expresión del pensamiento y el derecho a la información y su violación por la Sala Constitucional del Tribunal Supremo de Justicia', in Allan R. Brewer-Carías et al., 2001. *La libertad de expresión amenazada (Sentencia 1013)* (Caracas/San José: Instituto Interamericano de Derechos Humanos – Editorial Jurídica Venezolana, 2002), 17–57; and Jesús A. Davila Ortega, 'El derecho de la información y la libertad de expresión en Venezuela (Un estudio de la sentencia 1.013/2001 de la Sala Constitucional del Tribunal Supremo de Justicia)', *Revista de Derecho Constitucional* 5 (Caracas: Editorial Sherwood 2002), 305–325

587. *See Revista de Derecho Público,* 93–94 (Caracas: Editorial Jurídica Venezolana, 2003), 136ff. and 164ff. *See* comments in Alberto Arteaga Sánchez et al., *Sentencia 1942 v. Libertad de expresión* (Caracas, 2004).

decision.[588] The case is the most vivid example of the illegitimate collusion or confabulation between a politically controlled Judiciary and an authoritarian government in order to reduce freedom of expression and confiscate private property. For such purpose, it was the Constitutional Chamber of the Supreme Tribunal of Justice and the Political-Administrative Chamber of the same Tribunal that, in May 2007, instead of protecting the citizens' right of freedom of expression, conspired as docile instruments controlled by the Executive, in order to kidnap and violate them. In this case, it was the highest level of the Judiciary that covered the governmental arbitrariness with a judicial veil, executing the shout down of the TV Station, reducing the freedom of expression in the country, and with total impunity, proceeded to confiscate private property in a way that neither the Executive nor the Legislator, could have done because being forbidden in the Constitution (Article 115). In this case, it was the Supreme Tribunal, which violated the Constitution, with the aggravating circumstance that the conspirators knew that their actions could not be controlled. This case has also been recently submitted before the Inter-American Court of Human Rights.

Other cases of political persecution, also related to freedom of expression, are the cases against the principal shareholders of Globovisión, the other independent TV station that after the take-over of Radio Caracas Television, remained with a critical line of opinion regarding the government. They both were harassed by the Public Prosecutor Office and by the Judiciary, accused of different common crimes that they did not commit; they were detained without any serious base, their enterprises were occupied and their property confiscated. They both had to leave the country, without any possibility of obtaining Justice. Their cases have also been submitted before the Inter-American Commission of Human Rights.[589]

431. The Judiciary, particularly on criminal matters, has also been used as the government instrument to pervert Justice, distorting the facts in specific cases of political interest, converting innocent people into criminals, and liberating criminals of all suspicion. It was the unfortunate case of the mass killings committed by government agents and supporters as a consequence of the enforcement of the so-called Plan Avila, a military order that encouraged the shooting of people participating in the biggest mass demonstration in Venezuelan history on 11 April 2002, was asking for the resignation of the late President Chávez. The soothing provoked general military disobedience by the high commanders, in a way witnessed by all the country on TV, which ended with the military removal of the President, although just for a few hours until the same military reinstated him in office. Nonetheless, in order to change history, the shooting and mass killings were re-written, and those

---

588. *See* the Constitutional Chamber Decision No. 957 (25 May 2007), in *Revista de Derecho Público* 110 (Caracas: Editorial Jurídica Venezolana, 2007), 117ff. *See* the comments in Allan R. Brewer-Carías,. El juez constitucional en Venezuela como instrumento para aniquilar la libertad de expresión plural y para confiscar la propiedad privada: El caso RCTV', *Revista de Derecho Público*, No. 110 (Caracas: Editorial Jurídica Venezolana, 2007), 7–32.

589. Case Globovisión (Guillermo Zuloaga and Nelson Mezerhane). *See* Press Release. No. R119/10. Special Rapporteurship Expresses Concern Regarding Venezuelan State Intervention In Globovisión, 8 Dec. 2010, available at http://www.oas.org/en/iachr/expression/showarticle.asp?artID=827&lID=1.

responsible that everybody saw live on TV because government supporters were gratified as heroes, and the Police Officials trying to assure order in the demonstration, were blamed for crimes that they did not commit, and condemned of murder with the highest term of thirty years of prison.[590]

§2. The Use of the Judiciary to Facilitate the Concentration of Power and the Dismantling of Democracy

432. The Constitutional Chamber of the Supreme Tribunal, however, has been one of the most important instruments used by the government in order to reinforce the concentration of powers, not only adopting decisions, at the request of the Government, through which the Constitution has been 'mutated' (*see infra* paragraphs 715 et seq.) that is, changed by means of interpretation made by the Constitutional Chamber of the Supreme Tribunal of Justice as Constitutional Jurisdiction,[591] without a constitutional review procedure (*see supra* paragraphs 126 ff.); but through which the government has assumed direct control of other branches of government, as happened in 2002 with the take-over of the Electoral Power, which since then has been completely controlled by the Executive.

This began in 2002 after the Organic Law of the Electoral Power[592] was sanctioned and the National Assembly was due to elect, as an electoral body, the new members of the National Electoral Council. Because the representatives supporting the government did not have the qualified majority to approve such an election by

590. Cases *Simonovic and Forero*. A former Chief Justice of the Criminal Chamber of the Supreme Tribunal of Justice, general Eladio Aponte, confessed last year 2012 in a TV Programme (SolTV) in Miami, when answering about if there were political persons in prison in Venezuela, saying 'Yes, there are people regarding which there is an order not to let them free', referring particularly to 'the Police Officers', mentioning Officer Simonovic. The same former Justice, answering a question about '*Who gives the order*', simply said: 'The order comes from the President's Office downwards', adding that 'we must have no doubts, in Venezuela there are no sewing point if it is not approved by the President'. He finally said, answering a question if he '*received the order not to let free Simonovis*' he explained that: 'the position of the Criminal Chamber' was 'To validate all that arrived already done; that is, in a few words, to accept that these gentlemen could not be freed.' To hear this answers given by one who until recently was the highest Justice in the Venezuelan Criminal System, produce no other than indignation, because it was him, as Chief Criminal Justice, the one in charge of manipulating justice, in the way he confessed; condemning the Police Officers to thirty years in prison, just because obeying orders from the Executive. *See* the text of the statement on, in *El Universal*, Caracas 18 Apr. 2012, available at: http://www.eluniversal.com/nacional-y-politica/120418/historias-secretas-de-un-juez-en-venezuela.

591. *See* Allan R. Brewer-Carías, 'El juez constitucional al servicio del autoritarismo y la ilegítima mutación de la Constitución: el caso de la Sala Constitucional del Tribunal Supremo de Justicia de Venezuela (1999–2009)', in *Revista de Administración Pública*, No. 180, Madrid 2009, 383–418; 'La fraudulenta mutación de la Constitución en Venezuela, o de cómo el juez constitucional usurpa el poder constituyente originario', in *Anuario de Derecho Público*, No. 2 Caracas, Centro de Estudios de Derecho Público de la Universidad Monteávila, 2009), 23–65; José Vicente Haro, 'La mutación de la Constitución "Bolivariana"', in Gonzalo Pérez Salazar & Luis Petit Guerra, *Los retos del derecho procesal constitucional en Latinoamérica, I Congreso Internacional de Derecho Procesal Constitucional, 19 y 20 Octubre de 2011*, vol. I (Caracas: Universidad Monteávila Funeda, 2011), 93–141.

592. *See Gaceta Oficial* No. 37.573 of 19 Nov. 2002.

themselves and did not reach agreements on the matter with the opposition, when the National Assembly failed to elect the members of the National Electoral Council, that task was assumed, without any constitutional power, by the Constitutional Chamber of the Supreme Tribunal itself. Deciding an action that was filed against what was considered an unconstitutional legislative omission, the Chamber, instead of urging the Assembly to comply with its constitutional duty, directly elected the members of the Electoral Council, usurping the Assembly's functions as an electoral body, but without complying with the conditions established in the Constitution for such election.[593] With this decision, the Chamber assured the government's complete control of the Council, kidnapping the citizen's rights to political participation, and allowing the official governmental party to manipulate the electoral results. The same was repeated in December 2014, when the Constitutional Chamber again usurped the role of the National Assembly as an electoral body and appointed new members of the Electoral Council all related to the official political party.[594]

Consequently, the elections held in Venezuela during the past years have been organized by a politically dependent branch of government, without any guarantee of independence or impartiality.

433. The Constitutional Chamber of the Supreme Tribunal has also been the instrument in order to erode the democratic principle, limiting the right to be elected, imposing non-elected officials as Head of State, or revoking the popular mandate of elected officials without having competency or jurisdiction. As aforementioned (*see supra*, paragraph 101 ff.), between January and March 2013, the Constitutional Chamber of the Supreme Tribunal, openly violated the democratic principle by imposing a non-elected official as head of State, during the illness of former President Chávez and after his death, in two decisions adopted, in addition, without proving anything. The decisions were issued after deciding interpretations of recourses of the Constitution: The first Decision No. 2 of 9 January 2013, was issued to resolve the legal situation of the non-attendance by the President elected to his Inauguration for the presidential term 2013–2019, refusing the Constitutional Chamber to consider that the situation was one of absolute absence of the elected President, and instead constructing, without proving anything on the health condition of the elected and ill President, a supposed 'administrative continuity' of Chávez, affirming that even been absent of the country (he was said to be in a Hospital in La Habana), he was supposedly effectively in charge of the Presidency, so

593. *See* Decision No. 2073 of 4 Aug. 2003, Case: *Hermánn Escarrá Malaver y oros*), and Decision No. 2341 of 25 Aug. 2003, Case: *Hemann Escarrá y otros*. *See* in Allan R. Brewer-Carías, 2003/2004. El secuestro del poder electoral y la conficación del derecho a la participación política mediante el referendo revocatorio presidencial: Venezuela 2000–2004, *Stvdi Vrbinati, Rivista tgrimestrale di Scienze Giuridiche, Politiche ed Economiche*, Año LXXI – (Urbino: Università degli Studi di Urbino, 2003), 379–436.

594. Decision No. 1864 of 22 Dec. 2014, available at: http://historico.tsj.gov.ve/decisiones/scon/diciembre/173494-1864-221214-2014-14-1341.HTML; and Decision No. 1865 of 26 Dec. 26, 2014, available at: http://historico.tsj.gov.ve/decisiones/scon/diciembre/173497-1865-261214-2014-14-1343.HTML. *See* the comments in Allan R. Brewer-Carías, 'El golpe de Estado dado en diciembre de 2014, con la inconstitucional designación de las altas autoridades del Poder Público', *Revista de Derecho Público,* 40 (Caracas: Editorial Jurídica Venezolana, 2014).

his non-elected Vice President (N. Maduro) was to be in charge of the Presidency.[595] The second Decision No. 141, of 8 March 2013, was issued after the announcement of the death of President Chávez, but without proving such fact or when it effectively occurred, in order to assure that the Vice President (N. Maduro), already imposed as President in charge by the same Supreme Tribunal, was to continue in charge of the Presidency; and additionally allowing him, contrary to the text of the Constitution, to be a candidate to the same position in the subsequent election, without leaving the post.[596]

434. In other decisions, also contrary to the democratic principle, the Constitutional Chamber of the Supreme Tribunal revoked the popular mandate of two mayors, a decision that according to the Constitution only can be adopted by the people that elected the officials by means of a referendum (Article 74). The Supreme Tribunal, ignoring such principle and provision, without having constitutional competency and usurping the jurisdiction of the criminal courts that are only competent to impose criminal sanctions to officials for not obeying judicial decisions, issued Decision No. 138 of 17 March 2014, condemning the Mayors by considering that they had committed a crime (not to obey a preliminary injunction), and imprisoning them, without guarantying a due process of law.[597] The common trend in this case was that both Mayors were from the opposition to the government.

435. In another case, the Constitutional Chamber of the Supreme Tribunal also revoked the popular mandate of a representative to the National Assembly, which also can only be revoked by the people through a referendum, issuing Decision No. 207 of 31 March 2014, in case that the Tribunal had already concluded because the action was declared inadmissible, proceeding the Tribunal to act ex officio, and interpret an article of the Constitution (Article 93), that prevent representatives from accepting another public position without losing their elected one. The initial petition that was declared inadmissible was a request for the Tribunal to condemn *the facto* actions of the President of the National Assembly to strip out the elected condition of one representative; being the result of the case, once declared the petition inadmissible, for the Tribunal, to ex officio decide to revoke the popular mandate to the representative that was supposed to be protected by the Tribunal. The reason for such decision was that the representative had talked as such representative, before

595. *See* the text of the decision in http://www.tsj.gov.ve/decisiones/scon/Enero/02-9113-2013-12-1358.html.

596. *See* the text of the decision in http://www.tsj.gov.ve.decisioes/scon/Marzo/141-9313-2013-13-0196.html.

597. Decision No. 138 of 17 Mar. 2014, available at http://www.tsj.gov.ve/decisiones/scon/marzo/162025-138-17314-2014-14-0205.HTML 2014; and Decision No. 245 of 9 Apr. 2014, available at: http://www.tsj.gov.ve/decisiones/scon/abril/162860-245-9414-2014-14-0205.HTML Véase también en *Gaceta Oficial* No. 40.391 de 10 de abril de 2014. *See* the comments in Allan R. Brewer-Carías, 'La ilegítima e inconstitucional revocación del mandato popular de alcaldes por la Sala Constitucional del Tribunal Supremo, usurpando competencias de la jurisdicción penal, mediante un procedimiento "sumario" de condena y encarcelamiento (El caso de los Alcaldes Vicencio Scarano Spisso y Daniel Ceballo)', *Revista de Derecho Público,* 138 (Caracas: Editorial Jurídica Venezolana, 2014), 176–210.

the Permanent Council of the OAS, in a session devoted to analysing the political situation of Venezuela, from the site of the representative of Panama that had invited her to do so.[598]

436. Finally, in another decision, the Supreme Tribunal, also in violation of the democratic principle, accepted that the right of a citizen to be elected, which is a constitutional right, could be limited by an administrative body as the General Audit Office when issuing decisions imposing public officials the sanction of disqualifying them to run for elected positions. In Decision No. 1265 of 5 August 2008,[599] the Supreme Tribunal refused to declare that such disqualification for the exercise of a political right was contrary to the American Convention of Human Rights, that in Venezuela had a constitutional hierarchy (Article 23). The lack of justice in Venezuela, lead the interested person, a former Mayor, to file a petition before the Inter-American Court of Human Rights, seeking the protection of his political right, the result being a decision of such Court of 1 September 2011 (case *López Mendoza v. Venezuela*), condemning the Venezuelan State for the violation of the Convention. Nonetheless, the response of the State was to fie before the Supreme Tribunal of Justice, at the initiative of the Attorney General, an action for 'judicial review' of the Inter-American Court decision, which was astonishingly admitted by the Constitutional Chamber, which through Decision No. 1547 of 17 October 2011,[600] declared the Inter-American Court of Human Rights as 'non-enforceable' in Venezuela, recommending the Government to denounce the Convention. This eventually happened in 2012 (*see infra* paragraph 735).

437. Unfortunately, the political control over the Supreme Tribunal of Justice that can be appreciated in these examples has permeated to all the judiciary, due mainly to the already mentioned fact that in Venezuela, it is the Supreme Tribunal the one in charge of the government and administration of the Judiciary. This has affected gravely the autonomy and independence of judges at all levels of the Judiciary, which has been aggravated by the fact that during the past years, the Venezuelan Judiciary has been composed primarily of temporary and provisional judges, without career or stability, appointed without the public competition process of selection established in the Constitution, and dismissed without due process of law, for political reasons.[601] This reality amounts to political control of the Judiciary, as

598. *See* Decision No. 207 de 31 March 2014, available at en http://www.tsj.gov.ve/decisiones/scon/marzo/162546-207-31314-2014-14-0286.HTML Also published in *Gaceta Oficial* No. 40385 of 2 Apr. 2014. *See* the comments in Allan R. Brewer-Carías, 'La revocación del mandato popular de una diputada a la Asamblea Nacional por la Sala Constitucional del Tribunal Supremo de oficio, sin juicio ni proceso alguno (El caso de la Diputada María Corina Machado)', *Revista de Derecho Público,* 137 (Caracas: Editorial Jurídica Venezolana, 2014), 165–189.

599. *See* the text of the decision in http://www.tsj.gov.ve:80/decisiones/scon/Agosto/1265-050808-05-1853.htm.

600. *See* the text of the decision in http://www.tsj.gov.ve/decisiones/scon/Octubre/1547-171011-2011-11-1130.html.

601. *See* Inter-American Commission on Human Rights, *Report on the Situation of Human Rights in Venezuela*, OEA/Ser.L/V/II.118, doc. 4 rev. 2, 29 Dec. 2003, para. 174, *available at* http://www.cidh.oas.org/countryrep/Venezuela2003eng/toc.htm.

demonstrated by the dismissal of judges who have adopted decisions contrary to the policies of the governing political authorities.

Part VIII. Other Branches of Government

438. Another innovation in the Constitution of 1999 (*see supra* paragraph 60) was to formally declare that the distribution of the Powers of the State, at the national level, that is, the National Branches of government, are not only between the National Legislative Power, the National Executive Power, and the Judicial Power but also between two new additional branches: the Citizen Power and the Electoral Power (Article 136).[602]

602. *See* Roxana Orihuela Gonzatti, 'El nuevo Poder Ciudadano', in *El Derecho Público a comienzos del siglo XXI. Estudios homenaje al Profesor Allan R. Brewer-Carías,* vol. I (Madrid: Instituto de Derecho Público, UCV, Civitas Ediciones, 2003), 933–980; María A. Correa de Baumeister, 'El Poder Ciudadano y el Poder Electoral en la Constitución de 1999', in *El Derecho Público a comienzos del siglo XXI. Estudios homenaje al Profesor Allan R. Brewer-Carías,* vol. I (Madrid: Instituto de Derecho Público, UCV, Civitas Ediciones, 2003), 982–995; José L. Morantes Mago, 'El Poder Ciudadano y sus órganos en la Constitución de 1999', in *Revista de Control Fiscal,* No. 142 (enero-abril) (Caracas: Contraloría General de la República, 2000), 15–51; Celia Poleo de Ortega, 'El Poder Ciudadano en la Constitución venezolana de 1999', in *Revista de Control Fiscal,* No. 143 (mayo-agosto) (Caracas: Contraloría General de la República, 2000), 15–46.

Chapter 1. The Citizen Power

439. The Citizen Power is exercised by three traditional constitutional organs of the State: two established in the Constitutions since the 1940s, the Office of the Comptroller General of the Republic (General Audit Office) and the Office of the Public Prosecutor; and another one created by the 1999 Constitution, the Office of the Peoples' Defender, following the general trend of similar institutions existing in many Latin American countries for the purpose of protecting human rights.[603]

The Citizen Power, as a branch of government, is to be independent, and its organs are conferred functional, financial and administrative autonomy, having a variable assignation within the annual budget (Article 273).

§1. The Republican Moral Council

440. According to Article 273 of the Constitution, the Head Officials of the three organs of the Citizen Power, sitting together, conform to the Republican Moral Council (Article 274), which has the following attributions: to prevent, investigate and sanction facts against the public ethics or the administrative morals; seek for the maintenance of good business practices by the State, and assure that the use of public property is made in adherence to legality; and seek for the respect of the principle of legality in any administrative activity of the State. The Council is also empowered to promote education as a means to develop citizenship, solidarity, liberty, democracy, social responsibility and work (Article 274).

441. The members of the Republican Moral Council are required to inform the authorities and officials of the Public Administration of any breaches in the fulfilment of their legal duties. In a case of a continuous failure to conform to the Moral Council's admonition, the President of the Republican Moral Council is to send information to the organ or government agency in which the offending official is assigned or employed, so that those corrective measures may be taken by that entity (Article 275).

In conformity with Article 278, the Moral Republican Council must also promote pedagogical activities directed towards developing knowledge and study of the Constitution, love of one's country, civic and democratic virtues, the most important values of the Republic, and the observance and respect for human rights.

§2. Election of the Head of the Organs of the Citizen Power

442. The election of the Comptroller General of the Republic, the Prosecutor General, and the Peoples' Defender is assigned to the National Assembly, acting as

603. Organic Law on the Citizen Power, *Gaceta Oficial* No. 37.310 of 25 Oct. 2001. *See* Allan R. Brewer-Carías et al., *Leyes Orgánicas del poder ciudadano (Ley Orgánica del Poder Ciudadano, Ley Orgánica de la Defensoría del Pueblo, Ley Orgánica del Ministerio Público, Ley Orgánica de la Contraloría General de la República)* (Caracas: Editorial Jurídica Venezolana, 2005).

an electoral body for such indirect popular election, which nonetheless, has no discretion for the elections because they can only be made from candidates nominated by a 'Committee for Evaluation of Nominations to the Citizen Power'. This Committee is to be convened by the Republican Moral Council, and according to the Constitution, must be exclusively composed of 'representatives from different sectors of society' (Article 279).

For the purpose of making the nominations, the Committee must initiate and lead a public process to select three names for each of the organs of the Citizen Power, to be proposed to the National Assembly. The Assembly, through a favourable vote of at least two-thirds of its members, must then elect one of each triad of nominees within a period of no more than thirty consecutive days. If this period elapses with no agreement reached by the Assembly, the Electoral Power will submit the triads to a popular vote for selection (Article 279).

Article 279 of the Constitution states, nonetheless, that in a case when the Committee for Evaluation of Nominations has not been convened, the National Assembly must proceed to elect the heads of the organs of the Citizen Power, but of course, as an electoral body by the same qualified majority. Nonetheless, in December 2014, this provision was 'mutated' by the Constitutional Chamber of the Supreme Tribunal, which interpreted that the National Assembly in such cases could elect the high officials by simple majority of votes of the representatives present in the corresponding session, as a legislative body, ignoring its character in this case, of indirect electoral body.[604]

443. Regarding the Nominating Committee for the proposal of candidates for the election of the head of the organs of the Citizen Power, the same as occurred regarding the Judicial Nominating Committee in the case of the Magistrates of the Supreme Tribunal (*see supra* paragraph 239) has happened, in the sense that its composition has been distorted by the 2001 Organic Law of the Citizen Power, and contrary to the participatory sense of the Constitution, has been composed with a majority of representatives of the National Assembly and not exclusively by representatives of the various sectors of society, as provided in the Constitution. In this case, the Committee has also resulted in just a parliamentary commission with some additional members designated by the same Assembly from non-governmental entities.[605]

444. However, as happens with all the non-directed elected heads of the branches of government, the Constitution states that following a declaration of the Supreme Tribunal of Justice, members of the Citizen Power may be removed from

---

604. Decision No. 1864 of 22 Dec. 2014, available at: http://historico.tsj.gov.ve/decisiones/scon/diciembre/173494-1864-221214-2014-14-1341.HTML available at: http://historico.tsj.gov.ve/decisiones/scon/diciembre/173497-1865-261214-2014-14-1343.HTML. *See* the comments in Allan R. Brewer-Carías, 'El golpe de Estado dado en diciembre de 2014, con la inconstitucional designación de las altas autoridades del Poder Público', *Revista de Derecho Público,* 40 (Caracas: Editorial Jurídica Venezolana, 2014).

605. *See* Allan R. Brewer-Carías, 'Sobre el nombramiento irregular por la Asamblea Nacional de los titulares de los órganos del poder ciudadano en 2007', in Revista *de Derecho Público*, No. 113 (Caracas: Editorial Jurídica Venezolana, 2008), 85–88.

their positions by the National Assembly in cases of grave faults (Article 279). In the 2007 rejected constitutional reform, it was proposed to allow the National Assembly to approve such dismissals with only a majority of votes.

§3. The People's Defender

445. The Office of the Peoples' Defender is in charge of promoting, defending and maintaining human rights and guarantees declared in the Constitution and international treaties, as well as over 'legitimate collective and diffuse interests of Citizens' (Article 280).[606] The activities of the Office of the Peoples' Defence are to be executed in accordance with the principles of cost-free service, public accessibility, celerity, informality and self-initiative (Article 283).[607]

446. The Head of the Office is the People's Defender, who is designated by the National Assembly for a term of seven years (Article 280) and cannot be re-elected. The elected must be Venezuelan by birth without any other nationality (Articles 41, 280), with manifest and demonstrated skill in human rights matters. Its functions have been regulated in the 2004 Organic Law on the Peoples' Defender.[608]

447. Within its attributions, the Peoples' Defender has powers to watch over the effective guarantee of human rights, investigating ex officio or at party request, the complaints filed before his office; to seek for the good functioning of public services, and protect the people's rights and legitimate interest, collective or diffuse, against arbitrariness, abuse of power or errors in their rendering, filing the necessary actions, if needed, in order to ask the State to pay the citizens damages caused

606. *See* José L. Villegas Moreno, 'Los intereses difusos y colectivos en la Constitución de 1999', in *Revista de Derecho Constitucional*, No. 2 (enero-junio) (Caracas: Editorial Sherwood, 2000), 253–269; Ana E. Araujo García, 'El principio de la tutela judicial efectiva y los intereses colectivos y difusos', in *El Derecho Público a comienzos del siglo XXI. Estudios homenaje al Profesor Allan R. Brewer-Carías,* vol. III (Madrid: Editorial ThompsonCivitas, 2003), 2703–2717, and in *Revista de derecho del Tribunal Supremo de Justicia,* No. 4 (Caracas, 2002), 1 a 29; Mariolga Quintero Tirado, 'Aspectos de una tutela judicial ambiental efectiva', in *Nuevos estudios de derecho procesal, Libro Homenaje a José Andrés Fuenmayor,* vol. II, No. 8 (Caracas: Tribunal Supremo de Justicia, Colección Libros Homenaje, 2002), 189 a 236; Flor M. Ávila Hernández, 'La tutela de los intereses colectivos y difusos en la Constitución venezolana de 1999', in *El Derecho Público a comienzos del siglo XXI. Estudios homenaje al Profesor Allan R. Brewer-Carías,* vol. III, *supra,* 2719–2742.

607. *See* Alberto Baumeister Toledo, 'Algunos aspectos de derecho comparado de especial consideración sobre la figura del defensor del pueblo en la Constitución de 1999', in *Tendencias Actuales del Derecho Constitucional. Homenaje a Jesús María Casal Montbrun,* ed. Jesús María Casal, Alfredo Arismendi y Carlos Luis Carrillo Artiles (Coord.), vol. II (Caracas: Universidad Central de Venezuela/Universidad Católica Andrés Bello, 2008), 53–64; Gustavo Briceño Vivas, 'La protección de los derechos humanos y su inserción en la Constitución de 1999', in *Estudios de Derecho Público,* ed. Román Duque Corredor y Jesús María Casal (Coords), vol. II (Caracas: Universidad Católica Andrés Bello, 2004), 51–86; Gustavo Briceño Vivas, 'El Defensor del Pueblo en la nueva Constitución. Análisis y crítica', in *Revista de Derecho Público,* No. 82 (Caracas: Editorial Jurídica Venezolana, 2000), 57–69; Jesús M. Casal H., 'La Defensoría del Pueblo en Venezuela', in *Revista de Derecho Constitucional,* No. 3 (julio-diciembre) (Caracas: Editorial Sherwood, 2000), 345–358.

608. Organic Law on the Public Defendant Office, *Gaceta Oficial* No. 37.995 of 5 Aug. 2004.

by the functioning of public services; fill actions of unconstitutionality, of *amparo*, of habeas corpus, of habeas data regarding the aforementioned attributions; request the Public Prosecutor to file actions against public officials responsible for the violations of human rights; request from the Republican Moral Council to adopt the needed measures regarding public officials responsible for the violations of human rights; and watch over the rights of the indigenous peoples and exercise the necessary actions for their guarantee and effective protection (Article 281).

448. The Peoples' Defender, according to Article 282 of the Constitution, is immune in the exercise of its functions, and cannot be persecuted, detained or prosecuted because of actions taken in the exercise of its functions. The Supreme Tribunal of Justice is in charge of deciding over the prosecution of the Peoples' Defender.

§4. The Prosecutor General of the Republic

449. The Public Prosecutor is under the guidance of the Prosecutor General of the Republic (Article 284), who is elected for a term of six years by the National Assembly and must comply with the same conditions established in order to be elected Magistrate of the Supreme Tribunal (*see supra* paragraph 413). Its functions have been regulated in the 2007 Organic Law on the Public Prosecutor.[609]

450. Within the attributions of the Prosecutor General, the following must be mentioned: to guarantee in the judicial process the respect of human rights and guarantees; guarantee celerity and good development of justice and the respect of due process of law rules; order and direct criminal investigations for crimes committed, in order to register the facts, circumstances and authors; file in the name of the State the corresponding criminal actions and persecutions; and file the necessary actions to make effective the civil, labour, military, criminal, administrative or disciplinary liability of public officials, because of the exercise of their functions (Article 285).

§5. The Comptroller General of the Republic

451. The Office of the Comptroller General of the Republic (Audit Office) is the auditing State organ responsible for the control, oversight and investigation of public revenue and disbursements, national public assets and property, and all transactions referred to them. The Comptroller General Office has functional, administrative and organizational autonomy, and is oriented towards the inspection of entities and organs subjected to control (Article 287).[610]

The Office of the Comptroller General of the Republic is under the direction, and is the responsibility of the Comptroller General of the Republic, who is also elected

609. *Gaceta Oficial* No. 38.647 of 19 Mar. 2007.

610. *See* José Ignacio, Hernández G., 'La Contraloría General de la República', in *Revista de Derecho Público,* No. 83 (julio-septiembre) (Caracas: Editorial Jurídica Venezolana, 2000), 21–38.

by the National Assembly for a term of seven years, and must be Venezuelan by birth without any other nationality (Articles 43, 288). Its functions have been regulated in the 2001 Organic Law on the Office of the Comptroller General of the Republic.[611]

452. Within the attributions of the Comptroller General Office, are the following: to exercise control, watch and supervise public revenues, expenses and property, as well as the operation related to them; control public debt; inspect and supervise the public sector entities subjected to control; execute the inspections, and impose the corresponding administrative sanctions in cases of corruption; request the Public Prosecutor to initiate the corresponding judicial actions regarding the faults and crimes against the public assets; control public management and evaluate the accomplishment of the public policies and decisions (Article 289); and direct the national system of fiscal control (Article 290).

611. *Gaceta Oficial* No. 37.347 of 17 Dec. 2001.

Chapter 2. The Electoral Power

453. Another innovation of the 1999 Constitution was the creation of the Electoral Power as another branch of government, by giving constitutional hierarchy to the organ assigned to oversight and control over electoral matters.[612] For such purpose, Article 292 of the Constitution provides that the Electoral Power will be exercised by the National Electoral Council, as the governing entity of this branch of government, as well as by the National Electoral Board, the Commission for Civil and Electoral Registry, and the Commission for Political Participation and Financing. Its functions have been regulated in the 2002 Organic Law on the Electoral Power.[613]

454. The functions of the Electoral Power under Article 293, in addition to the organization, administration, direction and oversight of all activities concerning elections for State public offices, include the power to organize labour union elections, as well as the elections held in professional guilds and associations, and organizations with political purposes. In the same way, the Electoral Power may organize elections for civil society organizations that so request it, or, upon the order of the Electoral Chamber of the Supreme Tribunal of Justice. This constitutes an inconvenient interference by organizations of the State into intermediary organizations of society.

455. Article 296 establishes that the National Electoral Council is to be composed of five persons with no ties to political organizations, elected by the National Assembly for a seven-year term, by a vote of two-thirds of its members. Three of them must be nominated by civil society, one by Law and Political Science Divisions of national universities, and one by the Citizen Power. The three members nominated by civil society are to have six alternates sequentially ordered, and each member designated by the Universities and Citizen Power is to have two alternates respectively.

For the purpose of nominating before the Assembly the candidates to the Electoral Council, Article 295 of the Constitution also creates, in this case, a Committee for Electoral Nominations that must also be constituted of representatives from different sectors of society. Also, in this case, as happened with the Judicial Nominating Committee and with the Nominating Committee for the Members of the Citizen Power, the Committee for Electoral Nominations has been distorted in the Organic

612. *See* María A. Correa de Baumeister, 'El Poder Ciudadano y el Poder Electoral en la Constitución de 1999', in *El Derecho Público a comienzos del siglo XXI. Estudios homenaje al Profesor Allan R. Brewer-Carías,* vol. I (Madrid: Instituto de Derecho Público, UCV, Civitas Ediciones, 2003), 982–995; Rafael Méndez García, 'Estudio del Poder Electoral (controles)', in *Bases y principios del sistema constitucional venezolano (Ponencias del VII Congreso Venezolano de Derecho Constitucional realizado en San Cristóbal del 21 al 23 de Noviembre de 2001),* vol. II, 355–383; Alfonso Rivas Quintero, *Derecho Constitucional* (Valencia-Venezuela: Paredes Editores, 2002), 517 et seq.

613. *Gaceta Oficial* No. 37.573 of 19 Nov. 2002.

Law of the Electoral Power, regulating it without compliance with the constitutional provision tending to guarantee political participation of civil society, converting the Committee into a parliamentary commission, with some additional members appointed by the same Assembly.

456. In any case, in 2002, after the sanctioning of the Organic Law of the Electoral Power, the National Assembly was due to elect the members of the National Electoral Council but failed in such duty basically because the representatives supporting the government could not achieve the majority required and did not want to agree on the matter with the opposition. The consequence of this omission was that the Constitutional Chamber of the Supreme Tribunal of Justice, when deciding an action filed against such unconstitutional legislative omission, directly elected the Members of the Electoral Council, substituting the National Assembly in its duty and usurping its functions as an indirect electoral body, without complying with the conditions established in the Constitution. Since then, the complete control by the government of such an important State organ has been assured,[614] such control reinforced in December 2014, by the election of the new members of the Electoral Council, again, by the Constitutional Chamber of the Supreme Tribunal, usurping the indirect electoral character of the National Assembly for such purpose.[615]

457. Finally, also in this case, the Members of the National Electoral Council can be removed from office by the National Assembly following a declaration by the Supreme Tribunal of Justice (Article 296). In the 2007 rejected constitutional reform, it was also proposed to allow the National Assembly to approve such dismissals with only a majority of votes.

614. *See* decisions No. 2073 of 4 Aug. 2003 (Caso: *Hermánn Escarrá Malaver y oros*) and No. 2341 of 25 Aug. 2003 (Caso: *Hermánn Escarrá M. y otros*) in Allan R. Brewer-Carías, *La Sala Constitucional versus el Estado Democrático de Derecho. El secuestro del poder electoral y de la Sala Electoral del Tribunal Supremo y la confiscación del derecho a la participación política* (Caracas: Los Libros de El Nacional, Colección Ares, 2004), 172; 'El secuestro del Poder Electoral y la confiscación del derecho a la participación política mediante el referendo revocatorio presidencial: Venezuela 2000–2004', in *Boletín Mexicano de Derecho Comparado*, No. 112 (México: Instituto de Investigaciones Jurídicas, Universidad Nacional Autónoma de México, enero-abril 2005 1), 1–73, and in Rafael Chavero G. et al., *La Guerra de las Salas del TSJ frente al Referéndum Revocatorio* (Caracas: Editorial Aequitas, 2004), C.A., 13–58.

615. No. 1865 of 26 Dec. 26, 2014, available at: http://historico.tsj.gov.ve/decisiones/scon/diciembre/173497-1865-261214-2014-14-1343.HTML. *See* the comments in Allan R. Brewer-Carías, 'El golpe de Estado dado en diciembre de 2014, con la inconstitucional designación de las altas autoridades del Poder Público', *Revista de Derecho Público,* 40 (Caracas: Editorial Jurídica Venezolana, 2014).

Part IX. The Constitutional System of Human Rights and Guarantees

458. After a long tradition on matters of human rights,[616] the Venezuelan 1999 Constitution, as in all recent Latin American Constitutions, introduced notable innovations not only by expanding the list of constitutional rights, adding to the more traditional civil and political rights, the social, economic (*see infra* paragraphs 527 et seq.), cultural, environmental and indigenous people's rights as fundamental ones, but also by establishing general principles to assure the guarantee of all such rights.[617] The Constitution also provides for constitutional duties.

616. Which was initiated in 1811, with the 'Declaration of the Rights of the People' approved by the general Congress of the Independent provinces. *See* Allan R. Brewer-Carías, *Los Derechos Humanos en Venezuela: Casi 200 Años de Historia,* No. 38 (Caracas: Academia de Ciencias Políticas y Sociales, Serie Estudios, 1990); *Las Declaraciones de Derechos del Pueblo y del Hombre de 1811 (Bicentenario de la Declaración de 'Derechos del Pueblo' de 1º de julio de 1811 y de la 'Declaración de Derechos del Hombre' contenida en la Constitución Federal de los Estados de Venezuela de 21 de diciembre de 1811)* (Caracas: Academia de Ciencias Políticas y Sociales, 2011).

617. *See* Jesús María Casal H., *Los derechos fundamentales y sus restricciones* (Caracas: Legis, 2010); Josefina Calcaño de Temeltas, 'Notas sobre la constitucionalización de los Derechos Fundamentales en Venezuela', in *El Derecho Público a comienzos del siglo XXI. Estudios homenaje al Profesor Allan R. Brewer-Carías,* vol. I (Madrid: Civitas Ediciones, 2003), 2489–2535; Rafael Ortiz-Ortiz, 'Los Derechos Humanos en la República Bolivariana de Venezuela. Apreciaciones generales y principios orientadores de su ejercicio', in *Revista de la Facultad de Derecho de la Universidad de Carabobo*, No. 1 (Valencia, 2002), 339–369; Agustina Y. Martínez, 'Los Derechos Humanos en la Constitución Venezolana: consenso y disenso', in *Estudios de Derecho Público: Libro Homenaje a Humberto J. La Roche Rincón,* vol. I (Caracas: Tribunal Supremo de Justicia, 2001), 549–572; Élida Aponte Sánchez, 'Los Derechos Humanos: fundamentación, naturaleza y universalidad', in *Estudios de Derecho Público: Libro Homenaje a Humberto J. La Roche Rincón,* vol. I (Caracas: Tribunal Supremo de Justicia, 2001), 85–108; Luis A. Herrera Orellana, 'Sobre el concepto y fundamento de los derechos humanos', en *Revista de Derecho,* No. 12 (Caracas: Tribunal Supremo de Justicia, 2004), 31–58.

Chapter 1. General Principles Regarding Human Rights and Constitutional Guaranties

§1. The Basic Principles Regarding Human Rights

459. Among the innovations of the Constitution on matters of human rights, it is important to highlight the inclusion in the constitutional text of express provisions regarding the principle of progressive interpretation of the constitutional rights, the open clause of rights and freedoms, the constitutional hierarchy given to international treaties on human rights; the principle of personal liberty and the principle of equality and non-discrimination.

I. Principle of Progressive Interpretation of Constitutional Rights

460. The first of the articles of the 1999 Constitution contained in the title devoted to 'Constitutional Duties, Rights and Guarantees', which is Article 19, proclaims as a duty of the State to:

> guarantee to every individual, in accordance with the progressiveness principle, and without discrimination of any kind, the not renounceable, indivisible and interdependent enjoyment and exercise of human rights. Their respect and guarantee are obligatory for the organs of Public Power, in accordance with the Constitution, the human rights treaties signed and ratified by the Republic and any laws developing the same.

This principle of progressiveness means that no interpretation of statutes related to human rights can be admitted if the result of the interpretation is to diminish the effective enjoyment, exercise or guarantee of constitutional rights (*see supra* paragraph 79); and also that in cases involving various provisions, the one that should prevail is the one that contains the more favourable regulation. This principle of progressiveness has also been called the *pro homines* principle of interpretation, which implies that in resolving a case, 'the courts must always prefer the provisions that are in favour of man (*pro homine*)'.[618]

The principle also implies that if a constitutional right is regulated with different contexts in the Constitution and in international treaties, then the most favourable provision must prevail and be applicable to the interested party.[619]

---

618. *See* Pedro Nikken, *La protección internacional de los derechos humanos: su desarrollo progresivo* (Madrid, 1987).

619. *See*, for instance, regarding the protection of rights of a pregnant public employee not to be unjustifiably dismissed of her job during pregnancy, the former Supreme Court of Justice of Venezuela on 3 Dec. 1990, in *Revista de Derecho Público*, No. 45 (Caracas: Editorial Jurídica venezolana, 1991), 84–85 and in *Revista de Derecho Público*, Nos 97–98 (Caracas: Editorial Jurídica Venezolana, 1996), 170.

II. The Declarative Nature of the Constitutional Declarations of Rights and Freedoms and the Open Constitutional Clauses

461. The second general principle that must be highlighted is the express provision in the Constitution that human rights protected and guaranteed are not limited to those listed or enumerated in its text, and in the international instruments on human rights, but also includes other rights that are 'inherent' to human being (persons) not expressly mentioned in them.[620]

This principle, which was contained in Article 50 of the 1961 Constitution, allowed the incorporation in it, by means of judicial decisions, of many rights non-enumerated in the Constitution, assigning them constitutional rank. This clause has also been incorporated and broadened in Article 22 of the 1999 Constitution.

462. These rights inherent to human persons, for instance, have been defined by the former Supreme Court of Justice of Venezuela in 1991, as: 'natural, universal rights which find their origin and are a direct consequence of the relationships of solidarity among men, of the need for the individual development of mankind and for the protection of the environment'. The same Court concluded by stating that:

> such rights are commonly enshrined in universal declarations and in national and supra-national texts, and their nature and content as human rights shall leave no room for doubt since they are the very essence of a human person and shall therefore be necessarily respected and protected.[621]

In the case of Venezuela, the open clause allows for the identification of rights inherent to human persons, not only regarding those not listed in the Constitution but also not listed in international human rights instruments, thus considerably broadening their scope. According to this open clause, for instance, the former Supreme Court of Justice of Venezuela, on judicial review, annulled statutes founding its rulings on rights not listed in the Constitution but listed in the American Convention on Human Rights, considering them as rights inherent to human beings.[622]

---

620. *See* Agustina Yadira Martínez e Innes Faría Villarreal, 'La Cláusula Enunciativa de los Derechos Humanos en la Constitución venezolana', in *Revista de derecho del Tribunal Supremo de Justicia,* No. 3 (Caracas, 2001), 133 a 151.

621. *See* decision of 31 Jan. 1991, Case: *Anselmo Natale,* in Carlos Ayala Corao, 'La jerarquía de los instrumentos internacionales sobre derechos)humanos', in *El nuevo derecho constitucional latinoamericano, IV Congreso venezolano de Derecho constitucional,* vol. II (Caracas, 1996), and in *La jerarquía constitucional de los tratados sobre derechos humanos y sus consecuencias* (México, 2003).

622. In this sense in 1996, the Supreme Court annulled an Amazon State Act regarding territorial divisions sanctioned without the participation and consultation of the indigenous peoples organization, considering that it violated the American Convention on Human Rights, Decision of 5 Dec. 1996, Case: *Antonio Guzmán, Lucas Omashi ey al.*, in *Revista de Derecho Público*, Nos 67–68 (Caracas: Editorial Jurídica Venezolana, 1996), 176 et seq. Other cases regarding discrimination and the application of the International Covenant on Civil and Political Rights, in *Revista de Derecho Público,* Nos 71–72 (Caracas: Editorial Jurídica Venezolana, 1997), 177 et seq.; and on political participation as a non-enumerated right inherent in the human person, in *Revista de Derecho Público,* Nos 77–80 (Caracas: Editorial Jurídica Venezolana, 1999), 67.

463. In addition, because of the incorporation of this open clause in the Constitution regarding human rights, the absence of statutory regulation of such rights cannot be invoked to deny or undermine its exercise by the people.

III. The Constitutional Rank of International Human Rights Treaties

464. The third important principle on the progressive protection of fundamental rights and freedom has been the process of constitutionalization of international law in matters of human rights. In this sense, the 1991 Constitution has expressly established the value and rank of international instruments on human rights, regarding the same Constitution as well as regarding statutes, even determining which shall prevail in the event of there being a conflict among them.[623]

This process has resulted in the incorporation in the Constitutions of a provision giving the international instruments on human rights regarding internal law, not only the traditional statutory rank or a supra-legal rank but most importantly, constitutional rank and even supra-constitutional rank.[624] For such purposes, Article 23 of the Constitution, as one of the 1999 constitution-making process innovations, provides that:

> Treaties, covenants and conventions referring to human rights, signed and ratified by Venezuela, shall have constitutional hierarchy and will prevail over internal legal order, when they contain more favorable regulations regarding their enjoyment and exercise, than those established in this Constitution and in the statutes of the Republic.

According to this provision, constitutional rank has been given to treaties, pacts, and conventions on human rights, having preference over the national Constitution and statutes if they should establish more favourable provisions. In addition, they have immediate and direct application by all courts and authorities of the country.[625]

623. *See* Allan R. Brewer-Carías, *Debate Constituyente (Aportes a la Asablea Nacional Constituyente)*, vol. II (Caracas: Fundación de Derecho Público, 1999), 111–115; Carlos M. Ayala Corao, 'La jerarquía constitucional de los tratados relativos a Derechos Humanos y sus consecuencias', in *Bases y principios del sistema constitucional venezolano (Ponencias del VII Congreso Venezolano de Derecho Constitucional realizado en San Cristóbal del 21 al 23 de Noviembre de 2001)*, vol. I, 167–240, and Lorena Rincón Eizaga, 'La incorporación de los tratados sobre derechos humanos en el derecho interno a la luz de la Constitución de 1999', in *Revista de la Facultad de Ciencias Jurídicas y Políticas de la UCV*, No. 119 (Caracas, 2000), 87–108; Innes Faria Villarreal, 'Los tratados Internacionales sobre derechos humanos en la Constitución venezolana', in *Revista de Derecho*, No. 13 (Caracas: Tribunal Supremo de Justicia, 2004), 297–326.

624. On this classification, *see* Allan R. Brewer-Carías, *Mecanismos nacionales de protección de los derechos humanos, Instituto Internacional de Derechos Humanos* (San José, 2004), 62 et seq.

625. *See* Larys Hernández Villalobos, 'Rango o jerarquía de los tratados internacionales en el ordenamiento jurídico de Venezuela (1999)', in *Revista del Tribunal Supremo de Justicia*, No. 3 (Caracas, 2001), 110–131.

465. This supra-constitutional rank given to international treaties, for instance, allowed the Supreme Tribunal of Justice through its Constitutional Chamber to decide cases by directly applying the American Convention. In this regard, for instance, the Constitutional Chamber, in 2000, gave prevalence to the American Convention regulations referring to the 'the right to appeal judgments before a higher court' (Article 8.2.h), considered as forming part of internal constitutional law of the country, regarding the provision of the Supreme Court of Justice 1976 Statute, which excluded the appeal in certain cases on Administrative Jurisdiction courts' decisions, interpreting 'that the latter is incompatible with the former, because it denies in absolute terms, the right that the Convention guarantees'.[626] Based on the aforementioned, the Constitutional Chamber concluded its ruling by stating that the right to appeal recognized in Articles 8.1 and 2.h of the American Convention on Human Rights, which is 'part of the Venezuelan constitutional order', is more favourable regarding the exercise of such right in relation to what is set forth in Article 49.1 of the Constitution; and that such provisions are of 'direct and immediate application by courts and authorities'.

466. But in spite of the constitutional provision, and of its application by the Constitutional Chamber of the Supreme Tribunal, in a Decision No. 1.939 issued on 18 December 2008 (Case *Gustavo Álvarez Arias y otros*),[627] the same Constitutional Chamber after declaring as 'non-enforceable' in Venezuela the decision of the Inter-American Court on Human Rights of 5 August 2008[628] (*see supra* paragraph 93; *infra* paragraph 735) in which the Venezuelan State was condemned for violations of the judicial guarantees of various magistrates of the First Court of the Contentious Administrative Jurisdiction, has declared that the aforementioned:

> Article 23 of the Constitution does not assign supra-constitutional rank to international treaties on human rights, so that in case of contradiction between a constitutional provision and a provision of an international covenant, it is the competence of the Judicial Power to determine which is the applicable provision.

IV. The Principle of Liberty (Freedom)

467. Article 20 of the Constitution establishes the general principle of liberty (freedom) as the basis of the whole system in matters of human rights (*see supra* paragraph 94), by stating that 'each person has the right to the free development of

---

626. *See* Decision No. 87 of 13 Mar. 2000. Case*: C.A. Electricidad del Centro (Elecentro) y otra v. Superintendencia para la Promoción y Protección de la Libre Competencia. (Procompetencia)*, in *Revista de Derecho Público*, No. 81 (Caracas: Editorial Jurídica Venezolana, 2000), 157 et seq.
627. *See* in www.tsj.gov.ve/decisiones/scon/Diciembre/1939-181208-2008-08-1572.html.
628. *See* Case (*Apitz Barbera y otros ('Corte Primera de lo Contencioso Administrativo') v. Venezuela*), in *see* in www.corteidh.or.cr. Excepción Preliminar, Fondo, Reparaciones y Costas, Serie C No. 182.

his personality, without limitation other than those deriving from the rights of others and from social and public order'.[629] This enunciation, as indicated in the explaining document of the 1961 Constitution, which contained the same provision, substituted the traditional norm contained in previous constitutions setting forth that everyone may do anything that does not harm others and no one is obliged to do anything that the law does not require, nor can be impeded from doing what the law does not prohibit.

V. The Principle of Equality and Non-discrimination

468. The principle of equality is another of the main principles regarding human rights in the 1999 Constitution, which has been included in a very explicit way[630] in Article 21, stating that all persons are equal before the law, and consequently, no discrimination could be permitted based on race, sex, religion, social condition or any other motive that in general terms could have the objective or the consequence of annulling or harming the recognition, enjoyment and exercise by everybody of the rights and liberties in conditions of equality (*see supra* paragraph 81).

469. For such purpose, the same Article 21 of the Constitution provides that the law must guarantee the juridical and administrative conditions in order to guarantee that equality before the law could be real and effective, and must provide for positive measures in favour of persons or groups that could be discriminated, marginalized or vulnerable; must specially protect those persons that due to any of the above-mentioned conditions could be in a circumstance of manifest weakness and must sanction the abuses and harms inflicted against them. In addition, the Constitution prescribes that no nobility titles and hereditary distinctions are recognized in Venezuela.

§2. General Principles Regarding Constitutional Guarantees

470. The 1999 Constitution has also incorporated a very important set of norms concerning the constitutional guarantee of human rights, that is, the legal

629. *See* María C. Domínguez Guillen, 'Alcance del artículo 20 de la Constitución de la República Bolivariana de Venezuela (Libre desenvolvimiento de la personalidad)', en *Revista de Derecho,* No. 13 (Caracas: Tribunal Supremo de Justicia, 2004), 13–40; Rafael Ortiz-Ortiz, 'Los derechos de la personalidad como derechos fundamentales en el nuevo orden constitucional venezolano', in *Estudios de Derecho Público: Libro Homenaje a Humberto J. La Roche Rincón,* vol. I (Caracas: Tribunal Supremo de Justicia, 2001), 39–82; María C. Domínguez Guillén, 'Innovaciones de la Constitución de 1999 en materia de derechos de la personalidad', in *Revista de la Facultad de Ciencias Jurídicas y Políticas de la UCV,* No. 119 (Caracas, 2000), 17–44; María Candelaria Domínguez Guillén, 'Aproximación al estudio de los derechos de la personalidad', *Revista de derecho del Tribunal Supremo de Justicia,* No. 7 (Caracas, 2002), 49 a 311.

630. *See* Luis Beltrán Guerra, 'Algunas consideraciones respecto a la igualdad y a la libertad como valores protegidos en el régimen de los derechos fundamentales', in *Temas de Derecho Administrativo: Libro Homenaje a Gonzalo Pérez Luciani,* vol. I (Caracas: Editorial Torino, 2002), 815–876.

instruments that are designed to implement and permit the effective exercise of these protected rights.

I. Prohibition of the Retroactive Effects of Law

471. The Constitution expressly establishes the prohibition of legislative provisions having retroactive effects, except when they impose a lesser penalty. In the case of procedural laws, they shall apply from the moment they go into effect, even to proceedings already in progress; however, in criminal proceedings, evidence already admitted shall be weighed in accordance with the laws that were in effect when the evidence was admitted, insofar as this benefits the defendant. When there are doubts as to the statute that is to be applied, the most beneficial to the defendant will prevail (Article 24).

II. Nullity of Acts Contrary to the Constitution

472. However, the 1999 Constitution, also following a long constitutional tradition, has established the objective guarantee of the Constitution by providing that any State act that violates or encroaches upon the rights guaranteed by the Constitution and by law is null and void, and the public officials ordering or implementing the same shall incur criminal, civil and administrative liability, as applicable in each case, with no defence on the grounds of having followed superior orders (Article 25).

III. Due Process of Law Rules and the Right to Have Access to Justice

473. The Constitution has also expressly enumerated the rules of the due process of law guarantees, and the right to have access to the system of justice. For such purposes, Article 26 of the Constitution establishes the general right of everyone to access the organs comprising the justice system for the purpose of enforcing his rights and interests, including those of a collective or diffuse nature, to the effective protection of the aforementioned and to obtain the corresponding prompt decision. In this regard, the State must guarantee a free-of-charge justice, which in addition must be accessible, impartial, suitable, transparent, autonomous, independent, responsible, equitable and expeditious, without undue delays and superfluous formalities.

474. Regarding the due process of law rules, requiring justice to be imparted according to the norms established within the Constitution and laws, Article 49 of the Constitution requires that 'due process shall be applied in all judicial and administrative acts', and consequently, declares legal assistance and defence as inviolable rights at all stages and levels during the investigation and process. Consequently, the same article establishes that every person has the right to be notified of the charges for which he or she is being investigated, to have access to the evidence and to be afforded the necessary time and means to conduct his or her defence. Any evidence obtained in violation of due process shall be null and void. Any person declared guilty shall have the right to appeal, except in the cases established by the Constitution and by the law (Article 49.1).

475. In addition, the same Article 49 of the Constitution enumerates the following other rules of due process of law rights: Any person shall be presumed innocent until proven otherwise. Every person has the right to be heard in proceedings of any kind, with all due guarantees and within such reasonable time limit as may be legally detained, by a competent, independent and impartial court established in advance. Anyone who does not speak Spanish or is unable to communicate verbally is entitled to an interpreter. Every person has the right to be judged by his or her natural judges of ordinary or special competence, with the guarantees established in the Constitution and by law. No person shall be put on trial without knowing the identity of the party judging him or her, nor be adjudged by exceptional courts or commissions created for such purpose. No person shall be required to confess guilt or testify against himself or herself or his or her spouse or partner, or any other relative within the fourth degree of consanguinity or the second degree of affinity. A confession shall be valid only if given without coercion of any kind. No person shall be punished for acts or omissions not defined under pre-existing laws as a crime, offence or infraction (*Nullum crimen nulla poena sine lege)*. No person shall be placed on trial based on the same facts for which such person has been judged previously (*Non bis in idem)*. Every person shall request from the State the restoration or re-establishment of the legal situation adversely affected by unwarranted judicial errors, and unjustified delay or omissions. This right is established without prejudice to the right of the individual to seek to hold the magistrate or judge personally liable, and that of the State to take action against the same.[631]

IV. Guarantee for Rights to Only Be Limited or Restricted by Statutes

476. Among all of the constitutional guarantees of human rights, without a doubt, one of the most important is the guarantee imposing the need for a statute to establish limitations and restrictions upon these rights;[632] that is, only through formal legislation can limitations be established regarding the enjoyment of human rights. And 'legislation' in terms of this constitutional guarantee can only be an act emanating from the National Assembly acting in its capacity as the legislative body

631. *See* Antonieta Garrido de Cárdenas, 'La naturaleza del debido proceso en la Constitución de la República Bolivariana de Venezuela de 1999', in *Revista de Derecho Constitucional,* No. 5 (julio-diciembre) (Caracas: Editorial Sherwood, 2001), 89–116; Antonieta Garrido de Cárdenas, 'El debido proceso como derecho fundamental en la Constitución de 1999 y sus medios de protección', in *Bases y principios del sistema constitucional venezolano (Ponencias del VII Congreso Venezolano de Derecho Constitucional realizado en San Cristóbal del 21 al 23 de Noviembre de 2001),* vol. I, 127–144.

632. *See* Allan R Brewer-Carías, 'Consideraciones sobre la suspensión o restricción de las garantías constitucionales', *Revista de Derecho Público,* No. 37 (Caracas, 1989), 6–7.

(Article 202). Thus, statutes are the only form of government action which can restrict or limit constitutional guarantees under Article 30 of the Inter-American Convention on Human Rights.

Nonetheless, this guarantee has been contradicted in the same 1999 Constitution, due to the broad provision it contains regarding the possibility for the National Assembly to delegate legislative power to the President of the Republic through the so-called enabling laws (Article 203), authorizing it to dictate 'decree-laws' with the same legal rank and effect of national legislation in any subject area (Article 236.8)[633] (*see supra* paragraphs, 65, 148, 268).

V. State Obligations to Investigate

477. Among the constitutional guarantees of human rights, Article 29 obliges the State to investigate and legally punish offences against human rights committed by its authorities. In cases of actions to punish the offence against humanity, serious violations of human rights and war crimes shall not be subject to statute of limitation.

Human rights violations and the offence of violating humanity rights shall be investigated and adjudicated by the courts of ordinary competence. These offences are excluded from any benefit that might render the offenders immune from punishment, including pardons and amnesty.

478. Article 30 of the Constitution sets forth the obligation of the State to make full reparations to the victims of human rights violations for which it may be held responsible and to the legal successors to such victims, including payment of damages. The State is also obliged to adopt the necessary legislative measures and measures of other nature to implement the aforementioned reparations and damage compensation. In any case, the State shall protect the victims of ordinary crimes and endeavour to make the guilty parties provide reparations for the inflicted damages.

VI. The Regime of Restricting Constitutional Guaranties in States of Exception

479. As aforementioned, another important guarantee of human rights set forth in the 1999 Constitution is the impossibility of 'suspending' fundamental rights and their guarantees in cases of States of Exception, the President of the Republic being authorized, in such cases, only to temporarily restrict them, with the exception of those relating to the right to life, prohibition of incommunicative detention or torture, the right to due process, the right to information and other intangible human

633. *See* Pedro Nikken, 'Constitución venezolana de 1999: La habilitación para dictar decretos ejecutivos con fuerza de ley restrictivas de los derechos humanos y su contradicción con el derecho internacional', *Revista de Derecho Público,* No. 83 (julio-septiembre) (Caracas: Editorial Jurídica Venezolana, 2000), 5–19.

rights. In any case of restriction, the President is obliged to enact the corresponding regulation of the restricted guarantee[634] (*see supra* paragraph 312).

VII. Judicial Guarantees of Human Rights

480. Finally, the Constitution also regulates the judicial guarantees for the protection of constitutional rights by means of the actions of *amparo,* and habeas corpus (Article 27), which have been developed in the Organic Law of Amparo of Constitutional Rights and Guarantees.[635] The Constitution also guarantees the action of habeas data, in order to guarantee the people's right to have access to the information and data concerning the claimant contained in official or private registries or data banks, as well as to know about the use made of the information and about its purpose, and to petition before the competent court for the updating, rectification or destruction in cases of erroneous records and those that unlawfully affect the petitioner's rights (Article 28) (*see infra* paragraphs 594 et seq.).

VIII. International Guarantees of Human Rights

481. The international scope of the constitutional guarantees is established in Article 31 of the Constitution which provides for everybody, on the terms established by the human rights treaties, pacts and conventions ratified by the Republic, the right to address petitions and complaints to the international organs created for such purpose, in order to ask for protection of his human rights.[636] This is the case of the Inter-American Court on Human Rights created by the American Convention on Human Rights (1969), whose jurisdiction was recognized by the Venezuelan State until 2012, when the country withdrew from the Convention.

The Constitution also obliges the State, in accordance with the procedures established under the Constitution and by the law, to adopt such measures as may be necessary to enforce the decisions emanating from the corresponding international organs. Nonetheless, before Venezuelan withdrawal from the Convention, the Constitutional Chamber of the Supreme Tribunal repeatedly decided that its rulings were non-enforceable in Venezuela. It was the case of the Decision No. 1939 of 18 December 2008 (Case: *Abogados Gustavo Álvarez Arias y otros*)[637] that declared that the Inter-American Court on Human Rights decision of August 5, 2008 (Case:

634. *See* Jesús M. Casal H., 'Condiciones para la limitación o restricción de derechos fundamentales', in *El Derecho Público a comienzos del siglo XXI. Estudios homenaje al Profesor Allan R. Brewer-Carías,* vol. III (Madrid: Editorial Thomson-Civitas, 2003), 2515–2534.

635. *Gaceta Oficial* No. 34.060 of 27 Sep. 1988. *See* Allan R. Brewer-Carías & Carlos M. Ayala Corao, *Ley Orgánica de Amparo sobre derechos y garantías constitucionales* (Caracas: Editorial Jurídica Venezolana, 1988).

636. *See* Carlos M. Ayala Corao, *Del amparo constitucional al amparo Interamericano como Institutos para la protección de los Derechos Humanos* (Caracas: Editorial Jurídica Venezolana, 1998).

637. *See* in *Revista de Derecho Público,* No. 116, Editorial Jurídica Venezolana, Caracas 2008, 88 ss. Also available at: http://www.tsj.gov.ve/decisiones/scon/Diciembre/1939-181208-2008-08-1572.html. *See* the comments in Allan R. Brewer-Carías, 'La interrelación entre los Tribunales Constitucionales de América Latina y la Corte Interamericana de Derechos Humanos, y la cuestión de la

Apitz Barbera y otros 'Corte Primera de lo Contencioso Administrativo' v. Venezuela) condemning the State for violations of human rights of a group of judges (*see supra* paragraph 99) was non-enforceable (*inejecutable*) in Venezuela (*see infra* paragraph 735), and asked the Executive to denounce the American Convention of Human Rights, accusing the Inter-American Court of having usurped powers of the Supreme Tribunal. The same occurred with the Constitutional Chamber Decision No. 1547 of 17 October 2011 (Caso *Estado Venezolano v. Corte Interamericana de Derechos Humanos*),[638] which also rejected the decision of the Inter-American Court on Human Rights of 1 September 2011 (case *Leopoldo López v. Estado de Venezuela)* that condemned the State for violating the political rights of a citizen, considering it as non-executable in Venezuela (*see infra* paragraph 735). In this decision, the Supreme Tribunal also asked the Executive to denounce the American Convention of Human Rights, which eventually occurred when the Executive formally communicated to the OAS the withdrawal of Venezuela from the Convention on 6 September 2012.

---

inejecutabilidad de sus decisiones en Venezuela', in Armin von Bogdandy, Flavia Piovesan y Mariela Morales Antonorzi (Coodinadores), *Direitos Humanos, Democracia e Integraçao Jurídica na América do Sul* (rio de janeiro, Lumen Juris Editora, 2010), 661–670; and in *Anuario Iberoamericano de Justicia Constitucional* No. 13 (Madrid, Centro de Estudios Políticos y Constitucionales, 2009), 99–136.

638. Available at http://www.tsj.gov.ve/decisiones/scon/Octubre/1547-171011-2011-11-1130.html. *See* the comments in Allan R. Brewer-Carías, 'El ilegítimo "control de constitucionalidad" de las sentencias de la Corte Interamericana de Derechos Humanos por parte la Sala Constitucional del Tribunal Supremo de Justicia de Venezuela: el caso de la sentencia *Leopoldo López vs. Venezuela, 201 1*', en *Constitución y democracia: ayer y hoy. Libro homenaje a Antonio Torres del Moral,* vol. I, (Madrid, Editorial Universitas, 2013), 1.095–1124.

Chapter 2. The Status of Persons and Citizens

482. The rights and guarantees declared in the Constitution in general terms correspond to every person. Nonetheless, there are some rights that only correspond to Venezuelans or nationals. For such purpose, the Constitution has established the general status of persons distinguishing between Venezuelans or nationals and foreigners, and within the former, those that are considered citizens and, therefore, able to exercise political rights. In this regard, Citizenship and Nationality are one of the fundamental elements of the political organization of the State, regulated in the Constitution.

In this context, Venezuelans or nationals are the persons that have a fundamental legal bond to the State and the country allowing them to be part of its political life. Consequently, in spite of the equality general principle established in the Constitution (*see supra* paragraph 468), foreigners do not have all the rights that Venezuelans have, particularly regarding political rights. That is why although the provision of Article 45 of the 1961 Constitution that established that 'Foreigners have the same duties and rights as Venezuelans, subject to the limitations and exceptions established by this Constitution and the laws', was not included in the 1999 Constitution, the same principle subsists within the provisions related to Nationality, Citizenship and Foreigners.

§1. The Constitutional Rules on the Venezuelan Nationality

483. The 1999 Constitution distinguishes two sorts of nationals: nationals by birth and nationals by naturalization (acquisition of the Venezuelan nationality);[639] and regarding the former the Constitution also distinguishes the two classical ways of acquiring the Venezuelan nationality by birth, according to the principles of *jus soli* and of *jus sanguinis*.[640]

I. Venezuelan by Birth

484. In this regard, Article 32 of the Constitution declares that people who are Venezuelan by birth are, any person born within the territory of the Republic, any person born in a foreign territory, and the child of a father *and* a mother who are both Venezuelans by birth; any person born in a foreign territory, and is the child of a father *or* a mother, who is Venezuelan by birth, provided they have established

639. *See* Allan R. Brewer-Carías, *Régimen legal de la Nacionalidad, Ciudadanía y Extranjería (Ley de Nacionalidad y Ciudadanía, Ley de Extranjería y Migración, Ley Orgánica sobre Refugiados y Asilados)* (Caracas: Editorial Jurídica Venezolana, 2005); Allan R. Brewer-Carías, *El régimen jurídico administrativo de la Nacionalidad y Ciudadanía venezolana* (Caracas, 1965).

640. *See* Eugenio Hernández Bretón, 'Nacionalidad, ciudadanía y extranjería en la Constitución de 1999', in *Revista de Derecho Público*, No. 81 (enero-marzo) (Caracas: Editorial Jurídica Venezolana, 2000), 47–59; Juan De Stefano, 'El principio de la nacionalidad', in *Temas de Derecho Administrativo: Libro Homenaje a Gonzalo Pérez Luciani*, vo. I (Caracas: Editorial Torino, 2002), 593–608.

residence within the territory of the Republic or declared their intention to obtain the Venezuelan nationality; and any person who was born in a foreign territory, and is the child of a father or a mother who is Venezuelan by naturalization, provided that prior to reaching the age of 18, they establish their residence within the territory of the Republic, and before reaching the age of 25 declare their intention to obtain the Venezuelan nationality.

485. According to this provision, the *jus soli* principle remains in an absolute way, in the sense that being born on Venezuelan soil is enough for having the Venezuelan nationality by birth, even if it is accidental, and no relation in the future is established regarding the country. According to this same provision, the *jus sanguinis* principle also remains in an absolute way, in the sense that the Venezuelan nationality by birth corresponds to those born in foreign countries from a father and mother who are Venezuelan by birth, even if they do not establish any subsequent relation with the country.

II. Venezuelan by Naturalization

486. With respect to the regime of the nationality by acquisition (naturalization), the regimen of the 1999 Constitution also follows the previous tradition, establishing that foreigners can acquire the Venezuelan nationality by obtaining a 'naturalization letter', providing they have at least ten years of uninterrupted residence immediately preceding the application date. Nonetheless, the Constitution provides that this period of residence shall be reduced to five years in the case of foreign nationals whose original nationality is that of Spain, Portugal, Italy, or a Latin American or Caribbean country.

487. The 1999 Constitution also expanded the cases of naturalization based on marriage, in the sense that it benefits not only women married to Venezuelan men as established in the 1961 Constitution but also men married to Venezuelan women, upon declaring their wish to adopt the Venezuelan nationality, which may be done at least five years after the date of marriage. Also, minors of foreign nationality, on the date of the naturalization of one of his/her parents who exercises parental authority, provided that such minor declares his or her intention of adopting the Venezuelan nationality before reaching the age of 21, and has resided in Venezuela without interruption throughout the five-year period preceding such declaration.

III. Dual Nationality

488. The most important constitutional innovation in these matters has been the acceptance of the possibility for Venezuelans to have dual nationality, in the sense that Venezuelans by birth and naturalization may now have another nationality without losing their Venezuelan nationality. This principle, established in Article 34, prescribes that 'Venezuelan nationality is not lost upon choosing or acquiring another nationality' and radically changes the preceding rule, under which according to

Article 39 of the 1961 Constitution, Venezuelan nationality was lost upon voluntarily choosing or acquiring another nationality. In accord with the spirit and purpose of the new regimen, which was, of course, that if Venezuelan nationality was made available through naturalization, there ought not to be a requirement that the interested party renounce his or her nationality of origin, insofar as Venezuela is concerned in such cases, the nationality of origin is retained in conformity with the requirements of that country.

489. The constitutional progress of permitting Venezuelans to have dual nationality is nonetheless limited with respect to the holding of certain high public offices, for which not only Venezuelan nationality by birth is required, but not having another nationality is also required. It is the case, according to Article 41, of the offices of President of the Republic, Executive Vice President, President and Vice Presidents of the National Assembly, Magistrates of the Supreme Tribunal of Justice, President of the National Electoral Council, the Attorney General of the Republic, Comptroller General of the Republic, Prosecutor General of the Republic (Public Prosecutor), the Peoples' Defender, Ministers in matters of National Security, Finances, Energy and Mining, Education; Governors and Mayors of frontier states and municipalities, and those regarding military positions established in the Organic Law of the Armed Forces.

IV. Loss and Recuperation of Venezuelan Nationality

490. As aforementioned, Article 34 of the Constitution sets forth that the Venezuelan nationality is not lost upon electing or acquiring another nationality; and Article 35 establishes that Venezuelans by birth cannot be deprived of their nationality. Nonetheless, the Venezuelan nationality by naturalization can be revoked only by a judgment handed down by a court in accordance with law.

491. However, Venezuelan nationality may be renounced, but the person who renounces it when by birth, may regain such nationality if he or she establishes a residence within the territory of the Republic for a period of at least two years, and expresses the intention of regaining the Venezuelan nationality. Naturalized Venezuelans who renounce their Venezuelan nationality may regain it by again meeting the requirements prescribed under Article 33 of this Constitution (Article 36).

§2. The Constitutional Rules on Citizenship

I. Citizenship and Political Rights

492. Citizenship is the political bond established between the person and the State that allows that person to participate in the political system. For this reason, according to the Constitution, a citizen is essentially a Venezuelan national. On this basis, Article 39 of the Constitution states that Venezuelans with the required age who are not subject to political impediment or civil interdiction, can exercise citizenship and therefore are entitled to political rights and duties in accordance with the Constitution.[641]

493. The age conditions for exercising citizenship differ regarding the corresponding political right to be exercised. For example, to vote, it is enough to have reached the age of 18 (Article 64), but to be elected Governor of a State of the federation, it is necessary to be over the age of 25 (Article 160); to be Congressmen to the National Assembly and to a State Legislative Council, it is necessary to be over the age of 21 (Articles 188 and 162); to be Mayor of any municipality, it is necessary to be over the age of 25 (Article 174); to be President and Vice President of the Republic, it is necessary to be over the age of 30 (Articles 227 and 238); as well as to be People's Defender (Article 280) and General Controller of the Republic (Article 288); and to be Minister, it is necessary to be over the age of 25 (Article 244). Furthermore, as regards the Justices to the Supreme Tribunal of Justice (Article 263), the Attorney General (Article 249) and the Prosecutor General of the Republic (Public Prosecutor) (Article 284), the Constitution requires to be over the age of 35, which is set forth in the conditions to exercise such positions.

494. The condition of Citizenship implies the exercise of political rights, like the right to vote, the right to be elected, the right to exercise public functions, which are reserved for Venezuelans. The only exception to this rule, according to Article 64 of the Constitution, is the right to vote given to foreigners in state, municipal and parish elections, who have reached the age of 18 and have resided in Venezuela for more than ten years, subject to the limitations established in the Constitution and by law, and provided they are not subject to political disablement or civil interdiction.

495. According to Article 42, anyone who loses or renounces Venezuelan nationality loses citizenship. In addition, the Constitution establishes the guarantee that the exercise of citizenship or any political rights can be suspended only by final judicial decision in the cases provided by law.

II. Equality Between Venezuelans by Birth and by Naturalization

496. With respect to the exercise of political rights, the constitutional principle of equality between those who are Venezuelan by birth and those who are naturalized is derived from Article 40 of the Constitution, with the exceptions established in the aforementioned Article 41 of the Constitution, which requires in order to be elected or to be appointed for some public offices, to be Venezuelan by birth without having any other nationality. Also, in order to be elected representative to the

641. This provision has been repeated in Art. 50 of the 2004 Nationality and Citizenhip Law specifying that 'Citizen are those Venezuelans not subject to political impediment or to civil interdiction and fulfil the age requirements foreseen in the Constitution and in the statutes.' *See Gaceta Oficial*, No. 37971 of 1 Jul. 2004. *See* Allan R. Brewer-Carías, *Régimen Legal de la Nacionalidad, Ciudadanía y Extranjería. Ley de Nacionalidad y Ciudadanía, Ley de Extranjería y Migración, Ley Orgánica sobre Refugiados y Asilados* (Caracas: Editorial Jurídica Venezolana, 2005).

National Assembly, or to be appointed Minister, Governors and Mayors of non-frontier states and municipalities, naturalized citizens must have been domiciled in Venezuela with uninterrupted residency for not less than fifteen years (Article 41).

497. Nonetheless, all these exceptions establishing some distinction between Venezuelan by birth and naturalized Venezuelans disappear in the cases of Naturalized Venezuelans who have entered the country prior to reaching the age of 7 years and have resided permanently in Venezuela until reaching legal age shall enjoy the same rights as Venezuelans by birth (Article 40).

§3. Constitutional Condition of Foreigners

498. All other persons in Venezuela not being Venezuelans are legally considered aliens or foreigners, as is expressly set forth in Article 3 of the 2004 Aliens and Migration Statute,[642] which provides that all those who are not considered to be Venezuelans, are legally considered to be foreigners or aliens.

I. Migrant and Non-migrant Aliens

499. Aliens, according to this same Statute, and regarding their access and permanency in the territory of the Republic, can be admitted in two categories: as non-migrants or as migrants. Non-migrant aliens are the people who enter the territory of the Republic to remain in it for a limited period of ninety days, without having the intention to establish with their family permanent residence in it. These non-migrant aliens cannot perform activities that involve remuneration or profit.

500. Migrants aliens are those who enter the territory of the Republic to reside in it, temporarily or permanently (Article 3), being classified into two categories: temporary migrants and permanent migrants (Article 6). Temporary migrants are those entering the territory of the Republic with the intention of residing in it temporarily while the activities that have originated their admission last (migrant workers, border migrants). Permanent migrants are those who have authorization to remain indefinitely in the territory of the Republic.

II. Asylum and Refugee Aliens

501. In addition to the status of migrant and non-migrant aliens, Article 69 of the Constitution sets forth in the section related to political rights, 'that the Bolivarian Republic of Venezuela acknowledges and guarantees the right of asylum

642. *See* in *Gaceta Oficial* No. 37.944 of 24 May 2004. *See* in Allan R. Brewer-Carías, *Régimen Legal De La Nacionalidad, Ciudadanía Y Extranjería. Ley de Nacionalidad y Ciudadanía, Ley de Extranjería y Migración, Ley Orgánica sobre Refugiados y Asilados* (Caracas: Editorial Jurídica Venezolana, 2005), 101 et seq. Also Allan R. Brewer-Carías, 'Migration law in Venezuela and its Applicability in the Context of an Authoritarian regime', in Marie-Claire Foblets and Jean-Yves Carlier (Editors), *Law and Migration in a Changing World,* (Springer, 2022), pp. 813–838.

and of refuge'. Therefore, in addition to the non-migrant and migrant aliens, two other categories of aliens can be identified: refugees and asylees aliens, with a status that according to Article 2 of the 2001 Organic Statute on Refugees and Asylees,[643] is governed by the following rules:

(1) Every person is able to file a refugee protection claim in the Republic, based on a well-founded fear of being persecuted by the reasons and the conditions set forth in the 1967 Protocol on the Refugee Statutes.
(2) Every person is able to make a refugee protection claim in the Republic as well as in its diplomatic missions, warships and military aircraft abroad, when persecuted for political reasons or crimes in the conditions set forth in that Law.
(3) No person claiming asylum or refugee protection shall be neglected or subjected to any measure that forces him or her to be repatriated to the territory where his or her life, physical integrity or freedom is jeopardized due to the reasons set forth in that Law.
(4) Authorities shall impose no punishment due to the irregular entry or stay in the territory of the Republic on persons that claim refugee protection or asylum, pursuant to the terms set forth in the Constitution.
(5) Discrimination based on race, gender, religion, political opinions, social condition, country of origin or those that in general lessen or annul the acknowledgement, enjoyment or exercise in equal situation of the refugee's or asylee's condition shall not be permitted.
(6) The unity of a refugee's or asylee's family shall be guaranteed, and specially, the protection of child refugees and teenagers without company or separated from the family, in the terms set forth in the Law.

502. Consequently, pursuant to Article 38 of this Statute, the asylum status is granted to aliens the State considers to be persecuted due to their beliefs, opinions, or political affinities, or due to acts that might be considered political crimes, or to common crimes but committed with political purposes. Asylum cannot be granted to a person accused, processed or convicted before ordinary competent Courts due to common crimes, or having committed crimes against peace, war crimes or crimes against mankind, as defined in international treaties (Article 41 of the Organic Law).

503. Asylum can be granted within the territory of the Republic, once the nature of such is qualified (Article 39) (territorial asylum); or can be granted to persons seeking it before diplomatic missions, Venezuelan warships, or military aircraft according to the applicable international treaties and conventions on the matter (Article 40) (Diplomatic asylum). All these provisions related to asylum, according to Article 24 of the Organic Law, shall be construed pursuant to the 1948 Universal

643. *See* in *Gaceta Oficial* No. 37.296 of 3 Oct. 2001. *See* Allan R. Brewer-Carías, *Régimen Legal de la Nacionalidad, Ciudadanía y Extranjería. Ley de Nacionalidad y Ciudadanía, Ley de Extranjería y Migración, Ley Orgánica sobre Refugiados y Asilados* (Caracas: Editorial Jurídica Venezolana, 2005), 117 et seq.

Declaration of Human Rights, and the 1954 Caracas Convention on Territorial Asylum and other provisions of international treaties on human rights, duly executed and ratified by the Government of Venezuela.

504. The same Organic Statute on Refugees and Asylees establishes, regarding the refugee status, that the Venezuelan State shall grant it:

> to every person recognized as such by the competent authority, in virtue of having entered in the national territory due to persecution because of his or her race, gender, religion, nationality, membership in a social group or political opinion, and is outside his or her home country and shall not or does not want to be protected by that country, or that, having no nationality, shall not or does not want to return to the country where he or she has his residence' (Article 5).

The main legal trend regarding the refugee status is that according to the Law, no person asking for refugee protection shall be punished due to illegal entrance or stay in the national territory, provided that he or she appears without delay before the national authorities, and pleads just cause (Article 6). Additionally, a person making a refugee protection claim shall not be denied admission or be subject to a measure forcing him or her to return to the country where his or her life, physical integrity or personal freedom is jeopardized. However, these benefits shall not be granted to aliens considered, due to well-founded reasons, a danger to the Republic's security or that having been convicted of a serious crime, he or she represents a threat to the community (Article 7).

505. According to the same Statute, every alien claiming Venezuelan State protection as a refugee shall be admitted in the national territory and shall be authorized to stay in it until his or her claim is decided, including a reconsideration period. However, an alien considered due to well-founded reasons, a danger to the Republic's safety or a threat to the community because convicted of a serious crime, cannot claim these benefits (Article 2).

506. The refugee protection shall not be granted to aliens in the following cases: when the alien committed a crime against peace, war crimes or crimes against mankind, as defined in international treaties; when the alien committed common crimes outside the country granting refugee protection that are not compatible with the refugee status; and when the alien committed acts against the principles of the United Nations Organization (Article 9). All these internal provisions related to the refugee status, according to Article 4 of the Organic Law, shall be construed pursuant to the 1948 Universal Declaration of Human Rights, the 1967 Protocol on the Status of Refugees, the 1969 American Convention on Human Rights, and other provisions of international treaties on human rights, duly executed and ratified by the Government of Venezuela.

Chapter 3. Civil Rights

§1. Right to Life

507. Chapter IV, Title III of the Constitution enumerates the 'civil rights' of all persons, also called 'individual rights', beginning with the right to life (*see supra* paragraph 89), which is set forth in Article 43, as 'inviolable', and therefore, the prohibition of the death penalty is expressly declared, in the sense that 'no law shall provide for the death penalty and no authority shall apply the same'. In addition, the article obliges the State to 'protect the life of persons who are deprived of liberty, are in military or civil services, or are subject to its authority in any other manner' (*see supra* paragraph 89).

§2. Right to Own Name and to Be Identified

508. Article 56 establishes the right of every person to have his own name, to have the name of his father and of his mother, and to know their identity. For this purpose, the State guarantees the right of everyone to investigate maternity and paternity situations. All persons have the right to be registered free of charge with the Civil Registry Office after birth, and to obtain public documents constituting evidence of their biological identity, in accordance with law. Such documents shall not contain any mention of classifying the parental relationship.

§3. Personal Freedom

509. Personal freedom is declared in Article 44 as inviolable, and in order to guarantee such inviolability, the following rights of everyone are enumerated: no person shall be arrested or detained except by virtue of a court order unless such person is caught *in fraganti*. In the latter case, such person must be brought before a judge within forty-eight hours of his or her arrest. He or she shall remain free during trial, except for reasons determined by law and assessed by the judge on a case-by-case basis. Any officer taking measures involving the deprivation of liberty must identify himself. The bail, as required by law, for the release of a detainee shall not be subject to a tax of any kind. Any person under arrest has the right to communicate immediately with members of his or her family, an attorney or any other person in whom he or she reposes trust, and such persons in turn have the right to be informed where the detainee is being held, to be notified immediately of the reasons for the arrest and to have a written record inserted into the case file concerning the physical or mental condition of the detainee, either by himself or herself or with the aid of specialists. The competent authorities shall keep a public record of every arrest made, including the identity of the person arrested, the place, time, circumstances and the officers who made the arrest. In the case of the arrest of foreign nationals, applicable provisions of international treaties concerning consular notification shall also be observed. The penalty shall not extend beyond the person of the convicted individual. No one shall be sentenced to perpetual or humiliating penalties. Penalties consisting of deprivation of liberty shall not exceed thirty years. No person shall remain under arrest after a release order has been issued by the competent authority or such person's prison term has been completed.

510. In this same regard related to personal freedom, Article 45 expressly prohibits public authorities, whether military, civilian or of any other kind, even during a state of exception, exception or restriction or guarantees, from effecting, permitting or tolerating the forced disappearance of persons. An officer receiving an order or instruction to carry it out has the obligation not to obey and to report the order or instruction to the competent authorities. The intellectual and physical perpetrators, accomplices and those covering up the crimes of forced disappearance of a person, as well as any attempt to commit such offence, shall be punished in accordance with law.

§4. Personal Integrity

511. The right to personal integrity is established in Article 46, as the right everyone is entitled to respect for his or her physical, mental and moral integrity. Therefore, according to the same provision, no person shall be subjected to cruel, inhuman or degrading penalties, tortures or treatment. Every victim of torture or cruel, inhumane or degrading treatment effected or tolerated by agents of the State has the right to rehabilitation. Any person deprived of liberty shall be treated with respect due to the inherent dignity of the human being. No person shall be subjected without his or her freely given consent to scientific experiments or medical or laboratory examinations, except when such person's life is in danger, or in any other circumstances as may be detained by law. Any public official who, by reason of his official position, inflicts mistreatment or physical or mental suffering on any person or instigates or tolerates such treatment, shall be punished in accordance with law.

512. Article 54 of the Constitution establishes the guarantee that everyone is not to be subjected to slavery or servitude. Traffic of persons, in particular women, children and adolescents, in any form, shall be subject to the penalties prescribed by law.

§5. Inviolability of Person's Home

513. Article 47 of the Constitution, also following the tradition of prior constitutions, guarantees the inviolability of a person's home and any of his private premises. They may not be forcibly entered except by court order, and only to prevent the commission of a crime or carry out the decisions handed down by the courts in accordance with law, always respecting human dignity in all cases. Any health inspections carried out in accordance with law shall be performed only after notice from the officials ordering or carrying it out.

§6. Inviolability of Private Communications

514. The Constitution also guarantees the secrecy and inviolability of private communications in all forms. The same may not be interfered with except by order of a competent court, with observance of applicable provisions of law and preserving the secrecy of the private issues unrelated to the pertinent proceedings (Article 48).

§7. Right to Petition before Public Authorities and to Obtain Due Answer

515. Article 51 of the Constitution sets forth the right of everyone to petition or make representations before any authority or public official concerning matters within their competence, and to obtain a timely and adequate response. Whoever violates this right shall be punished in accordance with law, including the possibility of dismissal from office.[644]

§8. Right of Association

516. The right of everyone to assemble or associate with others for lawful purposes is also provided in the Constitution (Article 52), the State being obliged to facilitate its exercise. The right is, however, limited in Article 256 of the Constitution, that prohibits judges from associating with one another, and in Article 294, that establishes the intervention of the State (National Electoral Council) in the internal elections of professional associations (guilds).

§9. Right of Meeting

517. Article 53 of the Constitution establishes the right of everyone to meet publicly or privately, without obtaining permission in advance, for lawful purposes and without weapons. Meetings in public places may be regulated by law.

§10. Freedom of Movement

518. Article 50 of the Constitution establishes the right of everyone to freely transit by any means throughout the national territory, to change his domicile and residence, to leave and return to the Republic, to move his goods or belongings

644. *See* Carlos L. Carrillo Artiles, 'El derecho de petición y la oportuna y adecuada respuesta en la Constitución de 1999', in *Estudios de Derecho Administrativo: Libro Homenaje a la Universidad Central de Venezuela,* vol. I (Caracas: Imprenta Nacional, 2001), 219–251; and Lubín Aguirre, 'Garantías procesales frente a la inacción administrativa' in *Estudios de Derecho Administrativo: Libro Homenaje a la Universidad Central de Venezuela,* vol. I (Caracas: Imprenta Nacional, 2001), 35–41.

within the country and to bring his goods into or remove them from the country, subject only to such limitations as may be prescribed by law. In addition, Venezuelans shall enter the country without the need for authorization of any kind and no act of the State may establish against Venezuelans the penalty of banishment from the national territory. According to Article 69, extradition of Venezuelans is prohibited.

§11. Freedom of Expression and Information

519. The right to free expression without censorship is guaranteed in Article 57 of the Constitution, which states that:

> Everyone has the right to express freely his or her thoughts, ideas or opinions orally, in writing or by any other form of expression, and to use for such purpose any means of communication and diffusion, and no censorship shall be established.

Anyone making use of this right assumes full responsibility for everything expressed. Anonymity, war propaganda, discriminatory messages or those promoting religious intolerance are not permitted. Also, the same Article 57 of the Constitution provides that censorship restricting the ability of 'public officials' (*funcionarios públicos*) to report on matters for which they are responsible is prohibited, a provision that is not applicable to judges.

For such purposes, Article 58 of the Constitution guarantees that communications are free and plural, and involve the duties and responsibilities indicated by law.

§12. Right to Be Informed and to Reply and Rectification

520. Article 58 of the Constitution also establishes the right of everybody to be 'timely, truthful and impartially' informed, without censorship, in accordance with the principles of the Constitution. In this regard, the use of these adjectives was widely debated in the 1999 National Constituent Assembly due to the dangers they could raise regarding the State's temptation to control or monopolize what 'truthful, opportune and impartial' is, and with this, the possible creation of some 'official truth'.[645] This matter has been regulated in the 2005 Radio and Television Social Responsibility Law.[646]

645. *See* Allan R. Brewer-Carías, 'La libre expresión del pensamiento y el derecho a la información en la Constitución venezolana de 1999', in *Anuario de Derecho Constitucional Latinoamericano* (Edición, 2002, Konrad Adenauer Stiftung, Montevideo, 2002), 267 a 276; Fernando Flores Gimenez, 'Las libertades de expresión e información en la Constitución de Venezuela: Análisis de una confusión', in *Revista de Derecho Constitucional,* No. 7 (Caracas: Editorial Sherwood, enero-junio 2003), 125 a 135; Jesús A. Davila Ortega, 'El Derecho de la información y la libertad de expresión en Venezuela (Un estudio de la sentencia 1.013/2001 de la Sala Constitucional del Tribunal Supremo de Justicia)', in *Revista de Derecho Constitucional,* No. 5 julio-diciembre-2001 (Caracas: Editorial Sherwood, 2002), 305 a 325; María Candelaria Domínguez Guillén, 'Las libertades de

The same Article 58 also guarantees the right of everyone to reply and to ask for rectification when they are directly affected by inaccurate or offensive information.[647] Children and adolescents have the right to receive adequate information for purposes of their overall development.

§13. Right to Have Access to Personal Information

521. Article 28 of the Constitution guarantees the right of anyone to have access to the information and data concerning him or her or his or her goods which are contained in official or private records, with the exceptions only established by law, as well as the right to know what use is being made of the same and the purpose thereof. This right implies, in particular, the right to petition (habeas data recourse) (*see supra* paragraph 480) before the competent courts for the updating, correction or destruction of any records that are erroneous or that can unlawfully affect the petitioner's right.

522. According to the same provision of the Constitution, everybody also has the right to have access to documents of any nature containing information of interest to communities or groups of persons. The foregoing right is without prejudice to the confidentiality of sources from which information is received by journalists, or secrecy in other professions as may be determined by law.

§14. Right to the Protection of Honour and Private Life

523. According to Article 60 of the Constitution, every person is entitled to protection of his or her honour, private life, intimacy, self-image, confidentiality and reputation. The use of electronic information shall be restricted by law in order to guarantee the personal and family intimacy and honour of citizens and the full exercise of their rights.[648]

---

expresión e información', in *Revista de derecho del Tribunal Supremo de Justicia,* No. 5 (Caracas, 2002), 19 a 72; Héctor Faúndez Ledesma, 'Las condiciones de las restricciones a la libertad de expresión', in *El Derecho Público a comienzos del siglo XXI. Estudios homenaje al Profesor Allan R. Brewer-Carías,* vol. III (Madrid: Instituto de Derecho Público, UCV, Civitas Ediciones, 2003), 2598–2664; Rafael Ortiz-Ortiz, 'Las implicaciones jurídico positivas del derecho a la información y a la libertad de expresión en el nuevo orden constitucional', in *Revista de la Facultad de Derecho de la Universidad de Carabobo,* No. 1 (Valencia, 2002), 163–246.

646. *Gaceta Oficial* No. 38.333 of 12 Dec. 2005. *See* Allan R. Brewer-Carías et al., *Ley de Responsabilidad Social de Radio y Televisión (Ley Resorte)* (Caracas: Ediáltorial Jurídica Venezolana, 2006). and Carolina Puppio, 'Libertad de Expresión vs. Ley de Contenidos. Reflexiones de cara a la aprobación de una Ley de Contenido en Venezuela', in *Revista de Derecho Constitucional,* No. 6, enero-diciembre-2002 (Caracas: Editorial Sherwood, 2003), 165 a 190.

647. *See* Allan R. Brewer-Carías et al., *La libertad de expresión amenazada (sentencia 1.013)* (Caracas: Editorial Jurídica Venezolana, 2001).

648. *See* Rafael Ortiz, 'Configuración del derecho a la intimidad como derecho civil fundamental', in *Revista del Tribunal Supremo de Justicia,* No. 5 (Caracas, 2002), 87–149; Cosimina Pellegrino Pacera, 'El derecho a la intimidad en la nueva era informática, el derecho a la autodeterminación informativa y el hábeas data a la luz de la Constitución venezolana de 1999', in *Estudios de Derecho Público: Libro Homenaje a Humberto J. La Roche Rincón,* vol. I (Caracas: Tribunal Supremo de Justicia, 2001), 143–216.

§15. FREEDOM OF RELIGION AND CULT

524. The Constitution expressly declares in Article 59 that the State guarantees the freedom of cult and religion. Consequently, all persons have the right to profess their religious faith and cults, and express their beliefs in private or in public by teaching and other practices, provided such beliefs are not contrary to moral, good customs and public order. Nonetheless, no one shall invoke religious beliefs or discipline as a means of evading compliance with law or preventing another person from exercising his or her rights.[649]

The autonomy and independence of religious confessions and churches are likewise guaranteed in the Constitution, subject only to such limitations as may derive from this Constitution and the law.

Fathers and mothers are entitled to have their sons and daughters receive religious education in accordance with their convictions.

§16. FREEDOM OF CONSCIENCE

525. All persons have the right to freedom of conscience, and to express the same, provided that its practice does not affect their personality or constitute criminal offence. Objections of conscience may not be invoked in order to evade compliance with law or prevent others from complying with law or exercising their rights.

§17. RIGHT TO PERSONAL SECURITY AND TO BE PROTECTED BY THE STATE

526. Finally, according to Article 55 of the Constitution, every person has the right to be protected by the State, through the entities established by law for the protection of citizens, from situations that constitute a threat, vulnerability or risk to the physical integrity of individuals, their properties, the enjoyment of rights or the fulfilment of their duties. The citizens' participation in programmes for purposes of prevention, citizen safety and emergency management shall be regulated by a special law.

The Constitution guarantees that the State's security corps shall respect the human dignity and rights of all persons; and set forth in an express way that the use of weapons or toxic substances by police and security officers shall be limited by the principles of necessity, convenience, opportunity and proportionality in accordance with law.

649. *See* Josefina Calcaño de Temeltas, *Aproximación a la libertad de conciencia, religión y culto en derecho comparado y en Venezuela* (Caracas: FUNEDA, 2011); Carmen Vallarino Bracho, 'Libertad de religión y derechos humanos en Venezuela', en *Revista de Derecho*, No. 30 (Caracas: Tribunal Supremo de Justicia, 2009), 309–319.

Chapter 4. Social and Cultural Rights

527. The 1999 Constitution contains very extensive declarations of social rights,[650] including family and social protection rights, right to health and social security, labour rights, educational and cultural rights, environmental rights and the indigenous people's rights; although in many cases, the declarations are more of aims or public policy regarding social welfare than specific justiciable rights.

§1. Family Rights and Rights to Social Protection

I. Right to Family Protection

528. The Constitution has established a series of social rights as people's 'rights to protection' or to be protected by the State, beginning with the protection of families. In this regard, Article 75 imposes on the State the obligation to protect families as a natural association in society, and as the fundamental space for the overall development of persons. According to the same constitutional provision, family relationships must be based on equality of rights and duties, solidarity, common effort, mutual understanding and reciprocal respect among family members. In order to protect families, the State must guarantee protection to the mother, father or other person acting as head of a household.

529. Children and adolescents have the right to live, be raised and develop in the bosom of their original family. When this is impossible or contrary to their best interests, they shall have the right to a substitute family, in accordance with law. Adoption has effects similar to those of parenthood and is established in all cases for the benefit of the adoptee, in accordance with law. International adoption shall be subordinated to domestic adoption.

II. Right to Motherhood and Fatherhood Protection

530. Article 76 of the Constitution provides for the full protection of motherhood and fatherhood, whatever the marital status of the mother or father. Couples have the right to decide freely and responsibly how many children they wish to conceive and are entitled to access to the information and means necessary to guarantee the exercise of this right. The State guarantees overall assistance and protection for motherhood, in general, from the moment of conception, throughout pregnancy, delivery and the puerperal period, and guarantees full family planning services

650. *See* Mercedes Pulido de Briceño, 'La Constitución de 1999 y los derechos sociales', in *La cuestión social en la Constitución Bolivariana de Venezuela* (Caracas: Editorial Torino, 2000), 15–28; Carlos Aponte Blank, 'Los derechos sociales y la Constitución de 1999', *ibid.*, 113–134; and Emilio Spósito Contreras, 'Aproximación a los derechos sociales en la Constitución de la República Bolivariana de Venezuela', in *Revista de derecho del Tribunal Supremo de Justicia,* No. 9 (Caracas, 2003), 381 a 398.

based on ethical and scientific values. This provision, particularly when protecting maternity from the moment of conception, implies limits to configured abortion as a right.

III. Right to Marriage Protection

531. Article 77 of the Constitution also expressly 'protects marriage between a man and a woman, based on free consent and absolute equality of rights and obligations of the spouses'. Also, a stable de facto union between a man and a woman that meets the requirements established by law shall have the same effects as marriage.[651] From this provision, according to the Venezuelan constitutional system, no same-sex 'marriage' is admissible.

IV. Rights of Children and Adolescents

532. Regarding children and adolescents, Article 78 of the Constitution considers them as full legal persons that shall be protected by specialized courts, organs and legislation, which shall respect, guarantee and develop the contents of the Constitution, the law, the Convention on Children's Rights and any other international treaty that may have been executed and ratified by the Republic in this field. The State, families and society shall guarantee their full protection as an absolute priority, taking into account their best interest in actions and decisions concerning them. The State shall promote their progressive incorporation into active citizenship, and shall create a national guidance system for the overall protection of children and adolescents.

533. However, Article 79 of the Constitution guarantees the right and duty of young people to be active participants in the development process. For such purpose, the State, with the joint participation of families and society, shall create opportunities to stimulate their productive transition into adult life, including, in particular, training for and access to their first employment, in accordance with law.

---

651. *See* Anabella Del Moral, 'Contenido y alcance del artículo 77 de la Constitución de la República Bolivariana de Venezuela, según sentencia de la Sala Constitucional del 15 de julio de 2005', in *Revista de Derecho,* No. 27 (Caracas: Tribunal Supremo de Justicia, 2008), 111–131; María C. Domínguez Guillen, 'Más sobre las uniones estables de hecho, según la Sala Constitucional del Tribunal Supremo de Justicia', in *Revista de Derecho,* No. 27 (Caracas: Tribunal Supremo de Justicia, 2008), 133–167; Gilberto Guerrero Quintero, 'La interpretación de la Sala Constitucional del Tribunal Supremo de Justicia del artículo 77 de la Carta Magna', in *Revista de Derecho,* No. 27 (Caracas: Tribunal Supremo de Justicia, 2008), 169–237; José Peña Solís, 'Análisis crítico de la sentencia de la Sala Constitucional No. 0190, de 28 de febrero de 2008: Interpretación de los artículos 21 y 77 constitucionales: derecho a la igualdad, uniones estables de hecho y extensión de los efectos del matrimonio a uniones concubinarias', in *Revista de Derecho,* No. 27 (Caracas: Tribunal Supremo de Justicia, 2008), 287–322.

V. Rights of Elderly Protection

534. Regarding senior citizens, Article 80 of the Constitution imposes on the State the duty to guarantee the full exercise of their rights and guarantees, providing that the State, with the participation of families and society, is obligated to respect their human dignity, autonomy and to guarantee them full care and social security benefits to improve and guarantee their quality of life. Pension and retirement benefits granted through the social security system shall not be less than the urban minimum salary. Senior citizens shall be guaranteed to have the right to a proper work if they indicate a desire to work and are capable of it.

VI. Rights of Disabled Protection

535. Article 81 of the Constitution sets forth that any person with disability or special needs has the right to the full and autonomous exercise of his abilities and to integration into the family and community. The State, with the participation of families and society, must guarantee them respect for their human dignity, equality of opportunity and satisfactory working conditions, and shall promote their training, education and access to employment appropriate to their condition, in accordance with law. It is recognized that deaf persons have the right to express themselves and communicate through the Venezuelan sign language,[652] and the televised media must carry subtitles and sign language translations for persons with hearing impairments (Article 101).

§2. Right to Dwelling

536. Article 82 of the Constitution also establishes the right of every person to adequate, safe and comfortable, hygienic housing, with appropriate essential basic services, including a habitat such as to humanize family, neighbourhood and community relations. The progressive meeting of this requirement is the shared responsibility of citizens and the State in all areas. The State shall give priority to families, and shall guarantee them, especially those with meagre resources, the possibility of access to social policies and credit for the construction, purchase or enlargement of dwellings.

§3. Right to Health

537. The Constitution also provides expressly for the right to health, as a fundamental social right, being an obligation of the State to guarantee it as part of the

652. *See* María C. Domínguez Guillén, 'La protección constitucional de los incapaces', in *Temas de Derecho Administrativo: Libro Homenaje a Gonzalo Pérez Luciani,* vol. I, No. 7 (Caracas: Tribunal Supremo de Justicia, Colección Libros Homenaje, 2002), 609 a 658.

right to life (Article 83).[653] Consequently, the State shall promote and develop policies oriented toward improving the quality of life, common welfare and access to services; and all persons have the right to protection of health, as well as the duty to participate actively in the furtherance and protection of the same, and to comply with such health and hygiene measures as may be established by law, and in accordance with international conventions and treaties signed and ratified by the Republic.

538. In order to guarantee the right to health, Article 84 sets forth that the State must create, exercise guidance over and administer a national public health system that crosses sector boundaries, and is decentralized and participatory in nature, integrated with the social security system and governed by the principles of gratuity, universality, completeness, fairness, social integration and solidarity. The public health system gives priority to promoting health and preventing disease, guaranteeing prompt treatment and quality rehabilitation. Public health assets and services are the property of the State and shall not be privatized. The organized community has the right and duty to participate in the making of decisions concerning policy planning, implementation and control at public health institutions. This is to say the health service is constitutionally conceived as being integrated to the system of social security, as a sub-system of it, and is conceived as being cost-free for its users and universally available. Moreover, the Constitution itself establishes that public health-related property and services cannot be privatized.

539. Accordingly, the financing of the public health system is the responsibility of the State, which shall integrate the revenue resources, mandatory Social Security contributions and any other sources of financing provided for by law. The State guarantees a health budget such as to make possible the attainment of health policy objectives. In coordination with universities and research centres, a national professional and technical training policy and a national industry to produce healthcare supplies shall be promoted and developed. Finally, Article 85 concludes its regulation in the area by stating that, the State must 'regulate public and private institutions of health'. This is the only place in which private health institutions are mentioned, but for the purpose of regulating them.

653. *See* Jesús Ollarves Irazábal, 'La vigencia del derecho a la salud', in *El Derecho Público a comienzos del siglo XXI. Estudios homenaje al Profesor Allan R. Brewer-Carías,* vol. III (Madrid: Instituto de Derecho Público, UCV, Civitas Ediciones, 2003), 2867–2886; Oscar Feo, 'La salud en la nueva Constitución', in *La cuestión social en la Constitución Bolivariana de Venezuela* (Caracas: Editorial Torino, 2000), 29–46; Belén Anasagasti, 'Caracterización de los principales rasgos del derecho a la salud dentro del marco constitucional de los derechos sociales del texto de 1961 y de 1999', in *La cuestión social en la Constitución Bolivariana de Venezuela* (Caracas: Editorial Torino, 2000), 135–152.

§4. RIGHT TO SOCIAL SECURITY

540. Regarding social security, it is also considered in Article 86 of the Constitution as a constitutional right,[654] providing for it as a non-profit public service to guarantee health and protection in contingencies of maternity, fatherhood, illness, invalidity, catastrophic illness, disability, special needs, occupational risks, loss of employment, unemployment, old age, widowhood, loss of parents, housing, burdens deriving from family life and any other social welfare circumstances. The Constitution imposes upon the State the obligation and responsibility of ensuring the efficacy of this constitutional right, creating a universal and complete Social Security system, with joint, unitary, efficient and participatory financing from direct and indirect contributions. Nonetheless, the lack of ability to contribute shall not be ground for excluding persons from protection by the system.

541. The Constitution also establishes that Social Security financial resources shall not be used for other purposes. The mandatory assessments paid by employees to cover medical and health care services and other Social Security benefits shall be administered only for social purposes, under the guidance of the State. Any net remaining balances of capital allocated to health, education and Social Security shall be accumulated for distribution and contribution to those services. The Social Security system is ruled by a special organic law.[655]

§5. LABOUR RIGHTS

I. Right to Work and State's Obligations

542. The chapter of the Constitution of 1999 containing social and family rights also incorporated a set of labour rights, following the orientation of the 1961 Constitution, but amplifying and making them even more rigid, by constitutionalizing many rights which by nature could exist at the level of ordinary law. Thus, the right and duty to work is expressly set forth (Article 87); work is considered a social fact and shall enjoy the protection of the State (Article 89), and freedom to work shall be subject only to the restrictions established by statutes.[656]

---

654. *See* María Bernardoni de Govea, 'Reforma de la seguridad social en Venezuela: un proceso inconcluso', in *Derecho y Sociedad. Revista de Estudiantes de Derecho de la Universidad Monteávila,* No. 3 (Caracas: Universidad Monteávila, Facultad de Ciencias Jurídicas y Políticas, 2002), 193–213; Pablo Pérez Herrera, 'El sistema venezolano de seguridad social', in *Revista Tachirense de Derecho,* No. 14 (San Cristóbal: Universidad Católica del Táchira, 2002), 143–158; Allan R. Brewer-Carías, 'Consideraciones sobre el régimen constitucional del derecho a la seguridad social, el Sistema de Seguridad Social y la Administración Privada de Fondos de Pensiones', in *Libro Homenaje a Fernando Parra Aranguren*, vol. I (Caracas: Facultad de Ciencias Jurídicas y Políticas, Universidad Central de Venezuela, 2001), 73–85.

655. *See* Organic Law on the Social Security System, and Social Security Law, *Gaceta Oficial* No. 5.891 Extra.of 31 Jul. 2008.

656. *See* Napoleón Goizueta H., 'Aspectos laborales en la Constitución Bolivariana de Venezuela y normas concordantes con la legislación del trabajo', in *Revista Gaceta Laboral* 8, No. 2 (mayo-agosto) (Maracaibo: Ediciones Astro Data, 2002), 251–282; Héctor A. Jaime Martínez, 'La nueva

543. The State must guarantee the adoption of the necessary measures so that every person shall be able to obtain productive work providing them with a dignified and decorous living and guaranteeing him or her the full exercise of the right to work and of being employed. The State must also promote employment, and measures tending to guarantee the exercise of the labour rights of self-employed persons must be adopted by statutes.

544. However, every employer shall guarantee employees adequate safety, hygienic and environmental conditions on the job, and the State shall adopt measures and create institutions such as to make it possible to control and promote these conditions.

545. Article 88 of the Constitution guarantees the equality and equitable treatment of men and women in the exercise of the right to work. The same provision recognizes work at home as an economic activity that creates added value and produces social welfare and wealth; and declares that housewives are entitled to Social Security in accordance with law.

II. Rights to Have Work Protected

546. The Constitution establishes that by statute, the necessary provisions must be established for improving the material, moral and intellectual conditions of workers. In order to fulfil this duty of the State, Article 89 of the Constitution enumerates the following principles: (1) No law shall establish provisions that affect the intactness and progressive nature of labour rights and benefits. In labour relations, reality shall prevail over forms or appearances. (2) Labour rights are not renounceable; consequently, any action, agreement or convention involving a waiver of or encroachment upon these rights is null and void. Concessions and settlements are possible only at the end of the employment relationship, in accordance with the requirements established by law. (3) When there are doubts concerning application or conflicts among several rules or in the interpretation of a particular rule, that most favourable to the worker shall be applied. The rule applied must be applied in its entirety. (4) Any measure or act on the part of an employer in violation of this Constitution is null and void and of no effect. (5) All types of discrimination because of political reasons, age, race, creed, sex or any other characteristic are prohibited. (6) Work by adolescents on tasks that may affect their overall development is prohibited. The State shall protect them against any economic and social exploitation.

Constitución venezolana y su influencia en la Ley Orgánica del Trabajo', in *Revista Tachirense de Derecho*, No. 12 (San Cristóbal: Universidad Católica del Táchira, 2000), 151–178; Gabriela Santana González, 'Normas constitucionales en materia laboral. De moribundas a bolivarianas', in *Revista Syllabus,* No. 1 (Caracas: Escuela de Derecho, Facultad de Ciencias Jurídicas y Políticas. Universidad Central de Venezuela, noviembre, 2000), 39–55; María C. Torres Seoane, 'Las normas laborales en la Constitución', in *Comentarios a la Constitución de la República Bolivariana de Venezuela* (Caracas: Vadell Hermanos Editores, 2000), 149–176.

III. Working Hours

547. However, the Constitution (Article 90) has also established provisions regarding working hours that shall not exceed eight hours per day or forty-four hours per week. Where permitted by law, night work shall not exceed seven hours per day or thirty-five hours per week. No employer shall have the right to require employees to work overtime. An effort shall be made to reduce working hours progressively in the interest of society and in such sphere as may be determined, and appropriate provisions shall be adopted to make better use of free time for the benefit of the physical, spiritual and cultural development of workers. Workers are entitled to weekly time off and paid vacations on the same terms as for days actually worked.

IV. Right to Salary and Other Benefits

548. Regarding salary, Article 91 of the Constitution establishes that every worker has the right to a salary sufficient to enable him or her to live with dignity and cover basic material, social and intellectual needs for himself or herself and his or her family. The payment of equal salary for equal work is guaranteed, and the share of the profits of a business enterprise to which workers are entitled shall be determined. Salary is not subject to seizure, and shall be paid periodically and promptly in legal tender, with the exception of the food allowance, in accordance with law.

549. The State guarantees workers in both the public and the private sectors a vital minimum salary which shall be adjusted each year, taking as one of the references the cost of a basic market basket. The form and procedure to be followed shall be established by law.

550. Article 92 of the Constitution declares that all workers have the right to benefits to compensate them for the length of service and protect them in the event of dismissal.

551. Salary and benefits are labour obligations due and payable immediately upon accrual. Any delay in payment of the same shall bear interest, which also constitutes a debt and shall enjoy the same privileges and guarantees as the principal debt.

552. The liability of the natural or juridical person for whose benefit services are provided through an intermediary or contractor shall be determined by law, without prejudice to the job and severance liability of the latter. The State shall establish, through the competent organ, the liability to which employers in general are subject in the event of simulation or fraud for the purpose of distorting, disregarding or impeding the application of labour legislation (Article 94).

V. Stability Rights

553. The stability of employment is regulated in Article 93 of the Constitution, setting forth that it shall be guaranteed by law, with provisions as appropriate to restrict any form of unjustified dismissal. Dismissals contrary to this Constitution are null and void.

VI. Trade-Unions Rights

554. Article 95 of the Constitution guarantees workers, without distinction of any kind and without need for authorization in advance, the right to freely establish such union organizations as they may deem appropriate for the optimum protection of their rights and interests, as well as the right to join or not to join the same, in accordance with law.[657] These organizations are not subject to administrative dissolution, suspension or intervention. Workers are protected against any act of discrimination or interference contrary to the exercise of this right. The promoters and the members of the Board of Directors of the union enjoy immunity from dismissal from their employment for the period and on the terms required to enable them to carry out their functions. For purposes of the exercise of union democracy, the bylaws and regulations of union organizations shall provide for the replacement of boards of directors and representatives by universal, direct and secret suffrage. Any union leaders and representatives who abuse the benefits deriving from union freedom for their personal gain or benefit shall be punished in accordance with law. Boards of directors of union organizations shall be required to file a sworn statement of assets.

555. With respect to this right to unionize, the intervention of the State into labour union functions must be mentioned, through the provision in Article 294.6 of the Constitution of the jurisdiction of the National Electoral Council, an organ of the State (Electoral Power), to 'organize elections in unions and professional associations'. As a result, in Venezuela, unions are not free to organize their own elections of representatives and authorities, since these elections are now organized by the State.

VII. Right to Collective Bargaining Agreements

556. Article 96 of the Constitution guarantees all employees in both public and the private sectors have the right to voluntary collective bargaining and to enter into collective bargaining agreements, subject only to such restrictions as may be established by law. The State guarantees this process and shall establish appropriate provisions to encourage collective relations and the resolution of labour conflicts.

657. *See* León Arismendi; 'Libertad sindical y elecciones sindicales en la Constitución de 1999', in *Revista Gaceta Laboral* 8, No. 1 (enero-abril) (Maracaibo: Ediciones Astro Data, 2002), 79–98.

Collective bargaining agreements cover all workers who are active as of the time they are signed, and those hired thereafter.

VIII. Right to Strike

557. Finally, regarding the right to strike, Article 97 of the Constitution guarantees it to all workers in the public and private sectors, subject to such conditions as may be established by law.

§6. CULTURAL RIGHTS

558. Cultural creation is considered in the Constitution as a free action, including as provided in Article 98 of the Constitution, the right to invest in, produce and disseminate the creative, scientific, technical and humanistic work, as well as legal protection of the author's rights in his works. The State recognizes and protects intellectual property rights in scientific, literary and artistic works, inventions, innovations, trade names, patents, trademarks and slogans, in accordance with the conditions and exceptions established by law and the international treaties executed and ratified by the Republic in this field.

559. In addition, Article 99 of the Constitution declares cultural values as the un-renounceable property of the Venezuelan people and a fundamental right to be encouraged and guaranteed by the State, efforts being made to provide the necessary conditions, legal instruments, means and funding. The autonomy of the public administration of culture is recognized, on such terms as may be established by law.

560. The State must guarantee the protection and preservation, enrichment, conservation and restoration of the cultural tangible and intangible heritage and the historic memories of the nation. The assets constituting the cultural heritage of the nation are inalienable, not subject to seizure or to statute of limitations. Penalties and sanctions for damage caused to these assets shall be provided for by law.

561. The folk cultures comprising the national identity of Venezuela enjoy special attention, with recognition of and respect for intercultural relations under the principle of equality of cultures. Incentives and inducements shall be provided for by law for persons, institutions and communities which promote, support, develop or finance cultural plans, programmes and activities within the country and Venezuelan culture abroad. The State guarantees cultural workers inclusion in the social security system to provide them with a dignified life, recognizing the idiosyncrasies of cultural work, in accordance with law (Article 100).

562. Regarding cultural information, the State must guarantee its issuance, reception and circulation; the communications media has the duty of assisting in the dissemination of the values of folk traditions and the work of artists, writers, composers, motion-picture directors, scientists and other creators of culture of the country. The television media shall include subtitles and translations into Venezuelan sign language for persons with hearing problems. The terms and modalities of these obligations shall be established by law (Article 101).

§7. Educational Rights

I. Right to Education

563. With respect to the right to education, Article 102 of the Constitution begins by establishing, as a general matter, that 'education is a human right and a fundamental social duty, it is democratic, cost-free, and mandatory'.[658] The consequence of the foregoing is that Article 102 itself imposes upon the State the obligation to assume responsibility as an irrevocable function of the greatest interest, at all levels and in all modes, as an instrument of scientific, humanistic and technical knowledge at the service of society.

Accordingly, every person has the right to a full, high-quality, ongoing education under conditions and circumstances of equality, subject only to such limitations as derive from such person's own aptitudes, vocation and aspirations. Education is obligatory at all levels from maternal to the diversified secondary level.

II. Education as a Public Service

564. Education is constitutionally declared to be a public service (Article 102), although the Constitution also states that, 'the State will stimulate and protect private education that is imparted according with the principles established in this Constitution and the Laws'. As a public service, education is grounded on the respect for all currents of thought, to the end of developing the creative potential of every human being and the full exercise of his or her personality in a democratic society based on the work ethic value and on active, conscious and joint participation in the processes of social transformation embodied in the values which are part of the national identity, and with a Latin American and universal vision. The State, with

658. *See* Gustavo J. Linares Benzo, 'Bases constitucionales de la educación', in *Revista Derecho y Sociedad de la Universidad Monteávila,* No. 2 (abril) (Caracas, 2001), 217–252; Gustavo J. Linares Benzo, 'La educación en el texto constitucional', in *Estudios de Derecho Administrativo: Libro Homenaje a la Universidad Central de Venezuela,* vol. II (Caracas: Imprenta Nacional, 2001), 91–120 and in *Revista de Derecho Público,* No. 84 (octubre-diciembre) (Caracas: Editorial Jurídica Venezolana, 2000), 5–25; and Mabel Mundó, 'El derecho a la educación en las Constituciones de 1999 y 1961: reflexiones sobre principios, recursos y aprendizajes para la elaboración de la política educativa', in *La cuestión social en la Constitución Bolivariana de Venezuela* (Caracas: Editorial Torino, 2000), 47–74; Suying Olivares García, 'El derecho a la educación como un derecho humano fundamental a la luz de la Constitución de 1999', in *Frónesis. Revista de Filosofía Jurídica, Social y Política* (Maracaibo: Universidad del Zulia, Facultad de Ciencias Jurídicas y Políticas, Instituto de Filosofía del Derecho Dr José M. Delgado Ocando, Ediciones Astro Data, No. 14, 2 (mayo-agosto), 2007), 11–36.

the participation of families and society, must promote the process of civic education in accordance with the principles contained in this Constitution and in the laws.

565. Education offered at State institutions is free of charge up to the undergraduate university level. To this end, the State shall make a priority investment in accordance with United Nations recommendations. The State shall create and sustain institutions and services sufficiently equipped to ensure the admission process, ongoing education and programme completion in the education system (Article 103).

566. The law shall guarantee equal attention to persons with special needs or disabilities, and to those who have been deprived of liberty or do not meet the basic conditions for admission to and continuing enrolment in the education system. The contributions of private individuals to public education programmes at the secondary and university levels shall be tax deductible in accordance with the pertinent law (Article 103).[659]

567. Regarding the content of education, Article 106 of the Constitution sets forth that environmental education is obligatory in the various levels and modes of the education system, as well as in informal civil education. Spanish, Venezuelan geography and history and the principles of the Bolivarian thought shall be compulsory courses at public and private institutions up to the education diversified level.

However, the Constitution also declares that physical education and sports play a fundamental role in the overall education of children and adolescents. Instruction in the same is obligatory at all levels of public and private education up to the education diversified level, with such exceptions as may be established by law (Article 111).

568. The communications media, public and private, shall contribute to civil education. The State guarantees public radio and television services and library and computer networks, with a view to permitting universal access to information. Education centres are to incorporate knowledge and application of new technologies and the resulting innovations, in accordance with such requirements as may be established by law to this end (Article 108).

III. Right to Educate

569. Article 106 of the Constitution guarantees every natural or juridical person subject to demonstration of their ability and provided it meets at all times the ethical, academic, scientific, financial, infrastructure and any other requirements that

---

659. *See* Carlos Eduardo Herrera M., *La educación en Venezuela: dos dimensiones de un derecho*, (Caracas, Editorial Jurídica Venezolana, 2022).

may be established by law, to be permitted to fund and maintain private educational institutions under the strict inspection and vigilance of the State, with the prior approval of the latter.

570. For such purposes, only persons of recognized good moral character and proven academic qualifications shall be placed in charge of education (Article 104). The State shall encourage them to remain continuously up-to-date, and shall guarantee stability in the practice of the teaching profession, whether in public or private institutions, in accordance with this Constitution and the law, with working conditions and a standard of living commensurate with the importance of their mission. Admissions, promotion and continued enrolment in the education system shall be provided for by law, and shall be responsive to evaluation criteria based on merit, to the exclusion of any partisan or other non-academic interference.

IV. Principle of the University Autonomy

571. The Constitution establishes and recognizes the principle of the autonomy of universities, as a principle and status that allows teachers, students and graduates from its community, to devote themselves to the search for knowledge through research in the fields of science, humanities and technology, for the spiritual and material benefit of the Nation (Article 109).

572. Autonomous universities shall adopt their own rules for their governance and operation and the efficient management of their property, under such control and vigilance as may be established by law to this end. Autonomy of universities is established in the planning, organization, preparation and updating of research, teaching and extension programmes. The inviolability of the university campus is established. Experimental national universities shall attain their autonomy in accordance with law (Article 109).

V. Science and Technology System

573. Article 110 of the Constitution recognizes as being in the public interest science, technology, knowledge, innovation and the resulting applications, and the necessary information services, the same being fundamental instruments for the country's economic, social and political development, as well as for national sovereignty and security.

In order to promote and develop these activities, the State shall allocate sufficient resources and shall create a national science and technology system in accordance with law. The private sector shall contribute with resources as well.[660] The State shall guarantee the enforcement of the ethical and legal principles that are to govern research activities in science, humanism and technology. The manners and means of fulfilling this guarantee shall be determined by law.

660. Organic law on Science, Technology and Innovation, *Gaceta Oficial* No. 39.575 of 16 Dec. 2010.

VI. Right to Sport

574. The right to sport and the right to recreation are also declared in the Constitution, as well as the right to recreation as activities beneficial to individual and collective quality of life. For such purpose, the State assumes responsibility for sports and recreation as an education and public health policy and guarantees the resources for the furtherance thereof (Article 111).

The State guarantees full attention to athletes without discrimination of any kind, as well as support for high-level competitive sports and evaluation and regulation of sports organizations in both the public and the private sectors, in accordance with law. Incentives and inducements shall be established for the persons, institutions and communities that promote athletes and develop or finance sports activities, plans and programmes in the country.

§8. Environmental Rights

I. Right to the Protection of Environment

575. The Constitution of 1999 is also innovative with respect to its regulation of constitutional rights concerning the environment,[661] declaring that each generation has the right and duty to protect and maintain the environment for its own benefit and that of the world of the future; and that everyone has the right, individually and collectively, to enjoy a safe, healthful and ecologically balanced life and environment.

The State shall protect the environment, biological and genetic diversity, ecological processes, national parks and natural monuments, and other areas of particular ecological importance. The genome of a living being shall not be patentable, and the field shall be regulated by the law relating to the principles of bioethics.

It is a fundamental duty of the State, with the active participation of society, to ensure that the populace develops in a pollution-free environment in which air, water, soil, coasts, climate, the ozone layer and living species receive special protection, in accordance with law (Article 127).

576. In order to guarantee the protection of environment, Article 129 of the Constitution prescribes that any activities capable of generating damage to ecosystems

661. *See* Fortunato González Cruz, 'El ambiente en la nueva Constitución venezolana', in *El Derecho Público a comienzos del siglo XXI. Estudios homenaje al Profesor Allan R. Brewer-Carías,* vol. III (Madrid: Instituto de Derecho Público, UCV, Civitas Ediciones, 2003), 2917–2923; Germán Acedo Payarez, 'La Constitución de la República Bolivariana de Venezuela de 1999 y los denominados "Derechos Ambientales"', *ibid.*, vol. III, 2925–2978; Alberto Blanco-Uribe Quintero, 'La tutela ambiental como derecho-deber del Constituyente. Base constitucional y principios rectores del derecho ambiental', in *Revista de Derecho Constitucional,* No. 6 (enero-diciembre) (Caracas: Editorial Sherwood, 2002), 31–64, and 'El ciudadano frente a la defensa jurídica del ambiente en Venezuela', in *El Derecho Público a comienzos del siglo XXI. Estudios homenaje al Profesor Allan R. Brewer-Carías,* vol. III (Madrid: Instituto de Derecho Público, UCV, Civitas Ediciones, 2003), 2995–3008.

must be preceded by environmental and socio-cultural impact studies. The State shall prevent toxic and hazardous waste from entering the country, as well as prevent the manufacture and use of nuclear, chemical and biological weapons. A special law shall regulate the use, handling, transportation and storage of toxic and hazardous substances.

II. The Land Use Planning

577. As a matter of public policy, Article 128 of the Constitution imposes on the State the duty to develop a land use policy taking into account ecological, geographic, demographic, social, cultural, economic and political realities, in accordance with the premises of sustainable development, including information, consultation and male/female participation by citizens. An organic law shall develop the principles and criteria for this zoning.

§9. The Rights of Indigenous Peoples

578. Another innovation in the 1999 Constitution, was the incorporation in its text of a set of provisions concerning the rights of indigenous peoples,[662] which constitutes an ethnic group not exceeding 1.5% of the population.

The chapter begins with a declaration that the State shall recognize the existence of indigenous peoples and communities, their social, political and economic organization, their cultures, habits and customs, languages and religions, their habitat and original rights to the territories they ancestrally and historically occupy and that are necessary to develop and guarantee their ways of life. It is incumbent upon the National Executive, with the participation of the indigenous peoples, to mark the boundaries of and guarantee the property collective rights of their territories, which will be inalienable, imprescriptible, unseizable, and untransferable in accord with the Constitution and laws (Article 119).

This declaration is a recognition of the existence of political communities within the State, in the sense of recognizing that there can be *a people* in the country, with its own *political organization* and its own geographic *territory*, being these elements (people, government, and territory) the essential components of every State. Nonetheless, in order to avoid problems with respect to the integrity of national territory, Article 126 of the Constitution states that the indigenous peoples, as cultures with ancestral roots, form a part of the Nation, the State and the Venezuelan people, which is unique, sovereign and indivisible. Consequently, the indigenous peoples have the duty to protect national integrity and sovereignty, and in no case, the term 'people' shall be interpreted in the sense that it has in international law.

662. *See* Ricardo Colmenares Olívar, 'Constitucionalismo y derechos de los pueblos indígenas en Venezuela', in *Revista LEX NOVA del Colegio de Abogados del Estado Zulia,* No. 237 (Maracaibo, 2000), 13–46.

579. According to Article 120, the State's use of natural resources within indigenous peoples' territories must be undertaken without violating the integrity of the inhabitants' culture, social and economic life. The use of natural resources within indigenous peoples' territories requires prior information and consulting with the relevant indigenous population.

580. Article 121 of the Constitution declares the right of indigenous peoples to maintain and develop their ethnic and cultural identities, cosmology, values, spirituality, sacred locations and religion. To this end, the State is obliged to promote the value and distribution of indigenous cultural manifestations. In addition, indigenous people have the right to their own form of education as well as to an intercultural and bilingual education, giving specific attention to their particular socio-cultural characteristics, values and traditions.

581. Similarly, Article 122 establishes the right of indigenous peoples to comprehensive health, while taking into account their own practices and culture. As a consequence, the State is obliged to recognize their traditional medicine and therapies, subject to principles of medical ethics.

582. With respect to economic activities, Article 123 of the Constitution establishes the right of indigenous peoples to maintain and promote their own economic practices based upon reciprocity, solidarity, and trade, their traditional productive activities, and in addition, their participation in the national economy, while defining their priorities for themselves. However, the State is also obliged to guarantee the enjoyment of rights conferred by labour law to indigenous workers.

583. Article 124 of the Constitution guarantees and protects the collective intellectual property of the knowledge, technologies and innovations produced by indigenous peoples and requires that all activities related to their genetic resources and the associated knowledge be linked to the collective benefit of the indigenous people who produce it. The Constitution prohibits the registration of patents on such ancestral resources and knowledge.

According to Article 260 of the Constitution, the legitimate authorities of the indigenous peoples could apply in their habitat, according to their ancestral traditions, and following their own rules and procedures, judicial means that could only affect their members, providing that they are not contrary to the Constitution, the law or the public order.[663]

584. Finally, Article 125 of the Constitution consecrates the right of indigenous peoples to political participation, which in particular is established in Article 182 guaranteeing, 'indigenous representation in the National Assembly and deliberating

663. *See* María E. León Álvarez, 'El sistema de justicia en la Constitución de Venezuela de 1999. Estudio crítico acerca de la jurisdicción especial indígena', en *Revista del Tribunal Supremo de Justicia,* No. 4 (Caracas, 2002), 369–377.

bodies of federal entities and of local entities where indigenous populations exist, in accordance with law'[664] (*see supra* paragraph 578).

664. *See* Ricardo Colmenares Olívar, 'El derecho de participación y consulta de los pueblos indígenas en Venezuela', in *Revista del Tribunal Supremo de Justicia,* No. 8 (Caracas, 2003), 21–48.

Chapter 5. Political Rights

§1. Right to Political Participation

585. The 1999 Constitution also declares a series of political rights that in principle are reserved to Citizens (*see supra* paragraph 492), beginning with the right to free political participation in all public affairs, either directly or by means of their elected representatives (Article 62), considering such participation in the formation, execution, and control of public affairs as necessary to achieve their complete development, collectively and individually, being an obligation of both the State and society to facilitate the creation of conditions most favourable for the practice of this participation.

586. Article 70 of the Constitution enumerates the means of the people's participation in the exercise of their sovereignty, as follows: *in political matters*, election of representatives to public office, vote in referenda, popular consultations, revocation of the mandate of elected officials, legislative or constitutional initiative, open town meeting, and Citizens' Assemblies whose decisions are binding; in *social and economic matters*, people's complaints means, workers participation in the management of enterprises, all forms of cooperatives, including financial cooperatives, cooperative savings banks, communitarian businesses, and other 'forms of associations guided by values of mutual cooperation and solidarity'.

§2. Right to Vote and Electoral Principles

587. The right to vote is declared in Article 63, but without qualifying it as a duty, as was conceived in the 1961 Constitution (Article 110). This right to vote belongs to all Venezuelans who have reached the age of 18, and are not subject to civil interdiction or political incapacity (Article 64). The Constitution has also specifically conferred the right to vote to members of the armed forces on active duty, although military personnel my not participate in propaganda, political militancy or proselytizing (Article 330). This was an innovation in the Venezuelan political process, in which the military traditionally did not have the right to vote.

588. The election of representatives must always be done by means of free, universal, direct and secret voting, combining the principles of the 'personalization of suffrage' and proportional representation (*see supra* paragraphs 168, 363). Citizens, on their own initiative, and associations for political purposes shall be entitled to participate in the electoral process, putting forward candidates (Article 67).

In this regard, Article 63 establishes two elements for the configuration of the electoral system of representatives: on the one hand, the 'personalization of suffrage', which requires nominal voting, that is, the voting for a named person, whether votes are counted from single constituency districts, in which case there is no possibility other than voting in nominal or personified way; or whether votes are cast in plurinominal constituencies, by means of lists, where voters cast nominal ballots for multiple persons to represent a single district. On the other hand, the article also guarantees proportional representation, as a system that absolutely requires a plurinominal constituency in which ballots are cast for more than one candidate per electoral district. Proportional representation *excludes* the possibility of single district representation for representative assemblies, implying the need for an electoral system where elections are carried out through lists, where multiple candidates are selected for each district, in a nominal form (*see supra* paragraph 173).

589. Being the political rights of Citizens, and thus, of the Venezuelan nationals, foreigners in principle do not have such rights. Nonetheless, Article 64 of the Constitution extends an exception to the rule, providing that foreigners who have reached the age of 18, and are not subject to civil interdiction or political incapacity, and who have lived in the country for more than ten years, can vote in the states in municipal elections.

§3. Right to Be Elected and to Exercise Public Offices

590. The text of the 1999 Constitution contains no equivalent provision to Article 112 of the 1961 Constitution that established the right of the citizen to be elected and perform duties of public office, that is, to hold public office. On these matters, the Constitution only establishes restrictions and prohibitions. Article 65 of the Constitution establishes that a person who has been convicted of an offence while exercising public office or convicted of an offence involving public funds, may not be a candidate for any popular election, during a time period based upon the gravity of the offence. Also, Members of the armed forces on active duty are not permitted to run in popular elections (Article 330).

591. Regarding the right to be elected, according to Article 67 of the Constitution, nominations for all elective offices may be made by own initiative (self-initiated) or at proposals made by political associations. In this way, all Citizens have the right to participate in electoral processes nominating candidates.

However, Article 66 of the Constitution consecrates the citizens' right to have their representatives render periodic and transparent accounts for their work in an office 'according to the programme submitted in the election' (Article 66). This implies that all candidates in elections must present to the electors their corresponding programme.

§4. Right to Be Associated with Political Parties

592. All Citizens have the right to be associated for political purposes, in political associations that must be governed by democratic means of organization, functioning and direction (Article 67) (*see supra* paragraphs 186 et seq.).

§5. Right to Demonstrate

593. Citizens also have the right to participate in demonstrations, peacefully without weapons, subject only to such requirements as may be established by law (Article 68). The same provision establishes limits to police interventions regarding demonstrations, in the sense that they cannot use firearms or toxic substances to control peaceful demonstrations. The activity of police and security corps in maintaining public order shall be regulated by law.

Chapter 6. Judicial Protection of Constitutional Rights: The *Amparo* Proceeding

594. Constitutional declarations of rights, in the Constitutions or in international treaties and covenants, would be of no use at all if those rights were not supported by a set of constitutional guarantees for their protection, and particularly, by the judicial guarantee, that is to say, the set of judicial means established in benefit of persons in order to assure not only the supremacy of the Constitution but the effective exercise and protection of the rights therein contained.

For that purpose, an effective Judiciary has to be built upon the principle of separation of powers. So, on the contrary, if the Government controls the courts and judges, no effective guarantee can exist regarding constitutional rights, particularly when the offending party is a governmental agency. In this case, and in spite of all constitutional declarations, it is impossible to speak of rule of law, as happens in many Latin American countries, and as has been the case of Venezuela during the past decade (2000–2011).

595. Nonetheless, regarding the general provisions of the Constitution and the means for protection of constitutional rights and freedoms, their judicial protection and guarantee in general terms can be achieved in two ways: first, by means of the generally established ordinary or extraordinary suits, actions, recourses or writs regulated in procedural law; and second, in addition to those general means, by means of specific judicial suits, actions or recourses of *amparo* seeking remedies specifically and particularly established in order to protect and enforce constitutional rights and freedoms and to prevent and redress wrongs regarding those rights.[665]

That is, the judicial guarantee of constitutional rights can be achieved through the general procedural regulations that are established in order to enforce any kind of

665. On the action of *amparo* in Venezuela, in general, *see* Allan R. Brewer-Carías, *Derecho y Acción de Amparo Constitucional, (Caracas, Editorial Jurídica Venezolana, 2021);* 'The Amparo Proceeding in Venezuela: Constitutional Litigation and Procedural Protection of Constitutional Rights and Guarantees', in *Duquesne Law Review* 49, No. 2 (Spring, 2011), 161–241; Gustavo Briceño V., *Comentarios a la Ley de Amparo* (Caracas: Editorial Kinesis, 1991); Rafael J. Chavero Gazdik, *El nuevo régimen del amparo constitucional en Venezuela* (Caracas, 2001); Gustavo José Linares Benzo, *El Proceso de Amparo* (Caracas: Universidad Central de Venezuela, Facultad de Ciencias Jurídicas y Políticas, 1999); Hildegard Rondón De Sansó, *Amparo Constitucional* (Caracas, 1988); Hildegard Rondón De Sansó, *La acción de amparo contra los poderes públicos* (Caracas: Editorial Arte, 1994); Carlos M. Ayala Corao & Rafael J. Chavero Gazidk, 'El amparo constitucional en Venezuela' in *El derecho de amparo en el mundo*, ed. Héctor Fix-Zamudio & Eduardo Ferrer MacGregor (Coordinadores) (México: Universidad Nacional Autónoma de México, Editorial Porrúa, 2006), 649–692; Hildegard Rondón de Sansó, 'La acción de amparo constitucional a raíz de la vigencia de la Constitución de 1999', in *Revista de la Facultad de Ciencias Jurídicas y Políticas de la UCV,* No. 119 (Caracas, 2000), 147–172; Richard D. Henríquez Larrazábal, 'El problema de la procedencia del amparo constitucional en el Derecho venezolano', in *Bases y principios del sistema constitucional venezolano (Ponencias del VII Congreso Venezolano de Derecho Constitucional realizado en San Cristóbal del 21 al 23 de Noviembre de 2001),* vol. II, 403–475; Víctor R. Hernández-Mendible, 'El amparo constitucional desde la perspectiva cautelar', in *El Derecho Público a comienzos del siglo XXI. Estudios homenaje al Profesor Allan R. Brewer-Carías,* vol. I, *supra,* 1.219–1.301.

personal or proprietary rights and interests, or it can also be achieved by means of a specific judicial proceeding established only and particularly for the protection of the rights declared in the Constitution. In this regard, it can be considered a general trend in Latin America to establish these specific means of *amparo*,[666] mainly because of the traditional insufficiencies of the general judicial means for granting effective protection to constitutional rights.

596. The habeas corpus recourse is also considered an *amparo* proceeding regarding the protection of personal freedom; and in addition, the Constitution has set forth for the habeas data recourse in order to guarantee the right to have access to the information and data concerning the claimant contained in official or private registries, as well as to know about the use that has been made of such information and about its purpose, and to petition the competent court for the updating, rectification or destruction of erroneous records and those that unlawfully affect the petitioner's right (Article 28).

§1. The Right of *Amparo* (to Be Protected)

597. The action or suit for protection, or *amparo*, as a specific judicial means for the protection of all constitutional rights and guarantees, has been constitutionalized in Venezuela since the 1961 Constitution. This provision implies the obligation of all the courts to protect persons in the exercise of their constitutional rights and guarantees. In the *amparo* suit decisions, judicial review of the constitutionality of legislation can also be exercised by the courts as part of their rulings.

Article 27 of the Constitution of 1999 establishes:

> Every individual is entitled to be protected by the courts in the enjoyment and exercise of rights, even those which derive from the nature of man that are not expressly set forth in this Constitution or in the international treaties on human rights.
>
> The amparo suit is governed by an informal, oral proceeding that shall be public, brief and free of charge. The judge is entitled to immediately restore the affected legal situation, and the court shall issue the decision with preference to all other matters.

As per the Organic Law on A*mparo* of Constitutional Rights and Guarantees of 1988,[667] in principle, all courts of first instance are competent to decide *amparo* suits.

666. *See* Allan R. Brewer-Carías, *Constitutional Protection of Human Rights in Latin America: A Comparative Study of Amparo Proceedings* (New York: Cambridge University Press, 2008).

667. *See Gaceta Oficial* No.33.891 of 22 Jan. 1988. *See* Allan R. Brewer-Carías & Carlos M. Ayala Corao, *Ley Orgánica de Amparo sobre Derechos y Garantías Constitucionales* (Caracas, 1988). *See also* Allan R. Brewer-Carías, *El derecho y la acción de amparo, vol. V, Instituciones Políticas y Constitucionales* (Caracas: Editorial Jurídica venezolana, 1998), 163 et seq.

598. Standing to file the action of *amparo* corresponds to every individual whose constitutional rights and guarantees are affected (whether individual, political, social, cultural, educative, economic, Indigenous peoples' or environmental rights), even those inherent rights that are not expressly provided for in the Constitution or in the international treaties on human rights that are ratified by the Republic. In Venezuela, such treaties rank on the same level as the Constitution, and they even prevail in the internal order as long as they establish more favourable rules on the enjoyment and exercise of rights than those established under the Constitution and other laws (Article 23) (*see supra* paragraphs 464, 465, 731).

599. In Venezuela, the action of *amparo* may be instituted against State organs, against corporations and even against individuals whose actions or omissions may infringe or threaten constitutional rights and guarantees. In all cases of *amparo* proceedings, if the alleged violation of the constitutional right involves a statutory provision, in his decision, the *amparo* judge can decide that the statute is unconstitutional and not apply it to the case.

600. Generally, the individual directly affected by the infringement of the constitutional rights and guarantees has standing in action for *amparo*. But by virtue of the constitutional acknowledgement of the legal protection of diffuse or collective interests, the Constitutional Chamber of the Supreme Court has admitted the possibility of exercising the action of *amparo* to enforce collective and diffuse rights. For instance, those rights related to an acceptable quality of life and also those pertaining to the political rights of voters, admitting precautionary measures with *erga omnes* effects.[668]

In such cases, the Constitutional Chamber has admitted that:

> any individual with legal capacity to bring suit, who is going to prevent damage to the population or parts of it to which he belongs, is entitled to bring the [amparo] suit grounded in diffuse or collective interests ...This interpretation, based on Article 26, extends standing to companies, corporations, foundations, chambers, unions and other collective entities, whose object be the defense of the society, as long as they act within the boundaries of their corporate object, aimed at protecting the interests of their members regarding their object.[669]

668. Decision of the Constitutional Chamber No. 483 of 29 May 2000 (Case: *'Queremos Elegir' y otros*), *Revista de Derecho Público*, No. 82 (Caracas: Editorial Jurídica Venezolana, 2000), 489–491. In the same sense, decision of the same Chamber No. 714 of 13 Jul. 2000 (Case: *APRUM*), in *Revista de Derecho Público*, No. 83 (Caracas: Editorial Jurídica Venezolana, 2000), 319 et seq.

669. *See* decision of the Constitutional Chamber No. 487 of 6 Apr. 2001, Case: *Glenda López*, in *Revista de Derecho Público*, Nos 85–88 (Caracas: Editorial Jurídica Venezolana, 2001), 453 et seq. In a similar case, ruled by the Constitutional Chamber in a decision dated 17 Feb. 2000 (No. 1.048, Case: *William O. Ojeda O. v. Consejo Nacional Electoral*), in order to enforce diffuse or collective rights or interests, it is necessary that the following elements be combined: '(1) That the plaintiff sues based not only on his personal right or interest, but also on a common or collective right or interest; (2) That the reason for the claim filed on the action of *amparo*, be the general damage to the quality of life of all the inhabitants of the country or parts of it, since the legal situation of all the members of the society or its groups has been damaged when their common quality of life was

However, regarding the general defence and protection of diffusc and collective interests, the Constitutional Chamber has also admitted the standing of the Defender of the People.[670]

601. In order to seek uniformity in the application and interpretation of the Constitution, Article 336 of the Constitution also grants the Constitutional Chamber of the Supreme Tribunal the power to review, in a discretionary way, all final decisions issued in *amparo* suits. The extraordinary recourse can also be raised against judicial decisions applying the diffuse method of judicial review, being the review power of the Constitutional Chamber of facultative, non-obligatory character.

§2. The Various Judicial Means for *Amparo*

602. This *right to amparo* can be exercised through an 'autonomous action for amparo'[671] that in principle is filed before the first instance court; or by means of pre-existing ordinary or extraordinary legal actions or recourses to which an *amparo* petition is joined, being the judges empowered to immediately re-establish the infringed legal situation. In all such cases, it is not that the ordinary means substitute the constitutional right of protection (or diminish it), but that they can serve as the judicial mean for protection since the judge is empowered to protect fundamental rights and immediately re-establish the infringed legal situation.

This last possibility does not presuppose in Venezuela that for the filing of an autonomous *amparo* action all other pre-existing legal judicial or administrative means have to be exhausted, as is the case, for instance, of the recourse for *amparo* or the 'constitutional complaint' developed in Europe, particularly in Germany and in Spain.

603. This right for *amparo* has been regulated in the 1988 Organic Law of Amparo,[672] expressly providing for its exercise, as aforementioned, not only by means of an autonomous action for *amparo* but also through other pre-existing actions or recourses already established in the legal system. This main characteristic of the Venezuelan *amparo* was summarized in a decision by the former Supreme Court of 7 July 1991 (*Case Tarjetas Banvenez*), as follows:

> The Amparo Law sets forth two adjective mechanisms: the (autonomous) action for amparo and the joint filing of such action with other actions or

unimproved; (3) That the damaged goods are not susceptible of exclusive appropriation by one subject (such as the plaintiff); (4) That the claim concerns an indivisible right or interest that involves the entire population of the country or a group of it [and] that a necessity of satisfying social or collective interests exists, before the individual ones.' *See* in *Revista de Derecho Público*, No. 83 (Caracas: Editorial Jurídica Venezolana, 2000), 375 et seq.

670. *See* decision of the Constitutional Chamber No. 487 of 6 Apr. 2001, Case: *Glenda López*, in *Revista de Derecho Público*, Nos 85–88 (Caracas: Editorial Jurídica Venezolana, 2001), 453 et seq.

671. *See* Allan R. Brewer-Carías, 'El derecho de amparo y la acción de amparo', in *Revista de Derecho Público*, No. 22 (Caracas: Editorial Jurídica Venezolana, 1985), 51 et seq.

672. *See Gaceta Oficial* No. 33.891 of 22 Jan. 1988.

> recourses, which differs in their nature and legal consequences. Regarding the latter, that is to say, the filing of such action of amparo jointly with other actions or recourses, the Amparo Law distinguishes three mechanisms: a) the action of amparo filed jointly with the popular action of unconstitutionality against statutes and State acts of the same rank and value (Article 3); b) The action of amparo filed jointly with the judicial review of administrative actions recourses against administrative acts or against omissions from Public Administration (Article 5); and c) the amparo action filed jointly with another ordinary judicial actions (Article 6, 5).[673]

The same Supreme Court also ruled that in these latter cases, the action for *amparo* is not an autonomous action, 'but a subordinate one, ancillary to the action or recourse to which it has been joined, thus subject to its final decision. Being joint actions, the case must be heard by the competent court regarding the principal one'.[674]

604. Regarding the first mean for protection, that is, the autonomous action for *amparo*, in principle, it can be brought before the first-instance courts, and has a re-establishing nature in order to return things to the situation they had when the right was violated and to definitively make the offending act or fact disappear. For such purposes, the plaintiff must invoke and demonstrate that it is a matter of flagrant, vulgar, direct and immediate constitutional harm, and the courts must decide based on the violation of the Constitution and not only on the violation of statutes because on the contrary, it will not be a constitutional action for *amparo* but rather another type of recourse, for instance, the judicial review action against administrative acts whose annulatory effects do not correspond with the restitutory effects of the *amparo*.

605. Regarding the second mean for protection, the right to *amparo* can also be enforced by filing an *amparo* petition conjunctly with other pre-existing actions, recourses and proceedings, for which the Amparo Law provides the following possibilities:

> First, according to Article 3 of the Amparo Law, it is possible to file an amparo petition against statutes, bringing the petition together or jointly with the popular action of unconstitutionality of statutes exercised before the Constitutional Chamber of the Supreme Tribunal of Justice. In these cases, when the popular action is founded on the violation of a constitutional right or guaranty by the statute, the Organic Law authorizes the Supreme Tribunal to suspend the effects of the disputed statute regarding the specific case and in some cases with general effects, pending the issue of the requested decision on the nullity of the statute. Since the amparo petition is subordinate to the nullity action

673. *See* the text in *Revista de Derecho Público*, No. 47 (Caracas: Editorial Jurídica Venezolana, 1991), 169–174.
674. *See* in *Revista de Derecho Público*, No. 50 (Caracas: Editorial Jurídica Venezolana, 1992), 183–184.

against statutes, the amparo decision in the proceeding has a preliminary character of suspending the effects of the challenged statute pending the Court's decision on the merits of the nullity of the statute.

606. Second, according to Article 5 of the Amparo Law, as already mentioned, it expressly establishes that the petition for *amparo* against administrative acts and against Public Administration omissions may also be brought before the corresponding courts of the Administrative Jurisdiction (*Jurisdicción contencioso-administrativa*) jointly with the judicial review of administrative actions' recourses (*see infra* paragraph 706).

In such cases, when the recourse is founded in the violation of a constitutional right by the challenged administrative act, the general admissibility conditions of the *contencioso administrativo* nullity recourse have been made more flexible, in particular referring to the need to previously exhaust the existing administrative procedures, and to the term for the filing of the recourse; conditions that have been eliminated when the petition for *amparo* is filed jointly with the nullity recourse. In such cases, in addition, the courts are allowed to adopt immediate steps for the reduction of procedure terms, and also have the power to suspend the effects of the challenged administrative acts while the nullity action is decided (Articles 5 and 6.5). Also, in these cases, the *amparo* protection is reduced to the suspension of the effects of the challenged administrative act pending the court's decision on the nullity of the challenged act.

607. Third and finally, according to Article 6.6 of the same Amparo Law, it is implicitly recognized that the claim for *amparo* may also be brought before the courts jointly with any other 'ordinary judicial procedures' or with the 'pre-existing judicial means', through which the 'violation or threat of violation of a constitutional right or guaranty may be alleged'. In these cases, for instance, the *amparo* petition can be filed jointly with the recourse of cassation when the claim against the challenged judicial decision is based on violations of a constitutional right or guarantee. In such cases, the Cassation Chambers of the Supreme Tribunal shall follow the procedure and terms established in the Organic Law of Amparo (Article 6.5) and the recourse will anyway have the effect of suspending the challenged decision.

All these cases of *amparo* petitions in Venezuela, do not substitute the ordinary or extraordinary judicial means allowing the *amparo* claim to be filed jointly with those other judicial means.

§3. The Universal Character of the *Amparo* Proceeding

608. From all these regulations, the Venezuelan right for *amparo* has certain peculiarities that distinguish it from the other similar institutions for the protection of the constitutional rights and guarantees established in Latin America. Besides the adjective consequences of the *amparo* being a constitutional right, it can be characterized by the following trends.[675]

First, the right of *amparo* can be exercised in Venezuela for the guarantee of *all* constitutional rights, not only of civil rights, freedoms or individual rights. Consequently, the social, economic, cultural, environmental, political and indigenous people's rights declared in the Constitution and in international treaties are also justiciable and protected by means of *amparo*. The habeas corpus *action* is an aspect of the right to constitutional protection or one of the expressions of the *amparo*. Until 2021 was regulated in the Organic Law of Amparo when a specific Law was issued regarding the protection of personal liberty and security.[676]

Second, the right to *amparo* seeks to assure protection of constitutional rights and guarantees against *any disturbance* in their enjoyment and exercise, whether originated by *public* authorities or by *private* individuals, without distinction. In the case of disturbance by public authorities, the *amparo* is admissible in Venezuela against statutes, and also against legislative, administrative and judicial acts, as well as against material or factual courses of action of Public Administration or public officials.

Third, the judicial adjudication on *amparo* matters as a consequence of the exercise of this right to *amparo*, whether through the pre-existing actions or recourses or by means of the autonomous action for *amparo*, is not limited to be of a precautionary or preliminary nature, but is conceived to re-establish the infringed legal situation by deciding on the merits, that is, the legality and legitimacy of the alleged disturbance of the constitutional right or guarantee.

Fourth, since the Venezuelan system of judicial review is a mixed one (*see supra* paragraph 675), judicial review of legislation can also be exercised by the courts when deciding action for *amparo*. This can happen, for instance, when the alleged violation of the right is based on a statute deemed unconstitutional. In such cases, if the protection requested is granted by the courts, it must previously declare the statute inapplicable on the grounds of it being unconstitutional. Therefore, in such cases, judicial review of the constitutionality of legislation (diffuse method) can also be exercised when an action for *amparo* of fundamental rights is filed.

609. Finally, it must also be mentioned that in the Venezuelan systems of judicial review and of *amparo*, the 1999 Constitution introduced an extraordinary means of review recourse which allows the Constitutional Chamber of the Supreme Court to issue final judgments in all cases of constitutional importance decided by lower courts. This extraordinary review recourse can be filed, in effect, against judicial final decisions issued in *amparo* suits and also, against any judicial decision issued

---

675. *See* Allan R. Brewer-Carías, 'La acción de amparo en Venezuela y su universalidad', in *Génesis, Desarrollo y Actualidad de Amparo en América Latina*, ed. José de Jesús Naveja Macía (Coord.), vol. I (Tijuana México: Ediciones Ilcsa), 109–141; 'El proceso constitucional de amparo en Venezuela: su universalidad y su inefectividad en el régimen autoritario', in *Horizontes Contemporáneos del Derecho Procesal Constitucional. Liber Amicorum Néstor Pedro Sagüés* (Lima: Centro de Estudios Constitucionales del Tribunal Constitucional, 2011).

676. *See* Ley Orgánica de Amparo a la Libertad y seguridad personal, in *Gaceta Oficial* No 6651 Extra. of 22 Sep. 2021.

when the diffuse judicial review method is exercised resolving the inapplicability of statutes because they are considered unconstitutional (Article 336.10).

The essential trend of this attribution of the Constitutional Chamber is the discretionary character that allows it to choose the cases to be reviewed. As the same Constitutional Chamber of the Supreme Tribunal pointed out in its Decision No. 727 of 8 April 2003:

> in the cases of the decisions subject to revision, the Constitution does not provide for the creation of a third instance. What has set forth the constitutional provision is an exceptional and discretional power of the Constitutional Chamber that as such, must be exercised with maxim prudence regarding the admission of recourses for reviewing final judicial decisions.[677]

677. Case: *Revisión de la sentencia dictada por la Sala Electoral en fecha 21 de noviembre de 2002*, in *evista de Derecho Público*, Nos 93–96 (Caracas: Editorial Jurídica Venezolana, 2003).

Chapter 7. Constitutional Duties

610. In addition to the enunciation of rights, the Constitution also enumerates constitutional duties, in some cases of Venezuelans, and in general of all persons. In this sense, Venezuelans have the duty to honour and defend their native land symbols and cultural values and to guard and protect the sovereignty, nationhood, territorial integrity, self-determination and interests of the nation (Article 130); but everyone has the duty to comply with and obey the Constitution and the laws and other official acts of the public entities (Article 131); to fulfil his or her social responsibilities and participate together in the political, civic and community life of the country, promoting and protecting human rights as the foundation of democratic coexistence and social peace (Article 132); to contribute with public expenditures by paying such taxes, assessments and contributions as may be established by law (Article 133); of rendering its services in the electoral functions assigned to them by law; and to perform such civilian or military service as may be necessary for the defence, preservation and development of the country, or to deal with situations involving a public calamity. Nonetheless, a guarantee is established in the sense that no one shall be subjected to forcible recruitment (Article 134).

611. In addition, the Constitution declares education as a fundamental social duty; therefore, it is free of charge and obligatory. For such purpose, the State must assume the responsibility for it as an irrevocable function of the greatest interest, at all levels and in all modes, as an instrument of scientific, humanistic and technical knowledge at the service of society (Article 102). In Article 87 of the Constitution, work is also considered as a duty of all persons, imposing upon the State the need to adopt the necessary measures so that every person could be able to obtain productive work providing a dignified and decorous living (Article 87).

612. Finally, Article 76 of the Constitution also imposes duties related to family, providing that the father and mother have the shared and inescapable obligation of raising, training, educating, maintaining and caring for their children; and also that the latter has the duty to provide care when the former is unable to do so by themselves. The necessary and proper measures to guarantee the enforceability of the obligation to provide alimony shall be established by law.

613. In all cases of obligations imposed upon the State according to the general social welfare objectives, according to Article 135, these obligations do not preclude the ones which, by virtue of solidarity, social responsibility and humanitarian assistance, corresponds to private individuals according to their abilities. Appropriate provisions shall be enacted by law to compel the fulfilment of these obligations when necessary. Those aspiring to practice any profession have a duty to perform community service for such period, in such place and on such terms as may be provided for by law.

Part X. The Constitutional Regime of the Economy

614. The 1999 Constitution, also following the general trend of the 1961 Constitution,[678] in addition to the political and social constitutions, contains an economic constitution in which are established the principles governing the economy, including the respective roles played by private initiative and the State in this field. According to these provisions, since the beginning of the oil exploitation, and particularly during the second half of the twentieth century, the economic system that has been developed in Venezuela is one of mixed economy or of 'social market economy',[679] which combines economic freedom, private initiative and a free market economic model (as opposed to the model of a State-directed economy), and the possibility of State intervention in the economy in order to uphold principles of social justice. This has been possible, particularly because of the special position of the State as owner of the subsoil and of the oil industry which since 1975 was nationalized[680] (*see infra* paragraph 661). This has made the State the most powerful economic entity in the nation, leading it to intervene in the country's economic activity in important ways.

678. *See* Allan R. Brewer-Carías, 'Reflexiones sobre la Constitución Económica', in *Estudios sobre la Constitución Española. Homenaje al Profesor Eduardo García de Enterría* (Madrid, 1991), 3839–3853; Ignacio de León, 'A cinco años de la Constitución Económica de 1999. Un balance de la gestión', in *Tendencias Actuales del Derecho Constitucional. Homenaje a Jesús María Casal Montbrun*, ed. Jesús María Casal, Alfredo Arismendi y Carlos Luis Carrillo Artiles (Coord.), vol. II (Caracas: Universidad Central de Venezuela/Universidad Católica Andrés Bello, 2008), 379–406.

679. *See* Henrique Meier, 'La Constitución económica', in *Revista de Derecho Corporativo*, 1, no. 1 (Caracas, 2001), 9–74; Ana C. Nuñez Machado, 'Los principios económicos de la Constitución de 1999', in *Revista de Derecho Constitucional,* No. 6 (enero-diciembre) (Caracas: Editorial Sherwood, 2002), 129–140; Claudia Briceño Aranguren y Ana C. Núñez Machado, 'Aspectos económicos de la nueva Constitución', in *Comentarios a la Constitución de la República Bolivariana de Venezuela* (Caracas: Vadell Hermanos, Editores, 2000), 177 y ss.; Jesús Ollarves Irazábal, 'La vigencia constitucional de los Derechos Ecónomicos y Sociales en Venezuela', in *Libro Homenaje a Enrique Tejera París, Temas sobre la Constitución de 1999* (Caracas: Centro de Investigaciones Jurídicas (CEIN), 2001), 159 a 192.

680. *See* Organic Law that reserves to the State the Industry and Commerce of Hydrocarbons, *Gaceta Oficial* Extra, No. 1.769 of 29 Aug. 1975. *See* Allan R. Brewer-Carías, 'Introducción al Régimen Jurídico de las Nacionalizaciones en Venezuela', in *Archivo de Derecho Público y Ciencias de la Administración*, vol. I, vol. III, 1972–1979 (Caracas: Instituto de Derecho Público, Facultad de Ciencias Jurídicas y Políticas, Universidad Central de Venezuela, 1981), 23–44.

Chapter 1. Principles of the Economic System

615. It is precisely within this context that Article 299 of the 1999 Constitution sets forth that the social-economic regime of the Republic shall be based on the principles of social justice, democratization, efficiency, free competition, protection of the environment, productivity and solidarity, with a view to ensuring overall human development and a dignified and useful existence for the community. For these purposes, this very Article of the Constitution expressly sets forth that the State must, 'jointly with private initiative', promote:

> the harmonious development of the national economy for the purpose of generating sources of employment, a high national level of added value, in order to elevate the standard of living of the population and strengthen the nation's economic sovereignty, guaranteeing legal certainty, solidity, dynamism, sustainability, permanence, and economic growth with equity, in order to guarantee a just distribution of wealth by means of strategic democratic, participative and open planning.

616. The economic system is therefore based upon economic freedom, private initiative and free competition, although in combination with the participation of the State as a promoter of economic development, a regulator of economic activity, and a planner, together with civil society. As the Constitutional Chamber of the Supreme Tribunal of Justice stated in its Decision No. 117 of 6 February 2001,[681] this is 'a socioeconomic system that is in between a free market (in which the State acts as a simple programmer (*programador*) for an economy that is dependent upon the supply and demand of goods and services) and an interventionist economy (in which the State actively intervenes as the "primary entrepreneur")'. The Constitution promotes, 'joint economic activity between the State and private initiative in the pursuit of, and in order to concretely realize the supreme values consecrated in the Constitution', and in order to pursue 'the equilibrium of all the forces of the market, and, joint activity between the State and private initiative'. In accordance with this system, the Courts ruled, the Constitution:

> advocates a series of superior normative values with respect to the economic regimen, consecrating free enterprise within the framework of a market economy and, fundamentally, within the framework of the Social State under the Rule of Law (the Welfare State, the State of Well-being or the Social-Democratic State). This is a social State that is opposed to authoritarianism.[682]

681. *See* in *Revista de Derecho Público,* Nos 85–88 (Caracas: Editorial Jurídica Venezolana, 2001), 212–218.

682. The values that are alluded to, according to the doctrine of the Constitutional Chamber, 'are developed through the concept of free enterprise' (*libertad de empresa*) which encompasses both the notion of a subjective right 'to dedicate oneself to the economic activity of one's choice', and a principle of economic regulation according to which the will of the business (*voluntad de la empresa*) to make its own decisions is manifest. The State fulfils its role of intervention in this context. Intervention can be direct (through businesses) or indirect (as an entity regulating the market).

Nonetheless, in practice, particularly during the decade 2000–2011, this framework has been changed, due to the authoritarian government that has been developed, inclining the balance toward the State participation in the economy, through a process of progressively 'statization' of the economy, reducing economic freedom and increasing the dependency of the country on oil exploitation.[683]

§1. Private Economic Rights

I. Right to Exercise Economic Activities

617. Title III of the 1999 Constitution on constitutional rights and guarantees also contains a declaration of the economic rights (Chapter VII, Articles 112–118), including, economic freedom, and the right to private property.

Regarding economic freedom, Article 112 of the Constitution declares the right of all persons to develop the economic activity of their choice, without other limits than those established by statute for reasons of human development, security, sanitation, environment protection and other social interests. In any case, the State must promote private initiative, guaranteeing the creation of wealth and its just distribution, as well as the production of goods and services in order to satisfy the needs of the population, freedom to work, and free enterprise, commerce and industry, without prejudice to the power of the State to promulgate measures to plan, rationalize and regulate the economy and promote the overall development of the country.

618. In 2007, by means of the Constitutional Reform Draft that was rejected by referendum held in December of that same year, the President of the Republic proposed to eliminate this constitutional provision guaranteeing economic freedom, substituting it with one provision that defines, as a matter of State policy, the obligation to promote:

> the development of a Productive Economic Model, that is intermediate, diversified and independent ... founded upon the humanistic values of cooperation and the preponderance of common interests over individual ones, guaranteeing the meeting of the people's social and material needs, the greatest possible political and social stability, and the greatest possible sum of happiness.

The proposal added that the State, in the same way, 'shall promote and develop different forms of businesses and economic units from social property, both directly or communally, as well as indirectly or through the state', According to this norm, additionally, the State was to promote, 'economic units of social production and/or

---

Ibid. See on the decision, José Ignacio Hernández, 'Constitución económica y privatización (Comentarios a la sentencia de la Sala Constitucional del 6 de febrero de 2001)', en *Revista de Derecho Constitucional,* No. 5, julio-diciembre-2001 (Caracas: Editorial Sherwood, 2002), 327–342.

683. As reported by Simón Romero in 'Chávez Reopens Oil Bids to West as Prices Plunge', published in *The New York Times* on 12 Jan. 2009, 1, in 2009 Venezuela 'reliant on oil for about 93% of its export revenue in 2008, up from 69% in 1998'.

distribution, that may be mixed properties held between the State, the private sector, and the communal power, so as to create the best conditions for the collective and cooperative construction of a Socialist Economy'.

The 2007 Constitutional reform proposals on economic matters, although rejected by the people in the referendum of December 2007, were nonetheless implemented in 2010, of course violating the Constitution, through the Organic Law on the Communal Economic System[684] (*see infra* paragraphs 664 et seq.).

II. Property Rights

619. Regarding the right to property, Article 115 of the Constitution, although following the orientation of the previous 1961 Constitution,[685] in the sense of guaranteeing the right to property, did not establish private property as having a 'social function' to be accomplished, as did the 1961 Constitution. Nonetheless, it provides that property shall be subject to such contributions, restrictions and obligations as may be established by law in the service of the public or general interest. However, Article 115 defines the attributes of the right to property that traditionally were only enumerated in the Civil Code (Article 545), that is, the right to use, the enjoyment and the disposition of property are now in the Constitution.[686]

This constitutional regime regarding property rights was proposed to be radically changed in the 2007 rejected Constitutional Reforms, in which the President of the Republic sought to eliminate private property as a constitutionally protected right, and substitute the right's conception by a recognition of private property only referred to 'assets for use and consumption or as means of production', altogether with other forms of properties, and in particular, public property. The proposed reform regarding Article 115 of the Constitution tended to recognize and guarantee 'different forms of property' instead of guaranteeing the right to private property, enumerating them as follows: public property, as the one that belongs to State entities; social property, as the one that belongs to the people jointly and to future generations; collective property, as the one pertaining to social groups or persons, exploited for their common benefit, use, or enjoyment, that may be of social or private origin; mixed property, as the one constituted between the public sector, the social sector, the collective sector and the private sector, in different combinations, for the exploitation of resources or the execution of activities, subject always to the absolute economic and social sovereignty of the nation; and private property, as the

684. *See* Organic Law on the Communal Economic System, *Gaceta Oficial* No. 6.011 Extra. of 21 Dec. 2010. *See* the comments in Allan R. Brewer-Carías, 'Sobre la Ley Orgánica del Sistema Económico Comunal o de cómo se implanta en Venezuela un sistema económico comunista sin reformar la Constitución', in *Revista de Derecho Público*, No. 124 (Caracas: Editorial Jurídica Venezolana, 2010), 102–109.

685. *See* Allan R. Brewer-Carías 'El derecho de propiedad y libertad económica. Evolución y situación actual en Venezuela', in *Estudios sobre la Constitución. Libro Homenaje a Rafael Caldera,* vol. II (Caracas, 1979), 1139–1246.

686. *See*, José L. Villegas Moreno, 'El derecho de propiedad en la Constitución de 1999', in *Estudios de Derecho Administrativo: Libro Homenaje a la Universidad Central de Venezuela,* vol. II (Caracas: Imprenta Nacional, 2001), 565–582.

one owned by 'natural or legal persons, only regarding assets for use or consumption, or as means of production legitimately acquired'.

620. Regarding expropriation, Article 115 of the Constitution establishes that it can be decreed regarding any kind of property only for reasons of public benefit or social interest, by means of a judicial process and payment of just compensation.[687] Consequently, the Constitution prohibits confiscation (expropriation without compensation), except in cases permitted by the Constitution itself, regarding property of persons responsible for crimes committed against public property, or who have illicitly enriched themselves exercising public offices. Confiscations may also take place regarding property deriving from business, financial or any other activities connected with illicit trafficking of psychotropic or narcotic substances (Articles 116 and 271).

621. Article 307 of the Constitution declares the regimen of large private real estate holdings *(latifundio)* to be contrary to social interests, charging the legislator to tax idle lands, and establish the necessary measures to transform them into productive economic units, as well as to recover arable land. The same constitutional provision entitles peasants to own land, constitutionalizing the obligation of the State to protect and promote associative and private forms of property in order to guarantee agricultural production and oversee sustainable arrangements on arable lands to guarantee its food-producing potential. In exceptional cases, the same Article requires that the legislature must establish federal tax revenue to provide funds for financing, research, technical assistance, transfer of technology and other activities aimed at raising productivity and competitiveness of the agricultural sector.

III. Quality Services and Good Rights

622. However, Article 117 contains a constitutional innovation in the economic area, providing for the right of all persons to access goods and services of good quality, as well as adequate and non-misleading information regarding the content and characteristics of the products and services they consume; to freedom of choice with respect to them; and be treated fairly and with dignity. The mechanisms necessary to guarantee these rights, the standards of quality and quantity for goods and

687. *See* the Law on Expropriation because public and social needs, *Gaceta Oficial* No. 37.475 of 1 Jul. 2002. *See* Allan R. Brewer-Carías et al., *Ley de expropiación por causa de utilidad pública o social* (Caracas, 2003); Eloísa Avellaneda Sisto, 'La expropiación en la legislación venezolana', in *Tendencias Actuales del Derecho Constitucional. Homenaje a Jesús María Casal Montbrun*, ed. Jesús María Casal, Alfredo Arismendi y Carlos Luis Carrillo Artiles (Coord.), vol. II (Caracas: Universidad Central de Venezuela/Universidad Católica Andrés Bello, 2008), 407–442; Karina Anzola Spadaro, 'La expropiación y la ocupación temporal en Venezuela', in *Revista de Derecho n 26* (Caracas: Tribunal Supremo de Justicia, 2008), 201–222.

services, consumer protection procedures, compensation for damages caused and appropriate penalties for the violation of these rights shall be established by law.[688]

IV. Popular Economy Rights

623. Article 118 of the Constitution also recognized the right of workers and of the community to develop associations of social and participative nature such as cooperatives, savings funds, mutual funds and other forms of association, in order to develop any kind of economic activities in accordance with the law. The law shall recognize the specificity of these organizations, especially those relating to the cooperative, the associated work and the generation of collective benefits. The State shall promote and protect these associations destined to improve the popular economic alternative.[689]

V. Limits to Private Economic Activities

624. Article 113 of the Constitution prohibits monopolies. Consequently, any act, activity, conduct or agreement of private individuals which is intended to establish a monopoly or which leads by reason of its actual effects to the existence of a monopoly, regardless of the intentions of the persons involved, and whatever the form it actually takes, is declared contrary to the fundamental principles of this Constitution. Also contrary to such principles is the abuse of a position of dominance which a private individual, a group of individuals or a business enterprise or group of enterprises acquires or has acquired in a given market of goods or services, regardless of what factors caused such position of dominance; or the case of a concentration of demand. In all of the cases indicated, the State shall be required to adopt such measures as may be necessary to prevent the harmful and restrictive effects of monopoly, abuse of a position of dominance and a concentration of demand, with the purpose of protecting consumers and producers and ensuring the existence of genuine competitive conditions in the economy.

625. In the case of the exploitation of natural resources which are the property of the Nation or in the case of public services rendered by private entities, on an exclusive basis or otherwise, the State shall grant concessions for a certain period, in all cases ensuring the existence of adequate compensation regarding public interest (Article 113).

688. Law on the Venezuelan System of Quality, *Gaceta Oficial* No. 37.555 of 23 Oct. 2002; Law on the Persons' Access to Goods and Services Defence, *Gaceta Oficial* No. 39.358 of 1 Feb. 2010.

689. The Law on the Promotion and Development of Popular Economy of 2008, *Gaceta Oficial* No. 5.890 Extra. of 31 Jul. 2008. was substituted by the Organic Law on the Communal Economic System, *Gaceta Oficial* No. 6.011 Extra. of 21 Dec. 2010.

§2. State Participation in the Economy Regime

I. State Promotion of Economic Activities

626. The Constitution also regulates various forms of State economic intervention that have developed in Venezuela in the last decades. In this regard, the Constitution regulates the State as a promoter, that is, without substituting private initiatives, to foster and order the economy in order to ensure the development of private initiatives. In this regard, Article 112 sets forth that in any case, the State must promote private initiative, guaranteeing the creation of wealth and its just distribution, as well as the production of goods and services in order to satisfy the needs of the population, freedom to work, and the free enterprise, commerce and industry, without prejudice to the power of the State to promulgate measures to plan, rationalize and regulate the economy and promote the overall development of the country.

627. In this same regard, Article 299 sets forth that the State, jointly with private initiative, shall promote the harmonious development of the national economy, to the end of generating sources of employment, a high rate of domestic added value, raising the standard of living of the population and strengthening the economic sovereignty of the country; and guaranteeing the reliability of the law, as well as the solid, dynamic, sustainable, continuing and equitable growth of the economy, to ensure a just distribution of wealth through participatory democratic strategic planning with open consultation.

628. Specifically, regarding agricultural activities, Article 305 of the Constitution establishes that the State shall promote sustainable agriculture as the strategic basis for overall rural development, and consequently shall guarantee the population a secure food supply, defined as the sufficient and stable availability of food within the national sphere and timely and uninterrupted access to the same for consumers. A secure food supply must be achieved by developing and prioritizing internal agricultural and livestock production, understood as production deriving from the activities of agriculture, livestock, fishing and aquaculture. Food production is in the national interest and is fundamental to the economic and social development of the Nation. To this end, the State shall promulgate such financial, commercial, technological transfer, land tenancy, infrastructure, manpower training and other measures as may be necessary to achieve strategic levels of self-sufficiency. In addition, it shall promote actions in the national and international economic context to compensate for the disadvantages inherent to agricultural activity. The State shall protect the settlement and communities of non-industrialized fishermen, as well as their fishing banks in continental waters and those close to the coastline, as defined by law.

629. Regarding rural development, Article 306 imposes on the State the duty to promote conditions for overall rural development, for the purpose of generating employment and ensuring the rural population an adequate level of well-being, as well as their inclusion in national development. It shall likewise promote agricultural activity and optimum land use by providing infrastructure projects, supplies, loans, training services and technical assistance.

630. Regarding industrial activities, the Constitution (Article 308) imposes on the State the role of protecting and promoting small and medium-sized manufacturers, cooperatives, savings funds, family-owned businesses, small businesses and any other form of community association for purposes of work, savings and consumption, under an arrangement of collective ownership, to strengthen the country's economic development, based on the initiative of the people. Training, technical assistance and appropriate financing shall be guaranteed. However, Article 309 provides that typical Venezuelan crafts and folk industries shall enjoy the special protection of the State, in order to preserve their authenticity, and they shall receive credit facilities to promote production and marketing.

631. On commercial matters, Article 301 reserves to the State the use of trade policy to protect the economic activities of public and private Venezuelan enterprises. In this regard, more advantageous status than those established for Venezuelan nationals shall not be granted to foreign persons, enterprises or entities. Foreign investment is subject to the same conditions as domestic investment.

632. Finally, Article 310 of the Constitution declares tourism as an economic activity of national interest, and of high priority in the country's strategy of diversification and sustainable development. As part of the foundation of the socioeconomic regime contemplated by the Constitution, the State shall promulgate measures to guarantee the development of tourism and shall create and strengthen a national tourist industry.

II. State Economic Planning

633. Regarding economic planning, Article 112 empowers the State to promulgate measures to plan, rationalize and regulate the economy and promote the overall development of the country. The President of the Republic must formulate the National Plan of Development and, once approved by the National Assembly, direct its execution (Articles 187.8, 236.18). Since 2007 a centralized system of planning has been established in the country[690] followed by the structuring of the Communal Economic System (*see infra* paragraphs 664 ff.).

690. *See* the Organic Law on Popular Planning *Gaceta Oficial* No. 6.011 Extra. of 21 Dec. 2010; and the Law on Creation of the Central Planning Commission, *Gaceta Oficial* No. 5.990 Extra. of 29 Jul. 2010. *See* on this planning centralized system Allan R. Brewer-Carías, 'Comentarios sobre la inconstitucional creación de la Comisión Central de Planificación, centralizada y obligatoria' in *Revista de Derecho Público*', No. 110 (Caracas: Editorial Jurídica Venezolana, 2007), 79–89.

III. State Direct Assumption of Economic Activities

634. No provisions are established in the Constitution in order for the State to promote highly qualified or heavy industries, and what is established is for the State the possibility to reserve for its own exploitation, through an organic law and by reasons of national convenience, the petroleum industry (already nationalized since 1975) and other industries, operations and goods and services which are in the public interest and of a strategic nature. The State shall promote the domestic manufacture of raw materials deriving from the exploitation of non-renewable natural resources, with a view to assimilating, creating and inventing technologies, generating employment and economic growth and creating wealth and well-being for the people (Article 302).

635. As aforementioned, based on a similar constitutional provision establishing the power of the State to reserve for its own exploitation services or resources (Article 97, 1961 Constitution), the oil industry was nationalized in 1975, being managed by a State-owned enterprise, *Petróleos de Venezuela S.A.*, regarding which, Article 303 of the 1999 Constitution set forth that for economic and political sovereignty and national strategy reasons, the State shall retain all shares of such public enterprise, but with the exception of its subsidiaries, strategic joint ventures, enterprises and any other ventures established or to be established as a consequence of the carrying on of the business of *Petróleos de Venezuela, S.A.* This last possibility has been considered as a loosening of the strict nationalization process carried out through the 1975 Organic Law that reserves to the State the Industry and Commercialization of Hydrocarbons.[691] In this regard, the 2000 Organic Law on Hydrocarbons allowed the establishment of mixed companies for the exploitation of primary hydrocarbon activities, although with the State as majority shareholder,[692] which was implemented in 2006–2007.[693]

---

691. *See* Allan R. Brewer-Carías, 'El régimen de participación del capital privado en las industrias petrolera y minera: Desnacionalización y regulación a partir de la Constitución de 1999', in *VII Jornadas Internacionales de Derecho Administrativo Allan R. Brewer-Carías, El Principio de Legalidad y el Ordenamiento Jurídico-Administrativo de la Libertad Económica* (Caracas: noviembre 2004). Fundación de Estudios de Derecho Administrativo FUNEDA, Caracas Noviembre, 2004 15–58.

692. Ley Orgánica de Hidrocarburos, *Gaceta Oficial* No. 38.493 of 4 Aug. 2006.

693. *See* Allan R. Brewer-Carías, 'The "Statization" of the Pre 2001 Primary Hydrocarbons Joint Venbture Exploitations: Their Unilateral termination and the Assets' Confiscation of Some of the Former Private parties' in OGEL Intelligence, www.gasandoil.com/ogel/ ISSN: 1875-418X, vol. 6, issue 2 (OGEL/TDM Special Issue on Venezuela: The battle of Contract Sanctity vs. Resource Sovereignty, ed. By Elizabeth Eljuri), April 2008; and 'La estatización de los convenios de asociación que permitían la participación del capital privado en las actividades primarias de hidrocarburos sucritos antes de 2002, mediante su terminación anticipada y unilateral y la confiscación de los bienes afectos a los mismos', in *Nacionalización, Libertad de Empresa y Asociaciones Mixtas*, ed. Víctor Hernández Mendible (Coordinador) (Caracas: Editorial Jurídica Venezolana, 2008), 123–1 88. *See also* Allan R. Brewer-Carías, *Crónica de una destrucción. Concesión, Nacionalización, Apertura, Constitucionalización, Desnacionalización, Estatización, Entrega y Degradación de la Industria Petrolera*, (Caracas, Editorial Jurídica Venezolana, 2018).

636. However, regarding public enterprises in general, Article 300 of the Constitution refers to the statutes to determine the conditions for the creation of functionally decentralized entities to carry out social or entrepreneurial activities, with a view to ensuring the reasonable economic and social productivity of the public resources invested in such activities.

637. All the aforementioned provisions regarding the participation of the State in the economy were proposed to be radically changed in the rejected 2007 Constitutional Reform Draft, in which the whole economic role of the State pretended to be reduced to promote and develop economic and social activities 'under the principles of the socialist economy' (Article 300). Nonetheless, this has been achieved through an extended process of nationalization and confiscation of private assets executed during the past years (*see supra* paragraphs 661 et seq.), and by the formal enacting of a Communal Economic System based on the social property of all means of production (*see infra* paragraph 664).

Chapter 2. Taxation Regimen

638. The Constitution also establishes the general principles of the taxation regimen, providing in Article 316 that the tax system must seek a fair distribution of public burden (taxation), following the principle of progressive taxation according to the economic capacity of taxpayers; for the protection of the national economy and the raising of the standard of living of the population, sustaining itself through efficient collections.[694]

639. The Constitution also establishes the general principle of 'tributary legality', that is, that all taxes must always be created by statute approved by the representatives of the people, which must also be the one to provide for exemptions, reductions and any other incentives (Article 317).[695] In addition, the principle that taxes shall never have a confiscatory effect is also expressly established.[696]

640. Almost all taxation powers have been attributed to the national (federal level of government) but in addition, Article 156.13 of the Constitution assigns the National Assembly the power to enact legislation in order to guarantee the coordination and harmonization of the different national, state and municipal government taxation power. Such legislation shall define appropriate principles, parameters and limitations; determine the types of taxes or aliquots of state and municipal taxes; and establish specific funds for the purpose of ensuring inter-territorial solidarity.[697]

641. But the Constitution also establishes some prohibitions for the states and municipalities in taxation matters. For instance, on matters of agriculture, animal husbandry, fisheries and forest activities, the states and municipalities can only tax

---

694. *See* Gabriel Ruán Santos, 'Principios substantivos de la tributación en la Constitución de 1999', in *Revista de Derecho Corporativo* 1, No. 2 (Caracas, 2001), 11–38; Moisés Ballenilla Tolosa y otros, 'El régimen tributario constitucional', in *Comentarios a la Constitución de la República Bolivariana de Venezuela* (Caracas: Vadell Hermanos Editores, 2000), 117–148; Alejandro R. Van Der Velde; Antonio Planchart Mendoza; Adriana Vigilanza García, 'El poder tributario antes y después de la Constitución de 1999', in *Revista de Derecho Constitucional,* No. 3 (julio-diciembre) (Caracas: Editorial Sherwood, 2000), 187–228; Juan D. Alfonzo Paradisi, 'El Poder Tributario y los derechos y garantías constitucionales como límites a su ejercicio', in *El Derecho Público a comienzos del siglo XXI. Estudios homenaje al Profesor Allan R. Brewer-Carías,* vol. III (Madrid: Instituto de Derecho Público, UCV, Civitas Ediciones, 2003), 3151–3184.

695. *See* Eduardo E. Meier García, 'Reflexiones sobre el sistema tributario y el principio de legalidad tributaria en la Constitución de 1999', in *Revista de Derecho Corporativo* 2, No. 1 (Caracas, 2002), 73–124.

696. *See* Allan R. Brewer-Carías, 'Les protections constitutionnelles et légales contre les impositions confiscatoires', in *Rapports Generaux. XIII Congrès International de Droit Comparé* (Montreal, 1990), 795–824.

697. *See* Manuel Rachadell, 'La distribución del poder tributario entre los diversos niveles del Poder Público según la Constitución de 1999', in *Revista de Derecho Administrativo,* No. 8 *(enero-abril)* (Caracas: Editorial Sherwood, 2000), 179–205; Adriana Vigilanza García, 'Menú para la armonización y coordinación de la potestad tributaria de Estados y Municipios. Algunas reflexiones', in *Revista de Derecho Tributario*, No. 99 (abril-junio) (Caracas: Legislec Editores, 2003), 9–26, and in *Revista de Derecho Constitucional,* No. 6, enero-diciembre-2002 (Caracas: Editorial Sherwood, 2003), 213 a 230.

them at the opportunity, in the form prescribed by, and through measures permitted by national statute. This is confirmed in Article 183 of the Constitution that prohibits states and municipalities from creating taxes on matters reserved to the national level of government; from creating customs or taxing the import, export or transit of national or foreign goods; taxing consumption goods before entering in their territories; taxing them in a different way as those produced in their territory. The Constitution also prohibits the states and municipalities from forbidding the consumption of goods produced outside their territory.

Chapter 3. Budgetary System

642. Within the innovations of the 1999 Constitution are a set of provisions governing fiscal and budgetary issues, the monetary system, and macro-economic coordination, not only applicable to the national level of government but also to the states and municipalities (Article 311).

§1. Principles of Fiscal Policy

643. Article 311 of the Constitution established the general principles governing the fiscal policy, which must be based on efficiency, solvency, transparency, liability and fiscal balance. Fiscal policy is to be balanced over a multi-year budget framework, in such manner that ordinary revenues shall be sufficient to cover ordinary expenses. The National Executive must submit for enactment by the National Assembly a multi-year framework for budgeting that establishes the maximum limits of expenditures and indebtedness to be contemplated in national budgets. The characteristics of this framework, the requirements for modifying the same and the terms for carrying out are established in the Organic Law of State Financial Administration.[698] The Constitution also establishes the principle that any revenues generated by exploiting underground wealth (hydrocarbon) and minerals, in general, shall be used to finance real productive investment, education and health. All these principles and provisions established for national, economic and financial management shall also govern that of the states and municipalities, to the extent applicable.

§2. Principles of Public Debt Policy

644. According to Article 312 of the Constitution, public debt limits shall be set by law in accordance with a prudent level in terms of the size of the economy, reproductive investment and the ability to generate revenues to cover public debt service. In order to be valid, public credit transactions shall always require a special law authorizing them, with the exceptions established under the Organic Law on State Financial Administration. The special law shall indicate the modalities of the transactions and authorize the appropriate budget credits in the pertinent budget law. The annual special indebtedness law shall be submitted to the National Assembly together with the budget law. The State shall not recognize any obligations other than those assumed by lawful National Authority organs in accordance with law.

§3. Principles of Budget

645. Regarding budget, in particular, Article 313 of the Constitution establishes the general principle that the economic and financial management of the State shall

698. Organic Law on the Financial Administration of the Public Sector, *Gaceta Oficial* No. 39.556 of 19 Nov. 2010.

be governed by a budget approved annually by law. The National Executive shall submit the draft Budget Law or statute to the National Assembly at the time prescribed by the same Organic Law on State Financial Administration. Nonetheless, if the Executive Power fails for any reason to submit the budget bill within the time limit established by law, or the bill is rejected, the budget for the then current fiscal year shall be applicable.

646. Regarding the Budget draft law, the National Assembly has the power to alter budget items, but shall not authorize measures leading to a decrease in public revenues or to expenses exceeding the estimated revenue amounts in the budget bill (Article 313). In the annual public expense budgets at all levels of government, the specific objective to which each credit item in the budget is addressed shall be clearly established, as well as the concrete results expected and the public officials responsible for achieving these results. The latter shall be established in quantitative terms, by means of performance indicators, where this is technically possible (Article 315). Also, in each annual budget, the Constitutional Contribution to the States (*Situado Constitucional*) must be calculated in an amount equivalent to a minimum of 15% and a maximum of 20% of total ordinary national income (Article 167.4) (*see supra* paragraph 239).

647. In submitting the multi-year budget framework, the special indebtedness law and the annual budget, the National Executive Branch shall explicitly state the long-term objectives of fiscal Policy and explain how these objectives are to be achieved, in accordance with principles of responsibility and a fiscal balance (Article 313).

648. According to Article 314, a balanced budget is a constitutional principle, so no expense of any kind shall be disbursed unless the same has been provided for in the budget law. Additional budget credit items may be ordered to cover essential unforeseen expenses or items that had not been adequately funded only if the treasury has resources to cover the expenditure concerned; this shall be done only following a vote in favour by the Council of Ministers and authorization by the National Assembly, or in its absence, by the Delegated Commission. The Executive Power shall submit to the National Assembly within six months of the close of the fiscal year the annual accounting and budget implementation balance sheet for such fiscal year (Article 315).

Chapter 4. Monetary System and the Macro-economic Policies

649. In addition to the above-mentioned provisions on the State economic regime, for the first time in Venezuelan constitutional history, the text of the Constitution incorporates a set of norms regulating the monetary system, and in particular, the autonomy and role of the Central Bank of Venezuela, as well as the State's macro-economic policies (Articles 318–321).[699]

§1. Autonomy of the Central Bank of Venezuela Regarding the Monetary Policy

650. The monetary policy of the State, according to Article 318 of the Constitution, is attributed in an exclusive way to the Venezuelan Central Bank, whose fundamental objective is to achieve price stability and preserve the internal and foreign exchange value of the monetary unit. The Venezuelan Central Bank is conceived in the Constitution as a public law juridical person with autonomy to formulate and implement policies within its sphere of competence. The Venezuelan Central Bank shall perform its functions in coordination with general economic policy, in the interest of attaining the higher objectives of the State and the Nation. In order to provide for the adequate attainment of its objective, the functions of the Venezuelan Central Bank shall include those of formulating and implementing monetary policy, participating in the design of and implementing foreign exchange policy, currency regulation, credit and interest rates, administrating international reserves and any others established by law.[700]

651. According to Article 319 of the Constitution, the Venezuelan Central Bank shall be governed by the principle of public responsibility, to which end it shall render an accounting of its actions, goals and the results of its policies to the National Assembly, in accordance with law. It shall also issue periodic reports on the behaviour of the country's macroeconomic variables and on any other matters concerning which reports may be requested, including sufficient analysis to permit its evaluation. Failure to meet the objective and goals, without justifiable cause, shall result in removal of the Board of Directors and imposition of administrative penalties, in accordance with law.

652. The Venezuelan Central Bank shall be subject to oversight after the fact by the Office of the General Comptroller of the Republic and inspection and supervision by the public entity that supervises banking, which shall send to the National Assembly reports on the inspections it conducts. The budget of operating expenses of the Venezuelan Central Bank shall require discussion and approval by the

699. *See* Isabel C. Medina Ortiz, 'Comentarios acerca de las normas constitucionales y legales que regulan el funcionamiento del Banco Central de Venezuela', in *Revista del Tribunal Supremo de Justicia*, No. 8 (Caracas, 2003), 357–389.
700. Central Bank of Venezuela Law, *Gaceta Oficial* No. 39.419 of 7 May 2010.

National Assembly, and its accounts and balance sheets shall be subjected to independent audits on such terms as may be established by law.

653. Nonetheless, in the 2007 Constitutional Reform which was proposed by the President of the Republic and rejected by referendum, the purpose of it on these matters was to eliminate the Bank's competencies and autonomy, and render the Bank totally and directly dependent upon the National Executive. To this end, the following reforms were proposed and sanctioned by the National Assembly regarding Article 318 of the Constitution: to require that the national monetary system be directed towards the achievement of the essential ends of the 'Socialist State'; attribute the conduction of monetary policies to the National Executive and the Central Bank; eliminate the autonomy of the Bank, proposing to establish that it was to be subordinated to general economic policy and to the National Development Plan in order to achieve the 'superior objectives of the Socialist State'; and remove from the Central Bank the exclusive competency to administer international reserves, by proposing to place it under the administration and direction of the President of the Republic as administrator of the National Public Treasury. Although the 2007 Reform was rejected by the people on December 2007 (*see supra* paragraph 36), the fact is that because of the political and legislative practice of the authoritarian government that has been consolidated during the decade 2000–2011, the Central Bank has been completely controlled. In addition, all such reforms were implemented in 2010 through the establishment of the Organic Law of the Economic Communal System,[701] based on a centralized planning economy and the State ownership of the means of production (*see infra* paragraph 661).

§2. National Currency

654. The monetary unit of the Bolivarian Republic of Venezuela is the Bolívar. Nonetheless, the Constitution provides that in the event a common currency is instituted within the framework of Latin American and Caribbean integration, it shall be permissible to adopt the currency provided for by a treaty signed by the Republic (Article 318). Nonetheless, the Law on the Communal Economic System has provided in a way contrary to the Constitution, for the existence of 'communal currencies' at the communal level of the Communal State.[702]

§3. Macro-economic Policies

655. Regarding macroeconomic policies, the Constitution also innovated by providing the general framework for its coordination. In this regard, Article 320 establishes the general principle that the State must promote and defend economic

701. *Gaceta Oficial* No. 6.011 Extra. of 21 Dec. 2010.
702. *Ibid. See* Allan R. Brewer-Carías, 'Sobre la Ley Orgánica del Sistema Económico Comunal o de cómo se implanta en Venezuela un sistema económico comunista sin reformar la Constitución', in *Revista de Derecho Público*, No. 124 (Caracas: Editorial Jurídica Venezolana, 2010), 102–109.

stability, avoid its vulnerability, and watch over the monetary and price stability, in order to assure social welfare (Article 320). In order to facilitate the attaining of such objectives, the Minister of Finances and the Central Bank must contribute to the harmonization of the fiscal and monetary policies, although the Central Bank in the exercise of its functions shall not be subordinated to the Executive directives and would not avail or finance fiscal deficits.

The coordination between the National Executive and the Central Bank must be formalized in an annual agreement of policies, in which the final objectives of growth and its social repercussion must be expressed, as well as the external balance and inflation, regarding the fiscal, exchange and monetary policies. It must also include the levels of intermediate variables and required instruments in order to attain the final objectives. The agreement must be signed by the President of the Central Bank and the Minister of Finance and must be published once the Budget is approved by the National Assembly. They are responsible for the policy actions to be taken to be consistent with its objectives, so the agreement must specify the attained results, and the policies and actions to be achieved.

656. The Constitution also created a Macro-economic Stabilization Fund in charge of guaranteeing the stability of the public expenses at all National, state and municipal levels, regarding the ordinary income fluctuations. The Law on the Macroeconomic Stabilization Fund[703] has defined the basic principles the Constitution enumerated for its functioning: efficiency, equity and non-discrimination between the public entities that contribute to it with resources (Article 321).

703. *Gaceta Oficial* No. 38.846 of 9 Jan. 2008.

Chapter 5. Constitutional Provisions on Public Domain

657. The 1999 Constitution declares all mining and hydrocarbons deposits, of any nature, including those under the ocean floor in territorial waters, within Venezuela's exclusive economic zone, and on the continental shelf, as 'public domain' or public property (Article 12).[704] Consequently, according to the terms of Article 453 of the Civil Code, this property is inalienable and not subject to status of limitation.[705]

658. The same provision of Article 12 of the Constitution sets forth that the nation's sea coasts are within the public domain, meaning those of the nation's shores that touch the ocean, that is, the beaches between high and low tides.[706]

659. Article 304 of the Constitution provides, further, that all waters constitute property in the national public domain, irreplaceable for life and development. The Constitution provides that legislation is to be enacted as necessary to guarantee: the protection of national waters, and their productive use and recuperation while respecting the phases of the hydrological cycle, and criteria pertaining to a territorial order.[707]

660. Municipal land *(ejidos)* is considered in the Constitution as inalienable and imprescriptible. The Constitution establishes the presumption that all land without specific owner located in urban areas is considered as such *ejidos* (Article 181), although without prejudice to the legitimate and validly constituted rights of third parties.

704. *See* Isabel Boscán de Ruesta, 'La propiedad de los yacimientos de los hidrocarburos. Evolución histórica', in *El Derecho Público a comienzos del siglo XXI. Estudios homenaje al Profesor Allan R. Brewer-Carías,* vol. III (Madrid: Instituto de Derecho Público, UCV, Civitas Ediciones, 2003), 3061–3105.
705. The principle has also been established in the Mining Law (Art. 2), *Gaceta Oficial* No. 5382 of 28 Sep. 1999, and in the Organic Law on Gaseous Hydrocarbons (Art. 1), *Gaceta Oficial* No. 36.793 of 23 Sep. 1999. *See* Armando Rodríguez García, 'Comentarios sobre el régimen de los bienes públicos en la Constitución de 1999', in *Revista de Derecho Público,* No. 84 (octubre-diciembre) (Caracas: Editorial Jurídica Venezolana, 2000), 63–68.
706. Costal Zones Law, *Gaceta Oficial* No. 37.349 of 19 Dec. 2001. *See* Allan R. Brewer-Carías, 'El nuevo régimen de las zonas costeras. Inconstitucionalidades, dominio público, limitaciones a la propiedad privada e insuficiencias normativas' in *Ley Habilitante del 13 Nov. 2000 y sus Decretos Leyes*, No. 17 (Caracas: Academia de Ciencias Políticas y Sociales, Serie Eventos, 2002), 245–294.
707. Waters Law, *Gaceta Oficial* No. 38.595 of 2 Jan. 2007. *See*, Allan R. Brewer-Carías, *Ley de Aguas* (Caracas: Editorial Jurídica Venezolana, 2007).

Chapter 6. The Progressive Nationalization and State Ownership of the Economy

661. Within the general framework of the economic mixed system established in the Constitution, and due to the importance of oil exploitation, and oil income in the Venezuelan economy, during almost all the past hundred years, the State has been the most powerful component of the economic system. In 1975, the Oil Industry was nationalized (*see supra* paragraph 635).

As aforementioned, this explains why the Constitution is not only manifestly statist in its economic provisions but also establishes extended State responsibility for the management and provision of health, education, and social security services, as well as that of public utilities, including water, electricity and gas. The State has derived, through the regulation of these tasks, a complete set of powers to plan and control the economy, with wide possibilities of intervention in the private sector in some aspects, missing the necessary equilibrium between the public and private sectors. The only protected or privileged economic activities in the private sector are those that are *not* basic to the generation of wealth and employment in the country, such as agriculture (Article 305); handicraft and craft work (Article 309); small and medium business enterprises (Article 308), and tourism (Article 310). Added to this are the constitutional rules of control and sanctioning, such as those norms governing monopoly and other economic offences (Articles 113, 114); the declaration of the country's subsoil, sea coasts and waters to be within the public domain (Articles 112, 304); the State's reservation of rights in the oil industry; the possibility of similar State control in other exploitations, activities and services of a 'strategic nature'; and finally, the constitutional provisions that provide for the planning powers of the State, on the national (Articles 112, 299) and local (Article 178) levels. As a result, the State is responsible for nearly everything and can regulate everything, and private initiative and investment seem both marginal and marginalized.

662. The result of the implementation of the constitutional text by an authoritarian government in the area of the economy, from a comprehensive viewpoint, has been the increase of the economic intervention by the State, with, for instance, the almost complete State ownership of the whole economy, by means of nationalizations and expropriations of industries and private enterprises, in many cases without compensation.

For instance, regarding the private enterprise participation in the exploitation of the Oil industry, after its nationalization in 1975, through the policy known as the 'Oil Opening' (Operating Agreements and Association Agreements), such participation was allowed by the 1975 Organic Law Reserving to the State the Industry and Commerce of Hydrocarbons.[708] Nonetheless, in 2006–2007[709] through the Decree

708. *Gaceta Oficial* No. 1.769 Extra. of 29 Aug. 1975.

709. *See* Allan R. Brewer-Carías, 'The 'Statization' of the Pre 2001 Primary Hydrocarbons Joint Venbture Exploitations: Their Unilateral termination and the Assets'Confiscation of Some of the Former Private parties' in OGEL Intelligence, www.gasandoil.com/ogel/ ISSN: 1875-418X, vol. 6, issue 2 (OGEL/TDM Special Issue on Venezuela: The battle of Contract Sanctity vs. Resource Sovereignty, ed. By Elizabeth Eljuri), April 2008; and 'La estatización de los convenios de asociación

Law No. 5,200 on the Migration to Mixed Companies of the Association Agreements of the Orinoco Oil Belt and of the Shared-Risk-and-Profit Exploration Agreements of February 2007,[710] and the Law on the Effects of the Process of Migration to Mixed Companies of the Orinoco Oil Belt Association Agreements and the Shared-Risk-and-Profit Exploration Agreements of 11 September 2007,[711] the private sector participation in the oil industry was reduced to being minority shareholders on public mixed enterprises controlled by the State, following the provisions of the 2001 Organic Hydrocarbons Law,[712] which was then applied retroactively to the Agreements entered into in the 1990s.

In addition, all the electricity companies, and the telephone company were assumed by the State, the Steel industry and the cement industry were nationalized,[713] as well as all the assets and services related to the hydrocarbon industry were also reserved for the State.[714] Finally, in September 2011, the activities of exploration and exploitation of gold, and its related and ancillary activities were also reserved for the state.[715]

663. Finally, it must be mentioned that with the approval in 2020 by the National Constituent Assembly of the 'Anti-blockade law for national development and the guarantee of human rights'[716] some sort of reversion in the conduction of the economy has been occurring, although in secrecy (*see supra* paragraph 149). With such law, the National Executive seeks to obtain 'additional resources' (Article 18), through the implementation of a 'change' in economic policy consisting of indiscriminately and secretly de-estatizing, denationalizing and privatizing the economy, and conducting new negotiations on public financing, to supposedly meet the needs in the country.

---

que permitían la participación del capital privado en las actividades primarias de hidrocarburos sucritos antes de 2002, mediante su terminación anticipada y unilateral y la confiscación de los bienes afectos a los mismos', in Víctor Hernández Mendible et al., *Nacionalización, Libertad de Empresa y Asociaciones Mixtas* (Caracas: Editorial Jurídica Venezolana, 2008), 123–188.

710. *Gaceta Oficial* No. 38.632 of 26 Feb. 2007.
711. *Gaceta Oficial* No. 38.785 of 8 Oct. 2007.
712. *Gaceta Oficial* No. 37.323 of 13 Nov. 2001. *See* Isabel Boscán de Ruesta, *La actividad petrolera y la nueva Ley Orgánica de Hidrocarburos* (Caracas: FUNEDA, 2002).
713. *Gaceta Oficial* No. 38.928 of 12 May 2008; and *See* in Víctor Hernández Mendible et al., *Nacionalización, Libertad de Empresa y Asociaciones Mixtas* (Caracas: Editorial Jurídica Venezolana, 2008).
714. *Gaceta Oficial* No. 39.173 of 7 May 2009.
715. *Gaceta Oficial* No. 39.759 of 16 Sep. 2011.
716. Véase en *Gaceta Oficial* No. 6.583 Extra. de 12 de octubre de 2020

Chapter 7. The Implementation of the Rejected 2007 Constitutional Reform Through Legislation in Order to Establish a Communal Economic System

664. As aforementioned (*see supra* paragraphs 261 et seq.), the 2007 Constitutional Reform Draft was rejected by the people through a referendum held in December of that same year, pretended to convert the mixed economic system established in the Constitution into a State-owned, socialist, centralized economy in which economic liberty and private initiative as constitutional rights were to be eliminated, as well as the constitutional right to private property. In substitution, it sought to confer the means of production only to the State, to be centrally managed. In such framework, the State was to be configurated as an institution on which all economic activity depended and to whose bureaucracy the totality of the population was to be subject.

In this sense, the reform established that the socialist economic model created was to achieve 'the best conditions for the collective and cooperative construction of a Socialist Economy' (Article 112), through 'socialist means of production' (Article 168) by constituting 'mixed corporations and/or socialist units of production' (Article 113), or 'economic units of social production' as to 'create the best conditions for the collective and cooperative construction of a socialist economy', or 'different forms of businesses and economic units from social property, both directly or communally, as well as indirectly or through the state' (Article 112).

The reforms sought simply to derogate and eliminate the right to the free exercise of economic activities as a constitutional right and economic freedom itself.[717] The reforms then referred to the 'socialist principles of the socioeconomic system' (Article 229) and to the 'socialist state' and the 'socialist development of the nation' (Articles 318, 320). All the reforms collided with the ideas of liberty and solidarity proclaimed in the 1999 Constitution and established a State that substitutes itself for society and private economic initiative.

665. As aforementioned, although the 2007 Constitutional Reform was rejected by the people, the government proceeded to implement it in an illegitimate way by means of legislation (*see supra* paragraph 275). Specifically, on economic matters, this implementing process began even before the draft reforms were even submitted to the National Assembly, when Decree Law No. 5,841 was enacted on 12 June 2007,[718] containing the organic law creating the Central Planning Commission. This

---

717. *See* Gerardo Fernández, 'Aspectos esenciales de la modificación constitucional propuesta por el Presidente de la República. La modificación constitucional como un fraude a la democracia', in *Revista de Derecho Público* 112 *(Estudios sobre la reforma constitucional)* (Caracas: Editorial Jurídica Venezolana, 2007), 24; Alfredo Arismendi, 'Utopía Constitucional', in *ibid.*, 31; José Antonio Muci Borjas, 'La suerte de la libertad económica en el proyecto de Reforma de la Constitución de 2007', in *ibid.*, 203–208; Tamara Adrián, 'Actividad económica y sistemas alternativos de producción', in *ibid.*, 209–214; Víctor Hernández Mendible, 'Réquiem por la libertad de empresa y derecho de propiedad', in *ibid.*, 215–218; Alfredo Morles Hernández, 'El nuevo modelo económico para el Socialismo del Siglo XXI', in *ibid.*, 233–236.

718. *Gaceta Oficial* No. 5.841, Extra. of 22 Jun. 2007.

was the first formal State act devoted to building the Socialist State.[719] Later, once the 2007 Constitutional Reform was rejected in referendum, on 13 December 2007, the National Assembly approved the 2007–2013 Economic and Social Development National Plan, established in Article 32 of the Decree-Law enacting the Planning Organic Law,[720] in which the basis of the 'planning, production and distribution system oriented towards socialism' is established, providing that 'the relevant matter is the progressive development of social property of the production means'. For such purpose, the proposed 2007 rejected constitutional reforms to assign the State all powers over farming, livestock, fishing and aquaculture, and in particular the production of food, which was then materialized in the Decree Law on the Organic Law on Farming and Food Security and Sovereignty.[721] That law assigned to the State power not only to authorize food imports but also to prioritize production and directly assume distribution and commercialization. The law also expanded expropriation powers of the executive violating the constitutional guarantee of the previous declaration of a specific public interest or public utility involved and allowing the State occupation of industries without compensation,[722] what has repeatedly occurred during the past years.[723]

666. Another Decree Law, No. 6,130 of 3 June 2008, enacted the Popular Economy Promotion and Development Law, establishing a 'socio-productive communal model', with different socio-productive organizations following the 'socialist model'.[724] In the same openly socialist orientation, Decree Law No. 6,092 was also

719. *See* Allan R. Brewer-Carías, 'Comentarios sobre la inconstitucional creación de la Comisión Central de Planificación, centralizada y obligatoria', in *Revista de Derecho Público* 110 (Caracas: Editorial Jurídica Venezolana, 2007), 79–89; Luis A. Herrera Orellana, 'Los Decretos-Leyes de 30 de julio de 2008 y la Comisión Central de Planificación: Instrumentos para la progresiva abolición del sistema político y del sistema económico previstos en la Constitución de 1999', in *Revista de Derecho Público* 115 *(Estudios sobre los Decretos Leyes)* (Caracas: Editorial Jurídica Venezolana, 2008), 221–232.

720. *Gaceta Oficial* No. 5.554 of 13 Nov. 2001.

721. *Gaceta Oficial* No. 5.889, Extra. of 31 Jul. 2008. *See* José Ignacio Hernández G., 'Planificación y soberanía alimentaria', in *Revista de Derecho Público* 115 *(Estudios sobre los Decretos Leyes)* (Caracas: Editorial Jurídica Venezolana, 2008), 389–394; Juan Domingo Alfonso Paradisi, 'La constitución económica establecida en la Constitución de 1999, el sistema de economía social de mercado y el decreto 6.071 con rango, valor y fuerza de Ley Orgánica de seguridad y soberanía agroalimentaria', in *ibid.*, 395–415; Gustavo A. Grau Fortoul, 'La participación del sector privado en la producción de alimentos, como elemento esencial para poder alcanzar la seguridad alimentaria (Aproximación al tratamiento de la cuestión, tanto en la Constitución de 1999 como en la novísima Ley Orgánica de soberanía y seguridad alimentaria)', in *ibid.*, 417–424.

722. *See* Carlos García Soto, 'Notas sobre la expansión del ámbito de la declaratoria de utilidad pública o interés social en la expropiación', in *ibid.*, 149–151.

723. *See*, in general, Antonio Canova González, Luis Alfonso Herrera Orellana & Karina Anzola Spadaro, *¿Expropiaciones o vías de hecho? (La degradación continuada del derecho fundamental de propiedad en la Venezuela actual* (Caracas: Funeda, Universidad Católica Andrés Bello, 2009).

724. *Gaceta Oficial* No. 5.890, Extra. of 31 Jul. 2008. *See* Jesús María Alvarado Andrade, 'La desaparición del bolívar como moneda de curso legal (Notas críticas al inconstitucional Decreto No. 6.130, con rango, valor y fuerza de la ley para el fomento y desarrollo de la economía comunal, de fecha 3 de junio de 2008', in *Revista de Derecho Público* 115 *(Estudios sobre los Decretos Leyes)* (Caracas: Editorial Jurídica Venezolana, 2008), 313–320.

issued enacting the Access to Goods and Services Persons Defence Law,[725] which derogated from the previous Consumer and Users Protection Law,[726] with the purpose of regulating all commercialization and different economic aspects of goods and services, extending the State powers of control to the point of establishing the possibility of confiscating goods and services by means of their take-over and occupation of private industries and services through administrative decisions,[727] which has also repeatedly occurred during the past years.[728]

667. Finally, in December 2010, as aforementioned (*see supra* paragraphs 232 et seq.), the National Assembly approved a set of organic laws through which it has not only defined a legislative framework for a new Communal State, exercising the Popular Power, by-passing the Constitution and in parallel to the Constitutional State, but also a new economic system called the Communal Economic System, based on the Socialist doctrine and subjected to a centralized system of Public and Communal Planning. For such purpose, in addition to the Laws on the Popular Power, the Communes and the Communal Council, an Organic Law on the Communal Economic System was sanctioned.[729]

This Communal State is then structured through the Communes', with an economic model of social property and endogenous sustainable development that allows reaching the supreme social happiness of the Venezuelan people in a socialist society' (Article 8.8),[730] with the socialist political ideology, for which purpose the Law defined socialism, as:

---

725. *Gaceta Oficial* No. 5.889 Extra. of 31 Jul. 2008; José Gregorio Silva, 'Disposiciones sobre el Decreto-Ley para la defensa de las personas en el acceso a bienes y servicios', in *ibid.*, 277–279; Carlos Simón Bello Rengifo, 'Decreto No. 6.092 con rango, valor y fuerza de la ley para la defensa de las personas en el acceso a los bienes y servicios (Referencias a problemas de imputación)', in *ibid.*, 281–305; Alfredo Morles Hernández, 'El nuevo modelo económico del socialismo del siglo XXI y su reflejo en el contrato de adhesión', in *ibid.*, 229–232.
726. *Gaceta Oficial* No. 37.930, of 4 May 2004.
727. *See* Juan Domingo Alfonso Paradisi, 'Comentarios en cuanto a los procedimientos administrativos establecidos en el Decreto No. 6.092 con rango, valor y fuerza de Ley para la defensa de las personas en el acceso a los bienes y servicios', in *Revista de Derecho Público* 115 *(Estudios sobre los Decretos Leyes)* (Caracas: Editorial Jurídica Venezolana, 2008), 245–260; Karina Anzola Spadaro, 'El carácter autónomo de las 'medidas preventivas' contempladas en el artículo 111 del Decreto-Ley para la defensa de las personas en el acceso a los bienes y servicios', in *ibid.*, 271–276.
728. *See*, in general, Antonio Canova González, Luis Alfonso Herrera Orellana & Karina Anzola Spadaro, *¿Expropiaciones o vías de hecho? (La degradación continuada del derecho fundamental de propiedad en la Venezuela actual* (Caracas: Funeda, Universidad Católica Andrés Bello, 2009).
729. *See* in *Gaceta Oficial* No. 6.011 Extra. of 21 Dec. 2010. *See* Allan R. Brewer-Carías, 'Sobre la Ley Orgánica del Sistema Económico Comunal o de cómo se implanta en Venezuela un sistema económico comunista sin reformar la Constitución', in *Revista de Derecho Público*, No. 124 (Caracas: Editorial Jurídica Venezolana, 2010), 102–109. On the Laws referred to the Popular State, *see* Allan R. Brewer-Carías et al., *Leyes Orgánicas sobre el Poder Popular y el Estado Comunal* (Caracas: Editorial Jurídica Venezolana, 1911) (should this be 1991?), 361 et seq.
730. The Organic Law of Municipalities, however, defines the Communal State as follows: 'From of sociopolitical organization, based on the democratic and social state of law and justice established in the Constitution of the Republic, whose power is exercised directly by the people through communal self-governments, with an economic model of social property and endogenous and sustainable development that achieves the supreme social happiness of the Venezuelan people in a socialist society. Forming the basic unit of the Communal State is the commune' (Art. 4.10).

> a mode of social relations of production, centered in coexistence with solidarity and the satisfaction of material and intangible needs of all of society, which has as fundamental basis, the recuperation of the value of work as a producer of goods and services to meet human needs and achieve supreme social happiness and integral human development. This requires the development of social ownership of the basic and strategic means of production, so that all families, Venezuelan citizens, possess, use and enjoy their patrimony, individual or family property, and exercise full enjoyment of their economic, social, political and cultural rights (Article 8.14).[731]

Within the areas of communal power, the Law has specifically regulated the communal economy that must be developed 'under communal forms of social ownership, to satisfy collective needs, social reinvestment of the surplus, and contribute to the country's overall social development in a sustainable manner' (Article 18). This area of Public Power has been regulated by the Organic Law of the Communal Economic System,[732] which must be exclusively developed through 'socio-productive organizations under communal social property forms' created as public enterprises, family productive units or bartering groups, in which private initiative and private property are excluded. This system radically changes the mixed economic system of the 1999 constitutional framework, substituting it with a State-controlled economic system, mixed with provisions belonging to primitive societies, and even allowing the creation of local or 'communal' currencies in a society that must be ruled only 'by socialist principles and values' that the Law declares to be inspired, without any historical support, on the 'Simón Bolívar's doctrine' (Article 5).

668. The socialist productive model established in the Law (Article 3.2) is precisely defined as a 'production model based on social property, oriented towards the elimination of the social division of work that appertains to the capitalist model', directed to satisfy the increasing needs of the population through new means of generation and appropriation as well as the reinvestment of social surplus' (Article 6.12).

This is nothing different than to legally impose a communist system by copying isolated paragraphs perhaps of a forgotten old manual of a failed communist revolution paraphrasing what Karl Marx and Friedrich Engels wrote 150 years ago (1845–1846) on the 'communist society',[733] precisely based upon those three basic

731. The same definition is found in Art. 4.14 of the Organic Law of the Communes. Many are the definitions of socialism, but in all, its basic elements can be identified: (i) a system of social and economic organization; (ii) based on collective or State ownership and administration of the means of production; and (iii) State regulation of economic and social activities and distribution of goods; (iv) seeking the gradual disappearance of social classes.
732. *See Gaceta Oficial* No. 6.011 Extra. of 21 Dec. 2010.
733. *See* in Karl Marx & Frederich Engels, 'The German Ideology', en *Collective Works*, vol. 5 (New York: International Publishers, 1976), 47. *See*, in addition, the pertinent texts in: www.educa.madrid.org/cms_tools/files/0a24636f-764c-4e03-9c1d-6722e2ee60d7/Texto%20Marx%20y%20Engels.pdf.

concepts: the social property of production means, the elimination of social division of work, and the social reinvestment of surplus (Article 1).

Part XI. Rule of Law and Judicial Review

669. The formal consolidation in the Constitution of the principles of the rule of law (*Estado de Derecho*), following the general trends of modern constitutionalism, has led to the reinforcement in the Constitution not only of the aforementioned principle of its supremacy, considered as the foundation of the juridical order (Article 7) (*see supra* paragraph 124) but also of various judicial means in order to guarantee such supremacy. In this regard, the 1999 Constitution follows a long tradition on the matter and the general trends already set forth in the previous 1961 Constitution,[734] by establishing a system of judicial review of the constitutionality of legislation; the already studied specific means for the judicial protection of human rights, known as the *amparo* action or recourse (*see supra* paragraphs 594 et seq.); and a system of judicial review of administrative action.

734. *See* Allan R. Brewer-Carías, *Instituciones Políticas y Constitucionales*, vol. VI: *La Justicia Constitucional* (San Cristóbal-Caracas: Universidad Católica del Táchira, Editorial Jurídica Venezolana, 1998); *Estado de Derecho y Control Judicial* (Madrid: Instituto de Administración Pública, 1985); *Judicial Review in Comparative Law* (Cambridge: Cambridge University Press, 1989); *El Sistema de Justicia Constitucional en la Constitución de 1999: Comentarios sobre su desarrollo jurisprudencial y su explicación a veces errada, en la Exposición de Motivos* (Caracas: Editorial Jurídica Venezolana, 2000); *Justicia Constitucional. Procesos y Procedimienos constitucionales* (México: Ed. Porrúa, 2007); and *Judicial Review. Comparative Constitucional Law Essays, Lectures and Courses (1985–2011),* (Caracas/New York, Fundación de Derecho Público, Editorial Jurídica Venezolana, 2014).

Chapter 1. Judicial Review System

670. As aforementioned (*see supra* paragraph 70), Article 334 of the Constitution provides for the diffuse method of judicial review allowing any court to apply the Constitution when deciding a specific case, when it considers that an incompatibility between the Constitution provisions and a statute exists. In addition to the diffuse method, in Venezuela, there also exists the concentrated method of judicial review being attributed to the Supreme Tribunal of Justice, as Constitutional Jurisdiction, exercised by its Constitutional Chamber, which has the exclusive powers to declare the nullity of statutes and other State acts issued in direct and immediate execution of the Constitution, or that have the force of law (statute) when a popular action is filed by any interested party (Article 334).

671. These provisions of the Constitution established the general framework of the judicial review of constitutionality system in Venezuela, which was particularly developed since the democratic system was consolidated during the second half of the twentieth century. It is important to insist that judicial review is above all an institutional tool essentially linked to democracy, understood as a political system not just reduced to the fact of having elected governments, but where separation and control of power and the respect and enforcement of human rights is possible through an independent and autonomous judiciary. It has been precise because of this process of reinforcement of democracy in Latin American countries that judicial review of the constitutionality of legislation and other governmental actions has become an important tool in order to guarantee the supremacy of the Constitution, the rule of law and the respect of human rights. It is in this sense that judicial review of the constitutionality of State acts has been considered the ultimate result of the consolidation of the *rule of law*, when precisely in a democratic system, the courts can serve as the ultimate guarantor of the Constitution, effectively controlling the exercise of power by the organs of the State.

On the contrary, as happens in all authoritarian regimes even having elected governments, if such control is not possible, the same power vested, for instance, upon a politically controlled Supreme Court or Constitutional Court, can constitute the most powerful instrument for the consolidation of authoritarianism, the destruction of democracy and the violation of human rights,[735] as has been the case in Venezuela in the past twenty years. With this important warning, the following are the general trends governing the very comprehensive judicial review system established in Venezuela, in many aspects, since the nineteenth century.[736]

735. *See* Allan R. Brewer-Carías, '*Quis Custodiet ipsos Custodes*: De la interpretación constitucional a la inconstitucionalidad de la interpretación', in *VIII Congreso Nacional de derecho Constitucional, Perú* (Fondo Editorial, 2005), Colegio de Abogados de Arequipa, Arequipa, September 2005, 463–489.

736. *See* Jesús M. Casal H., *Constitución y justicia constitucional: los fundamentos de la justicia constitucional en la nueva Carta Magna* (Caracas: Universidad Católica Andrés Bello, 2000); Jesús M. Casal H., 'Hacia el fortalecimiento y racionalización de la justicia constitucional', in *Revista de Derecho Constitucional,* No. 2 (enero-junio) (Caracas: Editorial Sherwood, 2000), 215–242; Antonio Canova González, 'La futura justicia constitucional en Venezuela', in *Revista de Derecho Constitucional,* No. 2 (enero-junio) (Caracas: Editorial Sherwood, 2000), 93–181; María A.

§1. A General Overview of the Systems of Judicial Review and the Venezuelan System

672. Judicial review can always be analysed according to the criteria established a few decades ago by Mauro Cappelletti[737] who, following the trends of the so-called North American and European systems, distinguished between the 'diffuse' (decentralized) and 'concentrated' (centralized) methods of judicial review of the constitutionality of legislation. The former is exercised by all the courts of a given country, while the latter is only assigned to a Supreme Court or to a court specially created for that purpose such as a Constitutional Court or Tribunal.

673. In the diffuse or decentralized method, all the courts are empowered to judge upon the constitutionality of statutes in specific cases and controversies, as is the case in the United States of America, where the 'diffuse method' was born. That is why it is also referred to as the 'American model' initiated with *Marbury v. Madison,* 5 U.S. 137 (1803), later followed in many countries with or without a common law tradition. It is called 'diffuse' or decentralized because judicial control is shared by all courts, from the lowest level up to the Supreme Court of the country. In Latin America, the only country that has kept the diffuse method of judicial review as *the only* judicial review method available is Argentina. In other Latin American countries, the diffuse method coexists with the concentrated method of judicial review (Brazil, Colombia, the Dominican Republic, Ecuador, Guatemala, Mexico, Nicaragua, Peru and Venezuela).

674. The 'concentrated' or centralized method of judicial review, in contrast with the diffuse method, empowers only one single court to control the constitutionality of legislation, utilizing annulatory powers. This can be achieved by a Supreme Court or a constitutional court created specially for that particular purpose when requested by a specific party. The concentrated or centralized system is also called the 'Austrian' or 'European' model because it was first established in Austria in 1920, and later developed in Germany, Italy, Spain, Portugal and France. This

---

Bonnemaison, 'El control constitucional de los Poderes Públicos', in *Bases y principios del sistema constitucional venezolano* (Ponencias del VII Congreso Venezolano de Derecho Constitucional realizado en San Cristóbal del 21 al 23 de Noviembre de 2001), vol. II, 233–260; Carla Crazut Jimenez, 'Progreso de la protección constitucional en Venezuela', in *Libro Homenaje a Enrique Tejera París, Temas sobre la Constitución de 1999* (Caracas: Centro de Investigaciones Jurídicas (CEIN), 2001), 273–289; José Vicente Haro G., 'La justicia constitucional en Venezuela y la Constitución de 1999', in *Revista de Derecho Constitucional*, Editorial Sherwood, No. 1 (Caracas: sep-dic. 1999), 137–146; Allan R. Brewer-Carías, *El Sistema de Justicia Constitucional en la Constitución de 1999: Comentarios sobre su desarrollo jurisprudencial y su explicación a veces errada, en la Exposición de Motivos* (Caracas: Editorial Jurídica Venezolana, 2000); 'La Justicia Constitucional en la Nueva Constitución' in *Revista de Derecho Constitucional*, No. 1 (Caracas: Editorial Sherwood, Septiembre-Diciembre 1999), 35–44, in *Derecho Procesal Constitucional*, Colegio de Secretarios de la Suprema Corte de Justicia de la Nación, A.C. (México: Editorial Porrúa, 2001), 931–961, and in *Reflexiones sobre el Constitucionalismo en América* (Caracas: Editorial Jurídica Venezolana, 2001), 255–285.

737. *See* Mauro Cappelletti, *Judicial Review in the Contemporaly World* (Indianapolis, 1971); 'El control judicial de la constitucionalidad de las leyes en el derecho comparado', in *Revista de la Facultad de Derecho de Mexico*, No. 61 (Mexico, 1966).

method has also been adopted in many Latin American countries, in some cases as *the only* form of judicial review applied (Costa Rica, El Salvador, Bolivia, Chile, Honduras, Panama, Paraguay and Uruguay). In other countries, as mentioned, it is applied conjunctly with the diffuse method.

675. It has been this mixture, or parallel functioning, of the diffuse and concentrated methods, which has given rise to what can be considered the 'Latin American' model of judicial review. This model can be identified in Brazil, Colombia, the Dominican Republic, Ecuador, Guatemala, Mexico, Nicaragua, Peru and Venezuela. On the one hand, all courts are entitled to decide upon the constitutionality of legislation by autonomously deciding upon a statute's inapplicability in a particular case, with *inter partes* effects; and on the other hand, the Supreme Court or a Constitutional Court or Tribunal has been empowered to declare the total nullity of statutes contrary to the Constitution when requested by a party.[738] The Venezuelan judicial review system is precisely one of the latter, combining the diffuse and the concentrated methods of judicial review since the nineteenth century[739] that in addition can also be exercised through a variety of other means.

676. According to the express provision of Article 335 of the 1999 Constitution, the Supreme Tribunal and specifically its Constitutional Chamber, has the duty to guarantee the supremacy and effectiveness of constitutional norms and principles, and is the final and authoritative interpreter of the constitutional text. For this reason, it is the Tribunal's duty to oversee the maintenance of uniformity in the Constitution's interpretation and application.

677. Accordingly, the Constitutional Chamber has been empowered to give to its constitutional interpretations on the content and scope or constitutional provisions and principles binding effects upon all the other Chambers of the Supreme Tribunal of Justice and all other courts of the Republic (Article 335). For such purpose, the Constitutional Chamber is obligated to declare in its ruling in an express way

---

738. *See* Allan R. Brewer-Carías, 'La jurisdicción constitucional en América Latina', in *La jurisdicción constitucional en Iberoamérica*, ed. Domingo García Belaúnde & Francisco Fernández Segado (Madrid: Edit. Dickinson, 1997), 117–161.

739. *See* Allan R. Brewer-Carías, *El sistema mixto o integral de control de la constitucionalidad en Colombia y Venezuela* (Bogotá, 1995); Manuel Arona Cruz, 'El control de la constitucionalidad de los actos jurídicos en Colombia ante el Derecho Comparado', in *Archivo de Derecho Publico y Ciencias de la Administración*, vol. VII (1984–1985), *Derecho Publico en Venezuela y Colombia* (Caracas: Instituto de Derecho Publico, UCV, 1986), 39–114; Antonio Canova González, 'Rasgos generales de los modelos de justicia constitucional en derecho comparado: (1) Estados Unidos de América', in *Temas de Derecho Administrativo: Libro Homenaje a Gonzalo Pérez Luciani,* vol. I (Caracas: Editorial Torino, 2002), 373–411; Antonio Canova González, 'Rasgos generales de los modelos de justicia constitucional en Derecho Comparado: (2) Kelsen', in *Revista de Derecho Constitucional,* No. 6, enero-diciembre-2002 (Caracas: Editorial Sherwood, 2003), 65 a 88; Antonio Canova González, 'Rasgos generales de los modelos de justicia constitucional en Derecho Comparado: (3) Europa Actual', in *Revista de Derecho Constitucional,* No. 7 (Caracas: Editorial Sherwood, enero-junio 2003), 75–114.

that it is issuing a binding interpretation.[740]. Thus, in these specific cases, these constitutional interpretations have the weight and value of precedent, and, as such, are mandatory in the other Chambers of the Supreme Tribunal, as well as in all tribunals or courts in Venezuela (*see supra* paragraph 155).

The constitutional interpretation of the Constitution, of course, is normally established by the Constitutional Chamber when deciding any of the aforementioned actions or petitions for judicial review that the Constitution has expressly enumerated.

678. Based on all the aforementioned constitutional provisions, judicial review of constitutionality in Venezuela can be exercised not only through the diffuse and concentrated methods, but also through a variety of other means. Judicial review may occur through any of the following means: (1) The diffuse method of judicial review of the constitutionality of statutes and other normative acts, exercised by all courts; (2) The concentrated method of judicial review of the constitutionality of certain State acts, exercised by the Constitutional Chamber of the Supreme Tribunal of Justice; (3) The protection of constitutional rights and guarantees through the actions for *amparo*; (4) The concentrated method of judicial review of Executive regulations and administrative actions, exercised by special courts controlling their unconstitutionality and illegality (*contencioso adminsitrativo*); (5) The judicial review powers to control the constitutionality of legislative omissions; (6) The concentrated judicial review power to resolve constitutional conflicts between the State organs; (7) The protection of the Constitution through the abstract recourse for interpretation of the Constitution; and (8) The Constitutional Chamber's power to remove from ordinary court's jurisdiction over particular cases.

§2. The Diffuse Method of Judicial Review

679. Since 1897, the Venezuelan Civil Procedure Code has regulated the diffuse method of judicial review,[741] which is currently set forth in Article *20.* This article prescribes that 'In the case in which a law in force, whose application is requested, collides with any constitutional provision, judges shall apply the latter with preference.' The principle of the diffuse method of judicial review also was more recently set forth in Article 19 of the Criminal Procedure Organic Code, as follows: '*Control of the Constitutionality*. The control of the supremacy of the Constitution corresponds to the judges. In case that a statute whose application is requested would collide with it, the courts shall abide [by] the constitutional provision.'[742]

---

740. *See* Allan R. Brewer-Carías, 'La potestad la jurisdicción constitucional de interpretar la Constitución con efectos vinculantes', en el Jhonny Tupayachi Sotomayor (Coordinador), *El Precedente Constitucional Vinculante en el Perú (Análisis, Comentarios y Doctrina Comparada)*, (Lima, Editorial ADRUS 2009), pp. 791–819.

741. Expressly established in the Civil Procedure Code of 1897. *See* Allan R. Brewer-Carías, *Judicial Review in Comparative Law* (Cambridge: Cambridge University Press, 1989), 127 et seq.

742. *See* Allan R. Brewer-Carías, 'El método difuso de control de constitucionalidad de las leyes en el derecho venezolano', in *Derecho Procesal Constitucional Americano y Europeo*, ed. Víctor Bazán (coord.) Edit. Abeledo-Perrot, 2 vols Buenos Aires, Rep. Argentina, 2010, vol. I, 671–690; José

680. Article 334 of the 1999 Constitution consolidated the diffuse method of judicial review of the constitutionality of legislation by setting forth that:

> In case of incompatibility between this Constitution and a law or other legal provision, constitutional provisions shall be applied, corresponding to all courts in any case whatsoever, even at their initiative, the pertinent decision.

Through this Article, the diffuse method of judicial review acquired constitutional rank in Venezuela as a judicial power that can even be exercised ex officio by all courts, including the different Chambers of the Supreme Tribunal of Justice.

This constitutional provision follows the general trends shown in comparative law regarding the diffuse method: it is based on the principle of constitutional supremacy, according to which unconstitutional acts are considered void and hold no value. Therefore, each and every judge is entitled to decide and declare the unconstitutionality of the statute they are applying in order to resolve a specific case. This power can be exercised in a specific case or controversy at the request of a party or at the judge's own initiative, having the decision of the judge only an *inter partes* effect in each specific case, being, therefore, of declarative nature.

681. The general judicial procedural system in Venezuela is governed under the 'double-instance principle', so that judicial decisions resolving cases on judicial review are subject to ordinary appeal. Therefore, the cases could only reach the Cassation Chambers of the Supreme Tribunal through cassation recourses (Article 312 Civil Procedure Code). Since this situation could lead to possible dispersion of the judicial decision on constitutional matters, the 1999 Constitution specifically set forth a corrective procedure, granting the Constitutional Chamber of the Supreme Tribunal of Justice the power to review at the request of a party final judicial decisions issued by the courts of the Republic on *amparo* suits and when deciding judicial review of statutes in the terms established by the respective organic law (Article 336.10).

Regarding this provision, it must be pointed out that it is neither an appeal nor a general second or third procedural instance. Instead, it is an exceptional power of the Constitutional Chamber to review, upon its judgment and discretion, through an extraordinary recourse, similar to a writ of certiorari. Such review is exercised against last-instance decisions in which constitutional issues are decided by means of judicial review, or in *amparo* suits. It is a reviewing, non-obligatory power that can be exercised optionally. The Constitutional Chamber is empowered to choose the cases which it considers convenient to decide due to the constitutional importance of the matter. The Chamber also has the power to give in an express way a

---

Vicente Haro García, 'El Control Difuso de la Constitucionalidad en Venezuela. El estado actual de la cuestión', in *Tendencias Actuales del Derecho Constitucional. Homenaje a Jesús María Casal Montbrun*, ed. Jesús María Casal, Alfredo Arismendi y Carlos Luis Carrillo Artiles (Coord.), vol. II (Caracas: Universidad Central de Venezuela/Universidad Católica Andrés Bello, 2008), 129–156; Jesús María Casal H., 'El control difuso de la Constitucionalidad y sus perspectivas en el derecho venezolano', in *Estudios de Derecho Público*, ed. Román Duque Corredor y Jesús María Casal (Coord.), vol.II (Caracas: Universidad Católica Andrés Bello, 2004), 303–336.

general binding effect to its interpretation on the content or scope of a provision of the Constitution, similar to the effect of *stare decisis* (Article 335) (*see supra* paragraph 156).

682. Nonetheless, the Constitutional Chamber has distorted its review power regarding judicial decisions, extending it far beyond the precise cases of diffuse judicial review and *amparo* established in the Constitution. The Chamber has extended its review power over any other judicial decision issued in any matter when it considers it contrary to the Constitution, a power that the Chamber has proceeded to exercise without any constitutional authorization, even ex officio and regarding the Constitutional Chamber's interpretation of the Constitution, or in cases in which it has considered that the decision is affected by a grotesque error regarding constitutional interpretation.[743]

§3. The Concentrated Method of Judicial Review: The Popular Action

683. The second traditional method of judicial review in Venezuela is the judicial power to annul unconstitutional statutes and other State acts of similar rank, which has been granted exclusively to the Supreme Court of the country since 1858. According to the 1999 Constitution, this power is now attributed to one of the Chambers of the Supreme Tribunal of Justice – the Constitutional Chamber – as Constitutional Jurisdiction (Articles 266.1, 334 and 336).[744]

For the purpose of implementing the concentrated method of judicial review, the Constitution has provided for different judicial means and, in particular, for the popular action of unconstitutionality that can be filed directly against statutes before the Constitutional Chamber by any citizen. The only case in which the Constitutional Chamber can initiate ex officio a judicial review process is against the decrees of states of emergency (Article 336.6). In addition to this main judicial review action, the Constitution also provides for various a priori judicial review means. Consequently, this method of judicial review can be exercised in three ways: (1) when the Chamber is requested through a popular action to decide upon the unconstitutionality of statutes already in force, (2) in some cases, in an obligatory way, or (3) when deciding on the matter in a preventive way before the publication of the challenged statute. In all of these cases, the Constitutional Chamber has the power to annul the unconstitutional challenged statutes with *erga omnes* effects following a judicial process in which the rules of due process of law must be respected.

---

743. *See* Allan R. Brewer-Carías, *Justicia Constitucional. Procesos y Procedimienos constitucionales* (México: Ed. Porrúa, 2006), 389 et seq.

744. *See* Román J. Duque Corredor, 'La Sala constitucional contemplada en la Constitución de 1999', in *Estudios de Derecho Público: Libro Homenaje a Humberto J. La Roche Rincón,* vol. I (Caracas: Tribunal Supremo de Justicia, 2001), 289–301; Rafael Badell Madrid, 'Competencias de la Sala Constitucional', in *Nuevos estudios de derecho procesal, Libro Homenaje a José Andrés Fuenmayor,* vol. I, no. 8 (Caracas: Tribunal Supremo de Justicia, Colección Libros Homenaje, 2002), 61 a 119; Rafael Badell Madrid, 'Las competencias de la Sala Constitucional', in *Derecho y Sociedad. Revista de Estudiantes de Derecho de la Universidad Monteávila,* No. 3 (Caracas: Universidad Monteávila, Facultad de Ciencias Jurídicas y Políticas, 2002), 13–48.

684. Based on this traditional method of exercising judicial review in Venezuela, the Constitutional Chamber has judicial power to annul statutes and other State acts of similar rank issued in direct and immediate execution of the Constitution. This power is granted solely to the Constitutional Chamber of the Supreme Tribunal of Justice, as the Constitutional Jurisdiction (Articles 266.1, 334 and 336).[745]

According to Article 334 of the 1999 Constitution, following a tradition that began in 1858, the Supreme Court retains competence 'to declare the nullity of the statutes and other acts of the organs exercising public power issued in direct and immediate execution of the Constitution or being ranked equal to a law, [which] corresponds exclusively to the Constitutional Chamber of the Supreme Court of Justice'. This judicial review power to annul State acts on the grounds of their unconstitutionality refers to: (1) National laws or statutes and other acts which have the force of laws; (2) State constitutions and statutes, municipal ordinances, and other acts of the legislative bodies issued in direct and immediate execution of the Constitution; (3) State acts with rank equal to statutes issued by the National Executive; and (4) State acts issued in direct and immediate execution of the Constitution by any State organ exercising the public power. The judicial decisions declaring the nullity of statutes and the other State acts have *erga omnes*, general effects, and in principle *ex nunc* or *pro futuro* effects unless the Constitutional Chamber disposes in an express way its retroactive effects.

685. Since the 1858 Constitution, constitutional jurisdiction was assigned to the Supreme Court of Justice in Plenary Session. Therefore, one of the novelties of the 1999 Constitution was to assign constitutional jurisdiction to just one of the Chambers of the Supreme Court of Justice, namely the Constitutional Chamber (Articles 262, 266.1). This chamber, like all of the other chambers, has the mission of 'Guaranteeing the supremacy and effectiveness of the constitutional rules and principles: it shall be the last and maximum interpreter of the Constitution and guardian of its standard interpretation and application' (Article 335). The specificity of the Constitutional Chamber in these cases, according to Article 335 of the Constitution, is that it can expressly assign to the interpretations made on the content or the scope of the constitutional rules, binding effects on the other Chambers of the Supreme Court and other courts of the Republic.

The most important feature of the concentrated method of judicial review under the Venezuelan system is that the standing necessary to raise an action resides in all individuals, being an *actio popularis*.[746] Consequently, any individual or corporation with legal capacity is entitled to file a nullification action against the abovementioned State acts on the grounds of the act's unconstitutionality. According to the doctrine of the Supreme Tribunal, the objective of the popular action is that anybody with legal capacity has the necessary standing to sue.

745. The Constitutional Jurisdiction is regulated in the Organic Law on the Supreme Tribunal of Justice, *Gaceta Oficial* No. 39.522, of 1 Oct. 2010, *see* Allan R. Brewer-Carías & Víctor Hernández Mendible, *Ley Orgánica del Tribunal Supremo de Justicia 2010* (Caracas: Editorial Jurídica Venezolana, 2010).

746. *See* Allan R. Brewer-Carías, *La Justicia Constitucional* (México: Ed. Porrúa, 2006).

This concentrated method of judicial review has traditionally been used in an extensive way, particularly by states and municipalities against national statutes, and conversely, by the Federal government against state and municipal legislation. Also, individuals have used this method against national, state and municipal statutes for the protection of individual rights.

686. One important feature of the constitutional process leading to judicial review of legislation is that the Constitutional Chamber, except when reviewing Decrees of State of Emergency, cannot initiate judicial proceedings ex officio, and, on the contrary, must always act following a party's request (*nemo iudex sine actore; ne procedat iurex* ex officio). This is the reason why Article 89 of the Organic Law of the Supreme Tribunal of Justice expressly establishes that the Supreme Court of Justice *must hear cases that fall within its competence 'only at the request of an interested party*' except '*in cases provided for by law*',[747] and Article 32 of the same Law set forth that: 'the concentrated review of constitutionality will correspond solely to the Constitutional Chamber in the terms provided for in this Law, *through a popular recourse for unconstitutionality*'. Nonetheless, according to the last provision, once the action has been filed, and because Judicial Review is considered a matter of public order (*public policy*), the Constitutional Chamber may then *correct,* ex officio, deficiencies relating to the complaint filed by the plaintiff.

On the other hand, being constitutional judicial processes, in all cases of the exercise of the concentrated method of judicial review of legislation, the Constitutional Chamber must respect all the due process of law rules provided in Article 49 of the Constitution, in order to guarantee a fair trial. In particular, in judicial review processes, as in all judicial processes, the right of every person to defence, as declared in the Constitution, is 'invioable at all stages and levels during the proceeding', including the right of every person to be 'afforded the necessary time and means to conduct his or her defense' (Article 49.1). Also, including in judicial proceedings, 'every person has the right to be heard' 'with all due guarantees and within the reasonable time limit legally determined, by a competent, independent and impartial court established in advance' (Article 49.3).

This means that once a Judicial Review claim has been filed before the Constitutional Chamber of the Supreme Tribunal, and the Chamber has ordered the initiation of a process pursuant to Article 34 of the Organic Law, the Constitutional Chamber must ensure respect for due process, in particular, the right to a defence of the interested parties.[748] For this purpose, Article 135 of the Organic Law of the Supreme Tribunal of Justice expressly provides the basic procedural rules that apply to all constitutional proceedings of Judicial Review (Article 128, referring to the

747. For situations provided by the law in which the Constitutional Judge can act ex officio *see* Allan R. Brewer-*Carías*, 'Régimen y alcance de la actuación judicial de oficio en materia de justicia constitucional en Venezuela', in *Revista IURIDICA,* No. 4 (Valencia, Centro de Investigaciones Jurídicas Dr Aníbal Rueda, Universidad Arturo Michelena, 2006).

748. *See* Allan R. Brewer-Carías, 'The Citizen's Access to Constitutional Jurisdiction: Special Reference to the Venezuelan System of Judicial Review', in *Cuadernos de Soluções Constitucionais,* No. 4, Associaçào Brasileira de Constitutionalistas Democratas, ABCD, Malheiros Editores, São Paulo 2012, pp. 13–29. Exhibit, Tab 20.

constitutional Judicial Review process established in Article 25.1-4, 7, 8, 17), setting forth that the Constitutional Chamber, in the corresponding admission decision (auto de admission), must (a) 'order the summons of the defendant party', which means, in the case of judicial review proceedings against statutes, to summon the representatives of the National Assembly to allow them to defend the constitutionality of the challenged statute; (b) notify the Prosecutor General, the Attorney General and the Ombudsman, as well as 'any other pertinent authority'; and (c) order 'to call all the interested parties' through a public notice, which, as provided in Article 137 of the Organic Law, must be published by the plaintiff in a 'newspaper of national or regional circulation', to guarantee such 'interested parties' the possibility to file written submissions 'for the defense of their interests', with an opportunity to put forward evidence (Article 139).

§4. Other Concentrated Judicial Review Means

I. The Obligatory Judicial Review of 'State of Exception' Decrees

687. Under the concentrated method of judicial review, particular emphasis must be made regarding the 'state of exception' decrees that can be issued by the President of the Republic. Pursuant to Article 339 of the Constitution, these executive decrees declaring a 'state of emergency' shall be submitted by the President of the Republic before the Constitutional Chamber of the Supreme Tribunal in order for its constitutionality to be reviewed. Additionally, Article 336.6, as aforementioned, sets forth that the Constitutional Chamber is entitled to, 'Review, in any case, even *ex officio*, the constitutionality of decrees declaring states of exception issued by the President of the Republic' (Article 336.6).

This judicial power of obligatory judicial review is also a novelty introduced by the 1999 Constitution, following the precedent of Colombia (Article 241.7), but adding the Constitutional Chamber's power to exercise judicial review ex officio.

688. By exercising this control, the Constitutional Chamber can decide not only the constitutionality of the decrees declaring 'states of exception', but also the constitutionality of its content. This control is exercised pursuant to the provisions of Article 337 and the Constitution. In particular, in case of restriction of constitutional guarantees, the Chamber must verify that the decree effectively contains a *regulation* regarding 'the exercise of the right whose guarantee is restricted' (Article 339).

II. The Preventive Judicial Review

689. In addition to the *actio popularis* and these cases of obligatory review, the concentrated method of judicial review can also be exercised by the Constitutional Chamber of the Supreme Tribunal in a preventive way regarding statutes that have been sanctioned but are not yet published. This preventive control can occur in three cases established as an innovation in the 1999 Constitution: (1) cases regarding international treaties; (2) cases involving organic laws; and (3) cases regarding non-promulgated statutes, at the request of the President of the Republic.

In the traditional system of judicial review in Venezuela, the sole mechanism of preventive concentrated judicial review of statutes was the Supreme Tribunal of Justice's power to decide the unconstitutionality of a statute that is already sanctioned, but not yet promulgated because of a presidential veto.

Presently, the Constitution of 1999 has expanded preventive control of constitutionality to cover treaties, organic laws and non-promulgated statutes when requested by the President of the Republic.

A. *Preventive Judicial Review of International Treaties*

690. With regard to international treaties, there is the preventive judicial review method, foreseen in Article 336.5 of the Constitution, which grants the Constitutional Chamber faculty to:

> Verify, at the President of the Republic's or the National Assembly's request, conformity with the Constitution of the international treaties subscribed by the Republic before their ratification.

It is important to point out that this provision originated in the European constitutional systems, like those existing in France and Spain, and was subsequently adopted in Colombia. This system was incorporated into the Venezuelan system of judicial review and permits the preventive judicial review of international treaties subscribed by the Republic, thereby avoiding the possibility of subsequent challenge of the statutes approving the treaty.

In this case, if the treaty turns out not to be in conformity with the Constitution, it cannot be ratified, and an initiative for constitutional reform to adapt the Constitution to the treaty may result. However, if the Constitutional Chamber decides that the international treaty conforms to the Constitution, then a popular action of unconstitutionality against the approving statute could not subsequently be raised.

B. *The Preventive Judicial Review of the Organic Laws*

691. The second mechanism of the preventive judicial review method refers to organic laws. According to Article 203 of the Constitution, the Constitutional Chamber must decide, before their promulgation, the constitutionality of the 'organic' character of the *organic laws* when qualified this way by the National Assembly.

Article 203 of the Constitution defines the organic laws in five senses (*see supra* paragraph 143): (1) those named as such in the Constitution; (2) the organic laws issued in order to organize public branches of government (Public Powers); (3) those intended to 'develop the constitutional rights', which implies that all laws issued to develop the content of Articles 19–129 shall be Organic Laws; (4) those organic laws issued to 'frame other laws'; and (5) those Organic Laws named 'organic' by the National Assembly, when they are admitted by two-thirds votes of the present members before initiating the discussion.

This last case of laws qualified as such by the National Assembly are those that shall be *automatically* sent, before their promulgation, to the Constitutional Chamber of the Supreme Tribunal of Justice. The Tribunal will make a decision regarding the constitutionality of the laws' organic character.

C. Judicial Review of Statutes Sanctioned Before Their Promulgation

692. The third mechanism of preventive judicial review of constitutionality set forth in Article 214 of the Constitution is established in cases when the President of the Republic raises before the Constitutional Chamber the constitutional issue against sanctioned statutes before their promulgation. Thus, control over the constitutionality of sanctioned but not promulgated statutes is set forth in a different way than the traditional so-called presidential veto of statutes, which involves a devolution to the National Assembly (Article 214).

III. Judicial Review of Legislative Omissions

693. The fifth judicial review method established in the 1999 Constitution refers to legislative omissions, empowering the Constitutional Chamber to review the unconstitutional omissions of the legislative organ.[749] This is another new institution in matters of judicial review established by the 1999 Constitution. In Article 336, the Constitution grants the Constitutional Chamber faculty:

> To declare the unconstitutionality of municipal, state or national legislative organ omissions, when they failed to issue indispensable rules or measures to guarantee the enforcement of the Constitution, or when they issued them in an incomplete way; and to establish the terms, and if necessary, the guidelines for their correction.

This provision has given extended judicial power to the Constitutional Chamber, which surpasses the trends of the initial Portuguese antecedent on the matter, where only the President of the Republic, the Ombudsman or the Presidents of the Autonomous Regions had standing to require such decisions. On the contrary, the Venezuelan Constitution of 1999 does not establish any condition whatsoever for standing; whereby regarding normative omissions,[750] standing has been treated similarly as

749. This institution has its origins in the Portuguese system. *See* Allan R. Brewer-Carías, *Judicial Review in Comparative Law* (Cambridge: Cambridge Univ. Press, 1989), 269.

750. It has been called by the Constitutional Chamber: 'legislative silence and the legislative abnormal functioning', Decision No. 1819 of 8 Aug. 2000, of the Political-Administrative Chamber, case: *Rene Molina v. Comisión Legislativa Nacional*

in *popular actions*. The rules that apply to thc constitutional process in these cases are the same as the ones established for the concentrated method of judicial review of legislation.

694. In many cases, the Chamber has been asked to rule on omissions of the National Assembly in sanctioning statutes, like the Organic Law on Municipalities which, according to the Transitory dispositions of the 1999 Constitution, was due to be sanctioned within two years following its approval. Even though the Chamber issued two decisions in the case, the National Assembly failed to sanction the statute until 2005.[751] In these cases, fortunately, the Chamber has not itself decided (in this case, to legislate) in place of the legislative body, as it has done regarding the election of the National Electoral Council. There, due to the failure of the National Assembly to elect those members with the needed two-thirds majority vote, the Constitutional Chamber, which has been completely controlled by the Executive, directly elected them in violation of the Constitution. This has occurred since 2004, and through those decisions, the Constitutional Chamber guaranteed the complete control of the electoral body by the Executive.[752]

IV. Judicial Review of the Constitutional Controversies

695. The sixth judicial review method refers to the power attributed to the Constitutional Chamber of the Supreme Tribunal to 'decide upon constitutional controversies aroused between any organ of the branches of government (public power)' (Article 336).

This judicial review power refers to controversies between any of the organs that the Constitution foresees, whether in the horizontal or vertical distribution of the public power. In particular, 'constitutional' controversies – those whose decision depends on the examination, interpretation and application of the Constitution – refer to the distribution of powers between the different State organs, especially those distributing the power between the national, state and municipal levels.

696. The 'administrative' controversies that can arise between the Republic, the states, municipalities or other public entities are to be decided by the Political-Administrative Chamber of the Supreme Tribunal (Article 266.4) as an Administrative Jurisdiction.

As the Supreme Court of Justice specified, in order to identify the constitutional controversy, it is required:

751. *See* the reference in Allan R. Brewer-Carías et al., *Ley Orgánica del Poder Público Municipal* (Caracas: Editorial Jurídica Venezolana, 2005).

752. *See* decisions No. 2073 of 4 Aug. 2003 (Caso: *Hermánn Escarrá Malaver y oros*) and No. 2341 of 25 Aug. 2003 (Caso: *Hermánn Escarrá M. y otros*) in Allan R. Brewer-Carías, in 'El secuestro del Poder Electoral y la confiscación del derecho a la participación política mediante el referendo revocatorio presidencial: Venezuela 2000–2004', in *Boletín Mexicano de Derecho Comparado,* No. 112 (México: Instituto de Investigaciones Jurídicas, Universidad Nacional Autónoma de México, enero-abril 2005), 11–73.

> that the parties of the controversy are those who have been expressly assigned faculties for those actions or provisions in the constitutional text itself, that is, the supreme state institutions, whose organic regulation is set forth in the Constitution, different from others, whose concrete institutional frame is established by the ordinary legislator.[753]

In any case, the standing to raise a remedy in order to settle a constitutional controversy only corresponds to one of the branches of government (public power) party to the controversy.

V. Recourse of Constitutional Interpretation

697. Finally, regarding the jurisdiction of the Constitutional Chamber, mention must be made of the faculty to decide abstract recourses of interpretation of the Constitution. This is a judicial means that the Constitutional Chamber created from the interpretation of Article 335 of the Constitution, which grants the Supreme Tribunal the character of 'maximum and final interpreter of the Constitution', in order for the Citizenship to seek from the Constitutional Chamber an abstract interpretation of the Constitution without referring to any particular case or controversy.[754]

In effect, before the 1999 Constitution was sanctioned, the only recourse of interpretation existing in the Venezuelan legal order was the recourse of interpretation of statutes in cases expressly provided for them, formerly established in Articles 42, 24 of the Organic Law of the Supreme Court of Justice, and exclusively attributed to the Politico-Administrative Chamber of such former Supreme Court of Justice.

It was according to this previous regulation that the 1999 Constitution also attributed to the Supreme Tribunal the same power to decide the recourses of interpretation regarding the content and scope of statutes (Article 266.6) but attributing it, not only to the Politico-Administrative Chamber of the new Supreme Tribunal but to all its Chambers according to their respective competencies (Article 266.6). This attribution was later repeated in the 2004 Organic Law of the Supreme Tribunal of Justice (Article 5, paragraphs 1, 52).

698. In the 1999 Constitution, therefore, no recourse for abstract interpretation of the Constitution was established to be filed before the Supreme Tribunal of Justice. Nonetheless, in the absence of any constitutional or legal provision, the Constitutional Chamber of the Supreme Tribunal, interpreting its character of 'maxim and last interpreter of the Constitution' (Article 335), created an autonomous recourse to seek for the interpretation of the Constitution in an abstract way,

---

753. Decision of the Political-Administrative Chamber No. 1468 of 27 Jun. 2000 of the Political-Administrative Chamber, in *Revista de Derecho Público*, No. 82 (Caracas: Editorial Jurídica Venezolana, 2000), 744 et seq.

754. *See* Allan R. Brewer-Carías, '*Quis Custodiet Ipsos Custodes*: De la interpretación constitucional a la inconstitucionalidad de la interpretación', in *Revista de Derecho Público*, No 105 (Caracas: Editorial Jurídica Venezolana, 2006), 7–27; 'Le recours d'interprétation abstrait de la Constitution au Vénézuéla', in *Le renouveau du droit constitutionnel, Mélanges en l'honneur de Louis Favoreu* (Paris: Dalloz, 2007), 61–70.

founded on Article 26 of the Constitution, which established the right to access justice, from which it was deduced that although said action was not set forth in any statute, it was not forbidden, either. Therefore, it was decided that 'Citizens do not require statutes establishing the recourse for constitutional interpretation, in particular, to raise it.'[755] Based on such preposition, the Chamber considered that no constitutional or legal provision was necessary to allow the development of such recourse[756] (*see infra* paragraph 739). This power of the Constitutional Chamber of the Supreme Tribunal to decide recourses of abstract interpretation of the Constitution, even though created by the Chamber, it was not incorporated in the 2004 Organic Law of the Supreme Tribunal of Justice, but only in the reform of the Organic Law of 2010 (Article 2.17). In any case, its main rules have been developed by the Constitutional Chamber in subsequent decisions on the matter, as a recourse of the same nature to the one provided for the interpretation of statutes, that is, as having the purpose of obtaining a declarative ruling of mere certainty on the scope and content of constitutional norms.

699. Regarding the standing to file such recourses on constitutional interpretation, the Chamber has only required for the petitioner to invoke an actual, legitimate and juridical interest based on a particular and specific situation in which he stands, which necessarily requires the interpretation of a constitutional applicable provision, in order to put an end to the uncertainty that impedes the development and effects of such juridical situation. In the petition, the plaintiff must always argue on 'the obscurity, the ambiguity or contradiction between constitutional provisions' justifying the filing of the recourse. The petition, if applicable, must also specify 'the nature and scope of the applicable principles', or 'the contradictory or ambiguous situations aroused between the Constitution and the rules of its transitory regime'.[757] The interpretation of the Constitution made by the Constitutional Chamber in these cases can be expressly declared as with binding effects[758] (*see supra* paragraph 156).

700. Even though this recourse for constitutional interpretation must result in the opening of a constitutional process in order to confront the different criteria on the interpretation of a constitutional provision, and thus the need for a public call for any interested party to participate in the process, the Chamber denied such contradictory character of the process, arguing that the conditions established for the standing are only to justify the filing of the recourse and to avoid the use of the recourse only as a means to seek advisory opinions from the Chamber. Nonetheless, the Chamber has the discretion to call to the process all those that could have something to say on the matter, according to their right to participate, extended to the

755. This criterion was ratified later in decision (No. 1347 dated 11 Sep. 2000), in *Revista de Derecho Público*, No. 84 (Caracas: Editorial Jurídica Venezolana, 2000), 264 et seq.
756. *See* Decision No. 1077 of the Constitutional Chamber of 22 Sep. 2000, Case: *Servio Tulio León Briceño,* in *Revista de Derecho Público,* No. 83 (Caracas, 2000), 247 y ss.
757. *Ibid.*
758. Decision No. 1347 of the Constitutional Chamber dated 9 Nov. 2000, in *Revista de Derecho Público*, No. 84 (Caracas: Editorial Jurídica Venezolana, 2000), 264 et seq.

judicial activities, due to the *erga omnes* effects of the decision.[759] In addition, the Constitutional Chamber's decision on these matters of deciding abstract recourses of constitutional interpretation, according to Article 335 of the Constitution, have the character of a 'true *jurisdatio,* providing that it declares *erga omnes* and *pro futuro* the content and scope of the constitutional principles and norms whose constitutional interpretation is requested by means of the corresponding extraordinary action'. The Chamber added that 'the general norm produced by the abstract interpretation has *erga omnes* effects, and is, as a true *jurisdatio*, a quasi-authentic or para constituent, that declares the constitutional content declared in the fundamental text'.[760]

701. This extraordinary interpretive power, although theoretically an excellent judicial means for the interpretation of the Constitution, unfortunately, has been extensively abused by the Constitutional Chamber to distort important constitutional provisions, to interpret them in a way contrary to the text, or to justify constitutional solutions according to the will of the Executive. This was the case, for instance, with the various Constitutional Chamber decisions regarding the consultative and repeal referendums between 2002 and 2004, where the Chamber confiscated and distorted the peoples' constitutional right to political participation[761] (*see infra* paragraphs 715 et seq.).

VI. The Constitutional Chamber's Power to Assume Any Cause from Lower Courts

702. Finally, mention must be made to the figure of the '*avocamiento*', that is, the authority of the Constitutional Chamber to remove cases from the jurisdiction of lower courts, at any stage of the procedure, in order for the cases to be decided by the Chamber itself.

This extraordinary judicial power was initially established in the 1976 Organic Law of the Supreme Court of Justice as a competence attributed only to the Politico-Administrative Chamber of the Supreme Court, which the Chamber used in a self-restricted way.[762] However, the Constitutional Chamber has now assumed

759. Decision No. 2651 of 2 Oct. 2003 (Caso: *Ricardo Delgado (Interpretación artículo 174 de la Constitución)* https://vlexvenezuela.com/vid/ricardo-delgado-283443499.

760. Decision No. 1.309 of 19 Jun. 2001 (Case: *Hermann Escarrá*) ratified in Decision No. 1684 of 4 Nov. 2008 (Caso: *Carlos Eduardo Giménez Colmenárez*, Expediente No. 08-1016).

761. *See* decisions: No. 1139 of 5 Jun. 2002 (Caso: *Sergio Omar Calderón Duque y William Dávila Barrios*); No. 137 of 13 Feb. 2003 (Caso: *Freddy Lepage y otros*); No. 2750 of 21 Oct. 2003 (Caso: *Carlos E. Herrera Mendoza*); No. 2432 of 29 Aug. 2003 (Caso: *Luis Franceschi y otros*); and No. 2404 of 28 Aug. 2003 (Caso: *Exssel Alí Betancourt Orozco, Interpretación del artículo 72 de la Constitución*), in Allan R. Brewer-Carías, *La Sala Constitucional versus el Estado Democrático de Derecho. El secuestro del poder electoral y de la Sala Electoral del Tribunal Supremo y la confiscación del derecho a la participación política* (Caracas: Los Libros de El Nacional, Colección Ares, 2004).

762. *See* Roxana Orihuela, *El avocamiento de la Corte Suprema de Justicia* (Caracas:Editorial Jurídica Venezolana, 1998); Allan R. Brewer-Carías, *Sobre el avocamiento de procesos judiciales por parte la Sala Constitucional (Una excepcional institución procesal concebida para la protección de*

for itself the *avocamiento* power in matters of *amparo* cases,[763] and eventually annulled the former Organic Law provision.[764]

In 2004, the new Organic Law of the Supreme Tribunal granted to all the Chambers of the Tribunal a general power to remove cases from the jurisdiction of lower courts, ex officio or through a party petition, and when convenient, to decide the cases (Articles 5, 1.48, 18.11).

703. This power has been highly criticized as a violation of due process rights, and particularly, the right to a trial on a by-instance basis by the courts. It has allowed the Constitutional Chamber to intervene in any kind of process, including cases being tried by the other Chambers of the Supreme Tribunal, with very negative effects. For instance, this Constitutional Chamber power was used to annul a decision issued by the Electoral Chamber of the Supreme Tribunal,[765] which protected the Citizens' rights to political participation. There, the Electoral Chamber suspended the effects of a National Electoral Council decision,[766] objecting to the presidential repeal referendum petition of 2004.

In this way,[767] the Constitutional Chamber interrupted the process which was normally developing before the Electoral Chamber of the Supreme Tribunal, took the case away from that Chamber, and annulled its ruling. Instead, the Constitutional Chamber decided the case according to the will of the Executive, restricting the people's right to participate through petitioning referendums.[768]

§5. Some General Conclusions

704. As above-mentioned, judicial review has played a very important role in the contemporary world and can be considered the ultimate result of the

---

'orden público constitucional', y que ha resultado en un instrumento político violatorio del derecho al juez natural, a la doble instancia y al orden procesal), (Caracas, Editorial Jurídica Venezolana, 2013).

763. *See* decisión No. 456 of 15 Mar. 2002 (Case: *Arelys J. Rodríguez v. Registrador Subalterno de Registro Público, Municipio Pedro Zaraza, Estado Carabobo*), in *Revista de Derecho Público*, Nos 89–92 (Caracas: Editorial Jurídica Venezolana, 2002).

764. *See* decisión Nos 806 of 24 Apr. 2002 (Case: *Sindicato Profesional de Trabajadores al Servicio de la Industria Cementera),*in *Revista de Derecho Público*, Nos 89–92 (Caracas: Editorial Jurídica Venezolana, 2002), 179 ff.

765. *See* decision No. 24 of 15 Mar. 2004)(Exp. AA70-E 2004-000021; Exp. x-04-00006); and No. 27 of 29 Mar. 2004 (Case*: Julio Borges, César Pérez Vivas, Henry Ramos Allup, Jorge Sucre Castillo, Ramón José Medina Y Gerardo Blyde v. Consejo Nacional Electoral*) (Exp. AA70-E-2004-000021 – AA70-V-2004-000006).

766. *See* Resolution No. 040302-131 of 2 Mar. 2004.

767. *See* Decision No. 566 of 12 Apr. 2004.

768. *See* Allan R. Brewer-Carías, *La Sala Constitucional versus el Estado Democrático de Derecho. El secuestro del poder electoral y de la Sala Electoral del Tribunal Supremo y la confiscación del derecho a la participación política* (Caracas: Los Libros de El Nacional, Colección Ares, 2004); and 'El secuestro del Poder Electoral y la confiscación del derecho a la participación política mediante el referendo revocatorio presidencial: Venezuela 2000–2004', in *Boletín Mexicano de Derecho Comparado*, Instituto de Investigaciones Jurídicas, No. 112 (México: Universidad Nacional Autónoma de México, enero-abril 2005), 11–73.

consolidation of the *rule of law*. Judicial review can contribute to the consolidation of democracy, which ensures control over the exercise of State powers and guarantees the respect of human rights. When exercised for those purposes, judicial review powers are the most important instruments for a Supreme Court or a Constitutional Tribunal to guarantee the supremacy of the Constitution.

But when used against democratic principles for circumstantial political purposes, the judicial review powers attributed to a Supreme Court or to a Constitutional Tribunal can constitute the most powerful instrument for the consolidation of an authoritarian government.

Consequently, the provision of various methods of judicial review and the corresponding actions and recourses established in a Constitution is not, alone, a guarantee of constitutionalism and of the enjoyment of human rights. Nor does the mere existence of such provisions guarantee that there will be control of State powers, particularly, that there will be the division and separation of powers, which today still remains the most important principle of democracy.

705. The most elemental condition for this control is inevitably the existence of an independent and autonomous judiciary and, in particular, the existence of adequate institutions for controlling the constitutionality of State acts (Constitutional Courts or Supreme Tribunals), which are the institutions capable of controlling the exercise of political power and of annulling unconstitutional State acts.

Unfortunately, in Venezuela – notwithstanding the marvellous, formal system of judicial review enshrined in the Constitution, combining all the imaginable instruments and methods for that purpose – due to the concentration of all State power in the National Assembly and in the executive branch of government, and due to the very tight political control that is exercised over the Supreme Tribunal of Justice, the *rule of law* has been progressively demolished with the complicity of the Constitutional Chamber. Consequently, the authoritarian elements that were enshrined in the 1999 Constitution have been progressively developed and consolidated, precisely through the decisions of the Constitutional Chamber, weakening the democratic principle.[769]

That is why, unfortunately, the politically controlled Constitutional Chamber of the Supreme Tribunal of Justice in Venezuela, instead of being the guarantor of constitutionalism, democracy, and the *rule of law*, has instead been a façade of 'constitutionality' or 'legality', camouflaging the authoritarian regime that has been installed in the country (*see supra* paragraphs 31 et seq.).[770]

---

769. *See* Allan R. Brewer-Carías, 'La ilegítima mutación de la Constitución por el juez constitucional y la demolición del Estado de derecho en Venezuela', *Revista de Derecho Político*, Nos 75–76, Homenaje a Manuel García Pelayo (Madrid, Universidad Nacional de Educación a Distancia, 2009), 291–325.

770. *See* Antonio Canova González, Luis Alfonso Herrera, Rosa Rodríguez and Giussepe Graterol, *El Tribunal Supremo de Justicia al servicio de la Revolución* (Caracas 2015); Allan R. Brewer-Carías, 'El juez constitucional al servicio del autoritarismo y la ilegítima mutación de la Constitución: el caso de la Sala Constitucional del Tribunal Supremo de Justicia de Venezuela (1999—2009)',, *Revista de Administración Pública*, No. 180 (Madrid, Centro de Estudios Constitucionales, 2009), 383–418.

Chapter 2. Judicial Review of Administrative Action Jurisdiction (Administrative Contentious Jurisdiction)

706. The most important consequence of the rule of law and of the principle of legality applied to Public Administration is the provision in the same Constitution of the existence of the Administrative Contentious Jurisdiction *(Jurisdicción contenciosa administrativa)* (Article 259) as well as the Electoral Contentious Jurisdiction (Article 297), both integrated in the general organization of the Judiciary for the purpose of controlling administrative actions.

With these constitutional provisions, the Constitution adopted the judicial system regarding the Judicial Review of Administrative Action (Administrative Contentious) Jurisdiction, departing from the French model and reaffirming the traditional tendency in the national legislation to assign to the Judicial Branch the power to control the legality of administrative acts.[771]

707. The difference between the 'Constitutional Jurisdiction' attributed to the Constitutional Chamber of the Supreme Court of Justice, and the 'Administrative Contentious Jurisdiction' attributed to the Politico-Administrative and Electoral Chambers of the Supreme Tribunal and to other special courts for judicial review of administrative actions, resides on the State's acts subjected to control: the Constitutional Jurisdiction is in charge of annulling unconstitutional statutes and other acts of similar rank or issued in direct and immediate execution of the Constitution; and the Administrative Contentious Jurisdiction is in charge of annulling unconstitutional or illegal administrative acts or regulations, with general *erga omnes* effects.

771. *See* Luis Torrealba Narváez, 'Consideraciones acerca de la Jurisdicción Contencioso Administrativa, su Procedimiento y Algunas Relaciones de éste con el de la Jurisdicción Judicial Civil', in *Anales de la Facultad de Derecho* (Caracas: Universidad Central de Venezuela, 1951); Hildegard Rondón de Sansó, *El Sistema Contencioso administrativo de la Carrera Administrativa. Instituciones, Procedimiento y Jurisprudencia* (Caracas: Ediciones Magón, 1974); José Araujo Juárez, José, *Derecho Procesal Administrativo* (Caracas: Vadell Hermanos editores, 1996); Allan R. Brewer-Carías, *Instituciones Fundamentales del Derecho Administrativo y la Jurisprudencia Venezolana* (Caracas: Universidad Central de Venezuela, 1964), 451 et seq.; *Estado de derecho y Control Judicial* (Madrid, 1985), 281 et seq., and *Contencioso Administrativo, vol. VII* of *Instituciones Políticas y Constitucionales* (Caracas-San Cristóbal: Editorial Jurídica Venezolana, 1997); Antonio Canova González, *Reflexiones para la reforma del sistema contencioso administrativo venezolano* (Caracas: Editorial Sherwood, 1998). *See also*, *El Control Jurisdiccional de los Poderes Públicos en Venezuela* (Caracas,: Instituto de Derecho Público, Facultad de Ciencias Jurídicas y Políticas, Universidad Central de Venezuela, 1979); *Contencioso Administrativo en Venezuela* (Caracas: Editorial Jurídica Venezolana, tercera edición, 1993); *Derecho Procesal Administrativo* (Caracas: Vadell Hermanos editores, 1997); *8ª Jornadas 'J.M. Domínguez Escovar' (Enero 1983), Tendencias de la jurisprudencia venezolana en materia contencioso administrativa* (Caracas: Facultad de Ciencias Jurídicas y Políticas, U.C.V., Corte Suprema de Justicia; Instituto de Estudios Jurídicos del Estado Lara, Tip. Pregón, 1983); *Contencioso Administrativo, I Jornadas de Derecho Administrativo Allan Randolph Brewer-Carías* (Caracas: Funeda, 1995); *XVIII Jornadas 'J.M. Domínguez Escovar, Avances jurisprudenciales del contencioso– administrativo en Venezuela,* 2 vols (Instituto de Estudios Jurídicos del Estado Lara, Diario de Tribunales Editores, S.R.L. Barquisimeto, 1993).

708. The courts of this Jurisdiction have the power to annul general and individual administrative acts when contrary to the legal order, including those issued with abuse of public power (*desviación de poder*). They are also competent to order the State to pay sums of money, and to repair injuries or damages caused by the Administration, to hear claims concerning the rendering of public services, and to rule as necessary to re-establish subjective legal rights affected by administrative acts (Article 259).

709. Regarding the standing to challenge administrative acts on the grounds of unconstitutionality and illegality, when referring to normative administrative acts or regulations, anybody can bring an action before the court by means of the popular action of nullity. Consequently, a simple interest in the legality or constitutionality is enough for any citizen to be sufficiently entitled to raise the nullity action for unconstitutionality or illegality against regulations and other normative administrative acts. This simple interest has been defined as 'the general right granted by law upon every citizen to access the competent courts to raise the nullity of an unconstitutional or illegal administrative general act'.[772]

710. As to the administrative acts of particular effects, the standing to challenge such acts before the Administrative Jurisdiction courts corresponds solely to those who have a personal, legitimate and direct interest in the annulment of the act. This was the general rule on the matter even though some decisions were issued by the Politico-Administrative Chamber of the Supreme Tribunal, giving standing to any person with only a legitimate interest.[773]

Additionally, in the case of Administrative Jurisdiction, even before the new Constitution took effect in 1999, the possibility of protecting collective interests was also made available. In particular, it is now widely accepted that a collective or diffuse right exists against city-planning acts.

Nonetheless, despite very impressive advances regarding judicial review of administrative actions experienced in the past decades, due to the political control of the Judiciary during the past seven years, the role of the Administrative Jurisdiction in controlling Public Administration has dramatically diminished in Venezuela, affecting the rule of law.[774]

711. The procedure and organization of the Administrative Contentious Jurisdiction, since 1976, had been transitorily regulated in the statute referred to the Supreme Tribunal: first, by the 1976 Organic Law of the Supreme Court of Justice

772. *See* decision of the First Administrative Court dated 22 Mar. 2000, Case: *Banco de Venezolano de Crédito v. Superintendencia de Bancos, Revista de Derecho Público*, No. 81 (Caracas: Editorial Jurídica Venezolana, 2000), 452–453.

773. *See* decision of the Supreme Court of Justice in Political-Administrative Chamber of 13 Apr. 2000, case: *Banco Fivenez v. Junta de Emergencia Financiera, Revista de Derecho Público*, No. 82 (Caracas: Editorial Jurídica Venezolana, 2000), 582–583.

774. *See* Allan R. Brewer-Carías, 'La progresiva y sistemática demolición institucional de la autonomía e independencia del Poder Judicial en Venezuela 1999–2004', in *XXX Jornadas J.M Dominguez Escovar, Estado de derecho, Administración de justicia y derechos humanos* (Barquisimeto: Instituto de Estudios Jurídicos del Estado Lara, 2005), 33–174.

in 1976,[775] and after the sanctioning of the 1999 Constitution by the 2004 Organic Law of the Supreme Tribunal of Justice. This transitory regime was substituted in 2010 by the Organic Law on the Administrative Contentious Jurisdiction[776] in which the judicial competence on the matter was distributed among the Politico-Administrative Chamber of the Supreme Tribunal, and the National Tribunals, the States Tribunals and the Municipal Tribunals of Administrative Contentious Jurisdiction. In addition, other special statutes attributed to other courts with special aspects of the Administrative Contentious Jurisdiction, as has happened with the Taxation Superior Courts for the taxation contentious recourses, and with the Agrarian Superior Courts, with the agrarian contentious actions.

712. The Constitution assigns to the Politico-Administrative Chamber of the Supreme Tribunal exclusive jurisdiction to totally or partially annul Executive regulations and other general or individual administrative acts issued by the National Executive; to decide administrative controversies between the Republic, a state, a municipality and other public entities, when the other party involved is one of them, except controversies between municipalities that can be attributed to other courts; and to decide recourses of interpretation of statutes (Article 266.5). Consequently, competencies to decide actions challenging administrative acts of the states and of the municipalities and any other public corporations of entity are assigned to the other courts of the Jurisdiction.

713. According to the provision of Article 259 of the Constitution, the Administrative Contentious Jurisdiction in Venezuela is governed by the following general principles:[777]

(1) First, the universal character of the judicial control of constitutionality and illegality exercised over any regulations and administrative acts, which means that it is made without exception regarding the challenged act and no matter the motive of the challenging action. The Constitution allows the challenging of those acts when 'contrary to the law'.
(2) Second, the multiplicity of recourses or means of actions to be filed against administrative acts seeking to nullify unconstitutional or illegal executive regulations and administrative acts, to which must be added those recourses of *amparo* seeking to obtain constitutional protection of human rights violated by the challenged administrative act; the actions against administrative omissions particularly regarding responses to administrative petitions; the recourse of interpretation of statutes; the various actions that can be filed against Public Administration seeking liability and compensation for damages caused by its

775. Organic Law Supreme Court of Justice, *Gaceta Oficial* No. 1.893, Extra, of 30 Jul. 1976. *See* Allan R. Brewer-Carías and Josefina Calcaño de Temeltas, *Ley Orgánica de la Corte Suprema de Justicia* (Caracas: Editorial Jurídica Venezolana, 1994).
776. *Gaceta Oficial* No. 39.451 of 22 Jun. 2010. *See* Allan R. Brewer-Carías y Víctor Hernández Mendible, *Ley Orgánica de la Jurisdicción Contencioso Administrativa* (Caracas: Editorial Jurídica Venezolana, 2010).
777. Véase Allan R. Brewer-Carías, *Nuevas Tendencias en el Contencioso Administrativo en Venezuela* (Caracas: Editorial Jurídica Venezolana, 1993).

functioning; the recourse for the solution of administrative conflicts between public entities; the recourses for the solution of conflicts regarding public contracts, whether between the parties to the contracts or in cases of actions filed by any interested person seeking the annulment of public contracts; and the actions filed because of the malfunctioning of public services.

(3) Third, the broad and extended power of control assigned to the administrative contentious judges of extended powers of control, not only to annul administrative acts but to decide on the various subjective rights or interests that the individuals could have regarding Public Administration.

Consequently, the administrative contentious system in Venezuela has not only been conceived as an objective process against administrative acts but also as a subjective process for the protection of personal subjective rights and interest of persons regarding Public Administration, including the protection of fundamental rights. That is why administrative contentious judges not only have the power to annul administrative acts, but to restore subjective individual situations harmed by administrative authorities.

714. Nonetheless, and unfortunately, the authoritarian regime instilled in the country during the past years since 1999, in practice, due to the political control of the courts, has neutralized the possibility of judicial control of administrative action, to the point that only a very small percentage of cases have been decided to condemn the State or annul illegal administrative acts.[778]

778. Véase Antonio Canova González, *La realidad del contencioso administrativo venezolano (Un llamado de atención frente a las desoladoras estadísticas de la Sala Político Administrativa en 2007 y primer semestre de 2008)* (Caracas: Funeda, 2008).

Chapter 3. The Distortion of Judicial Review and Constitutional Mutations

715. In accordance with the provisions of the 1999 Constitution, the Venezuelan Constitutional Chamber of the Supreme Tribunal of Justice is, without a doubt, the most powerful instrument designed to ensure the supremacy of the Constitution and the Rule of Law, which, of course, as guardian of the Constitution, must be submitted, as well, to the Constitution. As such guardian, and as it occurs in any Rule of Law system, the submission of the Constitutional Court to the Constitution is an absolutely understood preposition and is not subjected to discussion, since it would be inconceivable that the constitutional judge can violate the Constitution that he is called to apply and warrant. As a matter of principle, it could be violated by other bodies of the State, but not by the guardian of the Constitution. For such purpose and in order to ensure that this does not occur, the Constitutional Court must of course have absolute independence and autonomy because, on the contrary, a Constitutional Court submitted to the will of the political power, instead of being the guardian of the Constitution becomes the most atrocious instrument of authoritarianism. Thus, the best constitutional justice system, in the hands of a judge submitted to political power, is a dead letter for individuals and is an instrument for defrauding the Constitution.

Unfortunately, the latter is what has been occurring in Venezuela during the past two decades since 2000, where the Constitutional Chamber of the Supreme Tribunal, as Constitutional Judge, far from acting within the expressed constitutional attributions, has been adopting decisions in some cases containing unconstitutional constitutional interpretation,[779] not only about its own powers of judicial review but regarding substantive matters, changing or modifying constitutional provisions, in many cases in order to legitimize and support the progressive building of the authoritarian State.[780] That is to say, it has distorted the content of the Constitution, through illegitimate and fraudulent 'mutation'.[781] These illegitimate modifications to the Constitution, like the ones that derives from the examples that are mentioned below, of course, have been made by its maximum guardian, who has no one to

779. *See* Allan R. Brewer-Carías, '*Quis Custodiet Ipsos Custodes*: De la interpretación constitucional a la inconstitucionalidad de la interpretación', in *VIII Congreso Nacional de Derecho Constitucional, Perú* (Arequipa, Fondo Editorial Colegio de Abogados de Arequipa, 2005), 463–489; and in *Revista de Derecho Público*, No. 105 (Caracas: Editorial Jurídica Venezolana, 2006), 7–27. *See also*, Allan R. Brewer-Carías, *Crónica sobre la 'In' Justicia Constitucional. La Sala Constitucional y el autoritarismo en Venezuela* (Caracas: Editorial Jurídica Venezolana, 2007).

780. *See* Allan R. Brewer-Carías, *Constitución de plastilina y vandalismo constitucional. A ilegítima mutación de la Constitución por el Juez Constitucional al servicio del autoritarismo,* (Caracas, Editorial Jurídica Venezolana, 2022).

781. A constitutional mutation occurs when the content of a constitutional standard is modified in such a way that, even when said standard maintains its content, it receives a different significance. *See* Néstor Pedro Sagüés, *La interpretación judicial de la Constitución* (Buenos Aires 2006), 5–59, 80–81, 165 ff.; Salvador O. Nava Gomar, 'Interpretación, mutación y reforma de la Constitución. Tres extractos' in Eduardo Ferrer Mac-Gregor (Coordinator), *Interpretación Constitucional*, vol. II (México, Ed. Porrúa, Universidad Nacional Autónoma de México, 2005), 804 ff.; and Konrad Hesse, 'Límites a la mutación constitucional', in *Escritos de derecho constitucional*, Madrid, Centro de Estudios Constitucionales, 1992).

guard him, assuming a derived constituent power that does not belong to it, and is not regulated in the constitutional text. The eternal question arising from the uncontrolled power, *Quis custodiet ipsos custodes* has also acquired in this case all its meaning.

§1. The Acceptance of a Transitory Constitutional Regime Not Approved by the People

716. The first constitutional mutation regarding the 1999 Constitution was decided by the Constitutional Chamber of the Supreme Tribunal of Justice, a few weeks after the approval of the Constitution, by admitting the existence of 'Constitutional Transitory' provisions different to those approved by popular vote and embodied in the text of the Constitution. The 1999 Constitution was approved by referendum held on 15 December 1999, with a text that included transitory provisions. With the popular approval of the Constitution in principle concluded the mission of the Constituent National Assembly.

However, one week after the approval of the Constitution, on 22 December 1999, the Constituent National Assembly sanctioned a Decree of the 'Regime of Transition of the Public Power',[782] in order 'to give effect to the transition process towards the regime established in the Constitution of 1999', in which it decided without any attribution foreseen in the new Constitution, to eliminate the prior Congress along with its Senators and Deputies, and instead, to assign Legislative power to a National Legislative Commission not established in the Constitution; to dissolve the Legislative Assemblies of the States, and assign legal attributions in their place, to State Legislative Commissions which were not provided either in the Constitution; take control of the Mayor's Offices and Municipal Councils; eliminate the former Supreme Court of Justice, create new Chambers of the new Supreme Tribunal and to assign them a fixed number of judges – not established in the Constitution – and to elect them without complying with what the Constitution demanded; create a Commission for the Reorganization and Functioning of the Judiciary in order to take it over, removing judges from office without due process which, even in 2009, still coexists with the Supreme Tribunal, with its complicity; elect the high officials of the different Branches of government; and dictate an Electoral Statute without any constitutional provision supporting it.

None of these reforms was constitutional because they were not approved by the people. Consequently, the Transition Regime Decree was challenged before the Constitutional Chamber created it, based on the violation of the Constitution recently approved by the people. The result was that the same Constitutional Chamber decided in its own cause, considering that the National Constituent Assembly supposedly had supra-constitutional power to create 'constitutional provisions' without the popular approval, and that, in consequence, in Venezuela, there were

782. *Gaceta Oficial,* No. 36.859 dated 29 Dec. 1999. *See* the comments in Allan R. Brewer-Carías. *Golpe de Estado y Proceso Constituyente en Venezuela.* (México: Universidad Nacional Autónoma de México, 2002), pp. 239–242.

two transitional constitutional regimes: the one contained in the Transitory Provisions approved by the people when they approved the Constitution via referendum, and those approved by the National Constituent Assembly without said popular approval.

717. In Decision No 6 of 27 January 2000, the Constitutional Chamber decided that since the Transition Regime of 22 December 1999 was adopted by the Constituent Assembly prior to the publication of the Constitution on 31 December 1999, it was not subjected to this, or to the previous Constitution of 1961 still in force.[783] Later, in Decision of No. 186 of 28 March 2000 (case: *Allan R. Brewer-Carías* and others), when deciding the challenging of the Electoral Statute of the Public Power also adopted by the Constituent Assembly on 30 January 2000,[784] the Constitutional Chamber ratified his criteria that in order to create a new legal order and adopt a new Constitution, the Constituent Assembly supposedly had several alternatives to regulate the transitory constitutional regime: *One*, to incorporate Transitory Dispositions that would be part of the Constitution to be approved by the people via referendum; and *the other*, to dictate separate constituent acts, of constitutional scope and value, that would originate a parallel constitutional transitory regime, not approved by the people.

With these decisions, it was the Constitutional Judge the one that proceeded to illegitimately mutate the Constitution, violating popular sovereignty, by admitting that supposedly, the National Constituent Assembly could dictate constitutional provisions not approved by the people through referendum, in this way, beginning a long period of constitutional instability that, ten years later, has not ended; as it can be evidenced, for instance, with the survival of Judiciary interference Commission, exercising disciplinary functions over the judges, which the Constitution expressly demands to be exclusively done by 'disciplinary judges' members of a 'disciplinary jurisdiction' and through a 'disciplinary procedure' (Article 267). Thus, Venezuela has been under a transitory constitutional regime not approved by the people, by the grace of the Constitutional Judge who legitimized the usurpation of the popular will.

§2. THE TRANSFORMATION OF THE REPEAL REFERENDA INTO A 'RATIFYING' REFERENDA

718. As aforementioned, in Venezuela, Article 72 of the Constitution established, as a political right of the people, the revocation of mandates of all popular election offices, when the repeal is required after half of the term for which the official was elected, by popular initiative of a number no lesser than 20% of the electors registered in the corresponding constituency. The Constitution determined that when a number of electors, equal or higher than 25% of the registered electors have attended the referendum and '*a number of electors equal or higher* than that of those

783. *See* in *Revista de Derecho Público*, No. 81 (Caracas: Editorial Jurídica Venezolana, 2000), 81 ff.
784. *See* in *Gaceta Oficial*, No. 36.884 of 3 Feb. 2000.

who elected the official, vote in favour of the revocation', its mandate is considered as revoked and the absolute void must be covered immediately through by a new election.

That is to say, the necessary votes to proceed with the revocation of a mandate must be of a number *equal or higher than the votes of the electors who elected the officer*, independently from the number of votes cast against the revocation, as it was even ratified by the Constitutional Chamber in several decisions.[785] The matter provided in the Constitution is about a 'revocation' referendum of popular election mandates and not of a 'ratifying' referendum (plebiscites) of said mandates, which does not exist in the constitutional text. Precisely for this reason, there is nothing in the Constitution regarding the case where a number of electors, higher than the number of votes obtained by the official at the time of his election, could vote against the revocation, that is, for the 'no revocation'. This could occur, but according to the Constitutional text, it would have no effect at all because what the constitutional regulation establishes is revocation referendum: it is enough for the votes for the revocation to be equal, or greater, than those obtained by the official at the time of his election in order to be revoked.

719. Nevertheless, clearly in an unconstitutional way, in 2003, when a repeal referendum was first called by the popular initiative for the revocation of the President's mandate, the National Electoral Council issued a Regulation on the matter,[786] in which even though it was established that a mandate is considered to be revoked 'if the number of votes in favour of the revocation is equal or higher to the number of the electors that vote for the officer', the phrase: '*and does not result to be lower than the number of electors that voted against the revocation*' was added (Article 60), changing the constitutional provisions on the matter. With this addition – in a Regulation of sub-legal scope – the right of the people to politically participate through the revocation of popular mandates was restricted when establishing a condition not included in the Constitution regarding the vote for the 'no revocation', disrupting the 'revocation' nature of the referendum regulated by Article 72 of the Constitution, and in an evident fraud to the Constitution, turning it into a 'ratifying' referendum of mandates of popular election.[787]

720. What was without precedent in this constitutional fraud was that said illegitimate constitutional 'reform' was endorsed by the Constitutional Chamber of the

785. *See* decision No. 2750 of 21 Oct. 2003, Case: *Carlos Enrique Herrera Mendoza (Interpretación del artículo 72 de la Constitución* (Exp. 03-1989; and Decision No. 1139 of 5 Jun. 2002, Case: *Sergio Omar Calderón Duque and William Dávila Barrios,* in *Revista de Derecho Público,* Nos 89–92 (Caracas: Editorial Jurídica Venezolana, 2002), 171. The same criterium was followed in decision No. 137 of 13 Feb. 2003, Case: *Freddy Lepage Scribani et al.* (Exp. 03-0287).

786. *See* Normas para regular los procesos de Referendos Revocatorios de mandatos de Elección Popular, of 25 Sep. 2003. Resolution No. 030925-465 of 25 Sep. 2003.

787. See the commets in Allan R. Brewer-Carías, *La Constitución de plastilina y vandalismo constitucional. La ilegítima mutación de la Constitución por el Juez Constitucional al servicio del autoritarismo*,,(Caracas Editorial Jurídica Venezolana, 2022). pp. 273–300.

Supreme Court when it decided on an abstract interpretation recourse of the Constitution in Decision No. 2750 of 21 October 2003 (Case: *Carlos E. Herrera Mendoza, Interpretación del artículo 72 de la Constitución*) stating that:

> It has to do with some kind of re-legitimating the officer and, even, in this democratic process of majorities, *if the option of his permanence obtains more votes in the referendum, he should remain in office*, even if a sufficient number of people vote against him to revoke his mandate.[788]

In this way, an illegitimate 'mutation' of the Constitution was adopted by the Constitutional Judge. Actually, in a 'revocation' referendum there cannot be votes 'in favour' of 'the permanence' of the officer; what can exist are votes in favour of the 'revocation' of the mandate and votes for the 'no revocation'. The vote 'in favour' of the 'no revocation' of the mandate is a negative vote (No), and a negative vote cannot be turned into a positive one (Yes) for the permanence of the officer. With this mutation of the Constitution, the Constitutional Chamber changed the nature of the revocation referendum, ratifying the disruption of the nature of the revocation of mandate, turning it into a vote to 're-legitimate' or to 'ratify' mandates of popular election, when this was not the intention of the Constituent. The only issue regulated in Article 72 of the Constitution is the 'revocation' of mandates, and for that, the only thing it demands in regards to the voting process is that '*a number of electors equal or higher* than that of those who elected the official, vote in favour of the revocation'.

This illegitimate mutation of the Constitution, nonetheless, had a precise objective: to avoid the revocation of the mandate of the President of the Republic, Hugo Chavez, in 2004. He was elected in August 2000 with 3,757,744 votes, being enough for the vote in favour of the revocation to surpass this number in order to revoke his mandate. As announced by the National Electoral Council on 27 August 2004, the number of votes in favour of the revocation of the mandate of the President of the Republic, obtained in the referendum that took place on 15 August 2004, was 3,989,008; reason for which his mandate had been constitutionally revoked.

However, the Constitution had already been illegitimately mutated, and regardless of the fraud accusations formulated, the National Electoral Council (on 27 August 2004), because the option for vote 'No' obtained more votes (5.800.629), decided to 'ratify' the President of the Republic in his position until the culmination of the constitutional term in January 2007.[789]

---

788. Exp. 03-1989.
789. In fact, on the web page of the National Electoral Council of 27 Aug. 2004, the following note appeared:

> 'Francisco Carrasquero Lopez, President of the National Electoral Council, addressed the country in national broadcast, to announce the definite and official results of the electoral act that took place on 15 August *which ratified* Hugo Rafael Chavez Frias, *as President of the Republic* with a total of 5 million 800 thousand 629 votes in favour of the option 'NO'. 9 million 815 thousand 631 electors participated in the election, of which 3,989,008 voted in favour of the option 'YES' to revoke the mandate of President Chavez. The total showed that the option 'NO' represented 59.25% of the ballot, while the option 'YES' achieved 40.74% of the grand total,

§3. THE ELIMINATION OF THE CONSTITUTIONAL PRINCIPLE OF THE ALTERNATE GOVERNMENT SYSTEM

721. Article 6 of the Constitution establishes the fundamental principles of republican government, in a clause pertaining to those denominated 'rocklike', that states:

> 'Article 6. The government of the Bolivarian Republic of Venezuela and its political entities *is and will always be* democratic, participative, elective, decentralized, alternate, responsible, pluralist and of revocable mandates.'

Consequently, among the fundamental principles of the constitutional system that cannot be modified either by means of constitutional reform or amendment are these principles of government, and within them, the principle that the government must not only 'democratic' but 'elective' and also 'alternate' (*see supra* paragraphs 38, 67, 129).

This latter principle was incorporated for the first time in Venezuela's constitutional history as a reaction to continuism in power and, among other aspects, based on the very 'doctrine of Simon Bolivar', in which the Republic is based according to Article 1 of the Constitution, when expressing, in one of its statements, that:

> There is nothing as dangerous as to allow the long term permanence in office of a single citizen. The people gets used to obeying him and he gets used to rule over them ... our citizens must fear, with abundant justice, that the same Magistrate who has ruled them for a long time, rules them forever.[790]

According to this doctrine, as a 'Bolivarian' one must be considered part of the values of the constitution itself (Article 1); in the Venezuelan constitutionalism, the word used of 'alternate' government refers to 'alternation' in power regarding the public positions, has always had the meaning of the people having to *take successive turns* in said positions or that the positions had to be carried out *in turns* (Spanish Royal Academy Dictionary). As stated by the Electoral Chamber of the Supreme Tribunal of Justice in Decision No. 51 of 18 March 2002, the alternate principle means '*the successive exercise of a position by different persons, belonging or not to the same party*'.

---

with a 30.02% of non-participation. It must be said that for these elections, the Electoral Registry increased significantly, reaching a universe of 14,027,607 electors with the right to vote in the Revocation Referendum. On this Friday, August 27, based on the expression of the popular will, the National Electoral Council *will ratify* Hugo Chavez Frias *in the Presidency of the Bolivarian Republic* of Venezuela, whose constitutional term will culminate in the year 2006.' And in fact, during a solemn act that took place on the same day, the National Electoral Council agreed to 'ratify' the President of the Republic in his position, despite the fact that a number of electors, greater than those who elected him had voted in favour of the revocation of his mandate. *See El Nacional*, Caracas, 28 Aug. 2004, A-1 and A-2.

790. *See* Simon Bolivar, 'Discurso de Angostura' (1819), in *Escritos Fundamentales* (Caracas, 1982).

722. This principle of alternate government was historically conceived to face the perpetuation desires to remain in power, that is to say, 'continuism', and to avoid the advantages in the electoral processes of those occupying positions when being candidates to occupy the same positions. The principle of 'alternate government', thus, is not equivalent to that of 'elective government'. Election is one thing, but the need for people to take turns in office is another, and thus the principle has always been reflected in the establishment of limits to the re-election of elected officials, which is proper of the presidential government systems. This is what happened in the Constitutions of 1830, 1858, 1864, 1874, 1881, 1891, 1893, 1901, 1904, 1909, 1936, 1845 and 1947 in which it was established the prohibition of the re-election of the President of Republic for the immediate constitutional term.[791]

This prohibition, on the contrary, regarding the President of the Republic, during the democratic period that began in 1958 was extended in the Constitution of 1961 for the two following terms (ten years). The softening of the principle occurred in the 1999 Constitution, in which the possibility of the immediate presidential re-election was allowed, only once, for a new term. That is why President Chávez, after being 'ratified' in 2004, was re-elected in 2006.

The alternation of government, thus, is a principle of constitutionalism that contests continuism or the permanence in power by the same person; for this reason, any provision that would allow this from happening, would be contrary to it. Thus the principle cannot be confused with the 'elective' principle of government or with the most general 'democratic' principle established by Article 6 of the Constitution. One thing is to be able to elect government officials, and another is the principle of alternation that impedes the successive election of the same government official.

723. Thus, it is contrary to the Constitution to interpret, as it was done by the Constitutional Chamber in its Decision No. 53 of 3 February 2009, that the principle of alternation 'demands that the people, as the holder of sovereignty, has the periodical possibility to choose its government officials or representatives', confusing 'alternate government' with 'elective government'. For this, what the Constitutional Chamber stated was wrong when deciding that the principle 'would only be violated' if the possibility of election is impeded. With its decision, what the Constitutional Chamber has done, once more, is to illegitimately mutate the text of the Constitution, and contrary to what has been said, the elimination of the ineligibility cause for the exercise of public positions derived from its previous exercise by any citizen, does misrepresent the alternation principle in the exercise of power.[792]

Thus, contrary to what was decided by the Constitutional Chamber, the possibility of continuous re-election does alter the fundamental principle of the 'alternate' government, which is one of the democratic values that inform our juridical order. Said principle would be altered if the possibility of the continuous re-election of

---

791. Actually, in the constitutional history of the country, the prohibition of the immediate presidential re-election only stopped being established in the Constitutions of the authoritarian governments, that is, the Constitution of 1857; Constitutions of Juan Vicente Gomez of 1914, 1922, 1925, 1928, 1929, and 1931; and the Constitution of Marcos Perez Jimenez of 1953.

792. *See* the comments on the decision in Allan R. Brewer-Carías, 'El Juez Constitucional vs. La alternabilidad republicana (La reelección continua e indefinida)', in *Revista de Derecho Público*, No. 117, (enero-marzo 2009), Caracas 2009, pp. 205–211.

elective positions was to be established, which is different from the principle of the 'elective' government. Because having a 'rocklike' formulation in Article 6 of the Constitution ('is and always will be'), it cannot be the object of any constitutional reform, and in the event that it could be modified, that could not be carried out either by the proceedings of Constitutional Amendment or Reform, but only by means of the invitation of a Constituent National Assembly.

The Constitutional Chamber, in its Decision No. 53 of February 2009, actually mutated the Constitution by means of an interpretation, illegitimately modifying the sense of the principle of the 'alternate' government that the Venezuelans decided must always rule their governments.[793] In any case, with this decision, what the Constitutional Chamber did was to smooth out the road so the Referendum held a few days later on 15 February 2009 could take place in order for the people to vote for the approval or the rejection of a 'Constitutional Amendment' project proposed by the National Assembly regarding Articles 160, 162, 174, 192 and 230 of the Constitution to establish, in Venezuela, the principle for the possibility of continuous re-election of elective positions, antagonizing the constitutional principle of the republican alternation (Article 6). The 2009 Amendment was approved in the said Referendum, and after the illegitimate 'mutation' introduced by the Constitutional Chamber, the Constitution was then formally changed eliminating the effects of the principle of 'alternate' government that has just remained void and ineffective in Article 6 of the Constitution.

§4. The Modification of the Prohibition to Repeat Referenda on Constitutional Reforms on the Same Matter During the Same Constitutional Term

724. In the aforementioned decision of the Constitutional Chamber, No. 53 of February 2009 regarding the illegitimate change of the principle of alternate government, another illegitimate mutation to the Constitution was adopted, losing the prohibition set forth in the Constitution to call for a popular referendum regarding reforms to the Constitution already rejected by the people during the same constitutional term (Article 345).

Article 345 of the Constitution, in effect, regarding 'constitutional reform' procedures, establishes an express prohibition to submit to the National Assembly during the same constitutional term an initiative for constitutional reform when its matter has already been rejected by referendum. Notwithstanding, the Constitution nothing establishes regarding the effects of the rejection of a 'Constitutional Amendment', or if it is possible in case of a rejected 'constitutional reform' to submit the matter again to referendum but through the 'constitutional amendment' procedure.

In December 2007, a Constitutional Reform proposal sanctioned by the National Assembly was rejected by popular vote, in which one of the aspects that were proposed was the elimination of the prohibition established in the Constitution for the

---

793. *See* the comments in, Allan R. Brewer-Carías, *La Constitución de plastilina y vandalismo constitucional. La ilegítima mutación de la Constitución por el Juez Constitucional al servicio del autoritarismo*, (Caracas Editorial Jurídica Venezolana, 2022), pp. 205–230.

possible continuous re-election of the President of the Republic. Being the expressed popular will the rejection of the proposal for a constitutional modification, according to Article 345 of the Constitution it was not possible to submit during the same constitutional term, once more, the same reform to popular vote. Nonetheless, and notwithstanding this popular rejection, the same National Assembly on January 2009, took the initiative and approved this time 'Constitutional Amendment' with the same specific purpose of modifying Article 230 of the Constitution regarding the limits to presidential re-election, and also of modifying Articles 160, 162, 174, and 192 of the Constitution regarding the re-election of the other elective officials, also eliminating the limits established.

725. This constitutional conflict was another of the topics interpreted by the Constitutional Chamber in its aforementioned Decision No. 53 of February 2009, and instead of looking for the intention of the Constituent when establishing the rules for the non-repetition of multiple referendum on the same constitutional issues (Article 345), the Constitutional Chamber, confusing the sense of the prohibition, sustained that the provision established was not directed to fix limits to successive popular votes on the same matter, but only to provide limits regarding the National Assembly in the sense that it could not be asked to discuss twice in the same constitutional term modifications already rejected. The Constitutional Chamber forgot the fact that the constitutional restrictive principle was addressed to regulate popular expression of will in matters of modification of the Constitution and their effects, and not regarding debates within the National Assembly.

In fact, the purpose of the constitutional prohibition to re-submit a rejected constitutional reform to multiple referendums is related to the effects of the expression of the will of the people in the sense that it cannot be asked, again and again in the same constitutional term about the same constitutional modification once it has already being rejected. Consequently, the importance of the prohibition established in a Title of the Constitution devoted to 'Constitutional Reform' which, in Venezuela, can only refer to the effects of the peoples' expression as an original constituent power, and not to the effects of the debate that could have taken place in the National Assembly on the matter, a body that is not a constituent power, not even derived, since it cannot approve by itself any constitutional modification.

In this case, the Decision No. 53 of February 2009 of the Constitutional Chamber can be considered as another one defrauding the Constitution because the fact was that in 2007 a constitutional reform was sanctioned by the National Assembly through the 'constitutional reform' procedure in order to establish the continuous and indefinite re-election of the President of the Republic, which was rejected by the people; and that in the same constitutional term, in 2009, the same National Assembly also sanctioned a constitutional reform for the same purpose, this time through the 'constitutional amendment' procedure, only adding to the original proposal, perhaps in order to try to differentiate both proposals, all the other elected representatives.

The result was then that although the people rejected in 2007 the proposal for the continuous and indefinite re-election of the President, this modification same rejected modification of the Constitution was submitted again to referendum in 2009 and was approved. For such purpose, the Constitutional Chamber issued a constitutional interpretation of Article 345 of the Constitution ignoring that it has the purpose that once the people have expressed their choice, rejecting a modification to the constitutional text, citizens cannot be summoned during the same constitutional term, consecutively and without limits, to express its will on the same matter.

§5. Illegitimate Transformation of the Federal System, Changing 'Exclusive' Attributions into 'Concurrent' Ones

726. Article 4 of the Constitution of 1999 establishes that the Republic 'is a decentralized federal State in the terms expressed in this Constitution', a wording that contradicts the real sense of the constitutional provisions that allow the qualification of the State as that of a 'Centralized federation'.[794] But in spite of these limits, and notwithstanding the contradiction, the Constitution has expressly distributed some State powers between the various public and different territorial levels of government, that is to say, the Municipalities, the States and the National government, which cannot be changed but by means of a constitutional reform (Articles 136, 156, 164, 178 and 179).[795]

Specifically, regarding the infrastructure for circulation and transport, the Constitution provides that the conservation, administration and use of roads and national highways, as well as of national ports and airports of commercial use, exclusively correspond to the States; competency that they must exercise in 'coordination with the National Power'.

In the rejected Constitutional Reform proposed in 2007, one of its general purposes was to change the federal form of the State and of the territorial distribution of the competencies established in Articles 156 and 164 of the Constitution, centralizing the State even more by concentrating almost all the competencies of the Public Power on the national level. Particularly, one of the purposes of the reform was to 'nationalize' the referred attribution set forth in Article 164.10 of the Constitution attributing to the States the matters of the conservation, administration and use of national highways, roads ports and airports.[796]

---

794. *See* Allan R. Brewer-Carías, *Federalismo y Municipalismo en la Constitución de 1999 (Alcance de una reforma insuficiente y regresiva) (*Caracas-San Cristóbal, Editorial Jurídica Venezolana, 2001); 'El Estado federal descentralizado y la centralización de la federación en Venezuela. Situación y perspectiva de una contradicción constitucional', in Diego Valadés and José María Serna de la Garza (Coordinators), *Federalismo y regionalismo* (México, Universidad Nacional Autónoma de México, Supreme Court of Justice of the State of Puebla, Instituto de Investigaciones Jurídicas, 2005), 717–750.

795. *See* Allan R. Brewer-Carías, 'Consideraciones sobre el régimen de distribución de competencias del Poder Público en la Constitución de 1999' in Fernando Parra Aranguren and Armando Rodríguez García (Editors), *Estudios de Derecho Administrativo. Libro Homenaje a la Universidad Central de Venezuela, Facultad de Ciencias Jurídicas y Políticas, con ocasión del Vigésimo Aniversario del Curso de Especialización en Derecho Administrativo*, vol. I (Caracas: Supreme Tribunal of Justice, 2001), 107–136.

796. *See* Allan R. Brewer-Carías, *Hacia la Consolidación de un Estado Socialista, Centralizado, Policial y Militarista. Comentarios sobre el sentido y alcance de las propuestas de reforma constitucional 2007,* Editorial Jurídica Venezolana, Caracas 2007, 41 ff.; and *La Reforma Constitucional*

727. As it has been said, the 2007 Constitutional Reform was rejected by the people in the referendum of 2 December 2007, for which the attribution of the States established is the aforementioned Article 164.10 of the Constitution, remained without modification. However, the Constitutional Chamber of the Supreme Tribunal, in Decision No 565 of 15 April 2008[797] deciding an autonomous recourse for constitutional interpretation filed by the Attorney General of the Republic ruled modifying the content of the aforementioned constitutional provision disposing that the 'exclusive attribution' established in it *is not such exclusive attribution*, but a concurrent one that even the National Government can revert it in its favour, eliminating it from the States level. The Attorney General of the Republic considered that the provision 'was not clear enough to establish, in an efficient and precise way, the scope and performance of the National Executive, regarding the coordination with the States about the administration, conservation and use of national roads and highways, as well as ports and airports of commercial use'. The Constitutional Chamber decided, accordingly, that the National Public Administration 'in exercise of its coordination authority can directly assume the conservation, administration and use of the national roads and highways, as well as all ports and airports of commercial use', and that it corresponds to the National Executive (the President of the Republic in Ministers Cabinet), to decree its intervention and assume the rendering of services and assets when considering deficient or inexistent.

With this interpretation, what the Constitutional Judge did was to illegitimately mutate the Constitutional in the sense proposed in the 2007 rejected Constitutional Reform, usurping popular sovereignty, changing the federal form of the State by misrepresenting the territorial distribution system of powers between the National Power and the States, and particularly 'nationalizing' against what expressly establishes the Constitution, attributions that are exclusively assigned to the States. The result of the interpretation requested has been that the Constitutional Chamber, has 'reformed' the Constitution and has eliminated the exclusive competency of the States in the matter, turning it into a concurrent one, subjecting it to be possibly 'decentralized', and in such cases with the possibility to be reverted and reassumed by the National Government. The Chamber, in order to decide, has forgotten that if it is true that the specific attribution of the States according to the Organic Law for Decentralization, Delimitation and Competency Transfer of the Public Power, was decentralized in 1989, such attribution was transformed into an 'exclusive' one in the 1999 Constitution, which constitutionalized what the said Organic Law established in 1989. Nonetheless, the Constitutional Chamber without any constitutional or legal basis, disposed that 'it corresponds to the National Executive, to decree the intervention in order to assume the rendering of services and assets of national roads and highways, as well as ports and airports of commercial use, in those cases where, even though said competencies had been transferred, the rendering of the service, either by the States, is deficient or inexistent'.

---

de 2007 (Comentarios al Proyecto Inconstitucionalmente sancionado por la Asamblea Nacional el 2 de Noviembre de 2007) (Caracas: Editorial Jurídica Venezolana, 2007), 72 ff.

797. *See* decision of the Constitutional Chamber, No. 565 of 15 Apr. 2008, Case: Attorney *General of the Republic, interpretation recourse of Art. 164,10 of the 1999 Constitution of 1999*, available at http://www.tsj.gov.ve/decisio-nes/scon/Abril/565-150408-07-1108.htm.

728. After an illegitimate 'constitutional modification' of this nature carried out through a judicial interpretation, as the very Constitutional Chamber said in its decision, it 'generated a necessary revision and modification of great scope and magnitude of the current legal system', warning the National Assembly to 'proceed to the revision and corresponding modification of the legal provisions related to the obligatory interpretation established in this decision, and sanctioned statutes congruent with the constitutional principles derived from the interpretation established by this Chamber in exercise of its competencies'. That is to say, the Chamber forced the legislator to issue legislation against the provisions of the 1999 Constitution, and according to the illegitimate constitutional modification imposed. This provoked that, after the electoral triumph of opposition Governors and Mayors in key States and Municipalities in the elections of December 2008, substituting pro Government ones, the National Assembly in March 2009, diligently reformed, among other, the said Organic Law for Decentralization,[798] in order to eliminate the exclusive attribution of the States established in Articles 11, 3 and 5 of said Law; adding two new provisions allowing the National Executive to 'revert, for strategic reasons, of merit, opportunity or convenience, the transfer of attributions to the States, for the conservation, administration and use of assets and services considered to be of general public interest' (Article 8); and that the National Executive, could decree the intervention of the said assets and rendering of public services transferred in order to ensure users and consumers a quality service (Article 9). With this, the defraudation of the Constitution made by the Constitutional Chamber was completed by the national Assembly, resulting that a constitutional assigned 'exclusive' attribution was changed into a concurrent one.

§6. The Illegitimate Reform of the Constitutional Prohibition to Finance Electoral Activities of Political Parties with Government Funds

729. Article 67 of the Constitution of 1999 expressly establishes that the 'the financing of political associations with Government funds will not be allowed', a provision that emphatically changed in a radical way the previous regime of public financing to the political parties, established in Article 230 of the Organic Law of Suffrage and Political Participation of 1998. This Law sought to establish a greater balance and impartiality for the participation of the parties in democratic life and, especially, in electoral campaigns trying to mitigate the unbalances and perversions that could arise just with the private financing of the parties, with the risk, for instance, of the presence of 'drug-financing', and the eventual indirect, irregular and corrupt public financing, just intended for government parties,[799] which can magnify in a system where there is no fiscal nor parliamentary effective control of the

798. *Gaceta Oficial* No. 39 140 of 17 Mar. 2009.

799. *See* Allan R. Brewer-Carías, 'Consideraciones sobre el financiamiento de los partidos políticos en Venezuela' in *Financiamiento y democratización interna de partidos políticos. Memoria del IV Curso Anual Interamericano de Elecciones* (San José, Costa Rica, Instituto Interamericano de Derechos Humanos, 1991), 121–139.

exercise of power. The constitutional prohibition, by derogating such article of the Organic Law, eliminated any public funding of political parties, abandoning the inverse technique that predominates in the comparative law.[800]

This express constitutional prohibition regarding the public financing of political parties was also one of the matters referred to in the 2007 rejected Constitutional Reform,[801] in which it was proposed to modify Article 67, providing the opposite, that 'the State will be able to finance electoral activities'. As already mentioned, the aforementioned 2007 Constitutional Reform proposal was rejected by popular vote in the referendum of 2 December 2007,[802] with which the governmental financing of political parties regarding their electoral activities continued to be prohibited in the Constitution.

730. However, in spite of said constitutional prohibition and of the popular rejection of its modification, the Constitutional Chamber of the Supreme Court of Justice, in Decision No. 780 of 8 May 2008 (File No 06-0785), by means of obligatory constitutional interpretation, has illegitimately mutated the Constitution; substituting itself to the popular will and of the original constituent power, disposing that 'regarding the scope of the prohibition of public financing of political associations' contained in the said norm, it only 'limits the possibility to provide resources for the internal expenses of the different forms of political associations, but … said limitation, is not extensive to the electoral campaign, as a fundamental stage of the electoral process'.

That is the Constitutional Chamber, even facing a clear although censurable constitutional provision as the one contained in Article 67 of the Constitution, whose reform was attempted without success in 2007, in this precise decision has usurped the constituent power, substituting the people, and has ruled reforming the provision by means of its interpretation, in the same sense that it was intended in the rejected Constitutional Reform, expressly allowing the governmental financing of the electoral activities of the political parties and associations, that is, in the opposite of what is provided in the Constitution.

Therefore, the Constitutional Judge simply decided that the Constitution does not say what it says, but says completely the opposite; that when it says that 'the financing of political associations with Government funds will not be allowed', it is not what the Constitution establishes, but what it prohibits is solely 'the financing of current and internal expenses of the political associations with resources coming from the State'; and, on the contrary, that the expenses of the electoral campaigns

---

800. *See* in Allan R. Brewer-Carías, 'Regulación jurídica de los partidos políticos en Venezuela' in *Estudios sobre el Estado Constitucional (2005–2006)*, Cuadernos de la Cátedra Fundacional Allan R. Brewer Carías de Derecho Público No. 9 (Caracas: Universidad Católica del Táchira, Editorial Jurídica Venezolana. 2007), 655–686.

801. *See Proyecto de Exposición de Motivos para la Reforma Constitucional, Presidencia de la República, Proyecto Reforma Constitucional. Propuesta del presidente Hugo Chávez Agosto 2007; Proyecto de Reforma Constitucional. Prepared by the President of the Bolivarian Republic of Venezuela, Hugo Chávez Frías* (Caracas: Editorial Atenea, 2007), 19.

802. *See* Allan R. Brewer-Carías, 'La proyectada reforma constitucional de 2007, rechazada por el poder constituyente originario', in *Anuario de Derecho Público 2007* (Caracas: Universidad Monteavila, 2008).

of said political associations, can be financed with funds coming from the State. In order to arrive at this conclusion, in a decision unnecessarily packed with author quoting about interpretation techniques, the notion of democracy, and the advantages of the public financing of the electoral campaigns of political parties, concluded in the aforementioned distinction, that one thing is that the State finances 'current and internal expenses' of political parties, and another is that it finances 'their electoral campaigns', deducing, without any foundation, that what the Constitution prohibits is the first and not the latter.

It is an absurd conclusion, which against any democratic logic, derives from a false premise, in which, supposedly, in democratic systems, it could happen that the State could finance the current and internal expenses of the parties. The latter is not conceived in democracies, reason for which it does not require any prohibition. In democracies, what is financed is the operation of the parties, but always, with a view to the electoral campaigns, to the point of cancelling the financing if the parties do not obtain a certain percentage of votes in the elections.

The decision of the Constitutional Judge can be very commendable, allowing the financing of the electoral campaigns of the political parties with funds belonging to the State, but since it was expressly prohibited by the Constitution, just by reforming it is that the opposite could be achieved. And, in that case, that was what the Constitutional Judge did in Venezuela, that is, to reform the Constitution, usurping the original constituent power which corresponds to the people and, even against its own will expressed five months earlier by rejecting, precisely, said constitutional reform, establishing now the possibility to finance with public funds the electoral campaigns of the political parties.

§7. The Illegitimate Elimination of the Supra-constitutional Rank of International Treaties in Matters Human Rights

731. Following a contemporary universal trend, which has allowed constitutional courts the direct application of international treaties in matters of human rights for their protection, progressively widening their cast, in the text of contemporary Constitutions, the normative scope of said treaties has been progressively recognized, being possible to distinguish four different ranks recognized in the internal law: supra-constitutional, constitutional, supra-legal or legal rank.[803]

In the case of the Venezuelan 1999 Constitution, Article 23 expressly disposes the following:

803. Regarding this general classification, *see* Rodolfo E. Piza R., *Derecho internacional de los derechos humanos: La Convención Americana* (San José 1989); Carlos Ayala Corao, 'La jerarquía de los instrumentos internacionales sobre derechos humanos', in *El nuevo derecho constitucional latinoamericano*, IV Congreso Venezolano de Derecho constitucional, vol. II (Caracas 1996), and *La jerarquía constitucional de los tratados sobre derechos humanos y sus consecuencias* (México, 2003); Humberto Henderson, 'Los tratados internacionales de derechos humanos en el orden interno: la importancia del principio pro homine', in *Revista IIDH*, 39 (San José, Instituto Interamericano de Derechos Humanos, 2004), 71 ff. S*ee also*, Allan R. Brewer-Carías, *Mecanismos nacionales de protección de los derechos humanos* (San José, Instituto Internacional de Derechos Humanos, 2004), 62 ff.

> Article 23. Treaties, pacts and conventions regarding to human rights, subscribed and ratified by Venezuela, have constitutional rank and prevail in the internal order, as long as they contain norms about their enjoyment and exercise, more favourable than those established in this Constitution and in the laws of the Republic, and are to be direct and immediate applicable, by the courts and other bodies of the State.

Without a doubt, this norm is one of the most important ones in matters of human rights in the country, unique in its conception in Latin America, because first, it grants international treaties in matters of human rights, not only constitutional rank but *supra-constitutional* rank (*see supra* paragraph 139); that is, a superior rank regarding the Constitution itself, which must prevail over it in cases they contain more favourable regulations for their exercise. The article also establishes the principle of the direct and immediate application of said treaties by the courts and other authorities of the country. This provision of the Constitution was, without a doubt, a significant advance in the construction of the human rights protection framework, which has been applied by the courts for instance declaring the prevalence of the norms of the American Convention of Human Rights regarding legal and constitutional provisions. It was the case, for instance, of the right to appeal before a second judicial instance invoked before the contentious administrative jurisdiction in which, in some cases (autonomous institutions or independent Administrations acts), it was excluded in the former Organic Law of the Supreme Court of Justice of 1976.

732. The 1999 Constitution only establishes as a constitutional right, the right to appeal in matters of criminal procedures in favour of the person declared as guilty (Article 40.1); so regarding the aforementioned contentious administrative suit, there was no express constitutional guarantee for the appeal, having always been the appeal of the First Court of Contentious Administrative decisions as inadmissible. Nonetheless, the application of Article 23 of the Constitution in these cases finally led the Constitutional Chamber of the Supreme Court to rule in 2000, on the prevailing application of the Inter-American Convention on Human Rights, considering:

> that Article 8.1 and 8. 2, h of the American Convention on Human Rights, are part of the Venezuelan constitutional order; that its dispositions, containing the right to appeal judicial decision are more favourable, concerning the benefit and exercise of said right, than that foreseen in Article 49.1 of said Constitution; and that are of immediate and direct application by the courts and other State bodies.[804]

However, in Decision No. 1.939 of 18 December 2008 (Case: *Gustavo Alvarez Arias and others*), by declaring executable a decision of the Inter-American Court

804. Decision No. 87 of 13 Mar. 2000. Case: *C.A. Electricidad del Centro (Elecentro) y otra v. Superintendencia para la Promoción y Protección de la Libre Competencia. (Procompetencia)*, in *Revista de Derecho Público*, No. 81 (Caracas: Editorial Jurídica Venezolana, 2000), 157 ff.

on Human Rights of 5 August 2008 referred to the case of the former judges of the First Court on the Contentious Administrative matters *(Apitz Barbera and others ('First Court on the Contentious Administrative matters') v. Venezuela)*, the Constitutional Chamber has definitely resolved that:

> the aforementioned Article 23 of the Constitution *does not* grant supra-constitutional rank to international treaties on human rights, thus, in case of antinomy or contradiction between one disposition of the Constitution and a provision of an international pact, it would correspond to the Judicial Power to determine which would be applicable, considering both what is established in the referred provision, and in the jurisprudence of this Constitutional Chamber of the Supreme Court of Justice, paying attention to the content of Articles 7, 266.6, 334, 335, 336.11 *ejusdem* and to Decision No.1.077/2000 of this Chamber.

In order to base its decision, and reject the existence of superior values not modifiable by the authoritarian political project, the Chamber clarified the following concepts:

> On this subject, the Decision No 1309/2001 of this Chamber, among others, clarifies that law is a normative theory at the service of politics that underlines behind the axiological project of the Constitution, and that the interpretation must be engaged, if we want to maintain the supremacy of the Constitution when exercising the constitutional jurisdiction assigned to the judges, with the best political theory that underlines behind the system interpreted or integrated and with the institutional morality that serves as its axiological base (*interpretatio favour Constitutione*). The decision adds: in this order of ideas, the standards to resolve the conflict between the principles and the provisions have to be compatible with the political project of the Constitution (Democratic and Social State of Law and Justice) and cannot affect the force of said project with ideological interpretative elections that privilege individual rights decisively, or that welcome the supremacy of the international judicial order over national law at the sacrifice of the sovereignty of the State.
>
> The decision concludes that: 'a system of principles, supposedly absolute and supra-historic, cannot be above the Constitution' and that the theories that pretend to limit 'under the pretext of universal legalities, the sovereignty and the national auto-determination' are unacceptable.
>
> In the same sense, the decision of this Chamber (No. 1265/2008) established that when a contradiction is evidenced between the Constitution and an international convention or treaty, the constitutional provision that privilege the general interest and the common wellbeing must prevail, applying the dispositions that privilege the collective interests … (…) over particular interests.[805]

805. *See* in http://www.tsj.gov.ve/decisiones/scon/Diciembre/1939-181208-2008-08-1572.html.

733. With this decision, the Constitutional Chamber accomplished an illegitimate constitutional mutation, reforming Article 23 of the Constitution when eliminating the supra-national rank of the American Convention on Human Rights, in the cases containing more favourable provisions for the benefit and exercise of human rights regarding those foreseen in the very Constitution.

The matter has been so about an illegitimate constitutional reform, that it was one of the express reform proposals made in 2007 by the 'Presidential Council for the Constitutional Reform',[806] in which, regarding Article 23 of the Constitution, the intention was to completely eliminate the constitutional hierarchy of the provisions of the international treaties on human rights, and their prevalence over the internal order, proposing the reformulation of the provision just in the sense that: 'treaties, pacts and conventions related to human rights, subscribed and ratified by Venezuela, as long as they remain current, are part of the internal order, and are of immediate and direct application by the bodies of the Public Power'.

This proposal for constitutional reform, which luckily was filled before the National Assembly by the President of the Republic, was a hard blow to the principle of progressivity in the protection of the rights established in Article 19 of the Constitution, which does not allow regressions in their protection.[807] However, what the authoritarian regime was not able to accomplish through a constitutional reform process, which in the end was in 2007 rejected by the people, was carried out by the Constitutional Chamber of the Supreme Court throughout its long carrier at the service of authoritarianism.[808]

§8. The Elimination of Judges' Power to Immediately and Directly Apply International Treaties on Human Rights

734. In matters of human rights, Article 23 of the Constitution not only grants supra-constitutional rank to the provisions of the international treaties, pacts and conventions regarding human rights, 'as long as they contain provisions more favourable to their enjoyment and exercise as those established in this Constitution and in the laws of the Republic', which, as it has been seen, it had been illegitimately mutated, but it also expressly declare that they are 'of direct and immediate application by the courts and other bodies of the State' (Article 23).

Regarding this provision, the Constitutional Chamber of the Supreme Court, by reaffirming its role of maximum and ultimate interpreter of the Constitution and the treaties on human rights, has established in Decision No 1492 of 15 July 2003

806. *See Consejo Presidencial para la Reforma de la Constitución de la República Bolivariana de Venezuela, 'Modificaciones propuestas'*. The complete text was Published as *Proyecto de Reforma Constitucional. Versión atribuida al Consejo Presidencial para la reforma de la Constitución de la República Bolivariana de Venezuela* (Caracas: Editorial Atenea, 2007), 146.

807. *See* in Allan R. Brewer-Carías, *Hacia la consolidación de un Estado Socialista, Centralizado, Policial y Militarista. Comentarios sobre el sentido y alcance de las propuestas de reforma constitucional 2007* (Caracas: Editorial Jurídica Venezolana, 2007), 122 ss.

808. *See* Allan R. Brewer-Carías, *Crónica sobre la 'In' Justicia Constitucional. La Sala Constitucional y el autoritarismo en Venezuela*, Colección Instituto de Derecho Público No. 2 (Caracas: Universidad Central de Venezuela, 2007).

(Case: *Impugnación de diversos artículos del Código Penal*), that because those treatises having constitutional rank, the only one capable of their interpretation, of determine which one of their provisions prevail in the internal legal order; and of deciding which human rights, not contemplated in said international instruments, have force in Venezuela, is the Constitutional Chamber of the Supreme Tribunal.[809] With this unconstitutional decision, the Constitutional Chamber has also illegitimately mutated the Constitution, because, according to its Article 23, the authority to do so not only corresponds to the Constitutional Chamber, but to all the courts of the Republic when acting as constitutional judges, for instance, when exercising the diffused control of the constitutionality of statutes or when deciding cases of *amparo*. The intention of the Constitutional Chamber to concentrate all constitutional justice procedures is not in accordance with the Constitution and the judicial review system it establishes.

§9. The Denial of the People's Right for the International Protection of the Human Rights and the Non-Enforceability of the Decisions of the Inter-American Court on Human Rights

735. But besides the unawareness regarding the supra-constitutional scope of the American Convention on Human Rights, the Constitutional Chamber, in Decision No. 1.939 of 18 December 2008 (Case: *Gustavo Álvarez Arias and others*, or more accurately, *Case: Venezuelan Government v. Inter-American Court on Human Rights*), has ignored the effects of the decisions of the Inter-American Court on Human Rights, declaring them as unenforceable in Venezuela, contradicting the international regime of the treaties.[810]

With the said decision, issued in proceedings initiated by the Attorney General of the Republic as a dependant organ of the National Executive, the Constitutional Chamber declared that the decision of the Inter-American Court on Human Rights issued on 5 August 2008 in the case of the former judges of the First Court on Contentious Administrative that were illegitimately dismissed without any sort of judicial guarantees (Case *Apitz Barbera and others (First Court on Contentious Administrative matters) v. Venezuela),* was non-enforceable in Venezuela. In that decision, the Inter-American Court decided that the Venezuelan State had violated the judicial guarantees of the said judges established in the American Convention, by removing them from their offices without due process, and condemned the State to pay for compensations, to reinstate the judges to their former positions or to some similar, and to publish the verdict in Venezuelan newspapers.[811]

Of course, in the case of the American Convention of Human Rights, once a Member State recognized the jurisdiction of the Inter-American Court on Human Rights, according to Article 68.1 of the Convention, they must 'commit themselves

809. *See Revista de Derecho Público*, No. 93–96 (Caracas: Editorial Jurídica Venezolana, 2003), 135 ff.
810. *See* the comments in Carlos Ayala Corao, *La 'inejecución' de las sentencias internacionales en la jurisprudencia constitucional de Venezuela (1999–2009)* (Caracas, Fundación Manuel García Pelayo., 2009).
811. *See* www.corteidh.or.cr. Excepción Preliminar, Fondo, Reparaciones y Costas, Serie C No. 182.

to comply with the decisions of the Court in every case in which they are a part of'.[812] In addition, the Venezuelan Constitution expressly contains the right to have access to the international protection in matters of human rights, with the obligation for the State to carry out the decisions of the international bodies. To that effect, Article 31 of the Constitution establishes:

> Article 31. Every person has the right, within the terms established by the treaties, pacts and conventions on human rights ratified by the Republic, to file petitions or complaints before the international bodies established for such purposes, in order to ask for the protection of their human rights.
>
> The State shall adopt, in accordance with the proceedings established in this Constitution and statutes, the necessary measures for the enforcement of the decisions issued by the international bodies indicated in this article.

736. There have been States, however, that have resisted the decisions of the Inter-American Court, and have intended to avoid their responsibility in their enforcement. The decision of the Inter-American Court on the *Case: Castillo Petruzzi*, of 30 May 1999 (Series C, number 52), is proof of that, since after declaring that the Peruvian State had violated during a proceeding, Articles 20, 7.5, 9, 8.1, 8.2.b, c, d and f, 8.2.h, 8.5, 25, 7.6, 5, 1.1 and 2,[813] the Plenary Chamber of the Supreme Council of Military Justice of Peru refused to enforce the verdict, considering that it had ignored the Political Constitution of Peru, subjecting it to 'the American Convention on Human Rights in the interpretation that the judges of said Court can carry out *ad-libitum*'.[814]

812. As stated by the Inter-American Court on Human Rights in the decision of *Case Castillo Petruzzi*, on 'Enforcement decision' of 17 Nov. 1999 (Series C, number 59), 'the conventional obligations of the State party entail all the powers and bodies of the State'; (para. 3) adding 'That this obligation corresponds to a basic principle of international responsibility right of the State, endorsed by the international jurisprudence, according to which the States must comply with their conventional duties in good faith (*pacta sunt servanda*) and, as it has been mentioned by this Court, cannot, due to reasons of internal order, stop complying with the established international responsibility' (para. 4). *See* in Sergio García Ramírez (Coord.), *La Jurisprudencia de la Corte Interamericana de Derechos Humanos* (México, Universidad Nacional Autónoma de México, Corte Interamericana de Derechos Humanos, 2001), 628–629.

813. Consequently, in the decision, the Inter-American Court declared 'the nullity, of the process against Mr Jaime Francisco Sebastián Castillo Petruzzi and others, for been incompatible with the Convention' ordering 'the guaranty of a new trial with the complete observance of the legal due process', and also, 'the State to adopt the necessary measures in order to reform the provisions that had been declared to be against the American Convention of Human Rights in the present decision, and to ensure the benefit of the rights established in the American Convention on Human Rights to all the people under its jurisdiction, without any exception'. Available at http://www.tsj.gov.ve/decisiones/scon/Diciembre/1939-181208-2008-08-1572.html.

814. It is precisely, because of this decision of the Plenary Chamber of the Supreme Council of Military Justice of Peru regarding the non-enforceability of the decision of the Inter-American Court on Human Rights in Peru, issued on 30 May 1999, that the same Inter-American Court ruled its subsequent decision of 7 Nov. 1999, declaring that 'the State has the duty to promptly fulfil the decision of 30 May 1999 ruled by the Inter-American Court in the case Castillo Petruzzi and others' *See*, in Sergio García Ramírez (Coord.), *La Jurisprudencia de la Corte Interamericana de Derechos Humanos* (México, Universidad Nacional Autónoma de México, Corte Interamericana de

737. In 1999 Venezuela followed the same steps as the authoritarian regime of President Fujimori in Peru, and the Constitutional Chamber of the Supreme Court in the aforementioned Decision No. 1.939 of 18 December 2008 (*Case: Attorneys Gustavo Álvarez Arias and others*), has also declared the Inter-American Court on Human Rights of 5 August 2008 issued in the case *Apitz Barbera and others (First Court on Contentious Administrative matters) v. Venezuela*, as 'un enforceable' in Venezuela, accusing the Inter-American Court of usurping the power of the Supreme Court.[815]

The Constitutional Chamber, in its decision, quoting a previous Decision No. 1.942 of 15 July 2003, and considering that it was about an interpretation request formulated by the Republic, ruled that the Inter-American Court on Human Rights could not 'intend to exclude or ignore the internal constitutional order' and that it had ruled 'guidelines' on the government and administration of the Judiciary a matter that 'is of exclusive and excluding attributions of the Supreme Tribunal of Justice', and has established 'rules for the Legislature in matters of judicial responsibility of the judges, transgressing the sovereignty of the Venezuelan State in its organization and in the selection of its officials; which it considered as inadmissible'. The Constitutional Chamber even accused the Inter-American Court of having used its decision 'to intervene, unacceptably, in the judicial government and administration, which exclusively corresponds to the Supreme Tribunal', arguing that with the questioned decision, the Inter-American Court intended to 'ignore the strength and force of judicial and administrative decisions that have acquired the res judicata, by demanding the reincorporation of the judges that have been removed from office'. In order to make these affirmations, the Constitutional Chamber turned, precisely, to the aforementioned decision of 1999 of the Plenary Chamber of the Supreme Council of Military Justice of Peru, which considered unenforceable in Peru the decisions of the Inter-American Court of 30 May 1999 (Case: *Castillo Petruzzi and other*).

738. But the Constitutional Chamber did not stop there, but in an evident usurpation of powers – since the international relations are a matter of exclusive attribution of the Executive – requested 'the National Executive to proceed to denounce

---

Derechos Humanos, 2001), 629. This occurred during the authoritarian regime in Peru, during the mandate of President Fujimori, and which, two months after the decision of the Inter-American Court of 30 May 1999, drove the Congress of Peru to approve the withdraw the recognition of the contentious competency of the Court; which was submitted the following day before the General Secretariat of the OAS. This withdrawal was declared inadmissible by the Inter-American Court, in its decision in the case *Ivcher Bronstein* of 24 Sep. 1999, considering that 'a State party can only remove itself to the competency of the Court through the formal complaint of the complete treaty'. *Ibid.*, 769–771. In any case, Peru, later in 2001, derogated the Resolution of July 1999, completely re-establishing for the State the competency of the Inter-American Court.

815. The issue had been affirmed by the Constitutional Chamber in its known decision No. 1.942 of 15 Jul. 2003 in which, when referring to the International Courts, began stating that in Venezuela, 'above the Supreme Court of Justice and according to article 7 of the Constitution, there is no jurisdictional body, unless stated otherwise by the Constitution or the law, and even in this last possible case, any decision contradicting the Venezuelan constitutional order, lacks of application in the country'. *See* Case: *Impugnación de artículos del Código Penal, Leyes de desacato,* in *Revista de Derecho Público*, Nos 93–96 (Caracas: Editorial Jurídica Venezolana, 2003), 136 ff.

the Convention, in view of the evident usurpation of functions in which the Inter American Court on Human Rights has incurred into with the ruling object of this decision'. With this, the Venezuelan State concluded its process of separation from the American Convention on Human Rights, and of the jurisdiction of the Inter-American Court on Human Rights, using its very own Supreme Court of Justice for this purpose.

We must recall in fact that, in this same matter, the Constitutional Chamber has also decided to adopt another illegitimate constitutional mutation, by reforming Article 23 of the Constitution in the way intended in the 2007 proposal for Constitutional reform formulated by the 'Presidential Council for the Reform of the Constitution', by suggesting to add to Article 23 of the Constitution, also in a regressive manner, that it 'corresponds to the courts of the Republic to be decide upon the violations on matters established in said treaties', proposing to establish a constitutional prohibition impeding the Inter-American Court on Human Rights to decide on the violations of the American Convention on Human Rights. That is, with a provision of that kind, Venezuela would have been constitutionally excluded from the jurisdiction of said International Court, and of the Inter-American protection human rights system.[816]

On this matter, also, what the authoritarian regime could not do by means of a constitutional reform process like the one initiated in 2007, which in the end was rejected by the people, was done by the Constitutional Chamber of the Supreme Court throughout its long carrier at the service of authoritarianism.

§10. The Illegitimate Creation of an Autonomous Recourse for the Abstract Interpretation of the Constitution

739. Almost all of the aforementioned illegitimate mutations of the Constitutions, that have been adopted by the Constitutional Chamber of the Supreme Tribunal, have been made when deciding autonomous recourses for the abstract interpretation of the Constitution, which in its turn have their origin, also, in illegitimate mutations to the Constitution made by the same Constitutional Chamber. In other words, it has been this autonomous recourse for the abstract interpretation of the Constitution, which is not established either in the Constitution or in any statute, the one that has served as the main tool for the adoption of some of the most distinguishable and illegitimate mutations to the Constitution, which have not their origin in constitutional interpretations made by the Constitutional Judge when deciding a particular case or action of unconstitutionality or another mean to of judicial review. Instead, they have their origin in the decision on autonomous requests for the abstract interpretation of the Constitution, in many cases filed by the National Executive through the Attorney General of the Republic.

In this regard, notwithstanding that a recourse or action for the interpretation of statutes is the only established in the Constitution, the Constitutional Chamber of

816. *See* Allan R. Brewer-Carías, *Hacia la consolidación de un Estado Socialista, Centralizado, Policial y Militarista. Comentarios sobre el sentido y alcance de las propuestas de reforma constitucional 2007* (Caracas Editorial Jurídica Venezolana, 2007), 122.

the Supreme Tribunal in Decision No. 1.077 of 22 September 2001, formally created its own power in order to decide 'autonomous recourses for the abstract interpretation in the Constitution', establishing an unconstitutional interpretation of Article 335 of the Constitution, which assigns the Supreme Tribunal and not solely to the Constitutional Chamber, its character of being the 'maximum and last interpreter of the Constitution'.[817] This recourse, according to the criteria followed by the Constitutional Chamber, has similarities in nature to the one expressly established for interpretation of statutes, but in these cases, in order to obtain a mere declarative decision about the scope and content of a constitutional provision. The Chamber recognized standing to file this recourse to anybody when alleging an actual, personal and legitimate interest, derived from a particular and specific legal situation which necessarily requires the interpretation of a Constitution provision applicable to it, in order to put an end to the uncertainty that impedes the development and effects of said legal situation. The main condition for the admissibility of such recourse is the obscurity or ambiguity of the particular constitutional provision that must apply to the legal situation or the contradiction that could exist between constitutional provisions and principles including those contained in the transition constitutional provisions adopted by the National Constituent Assembly in 1999.

As was decided by the Constitutional Chamber, notwithstanding the constitutional process that originated when a recourse for constitutional interpretation is filed, there is no need to open a contradictory hearing in order to allow the participation in the debate of people with judicial interest in a particular interpretation of the Constitution, and in Decision No. 2651 of 2 October 2003 it denied the character of a constitutional process to the procedure stating that in these cases 'there is no *litis*, confrontation between parts, regarding which their defence has to be secured'.[818] In any case, the result of the procedure is the binding character of the decision adopted by the Constitutional Chamber, particularly regarding the nucleus of the case in study.[819]

The creation by the Constitutional Chamber of this instrument for the abstract interpretation of the Constitution, without doubt, has produced a constitutional mutation, amplifying the constitutional powers of the Constitutional Chamber, by attributing to itself the power to decide a recourse that is not established in the Constitution. However, this autonomous recourse for the abstract interpretation of the Constitution has no precedent in comparative law.[820]

As we have mentioned, an autonomous recourse for the abstract interpretation of the Constitution, in the hands of an autonomous and independent Constitutional Judge, can be, without a doubt, an efficient instrument to adapt the norms of the Constitution to the changes operated in the constitutional order of a country at a

---

817. *See* decision No. 1077 of the Constitutional Chamber dated 22 Sep. 2000, Case: *Servio Tulio León Briceño*. *See* in *Revista de Derecho Público*, No. 83 (Caracas: Editorial Jurídica Venezolana, 2000), 247 ff. This criteria was then confirmed in decisions of 9 Nov. 2000 (No. 1347), 21 Nov. 2000 (No. 1387), and 5 Apr. 2001 (No. 457), among others.
818. *See* Case: *Ricardo Delgado. Interpretation of Article 174 of the Constitution*
819. *See* decision No. 1347, of 9 Nov. 2000.
820. *See* Allan R. Brewer-Carías, 'Le recours d'interprétation abstrait de la Constitution au Vénézuéla', in *Le renouveau du droit constitutionnel, Mélanges en l'honneur de Louis Favoreu* (Dalloz, Paris, 2007), 61–70.

point in time. However, a recourse of that nature in the hands of a Constitutional Judge is absolutely dependant on the Executive Power, in an authoritarian regime like the one structured in Venezuela during the last ten years, deciding, particularly, the interested requests filed by the Executive through the Attorney General of the Republic, is an instrument for illegitimate mutation of the Constitution, used to modify it and adapt at will, in order to strengthen authoritarianism. That is what has happened in Venezuela.

§11. The Unconstitutional Assumption by the Constitutional Chamber of the Supreme Tribunal of Ex Officio Powers to Exercise Judicial Review over the State Acts Issued Within the Transition Regime Towards Democracy of 2019

740. In 2019, as it has been analyzed (*see supra* paragraphs 46 et seq.), in the absence of a legitimately elected President that could take his oath on the 10 of January of that year for the constitutional period of 2019–2025, the National Assembly, interpreting the Constitution began to implement a Transition process in order to reinstate democracy and reinforce the Constitution that was considered violated (*see supra* paragraphs 45 et seq.), assuming as Interim President of Venezuela the President of the National Assembly, Juan Guaidó. Subsequently, all the decisions of the National Assembly and all the acts issued by the Interim President were declared null and void by the Constitutional Chamber of the Supreme Tribunal, but acting ex officio, without being requested by nobody and without having heard anybody and respected the right to defence of any interested party or authority.[821]

As mentioned, the National Assembly on 10 January 2019, decreed an 'emergency due to the total rupture of constitutional continuity', and began to set the path for 'ceasing the usurpation', assuming Juan Guaidó, in his condition of President of the Assembly, the role of interim President of the Republic. Five days later, on 15 January 2019, the same National Assembly decided 'to formally declare the usurpation of the Presidency of the Republic by Nicolás Maduro Moros and, consequently, consider the de facto status of Nicolás Maduro as legally ineffective, and declared all the alleged actions of the Executive Branch to be null and void' (*see supra* paragraph 45).

741. Against the Resolution of the National Assembly of 15 January 2019, the Constitutional Chamber of the Supreme Tribunal of Justice, a few days later, on 21 January 2019, issued 'judgment' No. 3 of 21 January 2019,[822] formulated as a kind

821. *See* the reference to all the decisions in Allan R. Brewer-Carías, 'The Unconstitutional *Ex Officio* Judicial Review Rulings issued by the Constitutional Chamber of the Supreme Tribunal of Venezuela Annulling all the 2019 National Assembly Decisions Sanctioned within the framework of the 2019 Transition Regime Towards Democracy for The Restoration of the Enforcement of the Constitution', in *Respuestas del Derecho Procesal Constitucional a los Desafíos de Hoy, VII Congreso Internacional de Derecho Procesal Constitucional. Homenaje a Héctor Fi Zamudio* (Coord. Gonzalo Pérez Salazar, Luis Petit García, María Auxiliadora Gutierrez) (Caracas, Centro de Estudios de Derecho Procesal Constitucional, Universidad Monteávila, 2021), pp. 417–459.

822. *Ibid.*

of *unilateral declaration* rendered without any process, case or controversy, that is, without trial or parties, without anyone having asked for it, violating all the most fundamental rules and principles of due process of law, as set forth in Article 49 of the Constitution (*see supra* paragraph 683). The decision, in fact, was rendered ex officio, and relied only on a previous ruling issued by the same Constitutional Chamber two years before (No. 2 of 11 January 2017) in which it declared that the National Assembly, as an institution, as a whole, was in 'contempt', providing that the 'action of the National Assembly and any person or individual contrary to what is decided here will be null and void'. This was obviously unconstitutional because in Venezuela no contempt measure is admissible against institutions and can only be legally imposed upon individuals or public servants in a criminal proceeding.

742. Nonetheless, and in spite of the Constitutional Chamber decision, the National Assembly sanctioned on 5 February 2019 the *Statute that governs the transition to democracy in* order *to reinstate the Constitution of the Bolivarian Republic of Venezuela* (*see supra* paragraph 47), being such decision the subject matter of another *unilateral declaration*, also issued ex officio by the Constitutional Chamber of the Supreme Tribunal, Judgment No. 6 of 8 February 2019,[823] in which the Chamber, also without anyone having asked for it or having claimed it, and without any hearing, proceed to annul the Statute. In this case, the Constitutional Chamber relied only on its previous rulings No. 2 of 11 January 2017, and No. 3 of 21 January 2019.

743. According to the provisions of the 2019 *Transition Statute,* the Interim President, Juan Guaidó, appointed a Special Attorney general and an Ad-Hoc Board of Directors of the State Oil Company, *Petróleos de Venezuela* and the Central Bank of Venezuela. In response, the Constitutional Chamber, again acting ex officio, without being requested by anybody and without a fair trial, because it did not summon nor hear the Interim President nor the Ad-Hoc Members of the Boards of Directors of the aforementioned decentralized State entities, proceeded through rulings No. 39 of 14 February 2019, No. 74 of 11 April 2019 and No. 247 of 25 July 2019[824] to annul and declare null and void all the appointment decisions; and also through ruling No. 67 of 25 May 2020 proceeded to declare null and void the decisions adopted by the Ad-Hoc Board of Directors of the Central Bank of Venezuela appointed by Juan Guaidó, declaring valid the Ad-Hoc Board of Directors appointed by Nicolás Maduro. Again, all these rulings were issued without guaranteeing a fair trial, without hearing anybody, and relied only on the already mentioned previous decisions issued by the same Chamber Constitutional.

744. Finally, the Constitutional Chamber proceeded to issue another ruling No. 59 of 22 April 2019,[825] in which it decided on a recourse for constitutional interpretation, regarding the Board of Directors of the Central Bank of Venezuela, concluding with a declaration that the one appointed by Nicolás Maduro was the

823. *Ibid.*
824. *Ibid.*
825. *Ibid.*

legitimate one, without assuring a fair trial because failing to summons and to allow the participation in the proceeding of the Interim President and of the members of the Ad-Hoc Board appointed by Juan Guaidó, to defend their acts.

745. In Venezuela, as it has been explained (*see supra* paragraphs 683 et seq.), according to the Constitution, there cannot be any sort of judicial review process, except regarding state of emergency decrees, without the existence of a case or controversy, that must have been initiated before the competent court through a demand, action or request filed by an interested party. In Venezuela, no judicial review process can be initiated by the Constitutional Chamber of the Supreme Tribunal on its own initiative. That is why prior to 2019, when the present constitutional crisis in Venezuela arose, there had been no examples of any case of the application of the concentrated method of judicial review with the characteristic of unilateral ex officio declarations issued in violation of the most elemental rules and principles of due process guaranteed by Article 49 of the Constitution, like those contained in the aforementioned unilateral, ex officio declarations.

746. In Venezuela, according to the Law on Public International Law of 1998,[826] foreign judicial rulings could have effects only if the 'defendant has been duly summoned, with sufficient time to appear, and that he has been granted in general, the procedural guarantees that ensure a reasonable possibility of defense' (Article 53.5). This is a principle that applies in the modern world in all rule of law State, being the consequence that decisions like the one previously referred, issued by the Constitutional Chamber of the Supreme Tribunal, ex officio and without summoning any defendants, without giving them sufficient time to appear, and without granting the defendants any procedural guarantees that ensure a reasonable possibility of defence, would not be recognized in countries that apply the same principle.

747. And this was the case, precisely, regarding all the aforementioned Constitutional Chamber rulings issued mainly during 2019, annulling ex officio without a hearing, that is, without guaranteeing a fair trial, all the decisions adopted by the National Assembly and according to the Transition Statute it enacted. That explains why in a case developed before the Courts of the UK, to determine who controlled and could give instructions to the Bank of England and another financial institution (Deutsche Bank) of London, on the destination and management of Venezuela's international reserves administered by the Central Bank of Venezuela represented in gold deposited in these institutions, in which the Board appointed by Nicolás Maduro requested the Courts to recognize the effects of the Constitutional Chamber decisions previously mentioned, the *High Court of Justice. Business and Property Courts of England and Wales. Commercial Court (QBD)*, in its decision issued on 29 July 2022,[827] rejected the recognition of such rulings in the UK, and concluded affirming that 'the failings in natural justice in each case are serious clear breaches

826. *See* in *Gaceta Oficial No. 36.511 of 6 Aug. 1998.*
827. The text of the decision is also available at: https://www.judiciary.uk/judgments/deutsche-bank-v-central-bank-of-venezuela-and-banco-central-de-venezuela-v-bank-of-england/.

of natural and substantial justice and a denial of a fair trial under Article 6 of the ECHR (in respect of which the label "flagrant" is appropriate) and would render it inappropriate to recognize them' (paragraph 239).[828]

---

828. *See* the comments on this decision in Allan R. Brewer-Carías, 'Comentarios sobre la sentencia de la High Court of Justice. Business and Property Courts of England and Wales. Commercial Court (QBD), del día 29 de julio de 2022, en el caso del oro venezolano de Londres', en *Revista de Administración Pública*, No. 219, (Madrid, Centro de Estudios Constitucionales, 2022), pp. 167–188.

Selected Bibliography

Alfredo Arismendi. *Contribución a la Bibliografía del Derecho Constitucional y su Historia.* Caracas: Editorial Jurídica Venezolana, 2005.

§1. General Texts

Allan R. Brewer-Carías, *Tratado de Derecho Constitucional*, 16 vols., Caracas: Editorial Jurídica Venezolana, 2013–2016.

Allan R. Brewer-Carías. *Instituciones Políticas y Constitucionales.* 8 vols. San Cristóbal-Caracas: Universidad Católica del Táchira, Editorial Jurídica Venezolana, 1996–1998.

Allan R. Brewer-Carías. *Reflexiones sobre el Constitucionalismo en América.* Caracas: Editorial Jurídica Venezolana, 2001.

Claudia Nikken, *Consideraciones sobre las fuentes del Derecho Constitucional y la interpretación de la Constitución*, EJV y Cidep, Caracas, 2018.

Ernesto Wolf. *Tratado de derecho constitucional.* 2 vols. Caracas: Tipografía Americana, 1945.

Humberto J. La Roche. *Derecho Constitucional.* Valencia: Parte general, Vadell Ed, 1991.

José Guillermo Andueza. *Apuntes de Derecho Constitucional.* 2 vols. Caracas: Editorial Inquietud, 1982.

José Peña Solís. *Lecciones de Derecho Constitucional General*, Volumen I, Tomo I y II. Caracas: Universidad Central de Venezuela, 2008.

Román Duque Corredor. *Temario de Derecho Constitucional y de Derecho Público.* Caracas: Legis, 2008.

Tulio Alberto Álvarez. *Instituciones Políticas y Derecho Constitucional.* Caracas: Tomo I, Ediciones Liber, 2008.

§2. Constitutional History of Venezuela

Allan R. Brewer-Carías. *Instituciones Políticas y Constitucionales.* 7 vols. San Cristóbal-Caracas: Universidad Católica del Táchira, Editorial Jurídica Venezolana, 1996.

Allan R. Brewer-Carías. *Las Constituciones de Venezuela.* 2 vols. Caracas: Academia de Ciencias Políticas y Sociales, 2008.

Allan R. Brewer-Carías. *Historia Constitucional de Venezuela.* 2 vols. Caracas: Editorial Alfa, 2008; 2d ed.n, Caracas, Editorial Jurídica Venezolana, Colección Tratado de Derecho Constitucional, vol. I, 2013.

Allan R. Brewer Carías, and Rafael Badell Madrid (coords.) *El pensamiento político y jurídico de la* Independencia, Academia de Ciencias Políticas y Sociales, Editorial Jurídica Venezolana, Caracas 2021.

Allan R. Brewer Carías, *Documentos Constitucionales de la Independencia/ Constitucional Documents of the Independence 1811*, Editorial Jurídica Venezolana, Caracas 2012.

Ambrosio Oropeza. *Evolución Constitucional de nuestra República.* Caracas, 1944; *Evolución constitucional de nuestra República, y otros textos.* Caracas: Biblioteca de la Academia de Ciencias Políticas y Sociales, 1985.

Ambrosio Perera. *Historia Orgánica de Venezuela.* Caracas: Editorial Venezuela, 1943.

Elena Plaza y Ricardo Combellas (Coordinadores). *Procesos Constituyentes y Reformas Constitucionales en la Historia de Venezuela: 1811–1999.* Caracas: Universidad Central de Venezuela, 2005.

Jesús María Casal, *Historia y Pensamiento Constitucional*, ABediciones, Caracas 2022

José Gil Fortoul. *Historia Constitucional de Venezuela.* 2 vols. Berlin: Carl Heyman, 1907; 3 Vols. Caracas: Ministerio de Educación, 1953.

Luis Mariñas Otero. *Las Constituciones de Venezuela.* Madrid: Instituto de Estudios Políticos, 1965.

Ulises Picón Rivas. *Índice Constitucional de Venezuela.* Caracas: Editorial Elite, 1944.

Mariano Picón Salas et al. *Venezuela Independiente 1810–1960.* Caracas Fundación Mendoza, 1962.

Pablo Ruggeri Parra. *Historia Política y Constitucional de Venezuela.* 2 vols. Caracas, 1949.

R.J. Velásquez et al. *Venezuela Moderna, Medio Siglo de Historia 1926–1976.* Barcelona: Fundación Eugenio Mendoza, 1979.

Pedro Vivas. *Guía de Historia Constitucional.* Caracas: Universidad Santa María, 1985.

§3. 1999 Constitution Making-Process

Allan R. Brewer-Carías. *Asamblea Constituyente y Ordenamiento Constitucional.* Caracas: Academia de Ciencias Políticas y Sociales, 1998.

Allan R. Brewer-Carias. *Poder constituyente originario y Asamblea Nacional Constituyente (Comentarios sobre la interpretación jurisprudencial relativa a la naturaleza, la misión y los limites de la Asamblea Nacional Constituyente).* Caracas: Editorial Jurídica Venezolana, 1999.

Allan R. Brewer-Carías. *Debate Constituyente, Aportes a la Asamblea Nacional Constituyente.* 3 vols. Caracas: Fundación de Derecho Público, Editorial Jurídica Venezolana, 1999.

Allan R. Brewer-Carías. *Golpe de Estado y Proceso Constituyente en Venezuela.* México: Universidad Nacional Autónoma de México, 2002.

Allan R. Brewer-Carías. *Asamblea Constituyente y Proceso Constituyente.* Caracas: Editorial Jurídica Venezolana, Colección Tratado de Derecho Constitucional, vol. VI, 2014.

Allan R. Brewer-Carías. *Golpe de Estado constituyente y fraude constitucional. Lecciones de la experiencia venezolana con la Asamblea Constituyente de 1999*, Ed. Olejnik, Buenos Aires, Madrid 2021.

Carlos M. Escarrá Malavé. *Proceso Político y Constituyente. Papeles Constituyentes.* Maracaibo, 1999.

Claudia Nikken. *La Cour Suprême de Justice et la Constitution vénézuélienne du 23 Janvier 1961.* (Paris II), Paris: Thése Docteur de l'Université Panthéon Assas, 2001.

Hermánn Escarrá Malavé. *Democracia, reforma constitucional y asamblea constituyente.* Caracas, 1995.

Lolymar Hernández Camargo. *La Teoría del Poder Constituyente. Un caso de estudio: el proceso constituyente venezolano de 1999.* San Cristóbal: Universidad Catóilica del Táchira, 2000.

Lolymar Hernández Camargo. *El Proceso Constituyente Venezolano de 1999.* Caracas: Academia de Ciencias Políticas y Sociales, 2008.

Juan M. Raffalli Arismendi. *Revolución, Constituyente y Oferta Electoral.* Caracas, 1998.

Ricardo Combellas. ¿Qué *es la Constituyente?, Voz para el futuro de Venezuela.* Caracas, 1998.

Ricardo Combellas. *Poder Constituyente.* Caracas, 1999.

Ricardo Combellas (coordinador). *Constituyente. Aportes al Debate.* COPRE, Konrad Adenauer Stiftung. Caracas, 1999.

Roberto Viciano Pastor y Rubén Martínez Dalmau. *Cambio político y proceso constituyente en Venezuela* (1998–2000). Valencia, 2001.

Asamblea Constituyente: Salida democrática a la crisis, Folletos para la Discusión No. 18. Caracas: Comisión Presidencial para la Reforma del Estado, 1992.

Tulio Alvarez. *La Constituyente. Todo lo que Usted necesita saber.* Caracas: Libros de El Nacional, 1998.

§4. 1999 CONSTITUTION

Alfredo Arismendi. *Derecho Constitucional.* 2 vols. Caracas: Universidad Central de Venezuela, 2002.

Allan R. Brewer-Carías. *La Constitución de 1999.* Caracas: Editorial Jurídica Venezolana, 2000.

Allan R. Brewer-Carías. *La Constitución de 1999. Derecho Constitucional Venezolano.* 2 vols. Caracas: Editorial Jurídica Venezolana, 2004; 2d ed. 2022.

Allan R. Brewer-Carías. *La Constitución de 1999 y la Enmienda Constitucional No. 1.* Caracas: Editorial Jurídica Venezolana, 2011.

Selected Bibliography

Allan R. Brewer-Carías. *La Constitución de 1999: El Estado Democrático y Social de Derecho*, Caracas: Editorial Jurídica Venezolana, Colección Tratado de Derecho Constitucional, vol. VII, 2014.
Alfonso Rivas Quintero. *Derecho Constitucional.* Valencia, 2002.
Hildegard Rondón de Sansó. *Análisis de la Constitución venezolana de 1999.* Caracas: Editorial Ex Libris, 2001.
AAVV, La Constitución de 1999. Caracas: Academia de Ciencias Políticas y Sociales, 2000.
Ricardo Combellas. *Derecho Constitucional: una introducción al estudio de la Constitución de la República Bolivariana de Venezuela.* Caracas: Mc Graw Hill, 2001.

§5. Venezuelan Constitutional Process 2000–2022

Allan R. Brewer-Carías, *Estudios sobre el Estado Constitucional (2005–2006).* (Caracas: Editorial Jurídica Venezolana, 2007).
Allan R. Brewer-Carías, *La Constitución de plastilina y vandalismo constitucional. La ilegítima mutación de la Constitución por el Juez Constitucional al servicio del autoritarismo*, (Caracas Editorial Jurídica Venezolana, 2022).
Allan R. Brewer-Carías, *Estudios sobre el Estado Comunal o Estado del Poder Popular. O de cómo se desconstitucionaliza al Estado en fraude a la Constitución y a la voluntad popular*, Caracas,Editorial Jurídica Venezolana, 2021.
Allan R. Brewer-Carías, *La demolición de la independencia y autonomía del Poder Judicial en Venezuela 1999–2021*, Editorial Jurídica Venezolana, Caracas, 2021.
Allan R. Brewer-Carías, *The Collapse of the Rule of Law and Struggle for Democracy Venezuela. Lectures and Essays (2015–2020)*, Dade College, Miami, 2020.
Allan R. Brewer-Carías, *proyectos constitucionales del chavismo: para desmantelar la democracia y establecer un estado socialista en venezuela (del principio al fin: 1999–2019)*, Editorial Temis, Editorial Juridica Venezolana, Bogotá, 2019.
Allan R. Brewer-Carías, *Transición hacia la democracia en Venezuela. bases constitucionales y obstáculos usurpadores*, Iniciativa Democrática de España y las Américas, Editorial Jurídica Venezolana, Miami, 2019.
Allan R. Brewer-Carías, *Crónica constitucional de una Venezuela en las tinieblas 2018–2019*, Ediciones Olejnik, Buenos Aires, Madrid 2019.
Allan R. Brewer-Carías, El *'nuevo constitucionalismo latinoamericano' y la destrucción del Estado democrático por el Juez Constitucional. El caso deVvenezuela*, Ediciones Olejnik, Buenos Aires, Madrid, 2018.
Allan R. Brewer-Carías, *Usurpación constituyente 1999, 2017. La historia se repite: una vez como farsa y la otra como tragedia*, Jurídica Venezolana International, Caracas, 2018.
Allan R. Brewer-Carías, *lL inconstitucional convocatoria de una Asamblea Nacional Constituyente en mayo de 2017. Un nuevo fraude a la Constitución y a la voluntad popular*, Editorial Jurídica Venezolana, Caracas 2017.
Allan R. Brewer-Carías, *lL mentira como política de Estado. Crónica de una crisis política permanente. Venezuela 1999–2015*, Editorial Jurídica Venezolana, Caracas 2015.

Allan R. Brewer-Carías, *Estado totalitario y desprecio a la Ley. La desconstitucionalización, desjuridificación, desjudicialización y desdemocratización de Venezuela*, Editorial Jurídica Venezolana, 2d. ed. Caracas, 2015.

Allan R. Brewer-Carías. *Authoritarian Government v. the Rule Of Law. Lectures and Essays (1999–2014) on the Venezuelan Authoritarian Regime Established in Contempt of the Constitution*, Editorial Jurídica Venezolana, Caracas, New York, 2014.

Allan R. Brewer-Carías, *Dismantling Democracy. The Chávez Authoritarian Experiment*, Cambridge University Press, New York, 2010.

Allan R. Brewer-Carías and Carlos García Soto (Eds.), *Estudios sobre la Asamblea Nacional Constituyente y su inconstitucional convocatoria en 2017*, Editorial Temis, Editorial Jurídica Venezolana, Bogotá, Caracas, 2017.

Carlos Ayala Corao and Rafael Chavero Gazdik. *La Asamblea Nacional Constituyente de Venezuela (*2017*–2019): El Leviatán de la democracia*, Academia de Ciencias Políticas y Sociales – Editorial Jurídica Venezolana, Caracas, 2019.

Jesús María Casal, *Asamblea Nacional. Contribuciones democráticas y obstáculos inconstitucionales a la reinstitucionalización*, ABediciones, Caracas, 2021.

Jesús María Casal, *Los derechos fundamentales y sus restricciones – Constitucionalismo comparado y jurisprudencia interamericana*, Editorial Temis y Fundación Konrad Adenauer, Bogotá, 2020.

José Ignacio Hernández G. *Bases fundamentales de la transición en Venezuela*, Editorial Jurídica Venezolana, Caracas, 2019.

José Ignacio Hernández and Allan R. Brewer-Carías, *The Defense of the Rights and Interests of the Venezuelan State by the Interim Government Before Foreign Courts*, and their International Recognition 2019–2020, Editorial Jurídica Venezolana International, New York, 2021.

Ramón Guillermo Aveledo, Jesús María Casal, Daniela Urosa Maggi, (coords.), *Estudios Constitucionales y Parlamentarios 2018–2020*, ABediciones, Instituto de Estudios Parlamentarios Fermín Toro, Caracas, 2021.

Rafael Badell Madrid, *Del Estado Federal al Estado Comunal*, Academia de Ciencias Políticas y Sociales, Caracas, 2021.

§6. Proposed and Rejected 2007 Constitutional Reform

Allan R. Brewer-Carías. *Reforma constitucional y fraude a la Constitución (1999–2009),* Academia de Ciencias Políticas y Sociales, Caracas, 2009.

Allan R. Brewer-Carías. *Hacia la consolidación de un Estado Socialista, Centralizado y Militarista. Comentarios sobre el alcance y sentido de las propuestas de reforma Constitucional 2007*. Caracas: Editorial Jurídica Venezolana, 2007.

Allan R. Brewer-Carías. *La reforma constitucional de 2007 (Comentarios al proyecto inconstitucionalmente sancionado por la Asamblea Nacional el 2 de noviembre de 2007)*. Caracas: Editorial Jurídica Venezolana, 2007.

Estudios sobre la Reforma Constitucional, Revista de Derecho Público. No. 112 (octubre-diciembre 2007). Caracas: Editorial Jurídica Venezolana, 2007.

Héctor Turupial Cariello. *Texto Oculto de la Reforma.* Caracas: Fundación de Estudios de Derecho Administrativo, 2008.

Selected Bibliography

Manuel Rachadell. *Socialismo del Siglo XXI. Análisis de la reforma Constitucional propuesta por el Presidente Chávez en agosto de 2007.* Caracas: Fundación de Estudios de Derecho Administrativo, Editorial Jurídica Venezolana, 2008.

§7. Judicial Review and Its Distortions

Allan R. Brewer Carías, *La Justicia Constitucional (Procesos y Procedimientos Constitucionales),* (México, Editorial Porrúa/ Instituto Mexicano de Derecho procesal Consittucional, 2007).

Allan R. Brewer Carías, *Derecho procesal constitucional. Instrumentos para la justicia constitucional*, 3d. ed. (Caracas, Centro de Estudios de Derecho Procesal Constitucional, 2014).

Allan R. Brewer Carías, *Derecho de amparo y acción de amparo constitucional*, (Caracas, Academia de Ciencias Políticas y Sociales, 2021).

Allan R. Brewer Carías, *Práctica y distorsión de la justicia constitucional en Venezuela (2008–2012)*, (Caracas, Editorial Jurídica Venezolana, 2012).

Allan R. Brewer Carías, *La patología de la Justicia Constitucional*, 3d, ed, (Caracas, Editorial Jurídica Venezolana, 2014).

Allan R. Brewer Carías, *El golpe a la democracia dado por la Sala Constitucional (De cómo la Sala Constitucional del Tribunal Supremo de Justicia de Venezuela impuso un gobierno sin legitimidad democrática, revocó mandatos populares de diputada y alcaldes, impidió el derecho a ser electo, restringió el derecho a manifestar, y eliminó el derecho a la participación política, todo en contra de la Constitución)*, (Caracas, Editorial Jurídica Venezolana, 2d. ed. 2015).

Allan R. Brewer Carías, *La dictadura judicial y la perversión del Estado de derecho. El Juez Constitucional y la destrucción de la democracia en Venezuela* (Madrid, Editorial IUSTEL, 2017).

Allan R. Brewer Carías, *Consolidación de la tiranía judicial. El Juez Constitucional controlado por el Poder Ejecutivo, asumiendo el poder absoluto*, (Caracas / New York, Editorial Jurídica Venezolana International 2017).

Carlos Ayala Corao and Rafael Chavero Gazdik, *El Libro Negro del TSJ de Venezuela: Del secuestro de la democracia y la usurpación de la soberanía popular a la ruptura del orden constitucional (2015–2017)*, (Editorial Jurídica Venezolana, 2017).

Daniela Urosa Maggi, Daniela, *La Sala Constitucional del Tribunal Supremo de Justicia como legislador positivo*, (Caracas, Academia de Ciencias Políticas y Soces, 2011).

Gonzalo Pérez Salazar, *Diálogo jurisprudencial en Venezuela*, (Caracas, Editorial Jurídica Venezolana, (2020).

Rafael Badell Madrid, *Derecho procesal constitucional*, Academia de Ciencias Políticas y Sociales, Caracas, 2020.

Chavero Gazdik, Rafael, *El control constitucional de las decisiones judiciales*, EJV y Cidep, Caracas. 2018.

Index

The numbers here refer to paragraph numbers.

Index

Index

www.ingramcontent.com/pod-product-compliance
Lightning Source LLC
Chambersburg PA
CBHW071411230926
51846CB00001B/52